MW01054200

FROM AMERICA TO NORWAY

Norwegian-American Immigrant Letters, 1838-1914

FROM

AMERICA

TO

NORWAY

‑·‑≈◦≈‑·‑

NORWEGIAN-AMERICAN
IMMIGRANT LETTERS
1838-1914

VOLUME TWO: 1871-1892

EDITED AND TRANSLATED BY

Orm Øverland

Norwegian-American Historical Association
Distributed by the University of Minnesota Press
NORTHFIELD, MINNESOTA, 2014

THE NORWEGIAN-AMERICAN HISTORICAL ASSOCIATION

Copyright 2014
Norwegian-American Historical Association
Northfield, Minn. 55057
www.naha.stolaf.edu

Distributed by the University of Minnesota Press
111 Third Avenue South, Suite 290
Minneapolis, Minn. 55401
www.upress.umn.edu

A Cataloging-in-Publication record for this book
is available from the Library of Congress.
ISBN 978-0-8166-9325-2

CONTENTS

1892

PREFACE

The three-volume *From America to Norway: Norwegian-American Immigrant Letters, 1838–1914* is based on a Norwegian edition in seven volumes, *Fra Amerika til Norge* (1992–2011), which in turn is based on the collection of immigrant letters in the Norwegian National Archives (*Riksarkivet*), which sponsored the Norwegian edition. Readers of these letters must keep in mind that the texts are translations and that they are a selection from the large number of available letters. There are some aspects of these texts that cannot be translated but that readers should be aware of. Many letter writers were unused to writing and did not always master spelling, punctuation, grammar, or syntax. The translations of their letters, however, cannot and, indeed, should not attempt to convey their linguistic and literary limitations. Addressing this issue in the preface of the first volume I wrote: "My guiding principle has been that these writers' deficient education must not be understood as a deficient intelligence and that they deserve to be presented in a grammatically correct and readable English translation. It is an ethical imperative that both reader and translator approach these texts with respect."

Readers of this volume should consult the Preface as well as the Reader's Guide in the first volume for useful information valid for all three volumes. Some readers may expect to find an index of names of people as well as places—an index for all three volumes will be produced in conjunction with the final volume. A provisional index for this volume is available on NAHA's website.

ACKNOWLEDGMENTS

I am indebted to the late Steinar Kjærheim, coeditor of the first three volumes of *Fra Norge til Amerika* and for many years the head of *Kjeldeskriftavdelingen* (The Department of Written Sources), which has been a division of the Norwegian National Archives since 1991. Knut Sprauten, Tor Ulset, Halvor Kjellberg, and Jo Rune Ugulen, all at the national archives, were of special help in preparing the Norwegian volumes. Todd W. Nichol, King Olav V Professor of Scandinavian-American Studies at St. Olaf College, first suggested the making of an American edition and has been an encouragement in moments of despair. Amy Boxrud has been of invaluable assistance in preparing these volumes for publication, as has Jackie Henry, the administrative director of NAHA. My main support is Inger, my wife of more than half a century.

Orm Øverland
Aukra, Norway

LETTERS

1871 — LETTER 2:1

FROM: Ole Olsen Haugerud the Younger
St. Ansgar, Iowa, 6 February 1871
To: Guri Rustand, *Aadalen, Ringerike, Buskerud*

To my unforgettable mother and siblings,

I must, as your son and brother, take up my pen to let you know how things are here in the far West. We are all, praise God, in good health and are satisfied in our daily progress through this sinful vale of tears. We sincerely wish that these lines will find you in good health. Our loving regards to our dear mother with a prayer to God that we may be gathered in the heavenly mansions when our struggles here below are over. It is my most sincere prayer and admonition to you, dear mother, that you will hold on to your true Lord even should he lay his chastising hand upon you with illness and other difficulties that humans suffer on their pilgrim's progress through the world to the heavenly Canaan.

I will now explain my main concern here. When Ole H. Rodningsand was made administrator of the estate of our brother, the widow reported to the probate court that in about six months she expected a child, who would then inherit the estate. These six months have now passed and the inheritor has not arrived, and there will never be one. So we will inherit from our brother. The widow has a right to one third of the chattel and real estate, and the rest goes to us. The legal issues concerning real estate are not to our advantage. As long as our dear mother lives it will be very difficult to sell the property. Our mother has the right to two thirds of the income for life and no one therefore has the right to sell it. After her death, however, the heirs may sell the land as they wish. If you wish to sell the land before her death it can only be done in this manner: our mother and all our siblings must sign what in English is called a *quit claim deed* to someone who is a resident here. This will transfer all your claims on the property to another person. Such a document has to be set up here and then sent to you for your signatures. If the property is to remain unsold until our mother's death it will be necessary to write an authorization here in English and send it to her for signing. This will give someone the authority to act on her behalf.

You must decide on one of these two procedures. You may find it problematic to transfer all your rights to another person and it is indeed so that, should this person wish to make himself a scoundrel for the sake of a few dollars, it would not be impossible to cheat you. You, my dear mother and siblings, must make your decision as soon as possible as everything has to be ready for the probate court before August 1, 1871. If no acceptable document has been submitted before this date, I fear that the lawyers will take over (this is the law) and then most of the property would be expended in court costs. The widow has a right to do as she wishes with her part, to sell it or to have it separated from the rest of the property. If the whole farm could be sold this would no doubt benefit the heirs on both sides, as a division would diminish the value of the estate. Moreover, the land has only one site fit for building and this is where the present buildings are. If the widow were to claim her part of the property she would surely be awarded the buildings and the land around them. However, if it could be arranged that the farm be sold, then this could either be done in cooperation with the widow or by purchasing her rights and then selling the property on our own. However, if we don't take the necessary legal steps, we won't be able to buy the widow's share should she wish to sell it because it would not be clear when we would have the right to sell the farm. If we should take out our part of the chattel and pay for our part of the farm, we would still owe money to the widow. I think the chattel is altogether worth 1,200 dollars and the property is probably worth 30 dollars an acre or 5,200 dollars. I don't think it would be in the interest of the heirs to leave the land unsold. The taxes here are so high that the returns on the land would not be enough to pay the expenses if the interest on the value of the farm is taken into account. Here the rule is that when a farm is farmed on shares, the owner has one third and the user has two thirds of the harvest. The owner then has to provide housing and firewood as well as keep the property in good shape with fences and more.

I think I've written enough about this and I hope you'll let me know your decision as soon as possible. We haven't heard from our brother Erik since he wrote to us five months ago and then said he was in good health. He didn't know when he would be able to leave New Zealand. As I don't have more of interest I'll end my simple lines with loving regards to you all.

Please remember us to all our acquaintances. In conclusion, our most loving regards to you, dear mother and siblings, from your faithful son and brother.

OLE OLSEN HAUGERUD AND FAMILY

. ——— .

Enclosed with this letter was a brief note from his nephew, Iver Elling-sen Elsrud, to his parents. OOH wrote many frustrated letters about the mounting legal problems caused partly by the widow's attempt to have half, rather than one third, of the property and partly (perhaps mainly) by the decision of his mother (urged by her son Torgrim) to give an American lawyer power of attorney. On 5 June 1871, OOH sent a quit claim deed explained and recommended by Pastor C. L. Clausen (Nor. ed. III:85). On 14 February, 1 June, and 4 December 1872 (Nor. ed. III:114, 122, 136), he tried to explain the consequences of his family's actions and warned them against the Norwegian-American lawyers his mother had appointed. Later letters (2 March 1876, 1 August 1878, (Nor. ed. IV:24 and 75, and others in the Norwegian National Archives) tell of his deteriorating relations with his mother and confirm his warnings. On this sad note ends the correspondence from OOH in this edition. «I:156 NE III:76

. ——— .

1871 — LETTER 2:2

FROM: Paul Torstensen Vigenstad, *Burke, Wisconsin, 22 March 1871*

To: Simen Torstensen Vigenstad, *Dovre, Oppland*

⟶⟨≡⟩◯⟨≡⟩⟵

My dear brother Simen Vigenstad,

I'll write now even though I would have preferred to wait so that I could have given you precise information on where we'll be going this spring, as I'm expecting information from Thor at any time. I'll write again as soon as

I know whether we'll make our journey. I wish that Thor had remained in Norway. I certainly don't think it would be better for him in Norway and I'm sure that he wouldn't be satisfied with Norwegian conditions should he return; but when I think of the grief his absence has given you, then I must wish this, even though I believe there is no reason for your anxiety. I would be glad if he returns because this has been his desire. For me it would be difficult to leave America now. It would only be good for one thing (and this goes for Thor as well) and that is the company of relatives and friends. I beg you to consider whether there is any reason to believe that we have acted against the will of God and let us know what you decide as this would help us. God is my witness that I acted according to my best understanding and that I had pondered the will of God when I left Norway. I also thought of you but the word of God and my calling as teacher were paramount. As a teacher I've been happier in America than in Norway. The material returns were greater in Norway but such things are not important. It may be, however, that Thor and I will be able to make a good home for ourselves here. Enough of this.

I'm enclosing eight portraits of Thor that he has sent to me. Four are for you, one for Iver Tofte, one for Thor Tofte, one for Hans Langdalen, and one for Simen Haugen. I'm also enclosing two of myself. In Madison portraits cost one dollar a dozen, fifty cents for four and a shilling for one. The best ones cost three dollars a dozen, two for half a dozen and fifty cents for one. Those I'm sending cost one dollar a dozen. Since coming to America I've been given three portraits. One is of a girl. I would like to send it to Gudbrandsdalen to be compared with any beauties of the valley, but I don't have her permission so I'll keep it for myself.

There is much talk of new land in the western part of Minnesota, called the Red River Valley. A few boys here are talking of going there next spring and it's possible that Thor and I will go too, if Thor doesn't decide to remain in Texas, which I find unlikely. But our pastors, both Preus and Hovde, insist that we don't go and if Thor wants to stay here I would gladly do so, too. But he has only once and then not convincingly said anything about staying. Mostly he has said that a new place would be the best for us to start out. Our only advantage here is my income from teaching and there would not be much of this in a new settlement. But Thor is right in saying that it would be best to go west. It is especially convenient for us who are unmarried and also acquainted with the country and this is also the situation of the others who are talking of going, so they would be good company. The human heart may map its way but the Lord decides where it

FROM AMERICA TO NORWAY

will go. Perhaps it will only be with talk, but we all need something to think and talk about for our entertainment.

The snow is gone now and spring plowing is about to begin. Hans Blessum is working on a road in Minnesota and went there last fall. Simen Blessum is working for a tailor named Olsen in Madison. Lars Øien, the glazier, and Jacob Stampen are also in Madison. Johannes Stampen went to Texas last fall. I've recently had a letter from E. Bakke but it was written last fall. I haven't seen or heard from others from Gudbrandsdalen for a long time. I've been in exceptionally good health since late winter, but my health remains unreliable. School was over for this season one week ago, but two men have asked me to teach two of their children writing and arithmetic and this is what I'm now doing. Others have joined so now I'm teaching seven children, four boys and three girls. When you write you mustn't forget to tell me whether Mari Tofte received her ten dollars and whether you have the receipt for twenty dollars from Thor Tofte. My regards to relatives and friends, and to your father, Mari, Guri, and Rønnaug—all unforgettable! May the Lord be with you!

PAUL VIGENSTAD

· —— ·

Thor emigrated in 1868, and his older brother Paul followed later that same year. PTV was educated as a teacher in Norway (see note I:166). Thor did not join him but remained in Texas, where he was a laborer. Lars Øien emigrated from Trondheim in 1870 (Ulvestad 1913, 1004). The two pastors who wanted him to stay were Herman A. Preus and Brynjolf Hovde. Dovre is in the upper, northern part of Gudbrandsdalen. A shilling was twelve and a half cents (a bit). «I:166 »II:5 NE III:79

· —— ·

FROM: Svend Larsen Houg, *Elgin, Iowa, 11 April 1871*

To: Ole Larsen Haug, *Aal, Buskerud*

Dear brother Ole,

After much delay I must again try to send you a few words. I received your letter of May 6, 1870 on July 13 and your letter of March 10 on April 15. Thank you so much. You say that your family numbers as many as when you last wrote and that all are in good health. And I can answer with the same words. Oh what grace and what mercy that He grants us so much good, both worldly and spiritually, but where is our gratitude? I for my part am ashamed when I think of this. And what is God's purpose? Yes, that he may make us his children and give us the undeserved grace that is in Jesus Christ, our Lord.

You may ask what the situation is for the Christian faith in America, and I'll answer that there certainly is Christianity and the true fear of God here, but it must be admitted that the true Christians are few compared to the worldly majority. I don't dare say anything about the faith of others in my neighborhood so I will only write about myself and my family. I must tell you, brother, that I've often been troubled by doubt of the grace of God, but God be praised, he has shown me through his word that I may come to him even as the sinful and corrupt person I am and be given grace and the forgiveness of sins through faith in Jesus Christ alone. Dear brother, I can neither admonish nor encourage you but we have an abundance of the word of God among us and we should take note of it as a light that shines in a dark place until the morning star Jesus Christ enters into our hearts. These are words to cherish in these times of strife when we hear calls from all directions: Jesus is here and Jesus is there, yes, especially in this country. But it is written that we must not always believe in such voices but test them to find if they are of God.

You may ask whether we have a pastor. Yes, we've appointed one for a trial year. He has just come from Norway where he studied at the Stavanger

Mission School and was ordained here. I think I wrote that we thought of getting a Swedish pastor but this couldn't be, as it isn't always possible to have agreement even among Christians. I think he was a tool of God for the conversion of our souls and his work here was not without results, but he has now gone to Minnesota where he is pastor for a congregation of Swedes and Norwegians. This is the way it often goes when we try to have our way. God comes and tears down what we have built, as his wisdom is so much greater than ours.

I must return to myself and my family. We are all in good health and doing quite well even though luck is not always with us. All my children are here with me. Two of my sons were confirmed on the Fourth Sunday after Easter with an acceptable understanding of their Christian faith. Their names are Ole and Kittil. Yes, dear brother, it gives parents reason for thought when our children are to establish their covenant with God. When we look back upon our own lives and out on the world in general we see how low this costly covenant is held. The teacher that we've had for some time is leaving so we won't have a regular teacher. Friends have urged me to send my son Halsten, who is now nineteen, to a school so that he may be educated as a teacher in both the Norwegian and the English languages, but Halsten isn't yet quite sure about what he wants to do. Nor have I made up my mind and it may perhaps come to nothing, as there are so many difficulties to be considered. He could certainly acquire knowledge in different subjects but my concern is whether he'll have nourishment for his soul and this is what makes the project so doubtful, as there are as many temptations at a school as in other places. The boy is well behaved and both obedient and meek and I think that God's Spirit is at work in him. (He is a good student.)

You write that your daughter Ingrid will be coming home this spring. Thank her so much for the very nice letter she sent me with our brother's son Lars. I was glad to hear that God had made her recognize she was a sinner because when this has been done he can make us his children in grace in Jesus Christ if we only believe and trust in him. Dear brother, give her my loving regards, and my wife also greets her as a sister in the Lord. Thank brother Knud for his letter and for the gifts he sent us. I am not writing to him separately but let him see these simple lines if he so wishes. As for our brother's son Lars, I find no fault with him. He is much like other young people and more than this is not to be expected. He has been very good at laying aside some money and things have gone well for him till now. When he came to us last summer most people around here had already hired their help. I'd made arrangements for him but as he came so late someone else had been hired. So I had to take him in for a month. Then an American hired him for four months, and last winter he lived with Johannes Groth whose children are too small to be of much help. This spring Lars has worked for an American and has now been hired by Johannes Groth. He has surely written about all of this to his parents. Now I wish to thank you on his behalf for all you've done for him. I think I've done what I could and he'll probably straighten our account this summer.

I cannot really answer your question about Syver Groth's wife but I'll tell you what I believe her worries were. She was probably anxious for her soul and this may have been caused by others, but it was probably mainly because of their oldest daughter Ragnild. She was ill, in both body and soul, and was sorely tried before she entered into a firm and living faith in our Lord and Savior. I now hope she is serious in her faith. She is of weak health but carries her burden patiently. The reason Syver hadn't written the letter himself was that he doesn't write anymore and their daughter writes what is necessary.

I am sending these simple sentences to you, my brother. The words are confused and the letters poorly made, but you will have to correct my words. My best regards to you and your family. I and my children and my wife greet you with the words that we through grace will meet with Jesus our Savior. My regards to brother Lars and sister Guri. My old mother-in-law is still living. She sends her regards and I can also report that all from Groth live. This may be the last time we speak with each other so live well in God. This is the wish of your lowly brother,

SVEND LARSEN HOUG

A few more words. I will write a few words to our sister Mari before I mail this letter, so I will enclose it and ask you, my brother, to put it in an envelope and address it to her, as I don't have her address. I know that this will cause you both trouble and expense but I also know that you will gladly do it.

When I wrote about a schoolteacher I meant a teacher in the religious school held in our Norwegian language. The English school is required. It is owned by the state.

S. L. H.

Svend Larsen and Margit Halsteinsdatter Houg emigrated in 1852 (see I:34). There seems to be some confusion of dates as this letter is dated some days before he writes that he received the last letter. SLH does not at this time seem to be committed to any of the Lutheran synods among the Norwegian Americans. Hans Christian Rornes, who had studied in Stavanger, was a pastor in the Norwegian Synod and Fredrick Herman Carlson, a Swede, was a pastor in the Elling and Hauge Synods. Halsten S. Houg eventually studied at Augsburg Seminary and, after teaching in parochial and public schoools and at Augsburg Seminary, he founded the St. Ansgar Seminary in 1878 and was principal until he left academic life in 1898 to be county auditor of Mitchell County, Iowa until he died in 1910. The nephew who brought a letter was Lars Larsen Houg. «I:159 »II:53 NE III:81

1871 — LETTER 2:4

FROM: Arne Jørgensen and Karen Olsdatter Brager
Vermont, Wisconsin, 29 April 1871

To: Johan Olsen and Lisbet Brendhagen, *Vang, Hedmark*

Dear brother-in-law,

Thank you for your dear letter dated at Arnseteie August 19 of last year that we received about a month later. I must now write you some words in return so that you may hear how things are with us. But I'm ashamed dear brother that we've been so lazy and not sent you any greetings before this; one month has followed the other and it hasn't been done. I hope you will forgive me. We've been in good health for which we must praise God. Oh that we could receive all that comes from his hand in gratitude and learn to believe, love, and trust in him of a whole heart. And should he send us suffering and chastise us more than others we should accept his fatherly hand

and praise him and proclaim that we are undeserving and that we have brought upon us his anger and <u>disgrace</u> in our sinfulness and disobedience. He therefore does well in <u>chastising</u> us in his mercy so that we will not be damned. When we are tempted by impatience we should pray to him to strengthen us in his mercy, so that living of the will of God we may say, as did our Savior, should I not drink of the cup my Father gives me?

I've nothing of importance to tell you about our daily life as one day follows the other as we approach the last one. We and our parents are share-farming this year and we'll have half of what we produce. We have planted thirteen acres with wheat, four with rye and two and a half acres with corn, and we have an abundance of grass for hay. We did our spring plowing and planting in the first days of March. We have a cow that will begin to give milk in about a week and all else we need.

Dear John and wife. Tuesday April 4 my dear Karen gave birth to a beautiful little daughter into this sinful and wretched world. She was unwell for about a week and then her pains began at eight on Tuesday and at eight that evening the child was born, for which we are glad. We have much reason to thank God for his great kindness in giving us such a healthy child, yes a costly treasure. May God grant that our child may be to his glory and serve him till the end of her days! My wife is, praise God, now well after all this pain and I have all reason to be happy. You may wish to know what our little girl will be called. We have thought of calling her <u>Gunnild Amalie</u> and next Sunday we will take her to church. Our Pastor Fjeld is our neighbor. I won't write anything about the country as I hope you have heard about it before. We now have an unusually strong thunderstorm. It is usually dark by eight during summer. In conclusion, our loving regards from us both. When you write again please don't send such heavy letters as they are so expensive. Write as soon as possible. Our regards from your brother-in-law and sister and our little girl. Yours faithfully,

A. BRAGER AND KAREN OLSDATTER

[*In the margins*] It would be nice to hear about our sister Oline if you have any information for us. The enclosed piece of cloth is from my wife's wedding gown. I have two other new dresses.

· ——— ·

Karen Brager (born in Faaberg, Oppland in 1843) emigrated in 1870 and wrote to her brother a few weeks before she left Norway (Nor. ed. III:47). Arne Brager emigrated with his parents from Hedalen, Sør-Aurdal, Oppland. John N. Fjeld, from Sør-Aurdal, was pastor in

Vermont and several other congregations in Dane County, Wisc. Karen's sister Oline had recently been a patient in a mental institution. The pronoun confusion in the last sentence suggests that both are involved in writing. They note the early darkness in summer as summer nights are light in Norway »II:21 NE III:82

· —— ·

1871 — LETTER 2:5

FROM: Thor Torstensen Vigenstad, *Texas, 13 May 1871*

To: Paul Torstensen Vigenstad, *Madison, Wisconsin*

Dear brother,

It has been a long time since I last wrote and the reason is that I wanted to see how things would work out for me in Texas. I am, praise God, in good health and living much as usual. First I'll try to describe for you the labyrinth I've been in now as I sit beside a little creek deep in the silent woods listening to the song of small birds. It's beautiful here. I see oak and fir and in between there are small trees filled with red and white flowers, the most beautiful I've seen. Creepers grow up along the tree trunks and hang down from each branch, making a house when the tree has many branches. There are wild flowers down by the creek. When I wrote my first letter I was near Houston. I was there about a month and it is the worst place I've ever seen. Outdoors I had to wade in dirt far over my boots. People there were lazy, so lazy that they hadn't cultivated more than four acres where they grew corn, potatoes and some cotton. I didn't see a fruit tree or any garden produce. I'm now 200 miles from there and the land is quite different: a high prairie with scattered woods and small creeks. The daily wage on the railroad is from two to two and a half dollars and fifteen dollars a month for board. Farmers pay twenty-five and the brickyards pay thirty to thirty-five dollars a month. You may wonder whether wages may be higher and my answer is that a good man may make from three and a half to four dollars a day and moreover be his own master. When I'm more used to the so-called station work I'll have three and a half dollars and to top it off I'll be my own boss and work when I want and stop when I want.

As for our plans to take land in Minnesota, you should do as you wish. If you don't want to take land and begin to farm you will nevertheless have to go to Minnesota and buy land for the money we have because if you can find a place it will probably be settled in a couple of years and you'll soon have doubled the amount, and it won't cost you much to go there. If you don't want land you could try establishing yourself as a merchant in one of the small towns because I'll stay here until next spring. Best wishes from your brother,

THOR

When you come to Minnesota you must look up our friends there. Tell Johan Stanbuen that I went through Crosby where his brother lives but didn't have time to look him up as the train I was on derailed and we were therefore four hours late. I'm now four days from there.

· —— ·

Thor often wrote short letters to his brother, who sent many of them on to their family in Dovre. In Texas he seems to have moved around from one job to another, mostly working for railroads. He not only writes far better than most immigrants in this edition but enjoys describing what he has seen. Other letters not included here were sent 9 June, 23 July, and 19 August 1871. «II:2 »II:15 NE III:83

· —— ·

FROM: Elise Wærenskjold, *Four Mile Prairie, Texas, 27 May 1871*
To: Thomine Dannevig, *Lillesand, Aust-Agder*

⤚⟦⟧⤙

Dear Thomine!

Thank you so much for the interesting news about friends and acquaintances in your welcome letter that I received a couple of weeks ago. I was particularly glad to see that your dear Niels is alive and well since I hadn't heard anything about him since he was hospitalized. He looks very young; in his portrait he doesn't seem older than Otto. Thank you for the portraits! Yes, you became a mother long before me but I became a mother-in-law before you. Otto was married March 2 to Ophelia Florence Spikes, a clever, kind, and beautiful girl who is three months younger than Otto. The wedding was of course at the Spikes'. It was held in the evening before dark. But the next day we had a dinner party in our home followed by a dance in the evening to which 130 people were invited, some Norwegian, others American. They will live with me to begin with but as soon as possible a house will be built for them just north of mine. I think they will be able to move in by Christmas. You may find it strange that Otto is already married but I suppose it will be no less of a surprise to hear that Mrs. Bache ceased to be Mrs. Bache April 13 when she married a German widower, Oscar Pabst, who has two little girls of five and nine years. They are nice children but he is not at all good looking and very unprepossessing. But he is said to be wealthy. His sister is married to a brother of Lina Reiersen's husband. Mrs. Pabst is doing very well, has a large property and a good income from a hotel, sawmill, farm, horses, cattle etc. Ouline Reiersen is also comfortable but hasn't more than necessary for her nice but small home. Ole Johan lives with her and has put a little aside: two horses and the interest on some money. Her next oldest stepson lives with her but is about to move into a nice house that his uncle Carl R. has just built for him. They recently had a little son. Her youngest stepson died this spring of brain fever. Sigurd is quite fat. He is bookkeeper for Reiersen & Grøgaard in Shreveport and doing quite well for himself. H. J. Grøgaard came with his wife and a little daughter for Mrs. Bache's wedding on his way to visit his father-in-law Lassen Reiersen in Bosque. He is a very nice man but cannot speak Norwegian. He and his brother-in-law are doing a good business in Shreveport. Last year Helene and Reiersen went to visit his brother-in-law Vinzent in California. Thomas lives in New Orleans and has one or two children. Nicolai lives in Texas and has two children and one that is dead. Both of H. Jacob's children are dead. Emma has, I believe, six. They are all doing well. I mustn't forget Miss Maria who is with Mrs. Pabst. Hans Jacob has bought a lot in Prairieville and will have a nice little house built for her, for which she is very happy. Now she too has a suitor, a rather unprepossessing and simple fellow without means. I don't know what can come of this but they both want to marry. Mrs. Bache's brother, his wife, son, and daughter as well as Mrs. Kolstad were also at Mrs. Bache's wedding. Few attended, not even my children were invited, but they had a very nice table. The next Sunday we had a Norwegian church service in my home and Andersen's little daughter was baptized. All the visitors, the newly-weds, and Pastor Estrem came to my house for dinner. Estrem married the Pabsts. I would have liked him to perform Otto's marriage but we had not expected him to come until April and he was here March 4, the day after *"the infare."* I think that you now have all the news that can be of the slightest interest for you.

Poor Theresia! This must be very unpleasant for her. What was really the matter with her husband? There is a veterinary here, a Lambrechts, and he and his wife board with Mrs. Pabst. He knows him and says that he now lives in La Crosse, Wisconsin where he is on the editorial staff of *Fædrelandet og Emigranten* and is doing quite well. Mrs. Pabst, Ouline, Ole, and Miss Maria were all eager to hear the news in your letter and they send their regards to you and other friends and acquaintances in Lillesand, as do I and my children. Where is Gusta Hauge? Write and tell me about the festivities when your son and Miss Heyerdahl have their wedding. Give my regards to the doctor and your daughter-in-law. I think he will remember me. I'm glad that your mother and Mrs. Hammer are alive and well. I'll soon write to Sigurd and let him know all that you write about the Grøgaards and then he will pass it on to Helene. You must excuse me for not writing a letter as it should be, but I'm watching a kettle of cherries that I'm canning as I write this. Our cherries and plums are now ripe and so many people, black and white, acquaintances and strangers, come asking for plums. We have read more than enough about the Franco-Prussian

War in the newspapers and I see that the Norwegians have mostly favored the French. But do they now say that the French, after the war is over, still haven't had enough of misery and bloodshed? I would certainly have preferred that the French won rather than the all-devouring Prussians, but the fact is that I don't like either of them. We've read about the balloon and the bazaar in Christiania.

Please mail the enclosed letter to Tønnes Salvesen. Tell me, dear Thomine, what manner of man is he? Is he hardworking and with sober habits? But now I have come to the end of my sheet. Ask Thorvald to write to me and also my other correspondents who all seem to have fallen asleep. Write soon to your old friend,

ELISE WÆRENSKJOLD

Sigurd Ørbæk asks me to give his regards to his nephew and asks whether he received a letter from him a couple of years ago.

.   ——   .

Fragments of this letter are in Clausen 1961. EW dates this and other letters at Prairieville, where her letters were mailed, but she lived in Four Mile Prairie. Syversen 1982 is a helpful guide in identifying the characters in letters from Texas. Lina (Caroline Amalie) Reiersen's husband was Charles Vinzent. Ouline Reiersen was the widow of Johan Reinert Reiersen and Ole Johan Ørbæk was her oldest brother. Her stepson was Johan Heinrich Reiersen. Helene and Peder Georg Reiersen visited Lina and Charles Vinzent in California. Thomas Grøgaard was in New Orleans and Christian Nicolai Grøgaard was in Texas. EW used the terms *madam* and *fru* (both here translated "Mrs."), the former (as in *Madam* Bache, *Madam* Kolstad, and *Madam* Hammer) for a married woman that she did not consider to have quite her own social rank and the latter for herself, Thomine Dannevig, and other married women she thought of as belonging to her own class. Another distinction made in EW's letters is between those she mentions by their given name and those who appear with their family name. The intimacy of the first name is reserved for members of the Reiersen (for instance, Ouline), Grøgaard (for instance, Thomas), and Ørbæk (for instance, Ole Johan) families that were also known to her correspondent. EW used the English word *infare*, perhaps because she had no Norwegian term for a wedding reception. The word would not have made sense to Thomine Dannevig. "Poor Theresia" was the wife of Ferdinand A. Husher, former parish pastor in Nissedal, Telemark. His decision to leave the ministry and emigrate may have been caused by behavior considered scandalous. Niels Dannevig married Vilhelmine, daughter of Stener Heyerdahl, an army physician in Kristiansand. They settled in Tønsberg, and Thomine Dannevig eventually lived with them there. The revolutionary Paris Commune ended with bitter warfare and mass executions after the end of the Franco-Prussian War. On the balloon and bazaar see Clausen 1961, 102. «I:160 »II:34 NE III:84

1871 — LETTER 2:7

FROM: Jul Gulliksen Dorsett, *Bratsberg, Minnesota, 25 June 1871*

To: Torstein Gulliksen Daaset, *Flesberg, Buskerud*

Dear brothers,

I haven't heard from you since I last wrote so I thought I would send you a few words to tell you that I'm in good health and living as usual. As for the times, they are as usual and a lot of people are coming to this state from Norway and other European countries. If you think of coming it would be best to do it sooner rather than later because the longer you wait the further west you have to go to find cheap land. I won't advise you to come or not to come, but in my view you may as well come if you can sell what you have at a reasonable price. But I'll also note that there are some who are not satisfied here, but there are more who think it is good and who are satisfied. Naturally, one must work hard here as in Norway to prosper, but if one is diligent then he is better paid for his work here. Land here is expensive and almost all land worth farming has been taken so one must go two to three hundred miles further into the country. I haven't been there, but most people are satisfied. And I will also note that if any of you want to come then I want to know as soon as possible, because if you come then I plan to sell the land I have here and go further west to take land so that we could do this together.

I have no news. Paul Paulsen Klevan went further west a few days ago and there are many from around here who have gone this spring to take land further west and I hear that this is also true of many other places. I will conclude with a request that you write as soon as possible about how you are and what you plan to do. My best regards,

JUL GULLIKSEN DOSET

· ——— ·

The letter seems to have been dictated but he has signed his name, which is in the process of becoming Dorsett. «I:165 »II:20 NE III:88

· ——— ·

1871 — LETTER 2:8

FROM: Hellik G. Branson, *Eureka, Kansas, 10 July 1871*

TO: Ole Gulbrandsen Lande, *Flesberg, Buskerud*

⟿⟾

Dear brother and your wife,

I must now take up my pen and send you a few words to let you know that we are all in good health and doing well. I have nothing to write about that would interest you. We are glad that you have decided to come. You wonder whether I'll be coming to Norway but that won't be. I would have liked to but I have so much to take care of here. And I cannot leave my old mother as long as she lives. So you must not hope to see me there. I can tell you that our town Eureka is growing fast and that we (that is Eureka and Greenwood County) will build a courthouse that will cost us 30,000 dollars, as well as a school that will cost 15,000 and a steam mill for 16,000 and much more. So this year our little town will build for about 100,000 dollars. There is talk of four railroads coming here. We are quite sure about two of these but I don't think they will come so soon that you can come on them next spring.

But even so we find the times hard, as the prices for cattle and other products are so low that money is short. So emigrants who come next spring and who have a little capital may do well because they can buy cheap cattle. And it seems that we'll have a good year for all products so food will be cheap. And we believe that a territory between us and Texas will be open for settlement in a year or two and all agree that this will be one of the best states in North America and it is so close that I can drive there in two days, and my sons Gulbrand and Henry live only half a day from there. The Indian land that I have written to you about is now as densely settled as here and this is where my sons live.

As for Ole Mesunt you must ask Niri Kolkinn not to let him travel alone. There are so few who go straight here that he should wait until Niri is ready. And I must ask you to be so kind as to provide Ole with food. Do this quietly so people in Kongsberg don't get to know about it. You must take care that he has what he needs before he leaves. And you must ask Niri to be patient with him because I'm sure that Niri means well.

Our old mother says to tell you that she is in good health and doing well. She is now with our sister who has just had a little girl named Gunhilda Oline. Write as soon as you get this letter. No more except that all here send their regards and that you both are lovingly greeted from me and my wife and our children. Farewell from your always-faithful brother,

H. G. BRANSON

. ——— .

Branson is an Americanization of the patronymic Gulbrandsen. HGB, his wife Margaret, and their eleven-month-old son Gulbrand emigrated in 1843, first to Dane County, Wisc., and then on to the area near Eureka in 1858. HGB's mother, Sigrid Reiersdatter, had recently come to Kansas with her daughter and son-in-law, Kari Gulbrandsdatter and Gullik Gulliksen Bringe, and their three daughters. Ole Christensen Mesundt was only fourteen in 1871. In 1865 Niri Gudbrandsen lived with his parents on the husmannsplass (croft) Kolkinn. He was then twenty-five. The Oklahoma Territory was not opened for settlers until 22 April 1889. «I:130 »II:17 NE III:89

. ——— .

1871 — LETTER 2:9

FROM: Iver Ellingsen Elsrud, *St. Ansgar, Iowa, 23 July 1871*
To: Elling and Olea Elsrud, *Aadalen, Ringerike, Buskerud*

Dear parents and siblings,

It is so long since I last wrote that I feel it is my duty to write even though I don't really have time for it and my back aches and my fingers are so stiff that I can hardly hold my pen. Harvest is upon us. Many have done theirs and it seems to be a bad year for wheat. There are lots of oats. I'm in fairly good health and doing well, for which I owe thanks to God alone. There is uncommonly much illness abroad, mostly typhus and the ague that many die of. I can tell you that I've bought two one-year-old foals for 125 dollars. You may find this expensive but they were cheap considering the prices for horses here and they are unusually large and beautiful. I have driven Uncle's horses and mowing machine for two days and his horse and rake for half a day and in this time I cut and stacked fourteen tons of hay, more than enough for two foals, I think, but since I plan to buy some calves in the fall it is best to have enough.

Erik Lia sends his regards. He works for a farmer near us. Fingal and Syver Fosholt went west last spring to look for land, but the land was not yet on the market so they are working on the railroad until it can be bought, probably next fall. Then Erik and I will also go there to get land and become farmers. A few days ago Uncle had a letter from Erik Haugerud where he asks me to give you his regards and thank you for the letter you sent him. Uncle Ole sends his regards and says that he and his family are well. As I have nothing to write about that will interest you I must conclude with friendly regards to all my friends, hoping that you will all be well when you see this. Loving regards from your faithful son and brother,

I. E. ELSRUD

IEE emigrated in 1869 and lived with his mother's brother Ole Olsen Haugerud the Younger. His uncle Erik Olsen Haugerud was prospecting in Australia. IEE wrote frequent letters to his parents, siblings, and friends in Aadalen, and only a few of these can be included here. On 17 February 1873 he wrote a short letter to two brothers and gave them a brief survey of his recent income and expenses, and concluded: "Here you can see what incomes and expenses are like in America and I believe that he who will work can do well here, yes better than any other place I know of." «I:167 »II:26 NE III:91

1871 — LETTER 2:10

FROM: Kari and Johan Bergman, *Waco, Texas, 24 July 1871*

To: Peder Eriksen and Siri Kristiansdatter Furuset
Romedal, Stange, Hedmark

Dear parents and siblings,

I will take up my pen and answer your very welcome letter. I'm glad that you all are in good health and I can say the same from us. I see that you haven't received the letter I wrote last spring. I've been waiting and longing for a letter from you but not received any, so I thought that you had forgotten me. But I must now excuse you since you haven't received my letter. So I'll have to repeat some of it and tell you that I'm married to a Swedish shoemaker whose name is Johan Bergman. We've been married more than a year and have had a son who was a great joy for us! He was so big and clever. But he was called away from us and is now dead. Yes, it is very sad and difficult for us now. He was three months old. He had dysentery and was very sick for eight days. It wasn't easy for me as I was also sick the whole time with a breast infection. I often thought that I would have been so glad if mother had been here, but my wish could not be fulfilled and this is something I must accept.

I'll now tell you how we get along here. We first rented a house for ten dollars a month for nine months and then we bought a town lot for 275 dollars and built a brick house that cost us a thousand dollars. Yes, you will realize that the cent goes as fast as we can get it, but now we live comfortably in our own home. The Dahl people send their regards. They are all well and doing as usual and expect a letter from you. Remember us to Dillerud and Vold. Please write to us. Erik and Pauline could write and tell me what they are doing. I'll send our portraits the next time I write. Dear parents, please send us your portraits. This would greatly please us as we may not see each other more in this life. It would be something to remember you by as long as I live. Please write to us as soon as possible; I expect a long letter. I must end my simple letter with our regards to you all and in particular to you my dear parents,

JOHAN BERGMAN

· —— ·

This continues the series of letters from Texas to the farm Furuset in Stange in the first volume. It is the last letter from their daughter Kari, who died a few months after she wrote. She signed with her husband's name but the letter was hers. Emigrants from Dillerud and Vold in Stange changed their names to Dilrud and Wold in Texas. «1:162 »II:18 NE III:92

· —— ·

1871 — LETTER 2:11

FROM: Gunder Larson Graven, *Wanamingo, Minnesota, 3 August 1871*

To: Lars Holan, *Katval, Stjørdal, Nord-Trøndelag*

Dear brother in the Lord, Lars Holan,

I know that you appreciate hearing from us here on the other side of the ocean, so I'll again take up my pen to send you a few words and a heartfelt greeting. First I can tell you that we are, praise God, in good health. I've been well all the time since I came here. Marit was ill for some time last winter but has since been well. She likes it here and now I'm more satisfied than I was before. We have no concern for our bodily needs as there is plenty of food and the prices are low and wages are good even though I haven't earned much because I've traveled a lot and the railroads are expensive. Last winter I traveled for about a month in Minnesota. I visited Norwegian settlements and found quite a few people of faith who hold on to the old acknowledged truths that we loved and embraced in Norway. These are usually members of the Elling Eielsen Synod that is called the Evangelical Lutheran Church in America. I, too, am a member here as we cling to everything in the Lutheran doctrine that is in accordance with the Word of the Bible. For this we are for the most part scorned and derided. You know how it is in Norway, that he who is born in the flesh persecutes him who is born in the spirit, but this must be so that Scripture may come to pass; as the Lord has said, I will put enmity between you and the woman, and between woman's seed and the serpent's seed and this enmity shall not end as long as the Lord allows seed on the earth. It is therefore a poor sign of Christian faith when it is at peace and agreement with the world.

This summer I've traveled for about two months in the West as far as Dakota. I first went to Iowa for a Synod conference where many of our pastors and lay people were gathered, among them Eielsen from whom I can send greetings. He is as well as when he was in Norway and he is almost always on the road preaching the Word of God. I've just returned home. In Iowa I went 465 miles with a team of horses and for the most part I spent the nights in my wagon, but the weather was nice. I have greetings from the old believing friends there and in particular from Tommas Leren. He was in reasonably good health and was doing well in worldly matters but the most important was that I not only found him the true witness he has been but that he seems to have purified his testimony and this made me glad. I have more fear for Erik and Ole Hofstad because of the testimony of believing Christians who had heard and seen how he worked. It seemed that Tommas and Erik were enemies but I didn't get to know why.

I went about 120 miles to Dakota and back again, mostly on foot since they rarely have horses in such new settlements and their oxen are too slow when you have far to go and have to go fast. I met many well-known believers, mainly from Trøndelag, who have taken land there. And you may be sure that it was good for us to meet each other in this new and foreign land. All were not doing so well in worldly matters because it is difficult for poor people to go so far west and take land in the new settlements as all are in the same situation and cannot be of help to each other. Even though they get their land for almost nothing, all they need to cultivate the land, including hired help, is so expensive that it is difficult before they have returns from their land and their animals. But this year the land fed them. I was there for their harvest in July when all they had planted in February and March was ready for an early harvest. The soil up there is rich and bountiful even though it was very hot and dry this summer as it was the year before, and this has not been good for their harvest. From Dakota I took a train to Minnesota and this cost me about seventeen dollars in addition to my other expenses. In the course of two months I covered between nine and ten hundred miles and I met Norwegians almost everywhere. A few here and there were believing children of God but the others are either enemies of the Cross of Christ or worship their belly as their God and are unashamed of their love of the world. Moreover, people are exposed to an abundance of sects. We live in Goodhue County where there are many members of our synod. But we will probably soon go to Dakota as the friends there have prayed for our return. The land looks beautiful and harvest has begun here too.

You may wish to hear about Ylvisaker. As you know, he has joined the Norwegian state church pastors in the Wisconsin Synod and is opposed to us. Not long ago he complained that I held meetings in his congregation and tried to stop me. It seems that he is an enemy of the believers and opposed to the work of lay preachers so we are at odds and he no longer has the support of believers. So this is how it goes for those who come to America to be great and powerful.

Give greetings from us, my dear brother, to all friends you meet. Tell Marit Forbord and the widow in Stenvik that in Dakota I visited Eli and Mattias in their home. They had a nice farm. Eli was not in good health and I hope this will further her salvation. I have waited for a letter from you for quite some time but I now realize that I forgot to write my address when I last wrote. In conclusion, heartfelt regards from me and my wife to you and your wife,

G. L. GRAVEN

· —— ·

GLG (1831–1903) was from the small farm Gravanes in Øksendal, Møre og Romsdal. He had been a shoemaker and itinerant lay preacher before emigrating in 1870. In 1871 he was ordained in the Eielsen Synod and served congregations in the Dakota Territory. The handwriting makes it difficult to be sure of the name of Tommas Leren: The family name is a conjecture (Leren is a farm name in Stjørdal). Erik and Ole Hofstad were from Stjørdal, and Ole was a lay preacher in the Dakota Territory before he was ordained in 1873 in the Augustana Synod. Niels Thorbjørnsen Ylvisaker, born in Sogndal in 1832, had been an itinerant lay preacher before he emigrated in 1868. He was ordained in the Norwegian Synod and first served a congregation in Red Wing, Minn., where the Eielsen Synod had a school. NE III:93

· —— ·

1871 — LETTER 2:12

FROM: Gunder Helgesen Skare, *Minneapolis, Minnesota, 25 August 1871*

To: Helge Gundersen Skare, *Eggedal, Sigdal, Buskerud*

⟶⟫◦⟪⟵

Dear and unforgettable father,

It is so long since I last wrote to you that I cannot delay it any longer. As I now have both time and opportunity I must send you a few lines and let you know how I am in this new land America. I will first let you know that, praise God for his goodness, I've been in reasonably good health since I left you, and health is one of our best gifts in our earthly pilgrimage, and we must not forget to thank God for his great grace and mercy toward us poor sinners. I can tell you that my brother was ill last winter and had to keep to his bed almost until spring but he is now well and he and his family are in good health. I can also tell you that Gunder Johnsen Moen and his family are in good health, as are Ole Evensen Jellum and his family and your other acquaintances around here. For this we owe God our thanks.

I can tell you that I worked for my brother last winter. I cut wood and cared for his animals and this was only a little of what I did last winter. It is not as in the old country where the women tend the animals. Here the men have to do this because it is so cold in the winter that the poor girls cannot do it. I should tell you a little about what I've done. I bought some land two and a half years ago only one and a half mile from my brother's land. I bought it from a Norwegian and paid 490 dollars. It is good land with forest and prairie. I haven't yet broken any of it but I plan to break a good deal next summer as well as build a house and do some fencing. Much needs to be done on new land before it will yield anything.

Now I must tell you about the journey Johan Evensen Jellum and I went on last spring to look for land. We left on June first and wandered around for a full month and we were 400 miles from here looking for land. Two and a half years ago Johan sold his land to Gunder Johnsen Moen for 700 dollars and he now wanted to take new land and this was also my intention. We went as far west as Becker County and looked around there and then went to Clay County close to the Wild Rice River where there is some good land with prairie and forest, but it is not yet safe to live there as there are hundreds of thousands of Indians. We were close to the Red River Valley but we did not take any land.

I must now tell you that my brother bought the land of Ole Evensen Jellum last spring for 700 dollars and Ole bought new land about four miles from here and got better land in return. I must end these simple lines with heartfelt greetings to you my dear father and siblings. Give my regards to my brother and his family as well as to Steinar Klev and his family and Halvor G. Skadeland and his family. Fare well with God. Your faithful friend,

GUNDER HELGESEN SKARE

GHS also wrote to his father 8 September 1871 (Nor. ed. III:98) about his dissatisfaction with his new country, warning others not to emigrate. His brother was Halvor Gundersen Skare. As so often in these letters the spelling of place names is based on how they heard them pronounced: *Beækker Kounty, Elee kounty, VilRersrever,* and *Redreverdalen.* Clay County is a conjecture. «I:158 »II:35 NE III:96

1871 — LETTER 2:13

FROM: Barbro Tollefsdatter Sando, *Estherville, Iowa, 1 September 1871*

To: Randi Tollefsdatter Opheim, *Aal, Buskerud*

Dear sister and family,

At last I can send you some sentences. First I must ask you to forgive me for not writing earlier. One reason is that I cannot use the pen myself so writing is always postponed, but another is that we wanted to send you our portrait with my letter and until recently we've not had an opportunity to have one taken. I must also thank you for all your letters. In the last one we saw that you were all in good health and this made us glad. All of us are as usual in good health. For my own part I get weaker with the years and we must hope that God in his mercy will help us carry our cross patiently and believe that it will be to our good. I suppose I should tell you a little about our family now that it is so long since you've heard from us. Our oldest son Erik was married two years ago to a girl from Voss named Sigri Larsdatter Hovde. Last May they had a son they named Oliver Ludvik who is growing and thriving. Our second son Tollef was married last week to Birgit Halvorsdatter. Ole left home August 26 for St. Louis to study theology. His health isn't so good but with God's help he hopes to complete his studies. Halvor, Berthe and Gjermund are at home and in good health. Berthe will prepare for confirmation next winter. Our brother Ole the Elder moved last spring with his family to Rock County, Minnesota, about sixty miles to the west, where he and his three oldest sons found free land. We recently had a letter from them and they were all in good health and doing well. Lars Eriksen Sando, who had been in bed all of last winter with tuberculosis, died in his sleep last May 12, believing, we hope, in his Savior. He is survived by his wife and their eight children, the oldest of whom is sixteen. May the Lord, the defender of widows, be her support.

You must tell our brother Haagen that we had a letter from him some time ago. Thank him and say I'll soon try to write to him. Give my regards to Guri Bøygard and to Knut Trintrud, who perhaps will send us a few lines. Heartfelt regards to you and your family from your always devoted sister,

BARBRO TOLLEFSDATTER SANDO

You must excuse this short letter. An American is hardly capable of writing letters to Norway. Nevertheless, you and all relatives over there are sent friendly greetings from the writer of this letter, who is

HALVOR O. SANDO

· ——— ·

BTS has dictated her letter to her son Halvor Olsen Sando. Although the address is missing, the letter must be to her sister Randi Tollefsdatter, who was married to Sevat Bjørnsen Opheim. BTS's brother in Minnesota was Ole Tollefsen Opsata. His daughter Margit wrote to her uncle Haagen Tollefsen Opsata on 8 December 1872 (Nor. ed. III:137). Her brother Ole the Younger had emigrated to St. Ansgar, Iowa. Lars Eriksen Sando was her brother-in-law. In 1867 her younger brother Haagen (or Haakon) had taken over the family farm at Opsata in Aal. She also wrote letters to her sister Guri Tollefsdatter Bøygard. In the 1850s the Norwegian Synod began to send students to the Concordia Seminary of the German-language Missouri Synod in St. Louis, and from 1859 the Norwegian Synod had a professor there with a special responsibility for their students. This arrangement lasted until 1876–1878 when the Norwegian Synod established its own theological seminary in Madison, Wisc. «I:117 »II:62 NE III:97

· ——— ·

FROM: Ole Olson Lee, *Mount Vernon, Wisconsin, 14 September 1871*

To: Anders Olsen Lie, *Hedalen, Sør-Aurdal, Oppland*

To Anders O. Lie,

As time permits I will in all brevity and just for fun take up my pen to send you a few simple sentences even though I don't have anything to write about that can be of interest for you because there haven't been any changes and all is as it has been. I can tell you that we and all relatives are in good health and doing reasonably well and I hope we may receive the same information from you. We have recently completed our harvest so I'll tell you a little about our crops. Last spring was early so we planted most of our spring wheat in March and the good weather continued so we had the best of hopes for a good harvest. But we were unable to see far ahead and contrary to all our hopes we had a mediocre harvest as far as wheat is concerned. But barley, oats and corn turned out quite well. The wheat was damaged by drought and rust but even more by the bug that devoured it so it shriveled. But the bug was not so bad everywhere: in some places it took everything and in others very little; some didn't even bother to harvest most of their fields because it wouldn't be worth the labor. The so-called wheat bug is a very destructive plague. It is a tiny fly, smaller than a mosquito, black with a white stripe on its wings and it is so dense that at its worst it was like an anthill. It attacks the wheat in the root and sucks out the sap so that it dries up whether it is ripe or not. On my and our brother Guttorm's farm the plague was neither at its worst nor its best.

This summer was as dry as last year but we had a little more rain in spring. Later we had much less and this continues with a hot sun and wind. So if we don't soon get some rain we'll not be able to plow our fields this fall. This will be bad for us as the soil is so dry and hard that it is impossible to get the plow into it. I've plowed about fourteen acres but I could have plowed much more if this had been possible. My wheat harvest this year was 270 bushels, seventy bushels more than last year, but I had planted eight more acres of new field so I had less per acre. For fun I'll tell you that I no longer use oxen. I sold them and bought horses last winter, a mare and a horse, two-year-olds, full bodied and trustworthy and good workhorses, so I can drive faster now but they are expensive to keep. It costs four dollars just to get them shod and thirty-five for a plain harness and all else at comparable prices.

Guttorm and his family are in good health and doing well. Halsten Børtnes has been well and quite satisfied and he is glad that he came here. He says that Mikkel and Anders Lie are making shoes and I wish you all success in your work. I could need a pair of shoes and a pair of boots this fall, so perhaps you will come here and make them for me, but it has to be done before Christmas. I almost forgot my most important news. Marit H. Klemmetsrud is remarried to a widower from Gudbrandsdalen who has two children and a forty land. I know no more about it. I should have written more but there is no space. So I'll conclude with the wish that you'll write to us as soon as possible. Loving greetings from your devoted brother,

OLE O. LEE AND FAMILY

. ——— .

OOL had emigrated in 1865, his brother Guttorm in 1858. Their nephew Halsten Børtnes, a son of their sister Olea Olsdatter Børtnes, had just arrived from Norway. He had been preceded by his half-sister Olaug in 1867 and a brother Ole followed in 1873. Mikkel, who is making shoes with his father Anders on the family farm Søre Li, emigrated in 1881. The standard term for a fourth of a quarter section in these letters is *en førti*, that is "a forty." It is not clear whether the writer meant a fourth or "a forty," but the meaning would be the same: forty acres. «I:164 »II:52 NE III:99

. ——— .

1871 — LETTER 2:15

FROM: Thor Torstensen Vigenstad, *Marlin, Texas, 24 September 1871*

TO: Paul Torstensen Vigenstad, *Madison, Wisconsin*

⁘⇒◯⇐⁘

Dear brother,

You've probably been waiting for a letter and this is the third Sunday I have a sheet of paper before me trying to write so now I must do it even though my eyes are full of sleep as I've worked most of the night. I am, praise God, in good health and doing well. We've not yet had any rain and they say that at the *Sentnor* Railroad they have to go seven miles for water for their workers. It is difficult for me to say anything about what you wrote about those at home. If they come on our advice and are dissatisfied it will be tough for us. But I think that at least Ole could come; if he doesn't like it he can return.

This summer we had a lot of grapes and plums but like everything else here they were inedible because they were as sour as old whey. I haven't found any other fruit here. For some days it's been rather lively in town as the Republicans and Democrats are fighting. All whites are Democrats and all blacks are Republicans. It went so far on election day that the white shot at the black. Every white man brought his gun with him to the courthouse.

You wrote that I should buy some things in Chicago when I come but I think the price is just as good in St. Louis. I think I'll go by steamboat to St. Paul as this will be cheapest. Tell me a little about how things are when you write as I haven't seen a newspaper since I came here. Tell me how great the difference is between gold and paper money and if it seems that gold will fall in price. I will conclude with the best wishes from your brother,

THOR

· —— ·

When PV sent this and other letters from TV to his family in Dovre he noted in a margin: "Two or three of Thor's letters have disappeared and I have torn off parts of a few others for some notes and I cannot now find them." It is difficult to guess what may have been meant by the *Sentnor* railroad. It may be TM's poor English spelling or a mis-understanding by the person who has copied the Vigenstad letters. It could be the Texas Central Railroad. Thor also wrote from Marlin on 18 November 1871 (Nor. ed. III:104). «II:5 »II:19 NE III:100

1871 — LETTER 2:16

FROM: Rakel Tonette, Berent and Berte T. Allikson
Medo, Minnesota, 29 September 1871

To: Osmund Atlaksen Ovedal, *Sirdal, Vest-Agder*

Dear brother Osmund,

I must take up my pen to let you know that I'm doing well to this date, for which I must thank God. I would like to hear the same from you. I'm with Syvert as usual. I must tell you that our brother Berent and Berte came here August 5 and were a week with Sigbjørn before they came here. Berent has been sickly since he arrived but is now better and has begun to work a little. Thank you for the very welcome book you sent me. I've long thought of writing to you but nothing has come of it. I had a letter from Reinert, Sara and Siri August 6 and they are doing well. Siri visited Coon Prairie this summer and Sigbjørn and his family are doing well. I must tell you that Hans Øxendal left yesterday with his family to go about 100 miles to the west where he wished to take land. We've had very nice weather this summer and the crops are good. Syvert hasn't threshed yet. He has four oxen, five cows and two pigs. Fredrik Oftedal has bought land for 150 dollars and they moved on the twenty-fifth of this month. They are about two miles from Tønnes A. I have no special news. Since I haven't had a letter from you for a long time I'll ask you to write as soon as you receive this letter. Say hello to Olene and all relatives and friends. I must now conclude my simple letter with my sincere greetings.

R. TONETTE ALLIKSON

Dear brother Osmund,

I must take my pen to let you know that we've come to our destination and I like what I've seen up to now. I've been sickly since arriving but now I'm better. I only had to be in bed for two days. We've felt no longing. All went well on the journey. We came to La Crosse July 25 and to Coon Prairie on the twenty-seventh. We walked about thirty miles from La Crosse to Sigbjørn and many of the settlers were German. We were glad to find our brother Sigbjørn and Uncle Haavard and Gabriel Jødestøl and their families and they were all doing well. Sigbjørn Haavardson drove us back to La Crosse August 3 and then we went on a steamboat and then on the railroad and on August 5 we came to Sivert and I like it here in Minnesota. I've bought a small cow for twenty-six dollars and it milks twelve to fourteen quarts a day. She calved in April. There is an abundance of grass for hay here. Sivert has only cut grass around the house and between fields and the grass is so long that it goes above the knee. I bought the books you asked me to and they cost three dollars each. I must now conclude my simple letter with greetings from us both. Farewell.

BERENT A. ALLIKSON AND BERTE

·———·

These two letters are in the same envelope. Now that Berent has emigrated with his wife Berte, Osmund is the only remaining sibling at Ovedal. In 1865 there were three siblings living at Ovedal: Osmund, the farmer, was forty-five, Sara, the housekeeper, was forty-three, and Berent, thirty-eight, is listed as a cooper. They were all unmarried. In 1865 Berte T. Sigbjørnsdatter was twenty-two and lived on her father's farm Lindeland, in Sirdal As noted in Volume 1, there is at times a discrepancy in the age given in passenger lists and the census. Berent and Berte Ovedal sailed on *Nordens Dronning* (the Queen of the North) from Stavanger on 13 May 1871 and arrived in Quebec on 14 July. They are here listed as being thirty-nine and thirty-seven. Siri Allikson wrote to her brother from Eau Claire on 22 December 1871 (Nor. ed. III:107). She had sent him a subscription for *Kirkelig Maanedstidende*, the monthly published by the Norwegian Synod. Osmund Ovedal also corresponded with other former neighbors; only letters from his siblings are included here. «I:144 »II:24 NE III:101

·———·

FROM: Hellek G. Branson, *Eureka, Kansas, 28 November 1871*

To: Ole Gulbrandsen Lande, *Flesberg, Buskerud*

Dear brother and wife,

Thank you for your letter of August 21. You must excuse me for not having replied before. I'll try to answer your questions as well as I can. As for the climate sickness I think you, like others, will have it for a while. But we didn't think of it as a dangerous disease. We don't have a high death rate as only three Norwegians have died in four years; two of them of old age and the third of a stomach infection. I don't think it matters whether people are lean or fat. When Gullik came here Ragnhild was the fattest in their group and she has not had any climate sickness, so you may also go free. But you must be prepared for both eventualities.

As for your prospects, I'm sure that it will be better for you here than in Norway. As for work, you alone can cut and gather hay for two to four hundred head of cattle since all you have to do is sit and ride as if you were in a cariole. For stacking you would have to hire two men for one and a half months. That would cost you sixty dollars and you would have hay for two or three hundred head of cattle. Horses, wagon, harness, mowing machine, and rake would cost about 500 dollars. I'm writing this because when you come you should buy 200 Texas yearlings, heifers and bulls. They cost about four to seven dollars apiece and after you have had them for one year you will get about fifteen dollars apiece.

You may not know where you could cut all that hay, but you can do it on my land or on Gullik's land or on Ole and Hellik Kolkinn's land. You may cut as much as you want for free on my or my sons' land. But if you don't drive around yourself and throw out hay for your cattle during winter you will need to hire a man to tend the cattle and give them hay. I'm writing this so that you may place your money in a business right away and if you have a larger capital than this then you can place your money in a bank in Eureka and get interest and then you can take it out again whenever you have an opportunity to buy land or anything else. As for bringing some poor people with you I think you would be doing them a favor, especially old Gunhild and those in Soli. You must not believe that they will be of any use to you, but I don't think they will be a burden for you either.

Last summer there was more illness than usual all over America. There wasn't so much where my sons live sixty miles to the southwest from here. They are both home just now and send their regards. They are in good health. Kittil Funrud went eight days ago to visit family and friends in Norway and if you come here next spring I suppose you will go with him. If Kittil doesn't return to Kansas he can advise you on your journey. Well, I cannot advise you one way or the other even though we live in a free and fertile country, because we are still in the world and that has its troubles both here and on other continents. Your decision to go or not to go must be firm. There are people here pretty much as in Norway. If you come I'll help you with the buying and selling of cattle to the best of my experience. This also goes for land and machinery and whatever.

No more now except that all the Norwegians here are well as far as I know. Our old mother says that if you come you must bring a book on midwifery that she lent to Kari Berget. And Ragnild asks you to please tell her mother that she is in good health and that she has written to Wisconsin but not had any reply. You must ask her mother to write immediately about whether she has heard anything from Wisconsin. She is working for a very wealthy American but right now she is here on a visit. She has had her position for a year. When her mother writes she must let her know whether she has had any assistance from Wisconsin. Give her regards to all her relatives and friends and also to old Guri Kolkinn. Our old mother sends her regards to you both and says she is in fairly good health. I also send regards from Gullik and his family that they are in good health and doing well. First and last our loving regards from me and my wife and sons. Farewell.

H. G. BRANSON

. ——— .

HGB's sister Ragnhild was married to Gullik Gulliksen Bringe. They had emigrated with their three daughters and her mother Sigri Reiersdatter (who had been a midwife in Flesberg), probably in 1868 (see I:133). The Ragnhild mentioned in the last paragraph has not been identified. Gunhild Sjulsdatter, a widow aged fifty-eight in 1865, was head of the small household on Solid, a small husmannsplass that in 1865 also fed an unmarried mother and her daughter. Hellik Kolkinn was from the croft Kolkinn in Flesberg and is probably the Hellik Gulbrandsen who is listed in 1865 as a servant on the farm Lande, owned by HGB's brother, Ole Gulbrandsen, and who was a passenger on the *S. S. Oder* from Christiania to Hull in 1868. «II:8 »II:29 NE III:105

1871 — LETTER 2:18

FROM: Hendrik Olsen Dahl, *Norse, Texas, 10 December 1871*

To: Peder Eriksen and Siri Kristiansdatter Furuset
Romedal, Stange, Hedmark

Dear parents-in-law,

We have waited for a long time and not heard anything from you, so I'll send you a few words and tell you that we are all in good health and we hope soon to hear the same from you. On November 14 Christine had a big and beautiful girl and was soon well again. The child has not been baptized yet but her name will be Caroline. I assume you have received the sad news from your son-in-law John Bergman that your dear daughter left this world on October 23 after being in bed for fourteen days with an illness similar to typhoid fever. They let us know that she was very ill and Christine would have gone down and spoken with her, but she was expecting any day so she couldn't go anywhere. Should you demand a division of inheritance I think this may be done, but I don't think it will be worth the bother. They have had great expenses in the short time they had together. When their child died they owed the doctor 100 dollars and when Kari got ill they had two doctors and I have seen the bill from one of them and it was seventy-five dollars. He had not then seen the other one but he believed it would be a little less. The coffin cost thirty dollars. When they married he had between 200 and 300 dollars and Kari had about seventy and for this they bought a lot and built a nice little house and were very comfortable. But should he sell now in these hard times I don't believe he would get what it cost him. Kari had a nice rocking chair that she had given to Christine before she died and since then Bergman has sent us her suitcase with some of her clothes and some small things. Christine got a lock of Kari's hair and is sending you half. The small lock is from our little Caroline and this patch is from Kari's shroud.

We had a poor harvest this year so times are hard, but even though our crop was only half of what is usual, it was of excellent quality and there are high prices for all grains. Prices are low for horses and cattle but we can keep them until times are better. Our tax is higher than usual; I paid it yesterday and it was ninety-one dollars. There is no poor tax but we now have a free school for our children, something we didn't have before. Syverine is attending confirmation classes and there will be a confirmation service this winter. We've had a nice fall, so the wheat looks good.

Horses and cattle are still doing well. Jens sends his regards and asks you to remember him to his father at Fjæstad. His health is good and he hasn't been sick for one hour since he arrived. He is a good boy and will do well here if he continues to be healthy. I hope you'll write soon as we haven't heard from you for a long time. I don't know of more that will be of interest to you and will conclude my simple letter with loving regards to all siblings and relatives and first and foremost to our parents from your devoted children and grandchildren.

H. O. DAHL

I am thinking of coming for a visit next summer. Tell Anders Bryni that the boy he sent has arrived and is in good health.

. ——— .

> Jens Larsen Fjæstad and the boy sent by Anders Bryni are instances of the many single young people who emigrated with prepaid tickets for agricultural labor. HOD visited Norway in 1872 and the next letter in the Furuset series is from his wife Christine Dahl. «II:10 »II:25
> NE III:106

. ——— .

FROM: Thor Torstensen Vigenstad, *Marlin, Texas, 26 December 1871*

To: Paul Torstensen Vigenstad, *Madison, Wisconsin*

Dear brother,

As it's now Christmas I'll use my pen to wish you a Merry Christmas and a Happy New Year. Praise God for all the good he has granted us miserable sinners in the year that soon is past. May the mighty God bless and protect us in the New Year. May the grace and peace of our Lord Jesus Christ be with you! Dear brother, this is the fourth time I celebrate Christmas since I left our dear home. Here there is no Christmas to be seen. All stores are open and each and all tend to their work. There have been many accidents due to drunkenness. Two have been shot and killed and another one was shot in the knee and they had to take off his leg. One of the men who sleeps in the same tent as I do had his head cut with a shovel and two have been hurt in their faces and hands. We've had a long spell of very nice working weather but soon there will be no more work here and I don't know where I'll go then. As I have some money I hope that you write me as soon as you have this letter and tell me how I best can have it sent to you, as it is not safe to walk around with it here. I don't know when I'll come so it would be best to have precise information on how to send it. I have no more to write about now and will conclude with loving regards from your brother,

THOR VIGENSTAD

«II:15 »II:22 NE III:108

From: Jul Gulliksen Dorsett, *Bratsberg, Minnesota, 13 January 1872*

To: Torstein Gulliksen Daaset, *Flesberg, Buskerud*

Dear brothers,

A few days ago I received your letter of October 21 and I'm glad to hear that you are doing well where you are and that you don't think of coming here. Since you say that you are satisfied and have good prospects I'll not say anything for or against coming here. Because if one is to have a living here he cannot walk on roses or be lazy but must work hard, and it is not only the hard work that makes it difficult but the heat that we usually have late in July and in early August that can be as much as twenty-five or thirty or more degrees Réaumur, and then you may imagine that we sweat. But with a good health and strength and when you get used to it, it is all right. As for our harvest, we didn't have as much wheat as last year because of a long dry spell. Some say about half, others two thirds. But my corn and oats did as well as last year if not better, and this depends, as it does in Norway, on what kind of soil you have. Here we have both dry and rich soil and I have some of both.

As for politics it now seems that most people, and that means the Republicans who now are the governing party, are satisfied with our current President (Grant) and according to the president's speech at the opening of Congress it appears that the past year must be regarded as a good one for the United States. Every month several millions of dollars are paid on the immense debt that the country is in because of the great war that raged here a few years ago even though duties on many things have been considerably reduced so that some products are not as outrageously expensive as they were during the war. Coffee now costs between twenty and thirty cents, sugar twelve to sixteen cents, tobacco sixty to seventy cents, pork four to four and a half, butter twelve to twenty, all according to quality and for the pound. Cotton materials are not all that expensive and linen is fifteen to eighteen cents a yard. Wheat is now at one dollar and five cents, corn at forty cents, oats at thirty-three to thirty-five cents a bushel. But for these products prices vary.

I would be glad to hear from you soon and let me know if many have gone here from Flesberg since you last wrote. Please note that the terrible fires that raged in Minnesota and northern Wisconsin (that you probably know about from the newspapers) hardly did any damage in this area, for which we must thank God. The prairie fire and forest fire may be terrible here when it is loose because of all the dry grass. In the great forests it is not within human power to stop a fire until there is so much rain that it stops of itself. And with this I will conclude my story as I send you all my loving regards.

JUEL DOSET

. ———— .

In the Réaumur scale water freezes at 0° and boils at 80°. «II:7 »II:43
NE III:I I I

. ———— .

1872 — LETTER 2:21

FROM: Arne Jørgensen and Karen Olsdatter Brager
Black Earth, Wisconsin, 25 May 1872

To: Johan Olsen and Lisbeth Brændhagen, *Vang, Hedmark*

⋆⟾◎⟾⋆

Dear brother and family,

We were glad to receive your letter dated October 30 last December. You may, with good reason, be surprised that we haven't written to you earlier. This is due partly to my negligence and partly to my daily work. But I hope we are forgiven. We found your letter very interesting as it told us how things are in our dear home. Your account of your dear wife giving birth to a healthy girl who then died while you were away made us sad. But then we must join you in thanking the good God who in his wisdom does everything for our best and has called the child away from this evil world and up to the heavenly home where there is neither sorrow nor tears. For the kingdom of God is for such as them, says Mark the Evangelist.

I will to the best of my ability tell you a little about our present situation. You know that last year my father and I worked a small farm on shares. This did not go well as the harvest was poor and the prices low. We earned almost nothing and wasted our labor and money. I was a fool to take on another farm this year and I fear the result will be the same. We have something called a bug in English. It attacks the root of the wheat and sucks out the juice and it has already started to do its damage. The outcome is uncertain but we must lay all in the hand of God. I have nineteen acres of wheat, nine of oats, three of corn and half an acre of potatoes in addition to some grass for hay. My share is half of everything.

Next year, God willing and if we have life and health, I plan to go west or north in Wisconsin to look for land, as there are many areas that have not been cultivated and where one may have four forties or 160 acres according to the Homestead Law which says that anyone who is a citizen and twenty-one years of age may pay fourteen dollars for the first papers and then, after having lived on the land for five years, acquire the proper deed.

If you should plan to come here you must let us know. For my part I will not advise for or against emigration, but I do believe that it is easier for a laborer to support himself and his family here. But it is not as most people believe, that when you come to America there are riches and bounty for all. No, the world is always the world and it has its troubles. You ask about Karen's health and she has been well since giving birth to our first child and little Gunild has also been healthy. I on the other hand have been rather poorly these last six months. I've been to a doctor and received some medicine that has helped quite a lot. Little Gunild is big and is growing; she now runs on the floor as fast as she wants to.

I will give you a brief account of our animals. One cow and a calf, one pig with four piglets, and four hens are all we have. Will you please write some lines home to Anne and father and tell them how we are as we haven't written to them for a long time. Anne has asked for assistance but we cannot possibly do anything as money is short and we hardly have an income. We would like to know how things are for Oline and also Even and <u>old father</u> and little Christian. And in conclusion we must send you our best wishes wherever you may go. Our most loving regards from your always faithful sister and brother,

KAREN AND ARNE BRAGER

Next fall, if God grants us life and health, we will have our portraits taken and send them to you.

· ——— ·

«II:4 »II:28 NE III:119

· ——— ·

1872 — LETTER 2:22

FROM: Paul Torstensen Vigenstad, *Fergus Falls, Minnesota, 28 May 1872*

To: Ole Torstensen Vigenstad, *Dovre, Oppland*

My dear family there at home!

A long time has passed since I received your welcome letter but many things have kept me busy, in part things where I wanted to see the outcome. I'm still alone here as brother Thor has not arrived yet, but I expect him any day. I've planted about four acres with wheat, more than six bushels of potatoes and a little corn and garden vegetables. I've bought a cow with a calf; the calf was then about one month old. As you will understand, I now have far too much to do but I don't think I've ever been as persevering in my work as I now am. I hope you will appreciate that it is both necessary and desirable for me to get a helper. This has also been the advice of many friends and neighbors, and yesterday I was engaged to a girl from Toten in Norway. Her name is Johanne Maria Petersdatter Midtboe. I will not try to describe this costly treasure that I hope our Lord has given me but only say that she is extremely clever, very beautiful, and known for her goodness. But she is not wealthy. I wish to have your permission and my father's blessing in your next letter. Last Sunday I went to her parents to ask their permission to marry her because even though I've known her for half a year I had not mentioned this to her as I didn't wish to take a girl away from her parents. As her parents gave their permission without any objections I went yesterday, the day after I had been to her parents, here to Fergus Falls, where she is a cook at a hotel, to have her answer. And as I had hoped on the basis of our close relationship, I received a dear yes and her firm handclasp. So now we are, in the name of God, engaged. She will probably remain here in town for some time before we have our wedding.

On Pentecost Sunday we had confirmation and on Monday holy communion. Sixteen were confirmed. Fourteen were baptized Sunday and eighteen on Monday, but then it had been more than half a year since we last had been visited by a pastor. We have now called a candidate from Norway to be our pastor and if he accepts our call he will come in the fall. If he cannot come we hope to have one from St. Louis. This summer I will again have school for those who are to be confirmed but this will have to be on Sunday afternoons as I will be too busy the other days of the week. At the last meeting in our congregation it was decided to have a school. I was asked to be the teacher, and I accepted. Our settlement has three congregations and I will probably have the school in the central congregation. I live in the northern part of this congregation and have the pleasure of being able to visit two churches, both the northern and the central one. They are both not more than seven miles away.

Our weather is now excellent and our harvest is promising. We had a late spring but more than enough hay. Last year was a difficult one for America. I won't do more on my store until Thor comes as I cannot do it all without doing damage. Today I am going fishing with Peter (the father of the abovementioned Maria) …

. —— .

> The rest of the letter has been lost and one sentence in the last paragraph is unreadable. PV's home was in Norwegian Grove in Ottertail County. His congregation had been established in 1871 and was divided into Northern Immanuel (in Pelican Rapids) and Southern Immanuel (in Rothsay) congregations in 1872 because of the great distances. In Norway the Monday after Pentecost is still a holiday with church services. «II:19 »II:32 NE III:120

. —— .

FROM: Ole Toresen Lande, *Eureka, Kansas, 14 June 1872*
To: Ole Gulbrandsen Lande, *Flesberg, Buskerud*

⊷≈⊙⊂≈⊶

I will now write you a few words and tell you about our journey to America. As you know, we left Kristiania on May 17 and we were in Hull at two in the morning of the twentieth. We stayed on the ship until 8 o'clock and were then taken to a dining house where we had breakfast. At two in the afternoon we left by train and came to Liverpool that evening at eight thirty. We stayed there for three days. On the twenty-third we went onboard and sailed for about four hours, then we anchored for about three hours before we sailed a day and a night and stopped in Ireland where one hundred Irishmen came onboard. At four in the morning of June 3 we sighted land but we did not go on land until the fifth at eleven. We stayed there until midnight. On June 6 at three in the afternoon the railroad car I was in derailed. We were lucky that the train was then going slowly so no one was hurt. At six in the morning of June 7 we came to a town called Point Edward and from there we went on a steamboat across a little river. That only took us fifteen minutes and we came to a town called Port Huron where we parted company with K. Finrud. They left at five in the evening of the eighth but we stayed there that night until we left at seven in the morning. We were in Chicago on the tenth at 6 o'clock. We were there until nine in the evening and on June 11 at nine in the evening we came to Kansas City where we changed trains. On June 12 we came to a city called Topeka where we also changed trains and we left from there on the same day at one in the afternoon. From there we went straight to Emporia where we arrived at five in the afternoon. As we stepped down from the coach a man came up to us and asked if we were Norwegian and asked us if we were going to Eureka. We said yes and then he said that my name is Branson. You will understand that we were glad.

He met us with two horses and a wagon and we left town almost at once. We drove for some time until sunset and we stayed the night at the edge of a forest and we came to Eureka the next day at six in the evening. Old Ole and I were not sick on the voyage but Jøran was a little sick. I have not yet spoken with Gullik nor with Hellik and Jøran Kolkinn but I have met Ole. I must now end my poor letter with greetings to you and your wife.

We found them all in good health, your mother and your brother and his family, and have greetings from them to you and your mother says that she is in good health. You must for all the world excuse my poor writing and not let any stranger see it as it is done so poorly. This will have to be enough for now. Give my regards to Niri Kolkinn and his mother but as I have so little space it will only be this brief greeting this time. Give my regards to all at South Lande. First and last, my best greetings to you both. Please write as soon as possible.

OLE TORESEN LANDE

· ——— ·

OTL was a foster son of Ole Gulbrandsen Lande. In the margin he wrote, "I had almost forgotten to send my regards to your hired man Henrik." The transatlantic steamer seems to have brought them to Quebec or Montreal. In Kansas he has joined Hellik Branson and other members of Ole Gulbrandsen's family. The Branson who met him at the depot was probably a son of Hellik. Ole Gulbrandsen emigrated to Kansas in 1873. «II:17 »II:29 NE III:123

· ——— ·

1872 — LETTER 2:24

FROM: Berent and Rachel Tonette Allikson
Medo, Minnesota, 25 August 1872
To: Osmund Atlakson Ovedal, *Sirdal, Vest-Agder*

⊶⊷

Dear brother Osmund,

We sent you a letter a short time ago about different things as usual but though we hadn't planned to send you news so soon, the Lord now forces us to send you and our relatives and friends the sad message that our brother Sivert is dead. *Just* eight days ago he sat here at the dinner table and was healthier and stronger than any of his siblings and then, no more than two hours later, his soul-less body was laid on the same table where he had just eaten his last meal. On the twelfth Sunday after Trinity, or August 18, it so happened that awhile after dinner Sivert and Hans Madsen Josdal were out on a field and there was a sudden thunderstorm with lightning. Sivert and Hans immediately began to return home, and they were no further from the house than seven or eight stone throws when a lightning bolt struck and they both fell down. It seems that Hans may have been more frightened, so he ran faster and was ahead of Sivert. After Hans had lain unconscious for some time he regained his senses and was able to think a little and realized that the same thing may have happened to Sivert. So he began to look around and then saw that Sivert was lying almost beside him. When he recovered he got up and walked over to Sivert and shook him and also thought that he should call to him, but he realized that there was no life, and as Sivert's clothes were on fire he tried to put it out, and when he couldn't do any more he returned home. We realized that there had been an accident from the expression in his eyes. We asked what had happened and he answered that Sivert was dead. We immediately called on our neighbors and in a few minutes many were gathered, both Norwegians and Americans. Because of the strong heat we had to bury him the next afternoon. Many were gathered at the funeral. We now feel the loss of a dear brother—as we know that you also will. His struggles are over but ours are still with us, and the way we now make use of our precious time of grace will determine our destiny. Alas! The precious time of grace is so often belittled by us all. Now the Lord has given us a warning and we are as the grass that today is growing tall and tomorrow is withered and dead. So let us therefore wake and pray that the Lord shall not find us on the great Day of Judgment among the foolish maidens who did not have oil in their lamps when the call came.

BERNT A. ATLAGSEN   RAKKEL T. ATLAGSDATTER

· ——— ·

Berent, his wife Berte, and Rachel also wrote 31 July (Nor. ed. III:127). They had taken the name Allikson, but the serious occasion may have prompted them to use the Norwegian form. «II:16 »II:27 NE III:129

· ——— ·

FROM: Christine Dahl, *Norse, Texas, 15 September 1872*

To: Hendrik Olsen Dahl, *Romedal, Stange, Hedmark*

＊⇌◉⇋＊

My dear beloved husband,

I've received your welcome letter of August 14 and am glad to see that you've safely crossed the great Atlantic and look forward to seeing your mother. I see that you've been seasick but that you now, praise God, are in good health. I talked with O. Colwick today and he said that he was sure that the sowing machine we had ordered was in Waco so we'll have it in time for this year's planting. The wheat looks good and we haven't yet removed the wheat from our living room. We have so far harvested 840 barrels of corn. We think we'll have in all twelve to thirteen thousand and that we'll have done all the corn this week. Ole has taken over the big mule and broken it in. It is now gentle for riding and easy to handle. We've had very little rain. We have to go to the Walle mill with our grain. Horses and cattle are getting lean and when people go to Waco they have to bring fodder for the oxen as all grass has dried up.

I have the news that Johan Ringnes will be a bridegroom next Friday and the bride is Agnete Hol from Løten. It seems that Mrs. Ringnes is not in favor of the marriage. Ole Brunstad was recently here. He had sold his team to Carl Durry for 600 dollars and he bought mules and a wagon from O. Wold and went back to east Texas to work until Christmas. And O. Wold has bought two pack oxen for himself. This is my fourth letter since you left us; the first was addressed to New York and I hope you got it. I see in your letter that your ship was threatened by a storm. Our safety is in the hands of the almighty God but I also see that you wish you had an overcoat and this is entirely up to you to do something about. So, my dear husband, I will advise you not to expose your health to any danger or suffer any need that you can take care of with money. I can send the money you asked me to send to Galveston if you tell me how much to send and when to send it. I must conclude with loving regards to you my dear husband. Our little Caroline is not feeling so good and I don't know what the matter is, but I suspect she is teething. Except for this, everything is fine here. We are healthy and I wish the same for you. May the Lord protect you and guide you and grant you good health and a happy return journey home to me and your dear children. Give our regards to parents and relatives on both sides. But first and last you, my dear husband, are greeted from me and our children. May the Lord guide you safely home, this is the highest wish of your devoted wife

CHRISTINE DAHL

. ——— .

CD first wrote to her husband three weeks after he had left for Norway via New York about family health, work on the farm (plowing and haying), and, proudly, about their eldest son Ole's first ride on their horse, Symtor (Nor. ed. III:126). She sent frequent letters while Hendrik was in Norway but only two of these have been preserved. Hendrik left Christiania on 2 November 1872 and arrived at the Dahl farm on 22 December with a group of forty emigrants. He was ill on arrival and died 13 January 1873. «II:18 »II:45 NE III:131

. ——— .

1872 — LETTER 2:26

FROM: Iver Ellingsen Elsrud, *St. Ansgar, Iowa, 4 December 1872*

To: Elling and Olea Elsrud, *Aadalen, Ringerike, Buskerud*

⚬⟶○⟵⚬

Dear parents and siblings,

As it's almost a year since you've heard from me I think it is time to let you hear that I'm still alive and, praise God, in good health. I must first ask you to excuse me for not having written earlier and then explain the reason. I left my uncle's May 1 and went west through Minnesota to look at some free land almost up at the land owned by the English in America (Canada), and see whether I could find Fingal Fossholt. I found him on land he had taken in Dakota about 500 miles from here. You may imagine that I saw a lot on this journey, much more than I can tell you, but I will say a little about the Indians that I lived with at the time I worked on the railroad. You may think that the Indians are the enemies of the white man but this is not true because there are many tribes that are very good friends of the whites and one may live in greater safety among them than among the Irish, the shoemakers as Norwegians call them.

I haven't made much money this summer as I've spent it on traveling but I can say with the adage, that it is better with a sore foot than sore longing. As long as one has health, praise God, there is no reason for complaint. And should God punish me with illness I have as good a home as I could possibly wish for with Ole and Maren who are so incredibly good to me. I came here in early August and since then I've worked partly for uncle and partly for others so the only time I've had for writing has been on Sundays and then I have for the most part been to church or had other work to do and this is why I've delayed writing until now. But now all work has been done and my only duties are to tend the animals and chop wood. It is my plan to go to school for two or three months and then I don't know what I'll do because next spring my horses will be big enough for work, but what work? I don't have sufficient savings to buy land but I have thought of working some land on shares. The user of the farm gets two thirds and the owner one third of the harvest, but this is not so good for one who isn't married because it is very expensive to board with others.

Uncle sent me your letter of April 22 but I got it after I had met Fingal. I hope he has written home as he said he would when I saw him. I've also received a letter from Asle to Fingal but I haven't sent it on. I received the clothes you sent me with Ole Brubraaten. Thank you so much, much more than my pen can express! The clothes fit as if I'd been to a tailor. I also have news for you: Hans N. Viger is married to Maren Lunde, uncle Ole's widow. He was the one who brought the clothes for me because he was here courting her several times last summer and he is here now. Dear mother, I see that you want to send me more clothes if I should need them but I think I have enough for the time being. But there is one thing I'll ask you to send the next time you write: some sage seeds. You can put them in small packages inside a letter. You can buy sage seeds here but rarely some that will grow. Sage is sold at the druggists for two to three dollars a pound. Uncle Erik writes to us often and he is doing quite well. It was a fairly good year in America and good prices for farm products so we have relatively good times. Last fall I bought 110 bushels of oats and 100 of corn for which I paid forty-five dollars, a low price. The bill you sent me from Guri Kvernbraaten to Erik Hansen has been delivered but he says that he doesn't owe her anything as far as he knows since he paid for what he got from her in cash. So if she has anything owing from him she will have to be more specific. I would like to know who wrote this bill.

I would so like to visit you, see you and speak with you, but the distance is too great and my wallet still too light as it isn't worth coming home with only 600 dollars. I'll wait and see whether I can get a few more dollars and then I'll come looking for you. I've almost used up my sheet and I cannot scribble any more this time but I must conclude with some greetings. Give my regards to Tore Elsrud and his family. My regards to all at Rustand and first and foremost to my old grandmother. There isn't a day that I don't remember her and how good she was to me when I lived with her and went to school. Greetings to all friends but first to you my dear parents and siblings from your faithful son,

I. E. ELSRUD

I don't have to write about the difficulties with uncle's estate since my uncle is writing about this now and you'll see it all clearly in his letter. But there's one thing I'll ask of you dear father; make sure that grandmother signs the warrant of authority that uncle is sending you. It would be too bad if everything of uncle Ole went into the hands of strangers. Today Maren Lunde is moving home to her husband Hans Viger with all her things. Good luck to her! There is an awful horse disease here and there is hardly a healthy horse to be seen. It is similar to strangles but not fatal. I wish you all a Merry Christmas and a Happy New Year.

I. E. ELSRUD

This letter was enclosed with one from Ole Olsen Haugerud the Younger to his mother (who lived with IEE's parents) (Nor. ed. III:136). The letter IEE wrote before this one was dated 17 February 1882 (Nor. ed. III:115). The Asle who wrote to Fingal Fossholt was Asle Enger, a friend in Aadalen. IIE wrote to him 8 June 1873 (Nor. ed. III:157). Names may cause some difficulties in this correspondence: IIE's mother had two brothers named Ole who both lived near St. Ansgar and whose wives both were named Maren. The widow Maren (IEE uses her maiden name Lunde) had been married to Ole Haugerud the Elder. «II:9 »II:30 NE III:135

FROM: Reinert Aslakson, *Colfax, Wisconsin, 20 December 1872*
TO: Osmund Atlakson Ovedal, *Sirdal, Vest-Agder*

Dear brothers,

I must send you some words so you can have news from us. I and my two siblings here are in good health, for which we praise God, and as far as I know Rachel and Sigbjørn are also doing well and we wish to hear the same from you. You know of our brother Syvert's sudden death and also that brother Bernt has departed after a long illness. May the Lord teach us to contemplate our end so we may be prepared for his return. Bernt's wife wrote to us that it was his last will that all his possessions should go to her if his siblings didn't object. We have agreed for our part and you should let us know your view when you write to us. What our brother Syvert left behind is another matter—his farm, animals, farming implements and other chattel. As you know, this is ours in common after his debts have been paid. Rachel wrote to me and asked me to come and help her get things organized for our departed brother. I went by train and returned home the day before yesterday. We auctioned all the animals and other chattel. I saw no other way of doing it as the animals needed care and the other chattel would merely decrease in value by lying around. Moreover, there is a debt to be paid. As far as we know the total debt is 911 dollars and 66 cents. We made 245 dollars and 45 cents on the auction so the debt is now 666 dollars and 21 cents. Most of this year's crop of wheat, oats etc. has not been sold and is brought to town and sold whenever convenient. The farm has been let for next year but as there is a mortgage and neither I nor Sigbjørn are in a position to buy it, we think we'll have to sell it to whoever bids the most. But as Sivert cannot sign the deed all his heirs will have to do this. As one of his heirs you will also have to sign, but as it will be so complicated to send the deed to you it would be simpler for you to appoint one of us as your attorney to act on your behalf. Whatever may be left when all has been realized in cash and the debt has been paid will be divided between us all and you will have your share. Someone here must be given this power of attorney, Sigbjørn, I or Ole Tobias Midtfjells, as he and a Sjur Vig from Hardanger will take care of the auction money because we live so far away. The power of attorney must give the buyer all rights to the farm and you must write immediately and tell us what you will do. If you want us to send you the deed for your signature we will do this but this will delay and complicate matters. Write immediately and let us know your view. Our pastor says he has sent the Church Monthly to you and we wish to know if you have received it. Regards from me and my siblings,

REINERT ASLAGSON

. —— .

Rachel Tonette Allikson wrote on 30 December from Medo, Minnesota (Nor. ed. III:140). «II:24 »II:36 NE III:138

. —— .

1873 — LETTER 2:28

FROM: Arne Jørgensen Brager, *Black Earth, Wisconsin, 13 January 1873*

To: Johan Olsen Brendhagen, *Vang, Hedmark*

⋆⟹⟸⋆

Dear brother and brother-in-law,

Thank you so much for your welcome letter dated in November that we received in December. We are especially happy to see that you are in good health and doing reasonably well. These are great blessings for which we must be particularly grateful. Without them everything is a heavy burden for those who are unable to bear it patiently. But He who sends us the burden also has the power to give us patience so that it won't seem too heavy. As for my own health I can, praise God, say that it is a little better than before. I've been to different doctors and none agrees on my illness. The last one I visited was a German who is said to have studied in Germany and he ensured me that my lungs were healthy and that nothing was wrong with them but that I suffered from a weakening of the nerves and a fault in my heart that caused it to palpitate. I feel better since I began to take his medicines. Karen has, thank God, been in good health and little Gunild is healthy. She is growing big and often says she wants to visit Uncle and her cousins. You ask for our portraits but you must excuse us for not having had them taken yet because of Karen's pregnancy. On October 8 she gave birth to a boy who was christened Johan Albert. He has been well since.

You write that you have thought of going to Australia and this may be a good idea and the many possibilities that are offered are very tempting. But there may be many difficulties as the world remains the world wherever one is. Karen is glad that nothing came of it as she thinks that you may wish to come here. She would so like to see you again and it would be terrible to think that one goes there and one here never to see each other again.

I'll now make a few observations on legal and practical matters that this country offers immigrants as well as natives. An immigrant can get work as soon as he arrives and there is enough food to be bought for people as well as for animals. He may acquire his papers or swear his loyalty to this country and its government as soon as he wishes and then go west where there is homestead land and take out four forties or 180 acres without paying anything but three dollars for the paper work at the land office. There is some such land, good for farming, in Wisconsin, Iowa, Minnesota and almost every state of the Union. I've thought of staying here another year and then, if God grants me life and health, go west and get my own land. As I see it we'll have very good laws as long as we have a Republican government. Last fall we had quite a row when we had a Presidential election as we have two parties, Republican and Democrat. The Democrats wanted someone named Greeley and the Republicans wanted General Grant and Grant was reelected with a great majority. We can now be sure that the country's laws will be enforced justly, at least as far as I understand politics.

We have freedom of religion and I hope that the Norwegian Evangelical Lutheran Church will, through the efforts of its excellent pastors, have the strength to grow and expand with more members and more pastors as several new pastors get their degrees every year in St. Louis. We also have a theological school in Decorah and teachers there are Professor Larsen and Pastor Brandt and a professor named Schmidt. We have parochial schools in every congregation and fifty-three pastors in all. It is not my intention to praise this country in order to persuade you to come here because in this you must do as you think best. I would of course like you to be here but I'll not try to persuade anyone to come. Should you come to us we'll provide for you the first weeks until you are able to make money on your own. And then we could go west and take land and farm our own land. I won't advise you to go to Australia. I have read about Australia in my world history book and it does not have much praise of Australia as a very fertile land. Karen will not in any way advise you to go there but wishes to see you here. If you have decided to go to Australia then write to us before you leave home. If you haven't, then I hope you've planned to come here. If you do it would be best to take the same steamship line as Karen, the Allan Line and the A. Sharpe Co. It is not necessary to spend much on clothing as it is better to get this here. Please give our regards to all at home. We would also like to have information about our sister Oline. I conclude my letter with the hope that we will at some time see you and your children and we wish you the Lord's blessing and a happy new year. Dear brother-in-law, please tell us whether you plan to go to America or to Australia. I won't advise you to do one or the other. Karen sends her regards and little Johan and Gunild say hello to their cousins. In conclusion, regards from me and my wife.

ARNE JØRGENSEN

. ——— .

AJB's written Norwegian is influenced by the code switching that no doubt characterized his language and he writes *Homstat* land and *landaffisen* (the land office). The Norwegian Synod had an agreement with the German-language Missouri Synod to have some students and teachers at their theological seminary in St. Louis. Luther College in Decorah, Iowa, was a liberal arts college. The teachers mentioned are Laur Larsen, Nils O. Brandt and Friedrich A. Schmidt, a German American who played an important role in Norwegian-American church history. A. Sharpe was an agent for the Allan Line in Christiania; AJB wrote *Scjarpe*. «II:21 »II:39 NE III:143

. ——— .

1873 — LETTER 2:29

FROM: Gullik Gulliksen Bringe, *Eureka, Kansas, 20 January 1873*

To: Ole Gulbrandsen Lande, *Flesberg, Buskerud*

⋯⟾◯⟽⋯

Dear brother-in-law and wife,

Thank you so much for your letter of November 26. I was glad to see that you were in good health and we can tell you that we've been well all winter, but last fall my wife and four of our little girls were ill and I had to get a doctor. I and the youngest were quite well all summer. I have nothing to write about that will interest you. I am enclosing a column from a Norwegian newspaper about our state and it will give you precise information. As far as I know it tells the pure truth (I believe it is written by our pastor). None that I know has died. I must tell you that our girls are going to the English school close to our land. Anne thanks you for the spinning wheel you sent her, as do I, and thank you for sending us Ole and Jøran. I mustn't forget that Ole has written that I was on a long journey. A Norwegian boy had come from Wisconsin and taken a claim near me and I took him to the land office and was his witness. I must tell you that money is short now and the interest is high. If you had come last spring you would have had at least twenty-four to thirty percent if you had lent your money and this may last yet awhile. Since you have money you should come when the interest is high and the cattle are cheap.

I should tell you a little about myself. It is difficult now as we haven't yet grown anything we can sell. The cattle we have bred are too young to get a decent price and I have many expenses. I pay thirty dollars in interest, twenty-seven in taxes and twenty to the doctor, and a considerable sum is needed for clothes. As for the guns I have written about, bring me a shotgun and a rifle if you come. The rifle should be one considered the best in Norway and both should have as slender a barrel as possible. Jøran Kolkinn has bought a house in Eureka and says she will have coffee ready for you when you arrive. No more now except that you must give our regards to Anders Gjømle and Niri and Guri Kolkinn. Loving regards from us all. Write immediately and let us know whether you are coming. Bring some nice butter molds if you come.

G. G. BRINGE

. —— .

Ole is Ole Toresen Lande, the foster son of Ole Gulbrandsen Lande. «II:23 »II:33 NE III:144

. —— .

1873 — LETTER 2:30

FROM: Iver Ellingsen Elsrud, *St. Ansgar, Iowa, 14 February 1873*
TO: Elling and Olea Elsrud, *Aadalen, Ringerike, Buskerud*

Dear parents and siblings,

We received your welcome letter of January 13 yesterday. We were sad to hear that father is ill and that Torgrim's knee isn't better but I hope that all will soon be well. I'll first tell you how I have celebrated this winter, in particular at Christmas. Because I've been to one ball and that's all. I haven't been anywhere else except a few times for half a day in town, so you may imagine that Norway and America are very different when it comes to dances and entertainment. But since I'm not all that fond of fun and games this suits me well. We have had an unusually cold winter and so much snow that it has been sixteen or twenty years since there has been so harsh a winter here and it is no wonder that more than a thousand lives have been lost in a few days here in America. My main work this winter is to look after my foals and take them out for a ride now and then so they are fit to go wherever I want them to go.

As you have seen in uncle's letter of December 4, he has bought part of the land and chattel of Ole the Elder from the lawyer from Milwaukee (who has now moved to La Crosse). He should have had a deed right away but still hasn't received it. It seems that the authorization signed by grandmother was not good enough with just a signature in her name and therefore the deed had to be sent to Norway and it may then be that she was stupid enough not to sign it because it was for her own son. Dear father, I would so like to know whether she is going to sign it or not. I see that you've spoken with Torgrim about the authorization that uncle wrote about and that you don't think he will sign it if it is from us but that he might sign one from Ole Rodningsand. But I think the expenses involved would be just as large if not larger as no one in America does anything for nothing and this is something grandmother will find out in two or three years, because I think that then she and the others will see what all of this comes to. I hope that Torgrim will then find out who has been lying and who has agreed and that he has perhaps been the one and grandmother the other. I know Ole Rodningsand so well that I would not recommend him (nor would anyone else) because he is like a wolf in sheep's clothing, so I think it is best that he continues to do what he has been doing because I don't think they can demand anything from grandmother should the estate not have sufficient value to cover the expenses. When the first bill from grandmother's lawyer arrives I would like to hear how much it is for because I think it will be a nice sum for grandmother to give to the so-called fleecers and one that she could have avoided. She will never know how much half the estate of Ole Haugerud could have been worth if the case had been handled well and I won't write anything about it as she would then also believe that I was a liar. I have no more to write about this now but should anything come up I'll let you know. I'm sure that uncle will soon write to grandmother.

I've written to Marie Aalde and had a letter from her in return and I can tell you that she has married the widower. Dear mother, I could read your letter but there were some things there that I couldn't understand. Tell the people at Enger that I've had a letter from Fingal and that he is well. Erik Hansen's address is the same as mine. I'll conclude with friendly regards to all friends but first and foremost to my dear parents and siblings.

I. E. ELSRUD

IEE also wrote 7 June and 1 October 1873 (Nor. ed. III:157 and 164). Ole Haugerud the Younger had asked the family in Aadalen to authorize IEE to act for them. Guri Rustand, IEE's grandmother, had first given the power of attorney to a lawyer named Knud Johan Fleischer in Milwaukee, who had handed this business over to another Norwegian-American lawyer, T. J. Widvey, also in Milwaukee. One thing the family in Aadalen could not have realized was the considerable distance from Milwaukee to St. Ansgar and the large sum the lawyers would deduct for expenses for every visit. Ole Rodningsand in St. Ansgar was the court-appointed administrator of the estate and Torgrim Haugerud in Aadalen was apparently his mother's main advisor. «II:26 »II:41 NE III:146

·⸻·

1873 — LETTER 2:31

From: Fingar Helgesen Nerdrum
West Lake, Minnesota, 24 February 1873

To: Helge Gundersen Skare, *Sigdal, Eggedal, Buskerud*

⟶⟹⟸⟵

Dear friend and brother-in-law Helge Gundersen Nerdrum,

I'm ashamed that so many years have passed by without a letter and I must beg you to forgive me. As you know, it is difficult when you cannot write yourself and always have to go to others to get it done. I can tell you that I'm in good health and that I have some land to work on. I have taken eighty acres of government land and last fall I had my first harvest and it was only fair. On twelve acres I had 226 bushels of wheat and sixty-five bushels of potatoes and next spring I plan to plant twenty acres. I also have some animals, a pair of oxen and a cow.

I can tell you that our brother Nils is further down in the country but plans to come up here in spring to take land. As far as I know he is quite well and has two children! He uses land on shares and has two pairs of oxen and three cows. I'll also tell you that we've had a hard winter but now hope that the worst is over. It has been cold with drifting snow for many days and many have lost their lives or their health. Not so many have died in our neighborhood but the storm took its toll on January 7, 8 and 9 with the life of the wife of Ole Embrektson Søland. Halvor's wife was with her in the wagon and froze her hands and feet so there is fear that she too may lose her life or at least one of her hands. I've heard that Gunder Eriksen also froze to death. Amund Medalen sold his land and plans to return to Norway next spring and then you'll have better information about our situation. But I forgot something about the women who had frozen: it happened on my land, about 100 steps from my house.

My dear brother, one thing is always on my mind, that you are little Helge. You wanted to follow me to America and I wonder whether this is still your intention. I see in your letter that you would like to have my portrait, but you must excuse me. I cannot fulfill your wish now but I hope it will be more convenient the next time I write. I can say from Anders and his family that they are in good health and also from Gunder Moen that their little girl has begun to speak. And Gunder Skare is much the same but he is in good health. His land is next to mine, but he hasn't worked on it yet. Please give my regards to Sjur Kodalen and ask him to write to me as I would very much like to hear how he is. And you mustn't forget to write and tell me all news, especially about who plans to come to America next spring. Please excuse these unreadable lines. As I cannot now think of any more that can be of interest to you I must lay down my pen. My most friendly regards, sincerely,

FINGAR HELGESEN

Halvor here is Halvor Helgesen Skare. «II:12 »II:35 NE III:147

1873 — LETTER 2:32

FROM: Thor and Paul Torstensen Vigenstad, *Prospect Bluff, Arkansas*
25 November 1872 and Norwegian Grove, Minnesota, 8 March 1873

To: Ole and Simen Torstensen Vigenstad, *Dovre, Oppland*

Dear brother,

Grace and peace in the name of our Lord Jesus Christ. I will again send you a few lines to tell you how I am. I'm still at the doctor's but will move out in two days and try to work again. I'm still weak and have to take medicine three times a day. The doctor says that I may work a little if I'm careful. We have a very cold winter, yes, I feel the cold more here than I did in Norway. I don't yet know where I'll stay when I leave here as I must try to get some light work. I'll conclude with my best wishes to you from your brother Thor. May the grace and peace of the Lord be with you. Amen.

As I received a letter from you today I will add a few words. I will come next spring, God willing. What you write about *farming* is all according to my taste.

Written *at* Prospect Bluff.

Since Thor's letter, as you see, ends here, and since there is some space left on the sheet, I'll write a little since I'm so good at writing long letters. I've long thought of sending you a year's subscription to *Kirkelig Maanedstidende* and will try to do this soon. In addition to this journal published by our synod I also subscribe to a church journal in English and an entertaining Norwegian magazine called *For Hjemmet* which is similar to *Folkevennen* in Norway, and, along with two neighbors, also a newspaper, *Fædrelandet og Emigranten*. Since I came home from my teaching on Monday before Christmas I've hardly done anything but read, as taking care of a cow and a calf through the winter with hay and water is not much to speak of and hauling firewood is not so much either when the forest is close to the house. But there will be enough to do in spring. Today is March 8 and I must try to get this letter written as I think I'll have an opportunity to send it tomorrow.

I've thought a lot about Ole's words that we should come home. What should I do there? Farming is not what I like or am good at either here or there. Here it is merely temporary until Thor—as I hope—comes. Later I hope it will be something to do in addition to teaching. Teaching is what I would most like to do, and, as I have written before, Norway is at present not for me. Although the church at home and our synod here have the same confession, the situation, and to some extent the practice, are not the same. There has been some improvement in Norway since I left and this is to some extent due to our synod. I'm convinced that today it is the German Missouri Synod that holds high the banner of the Christian Church for all Christians in this country and our synod has long been in association with them. Recently we've entered into a synodical conference with them and four other Lutheran synods. America is certainly the land of sects. Yes, even many Norwegians have left their Christian faith and do not baptize their children or bring them up in the faith, but these are outside the church and the sects have their own synods. Those who wish to be with us must accept the word of God or leave. We have no other authority to answer to. But I won't say that I would not be satisfied in Norway nor will I insist that I won't return. We do not know how things may change.

Norwegian Grove, March 7, 1873

My dear ones at home!

Yesterday I received the welcome letters from Ole and Simen dated January 20. Letters take about one and a half months to get here, but when the settlements are older and things become better organized here in the West they will take less time. It saddens me that Thor hasn't written a letter home. He has not, however, yet received the last letter you wrote to us because a few days after I had forwarded it I had a letter from him where he said he had moved to another place. As you can see of the enclosed letter he plans to come here in the spring and the time when emigrants go west is soon upon us. I cannot now find your last letters but I'll copy them and send them to him and if he does not write before he comes here then I will certainly get him to write after he has arrived. It is reasonable that you find it strange that he doesn't write but I'll mention two things that may explain this. In the first place he does not enjoy writing letters and when he writes it is merely a few words, for instance a page, where he says where he is and what he does and a little about his health. Second, and this may be a reason that you cannot appreciate, there is such restlessness in this country and a tendency to get all involved in one's work. When you are used to being among people of all nations and moving from place to place you get to feel at home wherever you may be. And third, Thor usually left the writing to me when we both were in Wisconsin. It is not strange that you wonder why we are so far apart and this is because of a series of unrelated and unwilled causes; since the time we decided to go to America things have kept us apart. But I think all is well with him and that Thor has learned a lot from his journeys in this country. Our situation is not at all rare here and I've met many in this country who have brothers or other relatives here that they don't know anything about, not even where they live.

I came here to farm where I have no acquaintances because I went where it is best for farming. In Blue Earth County, where most of our acquaintances are, the land has already been taken and, moreover, Thor and I agreed that it would be good for us to be with other people and see and experience other ways. As you, dear Simen, have written two letters and had one from me, I'm sure that one of yours as well as one of mine have been lost, because I've always written for every letter I've received from you. There have been great changes here in the three to four years people have lived here. Last year people had to go seventy miles to a mill and we now have a mill only fourteen miles away and there is a sawmill only three and a half miles from here, in Pelican Rapids, and we soon expect one to be built here. In America farmers don't have their own mills. They are built by capitalists who are paid by the bushel. Last year we had church service two or three times a year and now we have our own pastor and church ...

· ——— ·

The concluding page of this letter has not been preserved. TV wrote from Grand Glaise, Ark., 1 July and 28 September 1872 (Nor. ed. III:125 and 132). In the second he writes of his illness. Since he went south to work TV had been sending money to his brother to invest in land or in the store they planned to have. On 28 September he wrote that he had had to pay much to the doctor and for medicine so he could "not send more than 120 in gold as I must hold on to the rest in case I am ill again..." His brother Paul wrote two letters on 7 and 8 March 1873, first his own letter and then, the next day, he filled in an empty space on his brother's letter, beginning with an explanation of his brother's English words: *farming* and *at*. The journals PV mentions are the "Church Monthly" (published by the Norwegian Synod), "For the Home" (published in Decorah, Iowa), "The People's Friend" (published in Norway), and "The Fatherland and the Emigrant," the latter a merger of the two newspapers named in the title in 1868 and published in La Crosse, Wisc., later moving to Minneapolis. In 1871 the Ohio Synod had invited the Norwegian, the Missouri, and the Wisconsin Synods to discuss a federation of the synods, and the Norwegian Synod accepted this in 1872 but eventually left the Synodical Conference in 1883 in an attempt to "restore its own inner peace" (Nelson and Fevold 1:183). There are no further letters from the two brothers in the Norwegian National Archives. What became of Thor is not known; Paul, the author of two books, married Anne Maria Jakobson in 1874 and was still living in Norwegian Grove when O. M. Norlie compiled his *School Calendar 1824–1924* (1924). «II:22 NE III:148

· —— ·

1873 — LETTER 2:33

FROM: Hellek G. Branson, *Eureka, Kansas, 29 April 1873*
To: Ole Gulbrandsen Lande, *Flesberg, Buskerud*

Dear and unforgettable brother and wife,

I must write you a few lines and tell you that we are all well and we hope this will find you in good health too. I see from a letter to Ole Kolkinn from Tofte Langrud that you have sold your farm for between 6,000 and 7,000 and this is good news indeed. I almost believed that you would wait selling the farm until bad times were around again, but there I was wrong and I now hope that you will also be here at the right time. Because that money can do much here, so I believe you are lucky selling when times are good there and coming here to hard times with a lot of money. I must tell you that we've had a cold and hard winter in Kansas, but it seems that we'll have a good year. Last fall I wrote that I had bought some yearlings and now I can sell them for more than twice the amount. I don't have any news, but a wealthy storekeeper from Wisconsin has been here to look around and he'll return this spring. He went back to sell what he has there and he knows your wife's family well and is from Numedal. May God be with you and may you have a good and happy voyage to America. Our loving regards to you my brother and your wife from me and my wife and all our children. Farewell.

H. G. BRANSON

. —— .

Ole G. Lande emigrated in 1873. He was then fifty-two and his wife Anne was forty-four. They had no children. There is an undated fragment of a letter he probably wrote to Niri Kolkinn in 1874 (Nor. ed. III:152). He did not Americanize his name and eventually returned to Norway. This letter also included brief notes from the brothers' mother Sigrid Reiersdatter, from their brother-in-law Gullik Bringe, and from Ole Mesunt, who thanks for all help and wishes them as pleasant a voyage as he had had. The price for the farm is in *speciedaler*, which had a slightly higher value than a U.S. dollar. «II:29 »II:66 NE III:151

. —— .

1873 — LETTER 2:34

FROM: Elise Wærenskjold, *Prairieville, Texas, 12–18 May 1873*

To: Thomine Dannevig, *Lillesand, Aust-Agder*

⊶⟹⟸⊷

My dear, good Thomine,

In the newspapers I see that you have lost your husband and I'm sending you these lines in deepest sympathy for you and your sons in your grief. How are you now, my dear old friend? I would so like to hear from you. Will you remain in Lillesand or will you move to Tønsberg? I would think that you will prefer to stay in your old home. Please write and let me hear how you and your sons and all other friends are doing. Is Mrs. Hammer dead? Olsen thinks she is. Where is Gusta Hauge? Can you give her and Kaja Poppe my regards? Both could write now and then. We are all getting old and soon it will be too late as death calls on one after the other. Your acquaintances here are doing well. Andreas Andersen is visiting in Prairieville with his wife and two children and today they are going to Bosque to visit her parents and siblings. I think that he and Mrs. Pabst are doing very well with the sawmill. Ouline Reiersen is doing well, but her brother Ole Johan is in bad humor—as usual when he is out of work. During winter he works at his sister's stepson's cotton gin and then he is happy. Ouline is quite fat and looks good, but both she and I have to apply ourselves to making a living. I have quite a lot of land but there are many expenses and not much income and this winter has been hard on all who have cattle. First late summer and all fall were very dry, then winter came early and was very cold and around Christmas we had a horse disease that was all over the United States. All of this caused much death among our horses, cattle, sheep, and pigs even though we used corn in addition to hay to keep them alive. My loss in dead animals and the extra use of corn was more than 200 dollars, not counting the losses of Otto and Niels. It also cost me a lot to help Otto get started. Last winter I had a visit from a son of my cousin (a son of mother's youngest brother) in West Virginia and his cousin from Sweden. They were two handsome and refined young people and it was an unexpected pleasure to have a relative here.

May 18

Here I was interrupted and in the mean time I've received your very welcome letter. Thank you so much for all the news about friends and acquaintances. I suppose you don't know the Olsen I have mentioned. He was a sailor on the same ship as Edvard Terkildsen and Henrik Normann, but I see that he has been misinformed about many things. He is from Mandal or around there so he does not know so much about people from Lillesand. Stina had advised him to get in touch with me and he is here now. I'm glad that your children are doing so well. This must make you glad but it's sad that they are so far from you. It would be lovely to see Thorvald on his big steamship. You must give him my regards and tell him that it would please the old woman that he once liked so much if he once again would write to me. Oh, the many times he crawled up the stairs to me and so clever he was as a two-year-old to remember the alphabet and the countries of Europe: "Italy like a boot and London where Daddy is." I remember so well how sweet and clever he was. My little son who died was also a little Thorvald. I baptized him myself when we saw that he would not live. The worst of it was that it was the carelessness of his own mother that caused his death. She gave him morphine to get him to sleep and this killed him. I had so looked forward to getting a little Thorvald again. Otto and his wife live quite comfortably in a nice little house not so far from mine. My husband's younger sister and her husband and children live just beyond Otto.

It is wonderful that your mother is still living, and now she has great grandchildren, or at least one. I'm also glad to see that Hansen is well. Give him and his wife my regards. I'm writing to him this week so it may be that both letters arrive at the same time. Isn't it strange that Nikolay and Conrad don't marry? How are your other brothers and Alida doing? Where do H. J. and Alida live? Who lives at Møglestue? I'm so glad that the beautiful garden hasn't been ruined. Has the woods with the walking paths been cut down or does it still exist? How are Lotte Speilberg and Wenche Dahl doing? I had a letter from Bina Møglestue last year. It was very nice of her to write because I hadn't written to her. Poor Mrs. Basberg. Things are difficult for her. Sine Arntzen has asked me to give her regards to all her friends in Lillesand. She is no longer running a school and lives in Copenhagen. How is Mrs. Strømme? Do you know whether Blia in Christiansand is still living? Do you know anything about Rosenkilde's children? I've heard his wife is dead. Do you know what has become of Peter Markusen and his sister who lived at Snøringsmoen? She was so terribly poor. I was godmother to one of her children, a wonderful little girl, and I've often thought of what may have happened to my goddaughter. Who now lives at Nygaard? I had so many delightful hours there. How are Stina's eyes? If they are good enough, then tell her that she may write to me. Do you know anything about Niels Møller and Salvesen's children? And you don't say anything about the Friedrichsens. As you can see, you could have written much before I had my fill. Ole Johan has been here since I started writing and sends his regards. He also asks to be remembered to his son. He just left me an hour before I received your letter. Give my regards to all old friends, your children, your mother, Hansen and his wife, and your other siblings, the Grøgaards, Mrs. Hammer, Kaja, Gusta, Mrs. Arentz, and all other acquaintances. I am writing to one of the Grøgaards. Fare well and write soon to your devoted friend,

ELISE WÆRENSKJOLD

Why doesn't Thorvald marry? Is he not able to find a girl he can appreciate? It must be nice for you to have a visit by your little granddaughter.

A fragment of this letter is in Clausen 1961. Thomine Dannevig was married to Lars T. Dannevig. She eventually moved to the home of Niels and Vilhelmine Dannevig in Tønsberg. EW's cousin in West Virginia was Emil Meldahl and his son Tony Meldahl (Clausen 103). Among those she remembers in her closing sentences are Kaja Poppe (a widow whose maiden name was Møglestue) and Gusta Hauge. «II:6 »II:102 NE III:153

1873 — LETTER 2:35

FROM: Anders Helgesen Skare, *West Lake, Minnesota, 19 May 1873*

To: Helge Gundersen and Halvor Helgesen Skare
Sigdal, Eggedal, Buskerud

Dear father and brother,

As times have changed I'll send you a few sentences about my present situation. It pleased God in his wisdom to take home my dear wife to a better life on April 14. She died in labor and the child was stillborn. This was a hard blow for me but the bad must be suffered as well as the good and may God's will be done. As for me, I'm in reasonably good health. This is also true of my children who are growing and doing well. We've done our planting and the weather has been quite good for some time. Last year's harvest was fair for all products. I can also tell you that Amund Helgesen Medalen has gone to Norway. He left home May 1 and I hope that you'll meet him as soon as he is there. Then you'll get all the necessary information from him that will be too much to write about here, about our horses and other animals and other things as I am quite discouraged and will therefore not write much.

For my part I don't have much to boast or complain about. The winter was very harsh with snow and cold weather and many lost their lives in the storm in January that began on the sixth and lasted to the ninth. I can say from Gunder Moen and his family that they are doing well and are in good health and he also sent his regards to you with A. Medalen and this is why he won't write until Elling Wold and his wife Mari have been up here and Anne Wold, Ole Wold's widow, will also be coming to visit us. They are expected on May 21 or so they have written to Gunder Moen. All acquaintances are in good health and doing quite well as far as I know. I can say from Fingar Helgesen that he is in good health and doing well. You must forgive me for not having written for so long but the reason is that when Even Glesne was visiting in Norway he gave you all necessary information about me. But my dear father and brother, please write to me as soon as possible as it would make me glad to hear from my old home and place of birth. In conclusion I wish you all luck in your work here on earth and eventually, after a good life, eternal bliss. From your devoted son and brother,

ANDERS HELGESEN SKARE

I have seven children, five boys and two girls. The youngest is three years and five months.

· ——— ·

«II:12 »II:65 NE III:154

· ——— ·

1873 — LETTER 2:36

FROM: Berte T. Allikson, *Medo, Minnesota, 15 June 1873*

To: Osmund Atlaksen Ovedal, *Sirdal, Vest-Agder*

⊹⇒○⇐⊹

Dear unforgettable,

Thank you so much for your letter of October 11. I received it one month after the death of my dear husband. I must ask you to forgive me for waiting so long before writing. This has its reasons. First my grief, then the harsh winter, and when summer finally arrived there was such an unusual amount of rain that I, being a woman, couldn't go to the person I wanted to write for me. Please write about how things are with you. I must now tell you who are so far away about my sad fate. I know that you have been told, but not by me. My husband was ill all the time after we came to America. At first he thought he would get better. God willing, we were decided on returning to Norway, but the Lord had other ways for us. It pleased the Lord to call away my dear husband and your brother October 23 last year. During his illness he first wished to be back in Norway but as he got worse he realized that he would soon be separated from me and he worried about how it would be for me in this strange country far from all relatives while he would go to an even more distant land on a far more dangerous journey and there be strong and well and live with his Lord and Savior Jesus Christ in the heavenly Jerusalem and stand face to face with the Father, Son, and Holy Spirit and remain there in eternity without sorrow or troubles and always live in joy and happiness and give thanks and praise to his God, hoping that we would come together there and never more be separated. Because—as he said and as certainly is true—this land surpasses all description and understanding. He was certain of dying and by my understanding and judgment he passed away believing in his Savior and God. Oh that I may live so that I may be gathered with him with God my Father in the heavenly Jerusalem. At the end he weakened day by day but I believe that his soul grew stronger for each day he lived in America.

A few days after the death of his brother Syvert we moved to Ole Tobias Midtfjell's from Flekkefjord. Berent died there and this is where I've since had my home. They are as friendly and loving as had they been my own parents. I must say that my grief has been a heavy burden but I'm grateful to my heavenly Father who helps me to bear it. He has promised to be the father of the fatherless and the judge of widows and this is certainly true. I will return to Norway as soon as someone can go with me but it cannot be this year. I wanted to go last spring but as no one who could support me was going I decided to wait. The Lord's will be done. The last two weeks I've been living with Osmund Lindeland taking care of his wife who recently had a son. I'm doing well and have good health. God be praised!

· ——— ·

BTA has evidently dictated her letter. There is no signature; she may not have been able to write her name. In Psalm 68:5, God is "a father of the fatherless, and a judge of the widows." «II:27 »II:38 NE III:158

· ——— ·

1873 — LETTER 2:37

FROM: Iver Sjursen Ystaas, *Locust, Iowa, 20 August 1873*

To: Thrond Sjursen Haukenæs, *Granvin, Hordaland*

⊹⇒⇐⊹

My good friend Th. S. Haukenæs,

As I have promised, I will take up my pen to tell you, my dear friend, how I have been since I left home. I assume you've read about my voyage in the letter I sent to my father so I won't repeat this here except to say that we arrived happily in New York on June 25 after twenty-two days of stormy weather and after two children had died and one had been born on the voyage from Bergen. All were well when we arrived. We left the ship the next morning and stood on American soil. We gloried in the wonders of the great and famous city of New York but not for long, because that evening we continued our journey up through the country by train. We went as fast as lightning and could hardly make out the objects we passed, but there were many stations, in cities as well as in the country, so we had a little time to look around and see the remarkably beautiful and fertile country around us almost everywhere we went. So I can say that we had a very nice journey. On the evening of June 28 we came to the famous and remarkable city of Chicago but didn't have time to look around because we continued that same evening to Milwaukee. There we had to wait two days before we could go on. On July 1, after we had said farewell to our traveling companions, I came with Lars Kvandal and Torger Folkedal to our destination, the town of Decorah, where we were kindly received by our many acquaintances there. I lived for some days with Knut Kjærland and then went out in the country about ten miles north of Decorah to Johannes O. Seim where I have lived since. I haven't worked much yet because to begin with I visited the many people from Granvin who live around here. Then I did harvesting for three dollars a day. It was hard work, especially for one who has little practice. It has been hot this summer and we've hardly had any rain since I arrived. It has been a good year for hay and wheat but in other places people complain of a poor harvest. I would like to have a letter from you before many weeks have passed. I'm doing well and am quite satisfied in America. Regards to your family. Your friend

IVER SJURSEN YSTAAS

. ——— .

ISY emigrated from Granvin in 1873 at the age of thirty-three. He and Thrond Sjursen Haukenæs (1840–1922) were contemporaries. Letters to Haukenæs are from a handwritten book of copies of letters he planned to publish, now deposited in the Norwegian National Archives. Haukenæs was a prolific author of local history. His copies may not always be accurate, and parts of some letters may have been omitted. »II:46 NE III:161

. ——— .

1873 — LETTER 2:38

FROM: Reinert Allikson, *Colfax, Wisconsin, 18 October 1873*

To: Osmund Atlaksen Ovedal, *Sirdal, Vest-Agder*

❖⟹⟸❖

Dear Brother!

I must again try to write you a few words. I received a letter from you through Sigbjørn but I cannot remember whether I've replied. I must let you know that we are doing fairly well. Siri is not quite well but we others are in good health and we wish to hear the same from you. Your other family at Coon Prairie and your sister in Minnesota are also doing well as far as we know. Things are pretty much as usual. We've done our threshing and had an average crop. This year I've broken six acres and planted them with winter wheat.

The main reason I write is that we have, as you know, been sending you our Church Monthly for two years. Some time ago we heard that you hadn't received it. You must write and let us know whether you have received these journals so that we can do something about it if you haven't.

Write whether you have had them this year. Our pastor has sent them and he wishes to know whether you have received them.

As for our brother Syvert's property, the farm has been let on shares this year. All chattel has been sold and his debts have been paid. The farm has not been sold yet and if we are unable to sell it this winter we will again let it on shares. Please write as soon as you can and let us know whether you have received the Church Monthly and whether you would like to have it for the coming year. It will then appear weekly. And give our regards to my old uncle as well as to all friends there at home. My sisters Sara and Siri are living with me. Siri is not in good health but she doesn't have to stay in bed. Rachel is in Minnesota. She has written that she would like to come here but we don't know whether she will go here or to Coon Prairie. Sigbjørn says you've written to me but I haven't had letters from you for a long time so they may have been lost in the mail. Here is my address as there may have been an error. Write: Reinert Aslakson, Colfax P.O. Dunn Co., Wisconsin, U.S. America.

Greetings from us all. Write soon with news from home. Regards from your brother,

REINERT ASLAKSON

. ——— .

«II:36 »II:42 NE III:165

. ——— .

1873 — LETTER 2:39

FROM: Arne Jørgensen Brager, *Modena, Wisconsin, 9 November 1873*

To: Johan Olsen Brendhagen, *Vang, Hedmark*

Dear brother and brother-in-law,

I'm ashamed that I haven't written to you for so long but I hope you will forgive me. I answered your last letter right after I had received it. The reason I haven't written is that I waited for a letter from you. Moreover, we have recently moved. Last spring in May we left Black Earth and went with my parents and siblings up here where my brother-in-law had bought a farm. We hoped to find what they call government land <u>but there was none left</u>. This summer I've worked on farms for from $1.25 to $1.50 a day. During harvest I was in Minnesota and was paid $3.50 a day. All in all I made $41.50 so my income has been much better here. We are now in Buffalo County about 200 miles northwest of Dane County, by the Mississippi River and about fifty miles from La Crosse. Karen and I like it here and for this we thank God. Last summer I harvested six tons of hay. When I came here I had a cow, a heifer and a calf and have now bought another cow for thirty dollars. I can also tell you that this fall I've bought forty acres of government land that I'll pay thirty dollars for next fall. I could have made use of my right as a citizen to get it but I didn't want to use my right for so little, as I can make use of it to get 160 acres for fourteen dollars. I'll build a house next spring and this winter I'll haul planks and break as much land as I can, perhaps twelve to fourteen acres. I haven't harvested anything but not far from here there is enough hay to be had in return for working half time. I'm now working as a shoemaker in the little village Alma so I'm away from my dear Karen as I write these lines. My home is about fifteen miles from here. I've worked here for about seven weeks and plan to continue all winter. I'm paid for the pair and usually make $1.25 a day. I go to my wife and children every two weeks. We live with others. We have a Norwegian Evangelical Lutheran church near us. Last summer they called a new pastor, F. W. Moller, a young candidate who has studied in Norway as well as here. Even though he is young, only about twenty years, he is a sincere pastor. Most in our congregation are from Luster, Valdres and Bergen. We have church service every third week. I and my family have been in good health all summer except that my dear Karen had one of her usual attacks. It was milder but of the same kind as before. The children have been well and are growing.

Dear Johan, you must let me know if you plan to come here. I assume you haven't gone to Australia so I hope you will decide to come to us. I don't think much of Australia but I won't advise against it if you have decided to go. I hope you will soon write to me about your situation. It is our sincere wish that some of our relatives should come here. If possible, I would have helped Anne, as she once asked for our assistance but this is not possible now as there is so much I have to pay for by next fall. Best regards to you and your family from Karen, and Gunild and little Johan send their regards to their cousins. Johan is now beginning to walk and he looks like his mother and is quiet and serious. May God grant that if we are not to see each other again in this life we will do so in the Heavenly Mansions. May God grant us the grace to do this for His sake. Regards to you and your family from me and my family.

ARNE JORGENSEN

. ——— .

This is the last letter by AJB in this edition. The next letter is by his widow Karen Brager. Fredrik Andreas Moller (born 1845) emigrated in 1856 and studied at Luther College and Concordia Seminary in St. Louis. From 1873 he served congregations in Buffalo County, Wisc. AJB is mistaken about his age. «II:28 »II:71 NE III:167

. ——— .

1873 — LETTER 2:40

FROM: Gullik Gulliksen Dorsett, *Leland, Illinois, 24 November 1873*

To: Torstein Gulliksen Daaset, *Flesberg, Buskerud*

Dear brother!

I received your welcome letter of October 27 on November 13 and was glad to see that you were all living in good health and I can also say that I'm in fairly good health. Thank you so much for your letter; I wish to hear often from my dear siblings in Norway. As for news, I don't have much. First I must tell you that three years ago I sold my chattel and let my farm on shares for three years and went with my brother Jul up to Minnesota to see his home and land there. His land was a valley with a creek and hills on both sides. He had twenty acres of good field and lots of hay for his cattle and enough forest for his own use. While there I went on a trip to Iowa and the land there was hilly much like in Minnesota. Then I went to the capital city St. Paul in northern Minnesota. The city was magnificent with large buildings of blue stone. Traveling in Minnesota I also met some relatives and friends such as Knut and Ole Juveli. They were doing well and had three forties of land each.

St. Paul is by a large river and along the river the land is hilly but further west the land is more flat and the quality varies. I came to Minnesota in the spring and was there for about a year to try out the good climate that we have heard so much about. The spring was long and cold but it got hot enough during summer. It could be up to 115 degrees in the shade but late in August when we were at work harvesting the wheat and oats we had such a hard frost that the roofs were white. The fall was long and cold but when winter came I saw something I hadn't imagined. We had snowstorms every day and we had to be careful to survive. Many people perish in the cold in Minnesota. When I left Minnesota to go home I went through Wisconsin and there I found that most Norwegians were prosperous. My journey through Iowa, Minnesota and Wisconsin and back to my home in Illinois cost me $300 and on my return I had to buy farm implements, a horse team and wagon and some cattle. [...]

Before I end my letter I must let you know that I'm in the same situation as before, without a family. My cousins Christopher and Jorn Førle live a mile from my home. They are in good health and doing well. My brother Ole and his family send their regards. They live about four miles away. I haven't heard from our brother Jul for a while. I don't know more to write about now and will conclude with loving regards from your loving

G. G. DAASSET

. ——— .

The Daaset letters are all poorly written and some are dictated. Minnesota is for instance written *Melesota* and *Melesa*, Wisconsin is *Væskons* and St. Paul both *Sante paul* and *Santol*. A sentence in the second paragraph could not be interpreted. Pages five and six of the letter are too damaged to be included. GGD's brother Jul lived near Bratsberg in Fillmore County. It may seem from GGD's account that Jul had not settled on the best farming land, but from his point of view he had the water, forest, and hay for the kind of agriculture he was used to in Norway. «II:20 »II:43 NE III:168

. ——— .

FROM: Iver Ellingsen Elsrud, *St. Ansgar, Iowa, 2 December 1873*

TO: Elling and Olea Elsrud, *Aadalen, Ringerike, Buskerud*

Unforgettable parents and siblings,

As it is now winter and I have free time I'll send you some sentences hoping that you will receive them by the end of the old year. You may imagine that I would like to be in Norway now that Christmas is soon here, but my wish will not be fulfilled this year either and God knows when it will be. This is the fifth year and the fifth Christmas is almost here and, oh, these have been five long years away from parents and siblings and relatives and friends in a foreign land where I have not mastered the language and don't quite know how to conduct myself. But when all is left to God he will do what is best for us whether we are in America or in Norway. God is everywhere and I hope he will guide me on the right path in spiritual as well as worldly matters. This will be my last winter here if I don't buy land, which I'm now thinking of doing, and should this come about I'll probably stay here yet a while. I'm thinking of taking my uncle's farm on shares because he wants someone to do it. I would then do it with Anders Høghaug because it is too much for one man. When I last wrote I hadn't yet threshed my oats. This has now been done and I had 250 bushels and 200 of corn and that was a good harvest. I have no more to write about. I haven't heard from Fingal Enger for a long time so I don't know where he is. Give my regards to all my friends. Regards from your son and brother,

I. E. ELSRUD

As for the land of Ole Haugerud, uncle still has not received the deed. Please let me know whether grandmother has signed it or not because I would like to know whether it is the lawyers here who are procrastinating. Give grandmother my regards.

I have a request for you at this time. Should anyone be going to America from Aadalen I would like to have something sent here, not for me but for my uncle's wife and this is a spinning wheel. Good spinning wheels are not available here. So this is my wish if anyone is coming, but nothing but a good one will do as there are enough bad ones here. When my debt to you gets larger I will send the whole amount. Let me know about this when you write.

I. E. ELSRUD

«II:30 »II:64 NE III:169

1874 — LETTER 2:42

FROM: Rachel Tonette and Reinert A. Allikson
Colfax, Wisconsin, 22 January 1874

To: Osmund Atlaksen Ovedal, *Sirdal, Vest-Agder*

Dear and unforgettable brother,

We received your letter of March 1 in April and learned that you were doing well, for which we must thank God. We can also, praise God, say the same for us. But when I got your letter I was working for an American and a few days later I became ill but not so bad that I couldn't be up and about but I couldn't work for a long time. When I got better I wanted to return to my work but three days after I had arrived I was washing clothes and spreading them on the grass to dry when I was poisoned by a kind of grass on my fingers and it spread to my entire body so it was all swollen and almost black, but it didn't last more than a week. The doctor came three times and it cost me eight dollars. Last summer I paid ten dollars for a doctor and medicine and it cost me fifteen dollars to go to Reinert. I hope you've heard that I'm now living with our brother Reinert. I sent greetings to you in a letter Tønnes A. sent to Peder Haughom the same day I went. You wish to hear about the storm in Minnesota last year. It was a terrible storm and I don't think that many had seen a worse one. Many were killed and many were injured by frost, but it wasn't so bad where I was. As far as we know all those we know in Minnesota are doing well. Our sister Siri is sickly but is well enough to work every day here at home. I must conclude my simple letter with regards from us all. Farewell.

RAKEL T. ASLAGSON

Dear brother Osmund Aslagson,

I received your very welcome letter dated December 11 on January 21 and I'm so glad to see that you are doing well. And I can, praise God, tell you the same in return. Sara has paid for *Kirketidende* for this year and it is now weekly as you will see if it comes to you. We have had mild weather this winter and enough snow to use a sleigh. I have no news since you don't know anyone here. So I will conclude my letter with regards from your brother

REINERT A. ALLIKSEN

I will ask you to write soon, and don't do as I did last year because then I put it off again and again. Give our regards to all relatives and friends. You are lovingly greeted from Sara and Siri. Please write about all news from Bakke parish as well as from Tonstad parish. Farewell.

RAKEL T. ALLIKSEN

· ——— ·

«II:38 »II:50 NE III:173

· ——— ·

1874 — LETTER 2:43

From: Ole Gulliksen Dorsett, *Leland, Illinois, 16 February 1874*

To: Torstein Gulliksen Daaset, *Flesberg, Buskerud*

Dear brother Tosten Gullekson Daaset!

I have received your welcome letter dated September 21 and see that you are all doing well and I can say the same for us, that we all are, thank God, in good health. I will tell you how many children we have and their names and ages. The oldest, Ambjørg is seventeen, the next, Ingeborg fifteen, the third, Gullik eleven, the fourth, Ragnil is nine, the fifth Margit six, the sixth, Halvor four, and the seventh, Even is two years old. The two oldest are now preparing for confirmation with the pastor and will be confirmed in about a month.

I must also tell you that for these last four years we have had what we may call the usual good year. I will here note last year's harvest. I had twenty bushels of wheat per acre, of oats fifty bushels per acre and of corn about thirty bushels per acre. I had no more potatoes than I need for our own use. I have about twenty fruit trees of different kinds so I have enough fruit for our own use. My farm is 120 acres and of this I plow seventy acres and the rest is for hay and pasture. I have fenced it in four parts. My farm is five miles from the town Leland. I have four horses and two wagons, one old and one NEW that I bought last summer for ninety dollars. I have nine milk cows and four heifers and eight pigs and about a hundred hens. We sell butter and eggs for 220 dollars a year. I must also tell you about the price of land. Where we live it has been about thirty-five dollars an acre and the price for grain has been about a dollar a bushel for wheat and for oats about thirty-five cents a bushel. We now get fifty cents a bushel for corn and for a horse you have to pay from one to two hundred dollars and for a milk cow it has been thirty-five dollars and for pork you get six cents a pound. You may imagine that with such prices we can accumulate lots of money but you must not believe it is quite so simple. All we buy is expensive and a farmer has to buy all his equipment in town and machines are expensive, and a family leaves a lot of money behind in town because we have to buy both shoes and clothes.

I would like to hear from my brothers Even and Hellik and about what they do and how they are there at home. I haven't yet had any letters from them and would like to hear from them. I will send you portraits of us and our three oldest children and would like to have some of all of you in return. I will now end my simple letter with loving regards to you all. My brother Gullik also sends his regards.

OLE GULLEKSON DAASET

· ——— ·

«II:40 »II:158 NE III:174

· ——— ·

1874 — LETTER 2:44

FROM: Olianna Olson, *Necedah, Wisconsin, 24 February 1874*

TO: Ole Olsen and Ragnhild Jakobsdatter Vigerust, *Dovre, Oppland*

Dear parents!

As the correspondence between me and my home has been unsuccessful I must again try my luck and send a few words to you, my so often remembered parents. We've written many letters but I realize that you haven't received them since we've had no reply. This must have happened to you too as I heard from Jacob when he arrived that you had sent many letters that I haven't received. I must first tell you that we are all in good health as usual and doing quite well. Hans and Jacob went up to the forest last fall in the middle of November and have been there since then. They are about sixty miles from here. They are thinking of returning in the middle of March. Their pay is low this winter—from twenty to thirty dollars a month and board. The reason for their low pay is the big money crisis all over America last fall, but we hope it will be better next summer. We've had an unusually mild winter with from six to twelve inches of snow. Food is quite cheap. Flour costs 140 cents a pound, pork twelve cents, butter twenty-five cents, beef ten cents, coffee forty cents, tea 150 cents, and eggs are twenty cents a dozen. One cent is about the same as a Norwegian *skilling*.

As Jacob says that my sister Ragnhild wants to come to America, I'll give you my view of the matter. I believe that if she likes it here she will do better here than in Norway. But I'm sure that she won't like it the first year. She must do as she wishes. Jacob thinks she should come and he may be right as he is in a better position to compare conditions in Norway and America. I can tell you that a maid usually makes from two to six dollars a week, eats as at parties in Norway and has very light work. As I don't have more that is necessary to write and my time is short I will ask you to give my regards to all acquaintances as I find it unnecessary to write their names. In conclusion, loving regards from your children in America and I hope that you will soon reply. In haste,

OLIANNA OLSON

· —— ·

Olianna and her brother Jakob from the farm Vigerust used their patronymic as their family name in America. Before emigration she was Oleanna Olsdatter. When she later married Hans Engebretsen Hjelle they must have found both his patronymic and his farm name unusable and took the name Hanson. She writes the English words for the various foods (*flour, pork, butter, bif*) and provides translations. There is a short undated note in the collection written soon after Jakob's arrival. She reports that he is miserable and "so thin that you wouldn't have recognized him," explaining that it will be better when he learns the language. »II:178 NE III:176

· —— ·

FROM AMERICA TO NORWAY

1874 — LETTER 2:45

FROM: Anne Pauline Pedersdatter Furuset, *Waco, Texas, 8 March 1874*

To: Peder Eriksen and Siri Kristiansdatter Furuset
Romedal, Stange, Hedmark

⊷⊸⊜⊶⊷

Dear parents and siblings!

I must now answer your welcome letter where I was glad to see that you are doing well. I can say the same to you. I've been in good health since I came here to America. I must tell you that I live in Waco. I've been here for three months. The first month I had six dollars, the second eight and the third I had ten. My work is to cook and wash and mend clothes for six people and do what is necessary in a house. I am with good people. You may think that it isn't so good to live with people when you cannot understand a word of what they say, but it is better than I thought. They want me to be here until July when they are going to their parents. I would also have liked to go to my parents but I'll have to be satisfied with going to my sisters in the settlement. I hear that you spoke to Dahl about living with them. I could have lived there but if I was to stay in America it would be good to learn a little of the language. I would not learn this if I had lived with Norwegians but now I have to learn a little as I don't hear anything but English. My days are long and my thoughts are with you every day but I am lucky that the people are so nice. I suppose they thought it was boring for me and the only thing they could do to entertain me was to have their oldest daughter play on the piano for me. So I like it here and you must not feel sorry for me. If God grants me health I plan to be here until July. I just barely talked with the boys who came so I would like to go to the settlement to hear more from Norway. My greatest wish is to hear from there. I was so surprised when I saw people I knew so well and that I didn't think I would see in America. I hope they'll be happy here because that is so important.

I can tell you that Gine Brunstad has married a Dane. None of us went to the wedding, as it was the day before Dahl died. Ole Brunstad married a girl from West Norway last fall. Her parents are neighbors of Dahl. Ottine Slagsvold has married a widower. He is a storekeeper with two children.

Christine Dahl has just been here and sends her regards. She said she would write when she came home. Christine says they are doing well at Dilrud. The little girls are healthy and growing tall. You can walk there from Dahl in a good half hour. They could have seen each other if it hadn't been for the hill between them. It is nice land if he farms it well. The houses are not much to look at but they'll do.

Dear parents, please forgive me for not having written to you earlier. I hope that these lines will make you as happy as yours make me. Please write as often as possible. I must now end my poor letter with regards to you all. Remember me to all acquaintances and my love goes to you my dear parents and siblings from your distant

A. P. P. D. FURUSET

You can read this letter yourselves. You don't have to show it to anyone.

· ——— ·

The PD in her signature is for Pedersdatter. Anne Pauline was twenty-one when she emigrated via Galveston in the spring of 1872. Her parents seem to have been worried about her and when Hendrik Dahl visited home later that year they asked him to let their youngest daughter live with his family. The "boys" she had met in the settlement had come with Hendrik Dahl when he returned to Bosque County. Gine and Ole Brunstad were her cousins, the daughter and son of her aunt Anne and Johan Brunstad. They married Peter H. Hansen and Annie Mathilda Canuteson. Johanne Ottine Slagsvold was married to Otto J. Johanson. Dilrud was the farm of her older sister Karen and Peder Dilrud, who had emigrated in 1872. In Norway their name was Dillerud. «II:25 »II:48 NE III:178

· ——— ·

FROM AMERICA TO NORWAY

1874 — LETTER 2:46

FROM: Iver Sjursen Ystaas, *Locust, Iowa, 24 March 1874*

To: Thrond Sjursen Haukenæs, *Granvin, Hordaland*

⋆⇌◯⇋⋆

Dear friend Th. S. Haukenæs,

Thank you so much for your long and very interesting letter that I received January 22. I hardly have to tell you that it was very welcome as there are still so many dear memories that lead my thoughts to my old home and my many relatives and friends there. So it is good to receive letters from a dear friend who can give a good report of the most important news and happenings so that it is as if I were present to see and hear what is going on. I was very glad to see that you and your wife as well as all my family were doing well.

I suppose you wish to hear how I am doing here in the much-praised America. So I'm glad to tell you that I'm doing well, in good health and quite satisfied. I only regret that I didn't come here many years ago. First, it is much easier to learn the language and understand the American ways when one is young. Second, it is much easier to earn money here than there at home for all kinds of work and especially during haying when you can have as much as two or three dollars and board a day. But work here is often hard because they only consider how fast something gets done and not how it gets done. But if you are strong and have good health and, moreover, are willing to work regularly and take whatever jobs are available you can make quite a lot of money in a short time because there is always work to be had. But if money can be made quickly it can also be wasted in a short time by those who are careless, in particular by those who want to keep up with the latest fashions because such fashions are extremely expensive, and for those who spend a lot of their time in saloons their money will go even faster as nothing is cheap there either. A glass of beer, about half a pint, costs five cents and a shot of whiskey ten cents and other drinks accordingly. So you may understand that far too many spend what they have and are unable to save much. As for clothes it is the women who are most exposed to fashionitis, as one wants to outdo the other in dressing up in finery. Indeed, this seems to take most of their time and it has gone so far that there is now no difference in dress between country girls and house-maids and the better class of young women in town. So it is no surprise that they are hardly able to balance their income and their expenses even though their wages are many times higher than in Norway. And their work is far lighter than at home. All they have to do is cook, do laundry and ironing and dress up. Here the cattle, that are out all winter, are taken care of by the men. So I think that women are far better off here than in Norway and I believe that if the girls at home had known how it is here, many of them would have come here.

I must tell you a little about what I've done this winter. At first I decided to go to an English school but then I and Johannes Olsen Nesheim and his brother John agreed to cut 250 cords of wood for an American at seventy-five dollars for every 100. He had oak, aspen, basswood and some kinds of trees that are unknown in Norway. Each of us was able to cut about one and a half cord a day. We only used axes, no saws, and we were done by the end of February. I then had ninety cords. As we provided our own food we built a little house in the woods. We dug about three feet down and then we laid logs of aspen and basswood much like they make hay barns out in the woods at home and had clay in between the logs to make it tight and then made a roof of straw. The house is ten feet long and eight feet wide and high enough for us to stand up. The three of us built it in one day, laying the logs, thatching the roof and furnishing it with a door, windows, beds, a table and benches, so you may imagine that it was a nice and elegant home. Many immigrants live in such houses because here people are not as par-ticular about houses as about food and drink. We paid about one dollar a week for our food and if we had taken our board at a farm we would have had to pay from one and a half to two and a half dollars a week.

The weather has been unusually nice all winter, no harsh cold and very little snow, so it hasn't been good for sleds and people have often had to use wagons and some are already thinking of beginning their spring work. Farmers have begun to hire help for the summer and they are offering from twenty to twenty-five dollars a month for six or seven months. It would be nice if you wrote soon. Kind regards to you and your family and may you all fare well.

IVER SJURSEN YSTAAS

· ——— ·

«II:37 »II:54 NE III:179

· ——— ·

1874 — LETTER 2:47

FROM: Gaute Ingebretsen Gunleiksrud
Stoughton, Wisconsin, 28 April 1874

To: Hans Ingebretsen Gunleiksrud, *Tinn, Telemark*

✦⟶▸══◎══◀⟵✦

Dear brother Hans!

A long time has passed without letters from either of us so I must write some sentences and send them to you, hoping that they will find you in good health. I can tell you that we've been granted good health till now, for which we must thank the Almighty. We read news from Norway in the newspaper every week and see that the winter has been unusually mild there, as it has also been here. But we now have an unusually long and cold spring. Today the fields are covered with snow. I've planted my wheat but still have oats to plant. We've had frost almost every night for a long time. As far as I know there is not much illness here even though death sometimes demands his victims. Old Ole Berg departed about a year ago. Tollef Gullstein died the day before yesterday on April 26, and there have been others unknown to you. How is my brother Erik? We would like to hear from him. We've heard that his wife has had triplets twice and twins once. We would like to have information about this when you write. You must also let us know how our relatives and acquaintances are doing.

Our daughter Guro and Jacobsen are doing well. They live about 170 miles from here in a town called Decorah in Iowa. They have a daughter named Anna. Jacobsen teaches at the Lutheran college there. Lars Hansen Gulliksrud visited us a short time last winter and it was a pleasure for us to hear from our home village. He said he had heard that my father Ingebret had been ill last summer. He returned to Minnesota. Johannes Olsen Marum is in Michigan this winter cutting lumber. I've had a letter from him and he is doing well. In conclusion, loving regards to my parents and my siblings and their families as well as all acquaintances.

GAUTHE INGEBRITSEN

This is the last letter from GIG in this edition. It was dictated to John Steinsen who added a few words of his own. GIG's son-in-law Jacob Daniel Jacobsen was one of the first students at Luther College in 1858. He taught there from 1872 until he died in 1881. He had immigrated with his parents from Gjerpen, Telemark, to Pine Lake, Wisc. in 1843. «I:150 NE III:187

1874 — LETTER 2:48

FROM: Christine Dahl, *Norse, Texas, 29 April 1874*

To: Peder Eriksen and Siri Kristiansdatter Furuset
Romedal, Stange, Hedmark

Dear parents and siblings,

As it is a long time since I've heard from you and as I've waited in vain for a letter I'll again put together some lines to let you know how we are, which I do not doubt will interest you. We are all, praise God, in good health and are doing quite well. We have no news that may be of interest to you as everything is as usual here. Pauline is at the same place and is well as far as I know. I was in Waco some time ago and spoke with her and she was happy. I expect her home in about a month. Peder Dilrud and his family are well and send their regards. Karen will soon have a little one if all goes well. We've done our planting for this year and the weather is fair but we had a late spring. The winter was good so cattle and horses have done well but then we had some spells of cold weather, even frost, so late that it did considerable damage to the corn that had been planted early, and damage was also done to the wheat that had come up too early because of the mild winter. When I was in Waco I spoke with Bergman about the money he had promised Hendrik he would pay you from Kari, but he refused to give anything so there will be nothing from him. We had lent them 300 dollars to build their house and to get the money back I had to buy the house from him at a relatively high price as there is little money here now. I paid 1,000 dollars for the house.

The people at Rogstad send their regards. They are in good health and doing well. Rogstad has been here and built me a kitchen at the end of my house, so now I've built as much as I plan to do in my time. We had a lot of rain this past winter so it doesn't look good for our harvest as there is rust on the wheat, so the old wheat and corn are expensive now. Wheat is sold for two dollars a bushel and corn for one dollar. This spring a cow with a calf is sold for fifteen dollars. Please remember me and my children to my sister Syverine. I will again send you our portraits as those you have are not any good. I'm sending you one of each of the children and one of Kari. I'll send you mine later. Wilhelm sends his regards. He is well and lives with us. I don't know of any more now and must therefore conclude with the hope that these lines will find you all in good health and that if it is not to be our fortune to see each other again here in this world, we may meet again on the other side of the grave where there will be no more separation. My most sincere greetings from me and the children. Your far distant daughter,

CHRISTINE DAHL

· ——— ·

CD's deceased sister Kari had been married to Johan Bergman, a Swede, in Waco. Her aunt Anne was married to Berger Rogstad. «II:45 »II:51 NE III:188

· ——— ·

1874 — LETTER 2:49

FROM: Sevath Sevathson, *Paint Creek Prairie, Iowa, 17 August 1874*

To: Haagen Aslesen Bøygaard, *Aal, Buskerud*

⊷⇒◉⇐⊷

Dear cousin!

As I must send a few lines to my old fatherland I'll make use of this opportunity to send you, my old friend, a brief account of my present situation. I've been in this country for more than twenty years and God has blessed me with an abundance of what we need in this world. You may remember that when I left Old Norway I had nothing, but now, praise God, I have house and home, many obedient and nice children and more than enough to provide for them. But alas! All these wonderful things are as nothing compared to what God recently has taken from me. Yes, he has indeed tested me but I must not despair but ask the Lord, my true comforter, to grant me the strength and patience to bear the burdens that he in his inscrutable wisdom has laid upon me. First my dear sister Guri was called away; she died in the middle of last February a few days after she had given birth to a daughter. She left behind seven children. But then on March 10 I received a heavier blow when the all-knowing Lord called away my dear and beloved wife Ingrid Helgeson. She died in peace and in faith in her Lord and Savior Jesus Christ after she the previous evening between eight and nine o'clock had given birth to two children who both are alive and doing well. But, my dear friend, this was not enough. Now, my oldest daughter Aagot, who was married last fall, was twenty-two when she was called away on July 31 from this worldly life and to what we must hope is a better one. She too died after giving birth to a little girl on July 30. But the Lord was again compassionate and took the child home on August 8. Yes, the Lord gave, the Lord took away, praise be the name of the Lord. I am happy in the hope that the Lord gathered them all in his home as they all had faith in God. Blessed are they who die in faith in their God and Savior.

I will also tell you how much I own. My farm is 280 acres and most of this is good land. I think I'll have about 500 bushels of wheat this year, 200 bushels of oats and 400 of corn. My home cost about $13,000 fully furnished. My cow and hay barn cost me $600. I have two horses, twelve cows, ten sheep, and fourteen hogs. In cash I have about $3,000.

In conclusion please give the enclosed authorization to Nils Olsen Sheel. And please give my regards to old acquaintances and relatives and in particular your old father, and my special regards to you and your wife and children. Loving greetings from your old friend,

SEVATH SEVATHSON

· ——— ·

Sevath Sevathson was born on the small croft Tveitejordet (part of the farm Tveito) in Aal in 1826. He married Ingrid Helgesdatter, also from Aal, after their emigration. Aagot, their first child, was born in 1852. NE III:212

· ——— ·

FROM: Rachel Tonette Rannestad
Willmar, Minnesota, 26 October 1874
To: Osmund Atlaksen Ovedal, *Sirdal, Vest-Agder*

⊷⫥◒⫤⊶

Dear brother,

As it has been some time since we wrote to each other I'll take up my pen to tell you how I am and what my situation is. I must tell you that I'm married to John Torkelsen Rannestad and we had our wedding June 6. I came here May 28 and I'm happy in my new situation even though there aren't many friends around here. Those we know are Asbjørn Rannestad and his family and Tore Lindeland who is married to Syverine Toresdatter Konstali as well as four of his siblings and Nils Tobias and Hans Øxendal who live about thirty-five miles from us. They say that Nils Tobias has been here in Willmar but I haven't seen him. We are living with John's brother Ole this winter. We don't have land yet but we have two cows and a calf and twenty-five chickens. We plan to buy land next spring. We have sold the land that belonged to our brother Syvert for 1,400 dollars. We were paid 1,200 at once, 100 this fall and 100 will be paid next fall. We won't know how much it will be all together, because Ole Tobias Midtfjells is taking care of it. I've received 153 dollars as my share and this includes half of your share, so I must thank you so much for having been as a father in father's stead for me. I cannot give you anything in return except our portrait as our simple gift to you and I would like to have your portrait in return as it is unlikely that we will ever see each other again.

I can also tell you that our brother Reinert has sold his land. He and our sisters Sara and Siri have returned to Coon Prairie. We recently had a letter from them and they are doing well. I don't know of any news about people you know except that we have a large Norwegian settlement and the congregation is well organized with a school and a monthly service and they are going to build a church that will cost 2,000 dollars. I don't know of more to write about except that Siri Gabrielsdatter Virak lives about twenty-five miles from here. So I'll conclude with loving regards to you my dear brother from your sister

RAKEL TONETTE

My address is John Torkelsen Rannestad, Willmar PO, Kandiyohi CO, Minnesota North America. Loving regards from me, John Torkelsen. Write soon.

· ——— ·

John Torkelsen Rannestad was also from Bakke, now in Sirdal, and emigrated on the ship, *Heros*, from Stavanger 27 April 1868. He was then thirty-seven. «II:42 »II:60 NE III:222

· ——— ·

1874 — LETTER 2:51

FROM: Anne Pauline Furuset, *Waco, Texas, 1 November 1874*

To: Peder Eriksen and Siri Kristiansdatter Furuset
Romedal, Stange, Hedmark

Dear parents and siblings,

I must write you some words and tell you a little about how I'm doing. I can first tell you that I have received your two welcome letters where I see that you are all well and this makes me glad. Then I can say that I was seven months at the same place in Waco and then I went to Dahl where I was about eight days and then I went to Dilrud and was there for a month. And Karen says to tell you that she has a girl child and her name is also Gine. She was born July 7 and Karen was soon up and about and I helped her during the time I was in the settlement, but now I have returned to Waco. I began work in a new place September 23 and I'm quite satisfied. I cook, wash, and iron for seven people and earn ten dollars a month.

But now I must tell you about my accident. I fell down the stairs and my right arm was put out of joint. I went straight to the doctor and set it right so it will soon be good. The man and his wife had just gone away for eight days so I haven't been free from work for a day because I thought I should remain until they returned. I had planned to go to Dahl but then I felt that it was getting better so fast and they thought I should stay. Now I earn ten dollars a month but I'm not to do washing or ironing but do other things instead.

I can greet you from the newcomers. I talked with Maren Tingstad's sister who said they were well but I didn't meet Gudbrand Brunstad so I didn't get to hear any news from you but I think I'll see him during Christmas. I saw in your letter that you were anxious for me and I must ask you to please, please lay this aside, because I think that my situation and my happiness here are better than you think. I can say that I'm happy here. But I must also say that I'm sad in my heart when I think of you, my dear parents and siblings, something I think is true of all who are so far away from family and friends. It could be that I'm alone in being divided in my feelings but if all were to write what they felt I think it would sound the same. I see that you want to know whether I'll be coming home. I cannot say anything for sure but I must at least stay here long enough to earn some money of my own. I have one request, that you'll all take a portrait and send it to us. This would make us glad. You must do this as soon as possible. I don't think you've written to Aunt Anne since you received their portrait. You should try to write as often as possible but I cannot expect this. I can tell you that Peter Dilrud hasn't received anything on the authorization. It is doubtful that he will get anything and I don't think it is worth the trouble. I have no other news of interest except that Syverine Dahl is soon ready to marry. I think I'll be at that wedding at Christmas. I wrote to Christine that Bergman was going to marry, but now I don't think so. I must tell you that Gine was buried on a Tuesday and Dahl on Thursday. They rest beside each other in the churchyard. Those at Dahl and Dilrud send their regards. I must now end with my loving regards to you all. Remember me to all acquaintances but you are first and foremost greeted from your

A. P. P. F.

· ———— ·

Anne Pauline has not written the year of her letter, but it seems to have been written in 1874. In the margin she wrote: "Do not show this to anyone." A daughter and a son at Dahl were both married 30 September 1875. Karen and Peter Dilrud's first child had died the year before and her name was also Gine. (Her burial is mentioned at the end of the letter.) The newcomers are probably those who had come with Hendrik Dahl in December 1872. Her aunt Anne had been married to Johan Brunstad upon their emigration in 1851. He died in 1852 and she married Berger Tollevsen Rogstad in 1853 and moved to Bosque in 1854. «II:48 »II:61 NE III:224

.　———　.

1874 — LETTER 2:52

FROM: Guttorm Olsen Lee, *Primrose, Wisconsin, 5 November 1874*

To: Mari Olsdatter Lie and Anders Olsen Lie
Hedalen, Sør-Aurdal, Oppland

⊷═◯═⊷

Dear mother and siblings,

Thank you so much for your welcome letter of July 15! I'm sorry that it has taken so long before you had a reply and I hope you will forgive me. I wanted to see what our harvest would be before I wrote to you. We were glad to see that you are all well, which is the greatest good in this life. As for this year's harvest, it was very poor for our wheat, oats and barley. A small fly in cooperation with a long and powerful drought destroyed it so that we will hardly have enough to live on until next fall. Many didn't get anything at all. But we had a good crop of potatoes and corn so at least we had something. It has been far worse in other parts of the country, as for instance Minnesota where the grasshoppers have destroyed everything. So the disaster is great in many places.

You ask for advice concerning the journey to America. It is truly not easy to advise you one way or the other but I will, as I have before, tell you my own view of the matter. Should you come and be happy here, then I believe that your young and clever sons would make a better living here since wages are higher, there are more possibilities and there is more to learn here than in Norway. But for the person who is somewhat advanced in years it can be both good and bad, depending on the circumstances and especially on whether you like it. I won't advise you not to come, nor do I dare advise you to come as it is best that you make your own decision. It is now easy to buy a farm here or other places as there are many who wish to sell—and sell cheaply. I have no news for you. Regards from Ole, our brother, and the sons of our sister who all say they are doing well.

As for me and my family, we thank God that we can say we are all well and busy every day. Gullborg O. Berg would like to hear from her relatives when you write as she has written several letters without getting any reply. Please write soon and let me know your decision about coming here to America and who wants to buy your farm. You must also let me know what our old mother thinks of you selling the farm and leaving as well as other news. My best regards to relatives and friends and to my old mother. Farewell all of you with greetings from all of us!

GUTTORM O. LIE

· ——— ·

Although GOL addresses his mother, Mari Olsdatter Lie, the envelope is addressed to his brother, Anders Olsen Lie, the head of the household at Søre Li. Although Anders Lie did not emigrate, his sister Olea Børtnes and three of his four sons did, as may be seen in later letters.
«II:14 »II:74 NE III:227

· ——— ·

1875 — LETTER 2:53

FROM: Svend Larsen Houg, *Elgin, Iowa, 11 January 1875*

To: Ole Larsen Haug, *Aal, Buskerud*

⊷═◉⊜═⊷

Unforgettable brother Ole,

I have long thought of sending you and my other siblings a few sentences but this has always been set aside. You may think that your brother in America is no longer alive since you don't hear anything from him. But this is not so. God still upholds me in this time of grace. It is all because of my own negligence and because I am so poor a writer. Please forgive me. I received your letter of February 22 on April 18 and your last letter to me has been misplaced and I don't know how this has happened as I have all the other letters you have sent me. But I know I received it at the usual time so thank you so much for being so good as to write to me and I can say in return that I and my family are in good health and that all is well with us.

I assume you would like to know something about church matters. You know that the Norwegians here have four Lutheran synods. I cannot write about them all in detail. That would be too much and, moreover, I don't know enough words and expressions. But I'll write a few words about the largest one called the Norwegian Synod, because it seems to me that they wish to suppress all Christian life even though they have a very nice church service as far as the superficial liturgical aspects are concerned. I don't know of any significant difference in the confession of the synods and their main differences are in their superficial traditions and customs. I think their purpose is to further a Christian life. Enough of this, but we have been admonished to examine ourselves and the profession of faith. When I now must address my own confession, I am but a lost sinner but in Jesus Christ I am saved and blessed by undeserved grace although I am often hidden in weakness and doubt. I will not develop this important point as my experience is too insignificant and my language too muddled but I will merely refer to the true word of God that we have in such abundance, first in the Bible that is God's own word, and then in all the witnesses of our faith who have written and explained the word for us. We do well in taking notice of this as a light that shines in a dark place until the light that is Jesus Christ enlightens us, for he has said I am the light of the world. But our nature is so corrupted by sin that we cannot understand that which is of God except that he through his Holy Ghost through the word explains Christ in our hearts so that we accept him as he has been given to us for wisdom, justification, sanctification and salvation, and then address ourselves to faith in his righteousness. I will not say more of this. I believe that you brother Ole have more experience and are more serious in your Christian faith than I, but it may nevertheless be good to share our confession of faith with each other.

You may like to hear more of my family. I am in good health and can work as my age permits as I was sixty just before Christmas. My wife is in good health except that she now and then suffers from headaches. My son Lars works for himself but when he is home with us he is as the others in our family. Halsten went to a Norwegian academy in February last winter and was there until June and in the fall he returned to this school and is there now. It is in a city called Minneapolis in Minnesota, 200 miles from here, and belongs to the synod that is called the Conference. I think it is a good school. The other children are at home with me. Ole, Kittil and Assor are grown up. Assor was confirmed last fall and Knud will be confirmed next spring. He who has many children will have many trials as the mind of youth does not sense more than what is of the flesh and even though this may not be carnal it is nevertheless nothing but sensuous pleasure. So it seems with the young generation here and so it will be in most places. But we are all in danger as the evil enemy stalks around us looking for whom he may swallow. This is how it so often seems to me when the storms blow so that the small vessel of faith is threatened by the waves, but when one holds on to the trustworthy captain Jesus then one can be led into the desired harbor.

With these poor and simple-minded lines I send my and my wife's best regards to you my dear siblings. It may be that this is the last time I write to you because my pilgrimage may soon be over. So it is my prayer to God that we may find each other at home with Jesus. I send greetings to you, brother, from our relatives here, first from Syver Groth. He is a kind man and is often a comfort and encouragement in my spiritual life. He often talks of you. Svend and Johannes Groth are very kind men. I believe they are serious Christians and they are the people I am closest to in both worldly and spiritual matters. My old mother-in-law Ragnil still lives and mostly lives with me. She was somewhat ill last spring but is now quite well for her age, but her memory is weakened. I must now correct an error. I said that I could not find your last letter. After I had written most of this letter I looked for it again and found it in a drawer among some letters that belonged to my sons. It was dated May 23, 1874 and I read it again with both pleasure and sorrow. With sorrow when I hear that in the land of my fathers there is disdain for the word of God, as if man did not have a costly soul that needed to be saved. And I was glad to read your confession that you do not seek your salvation in anything but undeserved grace in Christ. Regards to you and your family and our other siblings from me and my wife and our family,

SVEND LARSEN HOUG

. ———— .

SLH wrote far more letters to his brother than can be included here. A fragment of an 1876 letter is Nor. ed. IV:14. Many others are in the Norwegian National Archives. «II:3 »II:153 NE IV:3

. ———— .

1875 — LETTER 2:54

FROM: Iver Sjursen Ystaas, *Locust, Iowa, 8 March 1875*

To: Thrond Sjursen Haukenæs, *Granvin, Hordaland*

·→══◉═══→·

My good friend Th. S. Haukenæs,

I must now take up my pen and write a few sentences to you my dear, unforgettable and far distant friend in Norway. I must first thank you for your welcome letter of December 4 that I received January 25. I am happy to see that you and your family are well and that your family is increased with a big and healthy son. I wish him all luck and blessings and hope that he will grow to be big and strong so that he soon can be of help and assist you in your store with both scales and yardstick. I have also seen that you have completed your new home and I can imagine how magnificent it is with a beautiful view of sea and land and it would be wonderful to be home for a visit and see how beautiful and pleasant your home is.

As I don't have anything of interest to write about I'll tell you a little about what I've done since I wrote last year. Last spring I was a farmhand for two months at twenty dollars a month. During the haying season I earned $1.50 a day and later I took part in harvesting for three dollars a day, the regular wage during last harvest. Since then I've done some threshing for $1.50 a day. All wheat, corn and hay is stacked in the fields as they don't have buildings to put it in. When they began threshing I worked with a machine for some weeks and earned a dollar a day. After Michaelmas I contracted with a farmer to clear a piece of land of trees for forty dollars. After I had done this by mid-November I continued to work for the same man until Christmas cutting wood for eight cents a day. We had an average harvest. The wheat suffered from the intense heat and drought that lasted all summer, but the corn did well. In areas of the western states grasshoppers destroyed the crops and there is famine in many places, but food is sent every day from the eastern states to those who suffer need in the grasshopper areas.

During Christmas I visited Svend Endresen Folkedal and his wife Barbara Sjursdatter whom I hadn't seen since I came here. Christmas traditions are very different here and since there are all kinds of people there are all kinds of traditions. People from some nations don't celebrate Christmas or New Year or any other feasts. There are even many people of different nations who don't belong to any sect or church or who don't even have a religion and don't believe in anything. They don't keep Sunday or any other holiday but work all days. I haven't worked much after New Year because of headaches and spells of dizziness. The doctor claims that it is a kind of rheumatism called neuralgia. On no day have I had to stay in bed and since I'm much better I hope I'll soon be cured. But this winter it has been good to sit indoors close to the fire as it has been so cold after New Year that you can freeze to death as soon as you are out the door. Here are some words I've just read in a newspaper: "There have been terrible snowstorms and cold weather in January and February. Even though the wind may not have been as strong and violent as in the storm we had two years ago it has been colder and the snow has been deeper, stopping trains as well as other means of communication. Every day we hear of accidents involving both people and cattle caused by the cold. All over the western states reports say that this is the coldest and harshest winter people can remember." But the last eight days the weather has been mild so we must hope for an early spring after a hard winter. I must also tell you that I subscribe to the little newspaper *Vossingen* where I can read news from home. But I now fear that *Vossingen* has either frozen to death or been covered by snow because I haven't seen it since before Christmas. I hope it will be thawed by the spring sun. In conclusion, my loving regards to you all. Farewell.

IVER SJURSEN YSTAAS

· ——— ·

In the 1875 census Ulvik Thrond Sjursen Haukenæs is listed as a store-keeper for a co-op in Granvin (*Gravens Forbrugsforening*). His first son, Sjur, was born in 1874. Michaelmas was 29 September 1875. *Vossingen*, a weekly, was first published in Leland, Ill., from 1857 to 1860. The *Vossingen* that ISY subscribed to was published in Voss, a township next to Granvin in Norway, from 1869 to 1877. In 1920 Knut A. Rene began to publish *Vossingen* in the United States and it appeared irregularly until 1950. «II:46 »II:92 NE IV:4

· ——— ·

FROM: Jacob Tonning, *Jewell, Kansas, 21 May 1875*

TO: Paul Henriksen Tonning, *Herøy, Møre og Romsdal*

Unforgettable dear brother,

I received your letter of March 26 yesterday, on May 20, and I'm so sad to see that your dear Henrik has been called to eternity. I see that he was a good and well-meaning human being and I have all reason to hope that he died in the grace of God. Dear brother, as God had not given him more days we must be glad that he lies in his grave with honor rather than with censure and scorn that would have given you grief. So thank the good God who gave him the grace to achieve this. I well know and understand that your loss is great, but, my dear brother, you must with patient fortitude and acceptance of the ways of the Lord say, the Lord gave, the Lord took, may the Lord's name be praised. He surely governs all to the best.

I'll say a little about our situation. As for health, the situation is fairly good except that Gustav has been doing poorly since last fall because of a stomach illness. It seems that the doctors are unable to cure him but he is getting better. Henrik is big and fat, and I and my wife are quite well, thank God. My prospects for feeding my family have changed since I last wrote to you. I've planted five and a half acres with wheat, one fourth of an acre with garden vegetables and three acres with corn. The weather is very pleasant and everything grows and looks nice. I have two cows, one with milk. We expect the other one to calve in a month; she is a large and valuable cow that cost me thirty dollars. I sold my machine for forty dollars in cash and he will do my wheat harvesting. I bought the cow for thirty and bought seed wheat. I had to pay a man fifty dollars to plow land for the wheat. I have worked for one of my neighbors for sixty cents a day and he has lent me money to get my spring work done. This also added up to quite a sum, but what can I say: it cannot be done with a shovel and rake with this kind of soil. We've often feared for our daily bread but always managed. We've been through hard times but if we are spared such devastation this year we should be better off with provisions in the fall. May God grant that I can soon buy another team because it is difficult to hire out for everything we need, especially when wages are as low as they are now; but may the Lord's will be done.

In my letter to Kristoffer that you didn't get I wrote that I became precentor for our congregation last winter. I also asked him to send me a four-part hymnal. I forget the title but Martin Osnes has the one I need. It isn't the hymnal by Lindeman. Please do what you can about this. I don't want to cause you too much trouble but I miss it every time I have choral practice. Dear brother, don't worry too much about me; I'll work as hard as I can to succeed. God will help me. Please write; it gives me such relief every time I receive a letter from you. In conclusion, regards to you all from all of us. Your loving brother,

JAKOB TONNING

· ———— ·

In 1865 Paul H. Tonning (then thirty-five) had the farm Tjærvaag in Herøy, while his younger brother Jakob (then nineteen) lived with him and worked as a day laborer. Kristoffer, Paul's oldest son, was then ten. In the 1880 U.S. census Jacob and Merete Tonning are listed as Jacob and Marita Towning. They were both then thirty-three and had three children, all born in Kansas. (The two sons, Henrik and Gustav, mentioned here were then dead.) The couple died in Genesee, Idaho, in 1923 and 1916 and their names on their grave stones at the Genessee Valley Lutheran Church are Jacob and Meta Tonning. (Information provided by Maggie Rail who visited the churchyard 7 July 2000 with her camera.) The machine, apparently for harvesting, he sold for $30 is not specified and was probably mentioned in an earlier letter where he also seems to have written about his crop failure because of swarms of grasshoppers and the loss of a horse team. Ole Andreas Lindeman published a hymnal in 1838; his son Ludvig M. Lindeman's hymnal (1877), is better known. »II:56 NE IV:6

· ———— ·

FROM: Jacob Tonning, *Jewell, Kansas, 6 June 1875*

To: Kristoffer Paulsen Tonning, *Herøy, Møre og Romsdal*

Dear unforgettable Kristoffer P. Tonning,

For the second time I'll take up my pen to write you a few sentences in my poor hand as I promised in my letter to your father. I answered his last letter the day after I received it. My life here among strangers often seems difficult and lonely, but since the last letter from your father where we learned about the deaths there at home, I've had a heavier and deeper sense of loss. I assume that everything there at home is touched by a silence that I hope will have the good effect of reminding us of the transience of life and increasing in us our longing for eternity, which must always be on our mind. Dear Kristoffer, always think of our dear Jesus in faith, hope and charity and then all sorrow will leave you; for in Jesus there is no sorrow that can hurt your body or your soul because he has given his blood and what can then hurt us. To this you may reply, No, no man can hurt me when I have laid the anchor of my life in the arm of Jesus. Yes, my dear, call in hope upon the Lord and he will certainly help you.

As I still have space I will also tell you about some worldly matters. The crops now look quite good because of the nice, mild weather. The winter rye has formed spikes. There won't be much winter wheat this year, especially on high land. The spring wheat looks very good and is soon ready to form spikes. Corn and potatoes are also growing nicely as are garden vegetables. So may God grant that the terrible swarm won't afflict us again. It looks good so far. This week I've been blasting rock for the house I plan to build in the fall. I'll tell you more about this in another letter. I'm also working for an American who lives about one and a half miles from here. I've worked for him all spring.

On Pentecost Monday I and my wife got out of bed as usual. When she began to make breakfast I lay down again and fell asleep. She looked out the window and suddenly began to cry loudly, Oh God, have mercy on us, the Indians are coming. I leaped out of bed, still half asleep, and looked out on the road. It was as she said. I stood there until they arrived and then one of them got off his horse and came and shook my hand. Mette and the children were in the house, and you may imagine her fear. I wouldn't allow them to enter. If they needed anything I would take care of it where we were. But they behaved quite well. When they saw that I stood firm they said that they came in peace. Their leader asked me for a little food and I gave them bread and milk to drink, but they didn't like milk. They couldn't speak so much English that I was able to learn much about them. They spoke a little but mixed it with their own language so I couldn't understand all they said. They were going to Nebraska where they had some land with forest where they live during summer. During winter they are in the mountains in the southwest. These were the first Indians we've seen in Kansas.

I see that old Jakob Klungsøyr is dead. Please let me know how things are with his children and where they are. And let me know how things are with old Steiner and Maren Tjervaag and their children and also many others you may remember. It gives me great pleasure to hear about my friends. Please write immediately. Fill your letter with all news you may know. Regards to you and your siblings from Henrik and Gustav. Henrik is now visiting his grandparents. And regards to you and all your family from your loving uncle,

JAKOB TONNING

· ——— ·

Kristoffer Tonning is now twenty. His dead brother was two years younger. The first letter JT wrote to him is apparently lost. Mette is an informal version of Merete, his wife who became Marita in the United States. Steiner Ottesen and Maren Andersdatter Tjervaag lived on one of several crofts on the farm owned by Kristoffer's father. They were fifty-four and sixty-two in 1865. «II:55 »II:196 NE IV:7

· ——— ·

FROM: Anne Andresen Nordhus, *Marengo, Iowa, 8 October 1875*

TO: Peder Mortensen Nordhus, *Rennesøy, Rogaland*

Dear cousin Peder Mortensen,

This evening I'm so lonely and think only of you and I remember all the happy and fun times we had together in the days of our childhood. Pardon me that I take the liberty to write these lines to you now that I'm so far away from you. You spoke of getting to know what America was like when I came there. You will get to know this now. I think that for me and all boys and girls it is twice and yet again twice as good as in Norway. A boy may earn a hundred dollars faster than he can make twenty in Norway and isn't that pretty well done?

Dear friend, you mustn't forget me. Remember me. Come and let me see you again if you should ever come to America. You never leave my thoughts. I think I've had a very good time since I came to America. Well, you would also have thought so if you had been here. Time passes quickly for me this evening and soon it is time for me to go to bed and get some rest. I've had much to do today and tomorrow is Saturday. Then too I will have a lot of work but then it is Sunday and then I have nothing to do except to visit friends.

I must stop for now. I'll do better another time. Don't forget to write to me. Please remember this. You must tell me all the news you know there at home. Send me your portrait. Dear cousin, I don't know what news to tell you from here except that it looks very nice. It is as before with Bertel and Dorthe Iversen. Please give my greetings to my parents and siblings and to Uncle and all of Gonel and Serene's cousins. But first and last you are lovingly greeted from me, your cousin,

ANNE ANDRESEN

You mustn't be puzzled by this letter. It is just for fun and once it will have to be the first time I think.

Anne Andresen was Ane Andersdatter before her emigration from Rennesøy. In the 1865 census she is the eight-year-old daughter of the husmann (crofter) at Nordhusle, a croft under the farm Nordhus. Her father Anders Pedersen was a brother of Morten Pedersen, the farmer at Nordhus and father of Morten (twelve in 1865), to whom the letter is addressed. For a reading of this letter see Introduction, Volume One. NE IV:9

1875 — LETTER 2:58

FROM: Christopher Jacobson, *Tybo, Nevada, 11 October 1875*

To: Hans Jakobsen Hilton, *Ullensaker, Akershus*

Dear brother!

Again you've waited far too long for a letter from me and I must admit that I'm much too negligent. But whenever I start writing it seems that I've nothing to write about. I hear from you now and then and I get many letters from Gulbrand. If I write a few words to him I can get a reply in a couple of weeks as the railroad goes there. Hans and Gulbrand seem to be doing well. I often think of visiting Iowa but it's already too late for this year; I wouldn't dare go during winter as it's far too cold—not to speak of Norway where I'd probably be frozen stiff the first day. If I ever go it'll have to be in summer. I told you once that it would cost me five to six hundred dollars to go to Iowa and you thought that was very expensive and I suppose it seems so in Norway. But the truth is I couldn't go there and return for less than 1,000 dollars. It's far and the prices are high. It wouldn't cost me much more to go to Norway and it would be my greatest pleasure to see you all again and see the places where I spent my childhood. Yes, I think that many would wonder whether I was the same boy you had so much trouble with trying to keep home from balls and dances and from staying out at night. And even I would perhaps ask: is it I or is it not I? And many of my playmates, now old men and women, would probably say: is he the one who held his head so high and danced with us twenty-two years ago? Oh no, I'd probably join you all in saying: it is not he. We must stand back a little and when we look at those who are young now we'll have to admit, even though they may be rather wild: we've also done this. I've heard that people have changed in Norway and that they've become rather bold, etc. Progress and success are important reasons for this. In my hours alone I look back on the days that are gone, and the day when you pulled me over the fence so I lost half my coat now seems the happiest of them all. Could we but be so free from sorrow and trouble, my brother, how happy we then would be. If we today wouldn't care about our coat nor worry about where we could get another one, then this earth would be heaven for us. But no, Hans, we can't do this and I often ask myself "why?" But I have no answer. Back then I had my whole life ahead and today (because of my wandering life) I have at most about fifteen years left, and even so it seems difficult for me to take a thousand dollars (even though I would have two left) to go home to you and see you all. And this is the secret. A couple of thousand is not money in this country, so we strive for more, and in this strife we lose the little we have. You mustn't believe that I've become avaricious; no, had that been so I would've had a barrel of gold today. But whenever I have money, I also have poor friends and they will in their turn have money when I'm poor, and so it goes. Enough of this.

When I last wrote I think I was in Belmont. Now I'm in Tybo, thirty-five miles away, and I've been here for one and a half years. I had shares in a mine here and have made a little money. In a few days, perhaps tomorrow, I'll go into the mountains to find other mines. I'll be alone and four or five miles from any white man. Perhaps there'll be a few Indians. I've been there before and I know there is silver there but I don't know how much. If I can find enough to make it pay, I'll stay there for the winter. If not, I'll go somewhere else. I have two partners but they're in other places and if I find anything they'll come to me. If they find anything, I'll go to them. This is all I can say about myself except that my health is good for an old geezer. I was laid up a few weeks ago. A wild horse threw me but now I'm quite well. I sold him along with a rebellious mule for 200 dollars. Now I only have a dark brown mare and her one-year-old foal, but she has also been somewhat spoiled because some of the boys got drunk and rode her forty miles in four hours, but she is still good and can still keep up with the fastest ones.

Well, how are you and yours. You now have grown-up sons and a girl who soon is grown up too, I imagine. And how is our old mother? You must tell her that I'm well and happy. I suppose Lars is busy with his school and has no time to write. Give him my regards. You should let the boys do the work and take a day off and write me a few words about dear Norway. Give my regards to Kari Lystad. I'll write a few words especially for Allette Søli; please give them to her. Best regards to you and your family from your

C. JACOBSON

. ——— .

Tybo, in Nye County, is today a ghost town. Gulbrand and Hans Jensen Haga were shoemakers in Eldora, Iowa. This is where CJ's nephew, Jacob Hansen Hilton, first went when he emigrated in 1877. CJ's brother, Lars Jakobsen, was a teacher as their father had been. Kari Lystad was a sister and Allette Olsdatter Søli (born in 1851) was a niece. In 1875 she was living with her parents, Ole Larsen and Anne Jakobsdatter, at Søli. «I:163 »II:72 NE IV:10

. ——— .

1875 — LETTER 2:59

FROM: Martha Erickson, *Grove City, Minnesota, 5 December 1875*

To: Anna Stensdatter and Elsa Haavardsdatter Lothe
Kinsarvik, Ullensvang, Hordaland

⊷⟹⟸⊶

Dear brothers and sisters in Christ,

May the grace and peace of Jesus be with you, amen. I'll delay no more and write you a few words. Yes, dear mother, if you are still alive in this foreign land, and dear sister, I must ask your forgiveness for not having replied to your dear and welcome letter. It was such a great pleasure to hear that you are doing well and are healthy in both body and soul. I can also report the same grace and joy from God. We have so much to thank God for as he also this year has given us a good and bountiful crop. Yes, dear mother,

I think of how you are in body and in soul since I, your child, cannot give you any help. I so often think that had you been with me you wouldn't have been in need because I know it is difficult for you to have to work so hard when you are old. Though we are far apart in the flesh I hope we are not far apart in spirit. Yes, dear mother, seek all your comfort in the good God and your dear Savior Jesus our eternal high priest who sits at the right hand of the Father and who prays for us. There is true comfort in the words that we have such a friend and savior. I believe you are often with God in your prayers and we have his word that he who prays shall be answered and he who seeks shall find and it will be opened for him who knocks. Such is the word of God. Even though the distance is so great and I cannot help or comfort you, I will within my means send you some money, a bank draft for twenty dollars. I don't know what this is in Norwegian money. It isn't much but if we both live I won't forget to send you more. And you my dear sister Elsa, I haven't written a word to you yet but you'll have to excuse me this time. Write as soon as you get this letter and I'll reply at once. Until then, loving regards to you all, both relatives and friends, from me and my family. From your loving

MARTHA H. D.

Dear grandmother, if I may so call you. I must also send regards from Haavar and from me, his wife. We'll send you our portraits as soon as we have them taken. As I have written this letter you must please excuse my bad writing.

GEA MARIE (MICKELSEN)

· —— ·

ME was from the croft Gjerde under the farm Lote. She dictated her letters and different writers write her name in different ways. The H. D. in her signature is for her patronymic, Haavardsdatter. ME was unmarried when she emigrated with her son, Haavard, who took the name Mickalson and is now married to Gea Marie. ME's brother, Nils, emigrated in 1857 but later returned to Ullensvang. In 1865 ME's mother, Martha Stensdatter, was sixty-six and lived as a widow on a croft belonging to the farm Lote where she is listed as a day laborer. Her sister, Elsa, married to Sylfest Sjursen, lived on another croft under the same farm. They are in a "foreign land" in the sense that their homeland is heaven. ME's American-born daughter, Annie Oline, wrote to her cousin Sara Lote 9 February 1879 (Nor. ed. IV:88), her style and content strongly influenced by her confirmation classes in Norwegian. »II:132 NE IV:13

· —— ·

1876 — LETTER 2:60

FROM: John Torkelsen Rannestad
Medo, Minnesota, 5 January 1876

To: Osmund Atlaksen Ovedal, *Sirdal, Vest-Agder*

Dear brother-in-law,

At long last we must take up our pen to answer your welcome letter dated March 28, 1875 that we received May 1 and saw that you were doing well and that everything was as when we were there. We are so glad to hear from our old home. And we can also say that all is well and that we have returned to where we were because we didn't like it as much there as here and my wife wanted to return. We left my brother Ole May 24 and came here where Rakel used to live on June 2. We drove with oxen and brought everything we owned, including two milk cows, a heifer and two calves. We had a little son September 26, 1875 and christened him Theodore Christian. But the Lord has lain a small cross on him, giving him a slight harelip, but his mouth is fine so we have planned to have it fixed next summer if he lives that long and we think he'll be as fine as any other child. We recently had a letter from our sister Sara in Coon Prairie. They are doing well and Reinert has sold his farm and bought another one at Coon Prairie about five or six miles from our brother Sigbjørn. Siri is with him and she is as well as she has ever been. Sara moves between them and works for both. Sigbjørn's oldest daughter Berte was confirmed last fall. We must also ask whether you have received a book about the conflict in our church here in America. I asked a friend to mail one to you and one to Tore Rannestad but he may not have sent it to Rannestad. I will conclude with loving regards to you our dear brother and to all our relatives at Sandsmark, Konstali and Skibeli.

JOHN TORKELSEN RANNESTAD

JTR's "we" includes his wife, Rakel Tonette. They have been with his brother Ole Torkelsen Rannestad in Willmar. Sara Allikson is with her brother Sigbjørn in Coon Prairie, Wisc., where they have been joined by their siblings Siri and Reinert. The book referred to is August Wenaas, *Wisconsinismen belyst ved historiske kjendsgjerninger* (Wisconsinism as seen in the light of historical facts, Chicago, 1875). Wenaas was professor of theology at Augsburg Seminary. "Wisconsinism" referred to the Norwegian Synod and H. A. Preus came to its defense with *Professorene Oftedal og Weenaas's "Wisconsinisme" betragtet i Sandhedens Lys* (The "Wisconsinism" of professors Oftedal and Weenaas as seen in the light of truth, Decorah, Iowa, 1876). Rakel Tonette Rannestad wrote an undated brief note the next year, telling that they had been to a doctor with Theodore Christian and that the operation was successful. She complains that they hadn't yet had a reply to this letter. «II:50 »II:84 NE IV:15

1876 — LETTER 2:61

FROM: Christine Dahl, *Norse, Texas, 17 January 1876*

To: Peder Eriksen and Siri Kristiansdatter Furuset
Romedal, Stange, Hedmark

Dear parents and siblings,

I received your welcome letter of October 5 but since I'd written so recently I put off my reply. Then I got your second letter dated at Furuset December 13 where I see that you are all quite well except for mother, and this is sad as we are too far away to help her. Even though we know she has help this is not the same as having one of your own with you. I also see that you had much trouble getting the workers who arrived here January 15. Everything went well on their journey and so far they are satisfied. I must send you my deepest gratitude for your trouble. I don't think I'll ever be able to do you something in return even though this would be a great pleasure.

As for us, we are all, praise God, in good health and doing well. The health situation in our settlement is very good and the weather is mild and comfortable. We haven't yet seen snow and the grass is green, which is unusual for this time of year, and it has only been cold enough to freeze ice a couple of times this winter. Cattle and horses feed themselves and are doing well. Last fall I sold thirteen five- and three-year-old mules for forty dollars apiece and the money was paid before Christmas. I've bought more land, 320 acres, near Clifton for three dollars an acre. I gave half of it to Ole and he sold it and got a stone house and ten acres right next to his own land that used to belong to Syverine's father-in-law. The house and ten acres will cost him 1,800 dollars. He'll pay interest for some time on 1,000 dollars, 300 dollars have been paid in cash, and the rest is in a parcel of the land that I gave him and that he now has transferred to his father-in-law. Ole now has a good house that he can move into any time but I don't think he'll move this winter as he has to cut wood for fencing on our land where he has everything he needs in fodder and work animals. I have given him and Syverine two mules each so now I have four mules in addition to my workhorses. This year we got three 500-pound bales of cotton. The price now is from ten to twelve cents a pound.

The Rogstads send their regards. They were here for Christmas visiting their children and came to see us. They are all in good health and doing well. I also have regards from Pauline. She didn't come home for Christmas but Ole met her in Waco after Christmas. She is well and is satisfied. I can also tell you from Per Dilrud and his family that they are well. Please give my regards to the people at Bryne and tell them that Andres was here when his new hired man arrived. He hadn't expected him before spring and now he could take him home. They left today. I see in your letter that the ticket cost more than Hans Dahl says it would on the other line you had planned to send him on, the one the boys who came before this one used. You must let me know the full sum you have paid. And please give Hans Dahl my regards and tell him that I've received his letter of October 8 where I see that he's had a lot of trouble on my behalf and that I'm very grateful. Tell him that I'll soon write to him but not now so you'll hear from us more often. Give our regards to Syverine and her children and to all relatives and friends who may wish to hear from us. But you my dear parents and siblings are first and last greeted from me and my children.

CHRISTINE DAHL

CD wrote 26 October 1875 (Nor. ed. IV:11) about the double wedding of her two oldest children, Ole and Syverine to Gunde Hoff and Nels Jacob Nelson respectively. Ole and his wife were then still living with CD but she had given both couples land four miles north of the Dahl farm. She reports on running the farm and was evidently a competent farmer. She wrote this letter two days after the arrival of new farm workers, whose journey from Romedal had been organized by her brother there. Getting farm workers from Norway and the use of prepaid tickets is a regular theme in the letters sent to Furuset, also letters from outside the family. Syverine is also the name of CD's sister in Norway. «II:51 »II:75 NE IV:17

1876 — LETTER 2:62

FROM: Barbro Tollefsdatter Sando, *Estherville, Iowa, 18 January 1876*

To: Haakon Tollefsen Opsata, *Aal, Buskerud*

Dear siblings,

It is long since I've heard from you and even longer since I wrote, so I'll send you a few lines to let you know how we are. We are all doing well and in good health. As you probably have heard crops have been very bad for some years because these terrible guests, the grasshoppers, have visited us so often and eaten everything they could. But we have, with the help of God, not really suffered any want. We recently heard from our son Ole, who is a pastor, and they are all well. You may be interested in hearing a little about him. He was ordained when he was twenty-three and then went to his congregations 120 miles from here and was there for a year. About two years ago he stopped by and got married. His wife is a daughter of Erik K. Barskrind. Her mother is a half-sister of your wife. They now have a little son named Gustav Adolph. Ole is very busy, like all pastors here in America. He serves ten congregations. Our sons Erik and Tollef live near us. Erik has two children, a boy and a girl; the older will be five years next spring and is named Oliver Ludvig, the younger will soon be three and is named Berthe Andrine. Tollef has two girls; Barbro is soon four and Randine Louise is two. Our son Halvor now goes to college in Decorah and last summer he was here and taught English school. Our daughter Berthe Maria is soon nineteen. She is still home with us but occasionally works for the Americans. Gjermund, our youngest, is soon sixteen and was confirmed last fall. It is good to have him with us now that we are getting old and weak. My health is very poor but not so bad that I have to keep to my bed. Ole has been rather ill this winter and kept to his bed for a while but is now up again. It is only to be expected that we get weaker as we approach old age. We are only a short time in this world and should patiently bear the crosses God lays on us. Oh may we all live in such a way down here that we may meet again yonder with God in Heaven.

We recently had a letter from our brother Ole Opsata. They are doing well and had a very good crop this year. It isn't long since I wrote to our sister Randi. I must now end my letter. I hope you'll soon write to us and tell us how you and our relatives are. News from here would not be of interest to you. Give our regards to all relatives. Our most heartfelt greetings go to you my dear brother and sister and your families from your devoted sister,

BARBRO SANDO

I, the writer of this letter, should also use this occasion to send loving greetings to all my unknown relatives and ask your forgiveness for my bad writing.

BERTHE MARIA

. ——— .

Although BTS addresses her "siblings," it seems that the primary addressee is her brother Haakon (or Haagen). Surely her two sisters in Aal, Guri Tollefsdatter Bøygard and Randi Tollefsdatter Opheim, also read her letter. Since BTS could not write, it is one of her American-born daughters, Berthe Maria, who this time holds the pen and adds a few lines of her own. We may note that Norwegian was a natural language for the second generation in this American family. BTS writes about her high age and poor health; she was fifty-eight in 1876 and died in 1903. She was married to Ole Eriksen Sando. Her son, Ole

Olsen Sando, was a pastor in the Norwegian Synod and served congregations in Luverne, Minn., and Nidaros and Minnehaha in South Dakota. His uncle Ole Tollefsen Opsata also lived in Luverne (see the next letter) but belonged to another synod, the Conference. Members of the two families did not see eye to eye in theological issues. «II:13 »II:63 NE IV:18

· ——— ·

1876 — LETTER 2:63

FROM: Ole Tollefsen Opsata, *Luverne, Minnesota, 24 January 1876*

To: Guri Tollefsdatter Bøygard, *Aal, Buskerud*

⊷═◉ ◒═⊶

Dear sister and family,

It is time that I send you a few sentences so you can hear a little from us. It is long since I got a letter from you with an enclosed portrait for which I must thank you. We were so glad to see you again even if it was only on paper. It reminded us of days past. I am now glad to send you our portrait in return. It is not quite as natural as it should have been, in particular of me. I have aged in the ten years that have passed since we last saw each other. I am soon at the age when our father died; I think he was sixty-four and I was sixty last September. As I write this I am reminded of our dead siblings who were not as old as I am now. God knows how much time I have left in this vale of tears. I must say with the Apostle, my desire is to depart and be with Christ. With Christ! Note that when Paul wrote this there was much sin and tribulation among people even though he came to them with the message of peace: Have faith in the crucified Lord Jesus and you will be saved. They would not believe him and persecuted him. This was when he wrote that he would rather be with Christ. Yes, may God give me and all who are serious in their faith the strength to conquer all enemies of our soul in our faith in him, the Savior of all mankind but most for those who have faith.

It may interest you to hear how we fare with respect to pastoral care and education in our faith. Three and a half years ago all the Norwegians got together to organize ourselves in a Norwegian Evangelical Lutheran congregation named the Blue Mound Congregation, as there is a small mountain here with that name. In our constitution we included the true Word of God and all Luther's confessional writings as well as the texts that have been used in the Norwegian Church. We wrote to Gjeldager asking him to come and serve us with Holy Communion and baptism. He brought a candidate and after he had preached several times for us we called him to be our pastor. He is from Helgeland and was baptized and confirmed by Pastor Hansen who was in Aal some time ago. I believe he is a true Christian and a good man. We haven't been successful with our parochial or, as we say here, Norwegian school, as it is difficult to find a teacher. This winter we've had school for three months in our congregation. I assume Niels has written to you about the church we are building.

As for myself, I'm in good health and my present work is to tend our animals and cut wood and do a little carpentry. I am quite well off owning 160 acres of which fifty-one have been plowed. Last fall I had 500 bushels of wheat, 150 bushels of oats, 300 bushels of corn and more potatoes and garden vegetables than we can use. I own four horses, six cows, some calves and some pigs. I haven't counted my chickens. Every year we are assessed for tax and I've paid eight dollars and thirty cents. For the pastor I've paid four dollars, for the Norwegian school one dollar and I've paid twelve dollars for the new church we are building but this will add up to twice that before it is completed. As for my children, Tollef is married and has a son named Oluf. Ole is a bachelor and lives on his land. Thorsten is married and has a son named Oskar Albert and lives in Goodhue County about 200 miles to the east. Niels is working for me and Margit and Aagot are sometimes here and sometimes working for the Americans, mainly in order to learn the language.

I have no news as you don't know how things are here except that Turi T. Megaarden was married three years ago to a Thosten Larsen Noaas and came here the next spring. Thosten began to accuse her of adultery, first with one and then with another. Last fall they agreed that he should go with her to her father who lives in Estherville. Most think that he suffered from mental illness and all think she is innocent. In conclusion, my loving brotherly greetings to you and your family. All here send their regards and wish you well.

OLE T. OPSATA

Margit Opsata, a daughter of OTO, wrote 8 December 1872 (Nor. ed. III:137) about their new pastor. It may be noted that OTO does not mention that his nephew Ole Olsen Sando was pastor of a competing congregation in Luverne belonging to the Norwegian Synod. The candidate who accompanied Botolf Botolfsen Gjeldager was Hans Zahl Hvid, whose many letters to E. B. Kjerskow Zahl are not included in this edition. OTO quotes from Paul's Letter to the Phillippians 1:23.
«II:62 »II:81 NE IV:19

1876 — LETTER 2:64

FROM: Iver Ellingsen Elsrud, *St. Ansgar, Iowa, 28 February 1876*

To: Elling and Olea Elsrud, *Aadalen, Ringerike, Buskerud*

Dear parents and siblings,

I'm sending you a few words so you can see that I'm in good health and doing quite well, for which I must thank God. I don't have any news even though it may seem that I should. I'll begin by telling you that I'm about to sell my land for 2,000 dollars. As you know, I gave 960 dollars for it and I now owe about 500. If I deduct for the other things I own this should cover my debt and even leave me some. I've planned to return to Norway when I have 2,000 *speciedaler* but as you know, American money is about fifteen cents less on each dollar so it will be some time yet. What do you think a man could do with 2,000 *speciedaler* in Norway? That is something I would like to know. We should have had winter now, but we cannot call it winter as we haven't had more than two inches of snow and that has long since disappeared and we now have the nicest summer weather we could wish for.

And here is my news that I assume is not news for you: Uncle now has the deed for the land of Ole Haugerud or, rather, he has it from grandmother and her lawyer from La Crosse who has been paid 1,250 dollars and will have the remaining 500 in two months. So grandmother will be wealthy in her old age. But this is not all. As you know, grandfather was married twice here in America, first with the one he brought from Norway. Her daughter got the land he had in Iowa and he then went to Minnesota (Albert Lea) and married an old witch. I cannot remember her name but I think it was Anne. Well, the thing is that he had no money and uncle lent him 150 dollars that he still has the receipt for. When grandfather died uncle was in Wisconsin, and as he died of cholera he was not sick more than a day and he left all he had to his wife with witnesses present. When uncle returned he bought the right to have the land from the widow for 200 dollars and she gave him the deed. Uncle has had it for some years and paid the taxes, and the interest on what he had invested there amounted to more than 500 dollars and he sold it for 500 dollars to Andreas Sørensen and gave him the deed.

And then what do grandmother and her descendents in Norway, or rather their lawyer, do. Yes, they take Andreas S. or uncle to court for 2,000 dollars and 1,600 for the use of the land. Grandmother insists that as she was not legally divorced from him she was his legal wife even though he had been married several times. The lawyer includes your names in his subpoena. There is one thing that troubles me. I suppose grandmother thinks she didn't get enough from grandfather in Norway when he was alive and now wants it from his children here fifteen years after his death. The question is whether his testament will be found legally binding as there was no one present who could write and the testament is therefore only oral. The situation is that grandmother will now have a lawsuit in the courts here against her son and it is a strange situation because uncle won't pay. He would rather let the lawsuit argue away a few thousand, and Widvey may have some left of the money he got for the land he sold. Uncle went to Albert Lea a few days ago and we don't know when he'll be back. All of uncle's family are in good health and doing well and send their regards. I must now conclude with my best regards to all friends and most of all to you from your devoted son and brother,

I. ELSRUD

NB. Erik Hansen has married a rich widow. They have a son and live in Lanesboro in Fillmore County, Minnesota. I almost forgot to tell you that I think we'll have a post office here in Haugerud, but I'll write more about this later. I say it is grandmother who says this or does that because she has authorized Widvey to do just as he wishes and whatever he wants. Please write soon.

A letter IEE wrote 29 October 1875 (Nor. ed. IV:12) is not included here. T. J. Widvey, now in La Crosse, was the second of two lawyers used by Guri Rustand. There are many more letters about this matter than can possibly be included here. In 1876 for instance Gulbrand and Gunvald Jonsrud wrote about the case 26 and 29 February, 3 March and 15 August. «II:41 »II:68 NE IV:22

1876 — LETTER 2:65

FROM: Anders Helgesen Skare, *West Lake, Minnesota, 15 May 1876*

To: Helge Gundersen and Halvor Helgesen Skare
Eggedal, Sigdal, Buskerud

Dear and unforgettable father and brother, Helge and Halvor Skare and families,

It's long since I've written so I must let you hear from me. I and my children are in good health, for which we must thank God, and in your letter dated 03.13.76 I see that all is well with you and that you would like to hear from me. Perhaps I should tell you what animals I have and about my harvest. Of cattle I have twenty-six, among them twelve milk cows and a team of oxen and I have six workhorses and three foals, and twenty-three sheep. My land is 500 acres and of this I've broken 170 that I harvest. Last year I had 2,800 bushels of wheat and 1,600 bushels of oats. You may think this is a good crop and I suppose it is; we had a good year last year. Then I must let you know what I've done this past year. I need to have a housemaid and she is paid more than a hundred dollars a year and I also have to hire other help, so I'm sure that I pay 500 dollars a year. And for things such as clothes and other things for the house I think I pay 300 dollars a year. The tax on my land is about fifty dollars a year and then there are expenses for machines and other tools that need to be kept in repair, so much money is spent during a year. But I have no reason to complain or boast, but things have gone well up to now. I haven't written about my crops or what I have as I know that you don't know the situation here and think there is such an abundance and misunderstand my situation. But I've done this now since you asked about it. I must also tell you about my children. Helge and John are confirmed and Elly is preparing for confirmation. They have all been in good health. I have good help in my oldest children. This is short and simple-minded but I don't seem to have more to write about so I'll conclude with loving greetings to you from me and my children. Please send my regards to Uncle Halvor Skadeland and his children as well as to other relatives and acquaintances. From your devoted son and brother,

ANDERS H. SKARE

. ——— .

Halvor Gundersen Skadeland was the brother of Helge Skare. «II:35 »II:90 NE IV:26

. ——— .

1876 — LETTER 2:66

FROM: Ole Gulbrandsen Lande, *Eureka, Kansas, 28 June 1876*

To: Anders Olsen Gjømle, *Flesberg, Buskerud*

⊹⟹⇐⊹

Dear father-in-law,

Thank you so much for your letter of April 8 that we received some time ago. We see that you don't think we'll return to Norway but it is our serious intention to return if God grants us life and health. We also see that you think the journey must be difficult but we didn't find it so as everything went very well, so we are not anxious about our return journey. You should know that we'll be back as we otherwise would not have left behind the money we have entrusted to Niri Kolkinn. The reason we've bought more land is that we believe we can sell it more easily than we could our first land that was somewhat limited and had too little space for cattle.

We see that you've sold Gjømle to Nils and this made my wife sad since she has always believed she would have Gjømle and she didn't think you would sell it before we had returned. But we assume that your illness is behind this. I comfort her that if she doesn't get Gjømle she will get money and that there is always a farm to be bought. Moreover, we see in the letter from Nils that there still may be a possibility for her to get Gjømle. We also see that you are planning to sell your other farms and we also think this would be best as we are not interested in any of them and Nils and Marit are probably not very interested either. My wife would like to know whether Nils inherited Gjømle or bought it. We were sad to see that you were ill last winter and hope that you'll be well the next time you write. We are glad that your thoughts are on God. Our best regards and may the Lord's grace be with you.

OLE LANDE AND WIFE

. ——— .

Returning home is a theme in OGL's letters from Kansas. His successful years in Kansas illustrate that failure was not necessarily the motivation for an immigrant's return. Only a few of OGL's many letters are included. On the day he wrote this one he also wrote to his brother-in-law Nils Nilsen Liveland (married to Marit Andersdatter), who had just bought his father-in-law's farm. He wrote to his sister-in-law Marit on 1 November 1876 (Nor. ed. IV:34) that he was not ready to renounce his right to have the farm back. In 1900 Marit, a widow, is still the farmer at Gjømle. In his letter to his sister-in-law he writes that they miss not having a pastor: "There are enough Scandinavians here to have a pastor if they only could unite, but since they do not confess to the same synod we must be without a pastor." «II:33 »II:87
NE IV:29

. ——— .

1876 — LETTER 2:67

FROM: Svend H. Enderson, *Lee, Illinois, 28 July 1876*

To: Jakob Rasmussen Sandvik, *Kinsarvik, Ullensvang, Hordaland*

⊷⟹○⟸⊶

Dear cousin,

As I've just received such a welcome letter from you I must take up my pen to tell you about my situation. I can first tell you, praise God, that I'm doing well and in good health. My sister Marta has also been in good health since she came but she is rather unhappy and longs for Norway and her friends there. I had longing to begin with but I'm now getting used to things and beginning to like it here, as is my sister. It's worse to begin with when the people and the work are strange but now I'm getting to know the people and getting used to the work. Work here is different than in Norway. You mustn't believe it's easy. I'm working for Haldor Seglgjerd this summer. I've been invited to live here when I don't have work, as has my sister Marta. There is no work during winter and then we'll live here. This is the family that Jakob and Dorthea lived with. They are very nice people. I haven't been with kinder people.

I'm on a crew with a mowing machine and we cut hay much faster than in Norway. Two horses pull the machine and a man sits on it and drives the horses. They mow fourteen to sixteen acres a day and what they mow before dinner they take to the barn after dinner. They rake with a machine pulled by a horse. When the hay is raked they load it on wagons pulled by two horses and they have loads that are as big as houses and use forks to load the wagons. The hayforks are like the manure forks in Norway, but sharper. I've also worked with a machine that cuts wheat and it was a good deal faster than the scythes in Norway. They cut from twelve to fourteen acres a day. Four horses pull this machine. It leaves the wheat in bunches and we walk behind it and bind the wheat. This is hard work. You often have to change your shirt two or three times a day. We use clothes of cotton. You can wring the sweat out of your pants so I would call it hard work.

The heat is very strong and you may imagine that the work is tough when the day is at its hottest. It's been hot this summer. One week we had ninety-nine degrees. You cannot go into the woods when it is hot like we did in Norway and you cannot rest like we did in Norway. You have to be at it all the time like an ant.

It is usual to get up at four or four thirty to milk the cows. They have twelve, sixteen and up to twenty milk cows. And you have to tend the horses and they have six and up to twelve horses each and up to twenty hogs. We have to feed them on Sundays as on Mondays and when you've milked the cows and tended the other animals you can have breakfast. And then you work until dinner at twelve. Then you have an hour's rest but no sleep and then you work again until eight or nine and then it is dark. Nights are as dark as they are in fall in Norway. They light the fire every night all year round. They eat three times a day and they often have as many as six courses on the table at the same time and I can say that there is good food in America. They don't eat sour milk and porridge as in Norway but even so I must say that I liked things better in Norway. There we got more rest. Here they only rest one hour a day. They don't rest the horses and work all the time. They use two horses for all kinds of work. You don't have to carry things on your back but the work is hard. There is only a brief spell of light work in the spring when they plow in the corn. They plow in the corn for weeds and then they use a plow that you can sit on, and that is light work. But all other work is hard and it so happens that the hardest work is when the temperatures are highest.

I must say that work was lighter in Norway. But pay is better here so it is easier to earn money than in Norway. But no one should think of going to America if they want to make money without working. You can't sleep your-self into anything here. You must work hard to get anything and you won't find heaven on earth here either. I wouldn't advise anyone who makes a liv-ing in Norway to go to America but for those who must rely on their hands it is easier here than in Norway. Here a simple crofter can have as many as three cows that can graze along the road during summer because this is free here. This is called the post road. It's fenced and there is good meadow on both sides and cows graze there. They can also have three or four hogs so I must say that the poor live better here than in Norway so I don't think it is wrong for the poor to go to America. But those who have a farm and sell it to go to America do wrong. But if they have money when they come to America they can buy land at once and then it wouldn't be so bad for them and I see that anyone who has land, however little, does better than those with land in

Norway. But I also see that people are careful in buying because everything costs more. So if you want a lot of luxury it will be expensive here. For many it doesn't matter how much they may get paid; when winter comes and they have to pay for board they'll have nothing left. They can tend animals in return for board or they can pay two dollars a week for board and that is considered cheap here. At the hotels they pay three or four dollars for board. Board during winter was cheaper in Norway.

It's good for girls to be in America because they don't have to do outdoor work. All they do is cook, do laundry, iron, and help with milking. This is what Marta does in the home of Amund Laaming from Odda. He lives a short distance from Haldor. We meet every Sunday. We can also see Jakob and Dorthea every Sunday. They are not far from us. The landscape is quite flat and I can see six churches from one place. Our pastor is Johannes Tackle. He is very good. He is Haldor's nearest neighbor and he was the first Norwegian I met when I came to Lee. Lee is a town that is about four miles from Haldor Seglgjerd. That is the farthest I walk here. They have poor water here; there is no running water. They only have wells and when the weather is very hot the water is warm. The air is not as fresh as in Norway and there are so many flies and mosquitoes that sleep is difficult and there are also many different kinds of snakes.

I don't regret going to America as there is so much to see and learn, and for unmarried people it is easy to earn enough money for a return to Norway. I plan to stay for two or three years and make a little money and then return to Norway and live there, and you'll see me in Norway again in three years if I live and the Lord grants me health. I doubt that I'll like it in America; not many do. I think of you a lot. I had much fun in Norway that I don't have here. There isn't much opportunity to visit the girls here. I haven't been in a girl's bed yet and I don't know when it can be. They don't have such a custom here. The rules are strict and they are allowed to shoot those who come in to visit the girls at night so I don't think I'll be visiting the girls much until I return to Norway.

No more for this time. I can tell you that I'll be harvesting wheat, corn, oats, and hay. Please give my regards to my mother and siblings and tell them that I don't regret coming here, as it has been fun to see what America is like. I can also tell you that I've spoken to Josephus almost every Sunday and Iver Oppedal and Osmund Børve. He'll go to Norway in the fall and I've spoken with many others who want to return to Norway. I can't send you my portrait yet but you'll get it in the fall when I plan to have one taken. Best regards from me and my sisters. Give my regards to Haldor and

Sigri Bjotvet and to all acquaintances. And thank you for your portrait and your letter. Write soon and tell me what is going on. Farewell.

. —— .

> The letter has no signature. In the 1865 census SE is sixteen and living with his mother, a poor widow, and four siblings as renters on a croft under the farm Hus with another widow. At the time of this letter he has recently emigrated with his sister Marta. His mother, Sigrid Svendsdatter Hus, eventually emigrated around 1885. In his early letters SE used the farm name Hus and then experimented with different versions of his patronymic, Endreson, Endson, Endeson, and eventually seems to have settled on Enderson, using the middle initial H to represent his farm name. He wrote to Jakob Sandvik 29 September 1876 (Nor. ed. IV:32), about his work and girls; only a selection of his letters is included here. In 1865 Jakob Sandvik was eleven, living with his parents and five siblings on the croft Salthelleren under Sandvik. In 1900 Salthelleren is still his home. Dorthea, married to Jakob Svendsen Haugstvet, was SE's older sister. In many parts of rural Norway it was the custom for unmarried young men to visit unmarried young women after they had gone to bed. The visits were supposed to be social and both parties were to be fully dressed. It is sometimes difficult to interpret SE's writing and orthography and two sentences have been omitted for this reason. »II:69 NE IV:30

. —— .

1876 — LETTER 2:68

FROM: Iver Ellingsen Elsrud, *St. Ansgar, Iowa, 23 November 1876*

To: Elling and Olea Elsrud, *Aadalen, Ringerike, Buskerud*

Dear parents and siblings,

As time permits I'll send you some sentences so you can see that I'm alive and in reasonably good health even though I have a strong cold and must stay indoors. Uncle has been ill in bed for some time and it doesn't look good for him, but with God's help we must hope for the best. I'm beginning to fear for my own health as my back and indeed my whole body hurts almost all the time because I've worked too hard. You have to work hard here in order to make money. I have no news that will interest you so I'll tell you a little about this year's harvest. For wheat, barley and oats we had about one third of an average year but it was a good year for both corn and hay. I have about fifteen tons of hay and I wish I could have had that in Norway. As you know I let my land on shares last year and my share was 200 bushels of wheat. I won't let all of it next summer but keep enough to have work for two horses.

These are very hard times for both laborers and farmers with hardly a day's work to be had and almost no money among people, so I don't understand what this will come to. I have about 500 dollars owed to me that was due this fall but was only able to collect 200 and I owe some money that I should have paid but what can I do? I cannot make money. You know I had a mare that had a foal last spring and I tried to sell it but couldn't get a reasonable price, so I bought another one as it is as much work to take care of one as two and paid twenty dollars. (Last year a foal of that size was fifty dollars.) So you can see what the times are like here. I know nothing about the testament grandfather was supposed to have made and I think this is no more than lies and fabrications by evil people and they have it from uncle's widow. Don't believe any of it. I now have about 100 acres of field that I'll plant next spring and then hope to make some money. The price for wheat is pretty good, ninety cents a bushel, but this is of little use when I have nothing to sell. America has no wheat for export this year. If Russia goes to war with Turkey we'll have high prices for all grains and this would be good for us but not very welcome where you are. I'll conclude with friendly regards to all acquaintances, none mentioned so none forgotten, and most of all to you from your devoted son and brother. Give my regards to old grandmother. In conclusion my best wishes for a Merry Christmas and a Happy New Year. I hope you'll receive these lines before Christmas.

I. E. ELSRUD

· —— ·

IEE enclosed an account of his financial situation concluding with a balance of $3,270. Of this, $2,880 is his assessment of the value of his 160 acres. While many of the letter writers are focused on cultivating a farm or developing a business, IEE seems focused on cash that he can take back to Norway. He wrote 12 June 1877 about his land and the visit he was about to make to Albert Lea (Nor. ed. IV:46). In 1878–1879 he visited Aadalen, returning to Iowa in May. «II:64 »II:97 NE IV:35

· ——— ·

1876 — LETTER 2:69

FROM: Svend H. Enderson, *Lee, Illinois, 23 December 1876*

To: Jakob Rasmussen Sandvik, *Kinsarvik, Ullensvang, Hordaland*

⊷≫◉⟨≪⊷

Dear unforgettable friend,

I received your welcome letter December 22 and read it with great pleasure. I see that you are in good health and can write you the same in return, praise God. I'm not doing much as there is no work to be had during winter. I have a good time and my only work is to tend the animals and milk the cows here where I live with Haldor Seglgjerd. I board here, as do Jacob and Dorthea, so I must admit that I'm doing very well. I've decided to attend the English school after Christmas. I'll pay one dollar a month so it's a very cheap school. It's necessary to learn the language here. For eight days last summer I made a dollar a day. The pay is good. The regular wage for one day is a dollar. Last summer I was a day laborer and made about 100 dollars and I would have had to work a long time for that money in Norway. I've paid my travel expenses and have a little left over to pay for my board, buy some clothes, and pay for the English school. Marta will also go to the English school this winter. She longs for Norway but is better now. She'll visit Haldor after Christmas. She is working for a Norwegian and will come home to us for Christmas. Haldor has five children, two boys and three girls. One of his daughters is eighteen, another is now preparing for confirmation and the third is thirteen. His oldest son is twenty-one and the youngest is ten. A boy from Espe in Norway also boards here. We are good friends and have a good time with the girls. I must say that I wouldn't have had much time for women here if I had brought Kristi with me to America. No, I'll have to have what is available here or let it be.

Dear Jakob, thank you so much for all the news. It is as welcome for us to have news from Norway as it is for you to have information about America. It has been rather cold, so cold that we've had to use a hoe to hack loose the dung in the cow stable, so you may imagine how cold it is. It is either very hot or very cold. We haven't had much snow yet. The cows are outdoors all winter. There would have been much for you to see here, Jakob. You would have done better had you been in America but we also know that we are in the world wherever we may be. Things are better organized than in Norway. There is no drinking and messing around and no visiting the girls at night and no card games. These things are considered the work of the devil. There is church service almost every Sunday. The church is as well organized as in Norway and the service is almost the same as in Norway. There are two stoves in the church; you are as warm there as in a house. And people do much as they please.

Dear Jakob, please keep the portrait I sent you since you had to pay so much for the letter. I'm sending a portrait for you and the other one you should, as you know, give to her and ask her to send me her portrait as soon as possible. Give my regards to my relatives, to Svend, and to my mother and Inger and Ole Jaastad and his wife. Farewell.

SVEND ENDRESEN HUS

· ⸺ ·

Jacob is SE's brother-in-law and Dorthea and Marta are his sisters. Espe is a farm in Ullensvang. The Inger mentioned in the conclusion is probably his youngest sister. «II:67 »II:73 NE IV:37

· ⸺ ·

1877 — LETTER 2:70

FROM: Hellik Olsen Lehovd, *Salem, Minnesota, 5 January 1877*

To: Ole Helgesen, Knut Olsen Lehovd, and Jørand Olsdatter Aslefet
Flesberg, Buskerud

＊━━◉⊂━＊

Dear father, brother and sister in Norway,

I must take up my pen to write some words to you, but you'll have to excuse that it is short because writing is difficult. With a grieving heart I must tell you that it pleased the Lord in his wisdom to call away my dear and beloved wife in the night of December 15. So Christmas has been a time of sorrow instead of joy because it is difficult to part from those we love in this world. But I hope the exchange was good for her, as she surely has joined our already dead children with Jesus Christ our Savior. She was very weak towards the end but she was around the house and did her chores. She was with child and had only six weeks before she would give birth. And it began with bleeding. She was up the last day she was alive, but in the afternoon she was so ill that I had a midwife here and had medicine from the doctor, but nothing helped. I had help from Paul and Jørand. We had her funeral on the nineteenth and I am now alone with my five children. It is difficult for Julia. She grieves so for her mother and has to take care of her small siblings; the youngest one was only two on November 3. My children were also ill last fall and Julia had just become well when her mother died. They are now all well and I've been in good health since you last heard from me. It doesn't look good for me now but we must hope that we'll be helped. God will not forget anyone who trusts in him so we must take all from him in good and bad times.

This has been a bad year; I made less than half of what I did last year. I had 386 bushels of wheat and 225 bushels of oats but the price of wheat is a little higher this year. We must be satisfied with what the Lord gives us since we have our daily bread. I've seen a letter from you to Paul where you write about my brother Knut's wedding so I must wish you all luck and happiness in your undertaking. May the Lord bless you in your worldly as well as your spiritual life. With this I must conclude my letter and first send my regards to my dear old father. My regards also go to Knut and his wife with the hope that they may have a long and happy life together; and to Jørand and her husband Knut; and, finally, to all my relatives and acquaintances from me and my children with the wish that the Lord will protect you and preserve you wherever you may go and give you a blessed departure from this world to eternal life in heaven and that we there may be gathered with our dear and loved ones. May the Lord give you strength to bear these sad tidings from your unforgettable son and brother.

HELLIK OLESEN LEHOVD

. —— .

HOL's brother Ole wrote four days later from Kasson to his brother Knut about his wife's illness and other deaths in the neighborhood. There are two other letters by HOL in 1877 (27 May and 20 June). Paul and Jørand are HOL's brother and sister-in-law. «I:54 »II:78 NE IV:39

. —— .

1877 — LETTER 2:71

FROM: Karen Olsdatter Brager, *Modena, Wisconsin, 15 February 1877*

To: Johan Olsen and Lisbeth Brendhagen, *Vang, Hedmark*

⋆⇒◉⇐⋆

Dear unforgettable brother and family,

Some time ago I received your welcome letter of July 31. Please forgive me for waiting so long before replying. I have, praise God, the great pleasure of telling you that since I last wrote I and my children have been in good health except for three weeks at Christmas when I was so weak that I doubted whether I would regain my health and thought that if it was according to the will of God that I should leave this world and be with Christ then I would be satisfied. I didn't seem to fear death nor did it trouble me that I would leave my dear little ones if this was the will of God because I have seen so many examples of how wonderfully God provides for me and mine. So I had no fear but was glad that my time of redemption was near so I could sing the new song for God and the Lamb with my dear departed husband and all other believers. As for my daily life, time passes more easily than I could have imagined as the Lord always carries the heaviest end of my cross. Naturally I sometimes have dark moments that may bring on doubts and fears for both worldly and spiritual matters, but, praise God, it doesn't take long before the Lord through his Holy Spirit eases the darkness of my sorrow and lets my heart praise and thank him for all he has done for me. It was God's will that I should go to this country and here find my beloved husband and it was also God's will that I should leave him. I had received him as a gift from God and in his mercy I also gladly gave him back, so I owe thanks to God for all. God has in wonderful ways helped me through my worldly concerns. My haying was mostly done by helpful people and for my harvest sixteen people came one day and did it all. My parents-in-law are also in my neighborhood and are of much help and support, more than one could expect as they are getting old and weak. My harvest was 153 bushels of wheat, not much as we had a middling harvest this year. This winter I am feeding two cows and a heifer and one of the cows is about to calve. Last fall I sold a cow for twenty-nine dollars that I hope will be useful for my sister's travel expenses if it is God's will that she comes here. I wish that you my dear brother will write to me now and then. My best regards from me and my children to you and your wife and children. Your

KAREN BRAGER

· ——— ·

This is the last letter of this family's correspondence in this edition.
«II:39 NE IV:40

· ——— ·

FROM AMERICA TO NORWAY

FROM: Christopher Jacobson, *Watsonville, California, 6 March 1877*

To: Hans Jakobsen Hilton, *Ullensaker, Akershus*

Dear brother!

I should have written a long time ago, but I've been so busy since coming to this new place that I haven't had time until now. Another reason is that I cannot write Norwegian as easily as I used to. Since I never speak my mother tongue I cannot let my thoughts run so fast and there are often words I want to use but that I cannot remember. So you must excuse my incoherent letters and bad *grammar*. Nevertheless, I don't boast of my writing in English either as I make many mistakes. So of this you will understand that I've lost the one before I learned the other and can therefore write neither Norwegian nor English.

Well, Hans! I've left the silver mines and begun to cultivate the soil. This is something I know nothing about but I'm sure I'll do well. I live ninety miles south of San Francisco (five hours by train) near a small town called Watsonville four miles from the ocean with 2,000 inhabitants. We can always hear the sound of the waves. My farm is small. (Twenty acres—if you know how much land is in an acre; I don't.) But the land is very good. We have no winter; that is, we have no snow and rarely see ice. It rains now and then from December to April. In the other months it never rains, but we have a heavy fog that rises from the sea almost every morning. We planted grains about a month ago; potatoes, corn, beans etc. are not planted until April. We are two. I have a partner, an American, whose name is Hudson. He came from Nevada a few days ago while I came January 8 to get things going. I bought two small but lively horses and you should have seen me plow with horses that both trotted and galloped. My stiff legs were even stiffer at the end of the day. A week ago I bought a cow and a calf and you should see me milk the cow as well. It didn't go so well the first few days but I've improved. My partner says he'll take care of the cow. Tomorrow I may watch how he does it. We have about seventy-eight fruit trees: apples, pears, cherries etc.—more than we need, but we can sell what we don't. We have a little garden where we have some trees that give shade and all kinds of flowers that will be blooming in a month or so. Next fall I can tell you what our land will produce. But I know we can make a good living without too much work.

I got tired of running around in the mountains. My gray hairs began to show my age so I thought it might be best to settle down before I lost the few shillings I'd been able to save; as long as you're in the mines you'll always speculate and it's easier to lose than to win. But I don't know whether I'll enjoy this lazy way of life. I've never settled down since I left you at the train station at Kløfta but always wandered among all kinds of people. When I've gotten tired of one place I've moved to another. But now I can't just take my bed and go off so it may be that with time I'll feel that I belong here. But I can sell this place for more than I paid for it, but not just yet, so this will give me the opportunity to reflect more before I leave the known for the unknown. Right now there is no other place I think I would be happier than here. Well, perhaps Norway, but it looks so cold up there that it chills me to think of it.

I wrote to your son Jacob February 12 and sent him fifty dollars. I don't know whether this will be enough money for his journey. I hadn't then received his letter since it had been mislaid between here and Tybo. But I got it a few days after I had sent my letter and I was glad to see that you all were in good health. Well, Hans, there is no use going against it. Jacob has made up his mind about America and it is better to let him go while he is young. The separation will be difficult for you and Anne, but you know that this has to be so I think he should go now. It will be easier for him to learn the language and the American ways. I hope you aren't angry that I sent him a few shillings for his journey because I'm reluctant to oppose you as you are about the only one left who can give me words of comfort.

I'm in a good country. I have my health. I also have good friends, but because of my wandering I haven't taken a <u>wife</u>, who may, if you find the right one, be a good friend, comforter and help in life. So, brother! I'm alone when I get your letters and then I remember the old days when I ran so happily up to Gardermoen while you were there and when I ran in secret to a <u>dance</u>. Those days are past. Who would know me should I come to Norway? No one, because I'm not the same <u>Christopher</u>. I'm glad that I now and then hear from your children, but they belong to a new world and I don't know them. Tell Jacob to write to me if he isn't happy in America and I'll send him money for his return. Your

CHRISTOPHER

CJ admits that he finds it difficult to write Norwegian and this is evident, for instance, in his use of English idioms in Norwegian and substituting English words for Norwegian ones. When he for instance writes *sølver-minerne* for the silver mines this is neither English nor Norwegian but a mixture of both. CJ's nephew Jacob Hansen Hilton emigrated that spring and wrote his first letter to his father from Iowa 15 July 1877. «II:58 »II:86 NE IV:41

1877 — LETTER 2:73

FROM: Svend H. Enderson, *Lee, Illinois, 12 March 1877*

To: Jakob Rasmussen Sandvik, *Kinsarvik, Ullensvang, Hordaland*

Dear and always remembered friend,

I've received your dear letter and read it with great pleasure as I hear that you're all in good health and this is the best I can hear from you. I can tell you in return that we're also in good health, for which we must thank God. Yes my dear Jacob, thank you so much for sending me news and you may be sure that I'm glad to hear how things are in my old home. It's as if I'm given a new life when I have a letter from Norway. Our childhood home is the one we love the most. No matter where we travel and how much we enjoy ourselves, we can never forget our old home. This is how it is for me and I believe for others as well even though I'm happy here and don't wish to be in Norway. It's better here for those who had nothing in Norway. But you'll always miss something regardless of where you may be in the world.

I've just left the English school because I'm soon going to begin work. I liked being in school. There were thirty-seven children there but only three grown-up boys; the others were little boys and girls. I didn't hear anything but English spoken all day. I had thought it would be more difficult to learn the language but I didn't find it so difficult because now I can understand all kinds of things in that language. I've read two English books of the same size as your schoolbooks. My sister Marta hasn't gone to school because she has worked all winter. She is working for our pastor and next summer she is going to work for a Norwegian. I'm moving on March 17 so I'll get to know the people and my duties. My job begins April 1.

It's been rather cold and we've had lots of snow. I can tell you that this week two boys from Odda returned to Norway. They lived near here and I know them well as I've worked with them. They haven't done anything but drink and fight. And I can tell you that Svend Iverson Opedal hurt himself last month because a team ran off with him and he fell off the wagon and broke his arm. He is getting better but I don't think he'll be working this summer. Svend lives near me. I won a watch in a lottery, but not a very good one. We were thirty boys who bought tickets and each ticket cost thirteen cents and it so happened that I got the watch for 13 cents. I suppose it cost seven or eight dollars when new. I don't have much else to write about. I hope I'll have more when I've worked a while.

Please tell Torbjørg Sandvik that I'll send her my portrait as soon as possible. I had one, but I couldn't send it. Marta also promises to send her portrait to Torbjørg. Give them our regards. Please give my regards to all acquaintances and ask Svend if he won't soon join me. There is much here for him to see, above all the nice girls we have around us. I'm as popular with the girls here as in Norway. When I was in Norway I heard that there was no time for girls here, but that isn't true. You could have twenty if you wanted them. You should come here Jacob. Best regards. Write soon. Your friend,

SVEND ENDRESEN HUS

Please deliver the enclosed letter. Don't let anyone see it.

· —— ·

Odda borders Ullensvang. «II:69 »II:93 NE IV:42

· —— ·

FROM: Guttorm Olsen Lee, *Primrose, Wisconsin, 7 April 1877*

TO: Anders Olsen Lie and Mari Olsdatter Lie, *Hedalen, Sør-Aurdal*

Our dear and often remembered siblings and our dear old mother in Norway, which we have left but will never forget,

Yesterday we had the pleasure of receiving your letter so I'll sit down to write some brief and simple words in reply. We see that you are all in fairly good health and we can, thank God, tell you that we are in good health except that I am rather poorly. But I am, thank God, not so ill that I have to stay in bed. There has been much illness in our neighborhood this winter, especially this spring, and there have been some deaths but not people you know. We see that your son Ole plans to come to America and wonders whether we could send money to Quebec. We would of course do this but I think it would be better if he could borrow the money from one in his group of travelers or from an acquaintance there at home and then we would repay them as soon as they arrive. If you buy a ticket from Christiania to Madison it will be cheaper. If you don't write us until just before he leaves Christiania, he'll cross the ocean as fast as the letter and then he'll have to wait for the money and this will be both tiresome and expensive, so I'm sure it would be better if he could borrow money there. As soon as he arrives I can send a draft for the amount back to Norway. And if this should not be possible then you must write immediately about what line he will be taking and when he will be boarding, and I'll do my best to send the money in time. Tell me the name of the ship as well as of the captain.

I can't think of more to tell you now, except that you are welcome and I hope that God in his grace will be with you in your enterprise. I must give you our warmest thanks for the portrait; we were glad to see our relatives. As I can't think of any more to write about I must lay down my pen and end my simple letter with a humble prayer to God that he in his grace and compassion will help us in all the days of our lives and lead us on the path of truth and salvation to eternal life. Dear brother, remember me in your prayers. Regards from us all. Sincerely,

GUTTORM O. LEE

. ———— .

GOL's brother Ole wrote to Hedalen 10 January 1876 (Nor. ed. IV:16). GOL sometimes writes about his nephew in the third person and sometimes he addresses him in the second person. His nephew, however, did not come via Quebec but by steamer via England to New York, as did most immigrants by this time. «II:52 »II:76 NE IV:44

. ———— .

1877 — LETTER 2:75

FROM: Anne Pauline Furuset, *Norse, Texas, 4 July 1877*

To: Erik Pedersen Furuset, *Romedal, Stange, Hedmark*

⋆⇒⇐⋆

Dear brother,

I must answer your welcome letter that I received so long ago and that I've thought of answering all that time without doing it. So I'll set down a few words so you can see that I'm alive. I've been in Waco these last seven months. When the time came for me to go to the settlement, something I always look forward to, I went from my place of work to where I was to wait for the wagon that was to get me. When I saw them they gave me the sad message that our beloved father has left us. Oh, may he rest with God in Heaven. I had heard that our dear father was ill, but I comforted myself with the hope that I would soon hear that he was better. I hadn't seen our father's last letters. When I came to Dilrud I got to see them. Two days after I had come home, Christine came with the letter about his death and funeral. Oh, had I but been able to see him and speak with him during his last days. Oh, had I only written some words to him. Now I grieve that I was so thoughtless that I did not write more often, but my writing is so poor. Every day I think that I should write but nothing comes of it.

I've been here for eight days. I haven't been to Dahl or anywhere else and I'm not planning to go anywhere because Karen needs me. She is expecting a child again so there is much to do; but all are in good health. Today is the Fourth of July. Almost the whole settlement is gathered for dinner and celebration. They dance in the evening.

Yes, my dear brother, I see that you are determined to take over the farm and I will of my full heart wish you success and God's blessing in your undertaking. I also see that there will be something for each of us. I haven't thought of this but I'm sure it will be welcome, but I hope that you are not so generous that you won't have a good start with your farm. You must consider that the farm also represents the hard work of your youth. Poor mother, who is left alone with her sorrow in her old age! Don't let her have such days as our father. Don't let anyone mislead you. But I shouldn't be saying this as I've been disobedient to my parents. I think of this so much now. Many a time I've experienced the truth in mother's words. I know that you paid more attention to our parents than I did and I hope that you'll continue to do so. I'll now end my poor letter. Give my best regards to Syverine. All at Dilrud and Dahl send their regards. But first and last greetings to you from

PAULINE F.

Don't let any others see my letter. Just tell them about it. I would like to have a letter in return but I cannot expect this. Farewell.

· ⸻ ·

At the Dilrud farm APF was with her sister Karen Dilrud. It may be noted that she thinks of the homes of her sisters near Clifton in Bosque County as her home. Although Erik, as the only son, inherited the farm, he had to pay his siblings' share of its assessed value as their inheritance. «II:61 »II:85 NE IV:47

· ⸻ ·

1877 — LETTER 2:76

FROM: Ole Andersen Lee, *Mount Vernon, Wisconsin, 15 July 1877*

To: Anders Olsen and Kari Mikkelsdatter Lie
Hedalen, Sør-Aurdal, Oppland

⊷══◉═⊶

Dear and unforgettable parents and brothers as well as all friends and relatives in Norway that I have left but not forgotten,

We have come safely and happily to Uncle Guttorm and must send you a brief account of our journey even though we don't, after such a short stay, have much else to write about. We left Christiania June 22 at five in the afternoon and came to Kristiansand at five in the morning. Here the ship loaded more freight and received more passengers. We had land on both sides and we enjoyed sitting on deck and admiring the towns and the landscape, but now we entered the open sea and Norway's coast, that till now had smiled so kindly to us, stayed behind and gradually sank in the ocean. Soon we were only surrounded by heaven and sea. The weather, that up to now had been pleasant and nice, became more and more turbulent and at nightfall we had a strong storm. The sea washed many times across the deck with such power that it broke the ship's railing and filled the hold with water so that all our baggage (that is our chests; because our bedclothes and the other things we had placed in the bunks did not get wet as these were above the floor) were floating and were thrown here and there as the ship was cast about by the mighty waves. The fear was great among many of the emigrants and some were sure that their last hour had come. The crew, however, showed no fear and said that they had often seen it much worse. Most emigrants were seasick and those who were most affected kept to their bunks and wailed and moaned as they, one after the other, had to throw up in the bunk where they lay. This caused a terrible stench in the hold that in no small degree contributed to the sickness that ravaged onboard. We were also a little seasick but not so bad that we were not able to go up on deck and sit there and breathe fresh air. There was no better remedy for this ailment than to stay away from the awful stench as much as the weather permitted. But no one could stay on deck when the storm raged at its worst.

The strong wind calmed with the break of day and we had nice sunny weather. We came to Hull in England at two in the morning of the twenty-fifth. But we had to stay onboard until ten, when we were met by the line's agents who made sure that our baggage was taken to the railroad station while we were taken to a hotel to eat a dinner of meat soup and bread and butter. When we had eaten (of course paid for by the line) we were taken to the railroad station to go to Liverpool. We left Hull at half past eleven and went at great speed sometimes above and sometimes below the ground. It was very enjoyable to sit and look at this mighty England, now passing a town, now beautiful landscapes where large flocks of cattle and sheep were grazing on rich pastures; here and there we saw people and horses harvesting hay and everything told us that we were now passing through the mighty British island. After a pleasant ride we arrived in Liverpool at five o'clock and were met by agents who took us to the Star Line's emigrant hotel where we had supper and were shown our bedrooms. There were separate rooms for unmarried emigrants. We were to stay here until the twenty-eighth before we boarded the ship. So there was plenty of time to walk around and look at this magnificent city for those who so wished because there was an interpreter who went around with us and showed us much that was of interest. For my part I didn't find our stay pleasant, partly because of the great noise made by the never-ending traffic of these terribly large horses and their carts and partly because of the stench of rot everywhere in the streets. What impressed me most, in Hull and in Liverpool, were the enormous horses. I had never thought such large horses existed and no one who has never seen them can imagine how large they are.

We boarded on Thursday June 28. The *Adriatic* was large and well appointed; everything was clean and in order, the opposite of what we had experienced on the North Sea. There was a hustle and bustle as soon as we came onboard before everyone had been shown their bunks and most of this had to be mimed as one did not understand the other. When all was set we weighed anchor at half past twelve and left the port of Liverpool. After a pleasant voyage we came to Queenstown in Ireland at five in the morning of the twenty-ninth. Here we waited for a flock of Irish emigrants to board and weighed anchor at half past twelve and, distancing ourselves from the Irish coast, we sailed quickly out on the open and mighty Atlantic Ocean. Here we, thank God, had beautiful weather on the entire voyage and could sit on deck and amuse ourselves. There was not much seasickness on the Atlantic, but we were unable to eat much of the food provided by the ship and had to make use of our own chests of food; nor did the ship have special food for children.

After a most pleasant voyage we anchored in New York harbor at six in the evening of July 7. We had to stay the night onboard until we were let ashore the next morning and taken to Castle Garden. There was much we had to do there before we were through. Our baggage was inspected to see whether we had anything we had to pay duty on, and it was weighed and those who had more than was allowed for each passenger had to pay for excess baggage. Each passenger may bring eighty pounds free of charge and I had to pay one dollar and eighty cents, some more and some less depending on how much baggage they had. Here we also got our tickets to Madison. All of this went on until five on Monday afternoon of July 9 when we again were taken onboard a little steamboat that took us to the railroad station.

First and second-class coaches were intermixed and it didn't matter where we sat. We entered a first class car and were in all respects so comfortable that a king would have envied us. It would take too much time to describe all we saw of cities and landscapes as we traveled up through the New World as the letter is already getting too long. But I must say that I found America far more beautiful than I had imagined. We changed trains three times between New York and Madison and on the first and third we sat in first class cars and after a most rapid and pleasant journey we came to Madison at three o'clock on Thursday morning July 12.

We had been taken as far as we had paid and now had to find a way of going to Mount Vernon. We didn't understand what people said so we stood there for about an hour until we met a Norwegian who took us to a Norwegian hotel where we met many Norwegians and got one to drive us and our baggage to Mount Vernon, where we arrived at one o'clock that same day. There we met Olaug Børtnes and her family and she lived very comfortably and well, much better than I had thought. We stayed with her until the next day when Halsten Børtnes came and took us to Guttorm, where we arrived late Friday evening. Saturday we helped Guttorm with haying and on Sunday we went to church and heard John Fjeld preach. He was a wise and in all respects righteous preacher who explained the word of God correctly. At church I spoke with Gunnild, the wife of Uncle Ole, and when we came home Uncle Ole also came and he was just as I remembered him and he never tired of asking about Hedalen. On Monday morning Guttorm and Ole went to Mount Vernon, each with a team, and Guttorm drove our baggage home. I met Ole Børtnes in Mount Vernon and I hardly recognized him as he has grown so much. He gave me material for a pair of trousers, Guttorm cut it, and Olaug will be the tailor. Little Anders got a nice new shirt from Olaug when we arrived and is very handsome. From Uncle Ole and Aunt Gunnild I got material for trousers, Siri for a dress and Anders for a shirt. We haven't visited Uncle Ole but will go there soon. We've already spoken with many acquaintances from Norway, among them Gulborg Berg, who lives not far from here. On Saturday Marit Klemmetsrud's husband drove over to Uncle Guttorm and he was a nice and kind man. He asked me to send greetings to Klemmetsrud and say that they are doing well; Marit has had a bad toothache for some time. I've also met Torgrim's son Ole.

This is a brief account of our journey and I would have liked to write more about some things, but the letter is getting so long and heavy that I'll have to stop now with the promise to write more some other time. We can conclude saying that we were all well during our voyage except for the brief trial on the North Sea. Then we were sick the first two days on the Atlantic but after that we were all well. Little Anders wasn't sick a single day on land or on sea but he now has a cold and coughs now and then but we must hope that it is soon over. Farewell to you all. May the Lord guide us and lead us all on the path of truth to salvation. Amen. From your far distant son and brother

OLE ANDERSEN LIE AND FAMILY

We are enclosing pieces of the material given to Siri and Anders, the smallest one is from what Anders got from Olaug, the next largest is of the material he got from Uncle Ole, and the dark one is from Siri's dress material. Siri sends greetings to Synnøve Jensdatter and the girls at North Sørli that she is doing well, and also to Anna Klemmetsrud and Randi Lisbraaten.

· —— ·

OAL emigrated with his wife, Siri Mikkelsdatter, and their son, Anders. He dated his letter at "Lie," the name of the farm he had left in Norway and now also the name of his uncle's farm in Dane County. He describes his first days in the area around Mount Vernon like a homecoming. He wrote 7 December 1877 (Nor. ed. IV:55), with news about family and friends in Dane County, Wisc. The letter suggests that he wrote more letters than the many that have been preserved. There is a generational difference in the writing skills of OAL and his brothers and those of their uncles. Queenstown is now Cobh. Immigrants entered the United States through Castle Garden at the south end of Manhattan. Ellis Island was opened in 1892. Trains going west and south left from the New Jersey side of the Hudson River and passengers went on ferries from Manhattan. Olaug Børtnes, married to a shoemaker in Mount Vernon named Erik Eriksen, had been very poor before emigrating. She was a daughter of OAL's father's sister (Olea Olsdatter) who had lived at a croft named Børtnes and who later emigrated. Halsten and Ole Børtnes were Olaug's brothers. The pastor, John N. Fjeld, was from Valdres, a region that includes Hedalen. Marit Hermansdatter from the farm Klemmetsrud in Hedalen was the widow of Torgrim, the first to emigrate from Søre Li. «II:74 »II:79 NE IV:48

. ——— .

1877 — LETTER 2:77

FROM: Jacob Hanson Hilton, *Eldora, Iowa, 21 October 1877*

TO: Hans Jakobsen and Anne Olsdatter Hilton, *Ullensaker, Akershus*

⊹⇒◉⇐⊹

Dear parents and siblings,

I received your letter on the nineteenth and I'm glad to see that you all are in good health. You say you have a rainy fall but all the falls I can remember were rainy and harvesting was difffcult. America is very different, harvesting is not difficult nor does anyone worry about it. "If we only work as much as we can," they say, "it must go as it will." Summer is long, eight months of dry summer so you can get the harvesting done and work unhindered by the weather, because it rarely rains for more than a day at a time and usually only every eight or fourteen days and that is all they need. The farmers are prosperous; many have six to eight thousand dollars they have wrung from their farm with thrift and hard work. There are poor people too but this is their own doing because people who will work and who don't buy themselves poor have no reason to be poor here as long as they are healthy and able to work.

I'm glad I got out of Norway because there my future always seemed dark; whether I looked up or I looked down I could see no workable solution. It may seem rather self-important and strange that one so young should have any thought for the future. If I hadn't had a thought for my future I wouldn't have come here. Strangely, it may seem that your best days are over when you leave home, and this may in a way be true, as you are without worry as long as others take care of you, but when you have to support yourself something else is needed and then I think that the home may be too narrow in Norway. It is different here. Here you may work and struggle as well as you can but if you have anything saved up you can be sure there will be someone looking for a little extra. But enough of this. For my part I've been as comfortable as anyone could wish since I left Norway and I also believe that this will continue; if not it will surely be my own fault. I wish you were all here. I'm sure that you would like it here because all you see is as it was in Norway except that you get more for your work; it is a richer country and not so difficult to live in. You'll find pine, fir, maple and aspen here as in Norway and the friendly sparrow is here as well.

I asked Christopher in a letter whether I should advise you to sell out and come here and he answered that it would probably be good for you but even more for your children. But he doesn't think I should advise you to come as you've always had such a strong love for Ullensaker and would probably be homesick. On the other hand it's also possible that you would be happy with all your children here and, moreover, be making a better living and having a freer life, he says. So I cannot advise anyone to come as everyone will have to do as he wishes and then he will be responsible for the outcome. But I know that emigration would benefit your children and that you would like it too because all you would have to do here is to keep account of what has to be done indoors as well as outdoors and you wouldn't have to do any work yourself. Christopher says that I should tell you how large a farm you could have here for what you could get for your farm in Norway but I don't know how much you could get for your farm and therefore I can't tell. But I will in my next letter if you can tell me how much you could get for your farm and your chattel. The price for land in America is higher now and will continue to rise as long as so many people from other countries continue to come. So you will never lose money by buying land here as the price is higher every year.

You wish to know whether Christopher has anything left. You have no reason to be in fear; he has sold his farm and settled up with his partner. He was about to come to us when his itching feet led him astray. He has decided to go to Oregon and Washington Territory this winter as he thinks

Iowa would be too cold. I think he still has about four to six thousand dollars and this should be more than sufficient. He sent us his photograph, a large one more than twice the size of regular photographs, and he looks very old and has a large beard.

Mother wonders who does my laundry and mending and here is the information she requests: Marie has done my laundry since I began to work in the shop and before that, when I was out in the country, it was done by those I worked for. I haven't seen anyone do any mending here. I suppose you won't believe what I eat. I get white bread, butter, meat, pork, coffee, tea, cake and all kinds of jam every day as they don't know of anything else here. I've grown since coming here; I used collar size No. 14 ½ at home and these are now too small and I use 16. I'll conclude with regards to all, hoping that this letter finds you in good health.

J. JACOBSEN

· ——— ·

Enclosed were two bookmarks with quotations from the Bible and leaves of maple and lilac. JHH emigrated in the summer of 1877 with assistance from his uncle, Christopher Jacobson, some of whose letters are in this edition. His uncle advised him to use the name Jacob Jacobson, but after a while he reverted to the farm name Hilton. Writing about cake he writes *kek* and adds, "I suppose you don't know what this is, but it is exactly the same as sugar bread at home." His first preserved letter is dated 9 September 1877 (Nor. ed. IV:50). Here he writes that he has worked for a farmer and is now learning the shoemaker trade in the shop of two relatives, Hans (married to Marie) and Gulbrand Jensen Haga: "They have the largest shoe shop in town and have wares for about five or six thousand dollars and their business is good. Gulbrand plays in the town's brass band and often visits other towns and when there are dances here he also plays as he is the best fiddler in the towns around here." He also writes about seeing Indians "who are not as big as they said at home." »II:82 NE IV:52

· ——— ·

1877 — LETTER 2:78

FROM: Hellik Olsen Lehovd, *Salem, Minnesota, 30 November 1877*

To: Ole Helgesen, Knut Olsen Lehovd, and Jørand Olsdatter Aslefet
Flesberg, Buskerud

⋯⇒◯⇐⋯

Dear relatives and friends in Norway,

Thank you for your letter of July 29 that I received some time ago. I'm so glad to hear from family and friends in my old home. First I can tell you that I and my children have been well and healthy since you last heard from us, for which we must thank God. Julia began confirmation classes September 12. She also has to manage the household, so she has enough on her hands. The old people still live with me but they are so old and weak that there isn't much help from them, especially for Julia, so I must at times hire a young seamstress to make clothes for the children—when one is available. And I can tell you that we had an excellent year for all products and we also had excellent weather during harvest from the time of haying to when the wheat was stacked. Our wheat is full and shines like pearls, so the wheat is No. 1 this year. This fall I had 920 bushels of wheat, 250 of oats, and 170 of corn and some potatoes. Prices have not been bad, around ninety cents a bushel for wheat, thirty for oats, and forty for corn, so we must say that we have good times and there is more money and more movement among people than last year. In Norway you must think that we can now lay aside a lot of money but we also have many expenses. We have to provide for both pastor and sexton and pay for the pastor schools in Decorah and Madison and our parochial school, and we also have to support those who live in the grasshopper areas since several counties in the west were visited by grasshoppers this year and we help them with voluntary gifts. So for one who also has to hire a lot of help much money is needed.

I have no news for you as there have been no deaths or illness recently. I haven't spoken with my brothers Paul and Ole for some time but I know that Ole built a large house last summer. I'd also planned a new house but I've had to lay aside such thoughts for a time as my housekeepers are too

young to take on such an enterprise. A boy from Vangestad came last summer and I believe he lives with Paul. In letters and newspapers I see that you
had a late spring in Norway and that winter arrived early so you had a bad
year, but we've had nice fall weather and we could still plow six days ago.
But now the soil is frozen and we've had a little snow so winter is here with
its cold and strong northwesterly winds and snowstorms. Now I remember
that a man from Valdres who lives near here cut another Norwegian in his
throat with a knife last summer and was sent to prison for a year. I must
now end my brief and simple letter with loving regards to you my dear and
unforgettable father and to you my brother Knut and your family from me
and my children. Give my regards to my sister Jørand and her husband and
children and to all relatives and friends. My wishes for a happy New Year
from your loving son and brother in America,

HELLIK OLSEN LEHOVD

· ——— ·

"The old people" were mentioned in a letter dated 27 May: "an old
couple has moved in with me. The man is Paul Svendsen and his wife
is Aslaug Andersdatter. They are from Kviteseid in Telemark." They
were more than sixty and had only been in the United States a couple
of years. They came with two cows that grazed on Hellik's land and
the woman was paid to do housework, "because there are no Norwegian housemaids to be hired as they all want to go to the towns and
work for the Americans." Luther College in Decorah was not a "pastor school" but did have the function of preparing some students for
later theological studies. The Norwegian Synod's theological seminary
in Madison, Wisc., was established in 1876. «II:70 »II:80 NE IV:53

· ——— ·

1878 — LETTER 2:79

FROM: Ole Andersen Lee, *Mount Vernon, Wisconsin 7 April 1878*

To: Anders Olsen and Kari Mikkelsdatter Lie
Hedalen, Sør-Aurdal, Oppland

⊹⟫◉⟪⊹

Dear and unforgettable parents and brothers,

As it's some time since I had a letter from you I can no longer delay letting you hear from me. I can imagine that you long to hear from me. I hope you will pardon my long delay. I will now, in the name of the Lord, give you some news from me, your son and brother. We're all in good health, praise God, and doing well. I see that you have many questions that I must admit I haven't answered. So I'll first of all try to explain these things for you as well as I can.

You ask about church practice here. There are many kinds of church practice as there are many synods rather than one. Americans are divided into many sects that are served by their different pastors and follow their own practices and these can be very different. But I won't spend too much time and space on the teaching, practices, and rituals of other congregations as I haven't really arrived at an understanding of all aspects of their faith and teaching yet, so I can only say briefly and simply what I think and know about them. There are three synods here in Primrose (and a fourth, a small Methodist congregation consisting of only three or four families). These are the Synod, the Conference, and the Hauge Synod (also called the Ellingians). It is in the largest, the Synod, that we find our old and genuine Lutheran Confession, which is consistent with Holy Scripture as we have been taught by our parents and teachers in Norway. This congregation is served by Pastor J. N. Fjeld, the second by Pastor Gjertsen, and the third by Pastor Solberg. These three congregations started out as one and all belonged to the Synod. The first to break out were the Ellingians led by Elling Eielsen, whose name they have taken, and the Conference followed. These three congregations have recently put a lot of work into becoming united again and they may be able to agree if only some won't insist on a special form of worship but hold to Jesus their savior and only redeemer and not hold up their own good deeds as did the pharisees. I have been to the services of all these congregations and in their sermons I haven't been able to find why they should disagree because they preach one and the same faith and doctrine. I was also present at a discussion meeting in our church for all three congregations to see whether they could agree on faith and doctrine and there was full agreement on the questions that were raised. The pastors as well as the lay members of the congregations had agreed to this meeting, so I cannot see any reason for the two others to break away. In my opinion those who attempt to break up a congregation and tear down what others have built up may be likened to wolves in sheep clothing. I'll now return to our own congregation and let these swarming bees buzz as as they will but try to avoid their sting.

In our congregation we follow the same practice that I was used to from home except for a few superficial matters. They don't, for instance, use the so-called chasuble; the pastor wears his regular cassock for the entire service. And there is no one to assist the pastor; he takes his cassock on and off himself. The other duties of the pastor's assistant in Norway are either performed by the precentor or another member for the congregation. Our precentor is from Hallingdal, Henrik Damholt. He has a powerful but not beautiful voice. Moreover, he is rather advanced in years so he has lost some of his voice. Our church isn't large, but small and nice even though it isn't quite completed yet inside. We don't have church bells yet and to begin with I missed them but now I've become used to this. I'm sure we'll soon have bells.

You wish to know whether we have our own household. Until last fall we boarded with Uncle Guttorm but since then we've had our own board, which is what we prefer. I haven't had regular work as there isn't much work to be had in winter except for woodcutting. I've hired out for the day with different farmers for half a dollar a day and board. This is the regular pay around here. The work isn't very hard. This winter I also helped Uncle Ole cut timber for his house and we've now come so far that we're ready to lay the rafters, but we had to stop and begin spring plowing and planting. This was two or three weeks ago and most of it is now done except for the planting of corn and potatoes which isn't done before the end of April or in early May. We've had a nice winter. I've only seen snow a few times and it disappeared quickly—at the most the snow covered the ground for about a day. We now have nice weather and the fields are green and nicer than I ever saw them in May in Norway.

You wonder whether I've heard from Mikkel Sørli. I've corresponded several times with him since coming here and the last I heard he and his family are in good health. Although this may be old news, I'll tell you that Kari Mikkelsdatter has married a bachelor from Gudbrandsdalen named Gunder Hansen Nordrum. Their wedding was in November and they settled on land next to Mikkel according to a letter I've had from them. I've thought of going to Mikkel in Minnesota where land is cheaper. With time I may become an owner of land here too if God grants me health and strength, but land is expensive so it takes a longer time to save enough to buy a farm. There is neither homestead land nor land sold by speculators here.

You wish to know what Siri does, but she does so many different things that I cannot list them all. For about a month she worked for a woman from Drammen while she gave birth. And there is enough spinning and knitting here and the women are also busy making quilts, as they say in English, a blanket sewn of hundreds of small pieces of cloth of different colors. If they make more than they need these are easily sold.

I see that brother Iver has been visiting and that he's written to me. But I haven't heard anything from him except what I've seen in your letters. Give him my regards and ask him to write. Send me his address and I'll write to him immediately. Thank you so much for sending me the book I mentioned. I would like to have two or three other books but I'm reluctant to place such a burden on you. I know that you would do what you can for my sake; indeed, I know that you do more than you can for me, and therefore I'm a little ashamed to ask more of you. Could you send me my schoolbooks—Pontoppidan's Explanation, a Bible history and a Guldberg hymnbook, the same edition that your brother Mikkel had. Here books are very expensive; a cheaply bound hymnbook costs a dollar. Guldberg is the hymnbook they use here. If you get this letter before Ole Iljernstad leaves, then try to have him bring these books to me. I'll repay both him and you as well as I can. My brother-in-law Iver sends his regards; he now likes it here and is getting used to American ways. He has returned from the English school that he attended until March and has since then been working for farmers. He can already understand English and is about to decide whether to hire out for the month or the day, because now they are beginning to hire help. Our regards to you all. May we wander in peace so that we may meet again in glory. And may God in his grace help us in this for the sake of Jesus Christ, Amen. Sincerely,

OLE A. LIE

In a letter also signed by his wife, Siri Mikkelsdatter, 12 January 1878 (Nor. ed. IV:57), OAL wrote about the death and funeral of their son Anders and about how his Christian faith had helped him through this difficult time. His uncle Guttorm had made the coffin and paid most of the expenses. The Conference pastor was Melchior Falk Gjertsen, while the Hauge pastor named Solberg has not been identified. OAL's mother, Kari Mikkelsdatter, was sister of the father of Mikkel and Kari Sørli. «II:76 »II:100 NE IV:61

1878 — LETTER 2:80

FROM: Ole Olsen Lehovd, *Kasson, Minnesota, 14 April 1878*

To: Knut Gislesen Aslefet, *Flesberg, Buskerud*

Thank you so much for your welcome letter of July 30 of last year. I should have answered it before but you must excuse my negligence. We are all four in reasonably good health except that my wife is somewhat weak. Our children are growing and happy but Julia hurt two fingers between the wheels of a winnowing machine and this is so recent that we don't know how they will be. Ole is strong and a good worker but doesn't spare the horses when he harrows or plows. He has attended the English school and it seems that learning comes easily, but he hasn't learned much Norwegian yet. Last winter we hardly had any snow or cold weather. Roads are muddy and the weather is unhealthy. People began planting in March and were done around April 10, but we have rain and bad weather. I built a new house last summer for 800 dollars so I live well. Lumber was cheap in Kasson last summer, but now prices have gone up because there hasn't been enough snow to get lumber from the forests. Building is expensive but I've paid for everything and have lent 700 dollars at twelve percent. This is the legal interest rate here. I still haven't sold most of my wheat from last year. I had 930 bushels and 250 of oats. The price for wheat is now ninety-five cents a bushel and many are glad that the war in Europe continues because they believe that this gives better prices for wheat, but this is regrettable and proves that we have little love for other people.

I don't have any news as Numedal must be flooded with letters from all parts of America as so many have emigrated. It's been some time since I spoke with Hellik or Paul, and the honorable Ole Lindaas, who was so fine that he courted the daughter of Anders Holtan, isn't around either. He came here as a gentleman to see how common folks lived. I don't have as many animals as I used to since I've sold some. I now have three horses and twelve head of cattle, both big and small, and some hens, sheep and hogs. Last year I sold 524 pounds of butter from five cows and the price was fourteen to fifteen cents a pound, but you don't get paid in cash but in kind at the stores in Kasson. The town council has forbidden saloons in Kasson, so many Norwegians can no longer wet their dry throats as they are used to. In conclusion, friendly regards to you and my sister and all at Aslefet.

OLE O. LEHOVD

. —— .

OOL is writing to his brother-in-law, married to his sister Jørand. His wife is also named Jørand and his mother is Jørand Paulsdatter. Hellik and Paul Lehovd are his brothers. The war in Europe is between the Russian and Ottoman empires that had begun the year before. «II:78 »II:162 NE IV:62

. —— .

1878 — LETTER 2:81

FROM: Barbro Tollefsdatter and Berthe Maria Sando
Estherville, Iowa, 12–15 May 1878

To: Guri Tollefsdatter Bøygard, *Aal, Buskerud*

Dear Sister!

Thank you so much for your letter of December 16. I received it long ago and must again ask you to forgive me for being so late in replying. The reason is not indifference. Oh no, there can be no indifference for family however great the distance and how long the time between us may be. Oh, my dear sister, it is so difficult to live in this world so full of troubles, worries, and grief—one grief is almost always followed by another. Had we only been able to bear the grief God lays upon us <u>patiently</u> and, as you say, thank God for the bad days as well as the good ones and not forget to place our confidence in him as we from our heart pray, "Abide with me; fast falls the eventide." Things are well with us. My and my husband's health is as usual. Our youngest children Berthe and Gjermund live at home and our other children are doing well. I think I told you about them and their children in my last letter so I won't repeat it. We recently heard from our brother Ole the Elder and they are doing well. I haven't heard from Ole Roe for a long time. It's not so long since I had a letter from our brother Niels's widow and she is living comfortably with her daughter Margit Sagvolden. I don't know what to write about that could be of interest for you and you must excuse this short letter. Dear Sister, may we meet again up yonder where there is no separation, sorrow or illness. Give my regards to Haagen and Randi and their families and to our other relatives and friends. In conclusion you are all lovingly greeted from me, my husband and our children. Farewell! Your devoted sister

BARBRO T. SANDO

Dear Aunt!

I will again send you a little greeting. Please forgive me for not having answered you earlier because it is my fault that you had to wait so long for a letter from us. But I don't think I'm able to write as well as I would have liked to you so far away in Norway so it takes a long time before I finally decide to write. But you will have to excuse me and take my wish for my deed as they say. I often think about my relatives on the other side of the Atlantic and wish I could have seen them and spoken with them, but I don't suppose that will happen. Farewell my dear Aunt. You are lovingly greeted from your niece,

BERTHE M. SANDO

[*On a separate sheet*]

Estherville, May 14, 1878

Dear Cousin,

It was really cruel of me not to have answered your welcome letter that I received a long time ago. Thank you so much for your letter and for the beautiful gift you sent me. Your gift is all the more beautiful to me because it is from my fatherland! I have nothing that beautiful to send you. I am sending you my portrait but you must not imagine that I look as cross as I am there. It is not really well made but I cannot find a better one. I so often wish you were here. I'm sure you wouldn't find it boring, but I don't think we'll ever see each other. Give my regards to all our cousins. Tell your brother Asle and his young wife that I wish them all luck and happiness in their marriage. Please accept my loving regards and wishes for luck and prosperity in time as well as in eternity, from your devoted cousin

BERTHE MARIA SANDO

. ——— .

This concludes the series from BTS and other members of her family to siblings in Aal. She was married to Ole Eriksen Sando. Siblings in Aal were Haagen (or Haakon) Tollefsen Opsata, who had taken over the family farm, and Randi Tollefsdatter Opheim. She has dictated her letter to her daughter Berthe Maria, who corresponded with a cousin in Aal. The quotation is the first line of a religious song by Henry F. Lyte written in 1847. It is paraphrased in Norwegian in the letter, suggesting that BTS sang it in English. «11:63 NE IV:66

. ——— .

1878 — LETTER 2:82

FROM: Jacob Hanson Hilton, *Badger, Iowa, 18 May 1878*

TO: Hans Jakobsen and Anne Olsdatter Hilton, *Ullensaker, Akershus*

⊷⟾⟾⟾⊶

Dear parents and siblings!

My good father: I received your letter of March 5 on the thirty-first of that month and it surprised me to see that you are thinking of America. You say that you would appreciate a truthful account of conditions here and I'll give you as trustworthy an account as possible. As for the price of the size of farm that you want I'll have to say that you can have one at any price you wish to pay, from virtually nothing and up to fifty dollars per acre. If you want cultivated land, and this is the most profitable, there is quite a lot of it around Fort Dodge. There is also wild land but that is the most expensive over time as it takes a long time before you can harvest much. You can have nice houses, forest, fresh water (near the river), good soil and stone quarries etc. about ten miles from Fort Dodge if you come next spring. I know the people who want to sell quite well. They are Norwegian and the owner is sheriff in Fort Dodge. Last summer I worked on his brother's farm. I like the farm and I know that you and mother would like it too. I'm sure she would like it here as almost all around here are Norwegian. Many other places are for sale cheaply. This is the right time to come as the prices for land, horses, cows, implements and all else are so low that they can hardly be any lower, as the times are very hard. But no one here will ever see as hard times as you have in Norway. I get eighteen dollars a month and board, laundry and mending. This is the best pay you can get around here; many now work for ten and up to sixteen a month. But in Norway I don't think you even get as much as ten, not including board and laundry. Those who hire out for the day still have one to one and a half dollars a day and pay for their own food. So I don't think we have such hard times. I'm doing well and enjoying myself. I'll never return to Norway. But if you should wish to come, then I can get together enough for a return journey and come home for Christmas or some time next winter to help you as much as I can with your journey as I'm now quite familiar with it. I would like to see Hilton again and say goodbye to all friends. But I'm sure that I won't let fall a tear for old Ullensaker (as I did when I left it the first time) because then I hadn't seen anything better and thought it was the best. And you would agree if you were here.

You'll understand why I haven't saved much money yet when you hear how I work. The first summer in Eldora I did nothing for three months and in the fall I began my first year as an apprentice shoemaker for fifty dollars, barely enough for a change of clothes and a few other items. I was to have seventy-five the next year but as I realized that I had learned all I could, at least there, I left when Hans gave me only repair work for the same pay I should have for making new shoes. I saw that nothing would come of this. I was afraid of working for nothing and learning nothing. So I went to Fort Dodge and was paid ten dollars a month and free room and board. That was November 1. I was there until January 1 as they didn't need help after

FROM AMERICA TO NORWAY

Christmas and I had to move again. Crosby then entrusted me with some wares and I went to a small town called <u>Gowrie</u> where I made and repaired shoes on my own. I made enough to pay for my food and that is more than many did last winter. I was there for three months, until some time in April, and received your letter there. Since then I've worked on a farm <u>so I'll be used to it when you arrive</u>. So this is how the money went. I've traveled a lot and earned little. But I speak English well and know the ways and habits of many nations.

I wish you would come next spring, <u>the sooner the better</u>. There is no reason for delay as that is only a waste of time and money. This is the time for you to come, both you two who are old and the young ones. This is the experience of other good people: old and experienced Norwegian farmers, who have worked themselves up from nothing and who now prosper, say that those who have money to start with can do extremely well now that prices are low. Andreas Husmo from Nes, Malle's husband, sends his regards and says that you should come, as does August. They and Little Ole Ihle think you will succeed. But there's one thing I must say in conclusion: you don't have to worry about getting food since there is enough here and better than in Norway. You mustn't leave only because of what I've said. No one should go if they don't want to. I don't want to hear anyone say that I fooled them into coming. No one asked me to come; they told me how it <u>was</u> and I must admit that I found it was better than I'd been told. You and mother will probably find it difficult to sell horses and cows and all but here there is an entire world of such things that are just as good. I must end now but after reflection and with a good conscience I must again say, "Come." Think about it and you'll say the same. Enclosed is my photograph so you can recognize me when I come home for Christmas if you'll sell your farm in the spring. Write as soon as you have made up your mind. Don't fear the journey; it's a picnic; God will be your Captain on land as on sea. Tell the boys that if they wish to advance in this world they should come <u>here</u>. There are a hundred ways here compared to one there to make a good living. Tell mother that she has no reason to be afraid. Give my regards to all relatives. I'm doing well and enjoying myself in my new environment and it would please me if I could see you do the same. It's hard work but it bears good fruit, and you can work less and still live well if you so wish. This must be all for now. My loving regards to parents and siblings, hoping that this will find you all well.

JACOB

JHH wrote from Eldora, Iowa, 29 April 1878 (Nor. ed. IV:65) about his trade as a shoemaker and again encouraged his parents and siblings to emigrate. His spellings of Eldora and Gowrie (*Eldore, Cowru*) suggest that he cannot yet write English. Crosby is the shoemaker he worked for in Fort Dodge. August Halvorsen Hilton (from the South Hilton farm in Ullensaker) later became the father of Conrad Hilton. According to the latter's *Be My Guest* (1957) August was already corresponding with his future wife, Mary Laufersweiler, in 1878. Ihle is another farm in Ullensaker. Ole Ihle was not necessarily little. Both his grandfathers may have been named Ole and with an older brother named for one of them and he for the other, one would be Big Ole and the other Little Ole. Hans Jakobsen Hilton never emigrated. JHH's next preserved letter was sent from Boulder, Colo., 23 November 1879, to his brother Oluf. Here he writes, "As I see, no one will be coming here." He reports that a ticket agent in Christiania has offered him a free return ticket to Norway and four dollars for every adult and two for children he is "able to bring to his office to buy tickets." He is making good money, "from two to five dollars a day, paying four to five a week for room and board. This is more than anyone gets in Norway or in the East in the old states." His letters to Oluf are more gossipy than those to his father. «II:77 »II:107 NE IV:67

1878 — LETTER 2:83

FROM: Maria J. Killy, *Renville, Minnesota, 1 June 1878*

TO: Marie Fredriksdatter Thomter, *Dovre, Oppland*

Dear Marie,

Your long-awaited letter made a deep impression on us. It is sad to hear how poverty, illness and death are ravaging in our place of birth. It seems such a short time since we heard of golden times from Dovre and now all seems sadly changed, but we must consider that God has not promised us that we will always walk on roses in this life but that we must be prepared for all adversities that it may please the All-knowing to send upon us to encourage us to seek him. We must hope and believe that God is so gracious that he soon will send his help and change times for the better. Last summer it looked rather dark here too. The grasshoppers ate the wheat fields black in a few days. In our weak faith we thought there would be a famine. But God be praised, we haven't been in need and the grasshoppers haven't returned. So we very often, indeed every day, have instances of God's grace.

I see there are many who wish to come here but lack money for the journey. I'm sorry that we cannot send tickets as we are in the process of buying more land. We have lent money to farmers but as they didn't get any wheat last year there is no money to be had just now. Moreover, we've lost money on those we've paid for earlier and it seems that they'll owe us money as long as we live. Frans Fagerlien was an exception; he was honest and paid us back every cent in the course of the first year, and he's also been very helpful. But there aren't many of his kind. Almost all who have paid for people to come here complain that they've been cheated. This spoils the chances for others. It was good for Frans Peder and Ingebrigt Fagerlien to come here. They are good workers and honest and will soon improve their situation. All who have health and are able to work should be able to pay for themselves here. This is the best season for a worker to come. They should come early enough to take part in the haying and the wheat harvest. There is no work here during winter. Haying begins in July and the harvest at the end of July. If Ole Rykkhus had come with us when we left he would have had as much land as we have and been a prosperous man. If it had been possible Ole Rykkhus would have been among the first we had paid for, as I knew him in Norway as a hardworking and honest man. But you will understand that one doesn't have much money after a year with crop failure. It doesn't help much to be owed money if you cannot get it. But, as we have written before, we are ready to give as much help as we can to anyone who comes here empty-handed from Dovre and this is not insignificant as it is difficult to come here empty-handed and without family or friends here.

We've had an excellent winter. There was a little snow two or three times but the mild weather melted it as soon as it came and we could harrow and plow between Christmas and New Year. Planting could be done in early March and in many places the wheat was sprouting by the middle of March. The cattle could feed themselves by the first day of summer and now, praise God, it seems that we'll have a very good harvest. Work on the railroad is at full speed. It is supposed to be completed this fall. It won't go far from us and a town is being built about ten miles from us. There are already many stores and two mills there and more is being built. I see that the price for butter has gone down in Dovre but here it is even cheaper. It is now sold for eight cents a pound and that is very cheap. But calico is sold for seven cents a yard—and women hardly use anything else for their clothes. There have been great changes in Dovre since we left except for the pastors. We see they remain the same. It is sad that Dovre never gets a God-fearing pastor. Our old and charitable pastor died last New Year's Day and this was a hard blow for us, but we now have, thank God, a new one with whom we are very pleased. He is a man of God and the best preacher I have heard. He preaches so the sweat runs down his forehead and he is very concerned for the spiritual well-being of his fellow men. He held a service with Holy Communion in our home eight …

· —— ·

The last page or pages have been lost. Many letters from MJK have evidently not been preserved. She may be the Maria Hansdatter who in 1865 worked in the general store at Kirkestuen in Dovre. Marie married Paul Syversen Killi after their emigration and they became Maria J. and Paul S. Killy in the United States, but in her letters she signed herself Marie Killi. Maria Frederiksdatter and Hans Olsen Thomter had one of the Arneklev farms in Dovre in 1865. The *husmann* Ole Olsen Rykkhus was thirty-six in 1865 and he and his wife had three children. The first day of summer was traditionally 14 April. The pastor who had died was Lars Olsen Rustad (1818–1878) who had been a lay preacher before emigrating in 1869. The following year he was ordained in the Elling Eielsen Synod and he joined the Hauge Synod in 1876. He was succeeded by Bersvend Anderson. NE IV:68

· —— ·

1878 — LETTER 2:84

FROM: Rakel Tonette Rannestad (with an enclosed letter from her sister Siri Allikson), *Cerro Gordo, Minnesota, 30 July 1878*

TO: Osmund Ovedal, *Sirdal, Vest-Agder*

Dear and unforgettable brother Osmund,

About two years ago I had a letter from you and I'm so sorry that I've neglected to answer it. You were then doing well and we can, praise God, say that we too have been in good health. First I must let you know that we have another son. He was christened Albert Bernhard after our father and mother. Today he is one year and two months old. Theodore is also doing well and we can hardly see the clip in his lip. Last summer I had the pleasure of seeing our old uncle Haaver and his wife. They stayed with us for two nights. Uncle has aged but his wife is still quite youthful. Old Turi Haughom was also here for a night. I could hardly recognize her but her husband Haaver Jødestøl was much the same. Sigbjørn Haaversen had an accident and broke a leg before Pentecost but I have been told that the pain was not as great as may be imagined. He was kicked by one of his horses.

In March last year we moved to Fredrik Haaverson's and we've used twenty acres of his land. Fredrik and Tobias boarded with us. In February Tobias married Martha Christina from Voss. We were there until May 6 and went at least 150 miles further west. We now have 160 acres and have broken about fifteen. We paid 200 dollars. We have oxen, three cows, a heifer, three calves and fifteen chickens. I must also tell you that our sister Sara lived with us last year. She came in the middle of February and stayed until after we left and it was so good for me. We've had a letter Siri wrote herself, and she says that Sara came back on June 21. She has been in better health this summer than in many years. I'll send you the letter so you can see it yourself. It is better than I had expected as she has never written a letter before. All at Sigbjørn's are doing well. Rakel's oldest daughter is married to Charles Knudson Strømstad, Rakel's cousin. Berte says they are as tall as Siri. Alexander was confirmed last fall. John went to work in the harvest yesterday and will probably be away for two or three weeks. A little girl is living with me. I like it here in the West. I'll conclude my simple letter with loving regards from us all but first and last from your loving sister

RAKEL TONETTE

Dear sister Rakel Tonette,

I will write you a few words to let you know that we are doing well and wish to hear the same from you. I've been well all summer, for which I cannot sufficiently thank God. I'm with Reinert taking care of his home. Sara returned on June 31 and has been home since. I think she'll work for Reinert at harvest time. We were at the crossroads on June 26 and saw a circus with many people and animals. On Fourth of July there was a large gathering and we had two pastors, two lawyers and doctor Valle. Pastor Halvorsen from Coon Prairie, Pastor Meling from Coon Valley and the two lawyers, Widvey from La Crosse and one from Viroqua, all spoke and it was nice to be there. All are well at Sigbjørn's. Sigbjørn Haaverson has broken a leg and been in La Crosse since before Whitsun. I don't know whether he is home yet. He didn't have great pain. I must end my letter with regards to you all. You must write to me if you can read it. I have written it myself.

SIRI ATLAGSEN

. ———— .

RTR's parents were Atlak Amundsen and Barbro Sigbjørnsdatter Ovedal. Naming could be limited to using the same initial letter, here A (Albert) and B (Barbro). Her old uncle was Haaver Sigbjørnsen Ovedal, married to Karen Tonette. Turi Fredriksdatter, now married to Haaver Jødestøl (emigrated in 1876), had been a widow on the farm Haughom and was a sister of Karen Tonette Ovedal. Siri and Sara live with their brothers in Wisconsin. Their brother Sigbjørn's wife, Rakel, had been a widow, and Berte is one of three children from her first marriage with Sigbjørn Seland. Alexander and John are RTR's son and husband. The enclosed letter from Siri is dated 8 July. It is not easy to decipher and her spellings, especially of place names, are idiosyncratic, e.g. *veirok* (Viroqua) and *kornvæll* (Coon Valley). RTR wrote 29 March 1880 (Nor. ed. IV:137) about the birth of yet another son who they had feared would die, but now seemed healthy.
«II:60 »II:91 NE IV:74

. ———— .

1878 — LETTER 2:85

FROM: Christine Dahl, *Norse, Texas, 21 September 1878*

To: Erik Pedersen Furuset, *Romedal, Stange, Hedmark*

❖

Dear brother Erik,

It's long since we received your welcome letter of May 4. Thank you so much. I should have written earlier but different things have interfered, as we have had so much to do recently. Moreover, I wrote some time ago to Anton Bryni and asked him tell you that all was well with us and therefore I waited longer than I otherwise would have done. Please excuse my delay; I'll try to do better in the future. As for us, we are, thank God, in good health and doing well. Pauline is home and has the same cough but is quite well and does some housework. We are harvesting our cotton but this won't be such a good year as it was too dry when it blossomed. Moreover, there was a hailstorm over part of the settlement that destroyed much of the cotton and the corn, but it didn't touch us. We've picked between five and six bales. The price is low because of the yellow fever that rages in the eastern states; there is a quarantine in the ports where the cotton is shipped. Our corn crop was quite good; we harvested about 700 bushels on twenty acres. The wheat also did fairly well so we may say that we've had a fairly good year. The weather is now a little cooler. The summer was very hot but the health situation in our settlement has been good. We've had so much rain that the grass is getting green again.

Ole sends his regards. He and his wife and their little boys are doing well. Syverine and her husband also send their regards. They had a son two months ago and are doing well. I can say the same from P. Dilrud and his family. Dilrud recently had a spell of malaria, something he hasn't had since coming here. Aunt Anna and Rogstad send their regards. They are all well. I also have greetings from Ole Wold and his family. They had a bad accident last summer: a rattlesnake bit their next oldest son. He was the first Norwegian in our settlement to be bitten by a rattlesnake and as it was during the dog days, the hottest part of summer, it got so bad that his foot began to rot and they had to cut off the front part of his foot. Ole wrote to you a week ago and sent money for a hired man, the brother of the one he now has and who has written that he is ready to come as soon as he gets money. We hope you will take care of this. Ole also sent a draft for five dollars that the boy can have as travel money. I am enclosing the address of the agent in Waco. Please give it to the boy when he leaves. Tell him that he must go to this agent when he comes to Waco and he will see to it that he is sent right up to the settlement. Otherwise someone will take him to a hotel and this is expensive.

Please let me know if you have received the photographs of Ole and Jacob and their wives. I know I sent them to Syverine but I cannot remember whether you also got them. If you don't have them I'll send them immediately. Please see if they have them at Bryni, as I would also like them to have them. I don't know of more that will interest you. Give our love to Syverine and our dear old mother. Tell her that she is the great-grandmother of many children in America who probably will not have the fortune to see her. Give our regards to Anton Bryni and other relatives that my sheet will not allow me to list and, finally, you, my dear brother, are lovingly greeted from my children and me, your devoted sister

CHRISTINE DAHL

· —— ·

«II:75 »II:95 NE IV:78

· —— ·

1878 — LETTER 2:86

FROM: Christopher Jacobson
San Francisco, California, 23 September 1878
TO: Hans Jakobsen Hilton, *Ullensaker, Akershus*

⁂

Dear, dear brother!

Your last letter, dear brother, was so full of sorrow and worry that I thought it best not to write to you as this would again remind you of our innocent days of childhood when our future looked so bright, but I cannot put it off any longer. A letter from you, even a bad one, makes my blood run faster in my veins. I often hear from the boys in Iowa but their letters cannot be compared to those from my dear brother. I'm alone here—all alone—and a word from you is like a voice from heaven, so now, dear brother, I'll ask you to write to me as soon as you receive these sentences as I'll probably leave this place around Christmas.

I've been away from Norway for twenty-five years. I was barely twenty when I left, but in all this time I've had you in my thoughts every single day. For all these long years you've been at home among relatives and friends. It may be that your future at times seemed dark, but none of you can understand what the unruly Christopher has been through. But I must be thankful for good health and today I'm here in San Francisco and I'm not wealthy nor am I very poor. I have my health, so I can again go up into the mountains and earn my bread. I often think of my childhood days. I'm sometimes sorry that brother Lars hasn't had time to write to his younger brother. It may be that I wrote him many senseless letters in my youth but if he had had as warm a brother's heart as the prodigal son, he wouldn't have neglected to send him some comforting words. But please don't mention me to him or to any others as I'm as good as dead to them. Just let me hear from you as often as possible. The boys in Iowa are doing well. I hope these lines will find you and yours well. Regards from your distant but in his thoughts always present brother,

CHRISTOPHER

· ——— ·

CJ has given up his attempt at the settled life of a farmer and is again on the move. He is currently living in Cameron House on Sacramento Street, a boarding house or hotel. (This cannot be the Presbyterian Mission House, also on Sacramento, that started in 1874 but that much later was named Cameron House.) He writes more about the failure of the farming experiment in his next letter. The "boys in Iowa," Hans and Gulbrand Jensen Haga, now include his nephew, Jacob Hansen Hilton. «II:72 »II:94 NE IV:79

· ——— ·

1878 — LETTER 2:87

From: Ole Gulbrandsen Lande, *Eureka, Kansas, 6 November 1878*

To: Anders Olsen Gjømle, *Flesberg, Buskerud*

⟶⟹◉⟸⟵

Dear father-in-law and father!

Thank you for your letter of August 5 that we received a long time ago. I should have written earlier but this hasn't been possible. You ask whether we've had a good year and I can answer that it has been good for all grains. I had about 200 bushels of wheat and I don't know how much corn we had because I throw it to the pigs as soon as it comes from the field but I think I would have had about 1,000 bushels if I had measured it. I've already used much of it as I had to start giving it to the pigs quite early. I haven't planted wheat this fall as wheat isn't profitable with prices from fifty to sixty cents a bushel and it's far to the railroad. But it now seems that the railroad that has been talked about for so long will be coming to us: I've seen work on a rail bed between Emporia and Eureka. My wife and I went on a trip to Doniphan and Brown Counties a short while ago and I saw the work being done in Greenwood County.

I'll tell you a little more about our pleasure trip. Gulbrand Haugen wrote that we should come on October 13 for the consecration of the new Norwegian church in Brown County. We were a nice group since our pastor also went and we visited Gulbrand Haugen and his siblings. We were invited to the home of one of their friends and were very well taken care of. None there seemed to be in lack of food or clothes. On the contrary they had an abundance. You probably knew Tosten Gulliksen's situation when he left Norway and I'll tell you what it is like now. He has two horses and a foal, fourteen head of cattle and about thirty pigs. He has bought land but hasn't paid anything on it yet. He asked me to send you his regards.

You ask how far it is to our neighbors. The distance to our closest neighbor is like the distance between upper and lower Lande. This neighbor is an Irishman and the next closest is a Norwegian named Christen Ludvigsen. A Hansen lives to the east of my farm and Gullik Bringe lives about a mile from us but I can see his house from mine. It is ten miles to my brother. From Gullik Bringe to my brother is a little more than eight miles. A Norwegian family came from Minnesota last fall and they now live in Ole Kolkinn's house on my land. I see in your letter that you don't think much of Kansas. I don't have precise information but I've heard that we are better off than in the eastern states. A Norwegian near Eureka visited Wisconsin and Minnesota this fall and he says it's difficult for people to get ahead there so he was glad to be back in Kansas even though we complain of hard times. He says that we have no reason to complain. As for climate, there are many from the East who come here for their health and this was one of the reasons my brother came. Summers are much hotter in the East and the winter is harsher. There were some instances of sunstroke in Minnesota and Nebraska last summer. We don't get sunstroke in Kansas and there has been a large immigration from the East. Kansas has increased its population by 250,000 this year.

You ask whether I would exchange my farm for Bakke. I would have to have a fairly large sum thrown in since my farm is worth about 5,000 and Bakke cannot be worth more than 3,000. I sold steers last summer for 1,355 dollars. I bought them last year and paid about thirteen dollars a head and this year I got thirty-five a head so I was paid thirteen dollars a head for tending them for the winter. Before I sold them I thought I would send some of the money to Norway but since I had made good money on them I bought fifty young steers this fall. But I didn't use all my money as I need a lot to cover my expenses; I have to hire many men and pay large taxes. If I'd had children I would have been better off as I see that those who have children don't have to hire so many and they could moreover have learned the language and been of much help in that way as well, because language is the greatest difficulty here except for illness when it is serious. There has been much illness everywhere this fall but not many have died around here. My wife and I thought we had left the illness behind us but it returned this fall. I had bilious fever and my lungs were also attacked. My doctor was worried but I improved quickly after I got medicine. My wife also had bilious fever but she quickly regained her health and she has not been affected by the climate fever that has kept me from writing. I haven't had much climate fever but my wife has often had hard spells. I see that you were all in good health at the time you wrote and this made us very glad. We can report the same back to you. I'll soon write to Marit again. I'll conclude with friendly regards from us.

OLE G. LANDE AND WIFE

The animals he made so much money on may have been bulls or oxen. The letter uses a Norwegian word for bulls—*studer*—but it is more likely that steers are intended. There are many letters by OGL in the Norwegian National Archives. A few months before this one he wrote to his father-in-law and told him about his new barbed wire fence and complained about the expenses for the taxpayer of having a public school, which he did not think was necessary. As in other letters he writes about returning, and one reason seems to be that neither he nor his wife can speak English yet (Nor. ed. IV:69). He wrote to his sister-in-law Marit Andersdatter on 18 December 1879 (Nor. ed. IV:117) that he had sold horses, cattle, pigs, and farm machinery at an auction that fall and that he would be coming home as soon as he had the money the next spring. His last letter from Kansas is dated 16–27 February 1880 and here he writes: "The reason I'm coming back is that I cannot speak English. If I could then I would perhaps not return so soon, but it is so awkward when you have to use an interpreter for even the slightest thing. As it now is, I cannot travel around and trade. I must either have someone with me or send someone in my place." He returned in June of 1880. «II:66 »II:114 NE IV:80

1878 — LETTER 2:88

From: Paul Larsen, *Lake Park, Minnesota, 5 December 1878*

To: Ole Larsen and Turid Larsdatter Haug, *Aal, Buskerud*

⤙▚◉⊜▚⤚

Dear brother-in-law and sister,

It's been long since I heard from you and long since I gave you any information about my situation. I've been in good health and done a little farming on a small scale as most of what I've planted has been eaten by the grasshoppers! Last summer they finally left us. I had then planted twenty-five acres and harvested 232 bushels of wheat and 500 of oats. I have no other animals than draft oxen of which I now have six. I don't have a wife and mostly live with my brother Sven. I'm quite comfortable with my situation. I would have liked to see Norway again but that seems unlikely. My sister Rønnaug and her family send their regards. They are in good health and doing well. They live about two miles from here. My sister Margit and her family have all they need as well as good health.

Most people around here are Norwegian, so we could have had schools and churches if we who call ourselves Lutherans could be united. But we are divided in two parties; one calls itself the Synod and the other the Conference. We each have our own pastor and our own schoolteacher and a church each, so we are sharply opposed to each other. As you may know, the government pays for schools but these don't teach religion. So it is up to the parents and the congregations to teach the children this subject. But I shouldn't complain about church matters as we've always had pastors—and now we have also had laymen who explain the word of God. And we have a few weeks of school every year! All of this fighting between the synods may seem a sorry affair, but the Almighty may be able to awaken some who are asleep through these imperfections. My letter will be short as I cannot think of anything of interest to write about. Give my regards to relatives and acquaintances. It would be nice if you could send me a few words. Loving regards from

PAUL LARSEN

· ——— ·

NE IV:81

· ——— ·

1878 — LETTER 2:89

FROM: Hans Hansen Bjokne, *Osakis, Minnesota, 29 December 1878*
TO: Hans Jørgensen and Eli Johannesdatter Bjøkne, *Lesja, Oppland*

⋯⇒◉⇐⋯

Dear parents and siblings!

I received your letter of November 25 on the third day of Christmas and see that you are all well, and this is good to hear as we know what it's like to be ill. I can tell you that I'm well and like it here, and this is the best one may wish for. You say you would have preferred that I had gone to school but there you can only sit still without understanding what they say, so it's best to learn to speak a little first as you cannot learn to speak much at school, only to spell, read, and write. So I'll hire out to an Englishman first and learn to speak a little. It isn't difficult to get a little work in return for board during winter and even get a little money, but it's best to be careful the first winter as you get used to the climate as well as the work when you've been here a while. I'm still living with Johannes Hagen looking after the children and I think I'll be here most of the winter. I've learned many English words because both he and Mari, who has worked as a maid for the Yankees (that is the Englishmen), speak English. I don't want to leave them since I'm as comfortable here as a cat and I think I'll learn a little more of the language here because once one has begun to understand a little it all goes faster.

Father and brothers! You wanted to learn a little about how the farmer works here, so I'll try to tell you a little. But you mustn't expect too much information from me on paper as I don't know all that much and as I'm not among those who can speak easily and certainly not write! But the little I say will be true. I'll start with the spring even though I haven't been here during that time of year but I've heard about the work they do then and Johannes and Anders Andersen Hagen are here and if there is anything I'm not sure about, I'll ask them. In the fall they plow their fields so they can begin to harrow in spring. They harrow their fields twice and then they plant seeds with a machine called a "seeder." They can harrow six to seven acres in a day when they use oxen and about ten acres with horses. They use from one to two bushels of seed an acre and when the planting is done it is time to harrow again. They don't have a machine that spreads the seed so they use the harrow two or three times. They mainly plant wheat and oats and a little barley. They plant several fields of corn after the fields have been harrowed and fertilized. They set four seeds in each place with four or six feet in between since it is necessary to take care of the weeds so they don't grow too much. They also plant many other things that I can't ramble on about here.

When spring work is over they set up "fences" if they don't already have them. They don't use such tight fences here as in Norway. They have posts in the ground and fasten three "rails" on them with nails. They don't have them tight because it is not permitted to have "sheep" on the prairie except in a "pasture" with tighter fences. You can't have horses on the prairie at night either but only during the day as they "jump the fence." He who wants to "break" new soil during summer begins as early as possible. He uses two teams and an iron chain with a hook in each end and one hook is fastened to the plow and the other to the yoke. They break going both ways but they don't have the kind of plow that can be used both ways. They can break from one to two acres a day. Two men are needed, one to drive the oxen and the other to hold the plow. The plows are better than in Norway. You can hold on to it with both hands as it has two handles and you walk behind it in the furrow. There are a lot of stones in some places and it isn't easy to break there. A plow costs from twenty to thirty dollars. You can break for three months during summer. During breaking you also have to "fix" what has been planted so that it isn't killed by weeds. They don't pull the weeds here as in Norway but bury them. Later in summer they begin to cut hay.

I haven't had a letter from Bjørner but Erland Kjelshus writes that they are together. Give my regards to Lysbakken. You say that you would like to be in America but I would advise you to remain at home for another year because it's best to be an adult when coming here. I'm glad that I didn't come earlier because times have been hard but are now getting better. Johannes: you also say that you want to come but I don't think you will come this spring—perhaps all of you will come. Well, I'm not advising anyone to come, but for young people who have no prospects in Norway I say that it's easier to make a living here than in Norway. You have to learn how to do a few things, as it is expensive to hire, for instance, carpenters or smiths if you become farmers. A good smith makes the best money of all craftsmen but there is no use for a bad smith.

A little about houses in America. There are different kinds. The most common in the West are sixteen feet wide and twenty-four feet long and built of "logs" in two stories and a cellar. Houses are also built with planks or "lumber." They don't use benches and a table. Along walls they usually place America boxes. You can buy chairs and tables in the store. You can buy a "stove" with two pots, two coffee pots, a pan, an iron, trays for bread baking, and some other things. The roofs are not covered with turf but with thin pieces of wood. When I arrived I thought that the cow barns were the poorest things they had in this country. They are made of turf, straw, and hay. I have no more to say about them as they are not worth anything, but they are quite warm. I must now complete my poor and incoherent letter with loving regards to you and all my relatives. I have regards to you from all relatives and friends in America. They are all well. But you are first of all lovingly greeted from me.

H. HANSEN

. ——— .

This letter has been damaged and a few sentences in the translation are conjectures. Lesja is in the upper and northern part of the long valley of Gudbrandsdalen. HHB (born 1858) was from the farm Vesle/Lille Bjøkne (the little Bjøkne). His siblings were Anne (1862; emigrated in 1886 to marry Amund Bjorli), Johannes (1864; emigrated in 1882 and died shortly thereafter), Jørgen (1866; emigrated in 1886), and Jacob (1870; emigrated in 1892). Anne Bjorli settled in North Dakota, her brothers in Minnesota. In the Unites States Bjøkne soon became Bjokne but in their letters the brothers tended to write Bjøkne. HHB was an active correspondent. His first letter is dated 7 July 1878; in one dated 17 October 1878 he described his journey. He also wrote 15 February 1879 and 12 June 1879 (Nor. ed. IV:89 and 99). The many references to former neighbors in Lesja make clear that he lives among relatives and acquaintances in Minnesota. Only some of the many letters from him and his siblings are included in this edition. They also corresponded with each other. An "Englishman" is an English-speaking American. The use of English terms (often in quotation marks) suggests that he is among people where code-switching is common: *sider* (seeder), *fens* (fence), *rels* (rails), *skjep* (sheep), *paster* (pasture), *jumper fenset* (jumps the fence), *brække* (break), *tim* (team), *figse* (fix), *lomber* (lumber), *staar* (store) etc. When he writes *jog* and *jogget* (yoke and the yoke) he gives a detailed description of a yoke for oxen. "America boxes" were probably boxes used on the immigration journey. Bjørner Jakobsen Lysbakken and Erlend Olsen Kjelshus were both born in 1856. »II:99
NE IV:83

. ——— .

1879 — LETTER 2:90

FROM: Gunder Johnson Moen
Norway Lake, Minnesota, 20 January 1879

To: Helge Gundersen Skare, *Eggedal, Sigdal, Buskerud*

⋅⊶⫤◉⫥⊷⋅

To my unforgettable father-in-law and family in <u>distant Norway</u>,

I will now take up my pen to send you a few sentences from our distant home, America. We have the good news that all in our family are in good health and doing well, which is a great gift from God and we should re-member the Almighty with praise and gratitude for his goodness. We hope that this will find you in good health even though you must be troubled by the weakness of old age so we wish to hear that your situation is toler-able. We must always be satisfied and place ourselves in the hands of the Almighty hoping that he who governs everything will do all for the best. As you probably know through K. Frovold, we have moved from Iowa to our former home at Norway Lake in Kandyohi County where we will settle. I can tell you that we had an average harvest for almost all produce but the quality was not so good because of the strong heat and drought in the period of ripening which damaged the wheat so it got a low price. When the price is low for produce all complain about shortage of money and hard times, in particular those who are in debt. We had no crops this year because we came here last summer and plowed our fields for future use. Our farm is ready for spring and we've bought some cattle and a couple of horses, a wagon and machines, so we are just about ready to get started again. We've had a fairly mild winter till now but it was rather cold around New Year. We have almost no snow so we have to use a wagon.

Enclosed is a souvenir from us and our children: portraits made in Decorah, Iowa. The oldest is Ingeborg who was eight November 16 of last year, Elise Ionette was four October 14, Helge will be two in March; he is quick and clever and his grandfather can be proud of having yet another with his name in America. These portraits were taken more than a year ago and the children have grown since then. We have no other news of interest for you. Everything around here is as usual. All our relatives are in good health, at Anders Skare's as well as at Ole Evensen's. Gunder H. Skare was recently here and he is in good health as usual. Fingal Helgesen Nerdrum asks us to say that he is in good health and quite satisfied with his situation. We must now conclude with loving greetings from us all and pray that you will be held and protected by the almighty God until we meet again, which probably will not be until the other side of the grave where we hope to be gathered in the eternal mansions and never more be separated. We hope you'll soon make us happy with a letter and news from Norway! Your devoted son-in-law

GUNDER JOHNSON MOEN AND HIS WIFE AND CHILDREN

GJM was married to Eli, Ole Evensen to Ingeborg, both daughters of Helge Gundersen Skare. «II:65 »II:101 NE IV:84

1879 — LETTER 2:91

FROM: Siri Allikson, *Colfax, Wisconsin, 4 February 1879*

TO: Osmund Ovedal, *Sirdal, Vest-Agder*

Dear brother Osmund,

I'm writing you a few words to let you know how I am. I've been sickly for some years. This is often difficult but we must thank God for our cross and our suffering as well as for good days. I'm now better than I've been for a long time. Rakel sent us your letter. We got it January 31 and were glad to see that you were doing well. Rakel says that they are also doing well but last Christmas Theodore was so sick with the whooping cough that they thought he would die. He is now well. Albert is also well. I visited our brother Sigbjørn February 2. The four youngest children had the whooping cough last fall but it wasn't serious and they are all well now. They've had eleven children, eight are Sigbjørn's and three are Sigbjørn Seland's of which two are living. Ingeborg Christine is married to a man from Helleland. They have two children and live in Minnesota. Sofie Regine has been with her sister for about a year. The others are at home. Berte and Alexander are confirmed. Ole Tobias and Ingeborg Helen go to school. You probably know that Sivert is deaf and dumb but it is good to see that he has a good mind. Sigbjørn says that he is the cleverest of them all. He is eight and can write a little. When he is twelve they can send him to the dumb school. Berent Anton and Herman Joseph are too small to go to school. Reinert has fifty acres close to Springville, forty acres are cultivated and ten are forestland. He had 100 bushels of wheat and ninety bushels of oats last fall. He has four horses and two cows and a calf, seven pigs and twenty hens. He had thirty bushels of apples but most of them were damaged by a hailstorm. Many lost almost all their oats because of hail. Many crops have failed.

Sara was in Minnesota last summer visiting Rakel until she went to the West. She was six weeks with Syverine Midtfjellsaa. Since she returned she has for the most part lived with Reinert. This winter she has had difficulties with her eyes; they water and are sometimes red. All are well at uncle Haaver's. He is old now and has for the most part been indoors this winter and no longer looks after the animals. Karen Tonette is well. Sigbjørn broke his left leg last summer but is now well. Henrik and his wife are going to Minnesota next summer. I mostly live with Reinert. I must now end my letter with regards to you all. Farewell.

SIRI ATLAGSEN

. ——— .

SA's brother Sigbjørn lives in Coon Prairie. Theodore and Albert are sons of her sister Rakel Rannestad. The Sigbjørn with a broken leg is Sigbjørn Haaverson Ovedal. Henrik is his son. «II:84 »II:131 NE IV:86

. ——— .

1879 — LETTER 2:92

FROM: Iver Sjursen Ystaas, *Decorah, Iowa, 26 February 1879*
To: Thrond Sjursen Haukenæs, *Granvin, Hordaland*

Dear friend!

As you know about my land, I won't write more about it but only tell you about last year's crops, and I can truthfully say that they were very poor. Wheat failed but oats and corn did quite well. We had mild weather last winter so we could plant as early as March. At first things looked very promising but then we got extreme heat as well as lots of rain in late June and this made the wheat develop too fast. Moreover, it was damaged by rust as well as a kind of fly called the chinch bug that clung to the straw sucking the juice so it withered, making the wheat so small and light that a bushel of wheat didn't weigh more than forty to fifty pounds while it usually weighs sixty pounds. Wheat is sold by weight and never priced by the bushel. Last year I had planted four acres and harvested 275 bushels of wheat, 140 bushels of oats and 150 bushels of corn, but as the wheat was so light it went for a lot less.

This year I'll plant seven more acres that I cleared and broke last summer. Market prices are low so we have good reason to complain about hard times. Wheat has been priced at twenty-five to fifty cents, barley at twenty to forty cents, oats at fifteen to twenty cents, corn at fifteen to twenty cents, and pork at two to three cents, all of this by the pound, so you can see that this doesn't give much profit to us farmers when we have to pay high wages as well as interest and many have large debts. But we mustn't be discouraged but hope for better times. We have a horse team, a cow, a heifer, a calf, and six pigs as well as some chickens and a dog and a cat. I'll conclude my short letter with friendly regards to you and your family from us all, wishing you the best of luck and success in the future. Write soon.

IVER SJURSEN YSTAAS

This is the last preserved letter from ISY. «II:54 NE IV:91

1879 — LETTER 2:93

FROM: Svend H. Enderson, *Danway, Illinois, 23 April 1879*

To: Jakob Rasmussen Sandvik, *Kinsarvik, Ullensvang, Hordaland*

❖══◖══❖

My dear Jacob,

I received your letter of March 19 on April 18 and read it with pleasure. It is long since I heard from you even though I sent you and Svend a letter with my portrait last winter. But it seems that it hasn't arrived, as so often happens. I often think of you and I haven't forgotten the happy times we had together in Norway. I still hope to enjoy a good time with you. If the Lord grants me health my plan is to visit Norway when I have a little more money, so you can rely on my return. I saw that you were in good health and I can, thank God, tell you that I'm also in good health. I've been in good health since I came to America and must thank God for this because life is easy when he provides health even though I've had hard trials since I came to America.

I was deeply wounded in my heart when the girl and I were separated. We were secretly engaged for a year and you may imagine that we had many a good time together. But regrettably it didn't work because there are many temptations in this world that interfere and I can thank my own people for this. I had never expected or believed that he could be so mean a person. When he got to know that I was going there he began to slander me and lie about me and began to visit her himself. I understood this right away and revealed it to her parents and they chased him away. I got to know how he had spoken ill of me to the girl and I left them too. And the girl's parents have often said that it was a shame that he came between us because this was none of his business. I don't know of anything I've done to make him hate me. I didn't eat for eight days and only drank a few cups of coffee so it was very hard for me because my love was pure. The girl was ill in bed for a long time after this so she also found out what love can be. And I can thank Jacob for all of this and you mustn't think we are good friends again just because I wrote a letter for him up in Lee County: I've left him now and don't care about his letter. I'll hate him as long as I live and we are still enemies and he can be sure that he'll get no more help or advice from me since he has done me more harm than any other person. I wouldn't have cared so much if it had been someone else but imagine that one of my own people could do such a thing. I left Lee County and came here to Danway because I didn't want to be in his way. Now I'm fifty miles from him and don't go near him so often. I'll stay here as long as I am in America because it is the best place for work and other things.

Well dear Jacob, I'm no longer engaged even though there are good opportunities to be both engaged and married here because I'm still popular with the girls, but I don't care for them now as I've thought of going to Norway. I won't bother with women because I can have more fun when I come to Norway if I'm single. I'm just as happy and satisfied now and I let things of this world go their own way; when you rely on God and behave honestly and properly help will come from both God and people. It is best to hold to God because he will not desert anyone who seeks him sincerely. I'm still quite satisfied living with the man I've been working for since March 1. Last winter we had a lot of snow and cold weather, the coldest period I've experienced, and you may imagine that it is freezing here.

Dear Jacob, give my regards to my mother and thank her for her letter, and thank you for your own letter. I received it the same day I wrote to my mother. Thank Svend for the portrait he sent me last summer. I would also like to have a portrait from you in full uniform as a soldier and I'll send you one in return. Don't let anyone see or read this letter but keep it to yourself. Greetings to all friends and acquaintances but first of all to you. Don't mess with the girls before I come home. Farewell from your faithful friend,

SVEN ENDERSON HUS

. —— .

Jacob is Jacob Svendsen Hustvet, married to SEH's sister Dorthea. «II:73 »II:119 NE IV:94

. —— .

FROM: Christopher Jacobson, *Bodie, California, 22 May 1879*

To: Hans Jakobsen Hilton, *Ullensaker, Akershus*

Dear, dear brother!

I got your letter of November 13 before I left and I was again glad to hear from Old Norway. One thing puzzles me; you say you would rather have seen your son Jacob in his grave than in America. Life is dear for us all and it's surely as dear for him as it is for you and your other children. None of us knows what the "other world" may be. It is said that there we'll live without sorrow or trouble, but no one seems to be over eager to take the step over the dark valley. I know that when I went to America I went with a lighter heart than if I'd gone to the graveyard for my own burial, and even though I've lived through many dark days since then and even though my future doesn't look so promising, I still love life and I hope and wish that I'll be in this world a few more years. And when I—after all my wandering—still love life, what then of Jacob who is still so young? No, rid your mind of such thoughts, my brother, and don't wish your son in his grave as long as he has his liberty and his health and behaves well.

Let me tell you a few words about myself: everything went wrong after I left the mines and until I returned to them again. As you know, I bought a small farm in California, a truly beautiful place, and I thought I would live and die there. But I was unlucky in including a partner who only thought of himself and as he hardly had any money I was the one who had to pay. I thought he was an honest fellow and I had often supported him when we were up in the mountains, but as soon as I had helped him on his feet he showed his true self. When I realized that this would not be a good home for me I sold him my share and left.

I was unlucky again. In San Francisco I thought I would at least be able to pay my necessary expenses by speculating with the money I had left, but nothing succeeded and in the end I was almost destitute. This was my situation when I last wrote to you and I wasn't exactly full of hope. I see that you had guessed how things were with me. But it isn't my way to lay my sorrows on others. When I make my bed I lie on it. I keep my sorrows to myself and no one except you, my dear brother, could have seen me so clearly. None of my acquaintances here knew that I left with no more money in my pocket than to pay for my ticket. I had as nice clothes and was as merry as ever when some of my so-called friends followed me down to the wharf on December 20, 1878 (almost the same date that I first set my foot on the soil of San Francisco in 1859) where I went aboard a steamboat. My friends left and I sat down and thanked God that I was alone and could reflect on my past as well as my future days. I got off the boat in a small town called Vallejo where I took the train to Carson City, sixteen miles from Virginia City, Nevada. Here I took a stagecoach to my destination, Bodie, high up in California's mining region, 300 miles and a little more than two days from San Francisco.

Here I found a new mining camp and felt at home among the high mountains. I soon found acquaintances among those who own rich gold mines here, so I got work and get my four dollars a day—room and board costs nine dollars a week—enough for me to lay aside about seventy-five dollars a month (we work Sundays as well as Mondays). So things are not so bad for me now. My health is good as is my hope. In a year or two, my brother, if nothing untoward happens to me I'll again have some shillings in my pocket. This is the way with most of us in California, so we don't take it so hard if we now and then are poor.

This must be all for now. I should have written a longer letter but when I read through what I've written and see so many errors I feel ashamed that I've forgotten my mother tongue. Give my loving regards to all my siblings. I haven't heard from Jacob since I came here. I wrote to Gulbrand a few days ago. Write soon and I'll write back and let you know how I'm doing. Farewell to all from

CHRISTOPHER

· —— ·

«II:86 »II:112 NE IV:96

· —— ·

FROM: Christine Dahl, *Norse, Texas, 12 June 1879*

To: Erik Pedersen Furuset, *Romedal, Stange, Hedmark*

Dear brother Erik,

We received your very welcome letter of May 2 a few days ago. We were so glad to hear from you but it was sad to hear that mother is weak, but she is getting old and then I suppose we all will be weaker, especially those who have had heavy work all their lives, as she and so many of us have had. As for us, we are, thank God, in good health and doing well. I can tell you from both Ole and Syverine and their families that they are doing well. Ole now has four children, two boys and two girls. His wife had twins about two months ago, two girls who are healthy and strong. They are named for their grandmothers, Christine and Berte.

I was at Dilrud today and they send their regards. Karen has not been well since last winter. It is for the most part her old weakness. The others are quite well. Pauline is still in Waco. She is as usual. I expect her here soon for the summer. All the children are home as the American school is over and the Norwegian religion school that we have for a couple of months every summer has not yet started. Helene is preparing for her confirmation in three weeks, on the fourth Sunday after Trinity, so summer is here, but we have chilly days and haven't yet had any heat. The winter was cold and spring was both cold and dry, so now we need rain more than ever for our corn and cotton. Our wheat did poorly because of several hail storms after the wheat had set ears. We did, however, have some white wheat that comes a little later and it wasn't much hurt by the hail, but then we had a drought so it didn't turn out so good either. Our animals are doing fairly well. We haven't sold any yet this year but we have about thirty young calves. I don't know how many horses we have since the prices for them are so low.

As for news, there is none of any interest for you except that yesterday we went to the wedding of our Norwegian pastor who came to us last fall. He was married to a sister of my son-in-law Jacob Nelson. As for the money you mention for the parents of Ole and Christopher, I have spoken with them and they would be glad to help them. If you would be so good as to let them have thirty *speciedaler* they will repay me as soon as they can. So please send me a receipt or something written that I can show to the boys here so they can see that their parents have received this amount. The enclosed five *speciedaler* are not much but they could not send any more just now. As I am out of paper I must conclude with the hope that these lines will find you all in good health. Give our loving regards to our dear mother. She is often in our thoughts. And, finally, my dear brother, we send our regards to you.

CHRISTINE DAHL

. ——— .

CD wrote to her brother 25 March 1879 telling him of her work on the farm and their farm animals. The portraits she enclosed were ambrotypes (Nor. ed. IV:93). The two brothers were most likely Ole and Christopher Lund, who emigrated from Lundsbakken in Romedal in 1877 and 1878. «II:85 »II:109 NE IV:98

. ——— .

1879 — LETTER 2:96

FROM: Nels T. Olson, *Fort Dodge, Iowa, 13 June 1879*

To: Ole Olsen Torvetjønn, *Møsstrond, Vinje, Telemark*

⋆⇒◯⇐⋆

Dear father and siblings,

Today I've been three weeks in America. I long to hear from home so I must send you a few words. First I must let you know how we fared on our journey. At five in the afternoon Friday May 2 we left Kristiania and came to Hull in England at nine Sunday evening. At twelve on Monday we went by train across England and came to Liverpool at six in the afternoon. At seven in the afternoon on Tuesday we left Liverpool on the steamship *Republic* of the White Star Line. We were eleven days crossing the Atlantic and we had excellent weather all the way to New York. People who had made the voyage several times said they couldn't remember having had such fine weather. But even so many were seasick. Both Aase and I were sick the whole voyage and we sometimes had to throw up. You may imagine that the days were slow before we landed, especially for those who were sick. I must admit to this for my part and I'm sure that others will agree. You lose your appetite at sea and you also get poor food that isn't easy to eat for one who is sick. We couldn't drink the coffee; it was so sweet and disgusting that it almost made me throw up because it was mixed with syrup. The tea was almost the same. There isn't much to say about the soup for dinner. It was perhaps not so poorly cooked. It was made of fat and gristly beef meat, and eating this isn't pleasant for one who isn't used to eating fresh meat. I don't know how it would have been for us if we hadn't brought a little food with us. Salted and dried veal and salt sausage, *gammelost, surprim,* and unleavened bread are some of the things one should bring on the voyage. At least I would prefer such food.

Now I must tell you that the journey into the country went well. We were three days on trains from New York to Iowa. My address to Ole Haatvedt wasn't correct. I went on a train to Webster City instead of going to the town Fort Dodge in Webster County. It was difficult for us when we went off the train. We didn't understand anyone there and they couldn't understand us. Luckily a man from Kongsberg turned up. He saw that we were newcomers because of our clothes. This man had been ten years in America so he knew all the Norwegians around there. He knew nothing of Ole Haatvedt and said that I should have gone to Fort Dodge. As it was too late in the evening to go any further we had to stay overnight with this man. At four thirty in the morning we took the train to Fort Dodge. It was twenty miles and we had to pay one and a half dollars. If our address had been correct we wouldn't have had to pay anything extra. When we came to Fort Dodge we met a Swede who knew Ole Haatvedt. So then we were helped. He thought it would be best that we waited for awhile because he was sure that someone from there would be coming to town. After a short time Nils, Ole's brother came driving to town to buy a plow for his corn and he took us straight to Haatvedt.

We were there for two days and were very well taken care of. Then we went on to Ole and he received us in the same manner. Now we are with

Thor, and we'll live here this summer and perhaps also through the winter. Ole, Thor, Nils, and Knut live a short distance from each other. Bjørn doesn't have a home; he's almost always traveling. He has gone to school to be a pastor but he doesn't want a regular call. Knut hasn't built a house on his land and lives with Nils. None of my cousins are wealthy and they all have debts. Thor is doing best and he has quite a lot of cattle, thirty-four fully grown and twelve calves, about forty pigs and many chickens. Here it isn't as in Norway where they slaughter the calves; they keep all the healthy ones because there is enough fodder in winter as in summer. You can have cattle even if you don't own any land as there are miles on miles of land where you can cut hay at will. The grass is very high, much higher than in Norway; when you walk out on the prairie the grass goes above your knees or even higher. Thor gave us a cow, well really a heifer.

I've been away working for a few days but wages are low, it's difficult to find work and there is little money among people. A man can't make more than half a dollar a day. Money is almost as tight here as in Norway, but if we have a good year, as it now seems, times may change fast in America. My work has been to cut weeds and this is hard work. Yesterday I went to an Englishman to cut grass in his fields. For this I was to get a three-month old piglet. It was done in a day. This is not so bad. All in all, as much as I've seen of America, I don't think it is as good here as many have written. The food doesn't taste better than at home. They serve many kinds of food for every meal and I like some and some I don't like at all. I can hardly eat the wheat bread; it is quite dry and to me it has a bitter taste. And the climate is so hot and humid that it will take a long time getting used to it. I will now conclude my simple letter with friendly greetings to you all, asking you to write as soon as you hold this simple letter in your hands. Give my regards to Thor Bakken.

NILS OLSEN

· ——— ·

NTO was from the farm Torvetjønn (also Tarvetjøn and Torvetjern) in Rauland that is now part of Vinje. Not long after his emigration Nils Olsen Torvetjønn became Nels T. Olson. In a letter to his sister Svanaug Neset written 20 June 1906 (Nor. ed. VII:53) he explained his American name: "the reason I write myself N. T. Olson and not Nels O. Torvetjern is that the Americans can hardly pronounce Torvetjern. But I'm so fond of my old name that I took the T. out of Torvetjern and placed it in between as you see." Iver Elsrud (see next letter) was also on this voyage of the *Republic* and he wrote to his parents from New York on 18 May 1879 (unpublished), that "*Republic* is one of the smallest and poorest ships of the White Star Line." *Gammelost* is a rather pungent traditional cheese made of skimmed milk that can be stored for a long time. *Prim* is soft caramelized whey. Addresses and destinations were easily confused because of idiosyncratic spellings. He wrote *Vebster Citty* and for Fort Dodge he wrote *Fordats.* »II:103 NE IV:100

. ——— .

1879 — LETTER 2:97

FROM: Iver Ellingsen Elsrud, *St. Ansgar, Iowa, 26 June 1879*

To: Ole E. Blakkstveit, *Aadalen, Ringerike, Buskerud*

⊷⩴◑⩴⊶

Dear brother-in-law!

As time permits I'll send you some words so you can see that I'm alive and doing reasonably well. I've just settled on my farm and begun work: weeding my garden and taming my foals. This didn't take much time as they behaved like grown-up horses at once, which isn't strange as the mare is large and already has a three-month-old foal. I bought a one-year-old stallion from Maren Haugerud. It's a beautiful horse of French Norman race and if I'm lucky I'll have a horse worth $1,000 in a few years. I've bought a new harness for twenty-three dollars so you'll see that I've landed in the world on both feet. We have good growing weather with showers and warm sunshine. The thermometer shows from twenty-three to twenty-nine degrees Réaumur in the shade and everything points to a good year. But a few days of too much heat would spoil everything. The wheat has already set ears and stands three to four feet high. Farmers here need a good year as the times are very hard, but I think prospects are a little better now as there is more work to be had because the railroad companies are laying new tracks and we also have some new public works.

I've been to Albert Lea since I returned and met many acquaintances who send their regards, in particular Ellef Gravli and his wife. They still live with Peder Lunde but will soon move into their new house. All who came with me from Aadalen are around here and have for the most part found work, but I don't think any of them are really happy here and they wish they were back in Norway. But I don't think they have reason for complaint, as I know they are paid eighty dollars for five months. The journey here costs sixty so this gives them a surplus of twenty dollars the first year even if they only work five months. Tell Gjertrud at Jonsrud that they are in good health and have a new house. People here are very restless. All want to go west to Dakota and almost every farmer wants to sell as there is land for nothing in Dakota. You've never heard such boasting as I hear every day since Andreas Østensen and Anders Høghaug returned from a visit up there where uncle has taken land at Park River in Dakota. They were away for six weeks and the distance is 700 miles, so they went fast.

An after-dinner nap. I ate chicken drumsticks and fresh potatoes for the first time this year. My return journey was exceptionally good: only twenty days from Kristiania. But when I arrived everything was changed, especially at Haugerud as uncle had sold his farm and chattel and gone to Dakota while his family were still on the farm. Because of bad investments uncle was in a worse debt than I had imagined and all his creditors were at him when he was ill. To top it off a poor harvest brought on hard times and when he was forced to sell he didn't get more than half the value. He also had an enormous bill from the doctor so he didn't have much left. Maren is now with her parents but will be going to join him in a few days. I'll be worse off now as this has been my home. I'll have to settle on my farm and begin using it myself as Andreas Olsen is going west in the fall. Give my regards to all at Viker and say that Nils is working for a man from Bjoneskogen for eighty dollars for five months. The sun is now in the west and the shadows of the trees fall on me so I must conclude with loving regards to all at Blakkstveit, Elsrud, and Viker from me, your always devoted friend and brother,

I. E. ELSRUD

· ——— ·

Norwegian immigrants often gave their farms the name of the farm they had left in Norway and that also had become their family name. IEE has dated his previous letters at "Haugerud." Now that his uncle is no longer there he dates his letter at "Elsrud," probably with some pride. He has recently returned from a visit to Aadalen and he wrote

to his parents from New York on 18 May 1879 and from Iowa on
9 June 1879. «II:68 »II:108 NE IV:101

1879 — LETTER 2:98

FROM: Jens Herlef Ursin, *Chicago, Illinois, 27 August 1879*

To: E. B. Kjerschow Zahl, *Kjerringøy, Bodø, Nordland*

Mr. K. Zahl,

I finally came here about a week ago but I may regret that I went. Times
are bad and without a trade it is difficult to make the money necessary to
get along. I'm so sorry that I couldn't repay my debt and I thought that in
America I would soon get enough to send you something, but it doesn't
look good. But I'm glad that I haven't totally ruined my chances. The boat
I bought is still there as well as a few other things, but the worst is that I've
been ill and I cannot do hard labor. It's difficult to get regular employment
in less taxing work. I'll try another week and if I still haven't got anything
I'll go out in the country. To return to Norway is out of the question if I'm
not sure of a good position there. It's difficult to be alone and poor in a
strange country but I must believe that the Lord will help me. I've always
been unlucky whichever way I've turned in this world but I've had my good
health; without it it would be too difficult here in America.

Please excuse me for bothering you. There is only one thing worth thinking about at home and I've thought about it for a long time: a mill. We have
a large river on our farm. It isn't reliable all year but it runs from spring to
Christmas and in so populous an area I think it would be profitable. Would
you help me to set up a mill if I return to Norway? I could run it until you
were fully repaid. My poor father is getting weak and has no one to rely on

in his old age. He would like to see me again. It would be a happy surprise for me to receive a letter from you because I'm now very unhappy here. Please accept my regards. Sincerely,

JENS URSIN

· ——— ·

JHU emigrated in 1879. His parents had the farm Taraldsvik, now in Narvik. He had lost a substantial sum he had borrowed from E. B. Kjerskow Zahl, one of the wealthiest men in Nordland. JHU also wrote on 19 October 1879. There are many letters to Zahl from working class emigrants who had borrowed money from him for their emigration expenses either to explain why they hadn't paid yet or to report that a bank draft had been sent to him. »II:177 NE IV:107

· ——— ·

1879 — LETTER 2:99

FROM: Hans Hansen Bjøkne
White Bear Center, Minnesota, 7 September 1879
To: Hans Jørgensen and Eli Johannesdatter Bjøkne, *Lesja, Oppland*

⊷═◉═⊶

Unforgettable parents and siblings!

As several days have passed since I wrote to you I will now move my pen across the paper and tell you that I'm well. I suppose there is no need to tell you that I like it here as that has been my main theme in earlier letters. We are now done with the harvest and it went quite well. Syver Hagen reaped for Ole Bjokne and Lars Holen. We were six to bind the sheaves: I, Ole Bjøkne, Mathias, Lars and Ole Holen, and Ole Loftingsmo and his wife. These two were counted as one as they were unused to this work and that is how we made seven people count as six. We bound about ninety acres at Hagen, forty-six at Bjokne, thirty-two at Holen and some on land that Ole Jespersen Loftingsmo has bought near here. That was about 190 acres and you may imagine that we didn't have time to pick up every straw or have every sheaf even, but had to work fast. It may seem incredible but many have worked out that it is possible to bind as much in half an hour as we used to be able to do by breakfast at nine o'clock. The crop varies according to the quality of the soil. They say it is an average year in bulk but the quality is not the very best. The oats are somewhat better than the wheat and as it is the latter that the farmer lives on and uses to pay his debts and prosper, you often hear people complain. But there is no reason to fear for tomorrow in this country. Let today's trouble suffice for today, because when you work during harvest you can make so much in a short time that you can live well the whole year. And the end of the world comes, I suppose, when there is no more work. As long as the farmers and others have something to pay their workers they must surely have enough to live on, and so the farmer as well as the working man both live well in this country and the times look pretty good to me. Some have started to thresh but I haven't heard how large the crop is yet and I'll write about this some other time.

A couple of days ago I had a letter from Jakob Ekren and he says they like it here. He thinks they may come here next spring if his uncle comes home and I think he's there now. I've written him today and told him a little about life here. I must conclude with my regards to relatives and friends who may ask about me, but first and last to you my dear parents and siblings from your always-faithful son and brother.

HANS H. BJUKN

· —— ·

HHB's earlier letters were sent from Osakis on the border of Douglas and Todd Counties, while he now uses the White Bear Center post office opened in 1869, which was further south and west in Pope County. In 1882 the post office was moved to Starbuck, a new town created by the Northern Pacific Railroad. When writing about farms, he uses the names that the immigrants brought with them from Lesja. When he writes about "today's trouble," HHB is referring to Matthew 6:34. HHB wrote frequently, for instance, on 15 February and 12 June 1879 (Nor. ed. IV:89 and 99). «II:89 »II:104 NE IV:109

· —— ·

1879 — LETTER 2:100

FROM: Ole Andersen Lee, *Springdale, Wisconsin, 14 October 1879*

To: Anders Olsen and Kari Mikkelsdatter Lie
Hedalen, Sør-Aurdal, Oppland

To my often remembered parents and brothers, relatives and friends,

May the grace of God, peace in Jesus Christ, and the consolation of the Holy Spirit and welfare in the world as in heaven be with you! This is my heartfelt wish. It is with no inconsiderable shame of my own negligence and indifference that I now, finally, turn to my not yet executed labor of writing to you. Dear parents and brothers, I humbly confess that I've behaved badly by waiting so long to send you information about myself. I'm sure that I've given you a difficult time and many troubled thoughts. The loving hearts of parents are always in fear for their dear children, especially when they know that one of their dear ones is a pilgrim in a strange land, that he is in a part of the world where there is no lack of tempters and evil people, and is often lured and tempted to let go of the dear faith of his childhood and instead turn to some new false doctrine or even no doctrine or Christian religion at all. Dear ones, I have wronged you in waiting so long to write and hardly have the courage to beg your forgiveness. But I must do so believing and hoping that you will forgive these as you have forgiven my earlier transgressions. Believing that all has been forgiven I'll now, as well as I can, tell you what I and others you know have experienced of changes since I last wrote.

I'll begin with a little about myself. We no longer live with Uncle Guttorm. Just before Christmas, we moved to a house about a mile from Guttorm that I and my brother-in-law Iver rented for one and a half dollars a month. This is the same house that Uncle Torgrim lived in at the end of his life on earth and that he built himself. It has been much improved since he lived here. It is a large and spacious house with two floors and a cellar. The people who owned the farm are dead, the man twenty years ago and the woman three years ago. So this farm has been run by strangers who have lived here since the man died. Uncle Torgrim rented the farm from the widow. Now the heirs have just barely reached the age of maturity and are discussing what to do with it, whether some of them will take the farm or whether they will sell it and I think the latter will be done. As far as I know none of them is fit for farming. I don't know how long they will stay. The farm is in the town of Springdale near the border of Primrose where my uncles Guttorm and Ole live. So we don't have Pastor Fjeld as we did when we lived with Uncle Guttorm. The pastor in Springdale is A. Bredesen, an excellent man in his calling. We live about the same distance from three Norwegian churches: Pastor Fjeld's church in Primrose and Pastor Bredesen's in Springdale and Blue Mounds. We mostly go to the two latter as the roads are better.

We don't have many animals: one cow, two pigs and some chickens; I'm not quite sure how many but Siri says we have twenty-seven. Any others? Yes, we have a cat and a mouse and a lot of rats. We plan to slaughter one of our pigs this fall and will keep the other one through the winter. I should also tell you that on January 8 we were blessed with a girl child who was christened with the name Kari, and she is growing, is in good health, and is quite content. Actually we are all in good health and doing quite well. But times have been hard in America. Last year's harvest was very poor here because of the extreme heat and long drought along with the so-called wheat bug that ruined the good prospects we had in spring when we looked forward to a good year. Some were lucky and got a little more than they needed for their own use, others didn't get enough, while for others again the fields were so bad that they didn't find them worthwhile to harvest. Happily, it was a better year for hay and corn but the prices were so low that there was nothing to be had for what one had to sell. This led to lower wages and in many places there was no work to be had.

But now, praise God, it seems better. Here they had an average year for all crops and better prices compared to last year. This summer I hired out for one month during harvest for a man from Nore and was paid thirty dollars. During haying I worked for another man for one dollar a day, and after harvesting I continued to work for the man from Nore for six shillings a day (an American shilling is worth twelve and a half cents). My present work is grubbing. I suppose you don't know what grubbing is. This is to dig up the roots of trees so the land can be plowed with a breaking plow pulled by four horses. I, Iver and Ole Børtnes have bought a grubbing machine driven by the strength of our own hands and we can easily take up the roots of even the largest trees. We carry it ourselves from place to place and are quite busy. This kind of work is always by contract and our prices vary according to the state of the forest, from six to twelve dollars an acre. We paid forty-three dollars for the machine and we are quite satisfied with it since it allows us to work both faster and easier. We can continue this work until the ground freezes or is covered with snow and by that time there is very little work to be had around here and we will have to find other ways to amuse ourselves. Last winter I decided to become a student at a singing school in Springdale and this was a very pleasant way to pass the time as I got to meet so many nice people, and I've enjoyed their company many times since then. When I came to this school and asked to become a member of the singing association they had already had classes for some time and I feared that I would be behind the others. But I soon realized that I had nothing to fear. The most difficult thing for me was to learn the names of the notes in English and when this was done it was not difficult to follow the classes. This school didn't cost me more than my time because the teacher is a precentor in Springdale and had decided to train a choir at his own expense in return for getting to use it in his church and on other occasions. Our teacher, Ole Christensen Loftsgaarden, is from Nore in Numedal. We've decided to continue the singing school next winter and we practice on Sunday afternoons. It may seem unnecessary for me to write so much about this but this is my work during the part of the year when no other work is available.

I don't have any news of interest, but I can tell you that we have celebrated a fine wedding at uncle Guttorm's; his daughter Gunhild married Syver Nilsen Belgum, a master blacksmith. You may know the groom's father who is called Turi-Nils. He's from Valdres, either from North or South Aurdal. It was a wonderful wedding and many people had been invited. They were wed at home by Pastor J. N. Fjeld. The newlyweds live in Mount Vernon where he has his shop and does quite a good business. I think I may have written that Pastor Fjeld was a widower. I can now tell you that he is about to marry a young woman, hardly thirty. Pastor Fjeld is now an old and weak man so he is no longer able to serve his churches alone and has therefore appointed an assistant pastor. His name is Johannes Waage and he is a trustworthy and conscientious man.

My uncles send their regards. They are in good health and living much as before except that Guttorm has been weaker for some time and we don't believe that he can have much more time to live, but God alone knows. Olaug Børtnes and her family send their regards, as do the Børtnes boys. Halsten has been working as a carpenter and Ole has been with me in the grubbing enterprise while Andreas and Erik have done different kinds of work. Erik worked for a month during harvest for uncle Ole for fourteen dollars and then he hired out to another man for three months at nine dollars a month, a much better pay. I think Erik will do well in America but this is not the case for Andreas who still is as pig-headed and unreliable as he used to be. As soon as he came he hired out to a farmer for four months and was there for about one and a half month before he left and complained that the man had sent him off for no reason. But when I met this man, whom I know well, he explained that he had wanted Andreas to work for him as it was difficult to get help but that Andreas claimed that he couldn't stay if he was to remain alive and healthy. This was insolent, as this man is known as a good and reliable man who wouldn't harm anyone. Since he broke his contract Andreas has been hanging around, occasionally working a day here and a day there. It's possible that he may learn from this. We must hope for the best. I'll have to stop now and say farewell to you. Sincerely,

OLE A. LIE AND FAMILY

. —— .

OAL's uncle Guttorm Olsen Lie wrote on 20 November 1879 with news about the family (Nor. ed. IV:113): Halsten Halstensen Børtnes, married to OAL's aunt Olea Olsdatter, has been seriously ill. On 1 January 1880 (Nor. ed. IV:119) OAL wrote about his health problems and the help he had received from his uncle Guttorm, suggesting that his other uncle Ole is more careful about how he spends his money. Some cousins (often referred to as the Børtnes boys), sons of his aunt Olea, have arrived, and he has advice for his brother Iver who is planning to emigrate. Nore and Numedal are in Buskerud. «II:79 »II:113
NE IV:111

. —— .

FROM: Ole Aslesen and Ingrid Helgesdatter Myran
Decorah, Iowa, 8 November 1879

TO: Helge Gundersen Skare, *Eggedal, Sigdal, Buskerud*

⊹⊶⊜⊝⊶⊹

Dear parents,

As it's almost one year since we heard from home (we haven't heard anything since John Vold returned from Norway) we're sending you these sentences. When it's so long since we've written this is not because we have forgotten our family in Norway, but when one is busy every day with work and chores it isn't easy to write. But if there had been a letter for every thought we send to our old home there wouldn't have been many days without a letter from us. Although we must say that we are in good health it cannot be denied that we feel the weakness of old age as the years go by. Nor can our children be said to be as well as they could be. As we may have written before, our youngest son Anders is hard of hearing. This started with an infection in his throat. Helge hasn't been quite well and this may be caused by some disorder of his intestines. The others are well and we are all quite happy. May this find you with as few troubles and worries as possible.

Last summer our next youngest son Gunder was confirmed and we were glad to hear that he was well prepared, as our pastor assured us. This winter he'll live with my sister Mari so he can go to the English school. We should also tell you a little about our crops. Last summer we harvested 411 bushels of wheat, 427 bushels of oats, a lot of excellent hay, and a considerable crop of corn and potatoes. We now have six workhorses, eleven cows, and some pigs and sheep. The last two years in the Northwestern states have been lean years as wheat, which is our most important grain, has not done well and only yielded about half of an average year. Although this has not had so great an effect on us, it has hurt many of our nationality here and families often have to leave their farms.

As for Ingrid's siblings, we can report that Gunder lived with us for three years. He left us about a year ago and lives with my sister Ingeborg.

We recently heard from Anders and Eli. They've been in good health and are doing well, and Mari Vold and her husband also send their regards. She has recently been doing poorly. Our son Helge thanks you for the gift you so kindly sent him. Mari has received your gift and sends her most heartfelt thanks, especially to her stepmother who likely has had the trouble of making it. We'll end our letter with loving regards to you all with the wish that God may be with you and bless you in all you do. We would be glad to hear from you soon. Our loving regards also go to Halvor and his family. Please send my regards to Lars and Guri Nordmannsplassen and Elling Reisland.

OLE AND INGRID MYRAN

. ——— .

During the confirmation service the candidates would be examined in the catechism and other texts, so Gunder's parents had quite literally heard him perform. The service would have been in Norwegian. Mari was Gunder's mother Ingrid's sister, and she was married to Elling Ellingsen Vold. Both families had farms near Decorah; their letters are dated at "Myran" and "Vold" respectively, the names of the farms they had come from in Sigdal. "English school" was the name immigrants used for the regular public school. OAM's sister Ingeborg's married name was Flaagan. Halvor Helgesen Skare, Guri Helgesdatter Nordmannsplassen, and Elling Helgesen Reisland were siblings who remained in Sigdal. «II:90 »II:105 NE IV:112

. ——— .

1880 — LETTER 2:102

FROM: Elise Wærenskjold, *Prairieville, Texas, 1 January 1880*
To: Thomine Dannevig, *Lillesand, Aust-Agder*

⊷⇒◯⇐⊷

My dear, good Thomine!

It's so long since I heard from Lillesand that I can wait no longer and must try to revive your memory of my insignificant person so that you might sacrifice a little of your time to please an old friend who always remembers you with sincere love. I assume you'll read my letter to Kaja so I won't repeat its contents. Dear Thomine, you sometimes please me with a letter and I hope that you'll fulfill my wish and write as soon as you get this so I may have it in March. Husher, who is both publisher and editor of *Fædrelandet og Emigranten*, is so kind to send me his newspaper without charge and the first thing I look for are the death notices. As I haven't seen that any of my acquaintances in Lillesand have died I hope they are all alive. Helene Hammer must be very old now. How is she? And how is Bina Grøgaard? We've heard that they are not doing so well. I've always had affection for Bina since we were little girls. It would interest me to hear how she and her children are doing, as well as other old friends and acquaintances. Please send me Stina Normann and Gusta Hauge's addresses. I'm sure you can tell me a lot from Tønsberg. I haven't heard from Lovise Seeberg for ages. Who was the Miss Foyn whose embroideries had so much acclaim at the Paris Exhibition? Would you send me a portrait of your daughter-in-law and your grandchildren? It would be so nice to see them. I often wonder why Thorvald hasn't married. And I also wonder why Lovise and Milla Seeberg haven't married. Now, my dear Thomine, I'll conclude with loving regards to you and your children and other friends and acquaintances. Don't forget to write to your forever faithful

ELISE WÆRENSKJOLD

I wonder whether Helene H. and Bina G. will send me their photographs.

. —— .

This letter is not in Clausen 1961. It was probably enclosed with a letter to Kaja Poppe. The two mentioned in the final sentence are Helene Hammer and Bina (Jacobine) Grøgaard. Her interest in "Miss Foyn" was triggered by her name: EW's first husband was Svend Foyn. «II:34 »II:139 NE IV:120

. —— .

1880 — LETTER 2:103

FROM: Nels T. Olsen, *Callender, Iowa, 3 January 1880*

To: Tor Olsen Bakken, *Aamotsdal, Seljord, Telemark*

⋅-⟩⊜⟨-⋅

Dear brother,

It is long since we last parted in Seljord and it may be time to take up my pen to let you know how I'm doing in this distant and foreign land. I must first tell you that we have a child, a boy who was christened Ole after my father. He is five months but small for his age. He was rather sickly to begin with and beset with stomach troubles and we didn't expect him to get better, but now he is, praise God, quite well and is growing and thriving. Both Aase and I have been in good health since coming to America and for this we must thank God with all our heart. I recently had a letter from Torvetjønn, from Tallef, and saw that you are well but that your wife Anne has been ill and been in the care of a doctor in Seljord.

Dear brother, when we went down the Kivle valley to Seljord I had more or less given up on going to America, and we were quite merry when we left each other and didn't realize that it would be the last time we were together. Only God knows if we'll again be together here on earth and if not, we must live in the shining hope that after our work here on earth has been done we'll be gathered up there with God where there will be no grief or separation.

I must now tell you how I really am here in America. First, I don't in any way regret coming here and I think I was very lucky in not buying Myrbo, since I am convinced that it would have been much more difficult to get along there than here. If I retain my health and luck is on our side I'll be able to lay a little more aside here than there. If we should now be in Norway as we were when we came here I don't know how we would have acquired our daily bread, considering how the times there are now. When I came to America I only had eight dollars left of my travel money and what would it have been like to come to Norway with such a small sum when there is so little work and so little money. I've made eighty-two dollars since coming to America. I have two cows and a pig. One of the cows calved a month ago and the other will have a calf in May. For one I gave twenty-four dollars and the other is a gift from my cousin Thor E. Haatvedt. As you may have seen in my letter to Torvekjønn last winter I've rented a house from a widow from Valdres. We are to provide equal amounts of firewood as well as kerosene and matches and I am to tend her animals when it's cold and when I'm at home. She has four cows and four calves. As it's now getting late I'll have to end for now. I've just sent a letter to Tallef and you can see it when it gets to Torvekjønn. There I've talked about so much and told him things that I don't find worthwhile to write in the letter I'm sending you. I'll conclude this letter with friendly greetings to you and Anne. Farewell!

N. OLSEN

· —— ·

NTO's brother was married to Anne Aasmundsdatter who inherited the farm Bakken. «II:96 »II:143 NE IV:121

· —— ·

1880 — LETTER 2:104

FROM: Hans H. Bjokne, *White Bear Center, Minnesota, 4 January 1880*

To: Hans Jørgensen and Eli Johannesdatter Bjøkne, *Lesja, Oppland*

⚬⚬⚬

Dear parents and siblings!

This is the day to say farewell to the Old Year and look back on how we have used it, and I for my part have a clear conscience as regards breaking the law of the land. So I gladly enter the New Year wishing that all will go well for me and my relatives. There hasn't been much Christmas celebration as I've had enough to do tending the animals, and it has been so cold that it wasn't easy to go out and make a hullabaloo as they say. So I stayed home both the first and second days of Christmas until evening when I had looked after the animals. Then time went so slowly that I left the house and I happened to visit Hans and Marit Haugen who were alone so we didn't have much hullabaloo. We didn't have any liquor nor did we wish for any but we had a nice time nevertheless. On the third day of Christmas we had a service in the church and at Bjøkne we had a christening party. The center of attention was named Hanna and I believe this must be for Henrik Maatterud. She has grown to be big and nice. The godparents were: I, Hans, Marit, and Sigrid Haugen. After the service we were joined by the pastor, Tosten Hagen, all from Haugen and Marie Ulveholen, so we were nineteen people in this little house and you may imagine that it was packed.

January 4, 1880

On New Year's Day we also had a service and Ole Norderhus was there so I can give you greetings from that family. They are well but Paul and Anne are getting old and weak. Anders Hagen came New Year's Eve and they are all in good health and doing well. I can tell you that all relatives are well. Kari Teigen or Holen has recently had a daughter and they are both well as far as I've heard. If Anne wants to come to America she should write to me and let me know what line I should buy a ticket for. And you should confer with the others who are getting tickets from America so we buy tickets for the same line and as many as possible can go together. As I don't have any news I must conclude with the sincere wish that these simple sentences may find you well. Give my regards to all who may ask about me. My loving regards to you my dear parents and siblings from your faithful son and brother.

H. BJØKNE

. ———— .

The immigrants brought their farm names with them and these often became family names. When Kari is referred to as "Teigen or Holen" the readers would know that she was from Holen and that her husband was from Teigen (both are farms in Lesja) and that she used the name Teigen in the United States. HHB's sister Anne didn't emigrate until 1886, when she became Anne Bjorli. «II:99 »II:141 NE IV:123

. ———— .

FROM: Ole and Ingeborg Helgesdatter Evensen
Arctander, Minnesota, 12 January 1880

To: Helge Gundersen Skare, *Eggedal, Sigdal, Buskerud*

⊶⇒◯⇐⊷

Honored father-in-law Helge G. Skare,

I will make use of this opportunity to take up my pen to let you know how we are doing here in Minnesota. We are, thank God, in good health and doing well. As for our economic situation, I'll only note that we've moved twice for the good reason that we haven't had forest on our land and settlers in America have to go through many trials and tribulations. As we've had several major accidents it has been difficult to succeed. Five years ago we bought 120 acres of railroad land and this cost us 865 dollars and I now owe 400 dollars on our land and have to pay ten percent interest. In 1876 and 1877 we didn't harvest a single grain of any kind because of the devastation of the grasshoppers. I had built rather good buildings but April 26 we had a fire that burned down our new horse and cow stable with two calves, a heifer, harnesses for our horses, and all our farm implements. Our loss came to between four and five hundred dollars. So it will be rather difficult for us to manage our expenses if our luck doesn't improve. We now have very good land with some forest and a comfortable home. We have two horses and four cows. I must also let you know that we've had a fairly good year but since I haven't yet broken much of this land I still don't have much to sell.

I must also tell you that we have five children who are all growing and doing well. Berit is thirteen, Eli is ten, Even seven, Helge four, and Inger is three months old. We are enclosing our photograph. Had it not been winter we would also have sent photographs of our children but as it is about twenty miles to town and the weather is so cold we'll have to do this some other time. I can also say from your son Anders Skare that they are in good health and doing well. Should you receive these lines, I must ask you to write as soon as convenient. This must suffice for now. Our loving regards to you all. Farewell in the Lord.

OLE EVENSEN AND HIS WIFE INGEBORG HELGESDATTER

«II:101 »II:106 NE IV:125

1880 — LETTER 2:106

FROM: Anders Helgesen Skare, *West Lake, Minnesota, 5 February 1880*

TO: Helge Gundersen Skare, *Eggedal, Sigdal, Buskerud*

My dear old father Helge G. Skare,

It is long since I last wrote so it is a pleasure to let you hear from me. I can tell you that I'm doing well. We're all in good health and I hope that these lines will find you in as good health as your high age permits. I've heard from Knut Frøvold and the newly arrived Kristofer Bjørkerud that you are beginning to weaken, but I'll be glad as long as I hear that you are on your feet and can do a little work. It is only natural that you who are so old will feel weak. We must remember that you are a very old man and that you must therefore in a true Christian manner be prepared patiently to bear the burdens of age.

After the grasshoppers left us and we recovered from their devastations we've had two good years. Many farmers here had more wheat last year than this year but because the wheat then was so light in weight and the prices so low, they made much less then than this year. Last fall I harvested 2,475 bushels of wheat and a little more than 1,600 bushels of oats, which added up to about twenty bushels an acre. This must be considered a fairly good crop and now that the prices are rather high I'll be making quite a lot. For some time after Christmas we got one dollar and ten cents a bushel for wheat but it's now down to ninety-five cents. We think the price will go up in spring but this depends on how much wheat is needed in Europe. I have quite a few animals; nine horses including three teams of workhorses. I have twenty-five head of winter-fed cattle and thirteen milk cows and heifers bearing calves. I have quite a lot of land so I have both hay and pasture for my cattle in addition to my considerable field land.

My two oldest sons, Helge and John, are now home. They came from Iowa last year and have since then helped me with the farm and if the harvests are good they'll make more than if they hired out to others. This also means that they won't be exposed to so many temptations in their youth. Wherever you may be in this fallen world, there are many kinds of temptations and traps laid out for the thoughtless young, in particular here in America. As you know, I have many to bring up but with prayer and the help of God much evil can be avoided. Now my dear father, this is what I have to write about this time and as space permits. If I could have met you our conversation would no doubt have been both longer and more intense than this short letter. But as a meeting between us on this side of the grave is impossible, I will, as your son, earnestly ask you to turn away from the present and look to what is to be. We may be sure of death but not of when or how it will come. Lucky is he who at all times has his lamp lit and is ready to meet the bridegroom when he arrives. That you may be among those so that we may be gathered in God, this is the wish of your son,

ANDERS H. SKARE

· —— ·

This is the last preserved letter from AHS. «II:105 »II:145 NE IV:129

· —— ·

FROM AMERICA TO NORWAY

1880 — LETTER 2:107

FROM: Jacob Hanson Hilton, *Boulder, Colorado, 15 February 1880*

To: Hans Jakobsen and Anne Olsdatter Hilton, *Ullensaker, Akershus*

⋆⇒◉⇐⋆

Dear parents,

It's almost ten months since your last letter; I had one from Oluf last fall. So I must send you a few words to hear how you all are, hoping that you're doing well when you get this. Oluf wrote that you wrote one during the haying season but it hasn't arrived. I've been traveling since last spring, about 1,000 miles through Iowa, Nebraska, Wyoming and Colorado where I now am. I worked three months in Omaha, Nebraska last summer but got tired of the place, the worst pigsty I've been in, nothing but drunkenness and fighting that always ended with one of the parties getting a bullet. I left Omaha August 12 and went west through Wyoming and into Colorado where I now live in <u>Boulder City</u>, the most beautiful place I've seen on my journey. I'm still doing forest work and the money is good; I've been making from thirteen to twenty-three dollars a week since I arrived and it seems likely that this will continue as times are improving. I'm planning to begin farming, as this is the best business in America. I can't say for sure if this will be next summer but in a year's time I'll have a piece of land near Fort Dodge in Iowa if it hasn't already been sold. It was bought ten years ago for twelve dollars an acre, is 160 acres, and only two miles from Fort Dodge. I'm tired of being a shoemaker, as you have to be on the move all the time. It's difficult to get steady work because of all the large shoe factories; machines are now used for everything.

I have news for you. Malle Hilton is dead. She came to Colorado to be cured of her consumption but left us February 6. I sat by her bed until her last breath. She asked me to tell you that she died in faith in her dear Savior and Redeemer. These were her last words. Her earthly remains were buried on February 9 at the foot of the mountain outside the city where a beautiful slope has been set aside as a graveyard. Her husband and children are on their way back to Fort Dodge where he has his farm.

How are things at Aareppen or other places in the area? Any news? What about Ihle, Søli, Ullern and Salmakerstua? Are my uncles Gulbrand and Iver doing well? Is Ole Hunstad still there? Tell him and H. Jakobsen Ihle that they should come here. I think they would succeed here—at least if they came now when land prices are going up. Fort Dodge is growing. It now has four railroads; two have come these last two years. There is still land available near the town but large numbers of people are coming in and taking land as soon as they arrive. There are two large Norwegian settlements where everything is almost as at home and Christmas, Easter, Whitsun and May 17 and other Norwegian feasts are all celebrated there. And that is another reason why I want to return. I must now end my incoherent letter. Best regards to you all from your son,

JACOB

· ——— ·

It is not clear why JHH has stopped in Boulder, but as we see in this and later letters there were also others from Ullensaker there. He hasn't settled down, however, and he asks his father to address his next letter to a friend in Fort Dodge, Iowa. «II:82 »II:110 NE IV:130

· ——— ·

1880 — LETTER 2:108

FROM: Iver Ellingsen Elsrud, *St. Ansgar, Iowa, 25 February 1880*

To: Elling and Olea Elsrud, *Aadalen, Ringerike, Buskerud*

⟶⟦◯⟧⟵

Dear parents and siblings,

I've returned after a two-month visit to Minnesota where I met old friends. I last wrote from Fountain where I visited Olav Flaskerud. I then went to Erik Hansen where I stayed for a while with him and his brother

Gulbrand. Torine sends her regards and says they are doing well. Anton and Anders Tosholm were also there. And then I went to visit Ole Monsen but came there a few days too late for his wedding. He and his wife live with his parents and are very comfortable. But I wish that if I ever marry I would have a wife who was a little plumper because Lina was unusually thin and lean. I talked with Gustav and he is much as he was in Norway. From there I went to Hans and Ole Viger the Younger where I stayed for a week. Then I visited one of father's old friends Amund Gullubraaten who sends his regards. Then I had to go home. When I returned to Grand Meadow Torine Sandvik had had a son and I also stopped for a few days with Ole and Marie Viger. I had to give Marie the photograph of father and mother and I hope you'll send me another. From there I went to Rock Creek and found everything as it was two months ago. No, stop a little, my old flame, the girl that brother Edvard has a portrait of, had married.

Times are much better now than last spring. Prices for everything the farmer has to sell have risen by more than fifty percent. We have a fever here that you can hardly imagine: all who can raise the money want to go northwest to Park River where uncle lives. So many are leaving that if this continues there won't be many left. I plan to rent a railroad car and load it with horses, corn and oats because all such things are more expensive there than here and I think I should be able to make a little extra. Today I've been out shopping and I bought a wagon for fifty dollars. Now I'll begin hauling wheat that is at one dollar a bushel. I must end this now with regards to all friends but first and foremost to you at Elsrud, Viker and Blakkstveit from your son and brother,

I. E. ELSRUD

· ——— ·

IEE used the St. Ansgar post office when he lived on his uncle's farm. It may be, however, that his own land was closer to Rock Creek. «II:97 »II:III NE IV:131

· ——— ·

1880 — LETTER 2:109

FROM: Christine Dahl, *Norse, Texas, 11 March 1880*

To: Erik Pedersen Furuset, *Romedal, Stange, Hedmark*

⋅⇒◯⇐⋅

Dear brother Erik!

We have received your very welcome and much longed for letter of January 12 and were glad to see that you are all doing well and that mother is so well considering her age. Because I was waiting to hear from you I waited longer than I should to tell you about the change in our family since I last wrote: my daughter Marthe has entered the state of matrimony. The wedding was on the thirteenth of last month. Her husband is a stranger to you but he is a brother of Ole's wife. His name is Mikkel Hoff. The wedding ceremony was conducted in our home by our Norwegian pastor. I cannot say much about the wedding as all is unknown to you, but I must note that we had about 350 people to dinner. Some of them went home that night but most stayed over for the second day. The wedding was not as happy an occasion as it could have been under other circumstances, as the half-brother of Syverine's husband died two days before the wedding. He was our neighbor and our schoolteacher and is survived by his wife and two children. Otherwise the health situation in our settlement is quite good.

As for the money owing to us that you write about, I can say that I don't need it now and would rather that you keep it until we need another worker. Pauline says that she doesn't need hers either and as for Dilrud, I heard that he wrote for a laborer some time ago, but more than that I do not know. I assume he will write himself. Karen is doing poorly. She isn't bedridden but she cannot do anything. Her girls are good and do the housework. Pauline came home for the wedding and is now here. She has the same cough and isn't strong.

Winter is just about over and the grass is turning green and the weather is mild. We've had a very good winter but rather dry. The animals have managed well and now we've had a good rain so it seems that we'll have water in empty brooks that we sorely need. I have greetings from Aunt and

Rogstad and their family who say they are doing well. Pauline and I were up there last Sunday. Aunt's youngest daughter Gine and her family live in a town about eighty miles from us. They were there on a visit and had their youngest child baptized, since there isn't a Norwegian church where they live. They have two children, a boy and a girl. So I can send greetings from all of Aunt's children who had all come for the baptism and were gathered for dinner afterward at Rogstad. Aunt looks good and has become very fat.

As I cannot write a separate letter to Per Aasen you must please give him my regards as well as from Dilrud, Sinrud, Thingstad, Aunt, and Wilhelm, and also from Ole and Christoffer. Christoffer has been hired by my son-in-law Jacob for a year. The enclosed portraits of Marthe and her husband are for our dear mother. They are in their wedding clothes. You must also give my regards to my sister Syverine and her little girls as well as all friends and acquaintances that I don't have the space to list. My most heartfelt greetings go to you my dear brother and our mother from me and my children. Your devoted sister

CHRISTINE DAHL

· —— ·

The money CD writes about is the inheritance of the Texas sisters Christine, Pauline, and Karen. Rather than have it sent to them both, CD and Karen's husband, Peder Dilrud, have Erik Furuset draw upon it for tickets for farm laborers from Romedal who otherwise could not have afforded to emigrate. There are several letters from Peder Dilrud in the Norwegian edition about getting farm laborers from Norway. CD's father's sister, Anne, was married to Berger Rogstad. «II:95 »II:116 NE IV:133

· —— ·

1880 — LETTER 2:110

FROM: Jacob Hansen Hilton, *Boulder, Colorado, 28 April 1880*

To: Hans Jakobsen and Anne Olsdatter Hilton, *Ullensaker, Akershus*

❖══◉══❖

Dear father and mother,

I received your letter written on the Second Day of Easter on April 24. I'm so glad to see that you're all well and I can say the same for myself. I see that I've lost a letter from you that was returned to Norway, the first time I've heard of such a thing. I wondered what I might have done to offend you or what other reason you could have had for not writing to me. Now I see that it was just as I thought. Dear father, you were not entirely wrong when you said that I had now and then been irresponsible. This is true and cannot be denied and therefore I didn't get your letter last fall. I left Omaha, Nebraska on August 12 and your letter arrived a few days later. I'm now 700 miles further west, nearer San Francisco than New York, 1,000 miles from Chicago and 800 from Eldora and I don't know how far from Christopher. I've used a lot of money but I don't regret my journeys— I've always made more where I've come. If I hadn't found a place where I could make better money than in the eastern states, I would have gone right home again. I'm thinking of those who work for wages; if a man has his own business it's good enough there, but Colorado is the winner for daily wages. In six weeks here I've made about 600 dollars by hammering on my knees and making pine-pitched strings.

The main business here is mining gold, silver, copper, lead and some iron—mostly gold and silver. Millions are taken out of the mountains every day. Long lines of miners are going up into the mountains again after the snow is gone. Thousands will be coming from the East to pick up gold from the ground but they'll be bitterly disappointed and, in this new world outside of "civilization" where the rifle and the revolver are law and justice, many will find their death. They come here with the notion of becoming rich in a day or a week without doing much work, so when they are out of money and have to go to work they become like wild animals and begin to rob and murder those they believe have a few shillings. Some are shot here every week so a killing is no news. Two weeks ago a man was stopped in the street by two armed masked men who told him to hold up his arms. He did as he was told since they held a large revolver right in his face but they only found fifteen cents. They beat him up for not having more and when they let him go they sent a bullet through his thigh. This is life in the West. No, a man who comes here has to work hard, stay away from liquor and mind his own business. Then life here is as safe as anywhere else. The boys and girls I know here call me "Old Man" because I never go to parties or dances or other kinds of fun. First, it costs too much and second, it isn't safe to take a walk with a girl here. Now and then a bullet will come after you in the street and when they come they usually hit their mark. So I spend Sundays in my room. I don't plan to stay here for long but I'm making good money and I'll stay as long as this lasts—and then, goodbye to mountains. With God's protection you are never in danger.

I think I'll see Ullensaker again. If you knew me as I was then you'll know that money always burns in my pocket so it's best to get rid of it. I see that there is a large emigration from Norway this spring. Can you imagine that a total of 40,000 people come into New York every month, and there are millions of acres of uncultivated land and the settlers here in the West say to them all, "Welcome, we have room for more." If Streiff at Brotnu hasn't gone to America yet there is land enough for him and he would have made thousands if he had come here. There are places where they have seven to ten thousand sheep and cattle. They are out all winter since there is no snow to keep them from feeding themselves. A man may make money like grass if he has some to start with. You need money to make money here. It doesn't count for much if a man makes five dollars a day and saves a few hundred dollars. They'll say, oh, he doesn't have more than he works for. Give Streiff my regards and ask him to write me so I can hear how he is and whether he'll soon be coming or has decided to wait another year.

You ask whether I correspond with Asche, Christopher and the Haga boys. Well, I've heard from the Haga boys but had no letter from them since I left. I've written to them twice but had no answer, so I won't write any more and have no use for them. I have letters from Oluf Asche and Uncle every other week and keep up a regular correspondence. They are both doing well as far as I know. Give my regards to all relatives and friends—if I have any—and you, mother and siblings are lovingly greeted from your

JACOB

By now JHH's spelling and idioms reflect his life in an English-speaking environment. His correspondence with relatives in the United States is probably in English. JHH's next letter in this edition is from Socorro, N. Mex. but his last letter from Boulder has been preserved: 17 Oct 1880 (Nor. ed. IV:149). It is to Oluf who has returned home after his military service. He writes about going south with two relatives now in Chicago, Fritjof and Thomas Asche, "perhaps where white people have not yet set their feet, over a mountain where no one has yet climbed to the highest top more than 14,000 feet above sea level..." Pine-pitched string was used for sewing the parts of work boots together as well as for lacing them. Fridolin Streiff (from Glarus, Switzerland, and also known as Fredrik) had the large farm Brotnu in Ullensaker. It so happened that JHH's brother Oluf later married Streiff's only daughter and became the farmer at Brotnu. «II:107 »II:123 NE IV:140

1880 — LETTER 2:111

FROM: Iver Ellingsen Elsrud, *Sweden, North Dakota, 6 June 1880*

TO: Ole Ellingsen Elsrud, *Aadalen, Ringerike, Buskerud*

Dear brother Ole,

I've received your letter and see that your plans of coming to America this summer won't be realized and I think this is best. Times are not as they were when I came and it's not so good to come for one who doesn't have a lot of money as there is no work and little food. Should you decide to come it would be best for you to go to Henrik Bagge in St. Peter. I'm sure he will help you all he can and you could live with him until you get work. All land here is taken but I'm still waiting for a chance to get some for myself. Edvard says that the nose rings for pigs that I sent haven't arrived but you may have to pay duty. If so they may still be at the post office in Kristiania. Perhaps the postmaster in Aadalen could find out about this. I have no news that will interest you. When I returned to Haugerud everything looked very nice and still does. The weather has been wet and cold so growth has been a little slower than usual, but this can change. The land in the North is beautiful and bountiful but it is so flat that when the rivers swell some of it is under water. I have held on to Gustav's money and when you let me know the exact amount I will send it according to Gustav's directions. Give my regards to all my friends and in particular to old grandmother, and to all at Rustand, Blakkstveit, Enger, North Viker, and Elsrud, and first and foremost to you from your faithful brother,

I. E. ELSRUD

. ——— .

He calls his uncle's farm in the present North Dakota "Haugerud," as he did his farm in Iowa. «II:108 »II:120 NE IV:141

. ——— .

1880 — LETTER 2:112

FROM: Christopher Jacobsen, *Belleville, Nevada, 4 July 1880*

To: Hans Jakobsen Hilton, *Ullensaker, Akershus*

⊶⇒◐⇐⊷

Dear brother!

It is almost a year since your last letter. As brothers I think we should write more often as we are now on the downhill slope and will be in our graves in a few years; you in the graveyard at the old Ullensaker church and I—well that is more uncertain—perhaps here in the mountains where only wolves will let a tear fall on my grave because (as Thrane said) they can't get my skin, or perhaps in a more pleasant *spot*. But let that be as it may. As an old song says: our body may be thrown to the wolves but our soul will be in the blissful land of heaven. If this is true we'll probably meet again up there regardless of where our graves may be.

This spring and summer I've been running in my thoughts on my childhood paths and in May I seemed to hear the cuckoo sing its merry song from the tree tops. (There are no such birds in America.) I seemed to see the trees where I placed my snares and remembered how glad I was when I saw the poor thrushes hanging in them. It seemed that I could walk right up to those snares—oh, had I been there! But if I'd really been there, I would probably not have found any of them. The forest may be gone and with it the thrushes and the merry cuckoo. And I run home from school on a Saturday afternoon, jump over the fence by the old church, read the inscriptions on some stones, run on toward the parsonage, make a brief stop at the servants' quarters and continue down to the Hynne creek, over the bridge and up to Frogner. There I meet old Mother Frogner with some feathers in her mouth singing the hymn " My heart is heavy and my eyes run tears," and the tears are really in her eyes. I follow her around and try to comfort her and then I go into the kitchen and have fun with the girls. On Sunday I go to church and sit quietly on the teacher's bench. In the afternoon I go to Søli where mother has just finished a pair of stockings and Anne has cloth for my summer clothes in the loom, and I dance with Allette and when I leave I promise not to go to a dance that evening. Oh, but I break my promise because soon I seem to be at a ball where I'm swirling with the most beautiful girls in our neighborhood, and then I think: "Where are they all now?" I suppose many of them are dead and those who are living are old like me and have other things on their minds than dancing. But I suppose the younger generation is as wild as we were, and so it will be till the end of the world.

You seem to have a bad impression of San Francisco, but (even though this is where I lost all I'd made in twenty-five years) there isn't a place in the whole world where I would rather live and die. The climate is wonderful, not too cold and not too hot, and around San Francisco the land is extremely fertile. The people are not as dangerous as you seem to believe even though it cannot be denied that there are many dishonest people there—thieves, scoundrels and cheats—but they are everywhere, even in honorable Norway. I learned a lot there and at a high price, but I have no regrets. It may be that I've been lucky in how I was made because adversities do not weigh me down more than a week or so before I'm back to work with a bright look to my future. It might have been different if I had someone who relied on me for food and clothes, but as I have no one to share my joys or my sorrows with I wander as I wish on my own path and no one knows what may be hidden in Christopher's breast. I probably say more to you than to anyone else here on earth about such things.

I regret that I didn't take up farming when I was young because then it was easy to get land in America, in particular in the western states. Now most government land has been taken and much of it belongs to the railroad companies. My greatest regret is that I didn't buy the land in Watsonville, California on my own. Had I done so I would now have been living comfortably in one of the most beautiful places on earth. But I rarely have such thoughts. With the buzz of the world in my ears I forget all this and think only of the present. A man from Scotland who lives in Watsonville and who is one of my faithful friends there, wrote to me a few days ago and said: stay in the mountains as long as you are making money but when times get hard and the work is too heavy, then take what you may have saved and come down and settle here; because there are no problems for a man, Christopher, he says, who has your will to work and I only wish that we could be neighbors again. But I don't know.

Up to now I've been doing, you may say, well. That is, I've been making my four dollars a day. I left Bodie just after New Year because it was so cold and there was so much snow that I was tired of it. I went down to the state of Nevada again to a place called Candelaria, only eighty-five miles away. I found acquaintances there who gave me work as soon as I arrived. There are hard times in the mines now since so many come looking for work, and all over the coast there are thousands who are out of work, while I, and this may be the only thing I have going for me, can have all the work I want as long as I can move my old arms. The four dollars a day is only in Nevada and a few places in California. The regular pay is only two to three dollars and farmers in California only pay one dollar a day. If you read the newspapers you may have read about all the Chinese who come here. They work for little to nothing, so if the government doesn't stop immigration from China we'll perhaps soon have a civil war in California. The working class is rather restless and it gets worse year by year.

You seem to think that none of Jacob Frogner's *offspring* are *adapted* to America. You may be right and I'm sure that you know whether the others are as stupid as I, but I'm also sure, dear brother, that if we couldn't manage in America then we couldn't have made a living in Old Norway and we would have become a burden and a shame for our relatives. But we've come here and we're too proud to beg and too honest to steal, but we aren't too lazy to work, and as we are so far from any who know us we'll have to bear the shame and the burden of being an honest laborer alone. I know many here who had 100,000 dollars a few years ago but now work in the mines for a living. This is the way here, brother, one day rich, the other day poor. For my part I don't plan on getting rich, but I'm certain that if I have my health I can still put aside enough to live for a year or two in a more comfortable place than this.

Your son Jacob is doing well. I have warned him against the mines and I don't think he will go there. The Haga boys are doing well. I haven't heard from them for three months. Now brother, don't take any of this as an affront. You are quite right in what you write, but, you know, I have to defend myself and my relatives in America as well as I can. "In a hundred years all will be forgotten." So let's not worry about the few days we have down here. Don't wait so long before you write this time and I won't wait too long either. Farewell.

CHRISTOPHER

. ——— .

Thrane is the Norwegian labor leader, Marcus Thrane (1817–1890) who emigrated to the United States in 1862 after having served a prison sentence for his political activities. In his daydreams CJ is back in his childhood when his father, Jakob Larsen, was a teacher and lived with his wife, Anne Eriksdatter, and his family at Søli, on the Frogner farm. So he was therefore Jakob Frogner while his son Hans is Hans Hilton. Now it is CJ's sister Anne who lives at Søli as does her daughter, Alette Søli. Another brother, Lars Jakobsen, was also a teacher and lived at Ullern. Before his sister Kari became a widow, she and her husband had the farm Haga. She was the mother of the "Haga boys," Hans and Gulbrand, in Iowa. The mining camp at Candelaria was established the year before CJ arrived. For offspring and adapted CJ wrote *afspring* and *adoptet*, words that would not have made sense to his brother. «II:94 »II:137 NE IV:143

. ——— .

1880 — LETTER 2:113

FROM: Iver Andersen Lee, *Mount Vernon, Wisconsin, 11 July 1880*

To: Anders Olsen and Kari Mikkelsdatter Lie
Hedalen, Sør-Aurdal, Oppland

⊶⟫⟭⟬⟸⊷

Dear parents and brothers and all relatives and friends in old Norway!

I am now sitting far away from you in my brother Ole's house think-ing about the time that has passed since I left not quite a month ago. Even though the time has been short it has been rich in events. This is to be expected, as we all knew that the journey could not be compared to a trip to the city but it is impossible to imagine what it may be like in advance. I don't think I'm much wrong when I say that the journey is a series of con-fusing and unpleasant events interspersed with some lighter and entertain-ing moments of which some were quite attractive and inspiring but most were quite indifferent. Yes, now you'll probably be saying that I should give you an account of my journey where its different events would come alive before you. It's easy to say this and the request seems reasonable. For him to whom the request is made it's not quite so easy, partly because the journey, even for one who has taken it, is not as present in the mind after the journey as when you are still there and partly because this is a task that would require much time even of an experienced writer. Nevertheless, I won't neglect it entirely but will describe it in a few words as well as I can.

As you already know, Friday June 18 was the day I sailed from Kristiania. The heat was so oppressive that it was a struggle merely to be outdoors but this couldn't stop the traffic because the steamship *Angelo* was at the wharf for departure at four and then all had to be ready. Already by dinnertime one could see emigrants from all parts of the country come to the wharf to check in their suitcases and chests and they were so busy that they didn't even take the time to wipe off the sweat that was constantly dripping down their faces. Gradually the traffic became livelier and onlookers began to gather as usual. Close to 2:30 the suitcases and chests were in place but this didn't mean that things settled down because now the emigrants be-gan to stream onto the ship with their carpetbags, suitcases, sacks, rolls, mattresses etc. etc. looking for places for themselves and their families: a husband and wife dripping of the heat came down to their bunk with their baggage and their crying children, a couple of newlyweds, two lovers who have put off their wedding until the journey is over; but mainly the crowd is made up of single and unattached people of both sexes. For half an hour the throng below deck is worse than in an anthill: all want space and there is not enough of it, baggage is misplaced and all is chaos. But soon things settle down, the bunks are ready and many, especially the old and their children, are sitting in their places and guarding their baggage with the attention of a poodle guarding his master's property; others have ventured up on deck where people are swarming around as below. Many friends and relatives from towns and valleys have come onboard to exchange last words with emigrants who are about to leave for the New World (well, you'll understand that I'm not talking about Paradise; geographers have given this name to this country, so I'll also allow myself to use it). This traffic continues and then we hear the first call of the ship's bell signaling that time for departure is near. But there is still time and people don't seem to care much about it. But when the bell sounds again it's time for nonimmigrants to leave the ship; friends shake hands for the last time; some stand with tears in their eyes, others merely with a somber expression, while yet a few others even with a smile. Soon only emigrants are left on the ship; the bell sounds for the third time; the ship casts off and moves from the wharf with heavy groans. The crowd of onlookers, and there are several thousands of these, wave their handkerchiefs, hats or caps and are answered by a similar ceremony by the ship's crew that amounts to some hundred people. The waving continues as long as friends can be distinguished from strangers but it gradually comes to an end and the crowd of spectators spreads out and all go their different ways. Now we emigrants are left to ourselves; we are no longer on Norwegian soil and we no longer have the company of the inhabitants of the land of our birth.

We are now on the Kristiania Fjord; the wind has dropped and all have collected their wits and emotions after the last farewell scene. So now we have time to get acquainted and we pause with one, then with another asking about this or that. The most common questions are: What's your name? Where do you come from? Where are you going? What line are you going with? But our attention is with Kristiania that still can be observed from the deck. But the ship is gathering speed and soon the mountains are folding around the city and hiding it in their bosom. So now we can only observe the scenery as it passes us by. About six we sailed through the politically famous Drøbak sound with the city of Drøbak on the one side and

Kaholmen Island with the fortress Oscarsborg on the other. At seven our first meal was served: black coffee and sandwiches distributed from a kitchen door and even though all of this was done in an orderly fashion I cannot refrain from observing that it was similar to a flock of some hundreds of sheep given salt by their herders. Then it was dark and we went to bed and slept until morning. At six we got our breakfast that also consisted of coffee and sandwiches. At eleven we came to Kristiansand where we stayed several hours and took on some new emigrants before we sailed out again and were immediately in open sea with a strong wind. But it didn't take long before it dropped a little and all were still well and merry. We had our dinner at two and it consisted of fresh meat and potatoes and barley broth and was quite good even though it wasn't according to Hedal taste. After dinner we danced to a new tune, as seasickness made a discreet appearance. All were not attacked but I and many others were not spared for long. I must admit that it wasn't to my liking but it was never bad as the wind soon dropped and we had such nice weather all the way across the North Sea that we couldn't have wished for better. At about six on Saturday afternoon we sailed past Lindesnes, the most southerly point of Norway, and it was soon out of sight and our dear fatherland seemed to sink before our eyes in the billows of the North Sea. Air and water were now all we could look at and these were far too monotonous to hold our gaze for long and so we had to entertain ourselves with something else; some began to sing, others to dance and yet others turned to other pastimes. There was little seasickness, so people enjoyed themselves.

On Sunday afternoon we entered the Humber estuary that leads into Hull and in the evening we anchored in the harbor. We slept on board until Monday morning. Then the ship was unloaded and agents appeared and did what they could with our baggage but we were not entirely uninvolved as all our bed clothing was thrown into a pile on the dock and it took us some time to get it all separated and take what was ours and on such occasions it so often happens that there is more worry and anxiety than is actually called for. When all was in order the agents took us to the train station where after much hustle and bustle we got our train tickets and were arranged in groups according to the lines we were going on. So now we saw no more of those who were not taking the Inman Line and were placed with some Swedes who were going on the same line as us. At eleven the train for the Inman emigrants was ready for departure and we went off at high speed through long tunnels, cities, and fields. We got to Liverpool at six and here our agents led us through the city streets to our house of boarding where we were assigned rooms after a nourishing dinner. We were to stay here for the night and I slept like a prince as I had had rather restless nights since leaving Kristiania. Next morning there was a great hustle and bustle as the Inman Line's *City of Brussels* wasn't at the dock but anchored in the harbor so we and our baggage had to get onboard a smaller boat to get to it. Onboard the ship we didn't get organized until dinnertime and we had much more trouble and confusion than in Kristiania. In Liverpool we were united with different nations such as Germans, Englishmen, Danes and Finns and if we had been able to talk with each other we would probably have become quite friendly but we were excused and could neither reason with nor flatter each other.

Our ship was one of the smallest crossing the Atlantic but it was rather comfortably fitted. It had two between-decks that were partitioned into rooms that could take twelve to twenty persons each. Unmarried men and women had separate rooms and married couples were together and during the day you could go wherever you wanted regardless of whether you were a man or a woman. Although the ship was ready to leave at dinnertime we couldn't sail until four because of the ebb tide. So we just waited except that we had dinner at one. It consisted of fresh meat and barley broth. It was both better and more plentiful than what we got on the North Sea and the only complaint was that the meat wasn't really tasty and this was a fault of all dinners, which otherwise were good and above all plentiful. Every morning we got wheat bread with butter and coffee. I couldn't drink the coffee, nor could most others, so I preferred a cup of water. For supper we also had wheat bread and butter and either tea or barley broth. I usually chose the latter even though I could drink the tea.

After we had weighed anchor we sailed from Liverpool through the Bristol Canal and into the Atlantic Ocean. But before we set out on the ocean itself we had yet another harbor to visit—the city of Queenstown in Ireland where we arrived the next afternoon (Wednesday June 23). After the Irish had come aboard the cabin I was in had three Norwegians, three Irishmen, two Germans and four Finns. There were many nations and many languages but this was fine since we didn't have to fear saying bad things about each other. The people I was placed with were all pleasant and honest. I assume that the Irish were keen Catholics as they kneeled at their bed every morning and I suppose they prayed. All was well on Wednesday evening and the following night but at dawn the wind increased and when I woke up I was already seasick. I got up but the ship's movements were so violent that I stumbled from one wall to the other until I was able to hold on to something. I began to throw up and this continued as long as I had anything left to throw up in my stomach—indeed, much longer. The worst was that I couldn't touch food and for four days I lay there without tasting anything but a little water and it didn't take long before this too came up the same way it had gone down. What I've told you about myself was of course also true of many, many others, but there were many who weren't so strongly affected and there were indeed those who I don't think noticed seasickness at all. If we had had perfect nursing the seasickness may not have been so bad but there was regrettably nothing. I was told there was a doctor on the ship and two interpreters who could speak Norwegian but they were so busy that they only saw exceptional cases. We had stormy weather for four days and the waves often swept over the top deck of the ship. On Monday the wind dropped and thereafter we had nice weather and I was soon much better. Temperatures were quite comfortable all days at sea except on the day when we passed the icebergs. Then it was so cold that we could have used winter clothes had we had them.

We came to New York late in the evening of Friday July 2 after ten days on the Atlantic. On Saturday morning we were taken ashore with all our baggage and we had to find our chests so the customs officials could inspect them to see whether anyone was bringing illegal items. The inspection, however, was very superficial so they could well have done without it. Then we all had to go on board another steamboat to be taken across a small bay to the so-called Castle Garden, built for the emigrants. Here there was a variety of formalities for us as well as for our baggage. And then, after about five hours of continuous hustle and bustle everything was in order and we again had to get on board a steamboat to be taken to the railroad station where we spent another hour before we finally were ready to leave by train at dusk. We went fast both night and day with only a few short stops here and there except in Chicago where we came at five Monday morning and didn't leave until nine. And now we were close to my destination and at two Tuesday morning we were in Madison. I was the only one to get off the train here. It was as dark as in a sack and there were no people to be seen other than a couple of railroad officials I saw walk around for a few minutes. But my efforts to speak with them were futile. So I walked around for some time before I realized that there was free admittance to the station's waiting room. So I entered and lay down to sleep and when I awoke the sun was already up. So I got up and began asking the people I encountered but no one could give me a Norwegian reply. After passing some time in this manner I got the idea of walking into the city, which I did and I hadn't gone far before I saw the Norwegian Hotel. I entered and asked and was told that the mail to Mount Vernon would be leaving the other Norwegian hotel (there are two) in about an hour. I went there immediately and met the mail driver, a Norwegian from Reinli called Ole Bøle. He instantly agreed to take me and we left Madison at seven and came to Mount Vernon at one on Tuesday July 6. When we arrived the mail driver told me where Syver Belgum and Gunnild Lie had their home.

So these were the first I came to. I found Syver in his smithy but his wife had just gone to visit her parents, so he immediately took me in and served me food and drink. Then I went to Olaug Børtnes and her husband who lived right next to Syver and Gunnild. When I came there Olaug was visiting Uncle Guttorm but I met other people I knew, first Marit Klemmetsrud (well, I hadn't seen her before but I'll say I knew her anyway) and then Halsten Børtnes. A few hours later brother Ole came driving past in the street with Uncle Guttorm's son Ole. I went out and greeted them but Ole could hardly recognize me, mainly because he had no idea that I was anywhere near there. He hadn't expected me this year, he said. So he came with us to the home of shoemaker Eriksen, Olaug's husband, and after we'd been there a while Ole and I went to his home about two miles from Mount Vernon. There the same thing happened over again as Siri couldn't tell whether it was I or not since I hadn't been expected. It was not quite three weeks from the time I left you until I came to my brother, so that was quite fast and I didn't have to wait much at any place but went without pause both day and night. And this is good as the waiting on such journeys is very tedious.

I rested at brother Ole's for a few days and on Friday Ole and I visited our uncles and stayed with Uncle Ole until Saturday. Then we went to Mount Vernon and stayed with Olaug Børtnes until this morning when we left. There we also met Ole and Erik Børtnes. This summer they have hired out some miles from here but they came to visit and will be leaving tomorrow and won't be back until fall when they have made some money. I haven't met Andreas Børtnes. He has also hired out some distance from here. All I've met with the exception of Uncle Guttorm are in good health and doing well. Brother Ole has worked with a carpenter this summer and will be with Uncle Guttorm for the harvesting. I think I'll work for Uncle Ole. Ole sends his regards and Siri asks you to tell her grandmother that she would like to talk with her. From their daughter Kari I'm to say hello to you, mother. She says that she is well and big and wishes that you were here so she could get to know you. I'll now have to end my letter. I'll write more about my visits to people here some other time. In conclusion I must send you my regards and thank you for all you've done and ask you to give my regards to all friends. I hope you won't wait too long before replying. Farewell.

IVER ANDERSEN LIE

. ⸻ .

> IAL was the second of three brothers who emigrated from the farm Søre Li in Hedalen. The third followed the next year. They all wrote similar accounts of their journey and they all tended to write long letters. As in the previous generation, only one brother was left to take care of the family farm, first Anders Olsen, then Anders Andersen. In vocabulary, grammar, syntax, and spelling this second generation is different from their uncles in their literary education. In this letter the style of IAL is both longwinded and pretentious, but it is one of the most detailed accounts of the immigrant journey from Norway in the late nineteenth century. Before 1925 Oslo was Kristiania, also written Christiania. The alleged political fame of the Drøbak Sound may refer to the modernization of the fortress in the 1870s. On farms meat was usually salted, dried, or smoked so it would be specified when fresh. Queenstown is now Cobh. Reinli is in Sør-Aurdal. Gunnild Belgum was a daughter of IAL's uncle, Guttorm Lee. Marit Klemmetsrud was the widow of his uncle Torgrim Lee. Olaug was the daughter of his father's sister and was married to Erik Eriksen. «II:100 »II:115 NE IV:144

. ⸻ .

1880 — LETTER 2:114

FROM: Hellik G. Branson, Eureka, Kansas, 25 September 1880

To: Ole Gulbrandsen and Anne Andersdatter Lande
Flesberg, Buskerud

⸱⟴⟴⸱

Dear brother and wife,

I can no longer delay answering your letter that I received a long time ago. The reason I haven't written is that I wanted to know how it went with the land that Thom Nelsen was to take on your behalf. At last I now have your lease in good order and it was filed yesterday. Thom had lost his certificate of citizenship and this caused more difficulties than we had thought because we both had to go twice to Independence to get it done. Thom will pay the expenses for the last visit to the land office so you'll only have to pay for the first one. Thom did all he could to get the lease on the land and it had to be done this fall since there now is a new law that requires all to have a lease. And this saved you ten dollars since Thom now paid forty rather than fifty dollars. Ole Kolkinn hasn't done the breaking he was supposed to do. First he couldn't come at the agreed time and then it was so dry that breaking was difficult. And since he couldn't get the work done at the agreed time your renters didn't want to have it done at all. But I've learned my lesson and when I again rent out your farm I'll ensure my right to do breaking at any time I want. As for the harvest on your farm, it seems rather good even though there are a lot of weeds in your corn. You had about nineteen bushels of wheat per acre. I'm pretty sure that you'll get your rent this year. I can also report that I've sold Nelly and her foal to Mr. Berket in Upper Fall River for 100 dollars.

I can tell you a little about myself and my own business. We have been in reasonably good health since you left and we are much as before. I recently had a letter from Sam. He's in Oregon which he doesn't like better than Kansas but he has thirty dollars a month so he'll stay there. He asks about you in every letter and I've told him about your situation as well as I could. I can also tell you that I sold 150 oxen for $40.75 apiece. All in all I got $ 6,050. I've sold cows and pigs for more than 300 dollars. The pigs are at a better price now than when you were here. My son Henry still lives on his farm. This summer he went to Topeka for the state convention as a delegate from Cowley County. Martin has achieved his ambition and is a storekeeper. He bought a house and opened a store in a town in Cowley County by the railroad that goes from Independence to Winfield. Lincoln is now in Cowley to buy cattle on his own. I gave him 500 dollars for this. Sigel is now the only one of my boys who is at home. Our old Mother is as she has been. Gullik Bringe asks me to tell you that they are all well and that Anne and Sigri are working in Eureka. I have no more to tell you and will conclude with loving regards to you and your wife from me, my wife, and my sons.

H. G. BRANSON

Enclosed with this letter are the detailed accounts for HGB's expenses in connection with the land deal described in the letter. It seems that Thom Nelson is the "straw owner" of what is in effect OGL's land, probably because the latter could not wait to go through the formalities. HGB wrote again to his brother about his financial arrangements 22 December 1880. «II:87 »II:175 NE IV:147

1880 — LETTER 2:115

FROM: Iver Andersen Lee, *Springdale, Wisconsin, 16 October 1880*

To: Anders Olsen and Kari Mikkelsdatter Lie
Hedalen, Sør-Aurdal, Oppland

⊶⟲⊸⟳⊷

Dear parents and brothers, my old grandmother and all relatives and friends in Old Norway!

I'm writing even though I haven't had a reply to the letter I wrote right after my arrival. I've been waiting for a letter from you for almost a month and I can't wait patiently any longer as it's possible that you didn't get my first letter and that you are still longing to hear from me or that, what is worse, you have given up all hope of hearing from me and think that I'm dead and buried in the ocean waves. No, that is not the case; I'm alive and, what is more, doing far better than I had imagined. I choose to believe that you have read my letter about my journey. The reason I'm writing again without waiting for your reply is that I have news that I'm eager to tell you. I'll begin with news that gives reason for both sorrow and happiness; our dear and beloved Uncle Guttorm O. Lie is dead. I think I should use a few more words to tell you about this and it is a real pleasure for me to be able to say that he waited with longing for his passing and was gladly looking forward to his certain death. When I entered his house for the first time he wasn't so ill that he couldn't sit up now and then even though he was pale and emaciated. He liked to talk and took an interest in the farm and all that was related to it and was still the head of the family. In early September he was weaker than usual and he turned the accounts over to his wife and was no longer concerned with the affairs of the world. He was glad to do so because he was prepared. Indeed, I've never heard of anyone who went to his death with greater fortitude. His thoughts and his longing were for his redemption and he prayed as he died peacefully on Saturday afternoon on September 11. Although he was ravaged by illness in his last days he retained his mind and consciousness to the last. I must exclaim: "May we long honor his memory!" Few have been so highly loved and respected by family and acquaintances, and the participation and respect shown at his funeral witnessed to this. He was buried the following Monday and a large crowd of people gathered with horses and wagons to honor his memory by following him on his last journey. In this country they don't follow the tradition of only inviting relatives and neighbors and excluding others. No, here a death is publicly announced along with the time of the funeral. Thus everyone is free to participate, not for his own satisfaction and to eat freely of good food and expensive drink, but simply to honor the person who has passed away by being present at his funeral. After the funeral all return home except for some of the closest relatives who usually will go to the home of the deceased for a meal that concludes the funeral. Many came to Uncle Guttorm's funeral and among them were Pastor John Fjeld and his wife. Before the body was carried out from the home he gave a speech about the departed and said that with what he knew of this man he ventured to utter his certain hope that he had found the promised joy and, addressing the grieving widow and children, he expounded in warm and heartfelt words on how this was more an occasion for happiness than for sorrow. The body was taken to the church where it was again displayed and where Fjeld again spoke, whereupon it was taken to the cemetery to be buried. In conclusion I'll give you the deceased's last greeting to relatives and friends in Norway. He asked me to tell you about his passing as soon as he was dead. My reason for delay is that I awaited a reply to my letter.

I'll now tell you a little about myself and my situation in this new country. I'm in good health and doing well in all respects and to this day I'm far more satisfied than I had expected. Harvesting began about a week after I arrived and I hired out as a day laborer with Uncle Ole Lie. I was with him for about a month but during this time an accident gave me a swollen hand and I couldn't do anything for almost two weeks. We hadn't agreed on my wages in advance and I haven't yet returned to him for a settlement, so I don't know what to expect. Later I've done day labor for different people for seventy-five cents a day. The tasks have been many and I'll mention tobacco harvesting, cutting corn and threshing. I've made about thirty dollars since I left my uncle. There will still be plenty of work so I expect to make some more before I settle down for the winter. My home has been with my brother Ole. I've come to him every Sunday as well as on rainy days when it wasn't possible to work outdoors. We've had very nice weather this fall but these last few days it's been colder and with occasional snow. But people say we shouldn't expect winter yet and that we'll have a period of nice weather they call Indian summer. I don't know where I'll be this winter. Ole wants me to live with him as does Uncle Ole, but I've been thinking of working for an American and going to the English school because I think I'll then learn English much faster. I'm quite sure that this is what I'll do as soon as harvesting is over. Iver Mikkelsen asks me to give greetings to all acquaintances and say that he has a little son and is doing well. Other relatives and acquaintances send their regards and say they are in good health. In conclusion my best wishes to you and to all relatives and acquaintances. Farewell from your distant

IVER ANDERSEN LIE

· —— ·

IAL's brother Ole wrote a long letter 15 January 1881 (Nor. ed. IV:162) about his work as a carpenter's assistant and about the birth of a son who was named Anders (after his deceased brother) and much else. IAL was living with an English-speaking American and attending the public school as planned, but visiting his brother every Sunday.
«II:113 »II:121 NE IV:148

· —— ·

1880 — LETTER 2:116

FROM: Christine Dahl, *Norse, Texas, 13 November 1880*

To: Siri Kristiansdatter and Erik Pedersen Furuset
Romedal, Stange, Hedmark

⊷═◗ ◖═⊷

Dear mother and brother,

With a heavy heart I take up my pen to send you the sad message that our sister Pauline passed away on the sixth of this month. She was less than one day in bed. She had tuberculosis for about three years. She never wanted me to send you precise information about her illness but as you know, I've written enough to make you aware that things were not as they should be with her. I wrote in my previous letter that she had returned to Waco to work. I often tried to convince her to stay with us as I knew she wasn't well, but she insisted that she felt much better doing a little housework in Waco. I drove her down there myself and she promised to let me know if she felt any worse and that I could then come to get her. I heard from her now and then and she was always the same. She was at work until five days before she died. She then went to a Norwegian in Waco, a tailor by the name of Christiansen, where she used to stay between jobs and whose wife was one of her best friends. She had planned to stay there for a few days and perhaps get better or come home, but she got weaker every day. On the fourth day they came for me at four in the morning. I left at once and got there at two in the afternoon, but she had then been dead for three hours. She had asked for something that would make her strong enough to live until I came since she thought I wouldn't be there until four. The wife asked her if she felt worse but she only said that she was a little more tired.

Dear mother, you may imagine that it was difficult for me to go there alone and find her dead. I so wished to have been able to speak with her but I know that she died in her faith in her Savior and I hope that we'll all be with her on the other side of the grave where there will be no more separation. Do not grieve, dear mother; Pauline was prepared to die. She asked them to read and sing for her and she sang with them the last day she lived. She was given a respectable funeral; I would have taken her home but she had asked to be buried beside our sister Kari and since this was her last wish we did as she said. Her coffin cost twenty-five dollars and I paid ten dollars for the hearse, the regular price here. We had an American pastor at her grave and he gave a very nice funeral oration and many, both Norwegians and Americans, followed her to her last place of rest. The doctor had told her that there was no hope. The doctor and medicines and all that was needed for the funeral came to about fifty-four dollars. I paid for it all. When she died she had sixty-six dollars in cash and asked that this be used to pay for her funeral and that the rest should be covered by the money owed to her in Norway. But I won't do this. If there isn't enough left to buy a gravestone and a railing for her grave after the funeral has been paid for, I'll take care of it. She wished that what was owed to her in Norway should be distributed among her siblings.

The Dilruds send their regards. Karen is well enough to do a little around the house. I was there today. I also send greetings from our entire family who are, praise God, in good health and doing well. Please write when you get this and let me know whether Ole Rossing has decided to come. I haven't heard from him for a long time. Please ask Anton Bryni whether he has sent me anything concerning Lemek Huse's accounts. I haven't received anything. I must now conclude. Please give my regards to all relatives and acquaintances. Give my special greetings to Syverine and her little girls and, first and last, to you my dear mother and brother from us all. Your devoted daughter

CHRISTINE DAHL

PS: I am enclosing a lock of Pauline's hair. Say hello to Ingebret Domstadskjæret from his daughter Pauline. I spoke with her when I was in Waco.

· ——— ·

There is some uncertainty concerning the day of Pauline's death. CD seems to have written "the sixteenth," but this cannot be right. Nor could she have meant the sixteenth of the previous month. The date given here is a conjecture. CD had written a few weeks earlier (17 October 1880, Nor. ed. IV:150). Her main concern was getting a farm laborer from Norway for her son-in-law. She also noted that her brother-in-law Peder Dilrud had been unhappy with the last laborer who had come to him and who had left after three months. She was evidently worried whether Ole Rossing, whom she had promised to help, was coming to Texas or not. Pauline had then been with her but returned to Waco. Peder Dilrud wrote to Furuset ten days later (Nor. ed. IV:151) asking his brother-in-law to send him a new farm laborer. Lemek Huse apparently owed money to CD, and she had suggested that some of it could be used to buy a ticket for Ole Rossing. «II:109 »II:117 NE IV:152

. —— .

1880 — LETTER 2:117

FROM: Ole O. Rossing, *Norse, Texas, 25 November 1880*

To: Erik Pedersen and Beate Kristoffersdatter Furuset
Romedal, Stange, Hedmark

⟶➤◯⟨⟵

Dear Erik and aunt,

I have, thank God, safely arrived and I'll fulfill your wish and tell you that I've come to the Widow Dahl. I came to Waco on the twentieth so my journey took me twenty-two days. It was very fast, but I was sick most of the voyage. Mrs. Dahl and her son Peder met me in Waco. They had a wagon with four horses so you may imagine I had a fine ride. She has thirty horses, eighty cows, twelve pigs, six of them for fattening, and a tame wolf. And they have a lot of wheat, so much that it is wonderful for a Norwegian to see it all. And they have quite a few chickens and a tame squirrel. And the fields she owns look as if we were to stand right at the center of Romedal and look over all of it: that is what her property here looks like. She is now selling her cotton and wheat. I can tell you that there is a very nice and beautiful house here. She has a kitchen and three large rooms and many different other rooms. She has six children at home and three who have left. But I miss the most important person here who is Pauline. Had I been here eight days earlier I would have met her alive. And I can tell you that Karen Dilrud is said to be better. I can tell you that I'm very glad that I've already got work at a bakery in Waco. The reason why Mrs. Dahl wrote the way she did was that I was waiting in Waco and she didn't know that I was already there. This is why I wanted to write right away, but I'll write and tell you more later. I'll tell you that all are well here and we wish the same for you. Tell them at Tingstad that I'll write soon. We all send our friendly regards. I would like to hear from you about your Christmas celebrations. Give my regards to all at Furuset and all acquaintances. Farewell! I hope these lines will find you in the best of health.

O. O. ROSSING

. ——— .

This letter gives a newcomer's impression of Christina Dahl's achievement. Erik Furuset had married Beate Kristoffersdatter. She had a brother named Ole, and Ole O. Rossing may be his son (the Norwegian word for aunt here, *faster*, means father's sister). The only farm in Norway named Rossing was in Søndre Land in Oppland and OOR may have worked there before his emigration. «II:16 »II:122 NE IV:153

. ——— .

1881 — LETTER 2:118

FROM: John Olsen Leerfald, *Fergus Falls, Minnesota, 27 January 1881*

To: Karl Ludvig Olsen Lerfald, *Verdal, Nord-Trøndelag*

᛭᛫⟹⟸᛫᛭

Dear brother!

I haven't heard from you for a long time but this may be because I haven't written. Please forgive me. I'll briefly tell you of my movements since you last heard from me. As you know, I was in Minneapolis and I moved around there until I got tired of it. Then I went west and stopped here. With a partner I bought a butcher shop and began to sell meat and this went well, but when spring came along we sold it and Theodore Leerfald and I built a new shop and are now doing a good business. We've sold for as much as sixty dollars a day and that isn't so bad. I'll then tell you that I'm married. It was done at Christmas. On December 28 I married my beloved Hanne Christine Lyng. She is a daughter of Haldor Lyng from Verdal. You may know him. He lives nine miles from our town. She is about the same age as your Hanne was when you married her. Our wedding was held in the home of her parents. I live here in town and I've rented a house for six dollars a month, but I think I'll build one myself next spring. I've bought a lot for 250 dollars almost right in the center of town. I bought it about two months ago and since then the price has gone up by fifty dollars each month and I think the price will be even higher in the spring. You should visit us some time and look around. You would meet many from Verdal as almost the entire settlement consists of people from Verdal. I've recently had a letter from Juliana and Frelig who went to California last summer. She has been sick since they arrived but they are otherwise doing well. I'll conclude with loving regards from me and my wife to you and your family. Farewell and write soon to your brother

JOHN LEERFALD

. —— .

There are letters by members of the Lerfald family in Norway in Nor. ed. II and one from JOL (then in Big Rapids, Mich.) to his brother Ole Olsen Leerfald in Green Bay, Wisc., written on 5 December 1873 (Nor. ed. III:170). The family in Norway wrote their name Lerfald, but those who emigrated seem to have written it Leerfald. »II:130 NE IV:163

. —— .

FROM: Svend H. Enderson, *Danway, Illinois, 13 February 1881*

To: Jakob Rasmussen Sandvik, *Kinsarvik, Ullensvang, Hordaland*

Dear friend,

Your letter arrived a long time ago and I must now answer it as I've waited far too long. My dear friend, you are often in my thoughts and I often think that it would be nice to speak with you. I would have much to tell you about my situation. I'll first let you know that I and my sisters are in good health and I hope that you too enjoy this gift for which we owe thanks to God. I'm in Lee County for the winter living with my sister Marta where I pay for my board. I have good days; we do nothing during winter and my main work is to visit the girls. I have no fear, for if one should fail me then there are others. But I find that many of them are false; for the second time I've been betrayed by a girl, the one I wrote about in my last letter. It was good between us for a year but then she was tempted by another man and so our love was destroyed because she was too much with others while she was engaged to me. I don't want to have one who is with others. This girl was the daughter of a prosperous man and was nice and beautiful, but I won't yield, as it doesn't affect me so much now as it did when I was engaged for the first time and was betrayed. Now I don't care much whether it works out or not. But I'll try again because it is my greatest entertainment to talk with the girls because there are both false and faithful girls. There are many girls available here and I hope to find a faithful and honest friend and I've found one from Stavanger. We're engaged but I don't know how long it will last. If it works, this is fine, and if it doesn't then I won't care much.

Then I'd rather wait until I come to Norway and I believe this will be soon as I wish to see Norway again. I don't worry about the journey because it isn't as difficult as you all seem to believe in Norway. I suppose it's their concern for the journey that has made my mother and sister Ingrid delay their voyage. It may be just as well that they don't come because those who don't like it here have a difficult time so I won't advise any to come if they don't want to. But I'll say as I've said before that America is a better country than Norway. I don't wish to return to live there, nor could I have earned as much money there as I've done here.

Next summer I'll work for the same man I've worked for before; this will be the fourth summer. Jacob and Dorthea are going west to Iowa to work on their land. Christmas is over now but we had lots of fun with the ladies and we had lots of both beer and liquor. Liquor is a good thing to have, especially when you have been slandered. Farewell and give my regards to your brother Svend and to all friends and acquaintances. You mustn't let anyone see or hear this letter or I won't let you know anything another time. Write soon.

SVEND H. ENDERSON

. ——— .

SHE now uses the initial H for the farm name Hus. In a letter from Danway written 3 February 1880 (Nor. ed. IV:128) he mentions his plans to visit Norway when he has $600 "in my pocket," and writes about corresponding with a girl he met while visiting his two sisters in Lee County (he writes *Lekaunti*) for Christmas. His sisters both had children and his relations with his brother-in-law Jacob Svendsen has apparently improved. «11:93 »11:142 NE IV:164

. ——— .

1881 — LETTER 2:120

FROM: Iver Ellingsen Elsrud, *Sweden, North Dakota, 20 February 1881*

TO: Gulbrand Ellingsen Elsrud, *Aadalen, Ringerike, Buskerud*

⋅→≡◉⧯≡←⋅

Dear brother and family,

Had I been a pastor I would have chastised you for being lazy since it's so long since I've heard from you. I now expect a letter as soon as you've received this one. I have no news. This has been a fairly nice winter, a little on the cold side but not so bad that I haven't been out working every day. These last two or three weeks I've been with uncle Ole Haugerud as he's been ill, but next week I'll again begin my life as a hermit. I'll then be a carpenter and build a stall and a cow barn. This will be hard work since my logs are of oak, fifteen to twenty inches at the top and twenty-four feet long. I'll also dig myself a well and expect to have to go down about thirty feet. I'll do all this alone as I cannot afford to hire any help. So you can see that I'll be busy. I still haven't sold a horse but plan to do this as soon as I have an opportunity. Ole Nygaard has come to the West, probably to get some land, but there isn't much left around here. He's been ill with typhus in Fargo since last fall and he doesn't look good. Hans Granum also lives near here like all the other bachelors. Gulbrand Sortebraaten is also here and has taken land and is doing quite well. When you look out on these wide prairies and remember what it looked like a couple of years ago you can be quite astonished; then it was the playground of wandering redskins but now it has all been settled. Had you been here you would have seen many strange houses. Many are built of turf and are barely ten feet square. Others have dug a hole in the ground and hardly have a door and no windows while some have rather nice houses. But you can hardly expect things to be much better because almost all who come here are poor and the first thing they have to think of is food. Quite a lot is needed the first year because then everything has to be bought. But when you can begin to harvest, things get better. You don't have to pay more than 1,400 dollars for 640 acres of excellent soil and you get your deed when you have lived there for five years. When you consider how many in Norway have no land and see these enormous areas of excellent land, prairies as well as forest, that are uninhabited and unused then you may wonder why He who is almighty has divided the world so unevenly, but I suppose there is no use in pondering his secrets. Give my regards to Christian Oprud and to Elling. Say hello to little Olia from uncle Iver and of course also to Else, but first and formost regards to you and your wife from your devoted brother

IVER E. ELSRUD

· —— ·

«II:111 »II:134 NE IV:166

· —— ·

1881 — LETTER 2:121

FROM: Iver Andersen Lee, *Springdale, Wisconsin, 28 February 1881*

To: Anders Olsen, Kari Mikkelsdatter, and Anders Andersen Lie
Hedalen, Sør-Aurdal, Oppland

--➤◉⟵--

Dear parents and brothers,

Again a long time has passed since you last heard from me so I find it necessary to send you my regards and a report on my present situation. Since my last letter I've had the pleasure of receiving two letters from you, my dear brother Anders. Thank you so much; I was so glad to read your reports from home. I received the first letter on Christmas Eve, just in time to be my Christmas gift from home and it was truly a good Christmas gift as there is no gift so welcome as a report from home. Yes, a report from the close family circle shows that you have me in your thoughts and I can have no better gift. I received your other letter about fourteen days ago and again had the pleasure of seeing that you are all in good health.

As for my situation I can tell you that I'm in good health so I have no reason for complaint; you cannot complain so long as you have health and liberty even though your situation may be difficult. And if one can look forward to better times one does better by surmounting the difficulties than by complaining. But if one has no prospects it is better to try something else, because the world is wide and there is surely a suitable place for those who have their future in mind. This applies to any and all and if I consider my own case I'll say that in Norway I couldn't see how I could possibly achieve a situation that would answer to my expectations so I decided to go to a less crowded place to see what I was capable of. I was, thank God, not so naïve that I thought America was a paradise without difficulties and worries and had I had such expectations I would long ago have cursed both myself and America. But I cannot say that I've met with so many difficulties yet. My worst problem may be that it takes so long to learn the language. I've worked at it this winter and I've been attending an English school since last fall and to learn the language faster I've hired out to an American who lives near my brother Ole in return for board. I go to my brother every Sunday because his wife does my laundry and mends my clothes. Except for this I live with this American. I must say that I'm slow in learning their language but in other respects I'm quite comfortable with them. True, it can be awkward when I don't understand what they are saying to me, in particular at first when I didn't understand a word. Now I understand some of what they say. I think I'll live here until school is over in the middle of March. Then it is my intention to be with Americans until I either learn their language or find it impossible.

I see in your letter, dear brother, that thoughts of America are still alive there at home. This is natural at a time when almost all who cannot look forward to a home in their old age come here in order to get such a home. And as it's reasonable that those who are thinking of going would like to have our advice I will, as well as I can, let you know some of my views about this country. I'll first say that America is a more prosperous and fruitful land than Norway. Its soil is better and easier to cultivate. This is particularly true of uncultivated land and there still is an abundance of such land. All you need to do with such land is to plow and plant it and it will then bear forth wheat, corn and other grains without fertilization. Breaking such land cannot be compared to breaking uncultivated land in Hedalen. You can start plowing right away because the rocks that are so abundant and so troublesome there don't exist here. I'm of course speaking of the areas without forest, and most land that hasn't yet been taken is without forest. The conditions for acquiring such land are both cheap and simple so it's easy for people without means to get land. From a superficial point of view all this looks brilliant but if one looks at it more carefully one will surely see that there are many other difficulties. I've heard a little about the life of those who first settled around here more than thirty years ago. They were so far from towns or markets that they could hardly sell what they produced. There were no roads so if they set out on a journey to sell their produce they had to go through an unsettled wilderness. The journey could take several weeks and storms and bad weather could threaten their lives. As for today's settlers in the West we hear that the lack of firewood is one of their greatest problems, especially with the extreme cold of this winter, when the snow and cold came so early that people didn't have time to get enough firewood for the winter. According to a letter from the West to one of our neighbors the need has been so great that people have burned all they had and, as an example of the drastic measures taken, it told of a man who had chopped up his organ. If one is frightened by such stories,

America has many other trades and businesses so workers have more possibilities than in Norway, and as the pay is much better here it isn't difficult to lay aside a little fortune in the years one is able to work and thus ensure a carefree old age.

Another matter of concern is whether one will be happy in a foreign land. I cannot speak for others in this matter. For myself I can say that I don't fear that I'll be unhappy should I pass the days of my old age here; as for Norwegians around here who now are old, I can say that they don't appear to be unhappy. I've become acquainted with many of them and can say that they are more carefree than old people in Norway. One of the greatest concerns for poor people in our fatherland doesn't exist here—the concern for the necessities for the maintenance of life. The greatest difference between America and Norway is that while people in Norway often lacked the necessities of life even though they otherwise were quite well off, the situation here is the opposite: even those who are poor or weighed down by debt and other difficulties usually have more than enough food or at least what is necessary.

I also see that you've thought about whether you should all come or which one of you, my dear brothers, should come. As for the first, I must say that I find it difficult to advise you all to come and I also believe that you haven't really thought very seriously about this. First, the journey is too difficult for people as disabled as you are, my dear parents, and second, I think it would be more difficult for old people to like it here than for those who come when they are able to work. Work is a good physician for thoughts and other troubles and even if one isn't happy to begin with, work will disperse thoughts of the fatherland and this will be more difficult for those who don't have work. As I believe that one of you, my dear brothers, will stay with our parents in their old age, I think it would be best for our parents to remain in their home for the time they have left. It may be that you my dear brothers both believe it would be an advantage to come here and that he who stays home feels he will be more burdened with care for our parents. There may be good reasons for such thoughts but if time shows that he who stays will have greater difficulties in getting on than us others then I regard it as a dear duty to assist in the care of our dear parents to whom we all owe so much gratitude for all they have done for us in earlier years. As for who of you should come here I cannot say. If one of you has a greater desire to go than the other, then I would say that he who has the greater desire should go. It may be that there is no great difference in your desire to go to America and then I think that a decision should be based on a reasonable agreement. I think that both of you have the necessary qualities for success here—the will and ability to work. It may be that you brother Mikkel would wish to really develop your craft as a shoemaker and if so, you would have a greater opportunity for this here than at home.

I send greetings from brother Ole. He and his family are in good health and doing well and I can say the same for all our relatives here. As for Uncle Guttorm's widow, Berit, I think she is doing very well. Indeed she feels the loss of her dear husband but she has a good farm, is without debt, and her children are now all grown up. Her youngest, her son Ole, is about sixteen. Her four other children, who are all girls, are now adults. One of them, Gunnild, is as you know married and the others, Maria, Anne and Thorine, are sometimes at home and other times away in service. At present I can remember no more to tell you. In conclusion I must ask you to give my regards to all relatives and friends. And first of all you my dear parents and brothers as well as old grandmother are lovingly greeted from your respect-ful son and brother.

IVER A. LIE

As I know you are interested in hearing more about my brother Ole's fam-ily relations, I'm glad to report that I've found everything to be in the best order. The relationship between him and his wife is one of peace and love. I haven't noticed the least sign of coldness, indifference or disdain on her part for his earlier transgression. On the contrary, I think she is proud of him, and she has reason to be proud as I've often experienced that he enjoys much respect here. As an example I can mention that some young people tried to organize a singing school last fall and wanted Ole to be their teacher. I know he has written about the singing school we had last winter and it is this school they wanted to continue with Ole as teacher, as the old one couldn't continue. Ole was willing but because of the cold weather this winter with lots of snow it became too difficult to get together and noth-ing has come of it. My basis for writing about him is his behavior both in his family and in public. In particular I wish to emphasize his kindness to me and others. He's been so good to me since I came that I cannot possibly list all he's done, but I'll mention that when I came he bought me a new suit of clothes for fifteen dollars and last fall he invited me to live with him this winter. He didn't want me to live with Americans as he thought I'd be uncomfortable there. He didn't want as much as a shilling in return. So I must say that I'm greatly indebted to him and to his wife as she has also on all occasions been very helpful without expecting anything in return.

So I'll say that I've found his situation here as I had wished to find it and I feel it's an honor to be his brother and not a shame. I'll therefore say that you shouldn't be burdened by your memory of his transgression because his later progress and his kindness of heart demonstrate that it must have been something else that misled him and that his transgression cannot be regarded as a consequence of his natural disposition but is counter to it.

I. A. LIE

· ——— ·

IAL's brother Anders has taken over the correspondence from the Hedalen side. He remained in Hedalen while his brother Mikkel went to Wisconsin in the spring. The long paragraph that follows the signature is on a separate sheet. In this manner private matters need not be shared with all who were interested in reading letters from America. It seems that one reason for Ole's emigration was that he had fathered a child with another woman. In a later letter (Nor. ed. 2:204) Mikkel asks for information about Ole's son in Hedalen on a separate sheet. IAL's aunt Olea Olsdatter and her husband, Hallsten Hallstensen Børtnes, also emigrated later that year and joined their children who had all emigrated earlier. «II:115 »II:127 NE IV:168

· ——— ·

1881 — LETTER 2:122

FROM: Christine Dahl, *Norse, Texas, 2 March 1881*

TO: Siri Kristiansdatter and Erik Pedersen Furuset
Romedal, Stange, Hedmark

⁕═◖═⁕

Dear brother and mother,

We received your very welcome letter of December 20 some time ago and have waited for the laborers to come before we replied. They have now been here for about three weeks. They had a good journey and seem to be quite satisfied. I'm glad to see that you are all well and especially that our dear old mother still is so healthy that she can do housekeeping and this must be nice for her as long as she is up to it. As for us, we are all, praise God, healthy and doing well. Ole was ill last winter but is now better. Both Ole's wife and Syverine have increased the population. Ole had a son and Syverine a daughter about two weeks ago and there were only five days between them. I was at Dilrud today and all were well except that Karen remains weak. She is never quite well but she is nevertheless on her feet looking after the children. Her little girls are clever and can do all kinds of housework. She and her family send their regards. Aunt Rogstad is now a widow. Her husband died last December after having been ill for two months and in bed for two weeks. She and her children are doing well.

The newcomers say that you are sorry that Pauline died in Waco. But dear mother, it seemed preordained that she should go there and lie next to Kari, which was her last wish even though no one could have regretted this more than I. Both Karen Dilrud and I begged her to stay here and not go to Waco but she insisted that she preferred to be there and have a little work and we must believe that this was how she was meant to conclude her pilgrimage on earth. We have no news of interest for you except that there will be a new railroad about five miles from us and one mile from Ole and Syverine. The winter has been colder than for many years but the cattle and horses have done well. Now the weather is nice and we've started plowing and planting. I'm enclosing an authorization that I hope will make it possible for you to get the necessary signature on your bond. Tell the people at Jølstadengen that Wilhelm is here and in good health. I must now conclude with regards from all here, both children and grandchildren, to all our friends and relatives, but first and last to you and our dear mother. Your devoted sister,

CHRISTINE DAHL

· ——— ·

This summer Erik Furuset had at least two other requests for help in providing tickets for farm laborers: from Peder Jensen Hamarseie on 27 July 1881 and from Ole H. Dal on 6 August 1881. Peder Dilrud also wrote several times about this. CD's new grandchildren were Otto Dahl and Christine Nelson. Her widowed aunt was Anne Rogstad. Two sisters were buried in Waco: Pauline Furuset and Kari Bergman. Wilhelm Jølstadengen was one of the recent farm laborers.
«II:117 »II:128 NE IV:169

· ——— ·

From: Jacob Hanson Hilton, *Socorro, New Mexico, 17 April 1881*

To: Hans Jakobsen Hilton, *Kløfta, Ullensaker, Akershus*

Dear father,

I was glad to receive your letter of March 4 as it's a year since I last heard from you. The only letter I've had from Norway since April of last year is Oluf's with his photograph. This must be because of the post offices here in the distant West as well as my own restlessness, moving from one place to another. I'll now begin a more regular correspondence as I plan to live here if luck stands me by. I left Denver, Colorado on April 6 to go to New Mexico about 600 miles further south, a new world where white people have just begun to arrive. Now I'm among Indians and Mexicans and Spaniards and all three nations look alike and one is as dangerous as the other, but white people are coming in fast now that the railroad is here. It was built last year and these mountains and valleys, that once were inhabited by these lazy and useless people that live like wild animals, are now filling up with white people. I've never felt better since leaving home than I have after coming to this place. The birds sing in the morning as they did in Old Norway and there are all kinds of fruit trees—you can see oranges, apples, all the berries you can name, and grapes wherever you go. The fruit trees were in bloom when I arrived. There are flocks of thousands of sheep and cattle. They hardly have winter here. There may be snow one day but it's gone the next, so cows and sheep can graze all year. Gold and silver mines have been discovered and opened by white people and within a year all danger from the natives will be over as they'll have to retreat when the Americans come in.

There are enormous areas of government land that anyone can take as <u>homestead</u> land for virtually nothing. You can have 600 acres at twenty-five cents an acre down when you take the land and you can have it free from taxation for three years. Then you pay one dollar an acre and get a deed on your property. So we can have 600 acres for 150 dollars now and

600 in three years, a rather cheap piece of property. If a man doesn't want this much land he can have less on the same conditions; but right now this land is available at this price and in eight or ten years there won't be a spot left except to buy from others at a much higher price. Father, this is the time to make the leap to America with your entire flock. This place shall be my home if all goes well. I came here at the right time to be one of the first settlers in this New World. True, at first there may be many inconveniences and difficulties for a settler but as immigration grows and the land is taken, property prices will go up and civilization will bring in everything that is necessary for both farmers and miners. This is not an empty dream or a castle in the air; it has been built by white people all the way from the Atlantic Ocean in the East to the coast of California, from sea to sea. There are still millions of acres of land that haven't yet been trod on by white people but as immigration grows it will all in time be settled by whites. But this place has become my home. Let others go further. The climate here is excellent, the best I've experienced since leaving Norway. As everything here is new, prices are high. What do you think of three dollars a day for room and board? I opened a shoemaker shop here and rented a room for fifteen dollars a month where I work, cook, eat and sleep, so room and board only cost me half a dollar a day, since anything edible that is produced here is cheap, but whatever has to be transported is very expensive. I would have liked to have the little girls here to cook for me.

I get two dollars to sole a pair of boots, fifty cents for a patch, for patches over the toes one dollar a pair, for sewing soles two and a half dollars, and from twelve to twenty dollars for a new pair of boots. From next week I'll have a man to help me as there's more work than I can manage on my own. I saved between six and seven hundred dollars in eighteen months in Colorado with my pine-pitch thread and hammer and I've used my money to buy wares to open my shop and bought a few lots in town at a hundred dollars a lot but I plan to hold on to them for awhile and get three times what I paid for them. I came here on Saturday, bought lots on Monday and could have sold them for twice the amount on Tuesday. Land prices don't go up that much in places that have been settled for some time, only in new places where white people are coming in by the hundreds. Farmland, too, increases in value, but not as fast as town lots. But as I've been raised on a farm I prefer a farmer's life, at least here in America where a farmer can grow all he needs and not have to pay unreasonable taxes. Here they grow tobacco, cotton, all kinds of fruit, barley, oats, peas, wheat, corn, in brief anything that will grow on God's green earth. Raising cattle is the most profitable farming as it can be done with the least labor and expenses. You can buy a sheep here for fifty cents to one and a half dollars and a cow for fifteen to thirty dollars.

If you and the boys would like to come then do so before the best land is taken. I'll take 600 acres this summer if only I can get out of my shop long enough to look around. Do you think you can sell your farm at a reasonable price? If so, don't hold on to it. As soon as I hear that you've made up your mind, I'll come home and be of as much help as I can on your journey. For my part I'm not afraid of that journey as it is much more comfortable now than a few years ago. You mustn't fear for the journey; it is not as difficult as people in the Old Country think and God will protect you so you are as safe on sea as on land. I'll speak with all I know in the Old as well as in the New World and I'll quit being a shoemaker and we'll all take land together and whatever I can get of information from others will serve all of you as well as other Norwegians who would like to join us and take land in the same place. I know many in Denver, Colorado, both Norwegians and Swedes, who asked me to write to them as soon as I found there was good land to be had. I expect Frithjof Asche in a few days. He sent me a telegram yesterday that he will stay for a few days and make use of the New West. His brother Thomas in Denver will come this summer. August Hilton is with me and is just now putting the coffee pot in the fireplace to make us some supper. We live together here and he cooks one day and I the next. He has also bought some town lots. Tell Streiff at Brotnu that if he knew what this place is like he wouldn't stay another day at Brotnu. With his experience with cattle he would become a wealthy man in a few years. This goes for any enterprising man with an eye to the future; this is the place for hundreds of enterprising Norwegians. An entire colony, all of them Norwegian, are planning to come here from Wisconsin. They have an agent here to find a good place for them to settle. I'm expecting Ellison (a Norwegian agent) here in a few days and will get more information from him about where they will settle. I've soon used up my paper and must conclude. Write me as soon as you get these lines and let me know whether you'll go with me if I come. I can in good conscience say that you should come with your entire family. If I hadn't been convinced that you would do well here I wouldn't have said a word. Give my regards to all relatives and friends and to my brothers and sisters and to mother. There isn't a day that my thoughts don't go to Hilton. Every time I see a nice farm I think: "This would be a good place for father and the boys." Your son

JACOB

I had a letter from Uncle C. Jacobson a week or so ago. He asks why you don't write. He asks why my brothers don't come here where they could have good futures and whether they are learning a trade or taking higher education. I don't know the answers but I told him that none will come to America before you and mother come. Oluf once wrote that he would only come if you and mother came. So I haven't said anything about going to America in my last letters to him. But now I must again say how excellent an opportunity there now is to get good land cheaply here where the climate is excellent and fruit trees and all else grow and bloom. Why waste your time in Norway where there is nothing but poor food.

. ——— .

An unpublished letter from JHH dated 6 February 1881 was sent from Denver, Colo. He had just arrived so he had little to write about but he writes as if he has thought of settling there, and now, a few weeks later, he is in New Mexico, which did not become a state until 1912. The "little girls" are his sisters Dortea and Karen. He gets quite carried away in the course of writing and sees himself at the center of a large Norwegian migration to Socorro. With his four horses and forty-six cows in 1875, Fridolin Streiff's Brotnu was a large farm in Ullensaker. O. Ellison was a Scandinavian agent for the Atchison, Topeka, and Santa Fe Railroad and was very active in getting Scandinavians to settle in the Southwest. See Kenneth O. Bjork, *West of the Great Divide* (Northfield, Minnesota, 1958): Bjork 1958, 388–389. JHH's early letters from Socorro are discussed in two articles by this editor: "Becoming White in 1881: An Immigrant Acquires an American Identity," *Journal of American Ethnic History* 23:4 (Summer 2004): 132–141; "Intruders on Native Ground: Troubling Silences and Memories of the Land-Taking in Norwegian Immigrant Letters," Udo J. Hebel, ed., *Transnational American Memories* (Berlin and New York: Walter de Gruyter, 2009): 79–103. «II:110 »II:125 NE IV:171

. ——— .

⊷⇒◉⇐⊷

Dear Svend and wife,

Today I'll take up my pen to write you a few sentences and tell you how I am. I've been almost a year in America and I've had both good days and bad in this country. When I came last year I went far west in Minnesota and was there this past winter. It wasn't always all that much fun. The snowstorms were violent and not like those in Norway. It was so bad that it was impossible to go out to tend the animals. But when spring arrived all was forgotten. We had two feet of snow at Easter and it melted in three days. When the sun begins to shine it soon gets quite warm. The place I was last winter is called Sacred Heart. While there I attended school and learned enough English to get by. The only one from Sørfjorden in the West was Knut Berge and Jacob has written about him. There were some from Eidfjord and Voss but most were from Numedal and Valdres. They were all very friendly and when you visit you have to eat with them. I was on Minnesota's prairies, as they call them and I haven't seen anything so beautiful in my entire life. There were prairies that were 100 miles wide and excellent land for wheat. They harvested from twenty-two to twenty-five bushels an acre. Each man had from sixty to 150 acres. I cannot remember seeing such wide fields in Norway.

I suppose you want to have news and there is a lot of news from here. But as you don't know the people and the places it won't be of interest. But I can tell you that I've left the West and come down to Rushford and to Endre Jaastad and my brother. He has bought half of a pharmacy from his wife's uncle. The distance I traveled was 250 miles and it cost me ten dollars, almost all the money I had earned. I didn't come here at the best time for making money; I left home in the fall and it was winter when I arrived, but now that summer is here it will be easier to make money than in Norway.

Everything is more expensive here. But for people who are willing to work it is much better to get along than in Norway. I think it is nice here with valleys and open spaces as in the mountains in Norway but much nicer. I haven't had it as good before in America as here with Jaastad. They are so kind to me. I've done some carpentry for him and painted the outside of his house. He has a large stone house with 18 rooms. When you come to America you get used to many kinds of work. A pastor here is like a farmer in Norway. He is perfectly willing to go to the stable himself and tend to his horses. Here people don't distinguish between a pastor and a worker. It's not as in Norway where people doff their caps for the pastor. No, all are like farmers here.

People grow up faster here than in Norway. A boy or a girl is fully grown at fifteen. It's good for women in this country. I'll tell you how the American deals with his wife. He has to pull on her socks and hand her her clothes as she sits in bed and hold her jacket while she puts it on and stand with a piece of soap in his hand when she washes her face and bring in the water while she sits rocking on her chair. What I write is true! I've thought of writing to your brother Jacob but I suppose he is at Ulven. So I'll conclude for now. Excuse my poor writing. Give my regards to my parents and to yours and to my acquaintances. I've written to Lars Kinsarvik but had no reply. He may not have received it.

LARS L. URHEIM

. ——— .

LLU emigrated from Ullensvang in 1880. In 1895 he had a pharmacy in Eau Claire, Wisc. His brother Jakob Larsen Urheim emigrated in 1876 and became a physician in 1891 and practiced in Chicago. Endre Larsen Jaastad emigrated from Ullensvang in 1869 after his studies at the teachers training college at Stord. He was ordained in the Norwegian Synod in 1873 and became a pastor in Rushford, Minn. Sørfjorden is a branch of the Hardanger Fjord. Ulven was an army boot camp. »II:151 NE IV:172

. ——— .

FROM: Jacob Hanson Hilton, *Socorro, New Mexico, 7–28 August 1881*

To: Hans Jakobsen and Anne Olsdatter Hilton
Kløfta, Ullensaker, Akershus

❖⟩══◉══⟨❖

Dear parents, brothers and sisters,

Dear father: Thank you so much for your letter dated on St. John's Day that I received a few days ago. Nothing pleases me so much as letters from my dear place of birth that will always be the place I love the most. In my thoughts I often pay brief visits—over the foaming billows—but it's so far away and only a fantasy. I often send a wistful eye over the billows to the dear home, nice fields, beautiful woods, and many friends, to see if it's still like the place where I used to wander. These memories often call up a question from my heart: will I ever see these dear places again? These wonderful places of childhood? If God grants me life, luck and health I will with his help yet again see the blooming valleys of Norway—but not to live there. I am now immersed in my business and don't have time to go home, but as soon as time permits I'll try to take a pleasure trip over the rocking billows and again see the coast of Norway. This is not unlikely as Frithjof is a reliable person and can take care of the business for two or three months. I realize that you won't be coming to America. When I try to place myself in your position and consider what you write in your letter about selling everything you have, I can see how difficult this would be on top of our feelings for old Hilton.

August 28

I'll complete my letter now that I have a quiet evening by myself. The reason I didn't complete it then was that the Indians had raided in the mountains and reports from all over came to town with survivors, that they had shot, burned and pillaged, and murdered all they came across. They were as close to this town as from Hilton to the railroad station at Kløfta. They slaughtered seven men who were working in a quarry where they take stone for building. Gus Hilton and another Norwegian were partners in the quarry and had employed several men. Gus was the only survivor. He crawled under some large stones in the mountain so they couldn't see him and he hid there until an armed posse arrived from town. Seven murdered men were buried in one day in Socorro—in a white box instead of a coffin and without song or ceremony. I closed my shop (as Frithjof was in Chicago), rented a horse and rode off as fast as my horse could manage. I used my spurs till my boots were bloodied in order to get there and bring Gus Hilton back to town. He had already been five or six hours in his cave and could expect death any minute. I only had a revolver with seven bullets and a poor horse, and I had to go alone as no one would come with me without a larger group. So I went alone and came there in time and let August ride my horse to town as he was both hungry and frightened to death, and I walked down alone on my feet. The men killed by the Indians were the worst sight I've ever seen and I hope I'll never see such a butchery of men again. The red devils kill all they come across, sparing none. In three weeks they've put four to five hundred whites and Mexicans in their graves in this state around Socorro. In one place there are thirty-five new graves where the redskins made thirty-five civilized white men bite the dust. It is enough to raise the hair on a man's head and make him feel as if a lump of ice were drawn down his back from top to toe. The horses and cows they couldn't take with them they cut up in pieces. These are the "poor Indians" that people in the eastern states have so much sympathy for. My judgment on such people is that they should be in hell with broken backbones—both the Indians and those who feel such concern for them.

Business has been bad since this war began as all who could came into town and stayed here without working—and consequently without money. I hope it will soon be better as the cavalry is after them. As it soon is dark I'll end my letter. Give my regards to the little girls and tell them that I'll write to them later. I'm well and making good money. Give my regards to all my acquaintances, brothers, sisters and mother and loving greetings to you from your son

J. H. HILTON

Tell mother that she mustn't be afraid for me; there is no need. I am not in danger even here in the Far West. He who is protected by God is not in danger. Even at Old Hilton you are in as great a danger as I am in this wild, uncivilized and distant land. Farewell! Write soon.

JHH wrote frequently and at length. Some weeks earlier (Nor. ed. VI:173) he described his new life: "You can't find a man in this town who has been here one year; all are newcomers from all parts of the world. The American people flow like the water in a river, fast in some places, slower in others, all toward the New West where lots of gold and silver, copper and iron can be found in the mountains. Money can be made in these places where new discoveries are made every day of the year and this is why I followed the current like the other birds of passage who seek their fortune in this distant land outside of civilization where white people have only come in this last year. This place is not in the United States yet but will perhaps be a part of the United States of America in two or three years.... There are no regular laws here yet; every man carries the law in his belt (two large pistols and a long knife and a rifle). This is still the law here." He also wrote that Frithjof Asche had joined him in his business. St. John's Day is Midsummer Day, 24 June. Conrad Hilton writes about this incident involving his father in his autobiography *Be My Guest*. «II:123 »II:126 NE IV:175

1881 — LETTER 2:126

FROM: Jacob Hanson Hilton, *Socorro, New Mexico, 20 November 1881*

To: Hans Jakobsen and Anne Olsdatter Hilton
Kløfta, Ullensaker, Akershus

Dear father, mother and siblings,

Thank you for your letters dated the second, ninth, and the twenty-third. I'll begin with your first letter. As for my verdict on the Indians, I haven't changed my mind and you would have agreed if you had known more about their behavior. Ask Uncle C. Jacobson about this. Our business is sound and doing well. We've hired a shoemaker and will hire another as soon as we find one. I have all the shoe business in this town and came here when there were only fifty to sixty white men here. By now it has grown to 1,000 or so and is beginning to look more American.

No, father, no! I'll never forget my place of birth. It is the dearest place on earth for me where I lived my <u>happiest days</u> without a worry for tomorrow. Those days will never return. How could I ever forget them? Only a fool or madman can forget his dear birthplace. You say you were often hard on me. "<u>No!</u>" never without reason, father, because you know I was much too restless. The reason was that I couldn't see any future in Norway; I couldn't get it into my head—regardless of how and where I looked—how I could ever become useful for anything. My thoughts were in America where I built castles in the air. This is why everything seemed so boring and why everything I tried to do went so badly. So I behaved unreasonably whenever I was told to do something and it's a wonder you weren't harder on me than you were. So, my father, forget this and never bring it up again. I wasn't born to live in Norway; it was against my nature and my mindset, as you well know. You have some of this yourself, but I'm worse. Never will a king, bishop, pastors, deans or sheriffs ever have any influence on me as long as I live. These damned beggars are a great nuisance for Norway and they will keep it up until they eventually beggar themselves. They may paint America in as dark colors as they wish, but America will stand as a model and shine bright and clear as the sun while Norway shivers and falters in poverty and suffers under the government of these cowards who are not <u>men</u> able to earn their daily bread in an honest and honorable manner; they beg it and steal it from a poor working man. Fine people they are to govern a country! Send them to America where they would either die of hunger or take off their gloves and get to work. The pastor in our town couldn't live on his income and went around town with a list to get a little more. Do you know what he got as an answer? Go out with a pick and shovel like the others and work for your bread. This is how America pays its pastors. They are as great beggars as the Norwegian pastors but the people are different. They say: if a pastor can't manage on his salary then let him go out and work like us. And so our respected <u>pastor</u> had to take off his gloves and work on the railroad while he preached on Sundays. You should hear what the American people say about Norway giving (as they were told) a gift to the newly wed royal couple. They say they would rather collect enough money to buy gunpowder and send the entire court to Hell in smoke. And they would let them pay for their own marriage like other people or stay unmarried and wait until they had saved the money they need for their wedding. If these people had had any principles at all they would have been above begging.

I had planned to go home late in November in order to celebrate Christmas Eve at Hilton, but because of a brisk business and lots of work in the shop I won't be able to come this winter either. Just as I'm sitting here writing a man comes in the door and says that a man has been put in irons and jailed and will be hanged tonight. Two members of his band were hanged in a tree. They are horse thieves and murderers but as soon as they come near our little town they may as well say their prayers. I'll send you a portrait of the two hanging robbers in my next letter. <u>Hurrah for America!</u> This is the only way we can protect our lives and our property. We have laws, but money can buy anyone in this new land so every man has to have his own law: a good rifle and a six-shooter. These are the laws we have to rely on for our safety. We have two or four revolvers, two rifles and a shotgun. This is our daily life and we know of no other out here beyond civilization. A man who minds his own business and lets others do the same is in no danger and I'm as safe as at Hilton. I'm glad to see all who can get away from the slavery in Norway and leave those bigwigs to do their own work so they'll learn what it's like for the poor workers. They first work them like cattle and then give them miserable food (swill for swine here in America) and almost no pay. When I say that I make as much in a week as the best workers there make in a year, I suppose you won't believe me. And what is more, I live like a gentleman and get fresh-baked white buns, steaks, baked lamb and all the fruit you can name. I make about fifty dollars a week after expenses. Anyone who comes to America and is willing to work and save his money is in a better situation than the best landowner in Norway even if he has house and home. But you have to be prepared for many difficult days. C. Jacobson says that hope and happiness are fellow wanderers from childhood to old age, from the cradle to the grave; this is how it is and how it must be.

Hans Iverson Tveter came this fall after I'd written to him in Minneapolis. He's in a bad frame of mind because he doesn't have much work but he lives with us. He asks you to give his regards to his parents and siblings at Tveter. Hans is in good health and fat as a pig. Tell Ole Olstad that I would like to hear from him soon; give me his address so I can write to him. This photograph is of our house with our store in the end to the left. You can see the trees in front of the house and on the wall a boot and a shoe. This is my only Christmas gift and I hope it will get to you. I'll write a Christmas letter to the little girls. How are our neighbors, young and old? Give my regards to all, adults and children, relatives and friends. You my parents and siblings are lovingly greeted from your son and brother in this distant country.

JACOB HILTON

When JHH writes that Socorro "is beginning to look more American" he is referring to its former Mexican appearance. He has no regrets in displacing the town's formerly dominant population. His comments on pastors and labor are similar to those in the first letter in this edition: 1:1. «II:125 »II:136 NE IV:181

1881 — LETTER 2:127

FROM: Mikkel Andersen Lee, *Springdale, Wisconsin, 30 November 1881*

TO: Anders Olsen, Kari Mikkelsdatter, and Anders Andersen Lie
Hedalen, Sør-Aurdal, Oppland

Dear parents and brother,

My memory of you and the dear fatherland Norway I have just left urges me here in my brother Ole's house to send you a report on our journey as I know you are longing to hear whether we have arrived well and happy at our destination. We sailed from Christiania on Friday October 28 at three in the afternoon. We remained on deck until dark and then had to go down into the ship as there was nothing more to see that would satisfy our curiosity. We had our first meal of tea and bread and butter at six. This kind of food has so often been described by those who have gone before me so I won't tire my readers by repeating it. But I will say that we didn't eat the food we got as it wasn't prepared in the Hedalen manner. We had exceptionally good weather on the North Sea. Most onboard were well and in good form and played and danced most of the time. Some surely felt a little seasickness but not more than that they could walk back and forth on deck. Sunday evening at ten we anchored in Hull. We had to stay onboard until nine in the morning. Then our agent took us to a hotel where we had a dinner of fresh meat and soup with wheat bread. I ate as well as I ever have. When we had eaten we were taken to the railroad for further transportation. We left Hull at noon and went through England at great speed, sometimes over and sometimes under ground, and arrived in Liverpool at seven in the evening and were met by our agent who took us to a hotel where we were served supper and taken to our rooms where we slept as well as a little king who doesn't allow the labor and troubles of the world disturb him too much. We had to stay here Tuesday and the next day at four we went onboard for our voyage. In Liverpool we had time to look at the city but there was nothing there that attracted my attention other than the huge horses that you may remember that Ole wrote about, so for the most part I stayed indoors until we went onboard.

If we'd had nice weather on the North Sea it now changed to the opposite. When it became dark the gale was so strong that the ship was cast here and there with the wind and was ravaged by seasickness. Thursday evening we anchored at Queenstown in Ireland to take on passengers who were going to America. We heaved anchor at five and as soon as we were out at sea the gale was at us again. The ship was thrown about by the wind and while we were in our bunks we had to hold fast in order not to be thrown out. We had to tie down all our baggage. It was impossible to stand and we had to lie down holding on to the bunk for four days and nights while the gale remained undiminished. We were very seasick and in these four days we didn't taste as much as a drink of cold water, but then the wind dropped for two or three days and we could again be on deck. We were so much better that we could eat and drink a little but then the wind increased and we had a gale until we got close to land. The seasickness was not as bad as the first time but we were still sick. The unbearable swinging up and down lowers your spirit and empties you of all physical and mental energy.

On Sunday November 13 at three in the afternoon we anchored in Philadelphia where our baggage was inspected. But they were not so particular about it and no sooner had a chest been opened than they told us to lock it again. This went on until ten when we were taken to the train to be transported up through the country and we arrived in Madison Tuesday evening at four o'clock. This was as far as our tickets went so we had to leave the train and no one cared about us any longer and we had to take care of ourselves. I tried to talk to people but they didn't understand me, so I walked around and thought and deliberated until I finally met the well-known Anders Gjelde. Now I had someone to talk to and he helped me find a room for the night where he stayed himself. On Wednesday morning I went with him by train to a small town called Mount Horeb. This is where Christopher Brager lives (you were once his guardian, father) and Anders thought that Christopher could show us where brother Ole lived.

But when we came to Mount Horeb we met Andreas Kantum and he took us to brother Ole. And so we came here to Ole on Wednesday afternoon November 16 at three o'clock.

On Thursday I rented a team and got my baggage for which I paid half a dollar. Friday there was a large wedding at our next-door neighbor's and we had to attend. The bride was a daughter of Petter Brager. It was a large and wonderful wedding with no less than twenty-five teams attending and I rode with Petter Brager to and from the church. Pastor Fjeld officiated at the wedding and listening to him I had the impression that he must be a true servant of the Lord as I haven't heard anyone perform as well as he did and I don't believe that Pastor Fjeld had a more attentive listener than me because of the good reputation he enjoys in our fatherland. This was a day of joy for me as I for the first time had the pleasure of seeing and listening to John Fjeld and also had the honor of seeing the Springdale congregation with brother Ole as precentor. I believe that it was once far from your thoughts my dear parents that Ole should have the honor of having such a position but he has been called to be precentor by the Springdale congregation. It is not as in Norway where the great and high authorities appoint those who hold an office. Here it is the people themselves who elect their officials and every man, rich or poor, has a right to vote as soon as he is twenty-one years old, and whether he has a penny or not he is the equal of a millionaire and has the same rights. Last summer the congregation decided to dismiss their precentor because he had a tendency to drink too much whisky and they have called Ole to be his successor. They even want him to be their schoolteacher. He hasn't yet been willing, but I don't think he can avoid it as they are urging him so strongly that he will surely eventually accept this too. There are many that I know of around here who are better educated than Ole and who would like to be called (here in America they use the word "call" when they appoint someone). I could mention one from Sør Aurdal who has studied at the teacher's training school, Erik Eriksen Hagen, a nephew of Helge Hagen, but he was not considered. So you will realize that Ole is well liked and respected here and stands in a good light so the rumor that was circulated in Hedalen by gossips that he was quite mad in America was no more than a lie and an attempt to blacken his reputation. He is asked to be master of ceremonies at all funerals around here. Now I'll tell you a little about myself. I haven't worked much since I arrived. I took part in grubbing for four days at six shillings a day and I and Ole have agreed to build a stable for Halvor Bangsjordet and we have worked on this for two days. I think I'll work as a shoemaker this winter when the weather won't permit outdoor work.

I haven't visited our relatives yet as it is quite far to them from where we live after Ole moved. But Ole and Iver Børtnes have visited us so I've talked with them and also with brother Ole's brothers-in-law. Ole and Iver Børtnes have grown a lot since they were in Hedalen but I recognized them easily. Farewell for now and thank you for your most severe scolding as well as your most loving encouragement. Give my regards to Mikkel Sørli in Bertilrud and to Jorandby and to all who wish to hear from me, but first and last you my dear parents and brother are lovingly greeted by your distant son and brother.

MEKKEL ANDERSEN LIE

· —— ·

MAL's aunt Olea Olsdatter and her husband, Halsten Halstensen Børtnes, had emigrated earlier that summer and came to Springdale in late July. His brother Ole wrote a letter for Olea on 14 August 1881 (Nor. ed. IV:174) about their journey. Olea was the last of her generation from the farm Søre Li to emigrate and she and her husband needed assistance from other family members to do so. Olea was then fifty-seven and her husband, Halsten, was fifty-four. Now that MAL has joined Ole and Iver, their brother Anders Andersen Lie is the only remaining sibling at Søre Li. Olea's sons and her daughter Olaug Eriksen were also in Wisconsin. Olaug and her family are sometimes called Børtnes and sometimes Kantum, both for places where they had lived. MAL also wrote on 18 March 1882 (Nor. ed. IV:191) about visits to relatives, his life during the winter months, and advice to emigrants from Hedalen. His brother Ole had been appointed teacher in the parochial school and Iver was planning to go further west. Mikkel and Iver were both living with Ole. In a brief undated letter MAL writes that Halsten Børtnes had died after a long illness. The three brothers wrote similar letters about their emigration journey. MAL went on the S.S. *Domino* (of the Wilson Line of Hull) from Oslo to Hull and on the S.S. *Ohio* (of the American Line) from Liverpool to Philadelphia. A shilling (a bit) was 12 ½ cents. «II:121 »II:133 NE IV:182

· —— ·

From: Christine Dahl, *Norse, Texas, 3 January 1882*

To: Siri Kristiansdatter and Erik Pedersen Furuset
Romedal, Stange, Hedmark

✦═◉═✦

Dear brother and mother,

We've gratefully received your much longed for letter of October 10. We're glad to see that you are all in good health and doing well and in particular that our dear mother is still in such good health and so active. As for us, I can, praise God, report that we are now all doing well. We had a little accident before Christmas when Peder broke his leg. He was plowing and it so happened that as he was turning, the ground slanted and his plow turned over and broke his ankle and leg bone. But now, praise God, his leg is almost healed but still too tender for walking, but he is quite well and moves around on crutches. Otherwise all is well with us.

The seasons have not been of the best. We had too little rain last year, as often happens. A late frost ruined our wheat and it was too dry for the corn and cotton, so we only had half of a full harvest. The winter has been mild and pleasant and not cold enough to freeze ice more than three or four nights and the ice was quite thin. Our cattle and horses have managed very well without extra feeding but we nevertheless give fodder to most of them as we have such a large store because the winter has turned out so well. The wheat is beautiful now. Last fall we had an insect that ruined some of the earliest wheat and we had to plant again, but then the insect disappeared and the wheat grew fast and now looks very promising.

I must also tell you about another accident in our settlement. Eight days after Peder broke his leg Christoffer Tolerud fell down from the gallery of the building where they gin the cotton and where he was employed. He broke his leg about the same way that Peder did but he was so unlucky that he got a doctor who didn't know much about what he was doing. He didn't set the bones properly and the wound festered and another doctor had to cut off half his leg and he has had great pain. Of other news I can tell you that Johan Rogstad has married Per Hoff's youngest daughter. Martha Karlstad has married one of our neighbors from Western Norway called Colwick. She had been working for him for her ticket. He is well off. The emigrants you sent us arrived well and happy November 17. Thank you so much for all your trouble. The enclosed portrait is from Syverine and Jacob and is of their youngest child, a little girl named Christine. I send greetings from Jens Gillund who has returned in good shape. He has told us news from Norway. I also send greetings from auntie at Rogstad and her family. They are all well. Ole Brunstad's wife had twins last fall, a boy and a girl. They now have six children and are doing well. Ole Rossing sends his regards. He works for a baker who is married to Gine Brunstad and is doing quite well. As Christmas is over I wish you all a happy New Year. I must now end asking you to remember us to all our relatives and acquaintances that my sheet doesn't allow me to list and especially to Syverine and her little girls, and, finally my loving regards to you my dear mother and brother from me, my children and grandchildren. Your devoted sister and daughter

CHRISTINE DAHL

· —— ·

CD's Norwegian shows that her daily language now is English. Ove Torgersen Kjølvig emigrated from Jelsa in Rogaland in 1859. In Texas he and his family took the name Colwick. The baker in Waco was Peter H. Hansen. «II:122 »II:135 NE IV:185

· —— ·

1882 — LETTER 2:129

FROM: Even Nilsen Godager, *Moorhead, Minnesota, 29 January 1882*

TO: Even Martinusen Godager, *Hamar, Hedmark*

⤙═◯═⤚

Dear friend!

Thank you so much for the letter I received three days before Christmas. I got the photograph the next day and it was very nice and a good likeness. Give my thanks to all who are in it. Recently I had a letter from Uncle Osterhaus and all was well there. He had a family visiting and had placed them for the time being in a drawer. Uncle Paul arrived a few days before Christmas. He also wondered why Jens Gillund had left Norway in such a hurry.

I left *Red River-Posten* after the New Year because those damned Americans believed they could deal with Norwegians as they wished and placed us in a hallway and neglected to provide us with firewood etc. This is why Paulsen left before Christmas leaving me alone with the newspaper and I made three issues only helped by two boys in the evening. This was tough and I worked both late and early. I had promised to work for a Wesenberg who was moving his newspaper *Nordstjernen* from Grand Forks to Fargo but as he didn't come at the time he had said and gave me no reason for his delay I went to the other side of the Red River and took a share in the new newspaper *Red River Tidende*. Paulsen and I have arranged it so we only work evenings and can attend the Moorhead public school during the day. I don't know whether I did right or wrong in joining this enterprise but I've made certain that my loss won't be great if it doesn't succeed and if it does it may either give me a future or simply a little money. I can't promise that I'll remain a *"type"* forever and it may be that I'll one day become a farmer or something else remarkable. The *Posten* got an idiot, Møller, a son of Norway's gracious King Carl XV, as editor. With his lack of originality he is well qualified to translate their American newspaper and the Americans of course didn't realize that he had no idea of orthography. Brandt, who owned the newspaper when I came, is now editor of *Nordvesten* in St. Paul. It is very quiet here and rarely is there any kind of entertainment that I wish to take part in. When you write you should do something with Torkildsen and Halseth that we could use in the newspaper. We aren't as particular here as in Norway just as long as it is anything at all. You could write about how you have celebrated Christmas, about your plans for a summer on horseback, and about weddings and public and secret engagements etc. Vold who was with Paulsberg has married Agnete Paulsen, my colleague's sister, in Chicago. Yesterday I received a letter from home that had taken six weeks to get here, twice as long as yours. I'll have to conclude this. Give my regards to all acquaintances, in particular to Halseth, Torkildsen, Miss Kristensen, all at Norstad, and your father and siblings, and ask that brave and fearless agent to give my best to his employer and his wife and his shop assistant (my aunt). Kind regards from

EVEN N. GODAGER

ENG, a typesetter, is writing to his cousin who was a shop assistant in Ole Bredstue's store in Hamar. His father had several brothers, including Paul, and a sister Lina who was married to Ludvig Osterhaus. Three were in Texas. That his uncle placed his guests in a drawer is, of course, a faulty pronoun reference. Some Norwegian-American newspapers were solid enterprises, while others were ephemeral and journalists and typographers often had to move from one to another. Michal Wesenberg began his newspaper career as a typesetter for *Nordlyset* (the Northern Lights) in Northfield, Minn., in 1870 and was editor and publisher of several publications until 1887, when he began *Duluth Skandinav,* which he edited and published until 1932. In 1872–1873 he edited the short-lived *Minnesota,* and in 1878 he began the first Norwegian-language newspaper in North Dakota, *Red River Posten*, which he soon sold to the English-language *Fargo Argus.* He then began a new newspaper in Wisconsin, *Nordstjernen* (the North Star), which he brought with him to Grand Forks, N. Dak., a few months later. In 1881 the newspaper was again moved to Fargo, where it was sold in connection with an election campaign in 1882. This may be the unidentified *Red River Tidende* referred to in the letter. Møller has not been identified either. Kristian Brandt was the editor and publisher of several Norwegian-American newspapers. He came to Fargo as editor of *Red River Posten.* He bought it in 1880 and then sold it back to *Fargo Argus* the following year. Brandt bought it again in 1884 and merged it with his new newspaper, *Nordvesten* (the Northwest) in St. Paul. One reason for the brief appearances of some emigrant newspapers was that political parties found them useful for campaign purposes. As the letter suggests, it could be the Anglo-American owners and not the Norwegian-American editorial staff that controlled such newspapers. The most complete account of Norwegian-language newspapers in the United States is Odd Lovoll 2010. NE IV:186

1882 — LETTER 2:130

FROM: John Olsen Leerfald, *Fergus Falls, Minnesota, 27 February 1882*

TO: Karl Ludvig Olsen Lerfald, *Verdal, Nord-Trøndelag*

⋆⟾⟾⟵⋆

Dear brother!

It's very long since I heard from you so I'll send you a few words hoping to receive some in return. Please don't forget to write. I can tell you that I'm doing well and I hope to hear the same from you. I've been a butcher for two and a half years and I've done quite well since I began. I've made about 850 dollars. I've built a nice house on the lot that I bought. It cost me 800 dollars. As you know, I paid 250 dollars for the lot and it is now worth 810 dollars. I must also tell you that I have a little daughter and I've called her Alma Mathilde. She is about half a year old.

If you still have the tobacco tin that I forgot when I left you, please send it to me as it is the only reminder I have of my deceased father. He gave it to me when I left and I would like to have it in memory of him. It is not worth much for anyone except me. Ole Molden is in Dakota and has taken land there. As far as I know Hans Petter and his family are doing well. Theodore sends his regards and says he is doing well. Farewell. Write soon to your brother

JOHN O. LEERFALD

· ⸻ ·

Hans Petter Lerfald was a brother and Theodore was also a Lerfald.
«II:218 »II:138 NE IV:187

· ⸻ ·

1882 — LETTER 2:131

FROM: John Torkelsen Rannestad, *Madison, Minnesota, 4 April 1882*

TO: Osmund Ovedal, *Sirdal, Vest-Agder*

⊷⇛◉⇚⊷

Dear brother Osmund,

We have your letter of October 15, 1880 and see that you are doing well. We can, praise God, say the same. We've had many trials but the good God who governs all for our best has not forgotten us, even though God's ways may appear strange to us. First I must tell you how we were the winter before last. On October 15 and 16 in 1880 we had a terrible snowstorm that you may have heard about. I went to town with a wagonload of wheat on the fourteenth and got there that evening. I had sixteen miles to go home but I had only gone three when I had to stop at a house because I was so wet that I couldn't stand it any longer. It had become dark and there were few houses further on so I stayed there for the night. On the morning of the fifteenth the snowstorm was so powerful that we could hardly see anything. We were three men there in addition to the man of the house and it was difficult for us to get to the stable to see to our animals. When we got there my oxen stood in snow to their knees so I had to cut into their stall to get them out. We had to work hard all four for the animals to survive. I stayed there until Sunday morning when I started on my way home. But I didn't get far before I had to beg to get under a roof with my oxen because they were unable to go any further in the deep snow that was so hard that I had to break it up with my feet. When I came home on Monday, the fourth day after I'd left, it hadn't been any better for them and my own stable was full of snow. Luckily two women were visiting, Berte Guddal and Anne Lindeland. They went to neighbors and got them to help get the animals out on the second day. On the first day they couldn't go out themselves because of the storm. They had to take the life of our biggest cow because she was on her back covered by about five feet of snow and was barely alive. The others were taken to the neighbors and when I came home there was no one there, neither people nor animals, and it all looked very strange. The next day I got people to help me get the snow out from around my house and stable so both people and animals could come home. Then everything was all right except for the cow I lost. I was able to sell some meat for sixteen dollars and kept the rest for myself so the damage wasn't as great as it seemed at first. I was unlucky again last fall when my son Albert cut off his forefinger and hurt one of the others so we had to go to the doctor and this cost eight dollars. He is fine now and can work as before.

We must tell you that we have another son. His name is Steffen Gabriel. He was born November 7, 1881 and is doing well. The others are also healthy. I must also tell you about my land. When I came here four years ago I took 160 acres, but after I had come home from the land office I met a man who had already taken some of my land, but hadn't fulfilled the legal requirements. I had seven witnesses but nevertheless gave the case to a Norwegian lawyer who promised that the land would be mine and I paid him forty dollars to take care of my case in court. But he delayed it so long that I assumed it was too late. Last fall he came and said we should go to court but I preferred to lose what I had already lost, the eighty acres and the forty dollars I had given him, rather than continue to quarrel. So now I have eighty acres and this is what you must accept when you don't know better than to be fooled by lawyers, even though I looked as carefully into it as I could and asked about him before I let him have my case. So things haven't gone so well but I hope my situation will improve when I've settled down. We recently had a letter from our sister Siri. They are all doing well and send their regards. I have no further news except that we are doing well. Our uncle Haavar died last fall on September 3, as you may have heard. We've had excellent weather this winter, not so cold and with little snow so we could drive our wagon everywhere. I must end my simple letter with loving regards to you and yours and to our relatives and friends in our old and dear fatherland that we will never forget as long as we live in America. Farewell,

JOHN TORKELSEN RANNESTAD

· —— ·

JTR's wife, Rakel Tonette, wrote to her brother on 29 March 1880 (Nor. ed. IV:137) about the birth of their son Oscar Berent Severin. The letter Osmund Ovedal wrote in October 1880 was probably in response to his sister's letter. «II:91 »II:140 NE IV:193

· —— ·

FROM: Martha Erickson, *Grove City, Minnesota, 5 July 1882*
To: Elsa Haavardsdatter Lote, *Ullensvang, Hordaland*

⊷⟹⟺⊶

Dear unforgettable sister in Christ,

May the grace and peace of Jesus Christ be with you. I'm sitting here in my loneliness thinking of the long distance between us and I would so love to be able to talk with you. As this is impossible I'll have to take up my pen. First of all, thank you so much for your welcome letter that we received May 4. It's such a great pleasure to hear from you there at home. I see that many of my acquaintances have left this vale of tears. So I must let you know about my situation; my dear husband has moved to his home in the eternal mansions where there is no illness or grief, no death or need and where there will be no more separation. Dear sister, you know that separation is difficult and leads to grief, but God be praised for his grace and mercy. I believe with the grace of God that he fought the good fight, as it was his daily longing in prayer to go home to his dear Savior. On Sunday March 19 he began to get weaker and he continued to weaken until the morning of Sunday March 26 when he died quietly with faith in his Savior at half past eight. Yes, blessed be his memory. I can truly say that he was among the meek in the land. He was a loving and hard-working husband who cared for his family and told us that we must hold to God and his word. May the Lord give us grace and strength, as he surely will, as he has promised to be the support of widows and the father of the fatherless. He was buried on the last day of March and twenty-four teams followed him to his last place of rest. There were four to five people on each wagon and our Pastor Kleven held a funeral sermon in our home. When we came to the church the coffin was brought in and he gave a sermon there as well. Dear sister, you know how weak we are in our grief, so we must cast our sorrow on the Lord.

I'll tell you something about our daily life. We had a hired hand last winter until the end of May and now we are alone. But we must hire two or three men during harvest. Last spring I sold cattle for seventy-two dollars and I'll have to sell some horses in the fall as we have six. The weather has been rather rainy and cold this spring. We had snow on May 20. Some hundred miles to the west they had two feet of snow. The fields look miserable.

I send greetings from Nils and Haaver. They are in good health. Haaver had a daughter on February 26 and her name is Mattilda Emilie. He sends his regards to all acquaintances and in particular to Lars J. Midtun asking him to write soon. Loving regards to family and friends. I see in your letter that Margrete is poorly; may the Lord strengthen her faith and her patience so she may take up her cross and follow Jesus. Regards from your loving sister,

MARTA ERICKSON

. —— .

Nils Haavardsen Lothe is ME's brother and Haavard (or Haaver) Mickalson is her son, born in Norway before her emigration and marriage. The letter was dictated. «II:59 »II:172 NE IV:194

. —— .

1882 — LETTER 2:133

FROM: Mikkel Andersen Lee, *Springdale, Wisconsin, 23 July 1882*

To: Anders Olsen, Kari Mikkelsdatter, and Anders Andersen Lie
Hedalen, Sør-Aurdal, Oppland

Dear parents and brother,

I received your letter two weeks ago. Thank you so much. All news from my dear home is so welcome. Your letter had a request from a person unknown to me about the ticket that Gulbrand Ingemoen has offered to pay for a good and trustworthy worker. I've shown him your letter but as the person is unknown to him he won't do anything unless I guarantee for the money. I would like to do this if you could assure me of his honesty, and as he is married I would also like to see her agreement, because if she doesn't wish to come to America I would be taking responsibility for an unpleasant situation. But if they both agree and if there isn't any other possibility for them there, then I would be happy to do what I can for them. As he has some experience as a carpenter there is work for him here and carpenters are usually better paid than other workers. It's too late to have much of an income this year as the harvest has already started but if he's ready to go any time it's not a bad idea to come in the fall. Even though wages are not so high, there will be more time to become acquainted with American conditions before beginning with hard work. So you must think about it and if you can send me the necessary security I'll do what I can. Let me know his name and his age.

I'm in good health as are our relatives. I've worked steadily and made almost 100 dollars since coming here. Brother Iver went to Minnesota last spring to look for land. We've had a letter from him but he hadn't found land he liked. Halsten Halstensen Kantum passed away on June 23 and was buried on the twenty-fourth. He didn't have an honorable funeral; four teams and four men followed him to his last resting place and not a word was sung at his coffin. We were away at work at the time so we didn't get to know about it until after he was buried. I would like to have some Norwegian cabbage seeds that you could put in a letter and Gulbrand Ingemoen's wife asks if she can get some Norwegian butterwort sent with an emigrant. I don't have many animals, only one cow, two pigs and ten chickens. I've planted potatoes on the farm where we live and think I'll get so much that we won't have to buy any.

I hear that Halsten Lie and Marit Haugen have married and I would like to congratulate them. As I cannot remember anything else I must conclude for now wishing you all luck in your future progress. As I sat here writing we received a letter from brother Iver. He has met Torkel Fossholt and many others from Hedalen. He has bought land, so Iver visited him in his new home and he is doing very well. Ole Møller, Ole and Erik Kjensrud, Ole and Gulbrand and old Østen Busemoen and his old wife Taran died on their journey. He also mentioned Peder Goplerud, Kristofer Klemmetsrud, Asle, the American Ole Brenden, and old Østen Skinningsrud. But I think he has written to you and given you more information. Our little daughter Kari is growing and developing well. She is already such a talker that she says Pa Pa Pa Papa and she pulls my beard so much that I think I'll have to shave it off if I don't want it all messed up. She says to tell her grandmother that she is very good and that she'll send her portrait in the fall. Our portrait is enclosed. When Iver went to the West last spring I, Ole and Siri went with him to Madison so we could be photographed together. Give my regards to the Klemmetsrud boys and all my friends, in particular to Gulbrand Øverby. He is often in my thoughts as I remember how we played so innocently together. You are always in my thoughts along with my memories of my dear home. We must leave all in the hands of God. My love to Sørlie, Bertelsrud and Jørandby and first and last to you my parents and brother.

M. LIE AND FAMILY

· —— ·

> The letter has 13 August 1882 as the date for Iver's departure for the West, but since it also has him leaving in the spring this must be an error. The butterwort (*tette gress*) was used to make milk thicken as it soured. Torkel Jonsen Fosholt was from Hedalen and his wife was from Elsrud in Aadalen. Their family plays a role in two series of letters, to Søre Li and to Elsrud. In 1865 Østen and Taran Busemoen were fifty-seven and fifty. Siri was married to Ole. MAL also wrote on 12 February 1883 (Nor. ed. IV:216). He has had a letter from his brother Iver in North Dakota telling that he has acquired four forties (160 acres) and writes a little about his brother Ole's work as a teacher. «II:127 »II:148 NE IV:196

· —— ·

1882 — LETTER 2:134

FROM: Iver Ellingsen Elsrud, *Grafton, North Dakota, 13 August 1882*

To: Edvard Ellingsen Elsrud, *Aadalen, Ringerike, Buskerud*

Dear brother,

I received your letter a long time ago and was glad to see that you're in good health and enjoying yourself at weddings and with other fun. I'm also in good health and doing well but as for entertainment I'm doing very poorly, but I have no complaints. As long as you can make money, that is what counts. The reason I haven't written is that I haven't had any news and you may perhaps think that I don't have any now either but there you are very wrong. No, the news I now have is so great and so long that it may stretch all the way to Norway. I've sold my farm here in Dakota for 2,200 dollars cash. I don't have the money yet but the deed has been written and I've received 250 dollars to confirm the deal. I am to have the crop of twenty-two acres of wheat and twenty of oats and it looks so promising that I think I'll have 600 bushels of wheat and 1,000 bushels of oats. In return I'll have to plow it all this fall. I was in debt for 250 dollars on the land so I'll have 1,950—nineteen hundred and fifty—dollars and if the prices stay as they are I hope to have 1,000 dollars for my crop. You may think that I'm a speculator but remember that I also have four good horses to sell and they may bring me a similar sum. You may now wonder what I plan to do, and this is a question that I've asked myself and not yet been able to answer. But I think I'll go further west. Two weeks ago two of my neighbors went to Norway. They are from Bjoneskogen and will be visiting you. Receive them as my friends and they'll tell you what it's like here in my bachelor's cabin as they lived here before they went. Tell them about the sale of my land. I must conclude with regards to all my friends but first of all to you at Elsrud, Blakkstveit, and Viker from your brother and son,

IVER E. ELSRUD

. —— .

A letter IEE wrote to his brother Torgrim on 15 July 1882 says nothing about plans to sell his land. On the contrary, he writes optimistically about his prospects, both for his own harvest and his income from his new reaper and binder. In a letter to his three brothers in Aadalen written 8 October 1882 he tells that nothing came of his sale of land as the would-be buyer was unable to raise the money (Nor. ed. IV:204). His letters speak only of relations with other immigrants from Norway and it may be that IEE did not master English. In this letter his rendering of the English "bachelor's cabin" is *Beth Storse Cabyn*, words neither Norwegian nor American readers would have understood. «II:120 »II:174 NE IV:197

. —— .

FROM: Peder Olsen Dilrud, *Norway Hill, Texas, 18 August 1882*

TO: Erik Pedersen Furuset, *Romedal, Stange, Hedmark*

❖⟶◐⟵❖

My good Erik!

I'm very grateful for your readiness to help me and I have all reason to be satisfied with the farm laborers and servants you've sent to me. The last one, Anne Sandbakken, has been with me for some time and to my full satisfaction. I must again ask you to do me a service by giving the enclosed ticket to August Andersen and making sure that he makes use of it as soon as possible. I've spoken with his father Anders Nilsen who is with Peder Thingstad and he has already told him to be ready to go. He'll pay for his ticket by working for me for a year. There has been talk of Anders Nilsen's wife and youngest child coming with his son, but as he cannot send tickets I assume this will come to nothing. Anders is sending her a letter today asking her to try to get travel money for herself. So if you could pay for the child's ticket this would be a great service as I've said that if the woman could scrape together a sufficient sum for her own ticket, I would pay for the little one. But as nothing is decided I don't want to buy a ticket that may not be used. A short while ago I employed a man named Johan Jensen and on his promise to stay with me through the fall I gave him a note to you for ten dollars that he sent to his wife in Romedal. If you haven't already given her the money you should keep it as he hasn't fulfilled his contract with me. But it's quite all right if you've already given it to her. Please write to me about these matters as well as news from my old part of the country.

This year's harvest hasn't been so good as rye and wheat have done poorly, but the cotton remains to be harvested and if it turns out as nicely as it now looks I'll have the best crop I have ever had. Ever since I came here rain has been scarce but this summer there has been no lack of rain. Indeed, at times we've almost felt we had too much. All in my family are in good health and my wife is better than she has been for a long time. All the Dahls are well and send their regards. Marte Bryni came back from Norway two weeks ago and is now at Dahl. Friendly regards from us all,

P. DILLERUD

If August Andersen comes to Clifton, the closest depot, at a time when I'm not there, he should ask for Ole Dahl who lives close by. At the depot there will be many Norwegians who can take him there.

. —— .

POD was married to Erik Furuset's sister Karen. Other letters from POD to his brother-in-law are Nor. ed. IV:124 and 151. «II:128 »II:166 NE IV:198

. —— .

1882 — LETTER 2:136

FROM: Jacob Hanson Hilton, *Socorro, New Mexico, 3 September 1882*

To: Hans Jakobsen and Anne Olsdatter Hilton
Kløfta, Ullensaker, Akershus

Dear parents,

I'm home now and have already begun to work, but it's a little difficult now that my fingers are unused to it. All is well here. Business has been bad since I left in May. But Frithjof says that our sales have paid our expenses and brought in 1,200 dollars since I left, and this isn't bad in hard times. But we're used to making more. When I was home, I said that I wished the times would get worse so many of the other businesses would fail, and this is what has happened. Many have failed while I was gone. They sold on credit and this doesn't work here. We are on good ground since we only buy and sell for cash. Our prospects are good so I think we'll do a good business this fall and winter since the hard times during summer cleaned out quite a few <u>quick</u> businesses. Ole Halvorsen went to Chicago as soon as I came home. Professor Asplund (the Swede) had been fairly reasonable until the night I came home but then the Lysholm aquavit that I brought almost drove him mad. Today is his fourth day in <u>Paradise</u>. It'll take him at least a week to get through this. I came to Socorro August 30.

I left Liverpool on the tenth and came to Chicago on the twenty-fourth, to Kansas City the twenty-eighth where I stopped for a day, and then to Socorro on the thirtieth. I've been well all the time, not even seasick. Amundsen and the Tveter people did much better than I had expected; they threw up a little to begin with but after that they were well all the time. I had a letter from Olava yesterday. She says that the journey from Chicago to Denver had gone very well and that she had found Mrs. Hanson in Denver and was doing well there. I haven't heard from Amundsen yet. I left them all in Chicago. I didn't have much time in Norway; it all now seems like a dream. I can hardly believe that I've been there. Frederick Asche sends his regards from Chicago. (Oluf Frithjof Asche has changed his name to Frederick.) I stayed with him for three days on my way home and he sends special thanks to mother for the stockings. I'm sending the stockings and the box for C. Jacobson today.

In Canada the harvest wasn't more advanced than in Norway but the further into the country I came, the further they had come with the harvest. In Illinois, Missouri and Kansas they had harvested the wheat and were threshing and hauling it to town. But as I came further west, it began to look more like the situation in Canada; they were still cutting and hadn't begun threshing. They've only hanged two scoundrels here since I left, the last one was the week before I arrived. Soon we'll only have good people here. We haven't had rainstorms here this summer so the trains have run regularly. Mrs. Christiansen at Kløfta bragged so much of the wonderful Norwegian air and climate but I've yet to live in a nicer and better climate than here in Socorro. The climate in Norway and England can't compare with our New Mexican climate. Give my regards to all acquaintances and, in conclusion, my parents and siblings are lovingly greeted from your

JACOB HILTON

· ——— ·

JHH's decision to visit his old home seems to have been quite sudden. He sent a postcard from Liverpool on his way back on 9 August 1882 and said he would go second class to Quebec. A letter to his brother written 5 March 1882 (Nor. ed. IV:189) has no mention of a planned visit, only of the reasons why he can't leave his business. He wrote about Christmas in Socorro: "I can't say that Christmas was all that nice here; it was hardly noticed except that a man was shot dead and a policeman had his arm shot off. That was all the fun we had on Christmas Eve. Since then it has been quiet until the day before yesterday when the police took a robber and placed him in jail and last night they took him out and hanged him up in a tree; he was only seventeen. Hanging and shooting are so common here that we don't pay much attention." He also mentioned hiring a Swede named Asplund. «II:126 »II:144 NE IV:200

. —— .

1882 — LETTER 2:137

FROM: Christopher Jacobson, *Belleville, Nevada, 19 September 1882*

TO: Hans Jakobsen Hilton, *Kløfta, Ullensaker, Akershus*

-→=◦⊂=-←-

Dear, dear brother!

I received your letter of June 23 on August 2 and I'm glad to hear that you and yours are in good health and doing well. It's easy for me to *forgive* your long silence. You are surrounded by a large family and even though you sometimes think of those who are away it's only natural that your immediate concerns must have first place in your heart. A year runs by so swiftly. Had I been in your situation I'd probably have been even more negligent, but here I am entirely alone in the Nevada Mountains and my greatest pleasure is to hear from family and friends and write back to them. I correspond with many of my friends here on the Coast but nothing is like a letter from you as it reminds me of my childhood days. After reading a letter from you I usually take a walk around in Ullensaker, but the old paths and roads are not as easy to find now as they were in the past. For every year they seem to become dimmer and in some places they have quite disappeared. I now see Norway only through a cloud.

I'm quite sure, brother, that you've brought up your children in the best way possible and that they are honest workers. I think you worry too much about them, but then we all have our different views. It's easier to see the faults of others than our own. When we look back on our lives, we all think: Could I only start all over again, then I'd do it differently. But if we could have started all over again ten times, we would find as many missteps the tenth time as in the first. When you and Anne started out on your life together you first worked as hard as you could to accumulate as large a fortune as possible in order to build a Babylon where you and yours could live forever. As your flock of children grew you worked all the harder to increase your property for the new generation. I'm not surprised that you are worn out. Now you've brought up your children and there is enough work for them and, as you say, you don't any longer take part in the heaviest work. But let me say that I think you still carry the heaviest burden. Your concern for the future of your children weighs as heavily upon you now as it did when they were little. You are the foundation of your Babylon and its entire weight rests on your old shoulders and when the foundation crumbles and eventually falls, there will be disorder in Hans Jakobsen's Babylon and each and all will have to take up his own burden and we may then ask: Why couldn't they have done this before? I think it will be harder for them to let go of mother's apron strings when they are thirty than it would have been when they were fifteen. But I shouldn't say more about this. I don't have any children and cannot speak sensibly about it. But I will say this: Cast off as much as possible of your concern for the future of your children. You have fulfilled your responsibilities. They are big and strong. They'll make their way through this world as have our forefathers. They'll have failure and success, sadness and joy. When their time comes they'll each have a flock of children and will be as eager as you've been to build a Babylon. I wish they could build it in a land where they can have more space, yes, where with the love of work they have learned from you they could expand their frontiers, where their children and children's children could all be neighbors if they wished. I am referring, brother, to the great, free and wonderful "America." Too bad that we were born in Norway, brother, and even worse that we were born with such a love for our fatherland that being away from Norway disturbs our peace. Yes, Hans, it may be better for your sons to live and die at Hilton, even though in poverty, than to come to America with the viper of homesickness at their bosom.

I hoped that Jacob would return with a wife. If so he'd surely be happy here. But as he didn't I suppose he'll always have an eye on Hilton. You speak of returning, but what in the world should we do in Norway? I cannot see any way of making a living there except by having enough money to live off the interest—and if I had that much I could live without worries anywhere. Don't believe I look down on Norway. Not at all; I still love it. But neither the climate nor people's attitude would suit me and I would be a stranger in a strange land. A summer visit might be nice, but I'm reluctant to set out on so long a journey. I don't think much about the future but I suppose that when I've saved about 3,000 dollars I'll go up to Washington Territory or Oregon where there's still some government land left as well as some cheap railroad land. I could also, if I looked around, buy a partly worked up farm for about a thousand dollars and if I had a couple of thousand for horses, cattle, implements etc, then I think I'd have a good living even though I don't know much about farming. But in order to do all this I'd also have to get married and as I'm soon forty-eight I'd have to do so in a hurry. But be this as it may, I don't plan to sit here like a hermit for all of my days—if I have many days—because I do wish to come out among people at some time.

The San Francisco savings banks give little interest now, only four percent and this gives you a mere forty dollars a year for each thousand. You would have to be very careful to live on the interest of twenty thousand dollars in San Francisco and it is said to be almost the cheapest place to live in the world. So I'd have to have 20,000 dollars if I were to settle in Norway because the interest is probably no higher and the cost of living no lower. Moreover, I won't likely ever get my hands on 20,000 dollars again—at least not in this place. I suppose you're asking why I'm not rich when America is so full of money. There are millions in America poorer than I even though there seem to be riches enough for us all here. Right now I feel very rich as I'm in excellent health and have good wages and light work and I think I'll have the patience to stay here long enough to have three to four thousand dollars.

I can't explain our politics for you, at least not in Norwegian. I'll just say that there are hardly any who complain about high taxes. Only the newspapers and those who are seeking office fuss about politics. Common people don't complain. If you believe that Guiteau had any help when he killed Garfield, you are wrong. Sure, there was some disagreement between Garfield and other representatives of the Republican Party but Garfield's political enemies had nothing to do with the murder whatever the Democratic Party may say. The murderer was at more liberty during the trial than most murderers are allowed, but this was in order to convince people that he wasn't mad, as both he and his lawyer wanted us to believe. He was eventually hanged on July 30 and people all over the country are satisfied with this.

I suppose you know about what happens among your own neighbors. England uses bitter words about our laws and our government. But the English <u>Lion</u> doesn't dare set its paws on our soil again. She tried during our Civil War but retreated roaring with her tail between her legs. She may still believe that she has the best government in the world but I wouldn't change our administration for hers. What do you think about the murder in Phoenix Park in Dublin last spring? What do you think about Parnell and O'Connor who are members of the British Parliament but who come to America to get the Irish here to give money for the liberation of Ireland? And finally, do you think England is waging a just war in Egypt?

There is so little about Norway in our papers that I hardly know anything about your politics. It is only reported when the monkey—who you call King—comes to Christiania to open parliament and that he has a salary of 80,000 dollars a year that you poor Norwegians (only one and a half million) have to pay him and that he begs for more when his wife has a child. I think we now have about fifty-two million inhabitants and we pay our president 50,000 a year, and even so we sometimes complain and speak harsh words about our government. But when foreigners cast a *slur* on our free institutions we put up our back like cats and stand as one against foreign enemies. Well, I've said enough about this and I'm sure you won't be offended. I haven't been to the post office since the first of this month so I haven't heard from Jacob yet. But if he left Norway when he said he would, he should have been in Socorro for some time now.

You have one daughter more than I thought. I hadn't heard of Karin before. I wish she was here to cook for me. I see that Nicolaus Frogner is almost in his grave and I didn't realize that he was that old. It may seem difficult for a man who has so much of the world's glory to die, but both poor and rich have to accept reality. Give my regards to him and Netta when you see them. Are his sisters Kari and Maria still living? I had a letter from Gulbrand Haga about a month ago. They are doing well. They have a lot of work so they eat and drink well. Give my regards to Søli as well as to Lars when you see them. This won't be an interesting letter but as you've promised to write more often I'll try to write a better one next time. I hope this will find you and yours in good health. Best regards from

C. JACOBSON

When I came here to the P.O. I got a letter from Jacob as well as some gifts from you. I'll send you a letter the next time I come to town. That will be October 2.

· ——— ·

That CJ is unused to Norwegian is not only evident in constructions like *feil-steps* for "mis-steps" where the Norwegian word is *feiltrinn*, but also in spellings like *skjuldere* for "shoulders" where the Norwegian is *skuldre* and *krumbler* for "crumbles" where the Norwegian is *smuldrer.* He translates the idiom "apron strings" as *Faarklæd-Bonde* and this is not only a misspelling but is not a Norwegian idiom. CJ's nephew Jacob Hilton had been visiting Norway. President James Garfield was shot by Charles J. Guiteau in 1881. In 1876 Charles Stuart Parnell and John O'Connor Powers were on an official visit in the United States where they met the President, and Powers presented an address to the House of Representatives. They also met with nationalist supporters in America. There was a strong British presence in Egypt after they had helped the Ottoman Empire to battle Napoleon there. After a nationalistic uprising, the British bombarded Alexandria and occupied Cairo in 1882. CJ wrote as promised on 2 October 1882. «II:112 »II:149 NE IV:201

. ——— .

1882 — LETTER 2:138

FROM: John Olsen Leerfald, *Fergus Falls, Minnesota, 3 October 1882*

To: Karl Ludvig Olsen Lerfald, *Verdalen, Nord-Trøndelag*

❖⇒◉⇐❖

Dear brother!

Some time ago you wrote that you were waiting for a letter from me. I've been very negligent in my writing recently but I did write after you sent me the tin, but you may not have received it. So let me again tell you that I've received your letter and must thank you for what was enclosed. It made me glad to see my only remembrance from my father and it is very dear to me. I was in Minneapolis a month ago and send greetings from Hans Petter and his family. They are doing well. They have recently had a letter from Elen and she was also doing well. Several from Verdal have come here this summer. Among them are Olaus Vinne, Ole Lunden, Ellev Bye, a brother of Olaus Vinne, and some others and they all like it here and cannot imagine returning to Old Norway. I didn't do much last summer. We rented our shop last spring for forty dollars a month so I've had an easy time of it this summer but I'll soon have to begin again and then I'll be busy. You know that I bought a lot here for 250 dollars and now lots in this block are sold for 3,500 dollars so they have grown quite a bit in value in two years. I've been thinking of building a store on my lot next spring—at least if I can raise the money. We're doing well and I wish to hear the same from you. I'm enclosing a portrait of my little daughter Anne Mathilde. She is now learning to walk. She was one year old on the twentieth of last month. I must conclude with loving regards to you and your family from your brother,

JOHN O. LEERFALD

· ———— ·

Hans Petter and Elen were siblings. «II:130 NE IV:202

· ———— ·

1882 — LETTER 2:139

FROM: Elise Wærenskjold, *Prairieville, Texas, 10 November 1882*

TO: Thomine Dannevig, *Lillesand, Aust-Agder*

My dear and good Thomine!

Thank you so much for your very welcome letter that I received some time ago. It was especially interesting to read news about old friends and acquaintances, and I was particularly glad that you and yours are doing so well. But I don't quite like the idea of my dear Thorvald wanting to remain a bachelor. However successful Thorvald may be in other respects I'm sure that Niels is far more comfortable. I was very saddened by what you wrote about Mrs. Hammer who has been such a kindhearted and sensible woman, and I almost felt glad when I saw in the newspapers that she is dead. Poor Gusta and Bina! Their lot is not so light either. For me a failing vision would be among the worst things that I could experience. But why have things gone so badly for Bina who once was so well off. There is one of our old friends that you did not mention: Christine Normann. Do you know anything about her?

Last summer I again visited my dear Otto and some old friends in Bosque County. I went on the railroad both ways since the fare has been reduced to three cents a mile and the entire journey only cost slightly more than nine dollars. Otto and his wife have had a sweet little girl since I saw them here the summer before and they had built a house on a healthful site with a beautiful view. They farm sheep and sheep did well last winter. The first two winters he lived in Hamilton County sheep didn't do well, but now everything looked good and Otto wanted me to move to him. I decided to move next summer but this doesn't seem to be God's will. As soon as I'd left them their little child got ill and was close to death and then a disease spread among the sheep and Otto got afraid and decided to sell his sheep and, presumably, his land and house and move to the town of Hamilton and set up a small store. So I can no longer think of moving, as Otto will not be able to tend my sheep and cattle, which I now depend on for my living. Otto thinks I'm getting too old to go out every morning and evening to feed my animals. Moreover, my relations with Niels's wife are not at all good. But as long as I remain healthy I suppose I'll manage and there is little use in worrying about tomorrow.

I hope God will provide what is for our best. Doctors and lawyers ruin us here. The former rarely get anything from me but they get all the more from my children. The lawyers, however, have made me poor. Another difficulty for the farmers is that we cannot get help except by paying such outrageous wages that a profit is out of the question. So one may either rent out the farm or leave it unused. For most renters you not only have to provide a house but draft animals, tools and food for them as well as their animals and, for some, even clothes. If the renters are not hardworking and honest they'll often be in debt to the owner when they leave. Very often, when the time comes to pick the cotton, the renter realizes that he is so deeply in debt that the entire crop would be needed to pay it. So, if he is dishonest, he'll leave and pick cotton for another farmer where he's not in debt. This happened to Niels last year and then again this year. One left last year with a debt of seventy-five dollars and this year one family left owing him sixty dollars and another with an even larger debt. My son has a lot of unpicked cotton, about six bales I think, and four bales have been picked. This year has been good for all farm products—if you can only get your cotton picked. But the price for cotton is very low and the pickers make the best money as they are paid one dollar for one hundred pounds and a good picker can pick 200 pounds a day. That would provide a good income for many of your poor in Norway since also children can do this. Had I known last spring that the prices for cattle would go up so much it would have been much better for both your brother and me if I had waited until fall before I sold them as I then could have been paid twice as much for them. I sold yearlings for seven and a half dollars and now I could have had sixteen and twenty-seven for a cow and calf. I hope these prices will hold. We've had an extremely pleasant fall with summer temperatures but the trees have nevertheless dressed themselves in the many colors of fall, something I have always found so beautiful.

In Bosque County there are now about 2,000 Norwegians and many families there send money or tickets to people in Norway and thus pay for their journey. In return the immigrant must work a year for the person who has paid for him or her. Do you know of an honest male or female person who would come here on these conditions and be honest enough to fulfill their contract? I have nothing new to tell you about your acquaintances here. Ouline made a long visit to Bosque last summer and apparently had a pleasant journey. Give my regards to your sons as well as to your brother Samuel and other friends and acquaintances that you may see. If you are in Lillesand when you receive this you must be so kind as to give my regards to Kaja and Gusta. It happens that I dream that I'm in Lillesand but in real life I will never come there again. Farewell and write soon to your forever faithful

ELISE WÆRENSKJOLD

. ——— .

Fragments of this letter (and some interesting information) are in Clausen 1961 (116–117). After so many years with English as her main language of communication there are occasional anglicisms in EW's Norwegian, as for instance *pikker* for both "pick" and "picker." Although Thomine Dannevig's home was in Lillesand she spent much time with her son Niels in Tønsberg. The friends in Lillesand are Kaja Poppe and Gusta Hauge. Thomine's maiden name was Hansen, so her brother was presumably Samuel Hansen (and in some letters EW refers to a Hansen). «II:102 »II:146 NE IV:202

. ——— .

1883 — LETTER 2:140

FROM: Siri Allikson, *Colfax, Wisconsin, 3 January 1883*
TO: Osmund Ovedal, *Sirdal, Vest-Agder*

⚬⚬⚬

Dear brother Osmund,

I'm sending you a few words to let you know how we are. Sara and I live with Reinert where we are quite comfortable and do as we wish. My chest is too weak for hard work. Sara isn't as strong as she used to be either but she's always working. Reinert has let his land on shares to two neighbors, a Norwegian and an American, but he has his houses and does his own haying. He's sold his work horses and now has a foal, two cows, three calves, seven sheep, two pigs, and twenty-four hens. We had an average harvest. This winter has been very nice. Sara and I went to church on New Years Day and then to our brother Sigbjørn. They are doing well. Rakel was very ill two years ago and it seemed she might die, but she's now quite well and she and Ingeborg Helene do most of the chores. The two oldest girls, Sofie and Berte, have been working in Milwaukee for some time. They make three dollars a week but I think they'll be home soon. It's long since we had a letter from our sister Rakel. They're doing well and their children are in good health. Theodor herded the cattle last summer. Berte Tonette works alone on her farm. Uncle Haaver died more than a year ago as I suppose you have heard. Now Sigbjørn and his mother are alone and always have help. Omund Pedersen Tonstad lives about a mile from us. His two daughters were married last summer, Pauline with Bernt Berentsen Flika and Bergitte with Bernt Vermundsen Jødestøl. We hear that you've married. If this is true I wish you happiness in this life as in the next one. May we all wander so we may meet again with our Father in heaven where there will be no separation. Write and let us know how you and your neighbors are. Loving regards to all our acquaintances but first and foremost to our unforgettable brother Osmund. May the Lord bless you.

SIRI ATLAGSEN OVEDAHL

. ——— .

Osmund Ovedal had recently married Berte Tonette Larsdatter. Rakel
Tonette and Jon Torkelsen Rannestad wrote 1 April 1884 (Nor. ed.
IV:236). «II:131 »II:197 NE IV:210

. ——— .

1883 — LETTER 2:141

FROM: Hans H. Bjokne, *White Bear Center, Minnesota, 22 January 1883*

TO: Hans Jørgensen and Eli Johannesdatter Bjøkne, *Lesja, Oppland*

⊹⇒◯⇐⊹

Dear parents and siblings,

I must now take up my pen and send you a few words as it's a shame
how long it is since I wrote to you. First I must tell you that we are well
and healthy. We had an average good year even though the hail caused
some damage, but not so much for me. I had 246 bushels of wheat and 239
bushels of oats. This isn't much but I plowed and harrowed about twenty
acres last summer. I've also plowed my fields and fertilized some so I expect
a good crop next fall. We've had a good winter with some snow. But the
last two weeks we've had a snowstorm one day and a cold wind the next.
A few days it's been so cold that your nose would have frozen on the way
from the barn to the house if you hadn't kept your hand on it. We've often
spoken about our desire to see our parents and siblings again and thought of
visiting Norway, but that cannot be until we've become more prosperous. It
may be many years before it becomes possible to set out on such a journey
even if we should have good crops and the best of luck. But when we have so
much that we can go without risking all we've set aside for the future, then
we'll come if we still have our life and our health. I've often thought that
it would be better for you to come to America than to remain in Norway.
Land is expensive here but you could live with us as long as you wished so
you wouldn't need any land. Marit says that she often wishes that you were
here because soon my siblings will be coming one after the other and then it

will be sad to think of you alone among strangers in your old age. But you mustn't do as I advise but only do as you wish because it could happen that you didn't like it here and then that would be my responsibility.

Emma is very quick, good and funny. She hasn't begun to walk on her own yet but she crawls and pushes a chair along the floor. Ingeborg Haugen lives mostly with us but she recently visited Tosten and Johannes Hagen who live about three miles from us. They are all well. Everything is as usual here so I don't have much news. But I can tell you that Hans Haugen married a girl from Skien in Norway just before Christmas. Now there is almost no more paper so in conclusion I wish you all a Happy New Year from your son

HANS AND HIS FAMILY

· ——— ·

HHB has married Marit Olsdatter Haugen since the last available letter. «II:104 »II:147 NE IV:211

· ——— ·

1883 — LETTER 2:142

FROM: Svend H. Enderson, *Danway, Illinois, 8 February 1883*

To: Jakob Rasmussen Sandvik, *Kinsarvik, Ullensvang, Hordaland*

⊷═◉═⊶

Dear Jacob,

It's long since I received your letter, so I must send you a few words. First I must tell you that I'm doing well and in good health and I wish you the same blessing. This is the greatest good we have in this world and we must thank God because we are nothing without his help. I must also tell you that we've had a good harvest. And prices are good. We've had a very harsh winter, cold and much snow. We still have lots of snow and cold weather and they say this means a good summer. I made a lot of money last summer, more than any other summer since I came to America. I made two hundred dollars, much more than I could have made in Norway. Last fall I'd decided

FROM AMERICA TO NORWAY

to go to Iowa and buy land but there was too much snow so I'll let it be until next summer. Next summer I'll again hire out for the month with the same people and have twenty-four dollars a month. I think this will be the last summer I hire out for the month. I think it'll be better to work for myself, get married, and live the good life.

I must also tell you that I do as much courting as I can and hope I'll soon succeed. What about you? Won't you soon take the step? You'll have to hurry up or you'll be too old and it will be too late to get a wife. Nothing came of my plan to visit Norway last fall. I'll make no more decisions about the future. It's strange that my mother and sister are so afraid of coming to America. Everyone in Norway must believe that that the voyage to America is dangerous, but there are no dangers and I would like to cross the ocean every day. Give my regards to Svend and to all friends and acquaintances. Farewell. Write soon.

SVEND H. ENDESON

· ——— ·

SHE wrote a letter from Danway on 9 July 1882 (Nor. ed. IV:195) where he fears hard times because of a poor summer. He has been corresponding with a young woman in Ullensvang about coming to him in the United States, but after Jakob Sandvik has informed him about her relations with other men he has decided not to send her a ticket "because we have enough sluts here without her.... I'll have to find someone in America." SHE's written Norwegian suggests that he in his daily life is mixing his two languages. He thus writes *sain* rather than *tegn* for "sign" and *dis* rather than *denne* for "this."

«II:119 »II:156 NE IV:215

· ——— ·

1883 — LETTER 2:143

FROM: Nels T. Olson, *Callender, Iowa, 14 February 1883*
To: Aanund Olsen Torvetjønn, *Møsstrond, Vinje, Telemark*

⋗═◒═⋖

Dear brother Anund Torvekjøn,

I should have written when I got a letter July 12 and saw that you were all in good health. I can say the same for us, for which we must thank God. I'm ashamed that I haven't yet answered Tallef's letter. I tried to write to you three times but I couldn't get it into any kind of shape so I had to let it be. I sometimes wonder why you or Gisle don't write to us but I suppose you're waiting for me to write first. I suppose I should have more to write about than you but it's so good to hear from you and from Torvekjønn. I saw in Tallef's letter that there would be changes there and that you were going to buy the northern section and that our old father was moving to Bakken with Thor and that you would give him 400 *kroner*. So I long to hear about this and also about how you all are doing. I heard from Ole who lives in Haabistad that Svanoug had moved to Bø to work for Halvor Klausen Eika, so I suppose Gro is at home with you at Torvekjønn.

I must tell you that I've sent two tickets to our brother Ole and his daughter Margit. On the eigtheenth of this month it will be three months since I did this and I haven't yet heard from him. He could have been here several days ago if all had gone well. I had a letter from him at Christmas and he was then waiting for the tickets and was ready to leave as soon as the tickets arrived. But he also mentioned that his daughter Margit had been discouraged from going with him and that he couldn't force her. So he had written to Svanoug and asked if she wanted to go with him and she had answered that she wasn't unwilling. And if this is the case it will be long before everything is ready. I didn't like the idea of Svanoug setting out on the journey to America at this time of year because I know that her health isn't all that strong and the weather is colder and stormier now than during summer but all is in the hands of God.

I must tell you that last year I farmed the land of our cousin Nils who I'm living with. I didn't make much money because we had so much rain and cold weather from spring to late summer. We had very little corn. Corn and oats are common here. Wheat rarely succeeds and this year there was hardly anything so we have to buy the flour we need. I had luck last spring in buying two sows that have had ten piglets each. We sold the sows last week for $48.75 and two weeks ago we sold some of the piglets for $91.75. I'll have to sell the others soon because we can't feed them as we have so little corn. It's simple to keep pigs here compared to Norway. I think I'll get the same price for those I have left as for those I sold or perhaps more, and if we'd sold our corn we would have had less than a third of the money we got for the pigs. For fun I'll tell you how many animals we have: two two-year-old foals, nine cows, seven one-year-old heifers, two calves that we got around Christmas, and five we are expecting in the spring. For all this I'm in some debt to Aase's brothers Thor and Anund. I bought some cows at auctions and paid thirty-five and up to thirty-nine dollars.

In his letter Tallef asked me to tell you what I really thought about this country. First I'll say that I've done much better here than if I'd stayed in Norway and not say much more about it. In my opinion you should sell everything you have and come here. For my part I know that I wouldn't want to live at Torvekjønn if I had it for free. These words are especially for you, Anund, who have taken over. You shouldn't on any condition think of staying there. Sell it as soon as possible and come here. I wish I were so near you that I could talk with you about this, but I hope you'll accept my simple words as truly as if I'd been sitting there with you because I haven't changed my mind since I was at home. On the contrary, I understand things better than I did then. I hope you don't misbelieve what I've written and think that I'm talking nonsense. I can in good conscience say, my dear siblings, that that is not so. But I don't deny that memories of Norway and my dear home are always in my thoughts. If I had so much money that I could, for instance, buy a good and well appointed farm in Bø or Nes in Sauherad then I would have returned to Norway. But I wouldn't live in Aamotsdal or Møsstrond, no indeed, and I would never have gone back to cutting grass with a small scythe because here they don't even use the long one except for a little grass around the houses. They use a big machine they call a *mower* that they drive with two horses and in one day they can cut lots of hay and it falls right down and is spread out nicer than you could spread it with a rake. Such a machine costs from seventy-five to eighty-five dollars. A man who has his own farm with good buildings and the necessary machinery can have as nice a life here as in Norway.

True, it can be very hot in the summer but this is something you get used to. When it's too hot I don't have a good appetite, not only because of the heat but also because of all the flies, but we have better food here than in Norway, much better. Another thing I don't like in the summer is that after rain the soil is so wet and muddy that it isn't easy to walk on the roads. It gets stuck on your feet as if you were walking in clay. The soil is quite black and about three feet or more deep. But this kind of soil isn't everywhere. In Minnesota, Dakota and Wisconsin it is more sandy like it is in Norway. There are no dangerous snakes even though there are many snakes during summer. Some say that those called bull snakes are poisonous but there aren't many of them here. Not so far from here they have the dangerous rattlesnakes. We don't have many wild animals here. There are wolves and foxes and these are the only animals I know of that do any harm. Wolves here are no larger than an average dog. [...]

. ——— .

> The last pages are missing. This is one of the rare instances of a letter writer simply saying sell what you have and come. The cousin whose farm NTO uses on shares was Nils Haatveit. «II:103 »II:264 NE IV:217

. ——— .

1883 — LETTER 2:144

FROM: Jacob Hanson Hilton, *Socorro, New Mexico, 2 June 1883*

TO: Hans Jakobsen and Anne Olsdatter Hilton
Kløfta, Ullensaker, Akershus

⤙═◯═⤚

Dear parents,

Thank you for your letter dated April 23 that I received some time ago. I'm glad to see that you are all well and I can say the same for myself. I was alone with the store and shop after Asche went to Chicago and my shoemaker became difficult and left. I locked the building when I went to the hotel to eat. Now I have two shoemakers again and can relax more. My business is better than it's been the last year or so. You say that my letters suggest that I may be returning home. Well, as it looks right now you may soon see me coming down the road to Hilton. I'll tell you what I have in mind but it's still only a vague idea so it must remain secret. I have every reason to believe that we will soon get really good times in Socorro as a railroad is planned to be built here through new land that hasn't yet been trodden on by white people except for an occasional miner. They've discovered good silver and gold mines so with the building of the railroad and also right after it's been built, we'll have good times—but only for a short time. You see, they're going to build a large melting furnace to melt the metals out of the rocks and they'll need several hundred men to keep this going. All these railroad men and those working with the melting will need boots, so it will be quite lively. When the time comes I intend to have my hand in the barrel. I've built up a business here through solid work; I'm known by everyone and have a reputation as the best shoemaker in the West, so I'll get the best business. I'll make as much as possible in a short time and then, when it's at its best, I'll try to sell out at a good price before times again get bad, because then I won't even be able to give it away. So then it'll be thank you so much and goodbye to Socorro. But I must say that if I should remain in America, then Socorro is the place for me. It's a nice town and has an excellent climate. And now I'm off to sea again looking over the rocking billows until I can see the nice little town of Kristiania up in the hill over there and then the tiny stump of a railroad that goes as slowly as a muddy river until it finally and with some difficulty reaches Kløfta. But I doubt I could be happy at home after this busy and eventful life. I must end this now. Don't say anything about it. My regards to relatives and friends.

J. H. HILTON

· —— ·

JHH wrote on 3 December 1882 (Nor. ed. IV:208) about his problems with his employees as well as with his partner Frederick (Oluf Frithjof) Asche who moves back and forth between Chicago and Socorro. Kristiania is now Oslo. The railroad station at Kløfta was opened in 1854 as part of the first railroad in Norway. In an unpublished letter to his brother Oluf dated 14 February 1883 he wrote in greater detail about his business and his plans and prospects and advised his brother to come in the fall rather than in spring, and on 21 August 1883 (Nor. ed. IV:222) he wrote that he had sent money for his ticket, gave Oluf advice for his journey, and promised to meet him at the depot in Socorro. «II:136 »II:155 NE IV:219

· —— ·

From: Elling Ellingsen Vold, *Decorah, Iowa, 26 July 1883*

To: Helge Gundersen Skare, *Eggedal, Sigdal, Buskerud*

⤙⟺⤚

Dear father-in-law and family,

I've let too much time pass without writing. Please forgive me. I wanted to write when Mari had her accident but she said we should wait and see how things would develop. Then your son Gunder told us that he had written you about it so this is why I haven't written. In order not to repeat what he may have told you, I won't give you any details but say that the doctor visited her four times while she was in bed for seven weeks. This was a long and difficult time for her and she had intense pain from her fracture as well as from the rheumatism she already had in her legs, so you may imagine how difficult her situation was since she had to lie quite still. But God helped her to bear her burden until she gradually became better. Now she just barely, for the first time after her accident, can drive over to Ole Myran and then to the church and town. I suppose you've heard that I sold my land last spring so we could live with less worry in the future should God grant us life. I had an auction last spring for my farm equipment and animals so we now only have two horses and three cows. These are milked by a little foster daughter who also helps us, guided by Mari, with the other chores. We haven't yet bought another home but we have in mind a lot suited for the animals I've mentioned. As I believe that Gunder will be going home to you in a short while, there is no reason for me to write any more. Our heartfelt regards to you our father and your family.

ELLING E. VOLD

· —— ·

This letter concludes the series sent to Helge Gundersen Skare. It begins in 1852 with a letter from his two daughters, Mari (who later married Elling Ellingsen Vold), and Ingrid (who later married Ole Aslesen Myran), on 28 December 1854 (1:34). By 7 February 1855 his son Anders and daughter Ingeborg had also emigrated (1:53).

Yet another son, Gunder, wrote about his journey to America on 13 August 1862 (1:101) and a daughter, Eli, emigrated in 1866 and married Gunder Johnsen Moen in 1869 (1:157). Halvor Helgesen Skare and two other siblings remained in Norway. In the 1860 census Helge Gundersen is listed as sixty-three, so in 1883 he was eighty-six years of age. Margit Helgesdatter, his second wife, was then fifty-one.

«II:106 NE IV:221

· ——— ·

1883 — LETTER 2:146

FROM: Elise Wærenskjold, *Prairieville, Texas, 23 September 1883*

To: Thomine Dannevig, *Lillesand, Aust-Agder*

⊶≡◉⊂⊷

My dear, good Thomine,

Thank you so much for your very welcome letter and for the news about my old acquaintances. I'm not the only one who is made happy by your letters; they are also enjoyed by Ouline and when she gets letters from Lillesand I read them too. So you see that we are interested in everything about Lillesand. We've read Husher's travel epistles with great interest. But I'm sad to see that politics in Norway have led to so much bitterness and hatred. It is natural that there are different opinions in politics as in religion, but I think it is unchristian to hate each other for such reasons. I think I've told you that Husher is so kind as to send me his newspaper without charge and Mr. Relling, the printer, sends me his. I read everything about Norway but I skip everything about the elections in the North and the religious controversies among the Norwegian Lutherans in America.

I'm so glad, dear Thomine, that you are comfortable in your old age, enjoying your children and grandchildren and living in prosperity. My own fate has been so different. I'm poor and have almost as many children and grandchildren dead as alive. But I must thank God for my good health and my daily bread. Poor Bina Grøgaard! She has also had a difficult life. It is strange that the son of Tone, wife of a ship carpenter, should now be the owner of the one-time wealthy Grøgaard's house. I remember that I once set up a subscription list to help her build a little house. It must also be difficult for Christine Normann. I wish she would write. I've sent her two or three letters to New York but she may not have received them. Please tell Thorvald that he would be very kind if he sent me *Livsslaven* by Jonas Lie. Your son Niels once sent me *A Doll's House* and Lerche sent me a book by his son the painter. It is of great interest for me to see books by our new writers, but I cannot afford to buy them.

I must tell you a little about myself. I left home June 30 and had dinner with Mrs. Pabst in Will's Point, our nearest railroad depot about fifteen miles from here. That evening I took the train to Clifton where I arrived the next morning in time for breakfast. The distance between Wills Point and Clifton is 157 miles and it wouldn't take more than seven hours if we didn't have to change trains halfway and wait for several hours of the night in the depot, which is rather tiring. Clifton is in the large Norwegian settlement in Bosque County and since the railroad doesn't go nearer Hamilton than to Hico, twenty miles from Hamilton, I prefer to go to Clifton where I have many friends and acquaintances among the Scandinavians. It didn't cost me anything to get from there to Otto, to whom I came on July 7 and found both him and his wife ill. This was rather awkward, especially since Otto had written that he was well, but they were soon so well that he could take care of his business and she could take care of the house. They are not healthy, nor is my son Niels. While I was there they were also visited by her mother, two of her unmarried brothers, her oldest brother with his wife and their four children, and her oldest sister, so for a time we were sixteen people in the house. I was there for a month and then Otto drove me to the Norwegian settlement where I also stayed for a month, but on a round of visits from one to another of my acquaintances. I had a very nice trip. I suppose you saw in the newspapers that my son and his wife lost yet another little son in May. Five of their children are now dead, two boys and three girls. The three that live are in good health as is Niels's third child. They both have two girls and one boy. I don't think you know anyone in Bosque except for Andreas Andersen, Mrs. Pabst's brother. I was of course with them too and they are doing quite well. He has a pleasant and clever wife and many children. On May 17 they had a festive dinner and speeches in Bosque. The Norwegian pastor spoke in Norwegian and a Norwegian Professor Andersen from Austin, the capital of Texas, spoke in English. Both were said to be very good. Ouline is doing well but the Norwegian family that has lived with her, rented some of her field land, and helped her feed her cattle during winter will now be leaving her because they've bought their own farm. It's so difficult to hire help in Texas, particularly people who can be trusted.

Please remember me to any old friends and acquaintances you may see. Is Theresia joining her husband in America? It would probably be strange to see each other after so long a time apart. Does anyone hear from Osuld Enge, Peder Kalvehaven and Anders Holte, Christian Grøgaard's old friends? Give my regards to your sons when you write to them. If Niels's wife had had a son this time she had promised to call him Thorvald, but there may be another Thorvald some other time. Mrs. Pabst and Oline send their regards. Farewell and don't wait too long before you write to your old friend

ELISE WÆRENSKJOLD

. ——— .

Ferdinand Husher was publisher of *Fædrelandet og Emigranten* in Minneapolis and I. T. Relling's *Norden* was published in Chicago. Husher's estranged wife, Theresia, did not emigrate. In 1883 a major political conflict in Norway was coming to its conclusion with the impeachment of the conservative cabinet ministers in 1884 and the acceptance of parliamentary government. Bina (Jacobine) Grøgaard was the widow of Johannes Grøgaard, who in 1865 is listed as Danish vice consul in Lillesand. They then had no less than six servants. In 1865 Tone Olsdatter (then sixty-four) was married to a ship carpenter and two of her five adult sons were in the same trade as their father. In 1865 Christine Normann was married to a ship's captain and apparently prosperous. In 1900 she was a widow and lived with her married daughter Randi Nordvik in Larvik and was supported by her two sons in New York, Henry and Max Normann, owners of the shipping agency Benham and Boyesen. Jonas Lie (1833–1909) was one of the most prominent Norwegian novelists of his generation. *Livsslaven* (The Slave of Life) was published in 1883, the year of this letter. It has been called the first Norwegian naturalistic novel. The painter's book was *Med blyanten* (1874, With My Pencil) by Vincent Stoltenberg Lerche. Ibsen's *Et dukkehjem (A Doll's House)* was published in 1879. She uses a Norwegianized form of the American "the depot": *depotet*, a word probably not understood in Lillesand. The speakers at the 17 May celebration in Bosque were Pastor Jon K. Rystad and Professor Jon J. Andersen. «II:139 »II:161 NE IV:224

. ——— .

1883 — LETTER 2:147

From: Hans H. Bjokne, *Starbuck, Minnesota, 17 November 1883*

To: Hans Jørgensen and Eli Johannesdatter Bjøkne, *Lesja, Oppland*

Dear parents and siblings,

We recently received your welcome letter and see that you are in good health and doing well and we can say the same for us. Emma is lively and good. It hasn't been so good for her the last few days as she is being weaned, but she is getting used to it. We had very nice weather last summer and the fall has also been both long and nice. We had some early snow but it melted fast. The soil froze a few days ago. We had a good year for wheat around here, about twenty bushels an acre. I had a little more than twenty-two: 585 bushels on twenty-six and a half acres, 622 bushels of oats on fifteen acres, twenty-nine bushels of barley on half an acre. I must also tell you how many animals we have: two horses that will be four years next spring, four cows, four calves, two heifers, two draft oxen and a two-year-old ox, three hogs, two of them will be fed through the winter and the third will be slaughtered for Christmas. We also slaughtered a sow this fall.

Johannes has been here since summer and will live with us this winter too. He has a mare that will be four years next spring and two two-year-old horses. If there are any who are coming to America next spring I'll send one or two tickets. But you must write about it soon because tickets are cheaper in early winter than in spring. Kristen Kornkven visited us this evening. He has worked for Syver Hagen for four months and been in good health since he came. He sends his regards. We recently visited Trond Lillejordet. Anne is with him and they were both in good health and doing well. Mattias Holen has shortened his life by hanging himself. As I don't have more to write about I'll end my letter. Please give our regards to all relatives and friends. You are all lovingly greeted from your son and brother and his family.

HANS H. BJØKNE

HHB wrote to his parents on 30 November 1884 (Nor. ed. IV:253). He then had a second daughter Ida and his brother Jakob was also in Minnesota. HHB's brother Johannes (who became John Hanson in the United States) immigrated in 1882 and at first lived with his brother. He wrote home on 22 October 1882 (Nor. ed. IV:205).

«II:141 »II:159 NE IV:226

1883 — LETTER 2:148

FROM: Iver Andersen Lee, *Springdale, Wisconsin, 4 December 1883*

To: Anders Olsen, Kari Mikkelsdatter, Anders Andersen, and Ragnild Guttormsdatter Lie, *Hedalen, Sør-Aurdal, Oppland*

Dear parents as well as brother and wife,

Many days have passed since I last had the pleasure of writing to you and since then I haven't had a letter from home, but I've heard a story or two and it is my greatest enjoyment to hear from our home valley even though the reports may be incomplete. I've often thought of writing but nothing has come of it. I often ask myself what the reasons for my delay have been but without coming up with an answer. I hope that you will be able to forgive my faults as I now sincerely ask of you, ensuring you that I haven't forgotten my dear childhood home.

I'm glad to tell you that I've been in excellent health and had the pleasure of enjoying myself. As you know, I've been in Dakota for most of this time. I left Wisconsin in early April 1882 and was in the West until I returned to Wisconsin about two weeks ago. Now I'm with my brothers and plan to stay here until next spring when I'll return to Dakota. I went west to find free land as I thought it would be easier to get ahead in this manner than by staying in the old settlements where there is no land to be had except at very high prices. And I now have land in the West but I haven't settled on it yet so I cannot yet get a lease. I haven't done much work on it either. I've broken ten acres but that is about all I've done. I plan to settle there next spring because I have to live on the land for six months before I can get a lease. When I've satisfied the requirements I'll get my lease and then try to get more land. But there is no more land to be had just there so I may be traveling around a bit again.

I'll tell you a little about people from Hedalen I met in Minnesota and Dakota. Elling and Ole Brunbakke have land close to mine and are satisfied and doing well. I've spoken with Gulbrand and Ole Busumoen and their father. The two brothers have land and are doing well. Erik and Ole Kjensrud live nearby on their well-developed farms. I've spoken with Kristofer Rud, who you knew as Kristofer Klemmetsrud, and he asked me to give his regards to his old friend Anders Lie. He and his sons have taken land and are well situated. His health is weak and he can't do much but he's up and about and visits friends. I've spoken with all the children of Erik Vold except for his daughter Kjerstine who is in Minnesota. Siri and Oline, who are married to Anders and Harald Flatbraaten, have land nearby as does his son Nils. Tidemand and Erik took land east of there last summer, but they've been working in different places as have Gunhild, Inger, Ole Andreas and Tonette. I've spoken with Torkel Fossholt. I met him and his son John last spring out on the wild prairie as I was looking for land. They took land last summer and settled there. Ole Moen has taken land near them and I've spoken with him too. I've spoken with Ingrid Bergene and her husband. They took land last summer and plan to move there next year. Østen and Ingeborg Skinningsrud have moved to the West and live in Mayville with their daughter who is married to a blacksmith from Renli named Thore Skardet. I remember that your mother asked me to ask about Ingeborg Flaten and I didn't know that she was Østen Skinningsrud's wife and once when talking with her I thought that she might be able to tell me something about Ingeborg Flaten and she said that this was her name. I've spoken with her many times and each time she has mentioned you and I promised to give you her regards. She and her husband are in good health. Last spring I also visited Mikkel Sørlie, his siblings and his mother. They're all doing well and his mother Ragnhild is far more satisfied with America than she was at first.

Dear brother! I hear that you are married and I must send you and your wife my most heartfelt congratulations. I know that it was your heart's desire to enter into matrimony and that this is your best means of achieving happiness, peace and comfort in an existence replete with troubles. I've often felt how empty, worthless, and comfortless a life without a faithful and loving companion can be, so I've been observing how matrimony, when it is confirmed by mutual love, may be the only means to help one through longings and to sweeten much bitterness. In conclusion I'll proclaim my wish and hope that your matrimonial skies may forever remain clear and bright and never be darkened by stormy clouds and that the paths of your future life may always lie open and free before you and never be closed by adversity nor be embittered by sharp thorns. May the peace and help of God be with you both.

Dear parents! When I turn my thoughts to you and the home I've left I cannot but long for the happiness and pleasure it would give me to see you again in this life. But the road of fate is only traced in the book of the future that no one can read or write but the all-knowing God. I've heard that you are becoming weaker, which is to be expected at such an old age. The only certain point of relief for the weakness of old age is the end of the path of our life. And this is for our best; what earthly happiness can return to one who has completed his life and is weighed down by age and weakness! No, we must hope for liberation from all that is of this earth and from all troubles and adversities, and this can only be achieved in a blessed death. So I have no higher wish than to know that you've been redeemed and liberated from all earthly misery and become participants in that eternal peace and rest that knows no longing or disappointment. In this belief and in this hope I will forget my wish to see you in this life and turn all my efforts and all my thoughts to the achievement of this single and greatest goal and this single and greatest joy to be reunited with you in that place where the tears of separation will no longer flow. Should it so happen that I'm permitted to wander in a future life down here it would be a great pleasure for me to again stand on the ground where my childhood memories are rooted, but then you my dear parents will probably no longer be there. It will nevertheless be a great comfort for me to see the grave that encloses the remains of those beings that I have most to thank, after God, for my own being, the grave that holds the memories of my dear mother in whose arms I enjoyed my earliest care and at whose breast I slept so peacefully and safely. Dear mother, although I'm unable to return your goodness I can assure you that your admonitions have comforted me in my hours of despair and disappointment and your voice has spoken with greater strength than any other, warning me and urging me to be careful in moments of temptation.

Dear father, how often has your good example and your advice been a light for my foot and a lamp for my path and what greater happiness can I achieve in this world than to achieve the respect that you have prepared for me by passing on your name and your honor as my inheritance. Yes, you must believe me dear father that I greatly value this inheritance and will guard it as well as I can. Regrettably I can do nothing to repay you for your fatherly goodness but, dear father, I'm glad that you'll find your reward in God. With hope I pray and with joy I believe that you too will forgive me my transgressions against you.

I don't have any news. I've been around to several relatives since I returned. They are all doing well and enjoying health. My brothers are in good health as usual and their children are growing and thriving and have of course asked me to send greetings to their grandparents. As Christmas is approaching I won't forget to wish you a Merry Christmas and a Happy New Year and in this hope let us place our trust in God who governs the paths of fate because then we will, even in the darkness of adversity and grief, be given the strength to accept the bad as well as the good and not fail to see the hope that gives us the assurance of a happy reunion where we shall forever and ever praise the birth of the Savior Child and his coming to earth. In conclusion, loving regards from me and my brothers here,

IVER A. LEE

· —— ·

IAL's brother Mikkel wrote from Springdale on 12 February 1884 (Nor. ed. IV:216). His parents had written a note to Beret Lee, the widow of his uncle Guttorm, and although she apparently was unable to read it herself it had made her glad. Many of those in her generation who did not write were unable to do so. The three brothers from Søre Li all liked to write and both Mikkel and Ole at times attempted to do so in rhyme. In this they may be contrasted with the family of their father's sister, Olea Børtnes. She could or would not write herself but her son Iver wrote a short letter for her to Søre Li on 2 September (Nor. ed. IV:223) and he seems barely literate. Erik Tidemansen Vold was fifty-one in 1865, and in 1883 he and his entire family of ten children (three born after 1865) were in the Midwest, most of them in the same area. Mikkel Mikkelsen Sørlie was related to the family at Søre Li and wrote to them from his home in Rothsay, Minn., on 12 December and mentions Iver Lee's visit (Nor. ed. IV:229). In 1883 IAL's parents were seventy-one and sixty-seven years old. «II:133 »II:154 NE IV:227

· —— ·

FROM: Christopher Jacobson, *Belleville, Nevada, 13 January 1884*

TO: Hans Jakobsen Hilton, *Kløfta, Ullensaker, Akershus*

Dear brother!

I received your letter of November 20 on December 15 and as you say that you expect a letter from me before Christmas you will have waited a long time when you get this. I think you forget that it takes at least twenty days for a letter to get to Belleville and as I don't go there more than twice a month it can happen that a letter from you is at the post office a couple of weeks before I get it. I suppose I could have written before this but as I seemed about to lose four or five hundred dollars last month and was planning to leave this place, I thought it would be better to wait a little. Although I still don't know how all of this will work out I'll send you two or three hundred dollars as soon as I get to town tomorrow. I'll have to get a draft from San Francisco as there isn't any bank here that does business with foreign banks. This will take an extra three to four days. I would have to write a long letter to explain my possible loss and departure and you may think that I'm reluctant to help you. But this is not so. I'm quite sure that you'll soon have my money and then I don't care whether I leave this place or not. It is a lonely place and I'm a little tired of it but I had planned to stay another year or so. I'll know more about this when I get to town and then I may be able to inform you before I mail my letter.

So you are fifty-six, brother! Your children are old enough to take care of themselves, and you still have sleepless nights in fear of the future and a boundless anxiety for your sons who are almost middle-aged when they leave you. Oh no! I'm not laughing, brother! It makes me sad even though it seems unreasonable because children in America rarely live at home after they are sixteen or seventeen. The father may grumble that they leave just as they're old enough to be of use, but he continues to run his farm or other business and realizes that he once did the same thing. Their mother may miss them more but she'll soon hear from her dear *William*, *Jack* or *James* that he is doing perfectly well out in the far West and she looks forward to visiting her *William* and his sweet wife in the near future etc. But this is America.

Since I came to America the population has grown and spread out to the West. I immediately began to take such huge steps that before I knew it, one more would have taken me into the Pacific. So I had to take a step back up into the mountains. But what a country, what glory, and what wealth I blindly leaped over. I think that Chicago had about 60,000 inhabitants when I was there. According to the last census (1880) there were more than 500,000. It wouldn't have been difficult to get a lot on the outskirts of the city, a lot that today can't be had for money. I once went on foot from Batavia to Chicago (about thirty miles or so) and I couldn't see a single house. Now it is all a flourishing flower garden. In Wisconsin, where I worked in the saw mills by the Chippewa River, not so far from the Mississippi, the black soil smiled as if begging to be cultivated. But no thank you, not for me! And today the railroad cars roll up these valleys and across these prairies. There are enormous orchards that blossom in season and are overburdened with all kinds of fruit. We have wealthy farmers. There are large schools, good teachers, and thousands of healthy, happy and well-educated children running around during recess. And churches that all may visit if they wish—and lots of wolves! Oh, I'm sorry, I meant <u>pastors</u>, but <u>fire</u> and <u>brimstone</u> cannot scare the staunch American farmers or pale the rosy cheeks of his nature-loving children. Lucky the children who are brought up in such a land! The glories of nature are evident in their faces. The rays of happiness shine in their eyes and the Lord of Nature may here see his own image as he from the beginning meant it to be. But let me continue my wandering. I also scurried around up in Minnesota. St. Paul was an insignificant little town. I went up to St. Anthony Falls (nine miles from St. Paul), now Minneapolis. It couldn't even be called a town. In the last census (1880) it had more than 48,000 inhabitants. But I suppose you've read about these rapidly growing cities and the progress of America, and my knowledge also comes from reading, even though I now and then meet people who come from places I passed through blind in the days of my youth. And when I sit here in the mountains and think about how merrily I leaped over all of these glories, then the few hairs I have left on my head begin to stand straight up.

It isn't as easy for immigrants to get land now as it was in the past. But in <u>Idaho</u>, <u>Montana</u> and <u>Washington Territories</u> as well as in the State of <u>Oregon</u> there are almost boundless stretches of government and railroad land just waiting for good farmers, and in a few years there will be just as great progress and just as large cities and as much glory to astound us that we now see in the older states. All the inhabitants of Norway could find farms here and it would only be like a drop in the sea. And you are all—except for the King and his followers—welcome here. He too may come if he removes his crown and lays his hand on plough and spade and cultivates the soil as do some of our presidents when they leave office.

There is a stain on some of our members of government; a few years ago they gave away millions of acres of government land to the railroad companies, land that is untaxed as long as it isn't cultivated. These railroad kings, as we call them, are so rich that they have great political power. It's difficult for people to elect a representative who won't be bought for gold. These companies employ thousands or rather millions, mainly from the most ignorant class in America, the Irish and the dregs of other nations, and, as you know, after a short while they all have the right to vote. In this way the railroad kings can get their willing slaves to vote as they wish. Our beloved country is, in my opinion, far too free as far as the right to vote is concerned, but I suppose I shouldn't complain. The nation as a whole is wealthy. The railroad companies in *"the Northwest"* sell their land for two and a half dollars an acre, but as the emigrants arrive, the price goes up. But you don't have to pay it all in cash; you only pay one fifth of the price in cash, another fifth the next year, and so on. The interest on the unpaid capital is seven percent a year. This makes it possible for poor people to acquire a farm and a good home in a short time. But I mustn't forget to add that they'll have to work as hard as they can and be thrifty; they mustn't waste either time or money. You'll understand that I've only given you the bright side of America. I've only told you about the possibilities for working people that don't exist in other countries. But they have to make use of their possibilities wisely if they wish to improve their situation.

You ask whether I would like to go to see your sons in New Mexico. Oh, yes, I'd certainly like to, but we must accept our situation. Jacob is now doing so well that I couldn't be of any help there. I couldn't be there long without looking for work and then I would have to go to the mines. Wages there are lower than here while the living expenses are about the same. At my age a bird in the hand seems better than two in the bush, so I've decided not to look around for a mine of my own, because the work is hard and the expenses great and compensation is uncertain. Jacob hasn't given me much information about farming there, probably because he hasn't seen much of the country outside of Socorro. But I think the land is best suited for cattle. I suppose Jacob still has an eye on Hilton but he'll soon have all his senses focused on America and until I see or hear it, I won't believe that Jacob or Oluf would be so blind that they left America (forgive me, brother) to take over a farm that you haven't made profitable after thirty years of hard work. They will realize that if they work as hard and are as thrifty as you've been for thirty years they would be wealthy men. And wouldn't you like to see your sons and daughters married and have children? Won't you admit that it would be better for these children to be brought up in America? I'm sure that your sons will soon see this and be content. But I won't advise them one way or the other. It costs a little too much to take a pleasure trip to Socorro as I would have to go in the opposite direction to San Francisco before I get to the railroad that goes to New Mexico. This is a rather long journey and it would probably cost about 100 dollars. There is a railroad that goes by Belleville and it is planned to junction with the railroad that will go to Mexico through Southern California or the corner of Arizona Territory when it is completed. This will cut the distance to Socorro by half. I could go this way now but would then have to buy a horse to take me from one railroad to the other. This would be difficult because of the enormous deserts you have to cross and it may even cost more than the roundabout route. But when the time comes to leave this place the difficulties of travel will not keep me from going there. The small place I thought of getting in California is too expensive for me. It is only fifteen acres, a little Garden of Eden and enough land for me, but it costs 5,000 dollars and I don't have the money. If I went on my own I could perhaps find a place that was cheaper and just as nice, but as long as I'm making money here I'll try to hold out a little longer even though this place is both lonely and boring.

Well Hans! It's soon thirty years since I left Ullensaker where I thought we were all so happy. People didn't have much money but none of our acquaintances seemed to lack anything. We youngsters went gladly off to dances on Sunday afternoons. The old people sometimes got together and seemed to take pleasure in the merriness of the young. Servants and laborers seemed to have no difficulty in taking up their burden on Monday morning after having danced all night and all they spoke of was where we should meet next Sunday evening etc. The poor seemed to have no concern for the future and the wealthy had no reason to complain and at first in America I often thought how wonderful it would be to go there again to see, yes, to live and die among those happy people. But slowly a veil was drawn before my eyes. It became thicker and thicker year by year until I now cannot see the happiness that I thought was there. All of Norway has changed before my eyes to become what it actually may be, a vale of tears. You know that Lars wrote a few letters to begin with. They always began saying that Norway was a cramped country to live in and concluded that I should get down on my knees and pray to God for forgiveness for my sins. He was no doubt well-meaning but this gave little comfort to a youth wandering around in a strange country among people whose language he couldn't even understand. Then your letters began to arrive with a little more encouragement but you too had already thrown off the joy of youth. You too knew nothing any longer of merry parties and you all seemed pre-occupied with grief and poverty. Little Alette Søli eventually became old enough to write, but even in childhood she didn't have any fun she could write to me about and she didn't seem to have any school friends that she enjoyed. She spoke as if she had been brought up in a convent among nuns. After she was married she didn't write like a newly married woman and mother but as one who was ridden with grief and worry.

Because of all this, my brother, I seldom dare let my thoughts fly to Ullensaker because this brings tears to my eyes and it would break my heart to come there and see you all old and bent with grief and worry. It would be like waking up from my childhood dreams and suddenly seeing the world as it is. I've been born anew and America is my land of birth. To be wrapped up in the American flag and buried in American soil now seems the most wonderful burial I could wish for, but I don't see myself in my grave just yet. I'm healthy in body and in spirit and I'm satisfied with myself and with everything around me. And except for a sigh for you all, so far away there in the North, no sorrow rests in Christopher's breast. You mustn't feel hurt by this letter; I haven't meant to reproach you; I just wanted to show you how changed we become in heart and mind as we get older. May the happy drops of nature fill your glass to the rim and may you learn to drink it empty! This is the highest wish of your

CHRISTOPHER

· ——— ·

«II:137 »II:168 NE IV:230

· ——— ·

1884 — LETTER 2:150

FROM: Louis Nilsen Solem, *Lanesboro, Minnesota, 20 February 1884*

To: Ole Tobias Olsen Ødegaard, *Nannestad, Akershus*

⸱⇒◉⇐⸱

Dear cousin T. Olson,

I must first tell you who I am. I'm the son of Nils and Karen, your mother's sister, but we've never seen each other since I was born here. My name is Laurits and I'm twenty years old. I've often thought of writing to you as it is so strange to have relatives so far away. My parents, three of my brothers, my sister and I are visiting my brothers Christian and Carl who have farms where we used to live. They are married to women from Trondheim and Christian has a son. A week ago I had the sad news that my dear sister Martia is dead. She left behind her dear husband Peder F. Falla and eight children, four boys and four girls. The oldest girl is blind after an eye disease. I'll soon go there. I've been here this winter. It's quite nice where we live. It's as flat as a big street in Christiania. We have plenty of forest but we use coal as fuel. We all have land except my youngest brother Nicolai who is seventeen. My parents are in good health. They often speak of you over there. My father's sister Maria and her son live where we do. They are farmers. When you write you mustn't forget to send a portrait of yourself and your sisters and I'll send you mine. Please do this. It's so nice to see my relatives. We've had nice weather this winter, about three feet of snow. It was cold at Christmas. We had great fun at Christmas as there are many young people around here, but they are all respectable. Where we live most people are Americans. I don't have more to write about, so farewell my dear brother. All here send their regards. Give my regards to your parents and siblings. My writing is bad but please excuse me. Write again soon; don't forget, don't forget. May God be with you. Farewell.

MR. LAURIS N. SOLEM

Would you like to go to America? I've spoken with many who've seen you. Write soon.

The earliest preserved letter in this correspondence from the Solem family to Nannestad is dated 29 March 1874 (Nor. ed. III:181) and is from Nils Christophersen to his sister Maria Kristoffersdatter. He and his family then lived in Fillmore County, Minn., where they had bought a farm that the former owner had named Solem, most likely after the place he had left in Norway. In the Norwegian tradition they took the name of their farm as their family name, also after they had moved to Deuel County in S. Dak. His American-born son Louis, twenty, here signs himself Laurits, a Norwegian version of his name, and takes his father's name as his patronymic in the Norwegian tradition. His first language seems to be English and he has little understanding of Norwegian orthography. Two older brothers remained in Fillmore County. LNS wrote again on 12 December 1884 (Nor. ed. IV:255). He complains of the low price for wheat and the "rich railroad kings who own almost all of America," but hopes the situation will improve now that the Democratic Party has won the election. »II:170 NE IV:232

1884 — LETTER 2:151

FROM: Jacob Larsen Urheim, *Harmony, Minnesota, 22 March 1884*

TO: Jacob Rasmussen Sandvik, *Kinsarvik, Ullensvang, Hordaland*

Dear friend and cousin,

When my brother Lars got a letter from you I was reminded that it was rather long since we exchanged letters. It is, as you say, strange to look back on how fast the years pass by; soon childhood and youth are behind us and in a few years we are old and one after the other of us enters the grave. You're so lucky you are at home and satisfied with remaining single while I've made myself a home here, have a wife and child, and another child is buried. But I'm quite satisfied with my fate. As you may have heard, I have a pharmacy or what they here call a *drugstore* and I'm very satisfied with my business as it gives me pleasure as well as advantages. I built a new house last summer; it cost me more than 1,300 dollars and now I'm going to build a storehouse for heavier wares such as paint and oils. I'm even lazier now than when I trudged around in "Hetleskaaren" for firewood. Now I have it hauled and cut up for me at my door. As soon as I have an opportunity I'll send you a picture of our home. Lars says that your letter was the best he has had from Norway. I would like to hear the same of my letter.

I see you believe that J. Skaar spoke the truth. To this I can say that it was a twisting of facts. I've been out in the West where these outlaws were and I slept as safely as at home. I've never had an opportunity to see outlaws hanged as he describes and as for their moving into the cities it must be noted that cities such as Minneapolis and St. Paul have in twenty-five years grown from a village like Odda to a city with a circumference of forty-nine miles and of course there are different kinds of people there. With his narrow outlook on life J. Skaar couldn't appreciate America. He writes, for instance, that he lost his appetite. So what! When you've eaten too much you don't want to eat any more! This is what they say about J. S. Moreover, he judges America on the basis of a settlement of shopkeepers and we've never accepted this as the right standard for America. And if the water tasted like diluted lye, well I've only come across such water once even though I've traveled through Iowa, Wisconsin, Minnesota, and Dakota. One thing he said is true, that no one took notice of a bigwig from Norway even when the bigwig was named J. Skaar. And he must have felt that he was superfluous here as they say he has returned home to mismanage his old farm. Hans Skaar, John's cousin, is a regular drunk and some shopkeepers are like him. He gives such a misleading account of the situation here. How do you think I could have earned enough for a well-appointed home and the capital for a profitable business in Norway? But I didn't do as J. Skaar. I set out to work with the goal of succeeding and you know what this led to. It may be that I'll go to school again and become a doctor and then I'll come home on a visit.

My brother Lars works in my drugstore and I may be able to train him to become a pharmacist. You would hardly recognize him now and I've also changed a lot. I'm quite bald. I should tell you about relatives and friends but I haven't met any for a long time. Most here are from Telemark. I may go to Wisconsin to visit friends next summer. I see that our brother Tosten has had an accident. I don't think people are careful enough with guns. Around here we haven't had any serious accidents this past year. Business is doing well. Some of the corn froze however. Some prices are: wheat seventy-five cents a bushel, oats thirty, barley forty-five, rye forty-five, potatoes one dollar a barrel, butter fifteen cents a pound, eggs fifteen cents a dozen, pork five and a half cents a pound, a good cow thirty-five dollars. I have two horses, a cow and three pigs. My horses are only for driving around as I don't like to sit at home all the time. I'm going to Chicago in a few days and I haven't been there since I came to this country in 1876. We follow the news from Norway about politics and impeachment and received a telegram about the Selmer verdict the next day. Friendly regards to you all from your faithful friend,

J. L. URHEIM

. ———— .

JLU became a physician in 1891 and practiced in Chicago. His brother Lars, who emigrated in 1880, later had a drugstore in Eau Claire, Wisc. J. Skaar may be John Skaar from Øystese, a farmer who had some publications on local history and folklore in the 1870s. Johan Selmer was the conservative prime minister during the political struggles in Norway in the early 1880s. «II:124 »II:198 NE IV:235

. ———— .

1884 — LETTER 2:152

FROM: Anne Norsby, *Necedah, Wisconsin, 14 April 1884*

To: Marie Olsdatter Vigerust, *Dovre, Oppland*

◦⇒◦⇐◦

Dear Marie,

I received your letter some time ago. Please excuse me for not having replied. First I must tell you that we're in good health and I wish to hear the same from you. In your letter I saw that many were planning to marry and other interesting news, but I have no weddings to tell you about as you don't know any of the young Norwegians here. If you had known them I could have told you many entertaining things. Last Saturday evening Rønnaug and I were invited to a dance in the home of a Norwegian family. They had many Norwegian boys as boarders who had joined in buying beverages. We had fun dancing until three in the morning. We've bought a farm one and a half miles from town for 300 dollars. We also bought animals: three cows and three heifers and two sucking calves. Before this we had two cows, two sheep and four chickens. Father and mother moved to the farm two weeks ago. Jacob plans to be there this summer. He says that mother and father like it. But it must be rather boring as there are only three Norwegian families nearby. Many of the Norwegians here are speaking of buying land out there. A Norwegian family bought a farm close to ours. Last fall I wrote that Johannes Nørstebø and two other boys from Norway had come from Minnesota. They were in the forest last winter and now they are working in the sawmill again and boarding with us. Ole Snekkerlien has also lived here since he came from the forest. These four boys and my brothers Ole and Bjørner work in the sawmill. My brother Sivert will begin next week. I was home alone for a week but it was too much as we also do the laundry for all of them and it isn't as at Toftemo six to seven weeks between each washing. Here you have to wash them every week. You may think that there is no reason to wash that often but this is how it is. Rønnaug and I will be here this summer. It is quite lively when all are here except mother and father. It's worst in the morning because we have to be up at five or a little earlier and breakfast is served at six, dinner at twelve and supper at six.

I've often wished that you were here. It can't be much fun for you at home if your father is ill. When he gets better it will still be boring but if you'd been here we could have gone to a dance now and then and we would have chatted together as I know you liked to do before. Please tell me a little about Toftemo and Tofte and about what girls are working there now the next time you write. Today is Good Friday so you may imagine that these wild boys didn't want to go to work yesterday or today but they had to go both days. There were so many people around me yesterday evening that I wasn't able to complete my letter so I'll have to do it now. I've heard that Good Friday was properly celebrated in town as there was a Dane who shot a Swede and almost killed him. The doctor said he wouldn't live more than two hours but Sivert was in town today and saw him. He was then alive but Sivert thought he couldn't [...]

Please write me a long letter as soon as you get this. Don't write as little as you did the last time. Tell me all the news you know of.

ANNE NØRSTEBØ

· ———— ·

AN emigrated with her parents (Jacob and Marit) and siblings in 1882 from one of the Nørstebø farms in Lesja that borders on Dovre. In the United States their name became Norsby. They seem to have a boarding house in Necedah. In 1884 her parents were sixty-five and fifty-eight; she and her sister Rønnaug were twenty-eight and twenty-two. (Rønnaug added a few lines to this letter.) Her brothers were Jacob, Ole, Bjørner, and Sivert. Johannes Nørstebø was from another farm. Ole Olsen Snekkerlien was from Dovre. The emigrants from Snekkerlien first wrote their name Li and Lie but soon changed it to Lee. Toftemo was a staging inn in Dovre and it seems that both AN and Marie Vigerust had worked there. They were cousins; AN's father, who had come from Dovre, and Marie's mother were siblings. In Norway, Thursday and Friday before Easter Sunday are still holidays. »II:164 NE IV:237

. ——— .

1884 — LETTER 2:153

FROM: Svend Larsen Houg, *Elgin, Iowa, 29 April 1884*
To: Ole Larsen Haug, *Aal, Buskerud*

◦⫘◦

Dearly remembered brother,

I must again send you a small greeting from me and mine, but what manner of greeting can it be? I think it should be the apostolic greeting: Grace and peace to you from God our Father and our Lord and Savior Jesus Christ. Thank you for your welcome and well-written letter of March 25 that I received April 22. You speak so openly of your Christian faith. In this you speak as a true Christian because it is no different for a Christian; as long as we are in the flesh, we must go through light and dark and through strife and battle because even though the spirit may be strong, the flesh is weak. When I study myself in the light of the word of God I do not see anything but sin and weakness every day. And when the dark periods arrive what shall then, dear brother, sustain us? Yes, the faithful and unfailing promise of grace in Jesus Christ our Savior; it is truly told and a costly gift that Jesus entered the world to save sinners among whom I am the worst. But I have experienced mercy, and may God grant that I may learn better to praise and thank him for all his goodness, to my body and to my soul.

Brother Lars says you are in good health and doing well. I often wonder whether he has seen his own unredeemed state through the word of God so that he may be saved by grace alone for that is what we all must go through. Give him my loving regards. I hear that the situation for brother Knut is much the same. Oh, may God in his infinite mercy show him the way through Jesus Christ so that he may not perish in his wretchedness. I knew a little of the other matters you wrote about but not as much as now. It may be that only you and I have experienced a loving relationship in our married lives. I can now report that God has granted me good health for my age as I'm now in my seventieth year; I'm not working so much but I have a few things to take care of and that helps pass the time.

You may like to hear a little about my children but what can I say that won't make it seem too bright or too dark. I'll resort to a word of God: there is no fear of God before his eyes. Even though one does not live an openly sinful life one may have a sensuous and worldly mind. The young have received a worldly education. I'll mention those who still live at home. Assor, who owns and runs the farm, is not married and Ragnil and Elling work for him. Knud, who has the other half of the land, was married last summer. His wife is a sister of Ole's wife and they live here as they haven't yet built on their land. They had a girl April 22. Kittil taught English school last winter but has now gone to an institution of higher education. I'm not sure what he plans to study but it may be business. A few days ago Ole the Younger went to the Red River Valley in Minnesota. I think he'll work for Ingrid and Elling. Elling and Guri have lived with me until this spring. Elling has hired out and Guri has gone to the St. Ansgar School, so now I sit here alone in my single room and take my meals with the others.

My regards to you my brother in the flesh and in the spirit. We cannot do anything for each other but be frank in our confessions. I know that I have said that I was writing to you for the last time but now this is more to be expected as we have arrived at so high an age that we cannot have many days left in the world of tears. I must conclude these simple sentences. I may have written too openly about some things but the letter is for you alone. My best regards to you and your dear wife and children from your brother,

SVEND L. HOUG

Last summer a family that you know came here from Aal. His name is Knud Larsen and he grew up at South Holo and lived for some time at Øygarden. They had many children and were poor but people were good to them and gave them what they needed, even clothes and bedding. I did what I could for them and they were nice and satisfied. I've thought of making a visit to St. Ansgar this summer and I'll probably stay there for some time with my son Halsten. I cannot wait too long as my time may soon be over. Less than a year ago we had a change of pastors as the one we had was called to another congregation. We were somewhat anxious since he was such a good preacher but we are glad for the new one. He's one of the best preachers I've heard and also a very nice man. But it seems that the word of God has little effect on the young generation. We must hope that God is aware of this for he is as mighty as he has always been and he has all people in his hand and can bend them like brooks for he has bent hard hearts before this. I have written more than planned; I'll send you the whole sheet so you can correct my spelling mistakes and forgive my grammatical errors. In conclusion my wish for the grace of God and the community of the Holy Ghost for you and yours,

SVEND L. HOUG

· ———— ·

SLH wrote this letter over several days. The word of God he refers to in his third paragraph is from Psalms 36:1. His daughter Ingrid was married to Elling Tostensen Dokken. They had a farm near Eldred in Polk County. Ole Larsen Haug was married to Turid Larsdatter. The new immigrants from Aal were Knut Larsen Holo (born 1835) and Haldis Tolleivsdatter Opsata Øygarden (born 1842) and their children, here identified both by the names of the farms they hailed from and the farm they had lived on before emigrating. «II:53 »II:189 NE IV:238

· ———— ·

From: Ole Andersen Lee, *Springdale, Wisconsin, 4 May 1884*

To: Anders Olsen, Kari Mikkelsdatter, and Anders Andersen Lie
Hedalen, Sør-Aurdal, Oppland

⊷⟹⟸⊷

Dear parents and brother as well as relatives and friends in my old country Norway,

May God's grace and peace and the love of our Lord Jesus Christ be with you. It's long since you last heard from us and even longer since you had a letter from my hand. The reason I've been quiet for so long is that my brothers have written quite a few letters and given you the necessary information about me and my family. I'll try as well as I can to give you a brief account of my situation, hoping that you'll forgive my shortcomings. We are, thank God, in good health and doing quite well as far as our financial situation is concerned. When brother Mikkel last wrote to you we had planned to have someone work our farm, but this came to nothing as the man who rented the farm sold his good team and bought an old and worn-out one incapable of doing the required work. So he asked us to take back the farm since he wouldn't be able to work it with his horses. We agreed to take it back rather than let it be mismanaged and fall into neglect. It was too late to find another renter and we weren't equipped to do it ourselves, so we bought a three-year-old mare for 125 dollars and rented a horse from Syver Belgum (son-in-law of our deceased uncle Guttorm Lie). We are almost done with the spring plowing and planting and will continue in this manner through the summer.

You may be asking, "Are they both working on the farm?" No, Mikkel runs the farm and I'm almost always away teaching school or doing carpentry work. I've haven't taught regularly this winter because it's been too cold and it has often been impossible for children to use the roads, but as soon as weather permitted I began teaching regularly until a week or so ago when I began my carpenter work for the same man I've worked for before; his name is Iver Kleven. He's from Renli in Valdres and has his shop in a small town called Pine Bluff. He has a good business as he sells all kinds of lumber for building in addition to building houses for people. I've agreed to work for him this summer for $1.25 a day and this will be my main employment. I have about fifty days of teaching that must be done this school year but I've hired a substitute, a man you know well, S. Syversen from Renli. He came from Norway last fall and lives in this congregation. It doesn't look too promising for him here as he is quite unused to labor. Indeed, he is too old for hard work and the only thing he can do is teach. But it now appears that it won't be easy for him to get a school to teach in. There was an opening as teacher and precentor in the Blue Mounds congregation (next to ours in Springdale). I mentioned this to him and he asked me to help him get this position. I went to the pastor and told him there was a teacher who had just arrived from Norway who would like to be teacher and precentor in Blue Mounds. Since I knew him from Norway he was willing to appoint him but would first have to talk with him and test him in a little examination. The pastor found him qualified but he couldn't be appointed until the congregation had its annual meeting and that was still some time in the future. So I let him teach three weeks in my place to give him something to do, but he hadn't taught a full week before dissatisfaction was voiced and one after the other came to me and said that if I couldn't teach school myself I would have to find someone else to do it. They even went to the pastor and complained about him and all they had against him was that discipline was too lax. I didn't like this at all since I had recommended him. I thought he was qualified when I recommended him and I still think he is but the problem is that he is slightly deaf and perhaps somewhat indifferent, so some children made this an opportunity to fool around. I thought I would be able to fix this by talking with him about paying a little more attention and he said he would do this in the future. His excuse was that he was a stranger and had no experience with our conditions and had thought that he would do best in not being too strict. After a meeting with both the congregation and the pastor they agreed to hire him for some teaching. I don't know how it will work.

As for my own teaching I must say without boasting that it goes well. I've had good relations with the pastors as well as with the congregation and I haven't heard a word of dissatisfaction from anyone. I've been precentor in the Springdale congregation for three years; they all know me and I'm also well acquainted with the members because I've moved around from home to home with the school. Everywhere I've come people have been helpful and friendly and I've been met with love and kindness. I don't boast of this but thank and praise my God who has found me worthy of so holy and important a calling in his vineyard. Now that I've been met with so much love and kindness you may be thinking: Yes, then you must really enjoy being a schoolteacher. But I must admit that I haven't been so happy in my position. The reasons are various and it would take too much time to explain them for you now, but on some later occasion I'll write more about this. As my predecessors have left their position after a short period, I think that I'll also do the same. Indeed, I think I may resign soon. My time is short and I wish to write as much as possible so I must be brief. From what I've written you'll understand that Mikkel is home working the farm while I'm away at work. We share my income as well as what we make from the farm.

We are so sorry brother Anders for your loss of the faithful and devout spouse that God had given you. But we must take Job's words to mind: The Lord gave, the Lord took, the Lord's name be praised. However difficult it may seem to our sinful flesh and blood to praise and thank God when he sends us such difficult trials, this is how it must be, because if we consider Job's story we see that when his wife asked him whether he still believed in God in his suffering and great misery he replied: "Shall we receive the good at the hand of God, and not receive the bad?" He regarded this heavy cross as a loving gift from God. This is how it is when we think that God is at his harshest with us; but there is nothing but goodness in God. Job did not perish in his misery and God blessed him so that he not only got well again but twice as wealthy as before. Consider how strict Jesus was with the Canaanite woman. Not only did he refuse to answer her but he turned away and entered the house, and when he eventually responded, urged by his disciples, his words were so harsh and offensive that she may have despaired of any solace. But however strict and harsh he may have appeared, there was nothing but goodness in him because she was given what she had asked for. This is your situation, my dear brother. God has afflicted you heavily but his intentions are good and he will provide you with a glorious conclusion. We must not doubt this even though we as weak humans are unable to understand and grasp it, because my thoughts are not your thoughts and my ways are not your ways, says the Lord. So, my dear brother, do not despair but leave everything to him who can wound us and heal us, make us grieve and make us glad, break us down and raise us again. Hope and believe that he who has wounded you can yet heal you; he who has brought you grief may yet comfort you and make you happy. May the Lord help you in your grief and need and may he turn your sorrow to happiness and your affliction and your adversity to joy and glory for the sake of Christ, Amen.

I must conclude. It is late and tomorrow I'm going to work again. My letter is brief, but you must excuse me. I'll do better another time. I send greetings from all my relatives and friends; they are doing well as usual. Brother Iver has gone to Dakota again but we haven't heard from him yet. I often think of my family and friends and would have liked to see them and talk with them. Give them all my regards. Write when you can and tell me the news you know. Farewell in God.

O. A. LIE

. ——— .

OAL taught in the parochial schools of Springdale and East Blue Mounds until 1918, when they were probably closed. He was still precentor in 1924. Iver Kleven emigrated in 1867. A son, Knut Kleven, took over the lumber business in 1893 and with his brother Gilbert started the Wisconsin Silo & Tank Company in 1907. OAL's brother Anders had been married to Ragnild Guttormsdatter. Job's answer to his wife is in Job 2:10. «II:148 »II:186 NE IV:239

. ——— .

1884 — LETTER 2:155

FROM: Jacob Hanson Hilton, *Socorro, New Mexico, 4 May 1884*
TO: Hans Jakobsen and Anne Olsdatter Hilton, *Kløfta, Ullensaker, Akershus*

⊶⊷

Dear parents,

My good father: Thank you for your letter dated March 10. Uncle Christopher came to Socorro a week ago. I knew him from your descriptions as soon as I saw him in the door. He is a little fatter than you but not quite as grey-haired or as bald. I don't know what he'll do but I've suggested that he should buy Asche's part in the business and stay here but he hasn't given me his opinion yet. He wanders around, in and out, and thinks I stopped in a hell of a place to begin a business, a place where you can't get decent food. He says he can bake better bread and make better coffee than you get here. I think he would teach both mother and Aunt Søli to bake bread if he came to you. He, Oluf, Hans Tveter and one of the shoemakers rented a carriage and a couple of white and blue horses today and went to San Antonio to visit August and have a taste of his Trondheim aquavit. August sells beer and liquor and has just got in a barrel of the Trondheim drink that Uncle hasn't tasted since he was in Norway. I suppose they'll come back singing sometime tonight if they don't get lost on their way. He talks about going further east to the Haga boys but I don't think he'll get further east than he is now.

I see that people get married there but I can't understand why they would want to go to America now. Times here are no better than in Norway, at least not this past year, and they are getting worse. If I hadn't been well situated and built a solid business I would have gone home right away. As it is, I'm doing quite well. But if I had to begin here with hard work I wouldn't have stopped for twenty-four hours. A good worker can do better <u>right now</u> at home than anywhere in America. There are so many people out of work that wages have fallen to almost nothing. As I see it the impeachment of the Norwegian government was the right thing to do; to hell with the entire gang of scoundrels. Send them out of the country so people can live there and get something done. You seem to think that people can't live there any longer but I am of a different opinion: people will soon live better there than here in America or at least just as well and as long as you're satisfied you can live well anywhere. Give my regards to Karen and thank her for the photograph. I'll send her one in *return* right away, but I don't have time to write her a letter this time but will write a long one later. We have nice weather and all fruit trees seem to be doing well. In a few weeks we should have ripe cherries. Oluf is already becoming a good shoemaker. Uncle said yesterday that he didn't dare stay here too long because he feared that I would place him on a stool and teach him to mend shoes. He said it was difficult to teach old dogs new tricks but that he thought he would like to sell shoes since that would give him opportunities to fondle the ladies' legs when he buttoned up their boots. I have no more to write about now. Before he went off to see Gus this morning, Uncle asked me to give his regards to all at home. Loving greetings from us all, Yours

J. H. HILTON

· ——— ·

Two other members of JHH's family are now in Socorro: his brother Oluf and his uncle Christopher Jacobson, who did go further east, all the way back to Ullensaker to visit his old home. He returned to the United States but eventually settled in Kløfta as a merchant. The Lysholm distillery and maker of aquavit is in Trondheim. The failure of the Philadelphia and Reading Railroad in early 1893 marked the beginning of a depression period that lasted to about 1896. Karen is JHH's sister. «II:144 »II:202 NE IV:240

. ——— .

1884 — LETTER 2:156

FROM: Svend H. Enderson, *Radcliffe, Iowa, 25 May 1884*

TO: Jakob Rasmussen Sandvik, *Kinsarvik, Ullensvang, Hordaland*

⊷═◐═⊶

Dear Friend Jacob Rasmuson Sanvig,

As I've come to a new country I'll write you a few words and tell you that I like Iowa. I came here in March; it is 360 miles from Illinois to Iowa and that's far. There are people here from Sørfjorden and many other Norwegians so the land is quite settled. There is much good land and much cheaper than in Illinois, so I'll soon have a farm. But when you get land you also need a wife. I'm not married yet. I've often been close but without succeeding. I'm like you Jacob, I like them all. Neither you nor I have found the right one yet. The last one I had turned out to be false and I said goodbye to her after a year when I went to Iowa. I'll tell you more about her some other time. Say hello to your brother Svend and other siblings. I've heard that many are on their way to America but I suppose you won't ever come. Farewell. Write soon.

SVEND H. ENDRESON

. ——— .

SE writes the names of the states as *Iova* and *Illenoes*. Sørfjorden (the south fjord) is the innermost part of the Hardanger Fjord, going south from Ullensvang into Odda. «II:142 »II:233 NE IV:242

. ——— .

FROM: John T. Fosholt, *Ottawa, North Dakota, 8 June 1884*

To: Torgrim Ellingsen Elsrud, *Aadalen, Ringerike, Buskerud*

Dear friend,

Some time ago I had greetings from you in a letter from my grandfather. It was nice to hear from you and the best news was that your leg is getting better. I don't have much to write about of interest for you but I'll get down some sentences and send them to you so you can see how I live. I am, thank God, in good health and I'm reasonably well satisfied, and this is the best we can wish for. We've just started to break the soil and it's going quite slowly since we still only have oxen. We have a fourteen-inch plow that is pulled by three oxen. This year we planted about fifty acres, forty with wheat and ten with oats. We rented a team of horses for three days to pull the seeder and we used the oxen for the rest. We've had excellent weather and our fields look promising. I've just proved up my land so I won't have to live on it if I don't want to do so. I've planted about twenty-one acres of wheat and planted some trees on a small piece and potatoes on another, so I broke about twenty-two acres this year and last. This summer I've broken five to six acres and plan to break fifteen to twenty more.

Last Sunday all except Torval went to a church service. He stayed home to take care of the cattle since we don't have a *pasture* and have to keep them away from the fields. I may as well tell you what cattle we have. In all we have fifteen, including our draft oxen—four milk cows, four one-year-old calves and four born this spring (two of our cows milk well, about twenty quarts each time, the two others a little less). I almost forgot to tell you that we have joined a congregation; it is in the Conference and is served by Pastor Lundeby. We don't have churches as everything is so new and services are held in private homes. Ole and Torval go to an English school; we still don't have a Norwegian school. I see in the newspapers that you've had a <u>great</u> conflict about politics, that one cabinet minister after the other has been dismissed and that there are even fears of a coup. But we must hope that this gets better?

I haven't seen or spoken with your brother Iver for more than two years. He was in Iowa for the winter and I think he lives about 100 miles from here. We sometimes have letters from Onstad and Bjørn and all seem to have taken land. I see that you don't think it impossible that you may visit this country and should this happen I would enjoy seeing you. Well, I must limit myself and in conclusion ask you to give our regards to my grand-parents, my uncle and aunt and your parents and siblings. You and yours are greeted from

JOHN T. FOSHOLT

· ——— ·

JTF was born in 1860 and emigrated in 1879. His mother was a daughter of Tore G. Elsrud in Aadalen and his father, Torkel J. Fosholt, was from Hedalen in Sør-Audal. Three of his seven letters in the Norwegian National Archives are to Torgrim Elsrud. While JTF is mentioned several times in letters that another North Dakota set-tler, Iver A. Lee, sent home to Hedalen, JTF does not refer to Iver Lee since he would not have been of interest to readers in Aadalen. The letters do not give full information about the social life of the writers since they rarely mentioned people who were unknown to their read-ers. Farming was very different in North Dakota than in Norway, and JTF uses the Norwegian versions of American words that he was used to when he spoke: *brækkingen* (the breaking), *cideren* (the seeder), *proovet op* (proved up). As becomes clear in other letters, JFT and his father Torkel farmed together on different sections of land. Here he first uses the plural "we" in describing work on land he has with his father and then the singular "I" writing about his own preemption land. »II:176 NE IV:243

· ——— ·

1884 — LETTER 2:158

FROM: Ole Gulliksen Dorsett, *Bratsberg, Minnesota, 17 June 1884*

To: Torsten Gulliksen Daaset, *Flesberg, Buskerud*

❖⟹◉⟸❖

Dear brother!

I got your letter May 13 and we are glad to see that you and your family are in good health. For my part I can say that I've been sick for seven months but I'm a little better now and my family is all well. Our brother Gullik and his family have just been here and they were in good health. Old Christofer Gaaseberg who lives with Gullik is also well. This year was fairly good except for the corn that failed because the summer was too wet and cold. This spring has almost been too dry. Of news I can tell you that the two oldest daughters of Christofer Førli were married December 20, 1883; it was a very large wedding and more than enough to eat and drink. I don't know whether you have heard that my daughters are married. Ambjørg the oldest was married March 25, 1880 and Ingeborg September 30, 1880. They both have a son. There have been great changes here these last years. There is a new railroad only half a mile north of my house. When we sit at the window we can see it pass by. I can also tell you that my oldest son Gullik now is twenty-two and works on his own land. He has four horses. I could have written much more but I don't think it would be of interest for you. Thank you so much for the portraits. I would be very happy if you could pay us a visit. It would be a pleasure trip for you. My health is so poor that I cannot come to you, but I would like to. Our best regards from me and my family. Give my regards to my brothers. Please write to us. Farewell. Sincerely,

OLE G. DASET

· —— ·

«II:43 »II:181 NE IV:245

· —— ·

FROM: John Hanson (Bjokne), *Latimore, North Dakota, 30 June 1884*

TO: Hans Jørgensen and Eli Johannesdatter Bjøkne, *Lesja, Oppland*

⋆⇒◦⇐⋆

Dear parents and siblings,

I will now take up my pen and tell you a little about my life in America. I have come to the golden Northwest and I like it. I'm working on the railroad. They are building a new one but I'm working on maintaining the old track. We who work on the old track make $1.25 a day and the others make $1.75 a day. This is a great difference in wage but on a rainy day they make nothing and we are paid that day as for the others. You may find it strange that I left Hans but I got so tired of being there that I had to leave. You wanted to know why, but I'll write about it some other time as it's raining today and the house is full of people. It looks as if it will be a good year here so I think I'll make good money when they begin harvesting. I sold my horse for 100 dollars. I'll soon take my portrait and then I'll write more and send it to you. I'm glad, Anne, that you didn't come to America, because Marit so often told me how convenient it would be for you, as you could use her sewing machine and live there, but I heard many say that it wouldn't be for long. Jørgen, you asked if I had a watch. Yes, I have two. First I bought one in Pope County and when I came here I met an old man who was short of money and I bought one from him. It seems we'll have rain all day so we'll have our $1.25 for nothing. We have to pay four dollars a week for meals and a bed so that doesn't leave us that much money, but I don't care as long as I have my meals until harvesting begins. You must write as soon as you get this letter and tell me how things are at home. I must conclude with loving regards to you all. I send greetings from Ole Haugen. He and Bjørner are here. But first and last my parents and siblings are lovingly greeted from your far distant

JOHANNES HANSON

• —— •

JH had a brief life in the United States, and only this letter is included here. He evidently did not get on well with his brother and sister-in-law, Hans and Marit Bjokne. He has no Norwegian word for track and writes *træk*. «II:147 »II:193 NE IV:246

· —— ·

1884 — LETTER 2:160

FROM: Torine Iversen, *Silvesta, North Dakota, 8 July 1884*

To: Elling Olsen Elsrud, *Aadalen, Ringerike, Buskerud*

⊹⇒◉⇐⊹

Mr. Eling Elserud,

As I'm now at Iver Elsrud's I'll write a few words to tell you that Iver has paid Ole Haugerud the money I borrowed from you. He did it on Sunday. I didn't ask him to do it but he did it anyway and I'm glad he did. Now I owe him this money and he doesn't seem to need it now. I've lived here since I arrived but this evening I'm going to work for a family from Stavanger not so far from here. I'll make two dollars a week but will get a little more during harvest. Give my regards to Olea. I should have written to her but I won't do it until I've been here for awhile and have something to write about. I suppose I should tell you about my journey. We had nice weather but I was very sick so it was no pleasure trip, but it didn't take long, only three weeks from Kristiania to Elsrud. Thank you for lending me the money. I send greetings from your son Iver. He's at home now but is soon going to his land at Grafton. Greetings from

TORINE IVERSEN AND MY SISTER LISE ENGEBRAATEN

· —— ·

Inger Torine Iversdatter (born 1864) was from the small croft Havrebraaten in Aadalen and may have served at Elsrud before emigrating. At least it is clear that Elling O. Elsrud has lent her money for her ticket. Her sister Lise may have served at Engebraaten. Iver E. Elsrud had land at Grafton as well as at Silvesta, both in Walsh County, but it seems that in 1884 he was living on his land at Silvesta. Torine actually wrote that he was going to his land in *Manta*, so Grafton is a conjecture. Ole Haugerud was Elling Elsrud's brother-in-law. Olea and Elling Elsrud were Iver's parents. NE IV:247

· —— ·

1884 — LETTER 2:161

FROM: Elise Wærenskjold, *Prairieville, Texas, 18 August 1884*
To: Thomine Dannevig, *Lillesand, Aust-Agder*

⊷═◎═⊶

My dear, good Thomine,

I've written a letter to your son but am not sure of his address, so I'm sending it to you. Then I know he'll get it and you may be reminded to send a few lines to your old friend. When you write I get to know a little about my acquaintances; you are the only one in Lillesand that writes to me. Kaja, Gusta, and Christina Normann do not write anymore. In some ways I'm doing quite well: I'm in good health, and have good neighbors and my daily bread. But as long as I haven't paid all my debt I live in constant fear that my oldest son will be bankrupt. His business is in wheat and it will be difficult for many farmers to pay him this fall as the cotton crop will fail because of too much rain in spring and too little in summer.

I'm glad that our new relatives are so content and in good health as new-comers often are ill and dissatisfied. My son Niels and his wife had both a boy and a girl and they seem quite satisfied. I can greet you from Ouline Reiersen. I often visit her and it so nice to be there. We'll both miss her step-son. Johan Reiersen has let his house and land in Prairieville for three years because they want to move to a larger town with a better school for their children. Reiersen's wife is an American but a very pleasant woman and she is always kind to me. Mrs. Pabst never comes here. She doesn't go anywhere and stays at home with her unpleasant husband. She is wealthy and I am poor but I wouldn't wish to change places with her. I visit her every time I go to Otto as she lives near the depot closest to him.

You cannot imagine how excited we Norwegians have been keeping up with the recent developments in Norway. At times I feared that it would come to war and that would have been terrible. It was bad enough with the conflict between the Conservatives and the Liberals. I've never been able to understand why one cannot be good friends in spite of different political or religious opinions. Please give my regards to all old friends and acquaintances you may meet. How is Bina Grøgaard? It's so strange that she is now poor and I've not been able to understand what has caused it. I've never heard of any calamity that could have brought down the wealth of the Grøgaards. Dear Thomine! Please send me a long letter right away. I wish you and Thorvald would go to the exposition in New Orleans and then visit us. It would be so good to see you. Your always faithful

ELISE WÆRENSKJOLD

· ——— ·

This letter is not in Clausen 1961. In a letter EW wrote to Thorvald Dannevig on 14 July 1884 (Clausen 1961, 124–125), she thanks him for six books he has sent her and admits that she does not like Ibsen but is all the more fond of the Norwegian writers Jonas Lie, Kristofer Janson, Alexander Kielland, and Ole Kristian Gløersen. Two of the three who did not write to EW were Kaja Poppe and Gusta Hauge. Ouline Reiersen (born Ørbæk) was first married to Kristian Severin Reiersen and then to his brother Johan Reinert Reiersen. Her stepson Johan was a son of her second husband. His wife's name was Alice. In Norway a long political conflict had recently been resolved with the King (who was also king of Sweden) accepting a cabinet formed by the Liberal majority in the *Storting* (parliament). EW was not alone in fearing that the conflict could lead to a war between Norway and Sweden. The 1884 World's Fair, also called the World's International and Cotton Centennial Exposition, was in New Orleans. «II:146 »II:165 NE IV:249

· ——— ·

1884 — LETTER 2:162

FROM: Hellik Olsen Lehovd, *Rock Dell, Minnesota, 10 December 1884*

To: Knut Gislesen Aslefet, Flesberg, Buskerud

⊷⟞⟝⊶

Thank you for your letter of May 5 that I received a long time ago. It is so good for me to hear from old friends and relatives in my fatherland

Norway. I must ask you to excuse me for letting so much time pass before replying because I have so much to take care of, especially in summer, farming and taking care of my animals, and I am responsible for it all. I can tell you that I've been in good health as have my children, for which we must thank God. My daughter Julia was twenty-one last fall and is in Rochester working for an American family. My son Henry is nineteen. This fall he worked on a threshing machine. Berthea, sixteen, was confirmed last spring and is my housekeeper. The two youngest, Lovisa, twelve, and Helen Severine, ten, go to English school.

Last year was a good year for all produce, in particular for hay and corn, but prices for grains are lower now. For a bushel of wheat we only get forty-five to fifty cents, barley twenty-five to thirty-two cents, oats fifteen to twenty cents, pork three to four cents a pound and butter fifteen to twenty cents a pound, so times are hard and wages have remained high. This year I had 576 bushels of wheat, 381 of oats, 114 of barley, some corn, and more hay than I'll use this winter, but the weather has been so bad that I lost a cow and a thirteen-year-old horse died of hives, but we've been spared from tornadoes, had a mild fall and have had just enough snow for our sleds. Last summer they began work on a new railroad from Iowa to St. Paul and it will pass near my brother Paul. Both my brothers are doing well. I visited Ole a short time ago and they were in good health. We had a presidential election November 4 and next March 4 we'll have a Democratic president after having had a Republican government since 1860 when Abraham Lincoln was elected at the time war broke out between the Southern and Northern states. We'll see what the consequences will be.

I must conclude my simple letter with friendly regards to you and your family. It is many years since we went to school and to confirmation together and since then I've been tried in both success and in defeat, happiness and grief. When a man owns a farm in Norway large enough to feed himself and his family, he should be satisfied where he is and not leave his old home. Please be so kind as to give my regards to my old father and my brother Knut Lehovd. Best wishes for a happy New Year from your brother-in-law,

HELLIK OLSON LEHOVD

· ——— ·

«II:80 NE IV:254

· ——— ·

FROM: John T. Fosholt, *Cooperstown, North Dakota, 25 December 1884*

TO: Torgrim Ellingsen Elsrud, *Aadalen, Ringerike, Buskerud*

⋆⟶◉⟵⋆

Dear friend!

It is Christmas and as I sat here in peace reflecting on long gone days and my beloved land of birth I thought of you and many other childhood friends and I realized that I have a letter from you that I haven't replied to. That was long ago and I've lost the letter but I'll send you a few sentences so you can see that I'm still alive. We're all in good health and I hope to hear the same from you. We had nice weather last fall and it lasted far into winter, but for the past couple of weeks it has been very cold, so cold that it's been difficult to tend the animals and chop wood. We haven't hauled a single load of firewood since last winter and I think we have almost all we'll need. We haven't paid much for wood till now as there has been forest on some *railroad land* down by the river that hasn't been taken and quite a few have taken what they needed there. But it has all been cut and it'll now be more difficult as firewood is quite expensive. One cord usually costs three to four dollars for hard, good wood. A cord is a layer of wood that is eight feet long, four feet high and four feet wide. You can get it cheaper by cutting it yourself, buying trees or buying acreage. One acre of forest with good wood of oak, ash, elm, basswood and other hardwoods can be bought for forty to fifty dollars. There are no evergreen trees around here. We have forest about two miles from us. As for our harvest: Last year was what may be called a golden year and from forty acres we had 888 bushels of wheat, nine acres with oats gave us 430 bushels. We also had more than enough of potatoes, roots and garden vegetables. But prices were low and we now get forty-nine cents per bushel of wheat while we can hardly sell our oats and certainly not our potatoes and roots, etc. Last week we slaughtered one of our draft oxen that was too old. We had been fattening it with turnips, pumpkins and the like and last time I was in town I sold a thigh and a leg weighing 158 pounds for eight cents a pound and the skin that weighed 105 pounds was sold for four cents a pound. This may give you an idea of the prices we get. We buy five and a half pounds of good coffee and thirteen pounds of white sugar for one dollar; kerosene is thirty cents a gallon, chewing tobacco sixty cents a pound and a little more for smoking tobacco. Matches have been quite expensive until last year when the tariff was lowered, so now you can get six boxes for twenty-five cents and I think there are 250 matches in a box. They used to cost twice as much. Last fall I went to two funerals, the first one for a Yankee boy, one of our neighbors, who had been killed by a horse. We don't yet have a graveyard so they bury their dead on their own land. There are many accidents around here. I know of three who were shot to death this year because of their own carelessness; two were Yankees and one Norwegian. Two people froze to death last winter. As I can't think of any more to write about and since I'm in town today, I'll send this letter with a thousand greetings to you, your parents and siblings, indeed all at Elsrud and hope soon to hear from you again. Give my regards to my grandparents, and again you are greeted in friendship from me, your friend

J. T. FOSHOLDT

· —— ·

The code switching of his everyday speech is evident in words such as *kord*, *pampkins*, *jenkigut* (Yankee boy), and *jenkier* (Yankees). «II:157 »II:176 NE IV:256

· —— ·

From: Anne Norsby, *Necedah, Wisconsin, 12 January 1885*
To: Marie Olsdatter Vigerust, *Dovre, Oppland*

◦⇒◉⇐◦

Dear Marie,

It's almost a year since I wrote to you without a reply so I'll try again. I can tell you that we are all well and I hope you can say the same. Last summer Rønnaug and I enjoyed ourselves but we also had a lot to do. We had ten boarders until late fall. Then two or three left and my parents went home to the farm. It became too much for mother, so one of us had to be home. I went home and Rønnaug remained in town until the others had gone to the forest. Then she came here. My brothers were home this winter until after Christmas. Then Ole went to the forest but the others are still here. Rønnaug went to town to work as a maid the day before Epiphany. I think I'll be home until late March. On Christmas Eve we sat talking about how much fun they were having in Norway. Then two boys came to take us to a dance and all six went. They were all Norwegian except for an American who spoke Norwegian. There was plenty of beer and liquor and dancing. Ole and Sivert took turns playing and we were there until three or four in the morning. On New Year's Eve two Norwegian girls and a Norwegian boy came visiting from town. The next evening we were invited to a dance at one of our neighbor's, the next evening we had a dance, and the next Sunday evening there was a dance at another neighbor's. The visitors from town left when Rønnaug went. On January 12 we went to the funeral of a little boy of the family we visited on Christmas Day. It was done in the Norwegian manner and we were served both food and drink. We were there until evening.

I don't think I've told you about our animals. We have six cows, two three-year-old heifers, a one-year-old and a two-year-old ox, four sheep, three horses, eight chickens, two pigeons, and two pigs. Winter didn't begin until five weeks before Christmas when we had snow and wind. After Christmas it's been cold. I wouldn't like to live on the prairies of Dakota and Minnesota where there is little firewood. We have firewood next to our fields. I haven't seen your siblings since I was in town last fall. Bjørner was there after Christmas and they were then well. It's only five miles from us to your siblings as the crow flies but there is a river between us so it is about twenty miles for us to go. My brothers are tending the animals this winter. My outdoor work has been to feed two pigs, look after the chickens, milk the cows, fetch water and do some housework. I've also done some knitting and sewing as has mother. I cannot remember having had such an easy time with so many animals since I was old enough to work in the cow stable.

I often have letters from Oline Skaalgaard and I had one with a portrait before Christmas. She is doing well and asks me to give you and Ingeborg and Ragnhild her regards. I must now end my letter with loving regards to all of you at Vigerust from all of us at Norstebø. Were you invited to Anne Rise's wedding last fall? If you come this summer you must come in time for the Fourth of July so you can take part in the festivities. Last summer we had such fun on the Fourth of July. We were here on the farm with many visitors. If you write you must tell me a lot of news. I know that much happens in Dovre in a year. Give our regards to Haugen, Høye, Slette, Gurihaug and Dalen and not to forget, your sister Ragnhild and Mari Slette. But first and last you are remembered by me,

ANNE NORSBY

· ——— ·

The letter is dated 1 January 1885, but since the date 12 January is mentioned in the letter it was probably completed much later. Marie lived on the smaller of the two Vigerust farms. Ragnhild was a sister of Marie while Ingeborg Bjørnersdatter was the sister of the farmer on the other Vigerust farm, Jakob Bjørnersen. Another sister of Jakob B., Anne, was the wife on the farm Ekre in Dovre. They came from Lesja. Marie's siblings in Necedah were Jacob Olson and Olianna Hanson. It may be noted that after three years in Wisconsin, AN still finds it quite natural to do outdoor work on the farm, something her Anglo-American neighbors would have found strange, even uncivilized.
«II:1 52 »II:2 11 NE V:3

· ——— ·

FROM: Elise Wærenskjold, *Prairieville, Texas, 31 January 1885*
To: Thomine Dannevig, *Lillesand, Aust-Agder*

⊷⟹◉⟸⊶

My dear, good Thomine,

My best wishes to you and yours for a happy New Year. Thank you so much for your welcome letter. You had mailed it June 1 but it took so long to get here that it may as well have traveled around the world because I didn't get it until the end of November. It came to me in Clifton two days before I returned home and I was so sorry that I didn't have it two days earlier because I had just visited Andreas Andersen, Mrs. Pabst's nephew, and he said that he never heard from Lillesand, so he would have liked to read it. Mrs. Pabst read it when I spent a night in her home on my way back since she lives in the nearest town with a railroad depot. Ouline enjoyed it when I came home and now it is paying a visit to Sigurd. So you see how much people from Lillesand appreciate letters from home. I wrote to you and Thorvald before I went to Hamilton and Bosque and hope you have received them. If you haven't you must thank him so much for the books. You must be so happy, Thomine, being able to divide your time between your children and your home and all of you being so well off. My son Otto has had problems with his health and his business and I'm too poor to help him as I would have liked. Otto hasn't been well for a long time and when his wife wrote at Christmas he was bedridden. All here are well and my grandchildren are healthy. Otto's two oldest go to school.

I had a really nice visit to Hamilton and Bosque last fall and I was more than five weeks with Otto and more than four in Bosque. Summer was unusually warm and dry and this gave a poor harvest. We had a beautiful fall but had all kinds of bad weather at Christmas: frost, snow, rain, thunder, and lightning. I didn't visit anyone until New Year's Day when I attended a dinner party at one of our Norwegian neighbors whose son had been married the day before with a sister of Otto's wife. The newlyweds live with Ouline Reiersen and he has rented half of her field land and will feed her cattle once a day. They are a very nice family so this will be good for Ouline. If you received my letter you will know that several relatives of my husband came here last spring and I'm so glad they were satisfied. Husher is going to the Exposition in New Orleans this month and has said he will also visit Texas. I hope I'll be able to see him and will surely bother him with questions about Norway. I knew that Mrs. Hauge and Miss Grøgaard were dead because Mrs. Pabst had seen it in the newspapers.

January 31: This has been a long break and for a sad reason. I had a letter from Otto's wife and she thought he was dying so I packed my suitcase and went off the next morning. But, thank God, Otto was better when I arrived and could sit in a chair. His health is improving but he is unable to work and this is difficult for a man with a family that has to be fed every day. He was a storekeeper for a while but was unsuccessful. Then he was a butcher for a few months until he became ill and then that was over. God knows what he'll try now. This time my ticket cost fifteen dollars and I borrowed ten of them from Mrs. Pabst, and I sat all night in the waiting room at the depot and didn't even buy an orange that I'm so fond of. It isn't pleasant to travel under such conditions. Last fall I covered my travel expenses by selling subscriptions for Mr. Husher's newspaper. It takes two days to go from here to Hamilton or Bosque as you have to change trains about halfway and wait for eleven long hours on a hard bench. Well, those who can afford it can stay at a hotel. The weather was nice going to and from Hamilton but awful while I was there with ice, snow, slush and rain, all of which are a terror for us Texans as such weather causes great losses of cattle, horses and sheep. I wonder where you may be now—perhaps in Tønsberg or in Christiania? I'll send it to Lovise Seeberg and then it will surely find you. Of course, you were also called to your son's sickbed and I'm glad he got well. Give my regards to your children and to my old friends and acquaintances. If you see Mrs. Basberg then tell her that I wrote her in March and that I'm waiting for her reply. Ouline Reiersen and Mrs. Pabst send their regards. They are both doing well. Tell your brother Samuel that I was with him in my thoughts on his seventy-fifth birthday. Your faithful

ELISE WÆRENSKJOLD

. —— .

This letter is not in Clausen 1961. Andreas Andersen was a brother of Ingeborg Pabst. Sigurd Ørbæk was a brother of Ouline Reiersen. Otto Wærenskjold's wife was Ophelia and her sister was Ovie Spikes. Mrs. Hauge must be the often mentioned Gusta Hauge in these letters and

Miss Grøgaard may be a daughter or sister-in-law of Bina Grøgaard. Ferdinand A. Husher was editor of *Fædrelandet og Emigranten*. The letter thanking Thorvald Dannevig for the six books is in Clausen 1961, 124–125. The English EW used in her daily life sometimes interferes with her Norwegian as when she writes that the Dannevigs are *saa vel af*, thinking of the English "so well off" but not making sense in Norwegian. She also uses the Norwegian verb *gaa* as the English word "go" so that it seems that Husher plans to walk to New Orleans.
«II:161 »II:195 NE V:4

· ——— ·

1885 — LETTER 2:166

FROM: Christine Dahl, *Norse, Texas, 4 February 1885*

To: Erik Pedersen Furuset, *Romedal, Stange, Hedmark*

⋆⇒◉⇐⋆

Dear brother,

It's a long time since I heard from you so I'll send you a few lines and let you know how things are with us. I and my children and grandchildren are, praise God, all well and our family has grown by two since we last wrote. Ole has a little girl named Helma and Peder, a son who was born about three weeks ago and hasn't been christened yet. As for news I can tell you that Aunt Rogstad married off two of her children at once: Berendt and Marthea. Berendt's wife's name is Emma Andersen and Marthea was married to Johan Hoff, my son Ole's brother-in-law. We were all at the wedding. Thomas was married about two months ago to a girl named Martha Aas from Løten, so Aunt now only has one unmarried child, Pauline her youngest. Thomas does the farming and she will live with him.

Times are not the best as prices are low for what we can sell. There was little cotton last year. I sold three bales for nine cents a pound. The wheat did well but prices are low. I've sold about 700 bushels, some for sixty cents and some for fifty-eight cents a bushel. Oats are sold for twenty-five to twenty-eight cents a bushel. I haven't sold more than 100 bushels of oats. The weather is now very nice but winter has been cold and wet. The cattle and horses have managed well and if it doesn't get too cold I think we'll do well this winter. Many of the Americans' cattle and horses have died of hunger because they didn't have sufficient stores of fodder and the winter has been harsher than usual.

Karen sends her regards. Her health isn't so bad and her children are all well. The three youngest go to the English school. She doesn't have renters this year. We helped her plant some of her wheat and she'll hire help for the rest as her daughters can do much of the work that comes later. The woman you gave money for her journey has arrived and is very satisfied. Thank you so much for all the trouble you have taken and you must keep an account of all you give me. She is now with my son Peder. I've been expecting a letter from you as the woman said you would write, but I haven't received anything from you or other relatives in Norway. As I've written to them all I'll now only write to you, so you must give them my regards and let me know how they are doing. How is my dear old mother? I'm also beginning to feel old. Give her our regards, and also to Syverine and her children. Remember us to all relatives and acquaintances who wish to hear from us. Give my regards to your wife and children and you are greeted most lovingly from me and my children. Your devoted sister

CHRISTINE DAHL

· —— ·

CD's sister Karen Dilrud was a widow. The money her brother at Furuset used for tickets for poor emigrants who had agreed to repay by working for CD or her family came from CD's share of the inheritance from her father. «II:135 »II:171 NE V:6

· —— ·

FROM: Kari and Gunder Nordrum, *Rothsay, Minnesota, 21 February 1885*

To: Anders Olsen Lie, *Hedalen, Sør-Aurdal, Oppland*

•→══◎══←•

We received your welcome letter January 14 and see that you are all doing poorly but we can say that we, my mother and siblings and all our neighbors, are in good health. You don't know any of the people here as most are from Hadeland and Toten and other places. No one is from Hedalen but there are a few from Aurdal and Slidre. They are all nice people and wouldn't have been better had they been from Hedalen. We've had an easy winter with little snow but often quite cold. It's often hard to go to the cow barn but we don't have to carry water to the cows as in Norway. We let the cows out once a day and they go to the well and drink. Then we take half a bucket for our three sheep. It's often been so cold that the cow's teats have frozen. It's no further from the cow barn to the well than from your house to your barn and when it's so cold one of us lets out one cow at a time and the other draws water at the well. I don't do much with the cows except when Gunder is in the woods for firewood. We haven't had a hired man this winter but when my mother is here she likes to take care of the cows. She is now at Brenden and in good health, almost as fit as when she came from Norway.

It isn't far to Rothsay. It isn't very big; it has five stores, three elevators, two smith shops, many homes, and a schoolhouse. Next summer they are building a church for 4,000 dollars. The new church is four miles from our church and both are in the Synod. We have a service every Sunday and there is a service in the schoolhouse in town every third Sunday. The town is one and a half miles south of us and Mikkel lives halfway between us and town. Our land is next to his and we can see him from our doorway. Gunder's brother is our neighbor to the east. Gunder's parents have a house next to ours. They are both quite well for their old age; he is fifty-eight and she is sixty-three and he has six animals to look after. Peder and Karoline now have the farm he used to have. He has a small income from the interest on

600 dollars. They have four children. Mari is married to Anders A. Song from Hadeland. He says he knew Iver Lie and Gudbrand Gunderhuset when they were in Hønefoss. Oline is married to a man from Gudbrandsdalen. Father has given 100 dollars to each of his children and we can say that we are all well off. There are three farmers between us and Olaug. It is much better to be in service here than in Norway and after I married I've been very comfortable. I'm busy tidying and sewing. The clothes here are not as good as in Norway and we can't pay to have them sewn as we did there. That would cost more than the cloth. You mustn't think I'm so fine. I haven't had more than one new coat and a dress of grey calico, but I have the clothes I need and we have a good house with three rooms on the first floor and two upstairs. This winter Ole Eriksen Elmestuen from Haugsbygden made us a corner cabinet that cost us ten dollars. My only news is that a woman died so suddenly. She had been washing clothes and when she went out with the water she fell down dead. They saw her and carried her to her bed but there was no sign of life. Last summer a young man died in the same manner. He was quite well in the morning and went out after breakfast to lead his team to water, and when that had been done and he was about to harness them to his mowing machine he fell down dead. I often think of my father's sister who is so ill. I suppose she may soon leave this vale of tears. She has suffered much since I first met her. But you were patient and that is the best we can be. I think she will soon have a long Sabbath with Jesus. I hope I'll soon have a letter from you with news. I would be glad to pay for the letters as it is easier for us to spend some shillings than it is for you. Now I must end my simple letter with regards from us all.

GUNDER NORDRUM   KARI M. NORDRUM

I'm sending you a portrait so you can see our children. It was taken last fall. I've had a letter from Oline Sørli. Please thank her. And a special greeting to you, Inger Finnhert. When Anders writes you must tell me about your family and about my aunt if she is still alive.

· ⸺ ·

Part of this letter has been cut. KN, who wrote, was a daughter of Mikkel Mikkelsen Sørli, a brother of Kari Lie, the ailing wife of Anders Olsen Lie. So she was a cousin of Anders Lie, the next farmer at Søre Li, and his three brothers in the United States: Ole, Mikkel, and Iver Lee. After her father's death she and her mother, Ragnild Sørli, emigrated in 1876 as her brother Mikkel Sørli and sister Olaug Brenden had done some years earlier. In 1877 she married Gunder

Hansen Nordrum from Gudbrandsdalen. At Rothsay she is surrounded by members of her own and her husband's family and her mother can easily move from one of her three American children to another. Inger Olsdatter Finnhert was a servant at Søre Li and soon married the widower Anders. »II:213 NE V:7

. ——— .

1885 — LETTER 2:168

FROM: Christopher Jacobson, *Socorro, New Mexico, 29 February 1885*

TO: Hans Jakobsen Hilton, *Kløfta, Ullensaker, Akershus*

Dear, dear brother!

I've written to Karen as soon as I had an opportunity after I left Hilton so you'll know that I'm back in America. I thought I would delay writing until I was sure whether I would stay here or not but as this may take some time I didn't want you to wait too long so I'll write a few words today. Even though it won't be the letter I think I would have written if I had my thoughts in order, you will, I think, receive it with strange emotions as it comes from a brother who was lost and who appeared in the fullness of time only to disappear again. It all happened so fast and so strangely that I now and again pinch my arm to convince myself that it isn't a dream. But it is no dream; I still feel a little stiff after my last journey that was both cold and stormy and I now have two Norways in my mind. I didn't find the Norway of my birth and childhood that I had traveled so far to see and it will have to rest in my mind forever as a dream. But it still stands in my mind's eye as clearly today as it did more than thirty years ago and will remain until my eyes close for the last time. The other, the new Norway, is more real and my departure was more difficult than the first as I was now older and knew more of what it meant to tumble around in the cold world. I don't dare say more about this now as I cannot describe my emotions. For one who always has wandered around without family or friends it is strange to come among people who respect him and care for him. I'm glad

I've seen the new Norway and I believe that I behaved in such a way that you need not be ashamed for my sake and if it will be my fate never to see you again I'm sure that you all, the old as well as the children, will remember that the old "Uncle from America" was there.

The only change in Socorro is that Jacob has a larger and more convenient building for his business. I came February 22 and found Oluf and Jacob well and happy. I didn't have much news from Norway but I could tell them how things were at Hilton and this is of course the place most dear to them. Oluf has made his first pair of boots and they were good and strong. There isn't a shoemaker in Ullensaker who can make a better pair of shoes than Oluf. Three more are working in the shop. One is from Sørum, a very good shoemaker who does piecework, making eighteen to nineteen dollars a week. Rud, the man who was cut up last summer, is also good but has to enter "paradise" every now and then. The third is from Modum— sent by Asche—but Jacob says he is worthless and can do nothing well even though he supposedly is a "master" from Norway. He mostly does repairs. So we have a Norwegian colony here and days are quite merry in the shop. As I write Oluf is singing "The man came home from town drunk." He understands English quite well but hasn't begun to speak it yet. Hans Tveter is as before; the shoemakers had made such fun of him that he hadn't been in the shop for a couple of weeks when I returned and when he appeared the boys told him that he would have to treat them to six bottles of beer since I hadn't brought any of his brothers with me and he went to get the beer without a word. His brother in Denver is dead. Jacob wrote to Asche a couple of days ago about buying his share of the business. I can't say how this will work out until we have his reply. Jacob wrote that he could sell it or buy it and that he would prefer to sell. It will take some time before I know what will be done. We have a large supply of footwear but business is slow even though he has enough work for his shoemakers. Jacob and Oluf have their meals at different hotels while I go to various eating establishments where I get all I need for twenty-five cents, and as two meals and a couple of shots is all I need for one day I can get along for seventy-five cents a day, but this drains my pocket quite fast when nothing goes in.

I long for a good "cup of coffee" and every morning I wonder who has made the coffee at Hilton today. Let Karen wear out her new dress as soon as she can; it's not only poorly made but much too small and won't be of any use next winter if she grows even just a little bit. If I live I'll make sure she has material for new dresses until she has finished school. Give Anne and the others my and the boys' regards. We talk about you many times a day. Write as soon as you get this. I expect a letter from Karen first. Farewell. I cannot say more. Your

CHRISTOPHER

. ——— .

Frederic Asche, CJ's cousin, lived in Chicago where he had a dry goods store. In a letter to his brother on 6 May 1885, CJ writes that he had bought Asche's share in the Socorro business for $2,300 and that the full value of the business that he owned with his nephew Jacob Hilton was $6,000. «II:149 »II:179 NE V:8

. ——— .

1885 — LETTER 2:169

FROM: Hans Hansen Bjokne, *Starbuck, Minnesota, 11 March 1885*

To: Hans Jørgensen and Eli Johannesdatter Bjøkne, *Lesja, Oppland*

⚬⚬⚬

Dear parents and siblings,

We received your welcome letter of January 18 some time ago and we are glad to see that you are in good health and doing well. We have also been well. Emma talks a lot about Norway and her grandparents. Ida is growing and now knows us. It's been very cold but little snow so transportation has been difficult. The weather has been nice for awhile, the snow has mostly gone and the animals prefer grazing out on the prairie rather than eating hay even though they get as much as they can eat. When it was really cold many feared that they wouldn't have enough hay, because then the animals eat almost all the time, but if this weather continues it seems that all will have *plenty* as we say. Times are not as good as before in America. Almost everything we have to sell is cheaper than usual, as for instance wheat that we used to sell for about eighty cents a bushel was about fifty cents before Christmas and is now about sixty. Although the prices for other products such as butter, eggs and animals are not quite so low they are lower than they used to be. The things we buy are a little cheaper, but not much.

You may like to know a little about the school situation in a new country. The country around here is not really new as it is eighteen years since the first settlers came. We have nine months of school (English, naturally) and pay the teacher forty dollars a month. School is free from the age of five to the age of twenty-one. After that you have to pay a little. We only have Norwegian school for one to two months a year. The health situation is good and I haven't heard of any illness since Tore Rise died. He suffered from kidney stones, a disease that is difficult to cure. Johannes Dalen recently had a son. This is all the news I have. Relatives send their regards. Give my regards to all acquaintances. First and last you my dear parents and siblings are greeted from

HANS H. BJØKNE AND FAMILY

I sent you *Skandinaven* last winter. It was supposed to go to you for a year from January 1, 1885. Let me know whether you have received it. Please pass it on to Haugen.

· ——— ·

Only a fragment of a letter HHB wrote on 22 March 1886 (Nor. ed. V.39) has been preserved. He reports that he has not yet heard from his brother John in North Dakota and that he is enclosing a ticket for his brother Jørgen with the Star Line. «II:159 »I:190 NE V:10

· ——— ·

1885 — LETTER 2:170

FROM: Louis Nilsen Solem, *Norden, North Dakota, 15 March 1885*

To: Ole Tobias Olsen Ødegaard, *Nannestad, Akershus*

⟶⟹⟸⟵

My dear cousin Mr. Ødegaard,

I received your letter today and will reply to it right away. Thank you so much for the photograph of your fiancée. Everyone says that the photograph shows her as a very proper woman and that you look so alike that you could be siblings. I thought it was Karen before I read the letter. We sent the ticket to Karen along with ten dollars that she can use to buy a few necessary things. This was my parents' idea. We are now enclosing five dollars that will help her to get ready for her journey as soon as possible as this would be best for her. If she waits until the weather gets warmer the journey won't be good for her health, so I think she should try to go as soon as possible. She will be going with the America Line and they will take good care of her until she is in Gary, Deuel County, Dakota, where I'll meet her.

I'll briefly tell you what it's like in DT. It is quite simple here and all say that you needn't be afraid of having millions of dollars. Our neighbors are mostly Norwegian but there are also many Americans. We have no church and have meetings in the schoolhouse. Most houses are quite plain but it is better now than it was at first. All land has not yet been bought and is being sold all the time. Prices vary. This is all about DT.

How do you think Karen, who has so to speak grown up in Christiania, will like it here? I hope she will. I'll remind you and your mother that you mustn't worry because you can't see her; we will receive her as our sister. We know that God governs all our ways and all we do, and even though we are far apart in this life we must remember there is another one! Give my regards to your dear mother and tell her that she must remember this: I know that she is your only daughter and that it will be very painful for you to part from her, but when this is according to the will of God it will always be for the best. She is now an adult. I will again remind you that she will not be a stranger among us. Then I will conclude my letter with my heartfelt regards to all of you from all of us. Your cousin and friend,

L. N. SOLEM

Farewell. Best of luck in your enterprise! You will understand my meaning. Write soon.

· —— ·

LNS does not write Norwegian very well; it is clearly his second language and this translation is at times an interpretation. Indeed, there are sentences that would be difficult to understand for readers who did not know English. Karen did not emigrate until 1886. Her mother, LNS's aunt, was Maria Kristoffersdatter. The photograph was of Amalie Pedersdatter Nilsen and the "enterprise" referred to in the conclusion was no doubt the marriage of Amalie and Ole Tobias. LNS wrote to Ole Tobias on 10 February 1886 with advice for Karen's journey and on 18 April he wrote that he and Karen had become close friends but that she was still in love with a young man in Norway. «II:150 »II:185 NE V:11

· —— ·

1885 — LETTER 2:171

FROM: Christine Dahl, *Norse, Texas, 30 April 1885*

To: Siri Kristiansdatter and Erik Pedersen Furuset
Romedal, Stange, Hedmark

◦✥═◉═✥◦

Dear brother and mother,

I received your welcome letter of April 1 a few days ago and will answer it right away as I see that our dear mother was ill. If she is living when you get this I know she would like to hear from us yet once more. First of all, thank you so much for the letter. I had waited a long time for it as we are glad to hear from you even though the news about mother isn't so good. But she is so old that we cannot expect to have her with us much longer. I pray that the Lord may grant her reasonably good health in the time she has left. Tell her that all is well here and that children and grandchildren send their regards. Karen and her children are in good health and doing well. And I can say the same from Aunt and her family. They have an auction there today. Aunt has given up and will retire. The two youngest sons have divided the farm between them. It is the youngest who has demonstrated the greater concern for his mother. We don't know how much the auction will bring or how much each of them will get. The times here are not of the best as prices for all the farmer has to sell are low. Give my regards to Syverine and her children and tell her that I'm so glad that she is able to go home and help you take care of mother during her illness. I see that you are keeping track of what I get from you and subtract it from my bond. This is quite satisfactory and I'm grateful for what you've done.

The times are hard; we get little for what we have to sell and have to pay about the same wages. Winter has been hard and spring has been late and cold, and now there is so much rain that we cannot work on our corn and cotton. I also fear that our wheat will be hurt because with all this rain it is more exposed to rust. The grass is beautiful and our hayfields look promising if only it would stop raining. Our cattle and horses are beginning to look better, too, but they had a difficult winter. Our neighbors lost many animals but we were lucky and didn't lose any. But we had to use a lot of hay to keep them alive. The prices for cattle are very low compared to last year. Then we got thirteen dollars for a year-old ox. This year we are offered eight. We sell most of our oxen when they are one year old. This year we have thirteen to sell. We hope to make nine dollars on each but we don't know yet. We now have thirty-four calves and I don't know how many we will have in all, but we'll get many more.

We've had a solemn dedication of our church, but we've actually used it for several years. Our old pastor Ole Estrem and our pastor John Rystad and a pastor called A. Turmo and a dean called Koren were at the dedication. Several hundred took part and we brought dinners to the church and had a service both before and after dinner. I have no more paper. Give our regards to all relatives and acquaintances and, not to forget, our dear old mother.

· ——— ·

> The last lines are in tiny writing and she had no room for a signature. Estrem had been pastor in Clifton from 1869 to 1877 and Rystad served from 1878 until he retired in 1925. Andreas Turmo served in Luverne, Minn., and Ulrik Vilhelm Koren was then vice president of the Norwegian Synod and pastor of the congregation at Washington Prairie near Decorah, Iowa. «II:166 »II:183 NE V:13

· ——— ·

1885 — LETTER 2:172

FROM: Martha Erickson, *Grove City, Minnesota, 6 June 1885*

TO: Nils Haavardsen and Elsa Haavardsdatter Lothe
Kinsarvik, Ullensvang, Hordaland

⋄⇒◉⇐⋄

Dear and unforgettable brother and sister,

May the grace and peace of God and our Lord Jesus Christ be with you. I've been thinking of writing to you for a long time as I've neglected it for so long. I cannot delay it any more. First I must thank you for your welcome letter. It was such a pleasure to hear that you were all in good health and doing well. I'm glad to be able to say the same for us. May the Lord be praised and thanked for his daily grace and mercy. I can tell you that Anna has a son who was born November 29 and his name is Gotfred Casper. Haaver has another daughter born August 29 named Emma Almeira. All are in good health and doing well. I can say from your family that they are doing well. He has broken nine acres and fenced the woods for a pasture and now has eleven head of cattle. He has bought a grub. I can also tell you that Peder Lund recently married a widow who has been here for a year. We have just had a funeral for the oldest son of Ole Pedersen. He was sixteen. He was very ill for two months and was glad to go home to his Savior. He asked his father to live in such a manner that he would find him in heaven. He also exhorted his siblings and friends. Yes, blessed are they who die in the Lord. My dear brother, you are always in my thoughts. How are you now with your dear God and Savior? We know that we must seek the Lord and pray diligently for grace and forgiveness for our sins while we are in our time of grace. I don't know where you live now as you didn't say whether you are with your sister or not. When you write please let me know how you are, in your soul as in your body.

We can also tell you that Helge returned last fall and lives with Anders Olsen. Lars went to Christen Erickson's father Haaver and was there for four and a half months at twenty dollars a month and has now gone to the West. We haven't had any letter from him and he lives as before, no better. You say that Lars had written that there was a search for Haaver. There is no truth in this.

Dear sister and family; some words for you too. It's so long since I had a letter from you. I long to hear how you are in your soul as in your body. You know how much trouble and grief we have in this vale of tears. Let us not neglect prayer. Pray often to our dear Father to be enlightened by the Holy Spirit and he will hear our prayer. Only you, dear Father, know how many letters we may still send to each other. Thy will be done. I must conclude with loving regards to you all. Farewell in God. Please write as soon as you can. Your loving sister

MARTA ERICKSEN

·   ———   ·

ME's letters are dictated and the spelling of her name varies. Her brother Nils has returned to Ullensvang but his son Nils Lothe (here referred to as "he") has remained in Minnesota. The married name of her daughter Anna, who writes her name Annie Oline, is not known.

Her son Haaver's (or Haavard) family name is Mickalson. Lars may also be a son of Nils. «II:132 »II:250 NE V:14

1885 — LETTER 2:173

FROM: John Swenson, *Hammond, Wisconsin, 7 June 1885*
TO: Jakob Rasmussen Sandvik, *Kinsarvik, Ullensvang, Hordaland*

Dear friend,

I received a letter a long time ago. I've been lazy and haven't replied yet, but as you begged me to do so, I must now write. I had sent a letter and a book home a short time before I received yours so I thought it wasn't necessary to write so soon. I'm in good health and all your acquaintances are doing well. Mathis Frøines has bought a farm again: seventy-one acres and buildings for 900 dollars. He is now Hendrik Kolgrav's neighbor and lives a mile north of my uncle. He bought three cows with calves and six chickens. He already had two mules. These are bred by a male donkey and a mare and are part horse and part donkey.

We've had a late spring. People couldn't do their spring work until mid May. In early May we had snowstorms but the weather is now as nice as can be imagined with both sun and rain, and everything is growing beautifully: fields of wheat and grass as wide as an ocean; the flowers in the field look up to you in a friendly way, and the trees in the garden fold out their leaves and flowers over you and bring fragrance to your nose. Shouldn't we be glad for all this and thank and praise our maker who has done all so well and given us a country with so many riches? But many come here and think that we all walk on gold and sleep on gems. Gold, silver and gems are found here. But you'll have to take off more than one sweaty shirt and tire your arms more than once before you can get any of it because it lies deep in the ground. But you must be determined if you are to get ahead in this world. I think you will understand this.

Mr. Jacob, you ask about my situation and tell me to have your letter in front of me. I would need a full bottle of whisky to tell you about all my exploits, but as I don't have one I'll do it anyway. Dear Jacob, I told you that I didn't go here to get rich, and I'm not, but I haven't been without money. You don't have to work all that hard to make a decent living. The summer I worked in a sawmill I sweated and toiled for 118 dollars, four twenties in gold and the rest in silver and paper. With a glad heart I ran with my money in my fist to the damned store that I'm now going to tell you about. I was without experience. The man had behaved well all summer and had gained our confidence as we bought our clothes and other things there. He had worked in the same mill and made his cents and he then began a business with another man and they decided to each invest 1,400 dollars in their company and share the profit. This went to my head and that of several others and we thought we would soon be able to increase our capital and become businessmen to boot and this was confirmed by the good words we heard. That winter I went to the forest and when I returned he had failed and run off. His friend didn't have anything left either. Detectives were sent after him but to no avail. I was so disheartened that I couldn't go to work in the mill again. I decided that I didn't want to work that hard for my money any more and got work with a painter and stayed with him for five months at little pay. We were six boys who worked for him and at the end of the day we drank up what we had made and kept this up all summer. My uncle got to know how I lived. All I brought home for the entire summer was twenty-five dollars. They were so mad at me that they didn't want to see me and I almost decided to take in with strangers. But at last they relented. All is now well. When I came home I had to listen to a lot of criticism and I thought it would be best to go to town and drink until they were through. But now all is well. These are hard times for workers but I have all the work I can do. I'm a painter and contract for my work. I can make from $1.25 to three dollars a day but some days I don't have work. I've thought of going to Dakota this summer but I don't know when. I saw a lot of Iver Frøines last winter. He hasn't had steady work this summer and says that he wants to go to Norway next fall as he doesn't like it here. This is all I have to tell you. Please write all you know as soon as you can.

Bout fierde Time i nou rid you Letter i bring you Pitjers of my Gilr end i think i vil go to Mariede to nexte Spring. Reespectffulley your

JOHN SVENDSON

· —— ·

Jakob Rasmussen Sandvik (born 1855), from the croft Salthello on the Sandvik farm, corresponded with several emigrants. This is the first preserved letter from his cousin John Svenson (Aslak Johan Svendsen), who used different spellings of his name. JS is living in Hammond with his uncle Jacob Swanson (Jakob Svendsen) from Salthello. JS has failed in his business venture but has not given up. At the end of his letter he shows off his English. His intended meaning seems to be: "It is about the fourth time I now read your letter. I will send you pictures of my girl and I think I will be married next spring." »II:214 NE V:15

. ——— .

1885 — LETTER 2:174

FROM: Iver Ellingsen Elsrud, *Silvesta, North Dakota, 5 July 1885*

TO: A brother, *Aadalen, Ringerike, Buskerud*

⊷⟹⟸⊷

Dear brother,

I'll send you a few words to let you know I'm still alive. I've had difficulties with rheumatism all summer and have hardly been able to work except for housekeeping (I'm now alone), taking care of my foals and milking my cow, and this is about all I can do. I sold a couple of horses last spring so now I only have three workhorses and four foals. One of them was two years in May and I've been offered 300 dollars for him, but I won't sell at that price. He is big and beautiful so I'll use him for breeding and I think I'll make good money. Here in America one has to try out many things in order to make money easily. Lars came May 5 and has since worked for me and I like him quite well. He's now plowing on my farm at Grafton. He's also taken land. Fingal, Guri and Thorvald Runhaug are here. He's built a house and I think they are quite satisfied. I've talked with Karen; thank mother for what she sent me. Regina Onstad has been ill in town this summer and Lise has been there to take care of her. She is now better and they expect her home any day. Many here have had the so-called Red River fever caused by poor water. I've just had a letter from John Torkelsen Fosholt and they are doing well. They have planted 140 acres of wheat and oats and have an ox team and a horse team. The harvest looks promising and as we think we'll have better prices for wheat than last year (because the harvest has failed in many of the southern states) farmers are optimistic. Olstad has planted seventy-five acres of wheat this year. All was well at Ole Haugerud's when I last heard from them. As I have no more to write about I must stop and hope that you'll give my regards to my acquaintances and in particular to my parents and siblings from their faithful

IVER E. ELSRUD

. ——— .

IEE has paid for Lars's ticket in return for a certain amount of labor.
«II:134 »II:212 NE V:17

. ——— .

1885 — LETTER 2:175

FROM: Hellik G. Branson, *Eureka, Kansas, 19 July 1885*
TO: Ole Gulbrandsen and Anne Andersdatter Lande, *Flesberg, Buskerud*

Dear brother with wife,

Thank you so much for your letter of June 6. I was sad to see that you had been ill but saw that you were better at the time you wrote. We are doing much as usual. I must tell you that our house burned to the ground earlier this summer and we lost almost everything in it including our clothes and bedclothes so I and my wife and Sigel are left almost naked. This happened at night and when we realized the house was on fire it was too late to do anything. I have a new house under construction and it is somewhat larger than the old one. It is twenty-eight by twenty-eight feet and in two stories with double outer paneling that I have plastered so it is much more solid than most houses. Fully furnished it will cost me about 2,000 dollars. When we move in we've planned to have a little party for relatives and friends and I would like to see you and your wife there, but I suppose this won't be possible.

We've had a lot of rain this summer and more flooding than usual in Kansas. The water has done great damage and both lives and property have been lost. Up in Madison the water was so high that it swept away the depot platform. Martin's home was surrounded by water and the roadbed for the railroad in Madison, the one that goes from Fort Scot to us, was washed away so we were without mail for an entire week. I write about this because you know what it's like around Madison. Actually, the water was higher both south and north of us; here the water hasn't been as high as it has been earlier. Some of the grain on your farm was washed away but some looks pretty good, but it is much delayed because the fields were so wet last spring that they had to be planted three times. Oats and wheat are doing well, but very little wheat has been planted. I've fenced all your land as well as eighty acres that belong to a neighbor on the condition that he could use the pasture this summer. I'll have to divide it next spring so only your land will be included. As I did the fencing with my neighbors it wasn't so expensive and Gullik Bringe and Sigel worked in return for having their cattle there, so it won't cost you anything except for the barbed wire. I had to fence the land because cattle from all over were on your land and it was impossible to keep them out of the fields when they were so close. And people would come and take away loads of firewood but now this won't be so easy. Times continue to be hard and the price on all kinds of property is low. To my knowledge no farms have been sold around here, just a little uncultivated land for pasture. The prices are so low for cattle and pigs that I sold thirty pigs this summer for three dollars and twenty-five cents per hundred pounds. I haven't sold any cattle because of the low price and it will probably remain low because of the poor prospects for our harvest.

My sons and their families are all well and have farms and cattle and are independent, so I think they will manage. Henry has a share in the so-called National Bank of Winfield and is one of the bank directors. This summer Sam bought a share in a gold mine and is working there. He says that it seems very promising. He is also Justice of the Peace. I must end this now with loving regards to you from me and my wife.

H. G. BRANSON

· —— ·

OGL's farm in Kansas was large enough to have four who farmed it on shares, according to a letter from HGB written 11 April 1885. HGB wrote about financial matters on 7 March 1885. This concludes the correspondence from HGB who emigrated in 1843, first to Wisconsin and Minnesota before coming to Kansas in 1858. «II:114 NE V:19

· —— ·

From: John T. Fosholt, *Ottawa, North Dakota, August 1885*

To: Torgrim Ellingsen Elsrud, *Aadalen, Ringerike, Buskerud*

⊷══◐═⊷

Dear friend!

Some time ago I received a letter from you that I don't think I've replied to. I'll try to stitch together a few sentences so you at least may see that I receive your letters even though it may take some time before I reply. I have news for you but not very good news as we this summer have had what we may call calamities. But first I must tell you that we've been in reasonably good health and this is the best news I have, indeed the best I can wish for since with good health other things follow, first our daily bread. So we should see the importance of thanking and praising our creator and God for these great things. But our daily bread is not the only thing of importance; there must be something else if we have any concern for our immortal soul—for Jesus has said that man does not live by bread alone, so we must acquire the kind of food that he here refers to. But I must confess that I'm not a good person in this respect.

This summer we have had unruly weather with rain, hailstorms, thunder and lightning and in June lightning killed four of our best cattle, something you may already have seen in a letter to my grandfather. We had a greater calamity on July 14 when a terrible hail storm beat down most of our grains; for us about 120 acres were ruined. This year we are using seventy acres of another man's land and almost all of this was beaten down, leaving us only four or five acres that may be profitable to harvest. On my land and on my father's free claim we have about fifty acres altogether and half of this was beaten down and here on father's preemption land where we are living not much was destroyed, but this is the least of our properties. Here we had ten acres of wheat, about the same of oats, four acres of barley, and all our potatoes, roots, corn, and garden vegetables. And yet we must be glad that everything wasn't destroyed as so many of our neighbors lost all their grain in one storm and won't even have seed for next year. We've had all kinds of storms all over the United States this summer.

This summer I had a letter from your brother Iver where he says that his health hasn't been so good. This summer we've broken forty to forty-five acres; about twenty-five on my land and the rest on my father's. This fall or next spring we'll plant trees on five acres of father's free claim and that will be a lot of work. This summer we bought a mowing machine and a rake for 100 dollars together with our neighbor Ole Moen. It will be difficult to pay the installment for next fall as we have a large debt and expected a good crop. The next time I write I suppose I can tell you how much wheat we've had. Harvesting has started and then comes the threshing that is supposed to put money in the farmer's pocket. Ole and Torval have been to English school this summer. Ole stayed home when we began haying but Torval is still going to school. As I don't have more to write about I'll conclude with regards to my friends, in particular to my grandparents, uncle and aunt, your parents and siblings and, finally, you yourself from your

JOHN T. FOSHOLDT

· ——— ·

«II:163 NE V:20

· ——— ·

1885 — LETTER 2:177

FROM: Jens Herlef Ursin, *Chicago, Illinois, 17 August 1885*
TO: E. B. Kjerskov Zahl, *Kjerringøy, Bodø, Nordland*

Mr. K. Zahl,

It may seem to you that I've forgotten my debt as I write so seldom, but this is not the case. The only reason is that times are very hard and there is little to earn regardless of what one does. Moreover, my health is so bad that my doctor advises me to go to another part of the country where the climate is better. He says that my lungs are so poor that I may become consumptive if I remain here. He uses a machine that pumps air into my lungs.

He does this once a day so you may imagine that I know what it means to be under a doctor's care. But I can't think of going anywhere as it costs far too much money. Perhaps my pilgrimage on earth soon has come to an end. I'm tired of it all. It is difficult for a young man always to be ill.

I hear there's a good chance that work on the railroad will begin soon. My friend Julius Larsen wants to set up a business that should be profitable and he wants me to come and be a partner. If I did, would you extend my debt? Please don't misunderstand me. I hope you will from the goodness of your heart give me your advice. I don't dare tell those at home that I'm ill. My poor Aunt Erikke wrote and told me how kind you've been to her. May the Lord bless you in all your business. The weather has been changeable this summer, some days very hot, but most of the time so cold you could use a coat after sundown. Respectfully yours,

JENS URSIN

. ——— .

The planned railroad was from Narvik to Kiruna in Sweden and was opened in 1902. In 1900 Julius Larsen was still employed in his brother's store at Fagernes in Ankenes. «II:98 »II:187 NE V:21

. ——— .

1885 — LETTER 2:178

FROM: Jakob Olson, *Necedah, Wisconsin, 17 October 1885*

TO: Ole Olsen and Ragnhild Jakobsdatter Vigerust, *Dovre, Oppland*

⋆⟾⟾⟾⋆

Dear parents and sisters,

As time permits I'll write a few lines and tell you how we are. Because of my rheumatism I haven't worked for some time but with God's help I hope I'll soon be well again. My wife and children have been well. Jenny, Ole and Oscar go to English school. The schoolhouse has been moved and is now on my land. It's only a stone's throw from my house so the children come home for dinner every day. This winter we have six months of school from October first. We had an average harvest. Grains are cheap as are cattle. All things are cheaper than they have been and wages are also low, one dollar and twenty-five cents a day without meals. Some kinds of work are a little better paid. There are far too many workers.

Ole Snekkerlien has had a letter from his father Ole and I see that all are well, which we are very glad to hear. I see that they have lost a little girl at Snekkerlien and this must have caused more happiness than sorrow as we should not grieve for small children who are called from this vale of tears to the eternal rest. We have had a warm fall but there is snow today even though the ground hasn't frozen yet. I see that Ole Snekkerlien asks whether Ole has any information about Ole Slette and one of the boys from Bakken. Ole and Johannes Slette worked in Necedah all summer and visited me before they left. Ole Snekkerlien went with them to where Jørgen Bakken lives. I've heard that Andreas Bakken works on a railroad. Ole and his family send their regards. They are all well. Olianna and her family are well. I see that you've written two letters but these haven't come to us. Last spring it was one year since we received your letter about my father's death. We have written but not had any reply. I would like to know why the letters don't get to us. I have no more to write about. Give our regards to all at Snekkerlien. There are so many I would like to send greetings to that I don't have space for their names so give greetings from us all to all relatives and friends.

JAKOB OLSON VIGERUST

· —— ·

JO writes without any punctuation or capital letters so it is not al-ways easy to work out his sentences. He wrote from a lumber camp in Wisconsin on 23 November 1884 (Nor. ed. IV:252). The siblings from Snekkerlia used Lee as their family name in the United States; in Norway the name was written Lie. «II:44 »II:226 NE V:25

· —— ·

1885 — LETTER 2:179

FROM: Christopher Jacobson, *Socorro, New Mexico, November 1885*

To: Andor Hansen Hilton, *Kløfta, Ullensaker, Akershus*

⊹⇒◉⇐⊹

Dear Andor!

Your letter of September 13 arrived on time. I had one from Oluf a week before yours but as Jacob wrote to him I'll write to you first. I think I've replied to Karl's latest letter. I received Dorthea's letter a few days ago. <u>Iver is strange</u>. I haven't heard from him at all. I suppose Karen owes me a letter but she is a good correspondent. I don't know what Oluf wrote to Jacob but it seems to have been something he didn't like as he has said that we shouldn't go to Norway anymore. He may have been thinking that his father wouldn't be willing to step down yet. If so, Jacob wouldn't fit in there. It would be as impossible as flying for Jacob to come and work as you do. Jacob would want to use the horses and this would lead to endless quarrels. He would also want to run the farm differently. In short, your father and Jacob wouldn't agree and that would be awkward for all. So it may be best that he stays here for another three or four years. But the longer he lives here the less fit he will be to run Hilton.

I often think of your mother. She works more and worries more than necessary. You are young and strong and have no reason to worry; you can make a living wherever you go. But I suppose it would be best for you all to stay together for some time yet. Even if you don't have all that much money to spend you do have a good home and your work is for the future benefit of all. I miss Oluf but since he was never quite well I didn't dare try to convince him to stay even though he could have made more money here. And I knew he would be welcome at home. I would have liked to have at least one of you here but all you could do would be to learn the shoemaker trade. There is no profitable work to be had nor is there land of any value. For my part I've learned to be satisfied wherever I may happen to be but I can't say I'm particularly fond of this place; I don't like the shoe trade nor most people here. I suppose I'm not a good businessman but I hate unbuttoning the shoes of nasty old women and conceited young girls, especially now that there is no profit in it. The shoemakers have been busy for a while. We have three in the shop. The German (we call him "Old Charley" and Oluf knows him well) has worked for us for some time and mainly does repairs. He made eighteen dollars last week even though we now take less for repairs as well as for new shoes than when Oluf was here. If times improve we may try to sell out since I don't think the prospects for this town will improve. The mines are no longer profitable, so the only money made here is by the cattle ranchers and this won't be enough for the many businesses that have congregated here. One tries to sell cheaper than the other and there is no profit for anyone. We can manage as long as any others, indeed, perhaps longer as we've paid for all our goods and our rent is low.

I see you've had a lot of rain in Norway. Here too much rain is not a worry but we have at least had enough to wash in as we collect it in a barrel whenever possible. We have excellent weather. The heat of summer is past and I wear my woolen clothes, but I don't think I'll need my big winter coat. If Oluf had taken it with him as I said, he would have had something to keep himself warm when he went out hunting. Jacob has a nice little mare (three years old) that I think he loves more than anything else. He bought it before she had been used so he is taming her himself and she behaves reasonably well under her saddle now. He didn't think I would be able to manage her so to demonstrate that I wasn't entirely decrepit I got up on her one day and rode off. I returned after a couple of hours and then the sweat ran down her sides. But the boy got grumpy and said I shouldn't ride her too hard. So I told him that he was more like his <u>father</u> than I had thought. He and the other two shoemakers have been down to San Antonio a few times to shoot ducks, and they shot many. When this happens I usually get a couple that I bring with me to a Frenchman who lives next to us. He cooks them in the French manner and the two of us have a great dinner with wine etc. Going off on his horse is the only fun Jacob has and since I like to be in the store he can go off as much as he likes.

I realize it will soon be Christmas when you receive this letter and I hope you'll have a better harness next Christmas Day than we had when we drove to church last year. I wonder whether I'll ever drive down that road again. I seem to be getting old. However, I think I'll keep a stiff upper lip for an old man yet. I'll soon write to both Karen and Dorthea as well as to your father. Farewell. Heartfelt greetings from

C. JACOBSON

Jacob is at a temperance meeting. He is in good health.

Andor, Oluf, Jacob, Karl, Dorthea, Iver, and Karen were sons and daughters of CJ's brother Hans Jakobsen Hilton. Andor and Karl used their father's patronym, Jakobsen, while Jacob and Oluf used their patronym Hansen. This reflects the inconsistencies in naming in the late nineteenth century when patronyms gradually became family names in Norway. The letter has many anglicisms. Oluf had returned to Norway that spring and there is a letter to him from Jacob dated 11 June 1885 (Nor. ed. V:16). CJ returned to Norway in the fall of 1886. «II:168 NE V:27

1885 — LETTER 2:180

FROM: Svend Larsen Houg, *Elgin, Iowa, 4 December 1885*

TO: Ole Larsen Haug, *Aal, Buskerud*

⊷⇒◉⇐⊷

Dear brother,

I know you've waited to hear from me for a long time and there is no use in making up excuses because it is mere neglect. But what can I say? I got your letter of June 23 on July 13 when my daughter Ingri who lives 500 miles from us was visiting with her three children. I think she is a sensible woman as is her husband and they are doing well. What you wrote about brother Knud was strange, even sad. People who are so well off in material things should be comfortable in their life here. Their children have also done well. But we all have our trials and God knows best how much we need to be disciplined. I suppose this is what happens when willfulness is given free reign as was the case with his wife. May God look in grace to brother Knud and us all that our soul be redeemed. Then our suffering will be nothing compared to the glory that will be revealed for us. As for myself and my daily life it is all sinfulness and weakness; there is no goodness in my flesh and I cannot sufficiently deplore my corruption. Nor can I sufficiently thank God for his great love and charity for miserable sinners. I must say with the apostle that I do not do the good I want, but the evil I do not want is what I do. We must do battle with sin as long as we are enclosed in our mortal flesh. You may be thinking that your brother in America is a serious Christian and then I would say yes, but weak in my flesh. In myself I am a lost sinner but I believe that Christ on his cross gave his blood for my sins. Oh, that I may conclude with a comforting Amen; for it is very possible that this may be my last letter to you as my hourglass may soon be empty.

When people write to each other they usually speak of news and even though my news may be old I will tell it. Syver Groth has gone home to his Savior. In May 1884 he suffered a sudden pain in his head and I was sent for. He soon got better and was doing reasonably well until last April when the same illness returned and got worse and affected his understanding. It became difficult for him to speak and he couldn't read, but his wife read and sang for him and this made him glad. She said that he always asked about Jesus and that she should talk about Jesus. And when I visited and told him about God's grace in Christ he always thanked me. He was like a child and the Kingdom of God is for children. But he was up and about and dressed himself and went outdoors until his last week when he kept to his bed. I was with him the day before he died. He was then unable to speak and his ties to life were cut June 11. Thus the Lord plucks one after the other of the people who have come from our old Norway. When I now go to someone to speak about our salvation I go to Johannes Groth. He is a good man.

Perhaps I should say something about the large flock of children who have grown up here and are now beginning to be scattered. Hallsten still teaches at the school. Kitil is clerk and bookkeeper in a store in town. Assor and Knud have farms here. Ole the Younger and Elling still live with me but work for others. Ragnil and Guri have gone to St. Ansgar to work for others. Ragnil is housekeeper at the school and Guri has for the most part worked for Assor Groth. After Ragnil returned from a visit with her sister Ingri, Guri went there in July and then Ragnil kept house for Assor. He is unmarried and needs help. Ragnil would have liked to stay home this winter but Knud lives in one of our rooms with his child and wife and her mother and two brothers. Her mother and a brother came from Norway last fall and one has worked for Knud. I can say for all my children that none has become a criminal or is immersed in vice but I must also admit that there is no fear of God in them and this gives grief to an old father and I know that you also are well acquainted with such matters.

I see that most of your children live in their own homes and this is as ordained by God that they should be fruitful and multiply and fill the earth. Give my thanks to your son Sven for his photograph. He seems to be a handsome man. God has granted me good health since I last wrote to you. May I therefore be grateful for his grace. Should this be the last time I write to you I would like to thank you for your letters and all that has passed between us. My thanks go to God for his goodness to me in body and soul, in time and eternity. And finally, Amen, not in my name but in Jesus' name. Should you receive these lines and should you see our brothers then remind them that they have a brother in America who greets them with the grace and peace of God. And with this my last greetings to you and your wife. The foundation on which I have built is Christ and in his death I have found life. By myself I am worthless. With this my warmest regards to you and your wife and your other family from your brother

SVEN L. HOUG

. ——— .

SLH's daughter Ingri was married to Elling Tostensen Dokken. His unmarried son Assor has taken over his farm while Knut, who married in 1883, had half the land. Halsten founded St. Ansgar Academy in 1878 and taught there until he retired in 1898. The school closed in 1910, the year Halsten died. Ole Larsen Haug's wife was Turid Larsdatter. «II:153 »II:220 NE V:30

. ——— .

1885 — LETTER 2:181

FROM: Jul Gulliksen Dorsett, *Bratsberg, Minnesota, 27 December 1885*

To: Torsten Gulliksen Daaset, *Flesberg, Buskerud*

Dear brother!

I have received your letter of November 7 and see that our brother Hellik has left this world and that Kristoffer Landerud is dead. I can, thank God, tell you that I have my health and am doing well. I see that you've had a fairly good year for grain and hay but had a lot of rain and early snow this fall. Our wheat harvest was quite small, yes, less than we've had for many years. After we had planted our wheat last spring and the plants were a few inches high we had a hailstorm that destroyed the wheat, oats, corn and what else had begun to grow and our fields looked as if nothing had been planted. But after some time plants began to grow again and we had an average harvest of corn, oats and potatoes, but the wheat didn't ripen, partly because of a period of intense heat and partly because of rust. The price for pork is low and the best we can get is three and one third cents a pound, but we get better prices for cows and horses. When you write please let me know how Gullik Ødeberg and the other neighbors are doing. I have no news that will interest you, but can tell you that we've had a mild fall. A couple of weeks ago we had a little snow but it is now almost all gone so we have no snow for Christmas. But I must tell you that our vice president Hendricks is dead as well as the wealthy Vanderbilt in New York. Give my regards to all relatives and friends. My best regards to you and your family.

JUUL GULLIKSEN DAASET

· ——— ·

Vice President Thomas A. Hendricks died a short time after his inauguration with Grover Cleveland in 1885. William Henry Vanderbilt also died that year. «II:158 »II:199 NE V:32

· ——— ·

1886 — LETTER 2:182

FROM: Karen Olson, *Britton, South Dakota, 2 January 1886*

TO: Johan Henrik Rasmusen Geving, *Stjørdal, Nord-Trøndelag*

⊷══◖◗══⊶

Dear brother!

Thank you for the letter and the portrait. The best news is that you are alive and well. In our home the situation is serious. As you may know from a letter I sent to Nordgeving, our sister Gjertine has left this world of danger. John Vormdal from Orkdal, the boy who worked for us last summer, got sick before Gjertine and after about eight weeks he went the same way as she did. Gjertine was sick for five weeks and John for eight. So in three weeks we had two funerals and we are sorry to say that our little daughter Marie has had the same illness for five weeks. We hope she will come through but God alone knows. Since the beginning of October the light hasn't been out except for the night John died. When Marie got sick we had to sit by her and she has been very ill. She is hardly more than skin and bones. She sleeps well at night and eats well. The others could not sleep except with the help of sleeping medicine.

Ingebrigt's mother has been here since last fall and has been of great help as I was so worn down by sleepless nights and worry. May God grant that Marie gets well if this is his will. The doctor said that it isn't real nervous fever. Give our regards to father, Martha, Johanna and Petter. Ole isn't here this winter and is living with two other bachelors. He has grown a lot since he came and looks fine. I'll have to conclude but I'll soon write again and let you know how things are. I hope the Lord will have mercy on us and not give us a heavier burden than we can bear. Farewell from us all. Ingebrigt sends his regards.

YOUR SISTER KAREN

· ——— ·

KO, Johan Henrik, Gjertine, and their younger brother Ole were from the farm Sandferhus in Stjørdal. In 1865 Karen was thirteen, Johan Henrik four, and Gjertine one. At the time of this letter KO was married to Ingebrigt Olson. Since Johan Henrik uses the name

Geving, he is probably living on either the Geving farm where his mother's sister Johanna Josiasdatter was the farmer's wife, or the one where his father's brother Peder Johnsen was the farmer and his grandfather, John Rasmussen, also lived. Nervous fever was one of many names for typhoid fever. »II:188 NE V:33

. ——— .

1886 — LETTER 2:183

FROM: Christine Dahl, *Norse, Texas, 18 March 1886*

TO: Erik Pedersen Furuset, *Romedal, Stange, Hedmark*

⊷═◉⟅═⊷

Dear brother and family,

As it's so long since I've heard from you I'll send you some lines so you can see how we are. It's a long time since you wrote and I replied as soon as I got it and hope that you have received it. I don't really have any news that can be of interest to you but I can, praise God, let you know that all in our family are in good health. My married children live so close to me that I can visit them and my sister Karen in one day. Syverine and Gine were here last Sunday. Karen has been in good health lately and she and her children are well. I can tell you that the last of my children, Caroline, is preparing for confirmation, so all my children are almost grown up or at least confirmed. Karen's next oldest, Olava, is also preparing for confirmation this summer.

Times are fairly good. The winter has been nice but dry. The winter wheat still looks good but has frozen here and there. We've planted our corn. Cattle and horses have done well but we've had to feed them more than before as the area is getting more settled and there are more cattle and less pasture. Prices are rather low, especially for food, and we don't know what prices we will get for cattle this year. We mostly sell yearling calves. Last year we got eight dollars apiece but we fear that we'll get less this year. We have sixty-five calves, twenty-five of them bulls, for sale. So far we've had nineteen calves but many cows have yet to calve. The price for wheat is now seventy-five cents a bushel and we sold 800 bushels. Corn is sold for forty cents a bushel and oats for twenty-five. Last year we harvested seven bales of cotton and got from eight to nine cents a pound and each bale weighs between five and six hundred pounds. This is enough about our crops. I hope that when I write about this year's harvest we'll have had a good year.

I send regards to you from Aunt Rogstad. She and her family are in good health and doing well. Give our regards to Bryni and say that I send greetings from Anders and Marthe as well as from Christian. I had letters from them a few days ago and they are in good health and doing well. Say hello to Syverine and her children. I hope you'll find the time to send me a few words in return. Farewell, and our best greetings to you from my children and myself. Your sister

CHRISTINE DAHL

· ——— ·

CD's Sunday visitors were her daughter Syverine Nelson and her aunt Anne Rogstad's daughter, Gine Hansen. In rural Norway confirmation was a rite that signified passage into adulthood. Syverine was CD's sister in Norway. «II:171 »II:230 NE V:38

· ——— ·

1886 — LETTER 2:184

FROM: Halvor Hansen Ulsness, *Glenwood, Minnesota, 3 April 1886*

TO: Nils Andreas Olsen Brusli, *Tørdal, Drangedal, Telemark*

⋯⊸⊜⊜⊶⋯

Dear friend!

Thank you so much for your welcome letter dated the Second Day of Christmas. I should have replied long ago but I will, as usual, have to ask your forgiveness. One reason for the delay will be revealed later, but first I must let you know that we are all well. Our little daughter Nelle Olette is thriving. Hans and Synne have gone to school this winter but Mari has had to stay home to take care of the baby. This winter my work was as usual; I cut firewood in the woods near my house or worked in town. Spring is here and so I can make a little more money working on roads and farms. Last year was an average year for Minnesota. It was somewhat dry in some places but crops were good on swampy and flat land. Winter was good; only a few cold days in January and just enough snow for sleighs from late January to the end of February. The snow has gone. I slaughtered a cow right after Christmas since she didn't give much milk but I bought another one that calved in early March so we now have two that give milk as well as two one-year-old steers and a winter calf. Last fall I traded two steers and a heifer and forty-five dollars for a pair of nice foals who now are two years old (a mare and a horse). I'll be able to drive with them later this summer or in the fall.

The land I've been breaking and thought of moving to has been declared government land by the Supreme Court and is now free. So I could have had a homestead but another man got this information before I did and went to the land office to ask for the same land. Now the court will have to decide which of us will have the land. We met with witnesses at the land office in Fergus Falls 26 February. That is about seventy miles from here and this trouble has cost me quite a lot. We had expected an immediate decision but yesterday I had a letter from my lawyer that it would take some time as the case first had to go to the main office in Washington. This is why I haven't written to you as I first wanted to know the outcome since this concerns at least 1,000 dollars as there are many who would give ten to eleven hundred for this quarter section. I'll write when I have the court's decision.

I had a letter from Halvor Nordbø and he now seems to like it here. He may come visiting this spring. I suppose you've heard that Ole Graa is dead. I had three letters from him the short time he was here and he complained that he longed for Norway. He always said he would visit me. I can give you regards from Torbjørn and Guro. They are doing well and things are as usual. Gunnild lost her first daughter but last winter she had a son. She is doing quite well and has a good husband. Jørgen Torbjørnsen and his family are also doing well, as are Aase Busteraak and Elling and Mari and their family even though Elling is in rather poor health. Give our regards to all at Stigen and at Homlei and to all other acquaintances. And finally, greetings to you, your wife and children from your always faithful Halvor Hansen Ulsnes. I hardly have to tell you, Nille, how welcome your letters are.

H. HANSEN

. ——— .

HHU's wife was Margit. The receiver was married to Gunhild Johanne Nilsdatter (here called Nille). This letter begins the story of a long dispute concerning the ownership of a quarter section (160 acres). When

HHU explains that the Supreme Court had declared that the land was government land this may be because there had been questions about land ownership or, simply, that the land was now opened to the public under the Homestead Law of 1862. All that was required for the acquisition of 160 acres was a ten dollar registration fee and to improve the land and live on it for five years. The right to preemption, first stipulated in federal law in 1830, was also included in the Homestead Law and this is the right claimed by HHU. There were many such legal disputes in recently settled areas. »II:216 NE V:40

. ——— .

1886 — LETTER 2:185

FROM: Karen Olsdatter Ødegaard, *Norden, South Dakota, 26 April 1886*

TO: Maria Kristoffersdatter, *Nannestad, Akershus*

My dear mother,

I've sent many letters to Norway since I left but not to you and I'll do it now that I have time on my hands. You'll know from my letters to Tobias that I'm here, in good health and doing well. Even though I sometimes long for my old home I must admit that I'm quite happy here and I don't think there are many newcomers who lead as easy a life as I do. But there are not many who feel, as I do, that it is like being at home. I think I came just in time; my aunt has been so weak since I arrived that she has been unable to do any work and now she has been in bed for a week, so we haven't had a very nice Easter. We don't know how this will develop and right now she has a bad cough. Usually her greatest affliction is her rheumatism. So you will understand that I'm quite busy as there is a lot to take care of. I'll probably stay here till summer but next fall I think I'll go to Kristine. I've written to her but haven't had a reply yet.

I've gotten to know many around here. I've been many times to Per Falla who was married to Marthea. His next oldest daughter is called Hilda and will soon be eighteen. She is a good and nice girl. Klara is poorly and she is so pale that I think she has consumption; his other children are well. Marie, Nils's sister, and her son also live close by and she has asked me to give you her regards. Our nearest neighbor is Johan who lives next to us. He has two sweet little girls. They'll soon have Ida photographed and I'll send you one. His wife Ragnhild is from Trondheim. I've been twice to church service in the schoolhouse as there isn't a church here. The pastor's family are very nice people; I've spoken with them. The pastor has a choir but I don't think I'll have time to take part. Ole Melby is here just now and sends his regards. He is a close neighbor. At Pentecost I think I'll go with him to Jens Blekke who lives eight miles from us. There are many from Kjønstad here. I've met some but didn't know them; I suppose they've been here for a long time. I have so much to write about but I see that my page is too small. All here send their regards.

KAREN

. ——— .

In 1886 Easter Sunday was on 25 April. Karen was a frequent writer and wrote to her mother from Kristiansand on 7 March 1886 on her way to America. Her mother lived on the croft Flaen with her second husband, Olaus Olsen. Karen's friend Kristine Olsdatter Nelp lived in Peru, Ill. Kjønstad is in Nannestad. «II:170 »II:191 NE V:42

. ——— .

1886 — LETTER 2:186

FROM: Ole Andersen Lee, *Springdale, Wisconsin, 17 May 1886*

To: Anders Andersen, Anders Olsen, and Kari Mikkelsdatter Lie
Hedalen, Sør-Aurdal, Oppland

⊹⇒◉⇐⊹

Dear brother and old parents,

Grace to you and peace from God our Father and the Lord Jesus Christ. Amen. I received your letter today and when I see and understand the terrible suffering and pain our mother has endured I cannot but cry in heartfelt compassion for her and I could be tempted to criticize God and say: "Oh, good and gracious God, why do you do this? Why do you lay this upon one who had tried to live a respectable Christian life all her days and who as mother and wife has tried to bring up her children in fear of the Lord, who has lived with her husband in love and respect, obedience and support, in spirit and in body, as behooves a Christian wife and mother? She who always has had a noble and loving heart, tried to do the best for everyone according to her own ability and capacity, she who has always hated and punished evil, but loved and encouraged the good, in short, she who has always had the Word of God as her guide in her progress through this world—why should she be made to suffer so?" I could be tempted, I say, to criticize God and ask him: "Is this the mercy you have promised all who love you and keep your commandments?" These are questions that our reason may ask. The Devil would like us to believe that God is not the merciful God he says in his word that he is. Job sinned when he boasted of his righteousness and criticized God when he suffered and this would be true of us as well if we laid all our good deeds before God and said: See what I have done: do I deserve so much suffering? Surely, we do not suffer more than we deserve; when we consider how God chastised Job because he committed the sin of boasting of his own perfection, we will find that the ways of God with us may be incomprehensible but that all is for the best for those who love God—as we may also see in the example of Joseph.

I don't know whether these sentences will find our beloved and sorely tested mother alive. This seems unlikely from your account. If she lives I will remind her of some words of God for comfort and fortification, not because I believe that she doesn't know them but because God's word can never be heard too often. The first may be found in Psalms 27:14. Wait on the Lord: be of good courage, and he shall strengthen thine heart: wait, I say, on the Lord. The second is in Hebrews 12:5. My son, despise not thou the chastening of the Lord, nor faint when thou art rebuked of him: For whom the Lord loveth he chasteneth, and scourgeth every son whom he receiveth. (And read on in verses 7–11.) Psalms 30:5. For his anger endureth but a moment; in his favour is life: weeping may endure for a night, but joy cometh in the morning. Revelations 22:12. And, behold, I come quickly; and my reward is with me, to give every man according as his work shall be. 2 Timothy 4:6–8. For I am now ready to be offered, and the time of my departure is at hand. I have fought a good fight, I have finished my course, I have kept the faith: henceforth there is laid up for me a crown of righteousness, which the Lord, the righteous judge, shall give me at that day: and not to me only, but unto all them also that love his appearing. Hebrews 2:9. But we see Jesus, who was made a little lower than the angels for the suffering of death, crowned with glory and honour; that he by the grace of God should taste death for every man. Romans 8:18. For I reckon that the sufferings of this present time are not worthy to be compared with the glory which shall be revealed in us.

Yes, may the Lord strengthen you in your faith in his Word! May he give you fortitude and patience in your suffering to hold on until the end! May God help me and us all to fight the good battle of faith so we may all be gathered in him where there will be no more tears and sorrow! May God help us in this in his grace and for the sake of Christ! Amen.

I must tell you a little about myself. We are in good health and doing well. I can also give you the news that September 17 my family was increased with a little girl who was christened Mathilde. She is growing and thriving. Times are hard for all who are in debt. When I last wrote I hoped that I would be able to send you some money to help you in your difficult situation, but times changed so that which we were confident we would be able to sell can no longer be sold. This is our crop of tobacco: we still have not been able to sell last year's crop. This has caused problems for many and there is a great shortage of money. Prices for cattle are also very low, indeed it is difficult to sell any. Last year we went into a debt of about 100 dollars when we built a new *house* that we haven't been able to pay because of the hard times. But we hope that the situation will improve so we can sell our produce, and if it is in any way possible to send a little money for your support we will do what we can. I'm sorry that you are in such difficulties and I would have helped you had this been possible.

School was over three weeks ago so my work is now carpentry. I have taken on the building of new houses for Ole Børtnes and uncle Ole Lee as well as one for a man you don't know. This is more than I can manage on my own so I've hired a man I think you know to help me: Ole, son of Jens Baardsen. Mikkel is busy with spring planting and when he is done with a field of corn and the tobacco planting he may help me a little with the building.

Well, now I have no more time; they are waiting for me in the kitchen to get ready for work. It is Monday morning May 17. So I must conclude. There is much more I could have written about but I've decided that I won't delay writing anymore and will tell you things in greater detail later. In conclusion I can send greetings from Mikkel and his family and say that they are all in good health. I also send regards from all relatives and friends. Old Anders Skinningsrud who now lives in our congregation has asked me to send his regards to father and mother when I write home. With this, farewell in God and may the Lord strengthen you and uphold in you a true faith for the life eternal. Amen.

O. A. LEE AND FAMILY

. ——— .

OAL's opening words are from 1 Corinthians 1:3. He is building new homes for his cousin Ole Halstensen Børtnes (son of his mother's sister) and his father's brother. «II:154 »II:204 NE V:43

. ——— .

1886 — LETTER 2:187

FROM: Jens Herlef Ursin, *Chicago, Illinois, 26 May 1886*

To: E. B. Kjerskov Zahl, *Kjerringøy, Bodø, Nordland*

⤙══◐══⤚

Mr. K. Zahl,

I'm sure you were very surprised not to receive the money I owe you even though I had promised. I'm so sorry that I must seem unreliable, but I've been so unlucky recently and lost everything I owned. This is partly because of my own stupidity but mostly because of the evil of others that I cannot now explain. And this is why I've delayed writing so long. I can thank the Lord for giving me the strength to overcome this. Dear sir, please forgive me, I may have better days ahead, but this has been a difficult time for me.

Chicago is in a terrible uproar because almost all are striking for the eight hour day and no one dares to work even if he is eager to do so, because it is necessary to be very careful if you wish to hold on to your life. There have been many bloody conflicts and the worst was on May 4 when many people were assembled in an open street near where I live and a dynamite bomb was thrown into a group of policemen who had come to stop the meeting and fifty of them were hurt; one died immediately and now six are dead. Many others were killed too and since then we've heard of nothing but conflict and murder. So America is surely heading toward its downfall, but emigration is still so large that hundreds come here every week and many of them will no doubt suffer if no one helps them.

I won't write to my home until my situation has improved. I'm so sorry that they have such great losses. My aunt writes that it is likely that the railroad work in Ofoten will be started. I will soon write more about my situation. Respectfully yours,

JENS URSIN

. ——— .

JHU also wrote on 30 August 1886 (unpublished) and on 1 November 1886 (Nor. ed. V:58). In the latter he wrote that he did not think those who had been convicted would be executed "as there is fear of a rebellion." He has been involved in a court case where a former landlord has accused him of theft. «II:177 »II:201 NE V:44

. ——— .

1886 — LETTER 2:188

FROM: Ingebrigt H. and Karen Olson
Britton, South Dakota, 14 August 1886

To: Johan Henrik Rasmusen Geving, *Stjørdal, Nord-Trøndelag*

Dear brother!

We received your letter some time ago but it had taken a long time to arrive. We couldn't reply until we found out whether it would be possible to send you a rifle. It can be done but we cannot send it until we get an express office in Britton and they said it would open in about eight days. We'll first have to write to Montgomery Ward in Chicago and have them send it to Britton and then we'll send it by express to Norway, so you should have it later this fall. I'm sorry that you couldn't get it this summer as you had hoped but if you've bought one you should sell it because the Winchester rifles are said to be the best you can get.

We are in Britton today and Ingebrigt asked me to write for him as he's so busy. I must conclude. We are all well and busy with our harvest.

I should have written to father, Martha and Johanne and Nordgeving but you'll have to give them my regards. I've been waiting for the photograph but none has come yet. Ralph is crying so I must stop. Farewell.

INGEBRIGT AND KAREN

. ——— .

Ingebrigt had written about this rifle on 5 March 1886. There seems to have been some disagreement between Ingebrigt and his brother-in-law and neighbor Ole Rasmussen about who should send the gun. When Ole wrote about it to his brother in December and 26 January 1887, he reported that he had the rifle and had tried it. KO writes *Mongomeri Vord kompani* and *Vensjester*. «II:182 »II:248 NE V:49

. ——— .

1886 — LETTER 2:189

FROM: Svend Larsen Houg, *Elgin, Iowa, 29 September 1886*

TO: Ole Larsen Haug, *Aal, Buskerud*

⊷⇒◎⇐⊶

My dearly remembered brother,

In my thoughts I'm so often over there with you. So I must send you a few words right away as there may not be many grains of sand left in my hourglass. You have again honored me with a letter for which I'm very grateful. I received it September 21. I hadn't expected a letter since I had greetings from you this summer but it isn't the same to hear something through others as to hear from the person himself. Then you get the true situation and both the worldly and spiritual difficulties that I see that you've had more than your share of. Brother, it is too much when foolishness goes so far. I have till now been spared drunkenness and abusive language in my home even though we have our share of laughter, sensual pleasure, contempt for the word of God, and blasphemy. Yes, I call it contempt when it is not used other than in derision. But what can I then say for myself; when I look back on my youth this was also my way with the one difference that we now and then read the word of God. With a few words I'll tell you how things were with me. I read the word of God, struggled with sin, and wavered between belief and disbelief, but then God in his infinite goodness gave me faith in the forgiveness of my sins in the blood of Christ. But even though we may be on the road, we have not yet arrived but are in a struggle between the flesh and the spirit as long as we have our home here; and yet we may be sure that "he who has made a beginning will also complete among you this gracious work." And "he who comes to me I will not cast out." Let me use some words by a hymnist: "I have now discovered the rock on which I anchor my salvation; this rock is the wounds and death of Jesus from before the world's foundation. It is the eternal rock that stands when gone are heaven and all lands."

Yes, dear brother, I'm glad to hear your humble confession and that God has led you into his community of grace. For my part I know that there is so much that will disturb my peace of mind so that my nature and my inclination to evil so readily come to the surface. But it is written: "Trust in the Lord with all your heart, and do not rely on your own insight." And with this, my dear brother, my loving regards. It may be that there may be words here that are not wise even though they are well intended. For our knowledge is imperfect. May the love of God, the grace of the Son, and the community of the Holy Spirit be with you and your wife and your entire home. This is the wish of your lowly brother Svend L. Houg.

My health has been quite good except for the weakness of old age. I can do some chores every day, in particular now that Assor is away from home. This may need an explanation. Because of his health he went last winter right after Christmas to a place called Colorado. As his health became so weak that he could no longer work his farm he decided to try out a place with a different climate where many people go for their health. He writes that he feels much better. Last spring he took a trip to California and San Francisco, a distance of about 3,000 miles. He hasn't yet said when he will come home but he will have to come by next winter to look after his affairs. Now it is Kittil who takes care of the accounts.

You wish to hear about Kittil and Assor Groth. I haven't heard from Kittil recently but I'm sure he is well. Otherwise I would have heard. I heard from Assor last summer when my daughters Ragnil and Guri came home after living with him. Guri had been there for about a year and Ragnil had been there for nine months, not all the time with Assor but also with her brother H. Houg. They have now come home to take care of the household for Assor. The youngest four of our children are still part of the family when they are not working for others.

You wish to hear from our sister's son Engebret E. Houg. He came to us on the eighth of May and you may imagine how surprised I was when he introduced himself. He was here for some time trying to find work, but there was no work to be had. I let him do some work for Assor while he continued to inquire around here. He worked during harvest for Knud and then went to Goodhue County in Minnesota on August 10. I had a letter from him where he says that he has work. He could tell me a lot about my place of birth and I found him to be both clever and reliable for one so young. I expect he'll be back as he left some of his luggage. He was a very good worker.

As I'm writing about so many things I may as well say a little about the weather. This summer was drier and warmer than any have experienced since coming to America. We had a burning heat and hardly any rain from the middle of May to the beginning of September. But strangely, both wheat and oats did well while the corn varied depending on the quality of the soil. I must bring this to an end. I send greetings from the good man Johannes Groth and from the widows of Syver and Svend Groth. There may be things I have forgotten. For everything in us is imperfect but in Christ all is perfect. Loving regards from your brother

SVEND L. HOUG

· ——— ·

SLH has divided his land between two sons. The part with the family home is run by Assor and the other by Knud. In his 1884 letter he wrote that his son Kittil was studying business. His son Halsten was principal of St. Ansgar Seminary. His sister Guri Larsdatter married Embrik Embrikson, and they lived on the other of the two Haug farms in Aal. It was their son who surprised SLH on 1 May 1886. SLH is steeped in the language of the Bible and here refers to 2 Corinthians 8:6, John 6:37, Proverbs 3:5 and 1 Corinthians 13:9. He also quotes from a hymn by the Danish hymnist Hans Adolph Brorson. «II:153 »II:220 NE V:52

· ——— ·

1886 — LETTER 2:190

FROM: Jorgen Hansen Bjokne, *Starbuck, Minnesota, 31 October 1886*

TO: Hans Jørgensen and Eli Johannesdatter Bjøkne, *Lesja, Oppland*

⋆⊷⊜⊷⋆

Dear parents and siblings,

Yesterday I received your letter of September 27. I'm glad to see that you are in good health and I can say the same for myself. I see that you have waited long for a letter. We wrote when we came here and since then I've written one that you probably have by now. I haven't had a letter from Johannes but Kristen Kornkven has spoken with him in Devil's Lake and he said that he worked on a railroad and was doing well. The weather is nice and I think we'll have summer awhile yet. We've done threshing and they had a good year. This winter it seems I'll be a dairymaid but I would rather have hauled wood and moss than tended the cows. But here we don't have to be careful with the hay; they get more than they eat and they are also given a good bed of hay. I can tell you that there will be a district meeting here in our church on Wednesday and I think there will be a lot of people there. We are building a cow stable for the winter. We are digging into a hill and then we'll have three stone walls and one wall of boards and we encountered a rock that was so big that we'll have to use gunpowder.

You asked me to write a little about Ingeborg and I can tell you that she's in good health and doing well. She is now living at Knut Haugen's and says that since she didn't return to Norway last year she never will. Hans and his family send their regards. I can also tell you that John Storhaugen is mad and three men have kept guard on him. You mustn't tell anyone so they'll know you have it from me. Loving regards to you all,

J. HANSEN

· ——— ·

> JHB had emigrated earlier this year. He is not quite comfortable with milking and tending the cows that was woman's work in Norway. In Lesja they would have fed the cows moss in addition to hay in order to have enough feed for the long winter. Ingeborg Eriksdatter

Haugen was a daughter of a brother of Marit, Hans Bjokne's wife, and Knut Olsen Haugen was her uncle. John Engebretsen Storhaugen died later that year. «II:169 »II:193 NE V:56

· —— ·

1886 — LETTER 2:191

FROM: Karen Solem, *Norden, South Dakota, 31 October 1886*

TO: Ole Tobias and Amalie Ødegaard, *Nannestad, Akershus*

◂►═◐═◖◂►

Dear brother and sister-in-law,

A week has passed since I got the news of the birth of your son. You may say that I'm late in sending my congratulations, but my comfort is that I sent them in advance to make sure they arrived in time. Now that I am so happy to see that all has gone well and that your firstborn is a son I'll send you my congratulations a second time. May he always make you happy and proud! I like the names you are thinking of. If you call him Sigurd you should add Oscar after our father. He is born on the same date as Johan's little Ida who was two last September 27.

I hear that mother believes I'm in Peru but you will have understood from my last letter that I won't be going there soon. I think I've offended Kristine by not coming as she hasn't replied to a letter I sent her seven weeks ago. She should be reasonable, knowing what kept me from coming. I haven't yet visited Jens Engelstad and this is a shame since he doesn't live so far from here. But I'll try to go this fall before it gets too cold. I've visited his daughter Karen and you may remember her; she is married to C. Anderson, a tailor, and lives in Canby. I was warmly welcomed. She recognized me because I looked like mother. I've met so many acquaintances that I would have to write a book to mention them all, in particular a lot of old women who know mother and who send her their regards along with information about this and that. And there is Kristoffer Bjerkeg and his family; he's married to Kari Rovold, another friend from mother's youth. They live in Toronto where they own a *lumberyard*. They have two children,

Jenny and Herman, both in their twenties and both were at our wedding. We visit another family in Toronto that mother knows: two daughters of Kristoffer Døhlen in Holter. The older, Marie, is married to a man named Kristoffersen who isn't from Nannestad, the younger, Lava, lives with her sister and does tailoring. She made my wedding dress and was a bridesmaid. As I'm now in Toronto I can send greetings from another old acquaintance, Lars Evensen or Melbye as his name was. He was a corporal at Gardermoen. He works on the railroad, lives in town, and takes a glass of wine now and then. Let me also include Theodore Løvaas who is married to Karen Aamodt who was supposed to accompany me. Last summer they built themselves a nice new house and they had a son two months ago. I visit them when I'm in Toronto. Laurits and I were there recently and picked up our present from the band, a very nice chiffonier. We now have almost all the furniture we need, all of it gifts.

My aunt is in bed again. Last night she was so ill that we thought it was all over, but she revived. I think she is approaching the end. All the others are well. I've had a swollen finger and toothache but both are now well. Don't forget to give my regards at Holt and to all relatives and acquaintances. I'm glad to hear that the business is doing well. Give my regards to mother many times over. I am so glad that she still is well. Louis, Nicolai and all the others send their regards. Farewell, and don't forget to say hello to your little son from his aunt.

KAREN

· —— ·

KS has married her cousin Louis (also called Laurits) Solem. The letter that announced their marriage has not been preserved. In a letter to her brother the winter before she emigrated she wrote: "But Laurits must be a strange or quite original kind of American; could you imagine writing love letters to a cousin in America that you had never met? I don't think so. Well, I don't know what to make of it; in my last letter I commented on his manner of expression and now he responds in a rather self-important manner saying that he supposes he is allowed to love his family! And then he concludes with the remark, that he will <u>have me</u>, who he has never seen, as this is reasonable. Have you ever heard anything like this? ... I must admit that my first meeting in America with Lovis will be <u>awkward</u>. But, please dear brother, don't mention that I have <u>betrayed</u> him." Peru, the home of her cousin Kristine Nelp, is in LaSalle County, Ill. Canby is in Yellow Medicine County, Minn. Toronto is south of Norden. «II:185 »II:203 NE V:57

· —— ·

FROM: Guruanna Anderson, *Eau Claire, Wisconsin, 13 December 1886*

TO: Anne Olsdatter Sende, *Verdal, Nord-Trøndelag*

⊶⊷

Dear unforgettable mother,

We were so glad to receive your welcome letter where we see that you are living as usual and we can, praise and glory to God, say the same to you. We don't have any news but we hope it will be enough news for you to learn that we are in good health as that is the highest good in this world. Elling went to the forest about two weeks ago. Now Christmas is only two weeks away and I suppose this makes you quite busy in Norway, but here it doesn't make any difference. It would have been nice to pay you all a Christmas visit but it is too far. There is no use in talking about such matters but you must come and bring many friends because that would be nice now that the men have gone to the forest and we women have to sit home alone because it is the custom here every winter for the women to be alone. I send regards to you from my mother and sister. Mother is still well and strong. Give our regards to Moan and to Anemarte. Our son Karl was confirmed last fall and has grown to be almost as big as his father. We must now put aside our pen and ink hoping to have some lines in return as soon as possible. This is wished by all but first and foremost by your daughter-in-law

GURUANNA SENDE

· —— ·

Guruanna Johannesdatter (b. 1838) was from the farm Snausen and was married to Elling Andersen (b. 1832) from the farm Øvre (upper) Sende, both in Verdal. They emigrated with their family in 1880. Elling's mother, Anne Olsdatter, remained at Sende, where she had contractual care (*kaar*). GA's mother, Karen Karlsdatter Snausen, lived with her in Eau Claire. Although she and her husband often sign their letters with their Norwegian farm name, Sende, their American name was Anderson. Elling wrote to his sister Ingeborganna Andersdatter Lian on 14 November 1887 (Nor. ed. V:91) after he had heard of his mother's death. »II:234 NE V:60

· —— ·

1886 — LETTER 2:193

FROM: Anne Bjorli, *Bue, North Dakota, 14 December 1886*
To: Hans Jørgensen and Eli Johannesdatter Bjøkne, *Lesja, Oppland*

⊷═◉═⊶

Dear parents and siblings,

Thank you so much for the letter from my sister that arrived today. I'm glad to see that you all are in good health and that all is well at home. Amund is in town today to pick up his brother Lars. He got a letter from him today when I got yours, Guro, and they won't be home until tomorrow as they have to drive twenty miles. I wish that my brother Johannes would be with them when they arrive but I'm sure that he won't. I haven't heard from him since I came to America. We find it strange that he won't write to us or to his brother Jørgen. We would have been happy to receive him if he had come here last winter.

I haven't told you about our journey from Alexandria. Hans was with me until I left at three in the morning. There were no Norwegians on the train so I didn't speak a word. There was an American girl who wanted to have my company but as we couldn't understand each other it wasn't such great company. She looked at me and laughed and I did the same in return. She had a map that we looked at together and showed each other where we were going. She was going to Devil's Lake, further than I was. I came to Lakota at four in the afternoon. I had written to Amund and told him when I was coming but the letter didn't arrive until three days after I was there. He had been to town that day but had left. Matias Brandli came to the depot just as I arrived and he took me to Eli O. Kvam, Amund's cousin. I was only there for a short while; she wanted me to stay until Amund came but as I had company I wanted to continue as soon as possible and we came to Ole Bjorlivold that evening. He was the one who had driven me and he took me to Amund the next morning and I've been here since and enjoyed it.

Last Sunday we visited Syver Bjorlivold and were there till Monday evening. They had a girl who is a little bigger than Gyda who was with us and she stayed there till yesterday when we went to pick her up. Amund was helping them with haying and there are about four miles between us. I must end my letter as I don't have more to tell you; now I have to bake and tidy up before our visitors come. I'm almost afraid of their arrival as I know that it isn't very comfortable here. We don't have a large store of food for guests here as is common in Lesja. Loving regards to you my dear parents and siblings from your faithful daughter and sister Anne and my husband. Give my regards to Holen. Write soon. Excuse my haste.

· ——— ·

> AB emigrated in 1886 and married Amund Pedersen Bjorli. He had emigrated in 1879, and after his wife died in 1883 he visited Norway with his son Peder, who remained with his grandmother when Amund returned to the United States. Matias Niklasen Brandli was his cousin. In a letter (unpublished) dated 10 February 1887, AB asked her parents to write about personal matters on a separate piece of paper so that she could share the letter with others and still have part of it private. From this letter it seems that people had gossiped about her relationship with Amund and that they doubted he would marry her and that her parents had not been happy when she left to be with him. Her brother Johannes used the name John Hanson in the U.S. «II:190 »II:205 NE V:61

· ——— ·

1886 — LETTER 2:194

FROM: Ingeborg Larsen, *Blaine, Idaho, 19 December 1886*

TO: Henrik Olsen and Ole Henriksen Stokkenes, *Eid, Sogn og Fjordane*

⟴⟴

Dear brother and father,

I received your letter many weeks ago and my reply has regrettably been put off until now. Tonight my heart is much heavier than usual and I miss my sisters' and brothers' love, comfort and teaching. So I'm taking up my pen to lighten my heart. Religion was the reason we came here. Our worldly affairs were better where we were. But I've always believed: "For what will it profit them to gain the whole world and forfeit their life?" When we came here we met a Methodist pastor who had been sent by his conference. He began to preach in the schoolhouse, about a mile and a half from us. It is almost six miles to the Lutheran church, so we've been attending his meetings all summer. He started a Sunday school and had me teach one of the classes. I wasn't driven by ambition but by the thought that it would please the Lord that I helped to gather many neglected children under the banner of Jesus Christ and save them from the useless things they otherwise do on Sundays. The Sunday after I'd volunteered for the Sunday school he gave a sermon on absolution: a pastor couldn't absolve them from their sins, only God. His calling was not to make them Methodists but to have them live for God. I felt very uncomfortable and told him that I wouldn't be of use to him. In my view, the pastor, as God's servant on earth, had the authority to forgive the sins of a believer and if he wasn't truly repentant this would be his own concern. I referred him to Jesus and to Peter on the "authority of the key" but he insisted that the communion was a meal for true believers and that confirmation was a mere formality. If they are converted and have peace with God they don't need confirmation. And they don't baptize children because they are Satan's children, as the Lutheran pastors say, but because they are children of God. Jesus said that they belonged in the kingdom of heaven long before there was a baptism. We agreed to work together in the Sunday school and put these disagreements behind us. This has worked until now.

But now the children have come so far that they use books. When Latti comes with her Luther's Catechism she is told she is false. So I'll either have to submit to what they teach or quit and take my children out of this school. They are against Lutherans because they have denied their people Holy Communion because they hadn't been confirmed, not allowed their children to be buried in their churchyard if they hadn't been baptized, and refused to baptize their children because they themselves hadn't been confirmed. Tell me what you would have done in my situation. These people have prayer meetings every week where all are urged to confess the condition of their heart and say whether they've been converted to God or not, and also to pray to God. No one is accepted in the congregation before they've been converted and declare they will live for God. Children don't belong in the congregation until they've stood up and confessed that Jesus Christ has forgiven their sins and that they will live for God. They elect an assistant pastor for twelve people who meets with them every week and looks to their spiritual and material needs. I don't know any among the

Lutherans who are religiously minded when they go home from church. The last time we were there we had our wagon full of people from the islands west of Bergen and it was just like being in the fish market there.

Oluf was at the post office this week and one of the letters was from you and brought much interesting news. I'm glad to see that the Lord has opened his hand for the poor there at home. Praise be to his holy name. He loves all his creatures and wishes them well. May we use his gifts well and turn our backs on the evil of drink that corrupts both soul and body. Tell me, dear brother, are you thankful to God for having given you a good constitution? Has your heart been reborn in God to a living hope? If you, my dear father, become as old as grandfather I may see you before we die. If not, I wish that mother's wish may be fulfilled: She thought she saw you in heaven.

It is now five days before Christmas. Then the peace of Christmas will be with us. We have collected eleven dollars for the Christmas tree and we gave one dollar and thirty-five cents. Larsen worked at the church for six days. We thought we should give to the Lutheran church, but we haven't done so yet. You ask whether you should take some of the money in the bank and give it to the mission. I myself don't have any, as you know. Latti says you should do it if you want to. Last year Larsen and I had 550 dollars left of what we had earned. Here in Albion we cannot make any money and this is my fault because of my religious faith. Larsen thinks of going away again. It may be that I can get him to stay for the winter. He hasn't been as well as before. As soon as he gets depressed about something his old illness returns. Making a new home brings on sorrows and worries and there is no immediate harvest.

We now have frost and snow. The cattle have been outdoors till now. He has bought a cow and two calves and we now have six in all. Four horses and a foal ran away three weeks ago. The children have gone to school since September. Oluf is in the second grade; Latti has completed the fourth. She reads Norwegian well and understands it but she won't speak Norwegian—not outside the home. We've moved a distance of 400 miles. We wish you all a good and happy New Year. Give my regards to brother and sister. Loving regards from Paul Larsen and your sister and daughter

INGEBORG LARSEN

· ⸺ ·

IL (b. 1843) was first married to Lars Larsen Roti in 1872 and then, after his death, to his brother Paul Larsen in 1875. They emigrated in 1882. It is often difficult to interpret words and sentences and her code switching must have caused difficulties: *kamper ensom* (the conference), *apsuliationen* (the absolution), *paast ofisjen* (the post office). Albion may be in Whitman County, Wash. She uses the Blaine, Latah County, post office but she lived in Nez Perce County, where there were few Norwegian immigrants and no Norwegian Lutheran congregations. She quotes from Mark 8:36. Her reference to Peter and the key is to Matthew 16:19 "I will give you the keys of the kingdom of heaven, and whatever you bind on earth will be bound in heaven, and whatever you loose on earth will be loosed in heaven." The disagreement between IL and the Methodist pastor seems to be about who may admitted to the Holy Communion, IL contending that it was for all who had been confirmed and the pastor claiming that it was for those who had been converted as adults. "Latti" (Larsine) is IL's daughter from her first marriage. This may be her spelling of "Lotty." Oluf is a son. She refers to her husband as Larsen. »II:278 NE V:62

· —— ·

1887 — LETTER 2:195

FROM: Elise Wærenskjold, *Prairieville, Texas, 1 January 1887*

To: Thomine Dannevig, *Lillesand, Aust-Agder*

⊷⇒◉⇐⊷

My dear, good Thomine!

I'm so ashamed but I cannot remember whether I've answered and thanked you for your last very welcome and interesting letter. For a long time my mind has been so focused on money that I almost forget everything else. This has been the most disastrous year for Texas since I came to this country. All over the state we have suffered from varying degrees of drought so the harvest has been poor, in some counties so poor that they have had to beg for assistance. Moreover, the price for cotton was unusually low and it has been impossible to sell cattle. Regrettably, my husband's nephew speculated in cattle and last year he bought Ouline Reiersen's cattle for 400 dollars and tomorrow, he has to pay 500 on his land. Had he been able to sell his cattle this payment would not have been a problem. His mother-in-law has demanded some of the money I had borrowed from her in order to help him since he may lose his farm if he doesn't pay. Niels owes me as much as I owe to others but he cannot possibly repay me in such a year. Now he too has had to go up to a town to borrow money on his land. It is so disagreeable to be poor but I must thank God as long as I have food and clothes even though I live very simply. And I should also be thankful for my good health, in body as in spirit, and for my good friends both here and other places where I'm known.

Niels has moved into the house that used to be Otto's and I'm now quite alone in my old house, but after New Year a family who rents some of Niels's land will be moving into the other end of the house. I have a kitchen and living room for myself. The most awkward thing about the situation is that they have five small children who can be quite noisy, but it may be nice for an old woman. Ouline has sold her property for 2,000 dollars. She'll have an interest of ten percent of this amount as long as she lives. After her death the money will be owed to her three stepsons. She now lives with another Norwegian widow in our neighborhood. I'm so glad she decided to stay here as I had feared she would go to Bosque. Neither Niels nor Otto has been in good health. When I came to Otto in September he had been operated on for *piles* and was suffering a good deal. I hope he's been cured. Last fall he was made constable and then deputy sheriff. I don't know what the pay is for these offices, but they can be very dangerous and it isn't unusual that a deputy sheriff is killed as they have to arrest criminals and all disturbers of the peace and such people are not to be trifled with. I also visited old friends in Bosque and was away for almost three months. The tickets cost about ten dollars.

In Bosque I spoke with a friend who had visited the northern states last summer and met Husher. I asked about Speilberg and to my great surprise he mentioned another daughter, a Mrs. Sørensen. How can this be? Tell me all the news as you always do, my dear Thomine. I've read about the crisis in Arendal and have been annoyed with the bank manager who has caused so much difficulty. I see that Juliane Flørnæs was among the many failures. I'm sorry for her. How is my old friend, your brother Samuel? I suppose you are now with one of your sons. Please give them my regards. I'll send this to my godson Niels since I'm not sure where you may be. I wish I could spend an evening with you. I wonder why Mrs. Basberg never writes to me. I know that she received my last letter because I sent it with a letter to Dicta Aall and she wrote back. Poor woman! I believe she too is poor. I wonder whether her sons are good to her. My fire has died and it is a bitterly cold night so I had better go to bed. Thank God that I have a good and warm bed.

The morning of New Year's Day

I wish you and yours and all my dear ones in the unforgettable land of my birth a happy New Year! Yes I wish you and the entire country all luck and the Lord's blessing! Please give my regards to any old acquaintances that you may see and that are still a little interested in me. You would perhaps be interested in hearing something about the few Norwegians here that you know but I don't know much. I believe the Grøgaards are doing well but I hardly hear from them. A couple of years ago I wrote to Helene Reiersen but never had a reply. She has either forgotten or doesn't wish to remember how much I did for them in Norway. She and Hans Jacob and Lise's daughter live in New Orleans. Emma, who is married to a doctor and has many children, all boys except one, lives in Athens twenty-nine miles from here; I haven't seen her since she was twelve. I don't know whether Thomas and Nicolai Grøgaard are in Texas or in Louisiana. Sigurd is comfortable in Shreveport but is not making much money. Mrs. Pabst has an abundance of what this world has to offer, but an unpleasant husband; I would rather be poor than be Pabst's wife. But she seems to accept it. Now it is time to conclude my uninteresting letter. You must please me with a long one! Your always faithful

ELISE WÆRENSKJOLD

·   ———   ·

A few weeks before she wrote this letter, EW wrote a letter to *Fædrelandet og Emigranten* about the hard times in Texas and with news about the Norwegian settlements. It was published in the newspaper on 21 December 1886 (Clausen 1961, 126–128). Parts of the above letter are also in Clausen where it, however, includes parts of another letter written a year later, on 21 December 1887. The nephew was Adolph S. Wattner, a son of EW's sister. Mrs. Sørensen was a daughter of Ferdinand A. Husher and lived in Minneapolis. The other daughter was married to Christian G. Speilberg from Lillesand and was later divorced. In Arendal, Axel Herlofsen was the founder and director of Arendal Privatbank and was held responsible for the bank's failure in 1886 that caused great difficulties for many businesses. «II:165 »II:209 NE V:63

·   ———   ·

FROM: Jacob Tonning, *Blaine, Idaho, 2 January 1887*
To: Paul Henriksen Tonning, *Herøy, Møre og Romsdal*

⊷⇒◉⇐⊷

Dear unforgettable brother,

I should have done as you asked in your last letter and answered immediately. However, there were several reasons why this could not be. The most important one was that you had two requests, first that you would like to have our portraits. I really wanted to do this but immediately after receiving your letter I had to leave home for some railroad work and I was away for two months. When I was home and the time had come for our portraits, the photographer wasn't present and I haven't heard from him since, so that matter will have to wait until spring when we'll have our portraits taken as quickly as possible. The second was a question that was difficult to answer in a hurry: should Johan come to America? The question wouldn't have been so difficult had I known the situation for blacksmiths in Norway so I could have compared it to the situation here. I've spoken to many in this trade here and they all agree that it is the best trade an immigrant can come with to America and they've all advised me to let the boy come. I've made attempts to secure a good position for him in case he should decide to come, but this has been rather difficult as they don't hire anyone until they actually need a person. Moreover, I couldn't guarantee that he would come. But I've been promised that if he does come he'll be offered a position as soon as one is available. That is the best I could do.

So I've decided to answer your question in this manner. If it is your decision to let the boy come I would advise him to be satisfied with any kind of work he's offered until he has an opportunity to work in his trade. His prospects are very promising as the railroads are paying visits to us mountain folk, something that leads to the growth and proliferation of towns, in particular the railroad that will be built here next summer and will open a complete railroad system for us from the Atlantic to the Pacific. A branch of this railroad is planned to be built here next summer and the survey places it no farther from me than from you to Rafteset. When it is completed I'll be living between two railroads, one to the north and one to the south, so it won't be difficult to get transportation for our produce and they will also lead to higher prices for land and in general to better times for workers and farmers. There is a Dane here who has a blacksmith shop in Genesee, a small town only four miles south of here. It is quite possible that Johan may get work there, but I would prefer to have him work for an American because of the language because if he comes to a place where he hears no other language than pure English it will be easier for him to acquire it. This is the most important thing he has to learn. True, the work methods are different from those in Norway as are most of the tools, but it won't take long for him to learn them. I don't know what more to say about this. I would neither encourage nor discourage him; he must do as he wishes, but if he comes I stand ready to give him all the help I can. He will find himself welcome here with us whenever he wishes to be at home and it won't cost him anything. You mustn't take this to mean that I'm rich but as the old saying goes, where there's a will there's a way. And now in conclusion—if I in any way have misunderstood your question about whether there are good opportunities for blacksmiths here, then I must ask to be excused. But I've never seen a good blacksmith without work in America. If they haven't been employed by others they've been on their own and done a good business. I see that you also mention the situation for carpenters but I won't say anything about that right now.

Now I would like to turn to things that are more relaxing for my mind. I have to date been in good health and so has my wife. Since we came to Idaho she has always been well while she used to be quite poorly. My children are lively and fat as pigs except that my little Hendrik has a hernia. He is now a little more than two years old and he got it a year ago and we don't know what has caused it. Gustav, my oldest boy, works a lot. He plowed most of our fields last fall. He is now thirteen years and four months and we also have a little boy named Matthias who is a little more than nine months. We also have three girls. The oldest, Eline Gurine will be ten next May, Hendriette Mathilde will be seven next May and the third is Anne Marte who is four. So that makes six children in all who are living. I assume you know that I lost three boys in Kansas, among them my oldest son named Hendrik. It seems that I have no luck with boys named Hendrik and it has been no better for you who had to suffer the heavy loss of your Hendrik.

Our crop wasn't great last year but better than expected. We had a drought but those who got an early start in spring had a fairly good crop considering the terrible drought. For my part I got almost nothing since I started late because I had such problems with my team last year that I had to hire help and got delayed. But I did get enough for seed for next year. I grow flax as do many around here and we sell it to factories that make oil. The price is usually one dollar a bushel. I didn't plant any wheat last spring as it was so cheap that you could buy it for less than it cost to grow it, especially for me who had to hire all the help.

I must say something about carpenters. They don't do as well as blacksmiths. There aren't many carpenter shops but if one can get work in one of them the pay is quite good. I hear that you can get three dollars a day without board. But wages are not steady; they may go up and down. In this trade, as in all kinds of work, it is always worst before you become known. I would like to add, briefly but seriously and sincerely, that from what I see in the newspapers I think it would be better for all of you here than in Norway. But you will have to decide for yourself. Include God in your councils and then all will be for the best. In conclusion regards to you and your family from all of us and especially from your faithful brother,

JACOB TONNING

. ——— .

JT and his family must have moved from Kansas some time after the 1880 census. JT is listed as one of the officers in the small English-language Norwegian Lutheran congregation in Genesee, Idaho, when it was founded in 1898. This suggests that by this time (when most Norwegian Lutheran congregations still used Norwegian) he and his family preferred English. Johan Paulsen Tonning was twenty-four in 1887. «II:56 NE V:64

. ——— .

FROM: Siri Allikson, *Springville, Wisconsin, 10 January 1887*

To: Osmund Atlaksen Ovedal, *Sirdal, Vest-Agder*

Dear unforgettable brother Osmund and family,

Today is New Year's Day so I will wish you all a Happy New Year. This is a beautiful New Year's Day and the weather has been nice since fall. I hear that you are all doing well and have no need. But, my dear brother, we must not forget the coming life. May we live so that we may meet in joy at the throne of God because this is a world of danger that is always ready to lure us away from Christ and his word. We now have a good man to lead us in prayer, Henrik Hanson Oftedal, and we have no reason to turn down our Pastor Halvorsen. It is about seven miles to the church in Coon Prairie but now we have a new little church only a mile northwest of us and Pastor Halvorsen preaches there once a month.

Today is January 10 and on the fourth Sara and I went to the Coon Prairie church for the ordination of Christian, son of Mikal Larsen Fladestøl, and he left the same day for a call. We also visited our brother Sigbjørn and they were all in good health and doing well. I don't know if you've heard that Sigbjørn's oldest daughter Berte was married on March 20 three years ago and last spring, on March 19, she died leaving behind two children. The oldest was two in June and the youngest was eleven days when the mother died and he died too when he was five months. Berte lived in Minnesota and her sister Sophie went to her and arrived two days before she died. She was there for three months and took care of the children until the youngest was strong enough for her to bring them both here to her parents. I'm enclosing the alphabet letters that Syvert Sigbjørnson has learned. He is now in the fourth year and can both read and write. He's at school from September to June. The first two years Syvert went to school his sister Sophie was with him and worked in the same town. Sophie is their half-sister but she is a full sister in her relations with her parents as well as her siblings. She took care of Berte's children until last fall when she moved to town.

I must let you know how we're doing. I haven't been as well as I now am for a long time but I can't do any heavy work. Reinert and Sarah are well and we all live together here. Reinert asks you to give his regards to Henrik Skibeli. Give regards to all acquaintances and relatives there at home from us all. Berte Tonette, if you can write then please send us a letter. I hear that you now have two children so let us know how they are. I must conclude with friendly greetings to you all. Farewell!

SIRI ATLAGSON AAVEDAHL

· ——— ·

In a letter to her brother written 12 July 1885 (Nor. ed. V:18) SA for the first time signed herself Siri Allikson rather than Siri Atlagsen Ovedahl. This letter was begun on 1 January 1887 and was dated the day it was completed. For Coon Prairie SA writes *Konpræri*. This was a period of strife in many congregations of the Norwegian Synod and the one in Coon Prairie split in two the following year, in 1888. Halvor Halvorsen continued as pastor for the part that remained in the Norwegian Synod. Christian M. Larsen joined the group that broke away from the Synod. His new call was in Nebraska. Sigbjørn's daughter Berte was married to Gitle Torgersen Strømstad, who later married his sister-in-law Sophie (see the next letter in the series). Syvert was deaf and mute and had to leave home to attend a special school. Berte Tonette was the wife of Osmund Atlaksen Ovedal in Sirdal. Their daughters were Bolette and Ingeborg. «II:140 »II:241 NE V:65

· ——— ·

1887 — LETTER 2:198

FROM: Lars Larsen Urheim, *Eau Claire, Wisconsin, 6 February 1887*

TO: Jakob Rasmussen Sandvik, *Kinsarvik, Ullensvang, Hordaland*

Dear friend Jacob,

Today I have lots of time, is what we used to write in our letters when we were young, but this is something I've never been able to write in this country. But today I'll try to send you a few lines and tell you where I'm living and how I am. To make sure I'll have a reply I'll send it to you because I'm always glad when I get your letters. You always have lots of news. As for the past year, I must admit that I don't look forward to Christmas the way I used to do. No those days are in the past as are our Christmas customs. I almost laugh when I think of what Christmas was like there at home. We have some fun here too of course but old customs have been forgotten. And think that we had a Christmas vacation until the Thirteenth Day of Christmas. That was nice. I hope you won't forget it.

You mustn't believe that I've forgotten you just because I write so rarely but the time I could have had for writing must be used for other things and so it gets put off and put off and then you see what happens. There is a lot I could say about the time since we last saw each other but this can wait until you come here yourself and, moreover, I'm not good at getting it down on paper. But I can tell you that I'm in good health and that is about the best I can have and all else is a bonus. My family is doing well as I suppose yours is too. But it's a shame that so many of our friends have gone off and gotten married, one after the other, especially for one who is older than they are. But I can't do anything about it because I have a good excuse: no one wants me. I've gone unmarried for twenty-six years and I think this is fine and I've firmly decided to continue in this manner for the next twenty-seven.

As I suppose you know I'm working in a *drugstore* in Eau Claire, Wis. I think I'll stay here until fall when I'll go somewhere else to go to school because you can never learn too much and I don't like to work with people who know more than I do. My pay allows me to live well—thirty-five dollars a month—but in a couple of years I'll double that. This is as nice a job as I could wish for. My brother Torsten came here awhile ago. I have him studying every day as I'm thinking of making him a *druggist* too. He's a very good student and he also has a fiddle, and I think you would be surprised to hear him play, not like the old Urheim but perhaps like a relative. He plays so well that it's fun to listen to him. Brother J and Torsten don't get along since Jacob is too much of a church man for me and T. We're in a free country and think we don't have to go to church every Sunday but that it should be enough to do it as as often as the man who washed himself every spring and fall. Jacob is doing well. He and his family are in good health but it has been difficult for them now that both his father-in-law and mother died within a short time. Both were very nice people. I visited them last summer. His father-in-law died after being kicked by a young foal and his wife had been ill for some time. I haven't met anyone from home except Lars Tvedt. I saw him awhile ago and things are difficult for them as Lars lacks initiative. He doesn't get much done and they have many children to feed and clothe. I haven't seen other friends or relatives recently. I met Helge Kinsarvik last fall when he was in Harmony and painted my brother's house. He hadn't changed. We talked about old times and had a good time.

I'll have to conclude. Perhaps I should tell you about the weather. We've had a lot of snow and I mustn't forget that we have a Norwegian *Ski Club* with seventy-five members. On January 17 we had the largest ski meet ever held in Wisconsin with participants from Minnesota, Iowa and Dakota. It looked very nice when they marched in the street with their different uniforms and a band. Mikkel Hemmestveit, who had been the best skier in Norway, won the first prize and fifty dollars in <u>gold</u>. Give my regards to all there at home. I wish you all a good New Year. Give my regards to my old parents and my siblings. Greetings from your friend

L. URHEIM

· —— ·

Jakob Sandvik received many letters from immigrants who had belonged to his social group in Kinsarvik but who took different paths in the United States. About the same time he received this one he also had a letter from John Svenson (Nor. ed. V:66) who then was a day laborer in Crookston, Minn. The above letter mentions a specific local Christmas custom called *puttle skatten*, the giving of small gifts, in particular to children, at some time or other during Christmas. Such a gift could be expected but just what it would be was a secret. "The old Urheim" is probably Oddmund Urheim (1816–1895), a popular local songwriter and fiddler. The brothers Mikkel and Torjus Hemmestveit from Telemark won several national skiing competitions in Norway in the 1880s before emigrating to the U.S., where they continued to compete. «II:151 »II:265 NE V:67

· —— ·

FROM: Ole Gulliksen Dorsett, *Leland, Illinois, 12 February 1887*
To: Tosten Gulliksen Daaset, *Flesberg, Buskerud*

⊷⇒◑⇐⊷

Dear brother and family,

It's more than a year since I received your honored letter and you must excuse me for not having written before, but as none of mine can write Norwegian I haven't had an opportunity before now. We are all in good health and doing well. As you know, we have nine children. Two of the girls are married and have moved to Iowa where they enjoy themselves. I heard from brother Jul in Minnesota last fall. He's doing well. Brother Gullik is also doing well. His only boy is seven. Last year was rather poor. I had 1,300 bushels of corn, 700 bushels of oats, fifty bushels of potatoes, and fourteen bushels of wheat. I have seventeen head of cattle, nine horses, seven pigs, and 300 hens. The prices for what we sell have been low so it hasn't been easy to lay money aside. At first the winter was rather cold and we had a lot of snow until after Christmas, but then the weather turned mild and the snow disappeared and these last days we've had a lot of rain. Last summer we had so little rain that our crops suffered.

Christopher Førli is in bad health. Aslaug Bakke died a few days ago after more than a year in bed. She was eighty-four. As for church matters, there are many sects here even among the Norwegians. We have different kinds of Lutherans, Methodists, Adventists, Catholics, Baptists, Mormons, and free thinkers, and then there are the many who don't belong to any church. Two of my daughters are now preparing for their confirmation. In spite of the differences in religion there is friendship in our daily lives.

Thanks to Gullik for the portrait he sent us and in return our son George is sending his to you. We don't have any news of interest as everything is as usual with debates, choirs, and different kinds of social events for the young. We old people pass our time in our homes in winter with eating, drinking, and sleeping and looking after our animals as well as we can. With this I'll end my letter wishing that these lines will find you all well. Give greetings to

my brother Even and family and to Hellik's daughters as well as all acquaintances. It would have been nice to hear from you if this is possible. Farewell.

OLE DAASÆT

. ——— .

The style of the dictated Dorsett letters changes with the changing
writers. A note in the margin explains that there are four bushels in
one *tønde*. The Gullik who sent his photograph was a son of Tosten.
Hellik, one of the brothers in Norway, had died the year before this
letter. «II:181 NE V:69

. ——— .

1887 — LETTER 2:200

FROM: Ole and Nils Lind, *West Valley, Minnesota, 31 March 1887*
TO: Hans Nilsen and Helge Kristiansdatter Liubraaten, *Sigdal, Buskerud*

Dear and unforgetable ones there at home,

We received your letter dated February 21 on March 19 and were glad
to see that you were all in good health and I can tell you in return that we
are also in good health. I must reply to your letter at once and I think this
will be the last time I write to you as I hope it is the will of the Almighty
God that we will soon see each other and then the pen will no longer have
to do the speaking. I hope you'll have a good and happy voyage and that
the Almighty God will be with you and have his hand on the rudder. We
thought you were going with Engebret Sund but this is probably not the
case since you don't mention it in your letter. It would have been best for
you to be with someone who speaks English and knows how things are
done, but if all goes well you will surely arrive here regardless. When you
come to Warren you can ask for Grinder or the Northwestern Hotel where
we'll book a room for you if we are not there ourselves. I don't think we
have more to tell you since Nils is writing too. But you must be careful to
take note when this station is announced and get off the train at Warren
that is 30 miles north of Crookston. I think you will be in Warren by noon.

There is so much talk of carding combs around here that you must remember to bring four pairs. Turi Gren says you should bring all your skirts as these may be remade to underskirts. They are so good and warm, she says, because they are of wool. I have no news. Everything is as usual. The weather has been quite cold so there is a lot of snow left and we won't be able to do spring work before Easter. It's already late so this will have to be enough and I'll lay down my pen hoping that these lines will find you all well. I send greetings to you from Jens Gren who wishes you a good journey. Also from Ole and Turi Bjornerud. First and last, regards from me,

OLE H. LIND

Dear unforgettable ones there at home,

Since Ole is writing I'll also send you a few words and give you the good news that we are all well except that I'm driven by the same lord as before we left home. As you'll understand, I serve the king, but I'll soon have done my service as the great king has had to remove his crown and become a little more humble. But then I have three or four lesser ones even though they don't have quite the same power. Today Ole has been making an axe handle and then Ole Bjørnrud came to help him sharpen the axe and do some building. Ole Bjørnrud was here Saturday and made the foundation but then they had to work on the church for three days.

A few days ago I visited at Bagaas. They have a nice home and are quite comfortable. Anders asked whether you would buy a woolen undershirt and some bristle for him. But I think you'll have a lot as it is and you shouldn't be taking so much else. But you must do as you wish. I see in your letter that you've written *Varre* as the name of your stop, but this is wrong; it is Warren. And you don't write the full address on your letters; you leave out Minnesota. Our address is West Valley, Marshall Co. Minnesota North America. This may be the last time I write to you in Norway. So I'll wish you a good and happy journey and that God will be with you and bless you. Loving regards from me,

N. H. LIND

• ——— •

These two brothers emigrated from Sigdal in 1885. NHL soon left farming for study at Augsburg Seminary in Minneapolis. He was ordained as pastor in the United Church in 1896. In his letter he refers to his older brother as the king who orders him to work. OHL wrote the hotel name *Nordvesterrin Hottel*; *Grinder* may also be an idiosyncratic spelling like *Chrogston*. As the next letter in the series makes clear, the bristle NHL asks his parents to bring was for making or repairing shoes. Among his messages in the margins OHL wrote: "Knut Bagaas sends his regards. He has just bought a nice team and he tells me to ask you to bring a lot of girls. He is sleeping here tonight and the beds here in the West are only filled with boys and no girls." The parents of Ole and Nils emigrated soon after receiving this letter and the next one in this series is from them. »II:208 NE V:72

· ———— ·

1887 — LETTER 2:201

FROM: Jens Herlef Ursin, *Chicago, Illinois, 18 May 1887*
TO: E. B. Kjerskov Zahl, *Kjerringøy, Bodø, Nordland*

⊶⇒◯⇐⊷

Mr. K. Zahl,

I received your very kind letter on the twenty-first of last month and have noted what you wrote. I'm glad to see your great patience and I seemed to gain new courage. I think that God willing I will try to come home in the fall and try to begin with something there. America has shown its dark side to me. But I thank and praise God for having held his hand over me through the many temptations and adversities I've been met with. Honorable Mr. Zahl, it cannot be denied that a man may often act unwisely in his youth and that he must accept the sad consequences of his actions. But I have remained honest and faithful and this has made it difficult for me.

The times here are very hard. First all the carpenters went on strike to little purpose and now all the bricklayers have also been on strike, so we may soon expect great changes in Chicago. These so-called *unions* or worker's associations of all kinds are so angered that they would rather go hungry and make others go hungry as well rather than give in. The bricklayers went on strike because they had been paid on Mondays but now wanted their employers to pay them on Saturdays and when their employers refused, they went on strike. So this was a senseless strike. The weather has been quite cold. May 17 is celebrated by many here but it was so cold that people had to wear overcoats. So it is rather like Norway. Thank you so much for your comforting letter that almost gave me new life. Accept my friendly regards. Sincerely,

J. URSIN

. ——— .

The Norwegian of JHU has become influenced by the language he is surrounded by and American idioms are given literal Norwegian translations. In a letter dated 29 March 1887 (Nor. ed. V:71) JHU asked for a further extension of his debt if he should come home later that year and offers his part of the farm Taraldsvik as security. By the time of the 1900 census he had returned to Ankenes where he was a homeowner, married, and with three children. The oldest child was born in 1889. «II:187 NE V:75

. ——— .

1887 — LETTER 2:202

FROM: Jacob Hanson Hilton, *Socorro, New Mexico, 10 July 1887*

TO: Hans Jakobsen and Anne Olsdatter Hilton, *Kløfta, Ullensaker, Akershus*

⊷⟫⊜⟪⊶

Dear parents,

As it is long since I've heard from you I'll send some words to you today and as I finally have Olaf Bursum's photograph I'll enclose it. Olaf is an old-fashioned kind of man so such things take their time. He's big and strong and a clever fellow, so if August should lose him from his business it would probably not go very well because Olaf is the one who keeps the customers coming since Gus isn't so well liked after he got married. His wife is rather uppity, you see.

I have no news except that the town is dead. There is nothing to do and no movement in any kind of business. I could foresee this last spring and that is why I did as I did with uncle. If I hadn't he would have lost his money and I didn't want this to happen since I'd talked him into buying Asche's share in my business. So it was my responsibility to help him get out without a loss. He made a little while he was here as we then had relatively good days and as for me, I cannot become much poorer than I was when I came to Socorro. I'm now in a position to lose everything or make good money. If the town fails completely I'll lose all my money as it will be impossible to sell my business—even at half price—and I'll have to hold on to it and hope for better times. If I can hold on to it until things improve then I can both sell at a reasonable price and make good money if I keep on for a year or more. But if the situation improves and I'm able to sell then I may do so at the first opportunity, that is, when I get a reasonable price paid in cash. I don't owe anyone a dollar, neither here nor with any merchant company, so the goods are my own and I still have 700 dollars in the bank so there is no danger yet. But you should see how quiet it is now. There is no one in town whose situation is better than mine but if it continues to decline many will have difficulties. Most of the Americans, both businessmen and others, are leaving but that's the way I want it: the more that leave the better for those who remain. I'll have to end this as I have nothing of interest to tell you. My loving regards to father, mother, and siblings, hoping that you are all well.

JACOB

· —— ·

For some time JHH had been planning to return to Ullensaker. He wrote to his brother Oluf (who had returned to Norway) on 11 June 1885 (Nor. ed. V:16) about his business plans in Norway and about sending a carriage to his father from New York. His uncle Christopher Jacobson was back in Socorro but in a bad frame of mind: "*He say's* [sic] *that Socorro is the asshole of all Cuntry's* [sic]." In a letter to his father on 6 August 1886 (Nor. ed. V:47) his plans for taking over the general store at Kløfta are taking shape and he discusses details with his father as well as his brother Oluf. On 27 August 1887 (unpublished) he wrote to Oluf that his uncle Christopher Jacobson was returning to Ullensaker to prepare for a takeover of the general store and from his letter to his father on 18 November 1887 (Nor. ed. V:59) it seems that his uncle had already done a good deal to establish a business. By the time of the above letter, however, JHH is resigned to remaining in Socorro. He wrote to his brother Karl on 27 March (unpublished): "The town is almost deserted and we don't make as much in three to four days as we made in one day six months ago. It's impossible to sell a business here because if anyone comes and sees that nothing is happening, they'll leave for other places where the business is better. I must give up my hope of seeing Norway again this summer and wait and see what can be done in the fall." August Hilton married Mary Laufersweiler in Fort Dodge in 1885 and there may have been cultural differences between her as a Catholic German-American and August's Lutheran Norwegian relatives and friends. Their son Conrad Hilton was born in 1887. Olaf Bursum was August's nephew and had come from Iowa to help his uncle with his business in San Antonio. «II:155 »II:221 NE V:79

. ——— .

1887 — LETTER 2:203

FROM: Karen Solem, *Norden, South Dakota, 7 August 1887*

TO: Ole Tobias and Amalie Ødegaard, *Nannestad, Akershus*

⊷═◉⊜═⊷

Dear brother and sister-in-law,

Thank you for your letter that I received Saturday evening along with one from Sally with whom I still correspond. I'll try to reply with Marie on my lap as I'm sorry that I now write so seldom. If she will remain on friendly terms with the straw hat she is playing with I think it will go well. I'm so glad mother is well. This is always on my mind. You'll remember that I wrote in my last letter that our relatives from Peru were here. Now Kristine and her children have gone home. They were here for three weeks. Karen is here again and last Wednesday Uncle came too. Imagine; it's really true that Uncle Ole is here. I'll tell you about the evening he arrived. When we saw a wagon on the road we decided to fool Kye and tell her that it was her father. He hadn't written and when they came to the house we didn't imagine that it could be him and thought they were two agents. They asked to stay for the night but Kye and I had agreed that we wouldn't take in any Yankees. Nothing had been *fixed* as they drove up to the door. Kye went to the door to tell them that they couldn't come in but Uncle held out his big hand and said, "Nice to see you again, Karen." Before long she was hanging around his neck. He says that he'll never again go to Peru. He's now working for us but later he'll have enough work on Kristine's farm. As I wrote in my last letter, she had bought railroad land but then she traded with Per Falla. She gave him her land and 2,200 dollars for his farm and a couple of grey mares. Per can now repay his large debt.

You say you have a drought there at home and this is true of many places here too. Around where Christian lives fields and meadows have been ruined by drought and the "*chinchbug*," a kind of animal. We've had a lot of rain this summer so here everything is gowing nicely. The wheat harvest began before we were done haying so now we are doing both at the same time. The coffee crisis has come to us too and I hear it is also in Norway. Yes, the coffee is so expensive that we ought to say goodbye to it and we often talk about using less, but that is impossible. We have coffee three times a day. We pay thirty-five cents a pound for the best coffee. You can find out how much thirty-five cents is in Norwegian money and I can add that a pound here is less than a pound in Norway.

It is now August 7 and I still haven't finished my letter and I must now hurry up and do it as Johan is about to go to town. He had a little daughter a month ago and she'll be christened tomorrow. There is a lot I want to write about but I can't do it now. A town will be built three miles from us and you should come and establish a *store*, as we say. Kristine wants to start a hotel as she absolutely needs to *make money*. It would be nice to have mother here to take care of Marie, but I fear that she may be too heavy; she now weighs twenty-five pounds. Right now Amanda Falla is here to help me; she is only eight but is a nice and clever girl.

You had bad news from Gaarder. Well, with such a bad start a bad ending is to be expected. Send me news from Nannestad. Even if you don't think it is of interest it would entertain me. Are any there getting married? Kye wants to know whether the mad Engebret is married; she remembers him from Norway. All here send their regards.

KAREN

· —— ·

KS wrote on 2 May 1887 (Nor. ed. V:74) about the birth and christening of her daughter Marie and that Kristine Nelp, her cousin in Illinois, had become a widow. Many of her letters have been preserved but not the one she refers to above. Her uncle Ole Kristoffersen was a brother of her mother and of her husband's mother. His daughter Karen, or Carrie, was also called Kay (written both *Kai* and *Kye* by KS). In a later letter she is given the name Olsen. It may be that this is her family's last name in the United States (rather than Kristoffersen) or that KS has simply used the masculine form of her patronymic (Olsdatter). Uncle Ole may also be the father of Kristine (Olsen) Nelp in Peru. KS's brothers-in-law, Christian and Carl, lived in Fillmore County, Minn. Johan is another brother-in-law. «II:191 »II:210 NE V:81

· —— ·

1887 — LETTER 2:204

From: Mikkel Andersen Lee, *Springdale, Wisconsin, 2 September 1887*

To: Anders Olsen and Anders Andersen Lie, *Hedalen, Sør-Aurdal, Oppland*

⋇═◉═⋇

Unforgettable father and brother!

My memories of you and my place of birth often give me the desire to write home, but when I try it so often comes to naught because of my inability to express my feelings in the way I wish and so I have to give it up and merely let my thoughts go on a visit to you. Then at least I'm with you in my thoughts. I seem to see my father, his crutches by his side, with his bald head, his wrinkled face, the furrows in his forehead, his gnarled fingers, his trembling hands folded in a silent prayer to God. I seem to see my brother swinging his axe, hauling logs, hay and leaves from the mountain pastures, getting up at three or four in the morning and not getting to bed until nine or ten in the evening. I seem to hear the sound of the axe on wood, the rattling of chains, the sleigh runners on the snow, the thunder of falling logs, the powerful blows on the iron chains and see the steam of sweat from horse and man. I seem to hear the whirring of the grindstone, the scratching of the whetstone on the scythe, the sharp sound of the scythe hitting a rock, the rake moving in between bushes and rocks, the move up to the mountain pasture, the bellowing of the cows, the calls of the shepherd boys, the tones of the horns that come from a grove of firs and are answered from another grove and are then echoed and gradually expire between the mighty mountains, the braying of goats and sheep, the beautiful song of the birds and the green beauty of the woods on the hillside. The unruffled surface of the fjords, the clusters of farms, fields and meadows, the brooks and waterfalls, the mountains and not to forget, the ringing of the bells of the Hedalen church. All this gives me great thoughts of my fatherland and happiness in my heart that leaves even America in the shadows.

I must first of all tell you that we are all—big and small—in good health. Times are hard. It seems that this year will be worse than last because of the terrible drought that again has afflicted us. We've hardly had rain since the middle of April and we have moreover been afflicted by the chinch bug. In places many have mowed the wheat and barley for hay. I've harvested nine acres and this gave four small wagon loads of hay. I still have four acres to mow. Last winter I bought hay for twenty-five dollars because I couldn't sell any of my animals: the markets were overflowing with cattle. Farmers slaughtered as many as they could eat in the course of the winter but still had more than they could feed. This was also my situation. Hay was brought here from Minnesota and Dakota as conditions there were fine.

The only news I have is that on June 18 we were blessed with a boy child who has been named Albert. He is growing and thriving. All you know here are in good health and are doing well considering the drought. In conclusion, farewell, hoping that these lines will find you all well. I intend to write again as soon as I've done my preparations for the winter. Sincerely,

M. LIE

· ——— ·

> There are two enclosures. One gossips about a neighbor who has recently visited Hedalen. The other, a brief note, asks about an unacknowledged son of his brother Ole. Even though his family seems to accept that Ole has a son in Hedalen, MAL writes that "Ole has not yet spoken a word about this affair to me." MAL wrote on 9 February 1887 (Nor. ed. V:68) expressing his sorrow for his mother's death. His brother Iver in North Dakota wrote a similar letter on 26 January 1887. Both explain why they were unable to send money. «II:186 »II:217 NE V:84

· ——— ·

1887 — LETTER 2:205

FROM: Amund and Anne Bjorli, *Bue, North Dakota, 7 September 1887*

TO: Hans Jørgensen and Eli Johannesdatter Bjøkne, *Lesja, Oppland*

⊷⟹⟸⊷

Dear parents and siblings,

Thank you so much for your welcome letter that we received some time ago. We are glad to see that you are in good health and doing well. We are all, thank God, in good health and all is well with us. I'll now be alone for some time as Amund will be away threshing with T. Flagestad. We expect him either today or tomorrow. They are going about twenty miles further north and will be away for a couple of weeks since it's too far to go back and forth. I think I'll be rather lonely because I haven't been alone before for more than one or two nights. But I haven't heard of anyone who has been afraid so I'll have to be brave. I think Flagestad will be doing our threshing. He comes with his own people and food so there is no trouble for us. His sister and another girl do the cooking. They have a tent or a wagon I suppose but the men sleep outdoors. There are many threshing machines on the move around here and last week two that were competing for farmers met each other. They have to travel around and offer their work so the farmers don't have to beg them to come. Yesterday morning Kari Flagestad was here on a short visit. She had been to church on Sunday and stayed the night at Enstad. She was in a hurry. I made her some food and coffee when she came and she was soon ready to go on. I tried to get her to stay for dinner but she didn't have time. She sends her regards. She told me we were related and asked about many things from Lesja, but she seemed to know more than I did. The servant girl at Sønstebø had got it at a prayer meeting.

I see in the letter from sister Guro that you are sending me dress material or some woolen cloth. Thank you so much. I would rather have the woolen cloth if you are weaving anyway but don't bother doing it just for me and the color can be just as you want it. Here people are not at all particular about color and they use what they have. I've heard people say they thought I had nice and good clothes with me from Norway. It's the same whether it's checkered or all of one color or dress material or woolen cloth. Mother wondered what kind of food I made when we had so many guests. For dinner it was fried pork and eggs, butter, coffee, flatbread and regular bread, just common food that is usual around here. The women helped do the dishes as usual when we have visitors. In the afternoon, at coffee time as they say here, we had coffee, butter, bread and cake. Cake is like a snack that is baked with a little butter, egg, milk, sugar and something that makes it raise that is called baking powder when we use fresh milk and *soda* for sour milk, but I don't know whether it is what we call *soda* in Norway. It is like flour. And we have sauce. This is a kind of berry that is like lingonberries and it is cooked with sugar so it becomes like sugared water and this is poured on small tea saucers that they call sauce plates; there are many kinds of sauce. Once we had two families from Enstad and then I cooked a milk porridge and fish in addition to what I have just listed.

Guro Brøste gave birth to a boy last Sunday and Mari Enstad had one two weeks ago. People here bring each other *sengemat*. I visited Mari with a little porridge, which she said tasted like the one her mother made, and a cake. I don't go to many people with food but some go long distances with it. Loving regards from your

ANNE

I have now almost completed my letter and what I have left to tell you can wait till another time. It can be too heavy if we add more pages since Amund also has written. It is more than a week since we had your letter but we haven't had an occasion to go to the post office before now. Don't be afraid to ask if there is anything you want to know. And if you don't want Amund to know about it you can write it on a separate slip of paper and then I'll tell you everything. Today is September 7 and today *Skaute* gave birth to a bull calf. She is our best cow. The one we got in July that I mentioned in my last letter gives a lot of milk and her calf is thriving and getting fat. We have two cow calves and two bull calves. I now have five cows that give milk so there is enough to do. One of them belongs to Knut and Peder and they milk it themselves when they are home.

Dear parents-in-law and siblings,

Thank you so much for your welcome letter that we received some time ago. We are glad to see that you are in good health and we can say the same for us. We've done our haying but didn't get much, as we had a very dry early summer and those who waited to cut the grass got more as there was rain just after the haying season. We won't be getting much wheat as we had a strong frost just after the wheat came up followed by a long period of drought, but weeds thrived, especially on poor soil. No one here has threshed yet so we don't really know what we'll get. For our part we think we'll get as much as last year. The price for wheat is low but there is a rising tendency. There is a good price for horses while cattle are lower than they were last year. Wages are higher than they were last year. For a day laborer the wage is now two dollars a day and board. This is not for the whole year but from harvest and until threshing is over. So there are periods in between when there is no work and many go without work rather than work for the current wage and many go to the city and spend their hard-earned dollars rather than work for a farmer for seventy cents a day. After threshing I'll write and tell what we get. We have a lot of potatoes as well as rutabagas and carrots. Anne is also writing so this should be enough for now. Our loving regards and give our greetings to Berg.

A. P. BJORLI

Amund's initial "P" is for his patronymic: Pedersen. Anne wrote to her parents on 7 March 1887 (Nor. ed. V:70) about baking bread, their animals, and their relations with Amund's half-brothers Knut and Peder Engebretsen Bjorli. Her husband wrote on 17 April 1887 (Nor. ed. V:73), mainly about their farm. Amund's threshing partner was Tosten Pedersen Flagestad and Kari was his mother. AB had worked as a seamstress in Lesja, as she mentioned in a letter dated 10 February 1887 (unpublished). The cryptic sentence about the servant girl is surely a piece of gossip that made sense to her readers in Lesja. To distinguish bread (baked in the oven) and flatbread (baked on top of the kitchen range) she writes *stovbrø*. For cake she seems to have no Norwegian word and writes *kek* and *bekinpauder*, *soda*, *sas*, and *saspleiter*. The literal translation of *sengemat* is bed food, a traditional gift of food to women who had recently given birth. The idea was to help them revive after their ordeal. Traditional *sengemat* could be sour cream porridge, coffee and cakes, or meat dishes. *Skaute* was the name of one of their cows. Cattle were by tradition the women's responsibility in Norway and Anne regards them as her responsibility also in North Dakota. Knut and Peder were Amund's younger half brothers. AB did not always find time for writing. She began a letter at 7:30 p.m. on 27 September, writing that she was not sure when she would be able to send it, and although it is a rather short letter, it seems that it was not finished until about a month later (Nor. ed. V:88). «II:193 »II:206 NE V:85

1887 — LETTER 2:206

FROM: Hans Hansen Bjokne, *Lowry, Minnesota, 30 November 1887*

TO: Hans Jørgensen and Eli Johannesdatter Bjøkne, *Lesja, Oppland*

Dear parents and siblings,

I'll send you a few words even though I don't have anything special to say except that we are in good health and doing well. It's wonderful to think of how forbearing the Lord is who upholds us in his grace and lets only good befall us even if we sin against him. Far too often we forget to thank him for his goodness. It is now nine and a half years since I left home and I can say, "Till now the Lord has helped me." Yes, the Holy Spirit has always called me to turn to God and to walk in his path, but I have resisted him until about a year ago when he stopped me and I began to seek the Lord. Since then the Lord has been my help.

I wrote the above on Sunday and it is now Wednesday and it is my heavy duty to inform you that Johannes is probably dead. The first we heard of this was last week in a letter that came to Hans Haugen saying that we could get better information by writing to C. Haugen, Grand Forks. I wrote to him immediately and received the following reply: "I will give you the information I have, but I'm not entirely sure of the circumstances. The last letter I had from John was in June of last year. I sent him a pair of boots and some underwear and he was then part of a *"surface gang"* (a kind of railroad job) at Devil's Lake. Since then I haven't had a letter from him. I wrote to him several times but had no reply and I neither saw nor heard of him even though I'm employed by the same railroad. Then, five weeks ago someone told me that he had died while with a family from Stavanger, but he didn't know the man's name or anything else but had seen it in a newspaper. I cannot give you more information now, but if I hear more I'll try." This is the letter from C. Haugen and it is all the information I have. We've advertised in the newspaper and I've written to some pastors in the West to see if any of them have heard anything. It seems that he died a year ago last summer. I don't know whether I should believe it or not. If he is dead it is strange that he didn't make arrangements to have some of us notified and if he is alive it is just as strange that he doesn't write to us. But we must place this and all else in the hand of God and believe his word that all things are for the good for those who love God. We'll write you as soon as we have more information. With loving regards from your son and brother

HANS AND FAMILY

· —— ·

When HHB's younger brother Jørgen wrote to his parents 27 November 1887 he had no news about his brother Johannes (John Hanson) and wrote that they had advertised for him in *Folkebladet* (a Minneapolis newspaper). On 14 January 1888 Jørgen wrote to his sister Guro that they were not sure that the dead man actually was their brother "as there are so many who have the same name here. Most immigrants cast off their farm name and this is what he too has done." Hans Haugen was HHB's brother-in-law. The word of God he refers to at the end of his letter is from Romans 8:28. «II:205 »II:207 NE V:92

· —— ·

1887 — LETTER 2:207

FROM: Anne Bjorli, *Bue, North Dakota, 4 December 1887*
To: Hans Jørgensen and Eli Johannesdatter Bjøkne, *Lesja, Oppland*

⋯⇒⇐⋯

Dear parents and siblings,

As we've had the pleasure of hearing from you I'll right away send you a few words so you'll hear a little from us. I see that you're in good health and doing well and this makes us glad. Today we have full winter; it came last night with a little snow and today we have a wind. Till now the weather has been pleasant even though it has been quite cold. I understand that you've long had winter in Lesja but perhaps no colder than here in North Dakota.

I'm sewing a dress for Ingri Enstad, the wife of Peder Enstad. The material is fine; it is black and costs a dollar a yard. The work goes slowly. When you have to take care of the house you can't sit with it for long even though we only have three meals a day. You may think this isn't much but it's what we prefer and it saves time for the person responsible for the meals. This is not to save on food; it doesn't make a difference that way. I suppose you are now spinning all you can. I've also spun some yarn for knitting. I bought five pounds of wool at twenty cents á pound; quite cheap, but there is a lot of dirt in it so in the end it doesn't weigh that much. I'll be using it for socks and mittens. I see there has been an auction at Bjøkne. I suppose they had to do it. If you, brother Jakob, received the letter that Amund wrote to you last summer you must send him a reply. If you aren't used to writing, he won't care; the letters he gets from home aren't that well written. Peder and the little ones have written some and it's nice to have a few words. Could Mattias at least write enough for us to see his handwriting? I hope you are still a diligent student.

I've heard that Hans and Jørgen have advertised to find brother Johannes in a newspaper called *Folkebladet*. We don't subscribe to it but were told about it. It's been a long time since I had a letter from Jørgen and even longer from Hans, but I suppose I can't expect any when I don't write much myself. I don't have much to write about and I suppose this is how it is with them too. I haven't had a letter yet from Kari Berg. Please give them our regards. I must conclude now with loving regards to you my dear and often remembered parents and siblings from

ANNE BJORLIE AND HUSBAND

Father, you must write Mrs. and not Miss; the first means a wife and the other a girl.

. —— .

The spinning of wool was seasonal; the sheep were sheared in the fall. The auction was on another Bjøkne farm. Rønnaug Hansdatter Bjøkne was from yet another. AB is still unaware of her brother John's death. Her husband, Amund, had written to Jakob on 10 June 1887 warning him of the vices of alcohol and tobacco and telling him that "total abstinence associations do good work here and both young and old people take part." Peder was a son of Amund's first marriage and lived with his grandparents in Lesja. Mattias, addressed as "you," was Anne's youngest brother. Kari Berg was Amund's sister. Anne and Amund wrote a few weeks later, on 11 January 1888 (Nor. ed. V:100), that their newborn child had only lived one hour and seventeen minutes but had been baptized before he died. Anne wrote on 29 February without mentioning her child's death, and her brother Jørgen wrote on 14 January that he had been invited to live with Anne for the winter. «II:206 »II:215 NE V:94

. —— .

1887 — LETTER 2:208

FROM: Hans Nilsen Lind, *West Valley, Minnesota, 9 December 1887*

To: Sevat Olsen Vik, *Sigdal, Buskerud*

Dear friends Sevat O. Wiig and family,

We received your letter on November 5 but you must excuse my delay in replying; we've been so busy because the boys have been away working. Nils went on July 19 and was away till November 8. During that time he was home for three days and helped us stack the wheat. We used two teams so we could get it done in a hurry. It's no wonder that they wanted to be out at work as wages have been very good this fall; during harvest and threshing they got two dollars a day and now Nils has been making $1.50. Ole was at home until we had cut as much hay as we thought we would need and then he too went away to work and I was left to do the work here. I was to break land until the beginning of harvest but I didn't get anything done as I got ill and was too weak for five weeks. Ole Bjornerud and Ole Sætre had promised to reap our field for us as they have a selfbinder. I was to stack the wheat but this became too difficult for me. I had to sit down and rest all the time but thanks to the good lord Jesus I got a little better every day so I could do some work. Driving a heavy plow with three horses is tough when you are weak. I had plowed eight to nine acres when Ole came home and then we had to build a stable. But it was too late in the fall to get the lumber as it was too far away. Then Ole went to town and bought boards so now we have built a twenty-four-foot long and fourteen-foot wide stable only of boards. The cows and horses are in the same room. After a few days the threshing machine arrived in our neighborhood and then Ole had to go to work for others in exchange for them helping us. Fifteen men were needed and the machine was pulled by ten horses and the work for us was done in three and a half hours. We had seventy bushels of wheat, 217 of oats, and twenty of potatoes. This was on land that had just been broken and there the crop isn't so good. This is all we got this year and as they had to buy their seed it wasn't very profitable. Moreover, they had to pay for most of the breaking and this is quite expensive: two and a half dollars an acre and the work wasn't well done. Ole didn't buy a team until late fall last year, too late for plowing.

In your letter and in a letter from my brother Nils I see that you've had a long drought in Sigdal and I know that this will lead to grief in most homes and worry about how they will be able to feed themselves. But we don't have such worries here. In Marshall County we've had a blessed good year. Around the middle of July there was almost too much rain. We had just begun haying and one night there was so much rain that the stacks were almost covered with water on low land and for some time it was difficult to get dry hay.

It's nice to have letters and hear from Old Norway. I must thank you both. I was glad to hear that you were well and I wish that this letter will find you in the same good situation. I must add that I've been up past midnight several times in fear of a prairie fire that we've seen almost circle us, but at some distance, and we have praised God that we've been spared. We got two inches of the first snow on November 16 and on Sunday December 4 it snowed again and drifted so it was difficult to get out in the morning. Now we can use sleighs.

Please don't bother any more about the cobbler's bristle that you couldn't find because I only meant you to ask Haagen Velta to bring a little if you saw him. I've done what you asked concerning Jens Gren. I talked with him about it after I had your letter but had no answer. I gave him your note and since then I have talked with old Turi about it and she was rather upset. He had told her that he had paid his debt before leaving Norway but she said that it wasn't due until this year. They had thought of selling a cow last fall but prices were so low that they let it be. But they've already done a lot and are doing well. I can give you a fair report on their crop and livestock: 130 bushels of wheat, thirty bushels of barley, 153 bushels of potatoes, twelve cows large and small, two sheep and two pigs, one of which will be slaughtered for Christmas.

I almost forgot to tell you that we had three pigs and have already slaughtered one of them. It was pretty good. We bought it last summer for ten dollars and paid with one of our spinning wheels and a pair of carding combs and topped it with three and a half dollars. The other two are only six weeks old, and we'll feed them. The man who owned them couldn't sell them that late in the fall, so he wanted to kill them and we wanted to see if they would survive. I have no more to write about so I'll ask you to give our regards to all at Lower Vik as I don't have the time to write to them just now. It would be nice if you would let them listen to and see the letter. Give our regards to all at Ramstad and if you happen to go there it would be good if Ole Ramstad could see and hear it. Thank you Sevat for your goodness and for all the trouble you took upon yourself the last day we were in Norway. I'll never forget this as long as I live. Give our regards to Sergeant O. Gren, Sergeant H. Bjørnsen and Ketil Pilrud. And finally, regards from all of us here and our wishes for a happy New Year. Your friend

HANS NILSEN

. ——— .

HNL, who had only been in the United States a few months, is already codeswitching and uses English words such as *tim* (team), *ripe* (reap) and *stebel* (stable). He provides no translation so it seems that such words have entered into his spoken Norwegian and that he is not aware that they are English. «II:200 »II:237 NE V:95

. ——— .

1887 — LETTER 2:209

FROM: Elise Wærenskjold, *Prairieville, Texas, 21 December 1887*

To: Thomine Dannevig, *Lillesand, Aust-Agder*

⊹⇒◉⇐⊹

My dearly beloved Thomine,

Thank you for your welcome letter and news about our acquaintances. It must be nice for you to be able to visit your children every winter and that Thorvald comes to get you. We are both getting old for so much travel but it is nevertheless so precious for us to visit our children that we cannot sufficiently thank God for granting us the health to make this possible in our old age. Yes, God in his grace has done all for my best and that which seemed so black turned out to be a blessing. You know that I borrowed money from my sister-in-law to pay your brother; but then she demanded 150 dollars to lend to her son-in-law who owed money on his farm and could lose it if he did not get the 150 dollars. Niels owes me more than I owe my sister-in-law but he was unable to raise money and I had to try to get a loan and after many failed attempts a bank promised me a loan if someone with the necessary means would stand security. But this proved more difficult than I had thought; the man who was willing demanded security in my sheep and cattle and also set as a condition that I try to get a loan from Norway. So I wrote to Foyn and explained my situation and—imagine!—he was so extremely kind as to send me 400 dollars. There is not one in a thousand, probably not one in a million men who would do so much for a divorced wife as Foyn has done for me. I received his draft when I was visiting Otto and I was so happy that I hardly slept that night. Then I had to work out what I should do with the 200 dollars above the amount I had expected. For the 150 dollars I had borrowed from the bank I had to pay 168 dollars even though I had only had it for six months, and many demand a higher rate of interest. Otto had some debt at a very high interest so I gave him the 200 dollars in return for a monthly payment of twenty dollars for as long as I live and in addition to this ten dollars for some cattle that he took care of for me; so the annual sum will be thirty dollars, one fourth to be paid every quarter. Before I went to Hamilton I had let Niels have the sheep and cattle I own here in return for paying me twenty-five dollars each spring and fall when he sells the wool and in addition all the firewood I need and pork, mainly chops and ribs because I don't eat fat pork. We got a lawyer to set up a legal document so that this income will be mine whether Niels lives or not and this document also specifies that I have full ownership of half of the house and garden for life. It would have been very difficult to manage on fifty dollars but with eighty I should do quite well.

Please pass the enclosed letter on to Mrs. Basberg. In her letter she tells me how kind you and Hansen have been. It is strange that the Aall family does not help her but they may not know how difficult her situation is. I am quite comfortable in my old house. Everything here is plain and simple as are my clothes, but, as you know, I've never liked luxury. The only thing I miss is not being able to afford books; but it occasionally happens that I receive one as a gift. For Christmas I got *Amtmandens Døtre* by Camilla Collett from a Danish cousin who has sent me a book earlier and from Oscar Reiersen, the editor's oldest son, I received Bjørnson's *Det flagger i Byen og paa Havnen*. Kristofer Janson has sent me quite a few of his books and when I am in Bosque I can read several of the recent novels: *Kommandørens Døtre* and Gløersen's *Dagligdags*, both of which I found very interesting while I did not like Bjørnson's *Over Evne* much. I subscribe to *Illustreret Ugeblad* published by a Dane, C. Rasmussen, the best Norwegian American magazine I have seen. I will soon, as you may remember, be seventy-three and I am writing this without glasses but with a candle. In the evening I read and write; in the daytime I sew and if I don't have any work I help my relatives or visit neighbors. I have nice and pleasant neighbors, Norwegians and Americans. I have always been so lucky as to have good friends wherever I have been and this is a great blessing.

Please give all who care to hear from me my regards. To make a list of all who are of interest would be too much; but I must in particular ask you to remember me to your sons and your brother Samuel. I have not forgotten how sweet and intelligent Thorvald was and how much we loved each other and the many pleasant conversations I had with Hansen. I wonder whether Kaja may be unable to write any more; it is so long since I had a letter from her and it would be so good if she could send me some words. I think Stina Normann could have written if she wanted to. It must be difficult for them to have to depend on their children but it is nevertheless good that they both can and will do this. Do you know anything about the Hedemarks and Rosenvold, Peder Kalvehagen, Osuld Enge and Anders

Holte? I hardly even know whether these are their correct names as we for the most part called them the men from Eide Parish, but you will know who I am thinking of. What has happened to the Rosenkilde family? Not so long ago I dreamed I was in Lillesand and wanted to visit you. I never see any of Grøgaard's family, but I assume they are all well. Sigurd Ørbæk is in Shreveport, Louisiana and is happy there. Ouline R. and Mrs. Pabst send their regards. And now I must conclude with Merry Christmas and a Happy New Year! Your

E. WÆRENSKJOLD

· ——— ·

Parts of this letter are in Clausen 1961 (with several informative notes, 136) but the editor has included some of it in the letter EW completed on 31 December 1886 (128–130). Part of the letter she wrote to Mrs. Basberg on 20 December is in Clausen (134–135). Svend Foyn was EW's first husband. EW's friend Dicta (Elise Benedicte, born 1810) Aall lived with her husband Jacob Aall in Oslo where he was a high-ranking government bureaucrat. The authors and translated titles of the books she mentions are: Camilla Collett (1813–1895), *The District Governor's Daughters* (1855), Bjørnstjerne Bjørnson (1832–1910) *Flags Are Flying in Town and Port* (1884) and *Beyond Powers* (1883), Jonas Lie (1833–1908), *The Commander's Daughters* (1886), and Ole Kristian Gløersen (1838–1916), *Everyday Matters* (1886). Kristofer Janson (1841–1917) was a prominent writer who spent many years in Minneapolis where he continued to write poetry and fiction, some of it published by Christian Rasmussen, who emigrated from Denmark in 1873 and was a publisher of newspapers, journals, and books in Norwegian, first in Chicago and from 1887 in Minneapolis. *Illustreret Ugeblad* (Illustrated Weekly) began publication in 1881. In it she could read Drude Krog Janson's novel *En Saloonkeepers Datter* (*A Saloonkeeper's Daughter*), which began serialization the following year on 4 October 1882. «II:195 »II:223 NE V:96

· ——— ·

FROM: Karen Solem, *Norden, South Dakota, 25 December 1887*

To: Ole Tobias and Amalie Ødegaard, *Nannestad, Akershus*

Dear brother and sister-in-law!

It is rather late to wish you a merry Christmas so I must comfort myself with the thought that I did so in my former letter. First I must thank you for the letters I received yesterday. My congratulations and best wishes for the little one. Amalie is really good; I was expecting it as a little bird sang to me about it last summer. I think grandmother was right, Amalie, when she said that you should lay aside your old coat to make coats for the little boys, but I suppose you can afford new ones. It seems you are doing quite well and now that you have bought a horse you can go visiting during Christmas without extra cost.

We've just come home from a Christmas visit to a neighbor. There were many there so the house was full. We would still be there if it hadn't started to snow, but "snowstorm" is a word we have respect for. You may imagine how fast we went over the prairie with Cinch and Dolly who are well worth their 300 dollars. And they wore real bells, big ones that sound like the church bells in Nannestad. No, now I'm boasting again. Here is something I should have written first. I must report that grandmother has left us to enter into—as we must believe—the joy of her Lord. She died December 7. Her last days were difficult but she was at peace before she died. She lay there calling on God to come and take her home and we cannot imagine grieving for her; it was good that she was freed from her pain. A large flock was gathered at her deathbed—nineteen people including the children. It's so strange when death visits a home: we feel we are nothing and it is as if we wish to grasp God by force. But, alas, we soon forget this sensation and are again as before. It must be a strange God who has patience with us for so long. I'll return to my narrative. Friday before she died (on Wednesday) old Pastor Brandt was here and administered Holy Communion to her and that night we all took our farewells with her and from that moment someone was with her day and night as any moment might be her last. The last God's word we read for her was David's 103rd Psalm; that was an hour before she passed away. She died so peacefully that we hardly noticed that her spirit left its earthly prison. Tell mother she can thank God that her prayers are heard and she will meet her sister in the heavenly mansions. It was strange that she should pass away in my home; it was surely the will of God that I should come here to help her in her last days. We had the funeral on December 13. The entire neighborhood was invited as we knew that many wished to see her. Almost 100 people came to us. Both pastors Brandt were here and the old one gave the sermon. You may imagine all the crying and sobbing of her children and grandchildren. The hymn we sang was "Children of the Heavenly Father." We were very busy before the funeral preparing food for so many. Some returned home straight from the churchyard but many came back to us for the night and the next morning we had a snowstorm and we had them for dinner, supper and then break-fast the next day. Hilde Fella was with us all the time and she is very good at that kind of work. She was the one who dressed grandmother.

Grandfather and Nicolai are going to Fillmore County where Christian and Karl live. They should have left last Wednesday but couldn't because of the weather: we've had a snowstorm from Monday noon to yesterday. I suppose they'll leave tomorrow or Tuesday. We'll then be two less at the table and this is to my liking. I'm rather tired of having so many in our home, but we may need another hired hand as there is too much work for Laurits and Olaus.

Johan Møllerstad has gone to Norway and I suppose he'll have a lot to tell about Deuel County when he gets to Nannestad. Don't forget to send photographs as many are waiting for them. I'll distribute them. My letter has become rather long so it is best that I conclude. As you may understand, we've had a hard winter. We are all well except that one of Peder Fella's little girls (twelve years old) is doing poorly and it doesn't seem that she will grow up. Marie is so clever and I think she will soon be walking. All here send their best regards and wish you a happy New Year, as does your faithful

KAREN

· ———— ·

Pastor Nils Olsen Brandt was retired and lived with his son Realf Ottesen Brandt, pastor in Toronto, a small town south of Norden. The grandmother who had died was KS's mother-in-law, Karen Solem, a sister of her mother. Her father-in-law was Nils Solem. Nicolai, Christian, Karl, Olaus, and Louis (Laurits), KS's husband, were Nils

Solem's sons. Peder Fella, who had been married to a daughter of Karen and Nils Solem, was a widower. Hilde was one of his daughters. The hymn sung at the funeral, "Ingen er saa trygg i fare," was by the Swedish hymnist Lina Sandell (1832–1903) whose hymns and religious songs gained great popularity in Scandinavia. This one is translated into English as "Children of the Heavenly Father." KS wrote to her mother on 29 November 1887. Later she also wrote on 15 January and 20 March 1888 (Nor. ed. V:101 and 109). «II:203 »II:218 NE V:97

. ⎯⎯ .

1888 — LETTER 2:211

FROM: Anne Norsby, *Necedah, Wisconsin, 4 January 1888*

To: Marie Olsdatter Vigerust, *Dovre, Oppland*

◦⇒◦⇐◦

Dear cousin,

As it's long since I received your letter I must take up my pen to reply. I see you are all well and I can say the same from us at Norsby. As you know I was home last summer with Jakob, father and mother. Ole went to work in the forest one month before Christmas. Bjørner came home three weeks before Christmas and will be here until spring. Sivert worked in town until Christmas and after a few days he went to school in Northfield in Minnesota. They have three-month terms and I don't know whether he'll be home in three or six months. Christmas slowly vanished without any hullaballoo so we'll have to wait patiently for it to come to an end. Christmas Day I was on the farm and we were all invited to our nearest neighbor. The second day we had to go to town as Rønnaug and her husband went to visit his parents. They went Friday before Christmas and came back yesterday evening. I've been in town to look after our house. It has been as quiet as the grave. On New Year's Eve I and my brothers Bjørner and Sivert were invited to a Norwegian family here in town. I was the only unmarried adult woman but there were seven young men, two of whom played the violin and that was all the fun we had. So if you are thinking of coming here next spring you should expect that you have already celebrated your liveliest Christmases. It was very cold in the early part of Christmas but after a few days we had snowstorms that made it impossible to use the railroads in some places.

The harvest was poor. It looked promising in early summer but the early drought dried it all up before it began to rain so much that people could barely gather enough hay for their animals. And as if this wasn't enough, forest fires raged in our area and burned up both grass and hay. Your sister Olianna has been very ill. I was in town three weeks ago and we heard that the doctor had been there and Sivert and I went to see her. She was better then and was out of bed a few days later. I heard that she was ill again on Christmas Day but on the fourth day Hans came by and said that she was well. He was going to the forest the next morning. Your brother Ole was here yesterday and he said that she was quite well. He went to the forest today. Bjørner is now with his relatives and I'll let you know how they are when he returns.

As I couldn't get my letter done yesterday I'll continue on it today. Bjørner and your sister's son Edward were here yesterday evening. They are both helping to haul hay. Your sister is now well and out of bed, and your other relatives are also well. Ole Lee is in the forest in the same place as my brother. When I last wrote we didn't know where Anna Rudi lived but we do now. First she was in Dakota for a while and she wrote to H. E. Hanson and Bjørner asking for her sister Rønnaug's address. We've now had a letter from her son and she had then been with him for six to seven weeks. She says that she would have sent us money had she known our address. It seems it will be just like last winter when she said she would pay as soon as we sent a bill. I then told her that she knew what they had paid for the ticket and she was home for two or three weeks. There they would pay her whatever she wanted. But since then we've heard nothing. She knows our address so she is just making excuses. We wrote to Rise in early summer but have had no reply. If you see anyone from Hinden please ask them if they've received a letter from us. I suppose you've heard that Jakob Dalen ran away from his wife and children. A young man from Aalesund who has boarded with us went with Jakob and was in business with him. I think they ran it for one to two years and it was very successful. He was a nice boy and we got to know him so well that it was as if he belonged here. Last winter he visited us on the farm for several weeks. He spoke well of both Jakob and his wife. We had a letter from him after Jakob had run away; I don't remember how many thousands he ran away with but I think he took two thousand from his brother Ole. If you haven't heard about this then don't tell anyone.

Marie, I hope you won't wait as long before writing as I did. You must let us know whether you are coming or not. In my view you shouldn't wait any longer if you want to come. As I don't have more to write about I'll conclude with loving regards from us all. Rine and her husband send their regards. Say hello to Haugen, Høye, Gurihaug, Slette, Vigerust and Snekkerlien and all other acquaintances. Happy New Year from your friend and cousin.

. —— .

> The farm of Jacob and Marit Norsby was close to Necedah. Those mentioned in the first paragraphs are AN's brothers. The St. Olaf School began as an academy in 1874 and became a four-year college in 1889. AN's sister Rønnaug (called Rine) was married to Otto Christiansen Huslegard from Aasnes, Hedmark. Marie Vigerust's sister Olianna was married to Hans E. Hanson. Edward was a son. AN wrote more letters than can be included here, for instance one dated 23 June 1887. An undated letter, probably from 1888, gives information about the social life of immigrants in the Midwest: "We had good fun on July 4. We were on the farm and had many guests. You may imagine that we hadn't forgotten a fiddler. We were there from Saturday to Tuesday and danced every night and on the last day we danced all afternoon. Two weeks ago we had a loan party at the Norwegian church. You may not know what this is. They go around with a list where people write their names and what they will donate of food or drink. The day of the party the food and drink is collected and taken to where the party is held. This is the Norwegian church and the money is for the church as it is still in debt. That evening the church was used as an auction hall and not as a house of God, but you will understand that this was done for a good cause. Four tables were set up in the church and it wasn't necessary to ask people to come to the table. When people wanted to buy food and drink they sat at a table and one who was serving would come and ask what they wanted to have and this was brought to them. You would have to pay for your own food because all had to pay. And you had to eat more than was good for you as we wanted the church to have as much money as possible. You may imagine that there were many invitations. Rine and I were supposed to serve at the table but we didn't want to do this but we washed dishes until late at night when it was all over. There was an unusually powerful thunderstorm that night so there weren't so many people. There was so much food that they held a party the next evening in the home of a Norwegian family. We went and it cost ten cents for each person for supper. It was all sold for twenty dollars. There was of course no intoxicating drink, only coffee and lemonade. Some time ago Sivert won a nice bedcover at the ladies' aid." «II:164 »II:224 NE V:99

. —— .

1888 — LETTER 2:212

FROM: Iver Ellingsen Elsrud, *Grafton, North Dakota, 27 January 1888*

To: A brother, *Aadalen, Ringerike, Buskerud*

⋅⊷═◉═⊷⋅

Dear brother,

Some time ago I wrote to Edvard and asked him to see if there was a family who wanted to go to America in the spring. Enclosed is a draft for 446 *kroner*, and I hope you will do what you can to find a young couple who don't have too many children. I'll pay them a reasonably good wage either by the month or for the year. If I can get a reliable man to work for me next summer I plan to travel. Jan Raa, who worked for me last summer, recommended Martin, son of Aaste and Gudbrand, as a good worker and he has written many times to his people here for a ticket but they didn't want to help him. I'll leave the decision about who is to have the money for a ticket to you. If this isn't enough money I hope you'll make up the difference and I'll send you the amount as soon as possible. If you cannot find anyone who wants to go then you don't have to return the money right away. Please let me know if you find someone as soon as possible because if I cannot get someone from Norway I'll have to look around here. If anyone wants to come you should buy a ticket to Milton, Cavalier County, Dakota on the St. Paul, Minneapolis and Manitoba Railroad. Ole Huset is a butcher there and I'll ask him to meet them at the station. I would like them to come as early as possible, even to leave in the middle of March and that they let me know the day they leave for Christiania.

I have no news except that I've sold my horses and will now have to go east to buy fifteen or twenty new ones and if that goes well I can make five to six hundred dollars. We had a good year here so I got a little more money than I need so I'll try to speculate a little. It has been very cold and we've had a lot of snow so if this continues it will be the worst winter I've had in America. Fingal Runhaug is doing well here considering his age and now has enough wheat to pay his debt to me for the team of oxen I sold to him two years ago for about 150 dollars. All is well at Uncle Ole Haugerud's and

I can give you their regards. I assume you are bored with all this nonsense so I had better conclude with regards to my friends and in particular to those at Elsrud, Blakkstveit and Skognes from your devoted son and brother

IVER E. ELSRUD

· ———— ·

Gudbrand and Aaste lived on the croft Braaten, and Martin, their oldest child, was nine in 1865. IEE's letter to Edvard about getting a couple from Norway to work for him is dated 17 December 1887. He may not have been aware of the Foran Act of 1885 that made it illegal for immigrants to come with a contract to work in return for prepaid tickets. When IEE writes about going east he probably means Minnesota or Iowa. He may be compared to another immigrant in these volumes who returned, Ole G. Lande. Like him, IEE thinks more like a businessman, looking for opportunities to make money, than a farmer thinking of developing his farm that is also his home. There is one more letter from IEE in the third volume of this edition, the last one he wrote before returning to Aadalen, dated 11 July 1896. «II:174 NE V:102

· ———— ·

1888 — LETTER 2:213

FROM: Gunder and Kari Nordrum, *Rothsay, Minnesota, March 1888*

TO: Anders Olsen Lie, *Hedalen, Sør-Aurdal, Oppland*

◦⇒◦⇐◦

Dear friend and relatives,

I received your letter of August 20 a long time ago and my late reply is due to my neglect. We see that you are doing reasonably well and we can say the same for ourselves. Last year was a bad year because of a long drought and some frost in spring. We had 700 bushels of wheat, 200 of oats and 100 of barley. We use the barley to feed the pigs. We had no potatoes and bought them for forty cents a bushel. We now have five cows, two calves, five horses and two pigs. We slaughter two full grown pigs and a two-year-old heifer every fall for our own use. I don't know of any news to tell you as everything here is unknown to you. Last year two boys and two girls came here from Aadalen. We were recently at the funeral of an old man whose name was Anders Sveen. He was from Land in Norway and knew Anne Brenden. He was seventy and had been ill all summer and kept to his bed for about a month before he died. We had a hard winter with much snow and cold weather but it has been nice for some time and more than half the snow has melted. Last summer Anne's brother Iver A. Brenden visited us. He has been three winters in Minneapolis at the Conference's theological seminary. He came in April and worked for Mikkel for four months at twenty dollars a month and then he taught Norwegian school until Christmas. He then returned to Minneapolis and we think he'll return to teach school this summer. He was a good Christian teacher for our children. He was better than many believed before they got to hear him.

We haven't heard anything from your sons for a year. I've been expecting a letter from Mikkel and hope it will soon be here. I've also waited for a letter from Kari Bertilrud. We haven't had a reply to the note to her enclosed in the letter sent to you. Last year we said we would pay for her ticket but we assume that she doesn't want our money since she hasn't written yet. She may wish to go to her brothers and they may already have sent her a ticket so that she is on her way to Dakota. I would have liked to see her again. Give her our regards if she hasn't already gone and ask her to write and tell us what she wants to do. When you write you must tell us how many are going to America this spring. I would like to have news from Hedalen. I often think about my childhood home and it often comes to me in my dreams. Please give my regards to my aunt at Finhert if she still is alive. I suppose she is even older than you but I think she has had good health and that is a good help when we get old. Do her children send anything from America to help her? If these simple sentences find you alive I hope to receive yet another letter from you. They are all well at Brenden and Sørli and our old mother is in good health for her age. This winter she has mostly lived at Brenden. I must now end my poor and simple letter with regards to you from all of us, both big and small. Sincerely,

GUNDER H. NORDRUM   KARI M. NORDRUM

. ——— .

The letter has no date; the envelope is stamped on 24 March 1888 in Christiania. Enclosed was a brief note from KN to an "old friend of my youth" (probably Inger Olsdatter Finhert, who was maid at Søre Lie and soon married Anders Andersen Lie). Kari Bertilrud went to her brothers in Dakota (Nor. Ed. 2:229). KN's aunt Inger Mikkelsdatter

Finhert would have been eighty-three in 1888 and Anders Olsen Lie was seventy-six. Olaug Brenden and Mikkel Sørli were her siblings. Her mother was Ragnhild Olsdatter Sørli. «II:167 NE V:105

. —— .

1888 — LETTER 2:214

FROM: John Svenson, *Chippewa Falls, Wisconsin, April 1888*

TO: Jakob Rasmussen Sandvik, *Kinsarvik, Ullensvang, Hordaland*

⊶⟹◯⟸⊷

[...] and for a pig sty they have only set up a shed out in the field and covered it with straw on one side. But they take good care of their horses and keep them nice and fat and protect them as well as they can from the cold. Horses and cows are larger than in Norway but the sheep are very small. The cows are out every day and there is so much hay and straw that they can eat as much as they want and you will realize that this shows in the pail. And those who wish to live cheaply still have to make money but people here don't live cheaply but well. They don't build log houses but set up frames with wood siding on the outside and they either plaster or use unplaned boards and wallpaper on the inside. These houses are cold so they have to rely on firewood. They also have bedrooms set apart from the main room and on the walls they have paintings or other ornaments, and they wash before every meal and have nice and clean clothes. I can't say whether they keep their hearts clean, but they often drive past the church and go visiting while the pastor is preaching and on Sundays they plow or harvest; I've seen this myself. It is the so-called *Norvaygans* who do this, so Sundays and other holidays are no more important than other days. There is an adage that when the poor man becomes rich he becomes like the devil. Since there is no law here concerning the Norwegian religion and people do as they wish, many don't have their children confirmed or give them any religious schooling so they become like heathens. The Americans are strict about Sundays but they have no other holidays. I came here on Christmas Day and I saw them drive more than thirty wagonloads of provisions to the forest—now, that was my Christmas celebration. I had to go ten miles on a horse on Christmas Eve and when I came home I had two shots of whiskey and good food. These last eight days I've been quite comfortable, chopped firewood, kept the stove hot, made pancakes, cooked coffee, fried beef steaks and so forth. And you may be sure that I think of you all while I sit here alone. I have no news that may be of interest to you but you must write often as my best days are when I get letters from you.

You must get yourself a wife. Here there is a great shortage of girls. I've heard some say they would pay 200 dollars in cash for a wife. The single women here are useless as they know of nothing but gluttony and finery. They may be nice to look at but they cannot mend a stocking. The Germans and the English also want to have Norwegian girls and you should get yourself one and come to America. But what can I think of to fill the rest of my letter? Well I can write about the kinds of trees we have. The pines here are different from those at home and it isn't difficult to find a tree fit for a mast. The largest tree is the hemlock spruce; it's like a fir tree and much of this is exported to Europe. The tree we call a pine is like the Norwegian *furu*. Of hardwoods we have ash, aspen, birch and oak, all larger than in Norway, and we have elm, beech and wild plum trees. The only bird I've seen that we have in Norway is the crow.

I must tell you a secret but don't tell anyone because they told me not to write about it. Mattis and Sigri Brovold have decided to go home this spring, but they didn't want anyone to know about it because they didn't want them to expect them. I recently had a letter from uncle and they are all in good health, and I can say the same for myself. Give my regards to all relatives and friends and to my parents. But there is one thing you should know: if you were here you would make more money in one year than in ten at home. If you were here for two years you would make enough to pay your father's debt and still have money left over. If you would like to come I'll help you all I can. Why should you go around where there's so little space that you can hardly place your foot on the ground without having hands reaching up your legs trying to grab you. Come! Here there is space enough and no one stands in your way. If Svein Rasmussen had gone to America as soon as he got married it would have been the best thing he had done in his life. Give him my regards. Farewell,

JOHN SVENSEN

· ⸺ ·

The first part of this letter has not been preserved. A torn envelope is stamped 28 April 1888 in New York. Norway still has a state

FROM AMERICA TO NORWAY

church and at the time of this letter confirmation was more or less obligatory. It seems that JS doesn't think much of girls who have been brought up in the United States compared to "Norwegian girls." In another undated fragment, however, his views on women in Norway are negative: "Are the girls at home still just as proud and haughty. What reason do the girls there have to be proud, with their thick blue homespun clothes, or perhaps their crude Hardanger dialect as they make porridge and make flatbread of flour fit for pigs. No, here the girls are quite the opposite." There are more preserved letters from JS than can be included here. He wrote from Crookston, Minn., on 28 January 1887 (Nor. ed. V:66); although he had received several letters from Jakob Sandvik, some had evidently been lost and he writes about one railroad accident where all the mail burned and seventeen people were killed. Times are hard and there is little work to be had. He also writes about looking for the right girl and wants to have his rifle and some tools sent from Norway. He signs as John Sveinson. In another letter from Crookston on 28 October 1888 he has painted more than seventy buildings on a large "company farm" called Keyston covering fourteen sections and will have his own house next spring. Here he signs as John Svenson. «II:173 »II:236 NE V:112

. ⸻ .

1888 — LETTER 2:215

FROM: Anne Bjorli, *Bue, North Dakota, 25 April 1888*

To: Hans Jørgensen and Eli Johannesdatter Bjøkne, *Lesja, Oppland*

⸎

Dear parents and siblings,

We received your welcome letter some time ago and wrote the same day but it hasn't been sent yet so I'll have to write another one. The reason is that Amund didn't have time to go to the post office and now he can't go because the fields are so wet and we have to cross a river that is so large that we have to use a boat. I haven't been there either even though I've had many opportunities to do so. But now the roads are getting better. I'm glad to see that you are all in good health and doing well. We are also in good health and doing well.

Spring work is now being done. Amund is planting today. He has five horses and they have to go fast, but only three are used for the seeder. On April 17 we got a nice filly we've named Nelly. And Flory is soon one year old and they are both out in the field. He has a horse with Knut and Peder as he fears for the filly. Our seeder isn't like yours. It casts the seed on top of the soil so you also have to use a harrow. We don't use a roller; only a few do. A foal is quite expensive when it is newborn—ten dollars for each of ours. But if the mare doesn't get a foal you don't have to pay for using the horse, which can be from five to twenty dollars for each foal depending on the size of the horse. It seems that I'm writing mostly about cattle and horses and that is because I spend so much time with them. I do quite a lot of the work tending the animals and my husband is very good at taking care of what we have so things are going well. We didn't buy more than one cow last winter. This means one more that gives milk, so we have more butter than we can use. We sell butter and eggs and this pays for what we have to buy from town. And we don't think that's so bad. We don't have much hay, about the same as in Norway. It will be too little for many here but even though our cows haven't had hay for a long time they are doing quite well. They get some oats in the morning and evening and now the grass is getting green so it's quite good for the animals. The good weather was late in coming this spring.

I see that many have left this world. How did Oline Ekren take her husband's death? Perhaps better than we could expect? There haven't been any deaths here. Last night we had a visitor, a teacher from Telemark who had taught English school for two months in this district. Amund is school treasurer so she came to get her salary. She had thirty-five dollars a month, good pay for a young woman. It isn't as difficult to have visitors here as in Norway. There is no difference between people and a teacher and a farmer eat at the same table. I'll have to end for now. You've had to wait long for a letter but as I've told you, the reason is that we can't get it to the post office. Loving regards from your daughter and sister and her husband. The next time Jakob should write a little. Mattias can also write. Don't be afraid to write to us.

· ———— ·

AB explains that *røver* is the English word for river and writes *sideren* (a word her parents probably would not have understood) for the seeder. We may note that she is a little proud, both of having had a teacher at her table and of her husband who is treasurer for the public school. «II:207 »II:219 NE V:113

· ———— ·

1888 — LETTER 2:216

FROM: Halvor Hansen Ulsness, *Reno, Minnesota, 29 April 1888*

TO: Nils Andreas Olsen Brusli, *Tørdal, Drangedal, Telemark*

⤙⇒⇐⤚

Dear friend!

Thank you so much for your letter of February 25. In response you'll have these lines with loving greetings from me and my family. We are all well. I'm now a farmer living on my land. Even though I still don't have a secure right to own it I'm confident in my hope that it will soon be mine. I don't have much planted, only the four acres that I had already broken. I have planted wheat. This summer I intend to break twenty to twenty-five acres by shift breaking with another man, because you need two teams or four horses to break land and the best time for this work is from early June to mid July. This year I and a Swede have taken a quarter section with sixty-five acres of field on shares. We planted wheat on about fifty acres. We'll plant oats on the rest. We've had a very harsh winter, at times very cold with many snowstorms, and spring has been late. We still often have to feed the animals indoors and this rarely happens at the end of April. Some of the time I'm in Glenwood working for my old employer as Hans drives the team for spring planting. I need to make a little extra whenever possible. I have a nice quarter section and I think I could have more than 100 acres in a single field. From my house I can see eight farms as well as the railroad that runs through a neighboring section where there's a small town with a depot only two miles from my home. From my window I can see Torbjørn and Guro's home one mile from us. They are doing quite well. Guro has asked me to give their regards every time I write. His brother Jørgen who was so rich a time ago now has nothing. Aase Busteraak will probably lose a lot of money because of him. Aase, Elling and Mari and her family are doing well. Aase and Elling have some health problems but they are fairly well off and are careful and good people. I had a letter from Halvor Nordbø some time ago. He's getting on well and is glad to be in America. Since I have no special news I'll conclude with loving greetings to all friends in Tørdal. But first and last my regards to you and your family and, not to forget, your old Mother. Do you think we could take a dance together now, Old Gunhild, if we should meet again? Give my regards to Hans N. Stigen and the letter writer Karine and thank them for their letter. They shall soon hear from us.

HALVOR HANSEN ULSNÆSS

. ——— .

HHU is now on his homestead in Reno, a township in Pope County, Minn. At Brusli, Nils Andreas's wife and mother are both named Gunhild. «II:184 »II:258 NE V:114

. ——— .

1888 — LETTER 2:217

FROM: Mikkel Andersen Lee, *Mount Vernon, Wisconsin, 26 June 1888*
To: Anders Olsen and Anders Andersen Lee, *Hedalen, Sør-Aurdal, Oppland*

◦➤⟹◯⟸◂◦

To my unforgettable father and brother!

I've again had the pleasure of receiving a letter from you, for which I give you my most sincere thanks. I can tell you that we are all in good health and living as usual. We have wind and weather every day so this cannot be of interest even though it has varied greatly. The winter was extremely severe and people who have lived here for forty years say that it has never been this way before. Spring came late and has been cold. Spring work is done.

Pastor John Nilsen Fjeld died March 12 and was buried March 16 after being bedridden for about six months. His illness wasn't difficult. Indeed, he said that he felt no great pain but was faint and without strength and he gradually pined away. I took part in his funeral. As you already know, a death and the time of the funeral are advertised widely because the Americans think that the more people at the funeral the greater honor for the deceased. Even though I live twenty miles from Fjeld's home we got the news of his death in time. My wife and I drove off on Friday morning, March 16. The weather was very nice and lots of people had come for the funeral. His coffin was followed by 100 teams and there were people of all nations. In the Fjeld home Pastor Jacobson spoke in English because there were so many English there, Pastor Gundersen spoke in Norwegian and Pastor Krostu also spoke in English. I wasn't able to get close enough to hear anything because of the great crowd of people. There was also a well-rehearsed choir. Six pastors in their vestments bore the coffin out to the wagon that took it to the church where it was displayed for the last time. The six pastors then carried the coffin into the church accompanied by sorrowful music from the organ and the church was draped in mourning. Our pastor Syftestad then entered the pulpit (as had been requested by Pastor Fjeld shortly before his death) and gave a sermon on Simeon's words, "Lord, now lettest thou thy servant depart in peace, according to thy word; for mine eyes have seen thy salvation, which thou hast prepared in the presence of all peoples." Thereupon the body was lowered into the grave by the six pastors who consecrated it to its earthly sleep. Thus was Fjeld's funeral; may he long be remembered and may his dust lie in peace. Our pastor reminded us that Fjeld had ceaselessly preached the gospel for fifty years.

Ole Moen has also passed away. He visited Fjeld while he was bedridden and took farewell and when he got home he became ill, was put to bed, and died after four days. Anders Skinningsrud also died last spring of a sudden heart attack. He was working in the barn when he fell down dead. Anders Olsen Brenden has visited me twice since I came. He lives alone and is doing rather poorly, mostly, I believe, because he is rather simpleminded, as they say. Even though he hasn't been able to do much his children (as he has told me himself) have done much better. One of his sons, Iver, has now gone for three years to Augsburg Seminary and is said to be very gifted. He has asked to be remembered to you, in particular to father.

As for myself, I have about as many animals as when I last wrote except that I have six more pigs and I do all the many things a farmer does. I can remember, dear father, that you once wrote that you would like to write to us about spiritual matters. I would appreciate if you did this as I believe it would be very useful, entertaining, and educational and that your advice would be very valuable. I can send you greetings from your relatives; they are in good health. Father's sister is doing as usual. Give my regards to Sørlie and Jøranby and to all my acquaintances and, above all, to you my dear father and brother and to Inger Finhert. Hoping that you will soon be writing and praying that the Lord's peace and blessing may be with you and with all you do, I sign myself your son and brother,

MEKKEL ANDERSEN LEE

Pastor John Fjeld was from Sør-Aurdal. Pastor Jacobson is probably Abraham Jacobson who then lived on his farm near Decorah, Iowa. The other pastors mentioned are Severin Gundersen, Gunsten Gunstensen Krostu, Olaus Paulsen Syftestad, and Olaus Naess. Simeon's words are in Luke 2:29–31. Anders Olsen Lie's sister in Wisconsin was Olea Olsdatter Børtnes. Inger Olsdatter Finhert was the maid at Søre Li and soon married Anders Andersen Lie. A letter from MAL dated 6 January 1888 is largely concerned with an interpretation of King Melchizedek in Genesis 14:17–20 but also explains how expensive it has been for him to make a well. «II:204 »II:229 NE V:117

1888 — LETTER 2:218

FROM: Karen Solem, *Norden, South Dakota, 5 July 1888*
To: Ole Tobias and Amalie Ødegaard, *Nannestad, Akershus*

Dear brother and family,

Thank you so much for the letter I received three weeks ago. You must excuse me for not having written before; I've thought of doing it every day. I'll have to begin with the most recent event, the "fourth" which was yesterday. I don't really have so much to say about it since Louis and I decided to stay at home. I got so bored with the whole celebration last year that I thought it would be a long time before I repeated my experience. To be out among so many people with a small child is the least entertaining thing I know. Nikolai and Olaus of course had to go since Nicolai placed his fiancée (as I think we may call her) Mina Kjønstad in the *buggy* and drove off in style. A *buggy* is similar to a cariole at home except that it has four wheels and a folding top. It is a very convenient carriage that can be used with one or two horses; we only use one for ours. So that we wouldn't entirely neglect the day I baked a "*sweet cake*." We had bought *lemons* and we brought them in a basket to Auntie where we made *lemonade* and drank and ate cake all afternoon and had a nice time. No, this is far too much about the fourth so I'll stop.

We have fine summer weather with showers and sunshine so if we're ever going to have a good harvest it must be now. On Sunday June 24 we had confirmation here and Karen was confirmed. The next Wednesday she went to Fillmore County to visit Christian and Carl. She'll probably stay there for a couple of weeks and return to Peru. I've had a letter from her and she's enjoying herself. I'm alone now but probably not for long as haying begins in about a week and I'll then be in need of help. A spinster from Odalen who has recently come here has promised to stay with me for a while. Marie is big and clever but she still needs attention; as soon as the door is open she will get up and run out to the *stable* and everywhere else and since there are horses and cattle all over the place it isn't safe to let her go alone.

I talked with Ludvig Hetager the day he returned from Norway last week. Among other things he told me that you were doing a very good business at Sundby and I was very pleased. You must ask Amalie to continue writing to me even though I don't write specifically to her. When I write it is for you both. Our ladies aid is organizing festivities in a few days and I'll have to go. I've been pretty good at taking part all summer and also had a meeting in our home. It was amusing to hear that Johan Bidsler was married. The very day I received your letter I'd been visiting with Marthea Bidsler and there we agreed that the youngest Bidsler boys would probably never get married.

Give mother my regards. I think of her all the time and should have written something to her as well but I won't have time to do it. We thought of sending a ticket for one of them this summer if you could pay for the other. We would have good use for father here on the farm and I would so wish to have mother here whether she can do anything or not. Laurits was in Canby to find out about tickets but they are now so expensive (sixty-nine dollars) and the conditions for sending them from here are so difficult that we have decided to let it be for this summer. It may be that Nicolai will soon be married and move to the other farm and it would then be more quiet and peaceful around us and better to have them here. Yes, my letter is now so long that I'll have to conclude. Give my regards to all friends and relatives. You my dear brother and your wife and sons are all lovingly greeted from your devoted sister

KAREN

. ——— .

KS was married to Louis. Nicolai and Olaus were her brothers-in-law; Auntie was Maria Christopherson; Karen Olsen (also called Kye) was a cousin; Christian and Carl Solem in Minnesota were her brothers-in-law; Marie was her young daughter. Her mother was

Maria Kristoffersdatter: her father, Olaus Olsen, was actually her stepfather. Canby is in Yellow Medicine County, Minn. KS actually wrote the Norwegian definite form of the English word stable: *stabelen*. She also wrote on 12 August 1888 (Nor. ed. V:124). «II:210 »II:228 NE V:118

· ——— ·

1888 — LETTER 2:219

FROM: Anne Bjorli, *Bue, North Dakota, 8 July 1888*

TO: Hans Jørgensen and Eli Johannesdatter Bjøkne, *Lesja, Oppland*

⋄⟶≡○⊜⟵⋄

Dear parents and siblings!

Thank you for your welcome letter that we received some time ago. We sent our letter the same day we got yours and therefore we have put off our reply. For some time I've been busy sewing for the Fourth of July. I made three dresses and a jacket in one week; one was for me, of plain calico. We are in good health and all is well. I've been bothered by toothache for some days. I often feel it, but these three last days it's been bad. It has come and gone since I came here and now all my molars are affected. We have just walked around to look at our land. The fields are standing fine so if it continues as now we should have a good year, but it will be late compared to last year. We'll also have a good supply of hay. This summer Amund has built a granary and he's now plowing new soil. Haying will soon begin.

Father asks how we were on the Sunday before Pentecost. It was then two years since I left my home. It was a long day for me and I thought about you a lot. I began to write a letter but soon stopped; I couldn't. Friday we had lost two heifers and Amund went out early on Sunday morning to look for them. He heard that they had been with a German south of us and that was all he found out all day. I was alone and was sure he would be home for dinner, but he didn't come until three o'clock and then he took a horse and went out looking again. He saw no sign of them that day and came home late in the evening. Early in the day Knut and another man came by and around four in the afternoon the wife on the farm east of us was here to borrow some butter, but we had just sent butter to town a couple of days earlier so I didn't have any. Those people have now moved four miles further west. Today the husband was here at dinnertime. I liked them and he had a good wife so I miss them. Lars Bjorli bought their land. I must tell you about the heifers. They found them before dinner on Monday, not so far east of here. He came home for me and we drove off to get them. This is all I remember of May 13.

Some time ago we sent *Budbæreren* to you and now we want to send you the four issues we have. We also had a letter from Hans and Marit where they said that Mari Bjøkne had died and that mother's sister was often ill. Mari was only ill for a few days. It's long since we had a letter from Jørgen. I suppose he doesn't have time now that there is so much to do during summer. With this I'll conclude for now with loving regards to parents and siblings from your daughter and sister Anne Bjorli. My Amund also sends his regards.

· —— ·

For calico she writes *kalko* and for granary, *grønri*. Neither word makes sense in Norwegian. For the latter she adds an explanation in parenthesis, *(grønhus)*, but this would not have made sense either. Using the Norwegian word for green—*grøn*—instead of grain seems to have been quite common in immigrant code switching. Knut was Amund's half-brother; Lars, his brother. *Budbæreren* (the Messenger) was published in Red Wing, Minn., by the Hauge Synod. AB's aunt Guri Johannesdatter and Ole Jørgensen Bjøkne emigrated in 1867–1868 and their daughter Mari was born in 1882–1883. AB wrote far more letters than can be included here and many were written over several days, reflecting her busy life. She wrote on 21 September 1888 and on 14 October she began a letter than was not completed until 9 November (Nor. ed. V:134). On 3 March 1889 (Nor. ed. V:144) she wrote about her loneliness when Amund was visiting a brother in Minneapolis and about births, deaths, and illnesses among her neighbors from Lesja. She was afraid for Mari Enstad, who was ill, because she was the woman she had been closest to. On 1 April she began a letter she completed 18 April (Nor. ed. V:146) about work on the farm, a visit from a half-brother of Amund and the dresses she had sown. She enclosed pieces of the material for two summer dresses. «II:215 »II:227 NE V:119

· —— ·

1888 — LETTER 2:220

From: Svend Larsen Houg, *Elgin, Iowa, 30 July 1888*

To: Ole Larsen Haug, *Aal, Buskerud*

Beloved brother,

I know that you long to hear from me. When I walk around thinking of writing to you there is so much that I want to write to you but when I try to set something down on paper I have no words. This is the way it is with me. Thank you so much for your letter of June 24 that I received on July 12. It is encouraging to have a letter from a brother in the flesh as well as in the spirit when it comes with such a living faith in God's grace in Christ even though we all know that our flesh is weak. As for myself, I know that nothing good dwells in my flesh. For I do not do the good I want, but the evil I do not want is what I do. Wretched man that I am! Thanks be to God who has let me see some of the wretchedness of my sinful nature and also a small piece of his great and incomprehensible love for us sinful human beings that he gave us his Son. Not our renunciation, nor our repentence, nor our prayer can save us (even though these belong in a Christian life) but only the precious redeeming blood of Jesus can make us pure and free us from our sins. This is my brief confession of my faith.

Now I must tell you that God has granted me rather good health. I was in St. Ansgar from June 13, 1887 to March 13, 1888 and it was good to be there. In June I was visited by my son Halsten and his wife and children and old Assor and his youngest daughter and his oldest son and wife and two children. Most of my children have their home here and are in good health except that Ragnil has been a little weak. She now wants to go to her sister in the Red River Valley. Guri and Elling work for Assor who has the farm. Knud, who is married and has some of the land that I had, lives here in our house as he has not yet built one for himself. His wife has been ill in bed since last September and they have often expected death. That will be in the time set by the Lord. This is a little information for you.

I do not dare try to speak of the state of Christianity here as my description would be too dark. But God be praised, the word of God is taught and preached with life and strength. Yet it seems that the younger generation lay aside the word of God and have the reading of newspapers and novels as their religion. But we must hope that God may awaken some of them just as he drew us out of a life in sin, for God's grace in Christ is open for all. With this I send loving regards from your brother. God alone knows whether it will be the last time.

S. L. HOUG

As my sheet was too small I will take another little piece of paper as some have asked me to send their regards. I recently visited Knud Houg. He asked me to be remembered to you. He and his wife are good people. And regards from the widow Gro Groth, and from Johannes Groth. He is a good man. I go to him when I wish to visit someone and we talk together about sin and grace. I have not heard from Engebret Houg since last summer. I thought I would hear from him. Thank brother Lars for the portrait he sent me. I briefly mentioned our relatives who visited us from St. Ansgar, so I will add a little here. H. Houg has so much to do in addition to his school that it now and then seemed to me that he hardly had time to eat. He is a respected man. Assor Groth is in reasonably good health but has a limp.

As I was writing this little letter I heard that Kittil Groth was in the neighborhood and I waited to send it until I had spoken with him. So now I can send you his regards. He too is in reasonably good health but walks with difficulty. His wife died in the fall of 1886. He lives in faith in the Son of God. There is much more I could say but now I must conclude with loving regards to you and your wife and your other family. God willing, I will hear from you again. There may yet be some troubles and then an eternal life. That is the promise of God.

SVEND L. HOUG

· —— ·

SLH's guests all lived in or near St. Ansgar, where Halsten Houg was principal of St. Ansgar Seminary. Assor and Kittil Groth were his brothers-in-law. His daughter in the Red River Valley was Ingrid Dokken. SLH uses phrases from Romans 7:18–19, 24. «II:189 »II:263
NE V:121

· —— ·

1888 — LETTER 2:221

FROM: Jacob Hanson Hilton, *Socorro, New Mexico, 21 August 1888*
TO: Hans Jakobsen and Anne Olsdatter Hilton, *Kløfta, Ullensaker, Akershus*

Dear father and mother,

Thank you so much for your dear letter of July 31. I must first of all thank you for your congratulations. Dear parents, it was strange to read your letter; I've read it several times and each time I find something new in it, but this may be my imagination. Have I cast my anchor? No, not here in New Mexico, my longing for and my hope to see Old Norway are still as they have been; my marriage does not change that plan—on the contrary. The days of my childhood and youth have long gone; they disappeared when I sailed from Kristiania eleven years ago—even though I wasn't aware of this until later. Since then I've only met with adversities and troubles and always been among strangers and with no one I could rely on. This girl that I've decided to commit to is one who has learned what it is to work and not always have what you need, but in the course of all this she has nevertheless learned how to hold up among the better class of people as well as to milk the cows and drive the milk to town before working in her father's pharmacy the rest of the day. They came to Socorro February 1, 1882 without any money or a livelihood and she and her sister herded cows for others the first summer while their father first began as a doctor, then the milk business and later began a pharmacy. His only help was his two daughters who stood in as both hired man and maid. If she hadn't been that kind of a girl I would never have thought of marriage, but since she is used to doing so much she will be of great help. She is a good bookkeeper and can take care of the store so I can do without an extra man in the shop and thus save sixteen to twenty dollars a week. So I thought this was better than leaving it all as poor as when I came and now things may work out anyway the way things are looking now. One of the foundries here in town was sold and closed down and as a consequence fifty men lost their jobs and had to leave town. Our other furnace is also slowing down and this will make more than 100 men lose their work. Half of the buildings, both businesses and homes, are empty now so I don't really know how this will finally end. Perhaps it'll be as Uncle C. said: nothing but Mexicans left, just as it was when I came. Enough of this nonsense.

No, you don't have to say goodbye to your hopes. I haven't changed my mind. If I could sell my business for a reasonable price and before it all has been eaten, then it's still my intention to see old Ullensaker and Hilton again and—if there is money enough—live and die there. But, as you say, man may stake out his road but the Lord decides how it is used. This is true, but if I cannot fulfill my plan it will be because I don't have the means. It may be that I can save enough to make it possible to see Hilton and even to own it—who knows!

When I wrote that you should let the boys have the farm I didn't at all intend—nor do I think I suggested—that you didn't run it well enough, nor did I mean that you and mother could be seen as being in anyone's way. Indeed, I don't think any in our family would ever have such thoughts. The only reason I said what I said was that you and mother could be freed from the heavy work you've always had and let those who are younger take over, because if they can't do this now, they won't ever be able to manage on their own later. But I planned to come home when I rented the store from Christiansen and I had decided to sell what I had but when I only had half of my inventory left I was unable to sell any more—neither by auction nor privately. So this is why I sent Uncle the money for his share and if I hadn't he probably wouldn't have had it yet as there hasn't been any kind of business here since then and it is still going down month by month. So this is why I couldn't promise when I could come and didn't want you to wait for me since nothing is certain. For my part, I have no demands. Let those who have served you and worked with you share in it when the time comes. I'm no better off than anyone else in this town; we're all in the same boat. So I'm tied down. I would have left if I could—but how can you go without money?

Dear parents! You write as if I have said something that has been read in a different way from what was intended. In no way did I intend to dictate that you should do this or the other. I only meant that I thought you should be free for the rest of your lives and that since I couldn't do anything for you I thought that perhaps the others could. But enough of this! Give my regards to acquaintances and friends, if I have any. Also to my brothers and sisters; and first and last loving regards to you my dear parents from your son

JACOB

JHH has married Emily Kornitzer. The letter announcing their marriage has not been preserved. Their son Joseph Jacobson was born in 1889 and two daughters, Ann Dorothy (named for his sister Anne Dortea) and Bertha, in 1891 and 1893. He had written to his parents on 10 April 1888 that they should no longer consider him an heir to the farm and asked whether there were any papers he should sign. «II:202 »II:232 NE V:125

1888 — LETTER 2:222

FROM: Inger Hansen Berby, *Henning, Minnesota, 17 October 1888*

To: Hans Olsen and Berthe Marie Sandersdatter Berby
Varteig, Sarpsborg, Østfold

✥⭢▬◉◖▬⭠✥

I wrote to you eight days ago but since I'm not sure that it gets to you I'll write a little today as well. I am quite well as is my uncle. I enjoy my food and eat a lot and we eat as at a party every day. I drink *silesup* every day like a little calf. I liked *silesup* when I lived at home too. I can tell you that there is land for sale not so far from here for 400 dollars. It is good land and you could buy it if you came because it may be that they haven't sold it yet. You probably won't come until spring because it is now late fall and it is too cold. For a girl who is not yet a grownup the pay is one and a half a week while at home they get one dollar a month and here they only have to work half as much. Father, with the help of so many children you could become a prosperous man. Here they say that a man who has children to help him may, even though he is poor on arrival, be well off in a while.

I can tell you that a little girl died on the voyage. She was three years old. She was Swedish. She was strange. When I first saw and heard her I said that she wouldn't become old because she was so strange. She sang, and she sang beautifully, she sang a nice song. Yes, she was always singing it; she sang when she woke up in the morning and her mother asked her to be quiet, and she said that she had to sing about Jesus.

I hope you have received my portraits. When you write you must tell me whether Johanne has come home and whether Anna is grown up and other interesting things. You could write to me, Anna. Tell me all you know and write immediately. I must now conclude with dear greetings from me,

INGER HANSEN

Another time I'll write the song the little girl sang. I have learned the song and the melody.

· ——— ·

Ole Sandersen Belsby wrote to his brother-in-law, Hans Olsen Berby, on 7 August 1886 (Nor. ed. V:48) strongly suggesting that he emigrate with his family. He wrote of his own success and explained that a neighboring farm was for sale for $600. Nothing came of this but IHB, then in her late teens, emigrated two years later. In Norway she would have called herself Hansdatter; in the United States she used the male patronymic and became Hansen. Her letter is awkwardly written and not always easy to understand. *Silesup* was a dialect word for the warm milk right from the cow. IHB quotes the song by the Swedish girl, probably from memory, in a mixture of Swedish and Dano-Norwegian. In translation the refrain is: "Because I am saved in the blood from Golgatha and my sins have all disappeared in the sea, so I live in joy for Jesus." The song has not been identified. IHB wrote to her parents on 25 February 1889 (Nor. ed. V:143), mentioning that she has met the two Eriksen boys, Anders and Erik from Skofteby in Østfold, in Minnesota, and to her sister in Norway who will soon be confirmed. »II:243 NE V:127

· ——— ·

FROM: Elise Wærenskjold, *Prairieville, Texas, 20 October 1888*
To: Thomine Dannevig, *Lillesand, Aust-Agder*

⊷⟹⟸⊶

My dear, good Thomine!

Thank you so much for your very welcome letter of March 26. I had planned to reply long ago, but you know how it is when you begin to put off something. Then I decided I would write while I was visiting Otto because I always have so much time there as his wife never leaves the house; but then the little girl they got in January and that they loved so dearly got sick and died the day I left them. It was so sad that I had to leave them that same day but Niels was to meet me at the depot and from there it is sixteen miles to my home, so I had to go. Poor Otto! He is only thirty-seven and has had so much grief and illness. His wife suffered great pain from boils under both arms. Would you and your son Thorvald please get the enclosed notice into one of the most read newspapers? I had planned to write to you the day I wrote it but then Ouline Reiersen came to visit me for a few days and then Niels's wife got sick and I had to go to them every day to make dinner and supper. She has five little children and is expecting another one and has no help. It is almost impossible to get a servant girl now because in the cities they pay a girl from fifteen to twenty-five dollars a month and this is more than a farmer can afford to pay, so many wives are overworked.

So both Mrs. Basberg and Kaja have left this life; I suppose that is best for them. Life was not good for poor Mrs. Basberg! I see in your letter that Kaja had set up a will. I wish she would have mentioned me with a small thing however insignificant; it would have shown me that she had fond memories of me. It is so long since I had a letter from her even though I sent her several. I will never forget the nice times I had with her at Nygaard. Who lives there now? And Mrs. Stenersen's large house at Møglestue, who lives there now? Is the old parsonage still standing or has it had to make place for a new one? Do you know whether my mother's grave has been used for someone else or have they let their old pastor's wife rest in peace? I had an iron frame set up around her grave. Thank you for your information about the Aall family. Old Jacob Aall's wife was my father's cousin. His parents died when he was still a child and they were brought up together and loved each other like brothers.

Ouline and I see much of each other and we often speak about how nice and pleasant you must find your situation. Both you and your sons are well off and you can visit them every year and you still haven't lost a child or a grandchild. The only thing that is not quite according to my liking is that Thorvald still does not have a good wife. I often think of Thorvald, of how sweet he was as a small child and of how much we loved each other. Ouline is quite comfortable and she has very few expenses as she lives with another elderly Norwegian widow. But she does not have a room of her own and I would not have liked that. The widow lives with a grownup daughter so they are three women alone in the house. Ouline has an interest of about 200 dollars annually and the principal will go to her stepsons on her death. I have eighty, but then I also have my own house and garden and free firewood and as much pork as I need for as long as I live. Both Ouline and Mrs. Pabst send their kind regards. I visited with the latter for a few hours on my way home.

I have a liking for garden vegetables so I always have a good garden and I think it is healthy both to eat them and to grow them. I have a lot of asparagus and I can eat them every day from early March to early May and before then we have turnips, peas and carrots. Yes, we may have turnips and carrots and some other vegetables all winter. But there is one thing I miss: all the delicious fish that you have in Norway.

I've read the lawyer Arctander's lecture in the Labor Union Hall and it made me quite annoyed. I hope one of the Norwegians in America will make a response. He exaggerates so much. We read two journals from Norway. I subscribe to *Nylænde* and one of my relatives gets *Posten*, both edited by ladies. Do you read them? Our oldest pastor is now visiting us. We have two, one in Bosque, where there are two Norwegian churches, and one in Waco. One of them comes to us and then preaches on three Sundays and three weekdays on each visit and also conducts baptisms and weddings. For a long time we've had the most beautiful fall weather you can imagine so it has been ideal for the picking of cotton. On the whole this has been a good year but last winter was the worst one I've had here.

I almost forgot to tell you that Sigurd Ørbæk was so unlucky that the house that he has lived in for several years burned down and he lost everything except the clothes he had on. He also lost his employment as the family he worked for moved to Shreveport. God knows what he will do now.

If I had had as much money as Mrs. Pabst I would have sent him twenty dollars. He has always been so good to

The next day.

At this point I was interrupted by Ouline who came from Prairieville and we both went up to Niels. His wife is so much better today that she could get up and sit with us at the table. Today Niels took thirty cows to Wills Point where he will be able to sell them for 300 dollars. This is not much compared to what they were worth a few years ago but it is nevertheless better than it was two years ago when no one would buy cattle. Niels has more than a hundred including the young animals. Now neither Ouline nor I have any animals at all, not even a cat. Since we don't have a horse we have to walk when we visit our neighbors and I'm glad that I'm still able to walk to Prairieville and other neighbors in the morning and walk home again in the evening. It is three miles to Prairieville.

I don't know much about the Grøgaards, but I think they are doing well. Do you know anything about the Hedemarks and Rosenvolds that many years ago went to Ole Bull's colony? I later had a letter from them from New York. What has happened to the Rosenkildes? I once heard that the wife was on poor relief and that Bendix was at Mangelsgaarden. Here in Texas we always use *Madam* as we did in my time in Norway so that is why I am so unused to saying *Fru* or *Frøken*. We address all in the same manner and that is what I prefer. Please me with another letter soon, my dear Thomine and give my regards to your children and grandchildren and also to my dear old friend Samuel Hansen and to all who may have fond memories of me. But this can no longer be very many as death has winnowed out many among my relatives and friends. Farewell to you all,

ELISE WÆRENSKJOLD

· —— ·

Fragments of this letter are in Clausen 1961, 140–141. Kaja is Karen Poppe whose maiden name was Møglestue. The "old Jacob Aall" (1773–1844) played a prominent role in Norwegian politics and business. John W. Arctander (1849–1920) emigrated in 1870 and played a prominent role in the Norwegian-American society of Minneapolis. The lecture referred to was given in Christiania (Oslo). *Nylænde* (1887–1927, New Ground) was a feminist journal edited by Gina Grog. On *Posten* see the note in Clausen 1961, 137. The pastor who was visiting was John Knutsen Rystad. In the 1850s Ole Bull bought land in Pennsylvania for a settlement he named Oleanna. This venture was a failure. Mangelsgaarden, a former mansion in Oslo, was in

1812 made into an institution for the destitute. It seems that Thomine may have commented on EW's distinctions between *Madam* and *Fru* (both of which are translated as Mrs.) for married women and that EW's sense of who should be addressed as *Madam* and who as the somewhat more refined *Fru* had become old-fashioned among her contemporaries in Norway. Samuel Hansen was Thomine Dannevig's brother. «II:209 »II:251 NE V:128

. ——— .

1888 — LETTER 2:224

FROM: Anne Norsby, *Necedah, Wisconsin, 3 November 1888*

TO: Marie Olsdatter Vigerust, *Dovre, Oppland*

—◦═◦═◦—

Dear Marie!

As weeks and months have passed since I received your letter I must now send you a reply. We are all in good health and doing quite well even though we for some time have suffered illness and grief. Sivert had a major accident when the saw at the mill took three of his fingers. He kept his whole thumb but only a small stub of his little finger and worst of all was that this was his right hand. This was a hard blow but we must be patient and hope for the best. He was quite well again not more than a month after the accident. You may imagine that many felt sorry for Sivert as he's always been such a good boy. He's been lively but always kind so he has many friends. And now he's as lively and good humored as he's always been and he writes quite nicely with his thumb and the stub of his little finger. He also writes with his left hand. He's returning to school this winter but I don't know whether this will be before or after Christmas. He went to school last winter too.

I, father and Rine have been ill, but nothing serious. All are now well. Today Sivert paid the doctor; he took thirty-five dollars and that was quite cheap. Gina, Karen's daughter, was with Rønnaug while she was ill and is now working for a Norwegian family who are the neighbors of my sister. Today Karen has been in town and Gina also returned home this evening.

Jakob and Karen's youngest son is here on our farm. He's been here for two or three weeks and is doing well. I've been here with my sister for almost two weeks and will have to go home next week.

. ——— .

Sivert Norsby seems to have managed quite well. According to Ulvestad (1913) he became a merchant in Stewartville, Minn. AN's father was Jacob Norsby and her sister Rine (Rønnaug) was married to Otto Haslegard. Jacob Olson (brother of Marie Vigerust) was married to Karen; there are letters by Jacob Olson in this edition. «II:211 »II:239 NE V:131

. ——— .

1888 — LETTER 2:225

FROM: Jens A. Nilsen, *Tacoma, Washington, 5 November 1888*

TO: E. B. Kjerskow Zahl, *Kjerringøy, Bodø, Nordland*

⊹⊱≡◉⊜≡⊰⊹

Dear Zahl!

With this I must permit myself to ask you to be so kind as to do me the favor of sending me the money I have placed in Bergen Privatbank. As you may have heard, I was very unlucky upon coming here. I got work at a sawmill as soon as I arrived and after four days I had an accident. Some planks fell on me and made me fall down near a saw and my right hand was thrown against it. In a moment it cut into my fingers and three of them had to be removed. So now I only have a thumb and index finger left and I don't think that I'll have much use of them as they are still lame. The nerves leading to them have probably been damaged by the saw. I was in the hospital six weeks and since then I've done little or nothing. But many have been very helpful as my situation has made them feel sorry for me. So this is how the time has passed.

I've had to think of how I could make money other than by working and have sought the advice of people who are knowledgable about local affairs and bought a lot on which I plan to build a bouse. The lot cost 900 dollars; 300 in cash and the rest to be paid at my convenience at eight percent. If I could have my money to pay the 300 dollars on the lot and then build a house for seven to eight hundred dollars, such a house could be let for twenty-five dollars a month. I have thought that this would be the best way to pay for the lot. And if the city continues to grow as it has these last two years my lot will be worth twice as much in a couple of years. Many Scandinavians have made thousands of dollars on lots they bought a couple of years ago and now could sell at very high prices. So in this way I will try to earn a little. Excuse me for being so free as to ask you to please lend me so much money that I can have all of four thousand *kroner*, including the money I have in Bergen. This would be a great favor and I promise to repay you as soon as I can. In the hope that you will do me this great favor and send the money in the best manner and as soon as possible, I sign in great respect, yours faithfully,

JENS A. NILSEN FJÆRLI
2611 East C Str. Tacoma, Washington Terr. U.S. America

· —— ·

There are many letters to the merchant Kjerskow Zahl from people he helped with loans. Jens Antonius Nilsen (b. 1859) from Fjærlia in Kjerringøy had been employed by Zahl before emigrating. NE V:133

· —— ·

1888 — LETTER 2:226

FROM: Jacob Olson, *Necedah, Wisconsin, 7 December 1888*

TO: Ragnhild Jakobsdatter Vigerust, *Dovre, Oppland*

Dear mother and siblings,

I will again try my luck and see if these lines will get to you my dear mother and sisters. You may be thinking that I never write but I haven't forgotten you. But what is the use of writing when you don't get my letters. I must first tell you that we are all well to this date. Health is our greatest treasure in this world. Regina is big and well. She was two years September 24 and is named for mother. Ole Snekkerlien wrote to his parents some time ago and he has asked me to write a few words for him to his parents. He'll send them tickets next spring if they wish to come. Here they could be their own masters and not be the servants of others and now is the time for military service for Andreas so this would be to the advantage of all. Ole says that this is the last time he offers to send tickets and if they don't come he'll sell his land and animals and go somewhere else. This wouldn't be good for him or for his parents. He has good land, two draft oxen, two cows and two calves. My view is that since Ole and Anne are getting old and cannot keep on working for Jakob for long, Andreas will have to take over the croft and do you think that tiny piece of land can feed two families when he marries? If they come to America in the spring they can be sure that Ole will take care of them and they won't lack anything. If they make up their minds before spring they'll get their tickets. This will be an advantage for Andreas and Anna who are young. It must be better to make a dollar and a half a day than eight *skilling*. Ole will be away at work and his parents will be on his farm.

We had a presidential election November 6 and the Republicans won so the Democrats lost. The President is Ben Harrison and will be inaugurated March 4. Our harvest was fair so we can't complain but our summer was rather dry so it would have been better with more rain. Times are pretty much as they have been. We have eleven animals this winter and next summer we'll have six milk cows if nothing goes wrong. Brother Ole came visiting today. He and his family are well and send their regards. Olianna and her family are well and also send their regards. Hans is going to the forest Monday and Ole Snekkerlien has been there for three weeks. But how are you my dear mother? Are you coming to America next spring? I would like to see you before we depart from this world and my sisters won't come without you.

I have no more to write about now and will conclude with loving regards to you all from all of us. Our best wishes for Christmas and the New Year. Farewell. Give our regards to all in Snekkerlien and to all relatives and friends and to Karen's father from us all.

JAKOB OLSON WIGERUST

·———·

JO, married to Karen, and his sister Olianna, married to Hans Hanson, were from the farm Vigerust. Ole Olson Lee was from the croft Snekkerlien owned by the farmer Jakob Bjørnersen Vigerust. His parents were Ole and Anne Snekkerlien (or Lie). They did not

FROM AMERICA TO NORWAY

emigrate. His younger brother Andreas later emigrated and then became Andrew Lee. A Norwegian *skilling* was less than a cent. «II:178 »II:267 NE V:136

· ——— ·

1888 — LETTER 2:227

FROM: Hans Hansen Bjøkne, *Lowry, Minnesota, 23 December 1888*

To: Hans Jørgensen and Eli Johannesdatter Bjøkne, *Lesja, Oppland*

Dear parents and siblings,

I'm sending you a few sentences to tell you that we're all in good health and doing well. All fall and winter we've had the best weather we could wish for. One day we had so much snow that we could haul fertilizer on our sled but now the snow is all gone and temperatures are above freezing. You may find it strange that I say we hauled fertilizer since people in Norway used to say fertilizing the soil wasn't necessary in America. But both fertilizing the soil and letting it lie fallow is as necessary here as in Norway after it's been used for some years.

In one of your letters you ask whether we have a storage house and have planted trees. What you call a *stabbur* for food such as bread, meat and grain is here called a *granary* and is used for wheat and oats. Bread is kept in the house and is often baked once or twice a week and the Americans often do it for each meal. The climate here allows us to store such things longer. I built a kind of granary a few years ago by setting some posts in the ground and fastening boards on them for walls. I made the roof of hay and straw and the first year I had an earthen floor but later I laid on boards. Last fall I tore all this down and built a new one with real walls, floor and roof. It is twenty-six feet long, sixteen feet wide and twelve feet high and has two floors. It cost me more than 150 dollars and I still have to spend about fifty dollars on it before it is finished. It is expensive to build in America.

I've planted trees every spring for several years and next spring I'll plant 2,000 trees that I've already bought. They cost four dollars for the first thousand and three for the second. Our work this winter is to tend the animals and a few other chores. We are three men, I, Jørgen and Trond Stavem. Jørgen has a team of oxen and a cow and Trond has two oxen and he buys hay from Jørgen and Johan Sveen. We have twenty head of cattle and six horses (two of these are mares with foal) so we have thirty animals in all. The price for cattle is quite low and it's hard to sell any but fat ones for slaughter and good milk cows. I remember that father once said he couldn't go to America because there weren't any stones here but you should see a piece of land I have (about sixteen acres) and you would have found *plenty*. I broke four acres of this land last summer but then I tired of it. But I'll have to try again. I have a big slough on my land that looked like a lake when I first arrived but I've dried it out and now I have almost all my hay there and it is very good hay. Many things can be improved, even heaps of stone and sloughs.

We've heard that the farmer at Stavem has bought Sveen and that Marit will work for them and I'm surprised that she would accept such an arrangement. And I'm also surprised that her relatives didn't protest. Or perhaps they are living a better life now than they used to do but I haven't heard of any improvement in their situation. Last summer I decided to go to Norway with Ingeborg Haugen in the fall but she didn't want to go. She is now with Johannes Hagen. Guro Haugen lives with Tosten Hagen.

I've written a lot and must soon conclude, but first I must send you our Christmas greetings even though you won't get them until after Christmas. May Jesus whose birth we celebrate gain entrance to our hearts. I sent regards to you from Emma and Ida. They often speak of their grandparents. Give our regards to all relatives and friends up there in our mountain valley. Our thoughts are often there and we often speak of you. We can report that all is well with those you know here. Loving greetings to you all from me and my family.

HANS H. BJØKNE

· —— ·

HHB's brother Jørgen wrote the same day (unpublished). A storage house (*stabbur*) for grains, cured fish, and meat was a standard feature on Norwegian farms, and they were built so that rodents could not get in. The bread kept there would be unleavened (*flatbrød*). HHB explained the word *plenty*. Marit Jonsdatter Svee had recently become a widow; the sale discussed here was not realized. Ingeborg and Guro Haugen were daughters of his brother-in-law. «II:219 »II:238 NE V:138

· —— ·

From: Karen Solem, *Norden, South Dakota, 26 December 1888*

To: Ole Tobias and Amalie Ødegaard, *Nannestad, Akershus*

⊷⇒◉⇐⊶

Dear brother and sister-in-law,

It's too late to wish you a "Merry Christmas" so I'll just say that I hope you're having one. Here we've had a very quiet Christmas and today we've been quite alone, Louis, Nicolai, little Marie and I. Grandfather is in Fillmore Co. and Olaus is visiting neighbors; at the moment I don't know where he is. He may go where he wishes. We spent Christmas Eve with Per Fella and his children and tomorrow they will come to us for dinner with C. O. Holter and his mother. I'm not quite up to receiving guests right now (and I don't have any help) but we all help each other when we are together.

Everything in this world is changeable but the weather here in Dakota is the most changeable of all. We had very nice weather all fall and the day before Christmas Eve we had beautiful September weather; the sun shone so warmly on our bed in the morning that I must admit that this was something I experienced for the first time: a Christmas with sunshine and no snow. But goodness! We didn't get any further than to Christmas Eve before we had snow and a cold north wind that is still with us. But we still don't have so much snow that it amounts to a real storm. This must be enough about the weather.

I should tell you about some "business" we've had in the family. First grandfather bought the farm from Olaus for 1,000 dollars, then he set it out on shares for Louis and Nicolai, who are to have one third of the harvest each, and then he set his own farm on shares to Nicolai and sold his two horses to Louis for 250 dollars. So now he is free to be wherever he wants. Louis and Nicolai each have three fully grown horses and they will run it all and each pay half of the household expenses. After this we'll be more independent than before. I have no other news for you except that I got a new sewing machine last fall. Friendly regards to you all and my best wishes for the coming year. Don't forget to write soon. Your devoted

KAREN SOLEM

MS's father-in-law, Nils Solem, is visiting his sons Carl and Christian in Minnesota. Olaus (who lives with MS and Louis), Johan, and Nicolai are her brothers-in-law. Per Fella, a widower, had been married to MS's sister-in-law. Maria Christopherson, the mother of Christian Olausen Holter, was a sister of MS's mother. «II:218 »II:231 NE V:139

1889 — LETTER 2:229

FROM: Iver Andersen Lee, *Portland, North Dakota, 30 January 1889*
To: Anders Olsen and Anders Andersen Lie, *Hedalen, Sør-Aurdal, Oppland*

Dear Father and Brother as well as family and friends!

You may have been expecting a letter from me and I should have written earlier. The daily chores take up most of my time and the little leisure I have is often spent thinking of you and of writing to you. But you cannot see my thoughts; if you could you would have seen that my delinquency is not for lack of love for you. I still feel as strongly as ever the pleasure of thinking of my home, thinking of those with whom I've shared sorrows and happiness from the dawn of my life. But when you've been away from the childhood home for some time you become more and more concerned with the business of life where you are. Even if the heart is tied to the home, your mind has found a new field of activity. Consequently, it is more and more divided. You have the same warm feelings when you remember the home you've left but you don't necessarily feel a need constantly to correspond with it. Such is my experience and I've also seen it in others. I've heard many who have spoken tenderly about the childhood home even though they long have ceased to write. So you mustn't think that I've become indifferent to my childhood home just because I don't write so often.

Times are still hard for those who try to get ahead. Last year's crops were disappointing, here as in large parts of America. In spring and early summer it seemed that we would have a bumper crop. Indeed, hopes were great until harvesting began and we found that rust had done great damage. We still hoped for an average crop when a night of frost during harvesting gave us a fright. It caused considerable harm but not as much as we first feared. A few days later we had yet another night of frost, much worse than the first and in large areas of low land the crop was entirely destroyed. Some hadn't begun to cut their wheat but most had started, but after the second night of frost they all had to quit and begin plowing their wheat fields. On more elevated land where the wheat ripens earlier the situation was better, but as harvesting continued the effect of the rust became more evident. Still, the extent of the damage was not realized until threshing began when it appeared that the crop would be less than a third of an average year. For our part the result was somewhere between fair and bad. Because of the rust we had less than half of what is expected in an average year. About half of our field was untouched by frost, the other half more or less frost damaged—some to the extent that it would have been better not to have cut it. I should also report that wheat prices have been higher than last year and this has helped those who didn't get their entire crop destroyed by frost. When the extent of the frost damage became known wheat prices began to rise so much that in one month they went from seventy cents to 110 cents per bushel for the best quality wheat. They then fell a little and have since been between ninety cents and a dollar a bushel.

I don't have much news for you. For my own part I can say that I'm in good health and still live the life of a bachelor. We've had a lot of diphtheria this winter. For children it has in most cases been fatal and some adults have also died. It is very contagious. It has ravaged for some time in the family of Ole Kjensrud and has already taken two of his children. Now his third and last child is also said to be ill but it is still not known whether it will survive or not. His wife has also had it but is now said to be quite well. Erik Kjensrud's family has also been affected and yesterday I heard that one of his children had died. I don't know of any other news or changes of importance in families known to you. The Bertilrud family, that I'm living with this winter, are all well. Kari happened to be at Ole Kjensrud's when the illness began there. Kjersti is rather anxious for her and the doctors have forbidden her to go home or anywhere else until the illness has left the house. She is, however, quite well and unaffected till now. Syver, Iver and Anton are away this winter while the others are home. I think they are they are quite comfortable here everything considered. Kjersti thinks quite a lot about her old home and she may not be happy with many things that she had thought would be different or that she hadn't thought of at all. I think she'll be more satisfied with time. Gulbrand has some longing but I don't think this has caused any anxiety. Most often he speaks of the lakes where he used to go fishing in the northern hills and I think that such things are what he misses the most. Their little children are as free from worry as a litter of kittens. You may have heard as recently from Wisconsin as I have. The latest news I have from there is that Ole Børtnes has married. I don't know his bride but judging from the portrait she seems to be a pleasant and sensible girl. They wrote that she was from Western Norway and had emigrated four years ago. The other Børtnes boys are here in Dakota or at least they were all here last fall. Andreas has probably gone back to Minnesota. He came here from Wisconsin last summer. It is rather apparent that he is a descendant of Cain but whether this is his own fault or he is a victim of the curse laid on Cain may be more a matter of faith than of knowledge.

We've had nice weather this winter and until about three weeks ago there was no snow on the ground. These last three weeks we've had occasional snowstorms but it has been very nice in between. Indeed, this is one of the finest winters we've had for as long as I've been here. I cannot remember any more to write about and must therefore conclude with my best regards and my hope that you won't wait as long as I have before you write; I'll try to do better in the future. I hope you will give my regards to all relatives and acquaintances. It would have been nice to go with the letter and visit you in person, but this is not possible at present. I hope to see you again my old father, but this will have to remain a fond wish. Farewell! Sincerely,

IVER LIE

· —— ·

The bride of Ole Børtnes was Martha N. Hatleskog. «II:217 »II:242
NE V:140

· —— ·

FROM: Christine Dahl, *Norse, Texas, 2 April 1889*

TO: Erik Pedersen Furuset, *Romedal, Stange, Hedmark*

⊷⊶

Dear brother Erik and family,

I'm writing a few lines to you to let you know that we are all well and I hope this is the way it is with you too. I don't have much news since my last letter except that we've been to a wedding at Sinrud. It was a large wedding, because two couples were married at the same time. There were about 300 guests as the couples had many relatives on both sides. Nils was married to a cousin of my son Christian's wife and Anne's husband is the son of a Swede, a nice family who are neighbors of Sinrud. This year's harvest looks promising. The weather is fine and the grass has grown so that the cattle and horses can manage on their own.

I must explain why I'm writing so soon after my last letter. Edward P. Løken came to me and wanted to send ten dollars to his parents and wondered whether I had some money left with you so that he could pay them to me and you could give the money to his parents. I told him that according to my accounts I only had a little more than seven dollars that I had not thought of asking for. But they seem to need these ten dollars, so if you can let them have them we could say that my account is closed. But if this is in any way inconvenient for you, then just let them have the twenty-eight *kroner* and this will be fine with me.

Since I wrote to you such a short time ago I don't know of more to write about. If you have already responded to my last letter then please send me a few words in answer to this one as well. I must now conclude. I can send you regards from Aunt Rogstad and her family. She has not been quite well recently. Say hello to my sister and her children from us. I can say from Karen Dilrud and her family that they are doing well. Farewell and our best greetings from me and all my children. Your devoted sister

CHRISTINE DAHL

CD had written to her brother 18 March 1889 concerning the settlement of the estate of Ole Arneberg and enclosing the required papers and signatures. The money managed for her by her brother is from her share of the inheritance from their father. CD's sister, Karen Dilrud, wrote to her brother at Furuset on 20 June 1889 and 28 July 1892 (Nor. ed. V:253). This is the last letter from Christine Dahl in these volumes. She died in 1910. «II:183 NE V:148

1889 — LETTER 2:231

FROM: Karen Solem, *Norden, South Dakota, 19 May 1889*

To: Maria Kristoffersdatter, *Nannestad, Akershus*

My dear mother,

It is so long since I wrote to you. It is too bad that there is so much time between each letter but this is not as I wish. I have so much to take care of and so little time for writing, but I hope you will forgive me, mother. I often write to you in my thoughts and tell you a thousand things that never get on paper; when I sit down to write I can never remember what it is that I so wanted to tell you. We are in good health and doing well (except that we always have so much to do both indoors and out). Marie is now quite big and clever and runs around outdoors almost all day. The other day we got six goslings and you may imagine that she is fond of them. Little Nordt is also a good little boy and is growing and becoming both big and sweet. He resembles you much more than does Marie who is the spitting image of Aunt Karen, as all who see her say. Oh, that I had lived so close to you that I could have taken them to visit you every so often. During Easter Lars Evensen was here with his girlfriend. It was such fun to talk with him since he had been to visit you. He said that you had such a nice home and that makes me glad and also that you were in good health and that makes me even gladder. But you know that Lars isn't a "talker" so I didn't get to know more than I asked about. He said that he had brought a pair of stockings for one of the children but I haven't seen them yet. I'll soon go over to Ole Berger (or Melby) and get them there. His girlfriend is nice but I can't really say much about her as I don't know her well enough. But she didn't seem very refined and probably came right from the cow stable—but don't say this to anyone. They were married about a week ago—quietly and without a wedding party—by Pastor Brandt.

May 17 was celebrated in Toronto last Friday and it was convenient that this was the Day of Prayer as this day is not a holiday in this country. We were all in town but I was for the most part indoors visiting Mrs. Løvaas (Karen Aamotstuen). It isn't easy to be among so many people with small children. A while ago I sat with Marie and talked about "grandmother in Norway." (She knows that she has one grandmother in Norway and one in heaven.) I told her that Nordt's small socks were from you and then she asked if you couldn't knit her a pair as well and of course I had to say that I thought you would. You should have seen how big and clever she is and I must add that she is also good. Grandfather often scolds me for being too strict but I think this will be best for her in the future. Of course the boy is also clever. He is getting big and now has two teeth and he wants to stand up by the chair so I think he'll soon be more independent.

Yesterday was Sunday and we visited a O. H. Rostad who lives four miles from us. There we met a family that has lived in Kristiania. The husband's name was Kristian Grindager and he was from Bjerke. The wife was from Sweden. Tomorrow I'll go to the ladies' aid in the home of Christian Kjønstad. I'll take Nordt with me and drive the buggy with "Dudu." Imagine that I've had the great pleasure of receiving a letter from my dear teacher C. Olsen; it was so unexpected that I was overwhelmed. I've thought of writing to him so many times and nothing has come of it. If you should meet them then give them a thousand regards from me. You'll have to forgive me that I don't have a photograph of the children; it hasn't been possible to go to Canby yet but if it doesn't get too cold we'll go soon. Give Marie Toresen my regards; she must be angry with me for not writing but ask her to write to me with news from Nannestad. This is getting rather jumbled but it is late night and grandfather has to look after the children while I write. Give my regards to all relatives and acquaintances. Farewell and give my regards to father. Greetings from all here. Your daughter

KAREN

. ——— .

Aunt Karen, now deceased, had been married to Per Fella. Lars Evensen had been to Norway to bring back a bride. For "buggy" KS wrote *bogyen*; "Dudu" was her horse. The Day of Prayer (*bots- og bededag,* or the day of humiliation and prayer) has been the fourth Sunday after Easter since 1686. KS wrote more letters to her mother and brother than can be published here. On 3 February 1889 (Nor. ed. V:141) she wrote a note to her mother about the birth of a son. She often used many days to complete longer letters. On 17 March to 4 April she wrote to her brother about the christening of her new son, Olaf Nordt, and explained, "You may think Nordt is a strange name but it is genuine English. Many here have difficulties with their Norwegian names. I wanted to call him Norbert; you must remember that name from when we read *The River Queen.* But the name couldn't be pronounced in English." She wrote to her brother on 29 July and on 16 September (Nor. ed. V:156). «II:228 »II:247 NE V:152

．━━━━━．

1889 — LETTER 2:232

FROM: Jacob Hanson Hilton, *Socorro, New Mexico, 6 October 1889*
To: Hans Jakobsen and Anne Olsdatter Hilton, *Kløfta, Ullensaker, Akershus*

⊷══◉═⊱

Dear parents!!!

Since I haven't had a letter or written one in a long time I'll send you some lines today. I don't know whether I now owe you one or not, but I have news for you and must take the time to share it with you: a little "<u>Norwegian</u>" came to us last Sunday on September 29, a <u>big</u>, fat <u>boy</u>. And he is a Hilton boy from *top* to *toe* and all is well with both mother and son. I had planned to write a lot when I started this letter but now that I'm writing I can't think of anything new as I wrote to Karen a few days ago and then told her all I know.

Socorro is still going downwards, but for me and my business things have improved greatly these last two months. People need shoes and also to have them mended, and I have introduced some changes in my business that have contributed to the upswing: I no longer give credit to anyone and I have reduced my prices so significantly that the others who sell shoes here are unable to compete, first because I have very low expenses, secondly because I do much of my work in my shop that the others are unable to do, and thirdly because the others give credit and thereby lose about a third of their total turnover that will never be repaid, and therefore they have to sell at a higher price to make up for their loss. They have thousands in their accounts that they'll never see as much as a cent of. I also have some of these nonpaying gentlemen, but not many, perhaps four to five hundred dollars in all since I arrived here nine years ago, and if you divide that by nine it's not worth mentioning. I own my own home so I only pay rent for my business and that is very cheap, only twenty dollars a month; three or four years ago the rent was 100 dollars a month. I'm now going to have the entire shoe business in this town or ruin it for the others because I can make it pay whether I have a customer a day or none by mending old shoes while the others have to wait for their customers to come in. Gulbrandsen and I have worked all day recently and have as much as we can manage, so we don't have to rely on the store. If I'm able to sell some shoes, this is fine, but if not, it's also fine. And what I sell is, you understand, cash or else no shoes. I'll have to end for now with loving regards to father, mother and my siblings, hoping that you're all well. Best wishes from your son

JACOB

. ———— .

Although it may be a long time between letters to his parents, JHH evidently also corresponds with his sisters and brothers. «II:221 »II:284 NE V:157

. ———— .

1889 — LETTER 2:233

FROM: Svend H. Enderson, *Danway, Illinois, 20 October 1889*

TO: Jakob Rasmussen Sandvik, *Kinsarvik, Ullensvang, Hordaland*

Dear remembered friend,

As it is so long since I've written to you I'll make use of this opportunity to write a few words and let you know about my situation. I am, praise

God, in good health and I wish the same blessing on you and all others. I'm glad that my mother and sister have come to America and it would be even better if they will like it here. Everything is new for them yet and it is difficult to like it here the first year but I know that it will be better for my mother here than in Norway. She now lives with my sister Marta and Ingrid is working for some Americans and learning the language. I could hardly recognize them, especially Ingrid. I don't think I would have recognized her had I met her in a strange place and not known she was there.

Thank you so much, my dear friend, for the gifts you've sent me. I don't know what I can send you in return. Most of all I wish that you came to America. Then I would repay you even if all I gave you was a new girlfriend. I have again found one for myself and if everything goes well you'll receive our portrait next winter, but nothing is definite yet. You know how the girls are—sweet and pretty. I won't say more about this now. I've thought of moving to Iowa in the spring. Then my sister Marta is going to Iowa and my mother and my sister Ingrid will go with them. Ed and Marta have land close to Jacob and Dorthea. Ed is now in Iowa building a house and they plan to move in February. I must also let you know that we have had a good harvest this year and the prices are good for what they have to sell.

Dear Jacob, I always remember you as you were such a good friend when I was in Norway. It would be great fun to see Norway again. I have no fear of the journey but it would cost me a lot of money. I've spoken with many bachelors who have visited Norway and they all say the same: it would cost about two or three hundred dollars to visit Norway. So this is the only reason why I haven't come to Norway but if I live longer and have my health I'll probably see Norway again, because I still love my old fatherland. In conclusion I must now ask you to give my regards to your family and at Rinden and to Ole and Torbjørg and all at Sandvik and to all who may ask about me. Tell them that my old mother and sister are in good health. I think my mother will miss that she can't gather heather here or go down to the shore for seaweed because we don't have such things here. My friendly regards. Write soon.

SVEND H. ENDESON

· ——— ·

SE's mother and sister, Sigrid Svendsdatter and Ingrid Endresdatter Hus, emigrated in 1886. Sigrid wrote to her brother Rasmus Svendsen Sandvik on 25 May 1887 (Nor. ed. V:76). SE's sister Dorthea is married to Jacob Svendsen Hustvet; his sister Marta is married to "Ed." Torbjørg, a sister in Norway, is married to Ole Skrovik. «II:156 NE V:159

· ——— ·

FROM AMERICA TO NORWAY

FROM: Elling and Guruanna Anderson
Eau Claire, Wisconsin, 22 October 1889
TO: Johan Peter Eriksen Lian, *Verdal, Nord-Trøndelag*

Dear brother-in-law and family,

As a long time has gone by without a letter from you we'll send you a few lines so you can hear how we are and be reminded that it would be nice for us to hear now and then about relatives and friends in the old country. I hope that these lines find you in good health. With us things are as usual. We are in good health and we cannot ask for anything better. We are getting older and cannot expect to be able to get our work done as easily as in the past. This summer I've worked at the sawmill as usual and I plan to go to the forest this winter but not too early since a winter of toil and moil in the forest can be long for a man at my age. Our son Karl is also thinking of going to the forest this fall if he can get light work. Gustav was confirmed on the sixth of this month and is still so young that he should be at home.

I can give you greetings from our old neighbor Ole Eskilsen. He thought of visiting Norway last summer and I was to take care of his home, but he became ill and that was the end of his Norway visit. He has been ill all summer but is now getting better. I recently had letters from him and another old neighbor, Elling Moan, and you must give greetings to Moan and tell them that we are expecting a visit from Elling. And I must tell you that we have received *Nordenfjeldske Tidende*. Thank you so much for taking the trouble to have it sent to me. The first issue we received was for September 5 and since then it has come regularly. I have sent payment for one year to the newspaper's office and if you have paid anything yourself you may have it returned from the publisher. Please ask the editor to give me notice when my subscription is due. I send greetings from Anna and her husband and their little son. Little Odin is big and clever and his grandfather's favorite. We are enclosing a portrait so you may have some idea of what we now look like and we hope to have one from you—of yourself as well as your wife and children. This will have to be enough for this time. In conclusion you are all lovingly remembered by us,

ELLING AND GUROANNA SENDE

. ——— .

While EA seems to have dictated this letter, it was written by GA. The first person pronoun may refer to either of them. «II:192 »II:244 NE V:160

. ——— .

1889 — LETTER 2:235

FROM: Haakon Syversen Belle, *Salem, Oregon, 18 November 1889*

To: Syver Olsen Belle, *Lesja, Oppland*

Dear father!

We received your letter of July 30 on August 2. I should have written long ago but it has been put off from time to time. I assume that your winter has already begun. We still have warm weather with occasional rain. Grass and wheat are growing fast. We haven't sold our farm but a Swiss is farming it on shares. I still have three mares and two foals of one and two years, and two cows and a calf. The price of land is rising rapidly. Many farmers are now selling their farms as lots of ten to twenty acres at great prices and I think that I'll divide our land into lots of ten to twenty acres and sell them. In this manner I may get 100 dollars an acre and perhaps more if the land prices continue to rise as they have for the last six months. Many immigrants are coming all the time, in particular from Nebraska, Kansas, Iowa, Minnesota, Pennsylvania etc. The house and *lot* that we bought last fall for 2,730 dollars we can now sell for 4,500 dollars. Salem now has more than 10,000 inhabitants as compared to last year's 6,000 to 7,000. I don't have a business yet but this fall and winter I plan to buy a few houses and lots on speculation as I think this will pay better than any other business. We now have more than four miles of streetcar rails. Each car is drawn by one horse. It costs five cents to go from one end to the other or any other stretch regardless of length. They are now laying rails for a streetcar that will be run by electricity. This one will be about two and a half miles to begin with. All cars can take about twenty-two persons. Portland is growing at an incredible speed and now has about 70,000 inhabitants.

We are all well. Our little daughter is growing and thriving; she is now a little more than seventeen months. Claude was five on November 1; he is a big boy. Blanche was twelve on the thirteenth of last month; she is very tall for her age and is quite clever. Last September she was awarded three prizes at the city exhibition. One was for a picture, one for a dress she had made herself, and one was for a loaf of bread she had baked. These prizes amounted to five dollars in cash. In a few weeks I'll send you a bank draft as a little Christmas present. Who runs the post office in Lesja and where is it? I have no news of interest. Give my regards to Gunder Tøndevold and [...] Siem, to my brother and sister and her family, and to others who may ask about me. Farewell. Greetings from your son and family.

H. S. BELLE

· ——— ·

This letter exists in an edited copy. HSB (b. 1844) was from the northern of the two Belle (Belden) farms in Lesja and emigrated in 1867. His daughter Blanche wrote a letter that her father translated to Norwegian on 16 December 1888. HSB does not seem to have a Norwegian word for lot and for the plural form (lots) he writes *lodder*. »II:256 NE V:163

· ——— ·

1889 — LETTER 2:236

FROM: John Svenson, *Crookston, Minnesota, 3 December 1889*

TO: Jakob Rasmussen Sandvik, *Kinsarvik, Ullensvang, Hordaland*

Dear cousin Jacob,

I cannot understand what has come in the way of our relationship for so long. I haven't heard from you since February. Should I believe that you are all dead? Well, I'll let it pass as the post coach still rolls along and a five cent stamp won't break my neck. You may have believed the same of me, who was lost, died, woke up again, and have now been found. Do not go astray, says the pastor, as I am the shepherd who will find who is lost. Yes, He finds all those who have cents in their pocket—so he says he is glad for me because all want to have money. Last night we had Kristofer Janson give an excellent lecture on socialism. All his arguments are convincing.

Last summer we had dry weather so the crops suffered. Last summer I had a herd of cattle. I rented five sections for pasture, had 250 head of cattle and a horse for riding. I was boss and I hired a boy for fifteen dollars a month. But because of the drought there was no more water and I had to sell half the herd in August. I didn't make any money as I had high expenses. Now I'm doing my own housekeeping in town with my dog by my side keeping guard. I don't have a housekeeper. I hired one last summer but there is no one now. I haven't yet found a housekeeper for my future because everything bright is not gold. It probably won't be until I come to Norway and I don't think this will be next fall. I haven't decided what I'll do this winter, go to the forest or take a tour of another state, because there is nothing here at present. Winter has arrived with snow but it isn't so cold yet.

I have no news that would interest you, but my real reason for writing is to ask you to send me two spinning wheels as soon as possible. Two women have asked me to write for spinning wheels for many years but I've done nothing. It is easy to send freight here when it is boxed. I'll send you six dollars by express mail, but you had better write to me first if you can get them and number each part so I can see where it goes. Give my regards to mother and sister and say I'm doing well. I hope we'll see each other again sometime. Give my regards to all acquaintances, in particular the girls. Farewell. Your devoted and far distant cousin,

JOHN SWENSON

·———·

This is the last preserved letter by JS. He seems to have left his claim in Wisconsin. Both Jakob and his father, Rasmus Sandvik, were makers of spinning wheels. «II:214 NE V:165

·———·

FROM: Hans Nilsen Lind, *West Valley, Minnesota, 10 December 1889*

TO: Sevat Olsen Vik, *Sigdal, Buskerud*

Dear friend Sigvat O. Wiig,

Finally I'll have to try to answer your letter. It came to us August 14 with much news that we are grateful for. I don't have any news for you but I've heard from Sigdal that you are now enjoying good times which we were pleased to hear even though we cannot boast of this here and if the good Lord Jesus will punish us with more such bad years then almost every man here will go bankrupt. In addition we had a hailstorm last summer that beat down every little bit so that neither Ole Bjornerud nor our Nils got any ripe grain. There were of course many others that you don't know. Yes, eight acres were beaten down for our Ole and the fields of many others as well, including a great deal of mine. I'll tell you what we got. Ole had ninety-eight bushels of wheat, fifty of oats, thirteen of barley and twenty bushels of potatoes. I had fifty bushels of wheat, twenty-eight of oats, twenty-two of barley, and fifteen bushels of potatoes, and this was all we had.

My house is almost finished except that part of it still needs to be plastered. It has already been used as a schoolhouse for ten weeks for the English school. I haven't built a stable as we lacked lumber, so we haven't moved there yet. There are many fearful dangers to be experienced here such as the terrible prairie fire that rages here every spring and fall. Nine men battled a fire here April 13 and 14 and we just barely saved our houses. This was the first time Ole Sund was here and he took part in this terrible work. Last fall we lived through the same danger in early November and it wouldn't have been possible to save my house if I hadn't already plowed on two sides of it. But praise God! Those he will save he keeps from all damage and danger. This time we were only seven men and the fire came in the evening so we had to fight it almost the entire night. This time it didn't get to Ole's land.

I've wondered a lot why Ole Ramstad hasn't received my last letter that Nils wrote to him for I see no mention of it in your letter. I must stop for now with friendly regards and wishes for a merry Christmas and a happy New Year from all of us here. We are all fairly well to date and we hope that this letter will find you all in the same state. Farewell!

H. N. LIND

. ——— .

HNL's sons were Ole and Nils Hansen Lind. HNL again wrote *stæbel* (stable). He also wrote to Sevat Vik on 10 May 1888 and on 9 July 1890. «II:208 NE V:167

. ——— .

1889 — LETTER 2:238

FROM: Anne and Amund Pedersen Bjorli
Bue, North Dakota, 23 December 1889

To: Hans Jørgensen and Eli Johannesdatter Bjøkne, *Lesja, Oppland*

Dear parents-in-law and siblings!

Thank you for your welcome letter that we received a few days ago. We are glad to see that you are well. We can also report that we are in good health and doing well. The winter is mild, no snow yet except as a little frost. We don't have any news of interest but will send you a few sentences so you'll know how we are. Times are hard here for people who work and they will remain so until the next harvest. If we have a good year, times will improve, if not our situation will be quite bad.

We see from your letter that Hans is thinking of visiting Norway this winter and if he does we'll ask him to bring Peder back to us if he is willing to go with Hans when he returns. I suppose you've read in the newspapers about the bad situation in parts of Dakota, including Nelson County. I regret such unnecessary complaints. There are poor people in all countries, but those who work hard, are careful and healthy have no need for public support even though bad times and poor harvests may cause difficulties. But there are some scurvy sheep among us who don't want to work for their bread and just look for an opportunity to cheat honest citizens. Now that the harvest has failed I'm sure the situation is tough for such people and that hunger is unavoidable if they can't get enough attention with their loud calls. Such people are masters at getting attention. A public announcement has been made in the newspapers and the result has been a lot of rags and a few good clothes and committees have been set up to supervise the distribution. Those who have made the most use of this are Russian Jews and Finns. They have gathered around the distributors like vultures around carrion and tried to grab everything. The Jews are worse than the Finns and some Germans and Scandinavian wrecks are not above beggary. The Icelander is the worst scoundrel of all but perhaps not more of a beggar than the Jew. Regards to you all from us.

AMUND AND ANNE BJORLI

. ——— .

> Amund is the writer. Hans was Anne's brother in Minnesota and the American-born Peder, who lived with his grandmother in Lesja, was a son of Amund's first marriage. Amund and Anne each wrote their parts of a letter dated 13 September 1889 (Nor. ed. V:155). «II:227 »II:245 NE V:168

. ——— .

1889 — LETTER 2:239

FROM: Anne Norsby, *Necedah, Wisconsin, 31 December 1889*
To: Marie Olsdatter Vigerust, *Dovre, Oppland*

⋯⊜⊜⋯

Dear cousin Marie!

I will now take up my pen and write a few words to you and see if I'll get a reply. I wrote to you last spring and my only reply was a few words in a letter to Ole Lee and there you said you would soon write more, but I have waited and waited and there has been no letter. We are all well and I hope to hear the same from you. I've been working for my sister Rine since last spring. We had to take care of many men last summer—Rine's husband Otto, his brother and two of his cousins, Bjørner and Sivert. Since the mill closed we have only been Rine, her husband and I, but we now have one more in the family. Rine had a son November 15. Mother and father and Ole are alone on the farm. My brother Jakob is married and has a daughter. Last fall they built a house and a cowshed a small distance from home but on the same farm and they farm together. Last fall Sivert went to Indiana to go to school and he'll probably be away for a year. Bjørner is still working in town but soon both he and I will go home for the winter. Rine and Jakob's little ones are nice and healthy children.

We have celebrated Christmas. The little boy here was brought to church on Christmas Day and he is named Kristian for Otto's father and then we had our house filled with guests. In the evening we had a Christmas tree feast for the first time in the Norwegian church. I was lucky and got material for a dress, an apron and a nice pair of cuffs. The dress material and apron were from Rine and her husband but I don't know who gave the other gift because it only said who it was for and not who it was from. There were oranges, apples and candy for all who had contributed. All who saw the tree said it was exceptionally nice. The Americans had a Christmas tree in their church on Christmas Eve but those who saw it said that it wasn't as nice as the Norwegian one. Otto and Bjørner both worked on the second day of Christmas but in the evening we were all invited to our Swedish neighbors and on the third day of Christmas I was again at a party. Yesterday we were invited to a Norwegian photographer. We were six boys and five girls but it was great fun even though we were so few. We had food and coffee and all kinds of good things. We were there until three in the morning.

We have had exceptionally nice weather this winter and no snow. Last night we had a sprinkling of snow, but it is cold today. Christmas Day we had as nice a summer's weather as we could wish for. Rønnaug lives as comfortably as she could desire. They moved last fall because the house they lived in was too cold. They now have a small house but large enough for their family. It is both nice and warm and has a living room, two bedrooms and a kitchen and a pantry as well as a summer kitchen. Last summer mother wove carpets for her living room and bedrooms. If she has to manage alone laundry will be easy as she has a water pump in the hall. She has a kind husband who takes care of the cow and does all he can for her. If they continue to be in good health they have no need for anything better than they now have.

Your siblings were here not so long ago. Hans came in on Christmas Eve and wanted some of us to visit with them but that wasn't possible then. It may be that we visit them on our way home. I had a letter from Tholine Dahl just before Christmas and she urged me to visit them or work for them. I may go there and work for them next spring. We recently had a letter from Johannes Norsby with a portrait of him and his wife. I forgot to tell you the name of Jakob's daughter. I cannot say that it is such a nice name here in America; it is simply Marit. Dear Marie, I wish you were here now so you could have come home with me. Since I couldn't finish my letter yesterday I can send you greetings from your siblings. Edvard, son of Hans and Olianna, was here for dinner today and he said they are all well. Edvard is a big and clever boy. Father and mother have come today and will probably stay for a week or so. Bjørner and I will be returning home tomorrow. Mother and father are quite well and you may imagine how nice it would be if my parents and your mother could be together. Let me know as much as you can from Dovre and Lesja when you write.

The prices for what a farmer has to sell are very low. Pork is four cents a pound, meat four cents a pound, eggs twenty cents a dozen, but only ten in summer. Butter is eighteen cents a pound in summer but usually fifteen and sometimes less. Poor cotton material is very cheap but for good quality you pay more than in Norway. The harvest last year was exceptionally good, the best since we came to America. You must write immediately when you get this letter so I can receive it while I'm at home. Our three neighbors here are Norwegian, Danish and Swedish.

As I don't have more to write about I'll have to conclude with loving regards to you all. My parents and siblings and Rine's husband send their regards. Send me a very long letter with all the news you have. I, Anne Norsby, wish you a Happy New Year.

A. NORSBY

·⸻·

AN's parents, Marit and Jakob Norsby, had a farm near Necedah. Her sister Rønnaug was also called Rine. Ole Lee and his family were from the small farm Snekkerlien in Dovre and took the name Lee in the United States. An instance of codeswitching is *kændi* (candy), evidently an English word that has become part of their Norwegian speech. The next letter, from Johannes Spilde, gives a more detailed account of a Christmas tree feast. Marie Vigerust's siblings in Wisconsin were Jakob Olson and Olianna Hanson, who was married to Hans Hanson. AN wrote to her cousin on 7 November 1890 and commented on their infrequent correspondence. She had visited friends in Minneapolis and her brother Sivert had now gone there. She and her mother had picked blueberries for twenty-nine dollars in July. They are living among relatives and people they know from Norway and read news from home in their immigrant newspapers. «II:224 »II:267 NE V:169

·⸻·

FROM: Johannes Iversen Spilde, *Brownsdale, Minnesota, 1 January 1890*

To: Thrond Sjursen Haukenæs, *Granvin, Hordaland*

Dear friend,

Thank you for your welcome letter that came to me December 4. I was very glad to read it and was curious to find out what my good friend Thrond Haukenæs had to tell me. I see that you are doing a good business with your books. As for myself, I'm in good health and quite comfortable. I've recently moved but I'm still working for an American. It is a good place to be and I'm quite satisfied except that I would have enjoyed spending time with young Norwegians now and then. And I would also have enjoyed talking with my old friend Thrond Haukenæs about the times we were together in your home in Eide.

I must tell you how Christmas has been. On Christmas Eve I went to Brownsdale to see the Christmas tree that is usually decorated in the town's church and before the gifts are distributed it is usual that the town's school children each read a nice Christmas poem and we sing several Christmas songs, so it was an enjoyable evening. Christmas morning passed without prayers or readings. I could have taken a wagon to town and gone to church but I preferred being at home. On Christmas Day the food is the same as on other days except for the fine dinner. As for a Christmas shot, none was offered and I gave none, so I kept my money. That evening I went to a dance in a small town four miles from here and there were many young people there, sixty-five couples, and it cost one dollar a couple but if a boy came alone he had to pay seventy-five cents. The music was an organ, two violins and a horn. This was all the entertainment I took part in for Christmas. The second day of Christmas was a regular working day. The weather has been beautiful. We still don't have any snow and it isn't very cold. I plowed the week before Christmas. I have no news. Please write soon. I'll conclude with loving regards to you and your wife and children from your friend

JOHANNES IVERSEN SPILDE

Letters to Haukenæs, a popular local historian, are from a handwritten book of copies of letters that he no doubt planned to publish. It is deposited in the Norwegian National Archives. JIS had worked for Haukenæs 1882–1883 and emigrated in 1886. Other letters from JIS are dated 4 February and 9 May 1888 and 21 October 1889. NE V:171

1890 — LETTER 2:241

FROM: Siri Allikson, *Springville, Wisconsin, 2 January 1890*

TO: Osmund Atlaksen Ovedal, *Sirdal, Aust-Agder*

Dear and unforgetable brother Osmund and family,

Today is Christmas Day and it had been a real Christmas for our souls to be gathered with our Savior Jesus on the other side of the grave. Last summer I visited our sister Rakel for six months and I suppose you have heard that her husband and her son Oskar died last spring. Jon was buried April 6 and Oskar May 6. They died in faith in their Savior and it was a delight to listen to Oskar the last hour he lived. His last words were, now I am dying in the name of Jesus. Oskar died of diphtheria and Jon of pneumonia. He was already dead when I arrived. Theodor was confirmed last fall and they are now all well. Karen Bertine was also ill for several weeks and we thought that she too would leave us, but she got well again and has asked me to visit them next summer, but it costs too much to travel so far. It is 300 miles and it cost me seventeen dollars by train and it took a day. Ole Torkelson died in between Jon and Oskar and was buried April 18. Rakel has a large debt. Next summer she will learn whether she can keep her two quarter sections. She had two horses, six sheep, nine cows, and a pig. I spun and wove a hundred yards of material for Rakel. Remember her in your daily prayers.

Bernt's widow Berte Tonette visited us last summer when I visited Rakel. She gave Theodor five dollars when he was confirmed and she has four quarter sections. All at our brother Sigbjørn's are doing well. Sophie is married to Gitle Strømstad who was first married to Berte, the daughter of our brother Sigbjørn. Sivert is at school every day except for three summer months. Did you ever receive a sample of Syvert's writing? I've sent it to you. I and Sarah and Reinert are together here in Springville and are mostly at home. Now I'm with old Hans and Marte Skjerpe but they are not far away. We are all in good health. Reinert has let his land on shares as he is too old to work it himself. He tends the animals and chops wood so you may imagine that it is nice and quiet for us here. Today is New Year's Day and I'll send you my best wishes for Christmas and the New Year. May the Lord bless you all. I'm sending you this portrait of our brother Osmund that you had mentioned to Ingeborg Øxendal. Thank you for the painted bottle you have sent us. You must excuse my delayed letter. Not a day passes that I don't think of you. Bolette and Ingeborg may soon be so big that they can send me a letter. I would so like to have your portraits if this is possible. Give our regards to all acquaintances and relatives. Loving regards to you from all of us. Farewell.

SIRI ATLAGSEN OVEDAHL

. ——— .

SA lives with her sister Sarah and her brother Reinert. Her sister Rakel Thorkelson in Minnesota was married to Jon Torkelsen Rannestad. Oskar, Theodor, Albert, and Karen Bertine were their children. Ole Thorkelson was Rakel's brother-in-law. They all took the name Thorkelson in the United States. Berte Tonette had been married to SA's brother Bernt Andreas Allikson. Syvert was deaf and mute and had to live away from home at a special school. «II:197 »II:282 NE V:172

. ——— .

FROM: Iver Andersen Lee, *Mayville, North Dakota, 2 February 1890*

TO: Anders Olsen and Anders Andersen Lie, *Hedalen, Sør-Aurdal, Oppland*

⋆⇥⊜⇤⋆

Dear father and brother and other relatives and friends!

Again a long time has passed since I last had a letter from you, dear brother, and I still have not replied. I don't know whether I dare ask your forgiveness as you may see this as too much indifference on my part. My only excuse is that I'm often with you in my thoughts and that in this manner I've had many a nice visit with you even though you may not have noticed my visits since thoughts are much like elves and are neither seen nor felt where they wander. I've been in good health so I've managed quite well. This winter we've been visited by an illness called influenza. You probably know of it through the newspapers even if it hasn't paid you a visit. I as well as most others here, in towns as well as on farms, have had it. Around here, however, it hasn't been strong; I was rather poorly for a few days but not so bad that I could not do the chores. It has been worse for others but no one around here has died as far as I know.

I don't have much to tell you about relatives and acquaintances here. Last fall the Bertilrud family (except for Iver) went to Roseau River in Minnesota to take land. I've had a letter from Syver and they seem to like it there. Iver has lived with me this winter as has Iver Børtnes. Erik Børtnes lives with Ingeborg Bergene and her husband a little further west. I haven't spoken with Harald and Oline Sørlie. Oline and Anne Omsrud were around here last fall but I didn't meet them.

I see that I've forgotten to tell you that I've bought land here. The summer before last I bought 160 acres for 1,500 dollars. This is new land; the fields are unbroken and there are no buildings. It takes a lot of money and hard work to get going on such land. You want to know how much I owe so I'll have to list some of the most important things I've had to buy in addition to the land: two work horses for 300 dollars and a one-year foal for seventy. A wagon for fifty dollars, a mowing machine sixty, a horse rake twenty-five, a selfbinder 160, a breaking plow twenty-four, a regular plow eighty, a harrow fifteen, a seeder eighty dollars and so on in addition to the necessary houses that cost about 100 dollars without furniture. I paid thirty dollars for a stove. In all my debt is about 1,750 dollars. I've hired help for some breaking and done some myself. Last summer I planted about fifty-five acres and harvested 850 bushels of wheat and more potatoes and roots than I need. Last summer I broke another sixty-five acres so this spring I can plant about 120 acres. Next summer I plan to break the rest of my land. Things look better for me now than when I used Nils Vold's land without making much money. I almost forgot to mention the hay. In addition to the hay I need for myself I've sold hay for about ninety dollars.

Last year the crops in many places in Dakota were rather poor but they were pretty good around here. In many counties to the south and west there seems to be far too little rain. Indeed for the last three years they've had nothing to harvest. In addition to the drought these parts have difficulties with an animal called a gopher. It is somewhat similar to the weasel and it chews the straw. There are so many of them that they can destroy large fields in a few hours. There is famine many places because of the repeated bad harvests but it hasn't been so bad that I've heard of people dying of hunger. But this fall and winter people around here have come to realize that they'll have to help them to survive the winter. For this we have established assistance committees who go around to the farms and collect gifts that may be of help for those in need. There has been a regular stream of gifts and it seems that those who are in need may be able to survive this year and if they have a crop next year they should be able to stay on where they are. Otherwise they'll probably have to leave. With this I must conclude with my regards to all relatives and friends. Farewell.

IVER A. LIE

· —— ·

The Børtnes brothers were sons of IAL's father's sister. Roseau River is in northwestern Minnesota, near the Canadian border. There seems to have been no good homestead land available in the eastern part of North Dakota (which became a state a few months before this letter was written), so IAL has bought his land at the market price.
«II:229 »II:262 NE V:177

· —— ·

1890 — LETTER 2:243

FROM: Inger Eriksen (Hansen), *Henning, Minnesota, 8 February 1890*

To: Hans Olsen and Bertha Marie Berby, *Varteig, Sarpsborg, Østfold*

⋆⇒◉⇐⋆

Dear parents and siblings,

I received your welcome letter long ago and I see that you are all well, and I can also say that I am well and that also Uncle is well and that we live well. It hasn't been very cold this winter and we have little snow. Far to the east, in the state of Missouri, there has been rain that has caused floods. In one city the water was three feet deep in the streets and large railroad bridges were swept away, and far to the west there has been much snow that has killed several people. The snow has swept down great mountains, but here there is almost no snow and no mountains. Around here there are large forests and many work in the forests. Erik and Uncle work in the forest.

And I must tell you that I'm married to Erik. You may think I'm too young but this is the age when people here marry. Our neighbors' girl is getting married and she is only sixteen, so it isn't strange to get married when young, as it is at home. You know that love is above all else. I'm very satisfied with him. I've known him for more than a year and he is very kind and a good worker. He was away for about a month and made eighty dollars. He ran a threshing machine. There were three men who did this and he was first. There were eighteen in all at the machine and he was first of the three. It was a large steam machine. When he came home I met him in a town called Fergus Falls and he bought me new clothes from head to foot and a nice coat for ten dollars. He is very kind to me. I must now stop with friendly greetings from

INGER HANSEN

· —— ·

IE still signs herself Hansen as if she is not quite familiar with her new name as a married woman. Her naïve letter is characterized by poor syntax and spelling. «II:222 NE V:178

· —— ·

FROM: Guruanna Anderson, *Eau Claire, Wisconsin, 12 February 1890*

To: Anders Johansen Lian, *Verdal, Nord-Trøndelag*

Dear nephew,

I received your letter some ago but the reason I haven't written before is that I first had to send it to Elling and he is in the forest and has been there since Christmas. We see that you wish to go to America and would like to have a ticket from us and I think we should be able to help you with this because we know that it is difficult to resist this America fever once it has attacked. We've spoken with the agent about the price on the Inman Line and the White Star Line and it is forty dollars from Trondheim to Eau Claire. The agent will be at the station to receive you and take you where you are going if there is no one else to meet you but we'll do our best to meet you if this is possible.

And then we must admonish you a little: you must realize that you are leaving your father, mother, and brother and the place where you were born to go far out into the world to make your living. It is often not so good at first when one goes out into the world. There may be good times and bad and you will have to accept what comes whether this is happiness or grief or perhaps both. We hope that you have discussed this with your parents and that they are both willing to let you go, because when young people begin to think about leaving home they often do so without the consent of their parents. But I hope you have considered this and that it isn't necessary for us to admonish you. It is best that you are ready when the ticket arrives. For your own good we'll send it in March so you can be here when the sawmills begin to operate. Because if you're not here when they open up it will be more difficult to get work. I hope that everything will work out for the best and that you will arrive as planned. Give our regards to your parents and your brother and to all our old acquaintances from your

AUNT GURRUANNA SENDE

We want you to know that there are other lines that could take you here at a lower price but they are not as good as Inman and Star.

. ——— .

> Anders Johansen Lian was a son of GA's sister. Elling Anderson wrote
> to him from a lumber camp on 2 March 1890 (Nor. ed. V:181) about
> his ticket and journey. The two steamship companies were competi-
> tors. Both sailed from Liverpool to New York. Most ships taking emi-
> grants from Norwegian ports to Hull belonged to the Wilson Line.
> After coming to the United States Anders Johansen Lian became
> Andrew Lee. «II:234 »II:246 NE V:179

. ——— .

1890 — LETTER 2:245

FROM: Hans Hansen Bjøkne, *Lowry, Minnesota, 23 March 1890*

TO: Hans Jørgensen and Eli Johannesdatter Bjøkne, *Lesja, Oppland*

⋯⇒◠⇐⋯

Dear parents and siblings,

It's so long since I wrote to you that you may believe that I've forgotten you, but this is not the case. I'll first tell you that we are all well and living as usual. Marit has had some headaches this spring and last winter but only for two or three days at a time. There has been a lot of illness around here this winter and hardly a house has gone free. It has for the most part been "*influensa*." At Bjokne they have all been ill at different times. Ole was in bed for several weeks and spit blood that the doctor said came from his lungs. Guri has had rheumatism and one of her hands is almost stiff. Their children have been ill and some are still weak. Ingeborg Haugen lives with Knut Haugen and her son lives with Hans Haugen and is big and clever.

There was an auction at Tosten Hagen's on the eighteenth. He has sold three fourths of his land to Gunder and Matthias and now has one fourth and his house. Jacob seems to have been in charge there and the farm hasn't been run well. The debt was very large but not larger than they'll be able to pay. The times are worse than ever since I came here. The main reason is that the price for cattle is lower than it has been for many years. A cow can be bought for from ten to eighteen dollars, oxen for up to twenty for three-year-olds and that isn't much more than half of what it costs to feed them.

There is little church activity. We've been without a pastor since November and we don't expect one until July. Then we'll have one called Ruenæs who is just completing his studies at our school, Augsburg Seminary. Our temperance work also goes slowly even though there is some progress but what can you expect when they elect someone as unfit as me as president of the temperance society. We have achieved much here in Pope County as it is now illegal to have a *saloon* or sell whisky in the county. In other words, the *saloon license* has been voted down. A *saloon license* is permission to run a *saloon* and is more like a letter of indulgence than anything else. In conclusion I'll send you our most loving regards and ask you to write to us again. Your son and brother,

HANS H. BJØKNE AND FAMILY

. ——— .

In the margins HHB boasted that his daughter Emma was trying to write to her uncle Matthias and that her sister Ida could read. When HHB wrote "at Bjokne" he meant the home of Ole Jørgensen and Guri Johannesdatter Bjokne where he had lived after his emigration. Both Hans and his brother Jørgen wavered between Bjøkne and Bjokne in their letters but certainly used Bjokne in their daily lives. Gunder, Matthias and Jacob were sons of Tosten Hagen. No one with a name similar to "Ruenæs" graduated from the United Church's Augsburg Seminary in St. Paul. The new pastor for the Norwegian Evangelical Lutheran congregation in Lowry in 1891 was Hans Hansen Hagen. HHB was then secretary for the congregation, an office later held by his brother Jørgen. When HHB refers to a saloon license as a letter of indulgence he is harking back to Martin Luther's critique of the Roman Catholic Church before the Reformation. «II:238 »II:252 NE V:182

. ——— .

FROM AMERICA TO NORWAY

From: Anders Johansen Lian (Andrew Lee)
Liverpool, England, 22 April 1890

To: Johan Peter Eriksen, Ingborganna Andersdatter Lian
and Jakob Johansen Lian, *Verdal, Nord-Trøndelag*

⟶⟹⟸⟵

Now I've seen things you haven't seen and probably won't ever see. I came to Trondheim around five. I looked around, visited Kristiansten Fortress, now only a ruin, but you can still see how impressive it has been. I also visited the cathedral where there is a lot to see. Yes, Trondheim is worth a visit. Around noon on Thursday the steamship *Hero* left Trondheim. I would call it a little cattle ship. The food was very bad, the coffee undrinkable. We were treated fairly well but the three to four hundred passengers were squeezed in. I was reasonably well on the voyage, except for Saturday; I haven't fed the fishes yet. Many were sick. We saw the coast of England Sunday afternoon and there were many ships. I remembered the song: On the coast of England where the proud ships sail etc. We enter the harbor at about eight in the evening. We stay on board that night. On Monday morning someone comes and cries: Get off! We take our belongings and bedding and go down. The customs snoop is there and we have to open our boxes and bags for him. Do you have any tobacco? Do you have snuff? Do you have cigars? These are his questions. Also liquor. You can bring as much as you want of other things. Now comes the chest and it is inspected in the same manner. Huge crowds of people. A ship from Gothenburg in Sweden had arrived with 1,100 passengers. Suddenly someone comes and cries "The Star Line. Follow me." Others call out for the other lines. We follow him, first to an eating establishment where we get a little food and then to a ticket office where we get a railroad ticket from Hull to Liverpool. Very crowded; all nationalities. Now we enter the train compartment, eight in each and now we have fun I haven't seen the like of. I didn't look around in Hull. Sellers of apples and softdrinks everywhere. Yes, now we have entertainment. England seems to be one large city. It is about six hours from Hull to Liverpool and here we are in Liverpool. We leave the compartment and stand around for a while. Here come the agents and call out for their flocks. When we hear The Star Line we follow him up through the city to a hotel. Enormous crowds, all nationalities, Jews and Muslims! We have some food but there are not beds for all. We have to go further through the city and we have fairly good accommodations. Now we have returned to the hotel. It isn't sure that all will get out on the Atlantic. It wouldn't be nice to have to stay here for a long time. I haven't seen a single house of wood since I came to England. Only stone and brick.

ANDERS LIAN

• ——— •

«II:244 »II:249 NE V:184

• ——— •

1890 — LETTER 2:247

FROM: Karen Solem, *Norden, South Dakota, 25 April 1890*

To: Amalie Ødegaard, *Nannestad, Akershus*

⋅→▷◁←⋅

Dear Amalie,

I must hurry and write a few lines to you as I'm driving to Brandt this afternoon. First, thank you so much for your letter that arrived more than a week ago. All is well here; we are very busy with spring plowing and planting but it is far too dry. All are waiting for rain and I hope it will come soon; or else all our work has been useless. And now some news. Nicolai is married to Mina Kjønstad. They were wed here after the service in the schoolhouse on Palm Sunday (March 30). There was no wedding party; she returned with us and they will live here for the time being. It was a very hurried wedding and this was not what I had expected of them. Now that I have someone to help me we manage the work quite well. Grandfather doesn't take much part in outdoor work so I can use him to look after the children now and then, and he sometimes brings the midmorning meal and after dinner coffee out to the field, so you see that we follow the Norwegian custom with five meals a day. Marie runs around outdoors all day and Nordt would like to go with her but he has to be satisfied with standing in the doorway. I would have loved to have curtains like yours; I'm sure they'll be very nice. Give my regards to Josefine Olsen. Mina is a cousin of Allette Gaarder and she would so like to have her address. Josefine may know it and then you could send it to me. The newlyweds ask me to give you their regards. Now I must conclude with friendly greetings from all of us. Your loving

KAREN

Burn this!

· ——— ·

> KS is writing to her sister-in-law. Brandt is a small town in Deuel County. Evidently, her request that the letter be burned, no doubt because of her gossip about the newlyweds, was not acted on. Some other letters KS wrote in 1890 are dated 19 February and 8 June, both to her mother. «II:231 »II:257 NE V:185

· ——— ·

1890 — LETTER 2:248

FROM: Karen Olson, *Britton, South Dakota, 26 April 1890*

To: Johan Rasmusen Bjørgum (Geving), *Stjørdal, Nord-Trøndelag*

⟶⟹⟻⟸⟻

Dear brother!

I have received your letter and see that father is ill. You who are well must be patient with him and remember that we don't know when we ourselves may be in the same situation, as God's fatherly chastisement may be for the young as well as the old. Poor father! Pray for him. I think much about him and you.

Ole has returned to the West and is working on the railroad here. His foot is well. We haven't had much illness here compared to many other places. But we still haven't had any rain this spring even though many have already done their planting. It seems that we'll have another dry summer. We've had an unusual drought; there has been hardly any rain or snow for a couple of years but even so we had a good harvest last year. The worst thing is that there isn't enough grass or hay for the animals. This is how it is in the West. Almost all come here poor and now they have had a few good harvests, but when you come out on a bare prairie you cannot grow anything the first year and you need buildings and equipment, as it costs more to farm here than in Norway. So you cannot save much the first years. If you have to borrow money in a private bank they demand thirty to forty percent interest even though this is illegal and if you cannot pay in time they'll soon bring you to ruin. But we must accept the bad as well as the good from the Lord when it pleases him. This year two from Meldal are using one of our farms on shares. We have provided the seed and they'll do the work; we'll have half the crop and they'll do the fall plowing. We both do our own threshing.

I see there has been much illness in Leksdalen. Tell us all the news when you write, as all you write about is news for us. We love to hear about old Norway. Write soon so we can hear how things are with father and the others. Ole has just had a letter from Petter. Magnus Bjørgum arrived recently and is working for a farmer here. I've had two letters from Torsten Bjørgum since he came and all is well with him. Give greetings to Martha, Johanna and Petter from us all. Give our regards to all at Nordgeving and to all our acquaintances. Farewell and think first and last of father. Your sister

KAREN

. ——— .

Ole Geving is KO's brother. Johan Rasmussen has bought the farm Bjørgum and uses this name. There are several letters from Ole Geving to his brother in the collection. Several mention the difficulty of visiting Norway (see Nor. ed. V:206, V:259) «II:188 NE V:187

. ——— .

FROM: Anders Johansen Lian (Andrew Lee)
Eau Claire, Wisconsin, 10 May 1890

To: Johan Peter Eriksen, Ingborganna Andersdatter Lian
and Jakob Johansen Lian, *Verdal, Nord-Trøndelag*

⊷⇒⇐⊷

Dear parents and brother!

Here I am on the free soil of America! But what a long and uncomfortable journey! I assume you have received my letter from Liverpool. Unexpectedly, those who had arrived the day before in Liverpool didn't get to go with the Star Line's *Britannic*. It was packed; about 400 people had waited for eight days in Liverpool and these naturally had priority along with some Englishmen. So we were to wait for eight days in Liverpool—eight days in this awful city. Well, what could we do? Liverpool is an enormous city with huge factories everywhere. You may imagine that the agents were not popular, but our consolation was that we would then go on the *Majestic*, one of the best ships that cross the Atlantic.

So, we got to see Liverpool. Life is terrible in those dark, narrow streets; the worst sight is all the raggedy, half-naked, dirty children who roam around in the streets crying "tobacco." Well, we came to Liverpool on the twenty-first and looked forward to staying there for eight days. We were reasonably happy about this as we would be going on a good ship. But what then: on April 24 we are told that we will be taken by the Guion Line's *Arizona*. You may imagine the commotion and protests: "I have a ticket for the Star Line and I want to go with the Star Line!" Many would gladly have torn the agents apart; some Swedes protest against going on the *Arizona* and remain in the hotel waiting for the *Majestic*. The Norwegians go on the *Arizona*.

We were taken onboard the *Arizona* on the twenty-fifth. Much dissatisfaction, the agent doesn't dare come onboard. We are given our tickets at eight o'clock on the twenty-sixth. The ship leaves Liverpool at two in the afternoon and comes to Queenstown (Ireland) around six in the morning of April 27. Lots of Irish come onboard. There are many fruit sellers who come onboard to sell their wares at high prices. The ship leaves Queenstown around two and steams out into the Atlantic. By eight in the afternoon we can no longer see Ireland. I begin to get seasick.

We didn't have a good time on board. The Star Line people are packed together in a dark room under the foredeck next to Irishmen, Germans, Poles, Russians, Finns, Jews, and many others. They were not very clean people. Lice crawled all over them and there were a few vicious types. Luckily, we were twenty Norwegians in the same division. The food was rather bad and I couldn't drink the coffee or tea. For breakfast there was bread and coffee; for dinner raw meat, potatoes, and meat soup; for supper bread and tea. I would have starved to death if I hadn't had food from home. But the voyage was all right: I was well except for the first two days but it was boring and the water was poor. One day follows the other until May 5 when we come to land, and on the sixth the ship is at the dock and we debark.

Now the chests have to be opened and inspected and a check, a small brass plate on a leather strap, is fastened to the chest and another one on the owner. We are led to a barge and taken to Castle Garden. And here you may imagine that there was quite a commotion. We walked upstairs and downstairs (carrying our suitcase and bedclothes that you mustn't ever let go of) and we come to the ticket office where we hand over our tickets and are given a small receipt in return. It is very crowded. I have to go far up through the city to the main office to get my railroad ticket; my fellow passengers get theirs in Castle Garden. And then again this damned baggage: we need a new check on the chests and when this is done we go on a barge again to be taken to the railroad station. But what now? Well, my ticket is for another railroad than my fellow passengers. I'm taken to another barge and now I'm with total strangers. The barge takes us far beyond the steam ship docks and we come to the railroad station. We enter the coach and at great speed we go through a long tunnel. We are on the train all night until nine o'clock May 7 when we change trains and continue to Ogdensburg where we get off and are taken on a barge across a river and get on a train on the other side and it is now about three in the afternoon. At six we again change trains and now our journey continues through the night. On May 8 we come to Sault Ste. Marie. Here we have to get off, get new tickets, and continue our journey on the same train.

But I am unlucky at Sault Ste. Marie. Next to the ticket office is a store and I enter and buy a bread for twenty cents. I give them a five dollar bill and am given the correct change (four dollars and eighty cents); I put my wallet in my pocket, pick up my baggage and enter the railroad coach. And here my wallet and my money have disappeared. Someone must have had their fingers in my pocket. There is nothing I can do and now I am without money. I was surely not the first nor the last to have this experience. Luckily I had my ticket and my check in my pocket book. Now the train goes on through the night until we change trains at Cameron in the morning of the nineth and now it isn't far to Eau Clair. But there I'm left standing without knowing where to go. No one had expected me since I had come on the Guion Line. I heard that the agent wasn't home. But listen: ten minutes after I got off the train another one arrives from Chicago with several of those I had left in New York. I still don't know what to do. I see both Norwegians and Swedes at the depot but they don't know Elling Sende. But then I meet someone from Hestegrei in Værdalen and he offers to come with me. I leave my baggage at the depot. We walk down through the town, up one street and down another and we come to Water Street 725 and I enter. The first person I meet is Aunt Guruanna and she says they hadn't expected me yet. The agent had said I wouldn't arrive until Monday and this would have been correct if we hadn't gone on the Guion Line.

Karl and Elling work in the sawmill; they come home for dinner and I meet them. They have three men boarding with them and one of them is Ole Jermstad. I won't write more or make any judgments yet. It seems I'll get work at the sawmill. So this is a brief account of what has happened since I left home and you can now see that I have arrived. It isn't so hot here yet. It is good to come early before the heat gets stronger. I'll write more about conditions here when I've settled in and begun to work. With this, regards from me,

ANDERS LIAN

· —— ·

The shifts in tenses are as in the original. AJL writes *kjæk* (check), the first English word he tries to write. Crossing the river from Ogden took these immigrants into Canada and the train went through Canada to Sault Ste. Marie. His next letter is dated 26 May 1890 (Nor. ed. V:193). «II:246 »II:266 NE V:188

· —— ·

FROM: Martha Erickson, *Grove City, Minnesota, 14 May 1890*

TO: Elsa Haavardsdatter Lothe, *Kinsarvik, Ullensvang, Hordaland*

⁘⟶⟩◉⟨⟵⁘

Dear Sister and family,

I received your dear and welcome letter of August 7 a long time ago and I should have replied earlier. But it isn't so easy for me both because I cannot write myself and because I'm now old. When you have to ask others to do it, it tends to get put off, so I hope you will forgive me—yes, I'm sure you will, dear sister. I was so glad to hear that you and yours are doing well in both worldly and spiritual matters. When we have good health and our daily bread we must admit that we are doing well as far as the world is concerned and we owe gratitude to God. But there is a greater good for us that we cannot fully experience as long as we are in this world but that nevertheless gives us much happiness here, and this is to have peace with God; there is no greater good. This is why your letter makes me so happy. May we often be united in prayer to our Heavenly Father that we will be united in eternal joy in Him where there is no grief and longing. Yes, my dear sister, I often long to come home to Him as I'm getting old. I don't have much to live for but I must accept everything and patiently await the time that God has decided to take us home.

As for worldly matters, I am quite comfortable even though my health is rather poor. I have recently built a house for myself near my daughter so I am well taken care of. But as you know my foot has been painful for a long time. Last winter I was in St. Paul, seventy-five miles away, for three months in the care of a doctor named Bøckmann. This cost 125 dollars but I do not regret it as the wound has healed and I hope that I will be well with the help of God but I must accept what comes. I have no news as everything is as usual. All are well and healthy in my daughter's home and they send their regards. You have asked for their portrait and she asks me to tell you that she will send one as soon as possible. Haaver Mickalson and his family also send their regards. They are in good health and doing well. We have had a good winter but now we have a late and dry spring so things don't look so good. But I assume we will soon have rain. It is all in God's hands.

I have no more to write about. Please give my regards to all my old friends there at home such as Ingeborg and Torbjørg Utne as I always think of that place as a home, and to Margrete Midtun and tell them that I am doing well in body as in soul as I live with my God every day. Dear sister, don't forget me in your prayers but let us often fly on the wings of prayer to Him who has shown the way to bliss for us all without exception and let us hold on to what we have so that no one shall take our crown. And may the name of the Lord be our daily support and may they who seek Him be saved. And with this, my dear sister, I must end my letter with the wish that it may find you and yours well. I would be glad to receive some sentences from you soon. Loving regards from your dear and always faithful sister

MRS. MARTHA ERIKSON

. ——— .

Some of ME's letters may have been dictated to her daughter Annie Oline; in one letter (10 May 1889) she says that her former letter was written by Annie's husband, a Swede. Many immigrants preferred doctors from their own country, not only because of the language but also because they may have had greater respect for a degree from the old country. This doctor was Egil Bøckmann. In later letters (27 May and 26 October 1892) she continues to write about her failing health. Haaver Mickalson was her son. «II:172 NE V:190

. ——— .

1890 — LETTER 2:251

FROM: Elise Wærenskjold, *Prairieville, Texas, 16 May 1890*

TO: Thorvald Dannevig, *Lillesand, Aust-Agder*

⊷⟹⟸⊷

Dear Thorvald!

A thousand and yet a thousand more thanks for your welcome gift that you were so kind to send me and that will be a great pleasure both for me and for my friends. Ouline Reiersen immediately took three books home and my sisters-in-law also took three. I don't know how to thank you for your great kindness to an old lady that you may hardly remember from your childhood. It was such a pleasure to be able to read *Kong Midas* that I so often have read about in the newspapers. I really like Bjørnson's *Paa Guds Veie* much better than *Det flagger* that one of my friends, Oscar Reiersen, once gave me as a New Year's present. I have read a little here and there in *Nordens Natur og Folkeliv* and find it very interesting. But I regret that there is so much use of Swedish and, what is even worse, all the *Landsmaal*. Because although I am Norwegian in body and soul this is really too Norwegian for me and it is actually easier to understand Swedish. The Norwegian rural dialects are so different from one place to another that I cannot imagine how one can use them to construct a language to be understood by all. When emigrants used to come to Four Mile Prairie—the name of the prairie where we live—we often laughed at all the misunderstandings when people from western and eastern Norway spoke together. Everyone came to us and stayed here for a shorter or longer time.

Prospects are poor for our planned reading society. The most intelligent man among the Norwegians at Four Mile has moved to Tyler, a town about fifty miles from here, my brother-in-law now has a job in Dallas, and one man died of the grippe. Moreover, last year was a very bad year for us and it seems that this one will be worse as we've had much too much rain since New Year. On May 3 and 4 we had cloudbursts, hail, and a powerful windstorm that caused great destruction in both fields and gardens. But we must thank God that things were not worse for us since so many others have suffered great damages to their homes and many have lost their lives. In Wills Point only fifteen miles from here two people were killed, the large Methodist church, the schoolhouse, and the depot were destroyed and the other churches and many other buildings were more or less damaged, and things have been worse in many other places. I am anxious for news from Hamilton and Bosque. My oldest son lives in Hamilton and many of my friends in Bosque. I am sure that you understand English so I'm sending you a cutting from a newspaper that Ouline sent me.

Please remember me to your dear mother when you write to her and thank her for her letter. I'll reply to it later. My son Niels may sell his farm and move further west. If so I'll have to leave my old home and move to Otto's. This is not as I wish it but I hope that God does what is best for us. Your faithful and thankful

ELISE WÆRENSKJOLD

Much of this letter is in Clausen 1961, 148–149. Although EW lived at Four Mile Prairie her postal address was Prairieville, across the county line. Thorvald Dannevig was a naval officer. The books he sent were quite recent. Those mentioned are: Gunnar Heiberg's play *King Midas* (1890), Bjørnson's novel *On the Paths of God* (1889), and H. G. Heggtveit's *Scandinavian Nature and Society: A Selection of Poetry and Prose from the Writings of Various Authors* (1880). The most intelligent man at Four Mile Prairie was John Skjolden and EW's brother-in-law was Adolph S. Wattner. «II:223 »II:254 NE V:191

· —— ·

1890 — LETTER 2:252

FROM: Anne Bjorli, *Bue, North Dakota, 19 May 1890*

To: Hans Jørgensen and Eli Johannesdatter Bjøkne, *Lesja, Oppland*

⊷═◌⊏═⊷

Dear parents and siblings!

Thank you for your welcome letter that we received some time ago. We are all well and things here are as usual. Amund is doing spring work. I think he'll have his plowing done today and then only a little harrowing remains. He planted seeds before plowing as this is supposed to be best, especially for oats, and he has been doing oats for a long time. He has planted thirty acres of oats and I don't know how much of wheat. This has been a cold spring. We had a little snow on the seventeenth and yesterday there was some rain; today is much nicer. The soil is dry so rain followed by nice weather would be good.

We're going to Lee tomorrow. This is where there will be a change of mail drivers so we'll have to rent a room and board. Andreas will be taking the route. There is a general store there, so I'll go with Amund to buy some calico for a summer dress and some other trifles. I have almost six dollars of my own money that I've been saving since last fall. I've sold some butter and sewed a little for others and saved every cent. We don't have separate economies because then I would have been impoverished long ago, but it is good not to have to take from your husband's wallet when you're at the store. The last time I went with him we brought butter and eggs and this time we have eggs but they are now only eight cents a dozen. In the beginning of May we began to sell our cream. We have four cows; the fifth has been exchanged for a *pony* for the mail route. He exchanged our two-year-old mare and a cow for two small ponies. Flory, the three-year-old mare that cut herself last fall, is still not quite healed. This spring a Swedish horse doctor has treated the wound, cutting in it and burning it with a red-hot iron, so we must hope that she'll soon be fully restored. We used her for spring work along with the others and she didn't seem to favor her wound and looks quite good.

The boys had a letter from Jøda last winter and she said that Ingri had had an offer of marriage from a man from Lesja. Tell us who if you know of this. Don't let them know that I know about it and you mustn't ask any of their relatives if you haven't heard of it already. Write it on a slip of paper if you know who it was. I'll take good care of the slip of paper because I'm only asking for myself. Is Ingri good with her needle? It seems to me that she is a little slow. We had a letter from her last Saturday and she says that Marit Vangen is all over the place. What about those who were born again last year? If there are many backsliders you must tell me who was converted. Matthias says that some who are of his age have prayed at meetings and I don't know who that could be. Is Jøda Bjorli steadfast? She wrote a long letter to us last year and then I wondered how long it would last with her as she was so eager. I'll have to stop with all this nonsense. It's not long since we had a letter from Jørgen. He was then well. Loving regards to you my parents and siblings from your daughter and sister.

ANNE BJORLI AND HUSBAND

· —— ·

There has probably been a letter about Amund Bjorli getting the contract for a mail route. Andreas was Amund's half-brother, Jøda and Ingri his half-sisters. AB refers to his two half-brothers as "the boys." Matthias was a brother in Lesja. Her brothers Hans and Jørgen were in Minnesota. «II:245 »II:255 NE V:192

· —— ·

1890 — LETTER 2:253

FROM: Anders Johansen Lian (Andrew Lee)
Eau Claire, Wisconsin, 4 July 1890

To: Johan Peter Eriksen, Ingborganna Andersdatter Lian
and Jakob Johansen Lian, *Verdal, Nord-Trøndelag*

⋯⇒◯⇐⋯

Some time ago I received your letter of June 1 where I saw that you were well. I hope these lines will find you in good health. As for myself, my only difficulty is the horrible heat that at times is really a pest. Last week it was so hot that the Fahrenheit thermometer showed more than 100 degrees in the shade. There is no peace to be had night or day and I have no appetite. The sweat runs even when you sit in the shade or at night, and then you may imagine what it's like when you have to work as hard as they do here in America. But this week is a little cooler. Today is the American Independence Day. There is no work and the sawmill keeps closed tomorrow as well. Celebrations began last evening with fireworks in the streets.

It was a sad day when Gustav drowned in the river just below us on June 30. This is how it happened. At the time Elling and Guruanna went to church Karl and Gustav went down to the river to go swimming. At one of the mills there were rafts of boards and planks that were going to be floated down the river. They went out on one and Gustav, who was an excellent swimmer, jumped several times from a raft, swam under water, and came up again. The fourth time he jumped he didn't come up. A message was sent to the church for Elling and many came to search for him but he wasn't found until Monday evening not far from the place of the accident. The funeral was on Tuesday—the next day—and very many people came to follow him to the church and the grave. You will imagine the grief here better than I can describe it. With this Elling and Guruanna send you their message of their son's death.

I had no difficulties with the bells; they lay quietly at the bottom of my chest until I gave them to Ole Jermstad. The police in Hull and New York inspected my things but didn't see the bells; actually I don't think they would have bothered. I bought silver spoons in Trondheim and payed twelve kroner for half a dozen. The agent helped me to buy them and they were very nice. I must end with kind regards to you all from your son,

ANDREW LIAN

As a little illustration of how well informed we can be here in America I can tell you that about three weeks ago I heard a strange story about .... Could it be a lie? Elling laughed when he heard it. I'm not telling you who told me the story.

. ——— .

> The name of the person mentioned in the postscript has been deleted and cannot be read. A letter with such important news would be read by many so it is natural that the identity of the person gossiped about was kept secret. Elling wrote about the death of his son 17 July 1890.
> «II:249 »II:266 NE V:195

. ——— .

1890 — LETTER 2:254

FROM: Elise Wærenskjold, *Prairieville, Texas, 7 July 1890*
To: Thomine Dannevig, *Lillesand, Aust-Agder*

⊹⇒◉⇐⊹

My dear, good Thomine!

Thank you so much for your welcome letters and you must thank your brother for his demonstration of friendship in letting me know of his wife's death. It grieves me; I can well imagine his great loss but it will probably not be so long before he is allowed to come to her. Our hope to gather again with our loved ones in a better world where there is no illness, grief or separation is truly beautiful. How dark and hopeless it would be to look down into the grave if we did not have this happy consolation.

I should have written to you when I received your first letter but I've had so much sorrow since Christmas that I haven't been able to write. Since then my son Niels has kept a mistress and this is so sinful and shameful that it has caused me more grief than all I've been met with in my life. You may imagine that relations between him and his wife are bad but she is not without blame as she is quarrelsome and uses nasty language when she is angry and this is so terrible for the poor children because it has made the three oldest as much aware of their father's indecent relationship as us others. Niels's mistress was a nice girl and I believe she was decent when she came here with her father who last year rented Niels's land and lived in my house. Her mother died in 1888. Niels immediately began to court her and I soon saw that she liked him as well as he liked her and I warned both her and her father because Niels has earlier had an illicit affair; but that one didn't last long because when the girl realized that it was known she was willing to go somewhere else and she became an upright person. But this one rather left her father for the sake of Niels and he has spent at least 300 dollars on her. He and Florida are expecting their seventh child, so he should save what money he has for them rather than throw it away on a lecherous tart. Sadly, there is nothing to indicate that he will give her up. I would like this to be between us but you may tell your brother.

Things are now going well for my son Otto, praise God. All of last year his health was very poor, but he got himself an electric belt and it has performed wonders for him. He says that he feels as young again and can work as well as the next man, and an improved health leads to an improved income. God be praised that I don't have to be ashamed for my oldest son. I plan to visit him as usual this fall and look forward to being away from Four Mile for a while. All of my American friends with the exception of one family have moved and the relative that interested me the most, Johan Skjolden, and his wife and five children have moved to Tyler where their situation has greatly improved. The wife is a daughter of my husband's sister and an exceptionally clever woman. Another who has moved is Otto's mother-in-law. She is now in Kaufman. She was paid 6,000 dollars for her farm and this has been divided between her and her ten adult children. They all got 300 dollars each but they owe her a ten percent interest as long as she lives. Otto's wife was furious. It is so unpleasant at Four Mile now: many houses stand empty, fields are uncultivated, fences are falling down, and orchards are destroyed. The land has been bought for speculative reasons by large financial companies but I don't think they will make much money on it.

On May 3 and 4 we had the worst rain and hailstorm we've had in the forty-three years I've lived in Texas. It caused damage in many counties. In Wills Point, only fifteen miles from here, the depot, the schoolhouse and the best church were all destroyed and three other churches and many buildings were damaged and two people were killed. Many were killed in other places. There has been another disaster in Texas. Last year in Fort Worth they built a Spring Palace. It was very large and extremely beautiful and it was finely decorated on the outside as well as the inside of the building with everything that grows in Texas. All of this was very flammable, so no one was allowed to smoke or have a cigar, but some one had nevertheless dropped a match on the floor and when a boy happened to step on it something caught fire and it spread with great speed. Seven thousand were assumed to be in the building when the fire started but, amazingly, no lives were lost. But the man who worked till the very end saving women and children by lowering them with a rope sacrificed his life for them. When he had lowered the last one he tried to use the rope himself but it was so damaged by the fire that it broke and he and his clothes were so burnt that he died shortly afterward.

We have had a strange winter: when it was supposed to be winter we had spring and for spring we had winter. The peach trees had formed fruit that was all killed by the frost. So this year I will miss having peaches. Now the weather is very dry and warm. The thermometer has shown as much as 100 Fahrenheit. Ouline Reiersen sends her regards. She now lives in Prairieville with her stepson Johan Reiersen and is quite comfortable, but we don't see each other as much as when she lived with Mrs. Knudsen. It is three miles to Prairieville so it is a long walk there and back again in one day and I don't do such things as easily as I used to. I haven't seen Mrs. Pabst since last August. The storm in May caused no damage. Her youngest stepdaughter is happily married and has two children. The other one is at home. We've just had our pastor here with his wife and three children. Five youngsters were confirmed. All you write about old friends and all else from home is of great interest. It would have been so nice to see the old places again. Is the old parsonage in Moland still standing? Give my regards to all who may still have fond memories of me and in particular to your brother Samuel and your sons. Yours faithfully,

ELISE WÆRENSKJOLD

· ——— ·

An edited version of this letter is in Clausen 1961, 146–151: All mention of Niels and his mistress has been omitted. There are two other 1889 letters by EW: an edited version of one to Thomine Dannevig on 23 January is in Clausen 1961, 141–142 and one to an unknown recipient on 25 January repeats much of what she wrote two days earlier. In this second letter she wrote about being lonely in her house which is also inhabited by some of Niels's renters: "For two years a family that I knew well lived here but now some strangers came just after New

Year. They are kind people so I did not lose anything because of the exchange except company. He is a widower with six children, two of them adults. He now and then comes in to me in the evening but he bores me as he only talks about himself and boasts a lot." Thomine Dannevig's brother, Samuel L. Hansen, was a merchant in Lillesand. Electric belts and other quack cures were widely advertised in newspapers, also in Norwegian-American ones. The pastor and his wife were John Knudsen and Bergitte Rystad. «II:251 »II:269 NE V:196

. ——— .

1890 — LETTER 2:255

FROM: Anne Bjorli, *Bue, North Dakota, 11 July 1890*

To: Hans Jørgensen and Eli Johannesdatter Bjøkne, *Lesja, Oppland*

Dear parents and siblings,

Thank you for your welcome letter that we received a long time ago. We are glad to see that you're all well. We are well and living as usual so I suppose I can say that all is well with us. It seems that we'll have a good harvest. The wheat is coming into ear; on one field it's already done. There's been some good rain, enough rain I think, so it has been growing fast once it started to sprout, but it was late coming up because of the cold spring.

I'm spinning some yarn for knitting but I've quite forgotten how to use my spindle so it goes slowly; I don't always fill a reel in a day. I'm knitting stockings for myself, using wool from last fall. I've made two pairs and working on a third. It goes slowly. These are the first pairs I've knitted for myself here. Those I brought with me from home aren't worn out yet so I have no need, but it's good to have some extra. A short while ago I made three shirts, my first. I'll be able to use the trousers I brought with me from home for some time yet. I'm using everything I brought from home. I suppose you're not interested in all this but you'll have to excuse me; I have to fill the paper. Mother and Guro can see how things are with me through these sentences.

Our neighbor Mari Enstad has been in Minneapolis to see a doctor since the beginning of June. Her husband was also there for five weeks. He wouldn't leave his wife until she had been operated on. Her womb was broken in two parts. She was operated on by three doctors. It didn't take long, about one hour, Ole thought. She'll come home at the end of July. She has kept to her bed for one and a half years. It all happened when she gave birth. We've heard that Ole Rise is mad and is in an asylum in St. Peter where he is getting worse rather than better. It is not known over there so don't tell enyone, but I suppose they know it at Rise.

Our drivers began the mail route July 1. Andreas and Matthias Brandli are now the drivers but when winter comes Amund is thinking of driving himself. I suppose we may move to town but I don't really know. With this I'll have to end my simple letter with loving regards to all of you at home from your Anne Bjorli and husband. I had thought that Amund would be writing this time and so I've put it off. But he hasn't written. I suppose I haven't asked him when he's had the time. He'll have to write the next time.

· ——— ·

For her spinning AB used a handheld spindle (*haandrokk*). She seems to have thought that her account of women's work would not interest her father and then adds that her mother and sister may like to read about what she does. In a letter dated 16 August 1890 (unpublished) Amund Bjorli wrote: "I think we'll have a good profit on the mail route if we don't have any accidents. Is there a reliable driver we could get from Norway if we sent the ticket?" «II:252 »II:261 NE V:197

· ——— ·

1890 — LETTER 2:256

FROM: H. Syversen Belle, *Salem, Oregon, 14 August 1890*

TO: Syver Olsen Belle, *Lesja, Oppland*

⊷⫸◑⫷⊶

Dear father!

I received your letter long ago and should have replied before this but I've been quite busy and so I've put it off again and again. I'm now the manager of a *store* that belongs to the wool manufacturing factory in the enclosed photograph. We have all kinds of material as well as ready made clothes, all made in this factory. This building was built last fall and the whole factory costs about 75,000 dollars. It is owned by a company of capitalists that also owns the store where I am the manager. My present salary is twenty dollars a week but I'll soon have 100 a month. The harvest is over, even the threshing for the most part. Wheat gave a good crop and we had about thirty bushels an acre, but I haven't been there since the threshing. Some did even better. A neighbor threshed fifty-five acres of wheat and got fifty-five bushels an acre.

We are all well. I'm sending you a photograph of our three children. Blanche is a big and clever girl, and Claude and Lelah are also growing fast. My wife's sister, *Mrs. Doctor* Holmes, has been visiting us since they returned from Europe in May. The Doctor has his office in Portland and they are building there and will move this fall. I now have six horses, young and old, and I keep two for our wagon in town. We also have a cow in town and three pigs on the farm. The most important building being done here now is the bridge over the Willamette River that was taken by the flood last winter. It will cost 75,000 dollars. I have no other news for you. Hoping to hear from you that you are in good health, I am your devoted son with family,

H. S. BELLE

· ——— ·

«II:235 NE V:199

· ——— ·

1890 — LETTER 2:257

FROM: Karen Solem, *Norden, South Dakota, 12 October 1890*

To: Ole Tobias Ødegaard, *Nannestad, Akershus*

⁂

Dear brother!

Better late than never—so goes the old adage—but I don't know whether I have the right to use it here; I almost have a sense of fear when I now begin to write after so much time has passed since I should have written. This must be because there has been so much I could have written about that I haven't had the time. Now while Daddy and the children are taking an after dinner nap I had planned to scribble a note but my little boy has been so clever that he set the inkwell *upside down*, so I'll have to scrape it clean to have enough ink for one page. Well, right now the weather is so bad—it has rained all day—that all I want to do is sleep.

On July 4 the ladies aid organized a great feast at the Brandt depot with band music, speeches in English and Norwegian, a concert with piano, organ and flute, ball games, dinner and supper; but the best of it all was that we made 100 dollars cash and this means a lot for us who are working in our small way to collect money for a church that we plan to begin building soon. On July 12 Nicolai and Mina moved into the new nice house they had built on grandfather's farm. On the fifteenth we had a *"surprise party"* in their home; this means that their relatives on both sides and some neighbors had decided to surprise them with presents. In the evening after dark you could see wagons approaching on the road with presents and boxes with the most delicious food, including a baked turkey and a delicious cake. They knew nothing about it and were very surprised. The house was quickly invaded and you could say furnished: a huge dining table—a gift from two uncles—was brought in and instantly laid. And then we had a wedding feast through the whole night with between sixty and seventy people and the gifts were worth about ninety dollars. Mina's father gave them a Garland stove that doesn't have its equal on the entire prairie and it cost more than forty dollars. Then all went at its usual pace until October 2 when Mina gave birth to a son who will be christened in two weeks when also Mina's parents will have a daughter christened. (Now I've been really good getting all of this down in one sitting, so now I need a break.)

It is already late fall so it is best to be prepared for the tough winter. They should have had the threshing done around here but then this rain came and stopped it for some time. I've again done a little house *fixing*; I've painted the small room that I need as a kitchen in winter and I've painted and papered the living room that now is quite comfortable. When we've been to town and picked up the new stove that we've decided to buy this fall and placed it in our small kitchen it'll be quite nice for me. Then I'll begin sewing and this will take my time until Christmas as I've been to two different towns this fall and bought the material for a lot of clothes. I'm sending pieces of the material for my and the children's dresses; the reddish brown one is mine and the checkered one for the children; mine cost sixty cents a yard, the children's fifty cents. I got them to reduce the price by fifteen cents a yard for both pieces. I'll decorate them with silk ribbons in corresponding colors. I'll get Mina to help me with the sewing as she is quite a *dressmaker*. She has sewn a very nice *capote* for Marie of red silk with ruching. Amalie, you will understand that these words are for you.

Now that I've written about big things and small I should perhaps think of concluding. Give my regards to all relatives and acquaintances; don't forget Holth in Stensgaard. If mother comes to visit give her my regards as well. Greetings to Sigurd and Olaf from Marie and Nordt and, finally, greetings to you both from Louis and your always devoted

KAREN

· ⸻ ·

Although KS begins her letter criticizing herself for not writing more often she was a very active correspondent. On 21 September 1890 she wrote to her mother that she would have to conclude in order to write two other letters that same day. Her letters are sent from post offices in both Norden and Brandt, two small towns in Deuel County. The Lutheran church in Norden was built the next year and belonged to the United Church. A photograph shows a very plain wooden building without a tower surrounded by flat prairie land. Garland Stoves were manufactured in the late 1800s through 1955 by the Michigan Stove Company. KS wrote "*rushing*," a term as unfamiliar in Norwegian as the correctly spelled "ruching," a gathered strip of fabric used for trimming. There is no way of knowing how long a break she took writing this letter; it may have been some minutes, it may have been several days. KS wrote to her mother over several days beginning on 28 December and continuing on 19 January 1891 (Nor. ed. V:208). She also wrote a brief note to her mother on 4 December offering to send tickets to her and her stepfather if they wished to emigrate. «II:247 »II:259 NE V:203

· ⸻ ·

1891 — LETTER 2:258

FROM: Halvor Hansen Ulsness, *Glenwood, Minnesota, 24 January 1891*

To: Nils Andreas Olsen Brusli, *Tørdal, Drangedal, Telemark*

Niels A. O. Bruseli,

It seems that our correspondence has been shelved and forgotten. This is unacceptable. We'll have to take it up again. For my part I long to hear from you and other relatives and acquaintances in our dear Tørdal. First of all I want you to know that I and my family are all doing well and are in good health. My son Hans is in a town called Morris about twenty miles from here where he has worked for a storekeeper for half a year. To begin with he earned ten dollars a month when he didn't go to school but during winter when he goes to school he has no pay but free room and board (everything free except for books that he has to pay for) and he only works in the morning and evening and Saturdays. Last fall school began September first. Next spring he'll come home and live with us until summer. Signe has been away during summer but is at home this winter. She was confirmed last year in Glenwood. Mari goes to English school. The schoolhouse is on the land next to mine. Our son's daughter Helle is thriving and often asks to go to school with Mari.

You may remember that I had trouble for a long time with my quarter section that I have lived on for almost three years. The first two court decisions gave me right to the land. Finally, the other party appealed to a higher court and, can you imagine, to everyone's surprise they gave him the prior right to the land. This happened one year before last fall but all who are disinterested agree that this is *humbug* and that money has changed hands. I had to go to another lawyer who has been a candidate for Congress and who is said to be the best educated Scandinavian. His name is Knute Nelson. He looked into my case and said that it would cost me a lot and that I should first try to settle out of court and the other fellow finally renounced his right in return for a payment of 900—nine hundred—dollars. So the land is now mine and with God's help I hope to live in peace on it for the rest of my life.

We have been doing well as I have two good houses, good water and a short distance to town, less than two miles. I have two horses (seven years old next spring), a two-year-old foal, twelve head of cattle (big and small), two sheep, two pigs and about forty chickens. I don't have much farm machinery, only a mowing machine, a breaking plow, a harrow, and a wagon, but next spring I'll buy a seeder that will cost about fifty dollars. Last year was very dry so our crop was small, from ten to twenty bushels an acre. We've had nice weather this winter and there has been no snow yet so we still use our wagon.

Halvor Nordboe and Halvor Teigen visted us a year ago last fall. Margit asks me to send special greetings to your mother. Please also give our regards to Stigen and Homli and tell Lars Tvedt that I'm waiting for a letter from him. And give our regards to all our old acquaintances in Tørdal that you may meet. Last year I had a brief note from Andreas O. Porsmyr and I wrote to him but haven't heard anything since then. Give our regards to Ole and his family. Yes, dear Nils, write me a long letter filled with all kinds of news as soon as you get this. I would also like to know about those whose economic situation has changed since we left. In conclusion, my most loving regards to you and your family and your mother if she still lives. Your sincere friend,

HALVOR H. ULSNÆSS

Margit is HHU's wife. HHU wrote *storkiper* (storekeeper), *trubel* (trouble), and *sider* (seeder). «II:216 »II:276 NE V:212

1891 — LETTER 2:259

FROM: Karen Solem, *Norden, South Dakota, 1 February 1891*

TO: Amalie Ødegaard, *Nannestad, Akershus*

My dear Amalie!

It is Sunday evening and I've just put the children to bed and now I'll try to put together a few sentences for you. First I must thank you so much for your dear letter that arrived two weeks ago and you must also give my thanks to Tobias for the card I received for Christmas. I was so glad to hear that all is well with you and with mother; this is the best news I can have from Norway. All is well with us now but both Marie and Nordt have been quite ill after Christmas. They are now much better and just as good and clever as before. We've had very nice weather all winter until a few days ago when the cold arrived with a powerful north wind along with some snow flurries. We don't really have snow yet. Christmas has been peaceful and quiet; we've only been away visiting two or three times. At Fella they had a great party on January 20 for Carl's twentieth birthday. I suppose I should call it a ball as all the young people in our neighborhood, between fifty and sixty persons including a few children, were there. We were the only relatives.

We have been waiting for a letter from mother since we offered to send them tickets and we are now anxious to learn whether they have decided to come. We are sending you a few photographs (one from Johan to you two and one from us for mother). They are much too ugly to send to Norway but they are just for you and you mustn't show them to strangers. If mother has decided to emigrate she can give the photograph to whomever she wishes. I should perhaps explain the pictures but I think you will guess who they are. With Johan are his family, Louis and myself, Nicolai and Mina, Olaus, and Carl Fella who is sitting on the sulky plow in the background. In our picture you will see all the above and grandfather in his rocking chair, his sister Marie on another chair and right behind her, her son Christian Holter and in front of the door are Carl Fella, Almer Fella on a horse and, finally, little Ida Kjønstad, Mina's sister. We are all smiling rather nicely in the morning sun. I have visitors today too. *Miss* Johanne Hansen has returned and I think she'll stay a few days, but she is so engrossed in my English magazine *The Housekeeper* that I may as well write as I can't get a word out of her. Her parents are from Nannestad—Thorvald Hansen Lerberg and Dorthea Aanesruddalen; mother knows them well. They are a nice family; it is a pity that they live seven miles from us. I should have had much more to write about but I think I've forgotten it all. So I may as well conclude with my most loving regards to you from all of us, especially from Johan and Louis. Yours forever devoted

KAREN

PS: Thank you so much for the photograph. The little boys are so handsome that it is a delight to see them. Give our regards to all friends and acquaintances. The Indians are still very restless but we are in no danger as they are about 300 miles from us.

FROM AMERICA TO NORWAY

Per Falla had been married to the deceased Martea, KS's sister-in-law. Carl and Almer were two of their eight children. She no doubt thought of the photographs as "ugly" because they had not been dressed up in their best clothes. The photographs as described are rather typical Midwestern immigrant photographs showing off the house as well as furniture and farm implements. On 21 September the previous year KS wrote about this photograph: "We took a photograph of the house with the family outside last summer but it was done in such a hurry and we were so unprepared that it is not at all nice and Laurits says that I mustn't send anything so ugly to Norway." The massacre at Wounded Knee on 29 December 1890 marked the end of the wars against the Indians in this part of the country. «II:257 »II:270 NE V:214

1891 — LETTER 2:260

FROM: Gulbrand Rundhaug, *Milton, North Dakota, 10 February 1891*

To: Torgrim Ellingsen Elsrud, *Aadalen, Ringerike, Buskerud*

Dear friend,

As I now have time I'll write you some words, not because I have any news but for old friendship's sake and in the hope of getting a letter from you in return. I'll first tell you about our situation here now and it is bad. I'm in debt for about 800 dollars. The reason is that we have hardly had any crops for three years in a row because of drought, so times are difficult for people around here. I have 320 acres and ten miles from here I have ten acres of forest that I've bought from Iver Elsrud. I also have two horses that I've bought from him for 400 dollars. I owe Iver 300 dollars. Iver is owed about 7,000 dollars from people around here so he has done well in America, built himself nice houses and is good and helpful to all. He now has eight horses. I have eight cows and a selfbinder that I use with three horses. I have a seeder, a wagon, a harrow, and two plows. Our three little boys, Fred, Olavus and Gustav, are growing and thriving. Our home is built of sod and well lined with straw. Our stable is also built of sod but our granary is made of planks. My father owes Elsrud 100 dollars and that is all his debt. He has 160 acres, three draft oxen, four cows, a wagon, a harrow and two plows. Old Onstad is also my neighbor. He has a lot of land and much cattle but he has a large debt. The land is flat as far as you can see. We see no forest. It doesn't take much time to break land if you have good horses for your plow. And you may imagine that harvesting is quickly done here. One man with a selfbinder and three good horses can cut twenty acres a day. All the wheat is ripe at the same time and then it is important to get it down.

We live in constant fear of the Indians as they have begun to kill the whites. They have already killed and scalped many white people. They burn them alive in the most terrible manner. The soldiers are out to stop them and they have slaughtered many, and all people in Dakota who don't have guns are given them by the government. They are bad people; red as blood and worse than wild animals.

I could have sent greetings from many acquaintances. Please give my regards to your father and mother and to your brother Ole and to all acquaintances but first and foremost you are greeted from me and my family,

GULBRAND RUNDHAUG

Please write and tell me all the news you know and if there is anything you wish to know I'll tell you even though I suppose you get letters from Iver. Gulbrand Norby and a girl from Aadalen are now working for Iver. He has 800 acres and his house is made of fine planks that we call flooring. I must end now. I hope these words find you in good health and good spirits.

· —— ·

GR was from a croft at Rundhaug and emigrated in 1879. His father was Fingal Palmesen. Iver Elsrud was Torgrim Elsrud's brother. For a discussion of attitudes toward Native Americans in immigrant letters see Øverland 2009. Hansen 2013 is an excellent book on relations between Norwegian immigrants and Native Americans. NE V:215

· —— ·

1891 — LETTER 2:261

FROM: Anne Bjorli, *Lakota, North Dakota, 1 March 1891*

To: Hans Jørgensen and Eli Jørgensdatter Bjøkne, *Lesja, Oppland*

⊷⇒◉⇐⊷

Dear parents and siblings!

Thank you for your letter that we received some time ago. We are happy to see that you are all well. We are also well. Winter has arrived with lots of snow so we can use our sleigh. The mail driver has used a sleigh for two days. Elise is happy. She is a little restless but she likes to be with her mother. All I have time to do is for what she needs. I've been crocheting shirts for her. They were of fine woolen yarn. To begin with I used cotton but she now has woolen clothes next to her skin. Before she was born I knitted a fine white woolen shirt. Guro Haugen left us long ago. She has written to me but they weren't married then. I'm expecting another letter. She received a letter and a photograph from her parents while she was with us. Amund has also had one from his parents and Brit Ensrud is now with us and she also has one of her parents. I wish you would have your photographs taken so we could have one of my parents. Yes, please do this while you have a photographer so near. Guro, you must also have yours taken so we can have one of you, Jakob and Matthias too. Kristen Kornkveen gave me such a nice album so I would love to have photographs of all of you.

Brit Ensrud has been with us a week. She is attending English school. The woman she worked for went away on a visit so she will stay here until she is back and she helps me a little so I don't pay her anything while she is here. We've also had another girl here for three days but she left today. She knew us from the time we lived on the farm.

March 1—I must complete my letter today. All is well. It has been rather cold this week. Guro asked me to enclose pieces of the material for Elise's dresses in a letter but I forgot this the last time I wrote. You'll have them this time. Marit Bjokne sent us the white and checkered material that I used for her christening dress. The one marked with a G is from Guro Haugen. Most of the others were given by people you don't know so I won't list their names. When I mail this I'll also send a ribbon to Guro. If she gets it I'll send another one to mother later.

I see that Jakob has thought of going to America next spring. If he goes to Minnesota I'll go down to see him. This winter we've talked about my making such a trip next summer and I'll be sure to do so if Jakob comes so I can hear from you there at home. It is easier for me to do this now. If Elise comes with me Amund can manage on his own for a while. If you go Jakob, be sure to have some spending money. Many things are good to have for comfort on the journey. It was good to have a coffee pot and some roasted and ground coffee on the voyage. We didn't regret having it with us on the ship as the coffee they have there was tasteless. They can also bring some food because what they serve onboard is almost inedible. We also liked to have unleavened bread and it kept for as long as we had any left.

Regards from your daughter and son-in-law and my dear child. Please send us photographs of parents and siblings. I'll send you ours next summer. We must go to Grand Forks. I made two dresses for Elise of the white material before she was born. I'll sew three more next summer. I've made more dresses of calico than the enclosed samples but I don't have the material. The white woolen cloth was given to Elise for a skirt by a girl from Sel.

· ——— ·

The last paragraph was written in margins. AB's brother Hans Bjokne (married to Marit) wrote on 13 February 1891 (Nor. ed. V:216) promising to send a ticket for his brother Jakob and advising him to come as early in spring as possible because he needed help on his farm. He had a hired man but he "will drive cream to a butter factory we have here and cannot do work on the farm all summer." His brother Jørgen was cutting lumber for a new cowbarn. AB's husband, Amund, wrote to his parents-in-law on 11 May 1891, mentioning Anne's plans to visit her brothers in Minnesota. He wrote that he now made more on the mail route than on the farm. Kristen Guttormsen Kornkveen and Guro Eriksdatter Haugen married in 1889. «II:255 NE V:218

· ——— ·

FROM AMERICA TO NORWAY

FROM: Iver Andersen Lee, *Mayville, North Dakota, 2 March 1891*

TO: Anders Andersen and Anders Olsen Lie, *Hedalen, Sør-Aurdal, Oppland*

⊷≡◑◒≡⊷

Dear brother and old father and relatives and friends,

Time passes like a rapid stream and we, as the foam, must follow it in its wild course down roaring rapids, into whirling backwaters and then out on quiet pools where we are given a little time to collect our thoughts and cast an eye of remembrance on what we have experienced—on what is behind us. Life is now in a quiet phase. We are enclosed by winter and it forces inactivity upon us so we have more time to contemplate what we have neglected. I see that I should have written to you before and I am overwhelmed by a sense of shame. But please forgive me as it is not my ill will but my weakness that is the cause. It is so easy to put off things and then there are real obstacles and time passes and my intentions remain unfulfilled. But I mustn't get stuck in useless speculations on what has passed.

I live on the land I bought; last winter Iver Børtnes and Iver Bertilrud were with me but as you surely have heard, Iver Bertilrud died of typhoid fever last year, on March 16. He was a genuinely good man, excellent company, and a loyal friend. I miss him very much. May his memory be blessed. After his death I was alone for two months but then, on May third, I entered into matrimony with one of the neighbor girls. Her name is Karen Syversen and she was born and grew up in Brandval, about seven miles from Kongsvinger. She came to America with her parents eight years ago; her mother died three years ago but her father still lives. She has three brothers— two are married and one lives fifteen miles away and the other twenty miles and the bachelor lives near us—and three married sisters who all live near us, one as our neighbor. She is twenty-five years old, short and quite fat. We both enjoy good health. You may be asking how long we celebrated our wedding. My answer is that it is not so usual to have weddings here. Most marriages are performed with only two witnesses and the official who does the necessary formalities; this can be a pastor or a civil officer such as a judge or a justice of the peace. Our witnesses were the father of the bride and a brother-in-law and we were married by Pastor Allen of the Norwegian Synod.

Since last fall we had excellent winter weather until about two weeks ago and since then we have had snowstorms and cold weather. We had an average crop last year, for me and this area perhaps a little less than average. There was little rain during spring but more later in the summer and for awhile it looked quite promising but in the ripening period we had such an intense heat that much of the wheat dried up without getting ripe and this caused considerable damage in many places. We all got plenty of hay. In all I had 1,475 bushels of wheat, 140 bushels of oats, 80 bushels of barley, and 15 bushels of potatoes. I cannot give you the precise amount of hay but I have enough to feed my stock: four horses, two cows and a heifer. I've sold hay for thirty-five dollars. A man's annual income is decided by the size of his crop and the prices he gets. I don't sell any barley or oats as we use this to feed our horses and hogs. I don't even have enough and will have to buy about 100 bushels of oats to help me until the next threshing. For my own use for seed and flour I need about 170 bushels of wheat, so I can sell about 1,300 bushels. Early last fall, before we had done the threshing, the wheat prices were very good, up to ninety-six cents a bushel. But it then went down to seventy-five, a price that remained stable for about a week. I was still busy doing my fall plowing so I didn't get to town to sell more than 200 bushels before the price went further down and stopped at sixty-five cents. In this period I hauled and sold about 150 bushels before I quit and borrowed money on what I had left, hoping that the price would go up again. So now I have between 900 and 1,000 bushels unsold and I don't think I'll sell until after I've done my spring plowing and planting. I can't yet say just what my income will be in money for this year but I think I should be able to make more than 400 dollars after interest and expenses.

I had a letter from Wisconsin a couple of weeks ago. Siri has been bed-ridden since she gave birth this winter but is now better. Otherwise all was as usual. I can also tell you that I visited the Bertilrud people at their new homestead last fall. Syver was here doing harvest work and when he was to return home I decided to take a team of horses and go with him. They live about 150 miles from here and it took us almost five days to get there. I thought the landscape was quite pleasant so I think their prospects are pretty good. But everything is still too new to say anything for sure about what the future will bring; but at least they have hopes.

Apart from visiting the Bertilrud family my plan was to buy fish from the Indians and bring it back home. There is a large lake about forty miles from where the Bertilruds live. By this lake there is a large number of Indians who do a lot of fishing in the lake. I went to them and bought about 1,200 pounds of fish for two cents a pound. On my return I sold it for from six to eight cents a pound. I made *rakfisk* with some of it and it is now ready for eating and I haven't had *rakfisk* since coming to America. The Indians were rather nice people to visit. I had never been near their homes nor seen more than individual Indians before this. They live together in groups or in villages, partly in tents and partly in log houses. In most of their homes they had a stove but in some there were fireplaces. I must say that it was really nice to see a fireplace again, because I haven't seen one since I left you. The fire burned so brightly in their fireplace that I really felt at home. They had no chairs or anything else to sit on, nor did they use beds; they sat and they slept on the bare floor. There was quite a lot of trouble with the Indians last fall and winter and they've rebelled in many places; the government has made regular war against them. There have been several battles and several hundreds have fallen on both sides, but mainly Indians. There has been no uprising where I visited, but they are said to have done their so-called war dances some time after I was there and that caused quite a scare in the area where the Bertilruds live. In addition quite a few exaggerated and some completely false rumors were in circulation and this made the situation look much worse. Many left their cattle and homes behind and fled from the area. But the scare subsided when the exaggerations and false-hoods were revealed. The government is responsible for the unrest among the Indians. They are in a way the wards of the government. They do not farm the land but have fed themselves by fishing and hunting. So as the land has gradually been taken from them, their sources of livelihood have diminished and as compensation the government has agreed to supply them with food and clothes. This is done through government agents but these have been under so little control that they've made themselves wealthy at the Indians' expense. So the Indians have often suffered from hunger and this is what has led them on the warpath. It seems quite reasonable that they would rather fight for survival than die of starvation.

I see in your letter that you, brother Anders, have remarried. I must therefore wish you all luck and it is my hope that this time you will have a longer happiness in your marriage than the first time. It is my hope and my heartfelt wish that your good fortune will continue and that you will not again be overwhelmed by grief and adversity. Dear father! In concluding this letter I hope that it will find you satisfied with your life. I know that you have long been sitting by life's exit waiting for it to be opened by the gracious hand of

God. But I know that this last period of trials can be alleviated by every word of comfort and encouragement you have from us and I am therefore painfully aware that I haven't done my duty. Please forgive me and be ensured that my loving thoughts are always with you. May God grant you strength to wait in patience. With this, regards from us all for this time. Sincerely,

IVER A. LIE AND WIFE

. ——— .

IAL wrote *justis of the pease* and explained it with reference to a similar office in Norway. Their pastor was Hans Allen who was born in Iowa in 1863 and was pastor in Portland, N. Dak. 1886–1892. In Wisconsin, Siri was the wife of IAL's brother Ole. *Rakfisk* is fish, usually trout, that has gone through a two- to three-month fermenting process and then is eaten without further cooking. IAL's account of his visit to these Native Americans is discussed in Øverland 2009, 79–103. In Hedalen, IAL's brother Anders had married Inger Olsdatter Finnhert who had been housekeeper at Søre Li after his first wife had died. «II:242 »II:275 NE V:219

. ——— .

1891 — LETTER 2:263

FROM: Svend Larsen Houg, *Elgin, Iowa, 9 March 1891*

To: Ole Larsen Haug, *Aal, Buskerud*

⊶⟹⟸⊷

Beloved brother,

You have yet again written to me and this time I was surprised to receive a message from you. Thank you so much for your letter of the third that I received on the twenty-fifth of the same month. It is strange how God governs all things so that we may still hear from each other after thirty-nine years of separation. I am glad to hear that God maintains you in his grace and the true, living faith in the precious blood of his son Jesus Christ. For he who loves the word of God loves God, for God is in and with his word and God who began a good work in you will bring it to completion.

If I should say something of my children the picture would be too dark, in particular of some of the youngest for whom nothing but worldly wisdom, and politics, and sensuousness seem to be their entire religion, as it is for most young people here. (I hope it is better where you are.) But God has the power to wake up children from these stones. When I look at myself I am the greatest sinner but God be praised who has let me see and realize that I am a lost and condemned sinner but have been saved in Christ and in faith in his blood. For Christ has suffered for my sins, indeed for all sin in the world. May God through his Holy Spirit help me believe and hold on to this until my blessed end. But I am often weak as the devil shoots his glowing arrows at a Christian. But when we are given to wear the armor of which Paul speaks, the helmet of salvation, and the sword of the Spirit, which is the word of God, he will not be able to harm us with his cunning and artifice.

There have been some changes in this house since I last wrote. Assor, who owns the farm, was married last May. Guri went last fall to join her sister Ragnil. They are in a town called Mayville and their work is to sew clothes for women. They visited Ingrid and Elling Dokken last winter. Elling visited us last Christmas and they are doing well. Knud and his wife still live here. His wife has been ill these last four years and is now and then a little better. They have experienced the trials this world may offer us but she has learned the meaning of both sin and grace. They haven't been able to use their farm for two years, so Assor has used it. Elling will probably leave us and go west where Ole is a farmer. I assume he will try to find himself a home. But they tell me nothing. Kittil and the younger Ole do the same work they have done for many years. All you know from Groth are alive as far as I know, but I haven't heard anything from Assor or from St. Ansgar for some time. But I know that the Seminary in St. Ansgar is going with renewed strength and now has three excellent teachers.

Now I must conclude as my memory fails me and I know that I have often thought and said that this is my last letter, but this time this must be so as this is what our age tells us. So thank you for all the time we were together and the time we have been separated. May God protect me so that I may not be as the foolish maidens who only had their lamps but not the oil of faith. You, O God, will hear and grant my prayer for the sake of Jesus Christ. There are but a few steps left to us before we are gathered again, not in this vale of tears but in the mansion of joy. And with this my loving regards to you and yours. Your old brother,

SVEND L. HOUG

I don't know whether you will be able to read what I've written as I can only see a little with one eye. But thanks be to God for what is. I can read in the light of day. Lord, strengthen us in our faith. Grace and peace be with you in Jesus Christ. This is the apostolic salutation. Should you receive this you must try as well as you can to understand it.

. ——— .

SLH wrote to his brother on 3 August 1889 while visiting his daughter Ingrid and her husband, Elling Dokken, in Polk County, Minn. His daughter Ragnil was also there. Mayville, where Guri and Ragnil worked, is in Traill County, N. Dak. SLH uses phrases from Philippians 1:6, Ephesians 6, and Matthew 25:1–13. «II:220 NE V:221

. ——— .

1891 — LETTER 2:264

FROM: Nels T. Olson, *Callender, Iowa, 26 March 1891*

TO: Tor Olsen Bakken, *Aamotsdal, Seljord, Telemark*

⋯⇒◯⇐⋯

Dear brother,

As today is Maundy Thursday I will let you hear from us again and can first let you know that we are in good health and doing well and that we wish to hear the same from you. Health is one of the greatest worldly benefits we can wish for and we are far from sufficiently grateful for this. I should have written long ago but I have delayed it for too long. Thank you for your welcome letter and the nice photographs. It was a true pleasure to see you again. We were sad to hear that you haven't been so well and that Anne still has her headaches. It would have been great fun to talk face to face with you again as well as with our dear father but the journey is far too long and difficult to embark on now when we have so many small children. But it may be that I come home to see my old fatherland Norway in some years if all goes well. But I wouldn't come to stay but to see and speak with friends. I find it strange that Tallef won't write to me since he gets around so much and should have much of interest to tell me. When you see him you must urge him to write without delay. If you see Anund you must also ask him to write. I'll send him our photographs as soon as I get a letter from him. Perhaps he could best tell me about Møstrand. I suppose he lives somewhere there. I wrote to Gisle asking him to come if he had enough money and that Svanaug should do the same and I assured them that they would do better here than as crofters there at home. I also told them I was glad I had come to America.

I don't have much news so I'll tell you a little about our winter. It has been quite nice and not so cold. After February 1 we had enough snow for sleighs. There is still a little snow but not enough for sleighs. Spring is somewhat late. At this time we usually begin to plant oats but we can't do this for some weeks as the soil is covered with snow, ice and water. Anund and Margit Myrbøen are visiting and Anund will stay here this summer as I can't manage all my work alone. They ask me to give their regards to you and your wife and to dear grandfather. We now have another girl. She is one month old and was christened Anne after a sister of Aase's father. And now I must take you by the hand and say goodbye. Farewell Tor, Anne, and dear father and live well in God from me and my wife.

NELS OLSON TORVETJØNN

· ——— ·

NTO emigrated from Møstrand in 1879. His father was Ole Olsen Torvetjønn (written Torvetjern). Tor Olson was married to Anne Vetlesdatter Bakken and took the name of her farm. Tallef, Anund, Gisle, and Svanaug (married to Jon Jonsen Neset) were siblings. NTO's signature varies. He had been Nils in Norway. In a letter to Svanaug on 20 June 1906 he explained his American name: "The reason why I write N. T. Olson and not Nels O. Torvetjern is that the Americans can hardly pronounce Torvetjern. But I am so fond of my old name that I took the T from Torvetjern and placed it between my names, as you can see." «II:143 »II:272 NE V:222

· ——— ·

From: Jacob Larsen Urheim, *Chicago, Illinois, 30 April 1891*

To: Jakob Rasmussen Sandvik, *Kinsarvik, Ullensvang, Hordaland*

Dear cousin Jacob R. Sandvik,

I was glad when I saw that you finally had broken your silence and sent me a letter. After I started reading I soon realized why you wrote, so thank you for the letter. It is good to revive old friendships now and then and to hear how things are at home. I already knew that your old father had gone to his final rest. I suppose my aunt is quite old now. Indeed, I feel that my best years are behind me. I already have some grey hairs. This is our fate in life—at least I'm no longer young; the struggle of life has robbed me of enjoyment while there are no milestones that interrupt the flow of your years as I see from your letter that you haven't even married. Well, I don't have any advice concerning this, not even to get married to a rich girl and become a slave. But when I look back on the past I don't remember all that many rich girls who were ready to marry a poor boy even though he might be the best in the world.

To come to America <u>now</u>, after all your best years have been spent at home, to break a new path and take up the struggle for existence in a new country—this must be carefully considered before giving any advice on changing your address, especially when it is from one continent to another. I for my part have gotten so used to American conditions that I don't think I would get along at home for any length of time. Things are better for me here now as I have embarked on a new career. As you may have heard I have passed my final exams to be licensed as a doctor and I have begun my practice as a physician here in Chicago.

You wanted to know how I felt about my father's marriage. In short, my answer is that it is pointless. Father has his daughter Syniva to take care of him. I don't care whether father was thinking of getting rich or not and I wrote to him that she was probably good enough for him, but I didn't understand why he would wish to share his poverty with anyone. As for what I then wrote to him, this was his concern alone, and it isn't my fault that people thought he was getting so much from here. I've never written to anyone about what I sent or didn't send. That I have said that I would help either Johannes or him and Syniva to keep the farm is true. But consider that I've had to pay about 1,500 dollars for tuition to medical school and room and board and have just begun to have an income. Lars has a salary of 720 dollars and Torstein is also making good money, so we have hoped to be able to clear all debt on the farm for our brother. But our Christian love will not suffice if father wants to involve another in his life because it will cause unavoidable confusion when two interests are joined together. But I don't care that he is angry and complains about what I've written since I'm here. He thought it was wrong of me to write that a tie had been broken when mother died but that was the truth, and you know father well enough to know that I merely told him the truth. The phrase old billygoat horns is an old saying about old widowers who are eager to get married, and that I used the old adage, "Young and wild may easily be forgiven but old and wild is the work of the devil," actually suits the case because when an old man is anxious to get married then it seems that nothing can stop him. And father must accept that we say that he was a swine in his behavior to our mother as well as to us because—this is the truth. Of course we know that it isn't a crime, but the question is whether it is a wise decision for a sixty-six-year-old man to enter into wedlock. My experience is that this is wrong and I think that I've seen enough of life to say this. It may be an excuse that father is afraid that he hasn't been able to keep his children at home so that they could help him. He knows that Syniva's health will not allow her to go anywhere else.

Father believes that Marta's money will see both of them through. I know nothing of what she may have but I do know that I would rather see father lose the farm than that he should involve someone else in these affairs since a stepmother is usually a stepmother, especially when she has her own children. Whatever other people may have said, I'm sure that father's relatives have told him what they think. All I know is that Lars heard about it from one of his friends. My siblings haven't dared to write about it and this confirms that he is the same tyrant that he has always been. I'll help my sister to come here should father marry. Will you please read this letter aloud to my father and if he should misunderstand anything then tell him to understand it as it is written: a protest from his children against his wedding madness. Friendly regards to you, your mother, your sister and your brother. Your devoted

DR. J. L. URHEIM

JLU was a pharmacist in Harmony, Minn., before becoming a doctor. He later became a professor at Bennet Medical College in Chicago. Jakob Rasmussen Sandvik's father was Rasmus Svendsen Sandvik and his widow, JLU's aunt, was Gyrid Jakobsdatter Sandvik. Johannes was JLU's youngest brother. JLU's father was Lars Jakobsen Urheim. The marriage that upset his son does not seem to have taken place. In a letter from Eau Claire, Wisc., dated 3 October 1892, JLU's brother Lars Larsen Urheim was even more upset about his father's marriage. Here he also wrote about his brother Torstein's illness and death. «II:198 NE V:225

1891 — LETTER 2:266

FROM: Andrew Lee, *Eau Claire, Wisconsin, 3 May 1891*

TO: Jakob Johansen Lian, *Verdal, Nord-Trøndelag*

Dear brother!

I received your letter a couple of weeks ago and see that you are in good health and doing well. I can say the same for myself. I suppose you know that I came down from the forest at the end of March and then I had nothing to do for about a month. I have now worked at the sawmill for about a week. I have light work this summer and this is nice but the hours are far too long as it is a little too much to work eleven hours a day with one hour off for dinner. Well, I think things will go well this summer and I was lucky to get such light work.

You write that you haven't thought of going to America. Even though I can say that I like it much better here than I had imagined when I was in Norway I would not advise you to come here because things can be so different. Some don't like it here, others get sick, and others get hurt in different ways. I've been lucky and haven't experienced any of this but it may happen to anyone. The pay is good, especially in winter. One dollar a day is common and many have thirty to thirty-two dollars a month and more for experienced workers. During summer it is not as good and for common work in the mills it is thirty-six dollars a month and when you have paid thirteen dollars for room and board and another dollar for laundry you don't have much left. This is for common work in the mills, but you can make more working for the railroads and other kinds of work. So you will have to make up your own mind. If you come, I will help you as much as I can but I would rather that you didn't come.

The weather is nice. Fields and trees are beginning to get green but soon the heat will be a bother. Give my regards to old friends and, finally, my greetings go to you from me,

ANDREW LEE

· —— ·

In a short letter from an Empire Lumber Camp near Hayward, Wisc., on 24 January 1891 (Nor. ed. V:211) he wrote about his new name: "I wonder whether you soon could write my name Andrew Lee on your letters to me since I have difficulties in getting the letters as no one here knows me as Anders Lian." There is a sharp contrast between AL's detailed letters about his emigration journey and the later ones. He wrote frequently but briefly and he often writes either that he has nothing to write about or that things are so different in the United States that there is no point in writing about them. Other short letters from 1891 are dated 18 January, 1 February, 20 June, 26 July, 31 August, 3 October, 1 November, and 25 December. Winter wages in the lumber camps would be in addition to room and board. In farming areas, wages were considerably higher in summer than in winter. AL uses the English word "common" twice, spelling it *komment*. «II:253 »II:281 NE V:226

· —— ·

FROM: Olianna Hanson, *Necedah, Wisconsin, 5 May 1891*

TO: Marie Olsdattter Vigerust, *Dovre, Oppland*

Dear Sister,

I had a letter from you some time ago and see that you are well and this is also the case with us. Ole Lee has just received a letter from home and I see that they are coming here but that they haven't sold what they have yet, but I don't think they should delay their journey for that reason. They should come as soon as possible. I am glad to hear that my sister Ragnhild is coming and it would be good if you all came. If they have some combs for weaving or a tailor's scissors they should bring them. Also bring bedclothes and woolen skirts. If you have any material for dresses bring it as it is. If you haven't made shoes then only bring what you need for the journey. It is silly to have such things made. Don't bring white cotton shirts for the men as they only use dark shirts here. I must now end these lines with loving regards to you all from all of us, in particular from your sister,

OLIANNA

OH's cousin Anne Norsby (Nørsteby) has added a few lines at the bottom of the page urging her cousin to write. When OH married Hans Engebretsen Hjelle they probably decided that neither his patronymic nor his farm name were practical and simply called themselves Hanson. Ole Lee (Lie in Norway) was from the croft Snekkerlien.
«II:226 NE V:227

FROM: Sigri Nilsen, *Northwood, North Dakota, 3 July 1891*
To: Nils Nilsen and Aagot Larsdatter Gudmundsrud, *Aal, Buskerud*

❖━━◉◕━━❖

Dear parents and siblings,

A long time has already passed since I came to Dakota and I still haven't written to you, but the reason is that I didn't go straight to my destination. Uncle Ole should have bought my *tiket* to Northwood and not to Grand Forks. I came to Grand Forks June 24 and stayed at a hotel to the twenty-eighth. By then I thought I had waited long enough and bought a *tiket* to Northwood and it cost one dollar and sixty cents. As I arrived at the station Carl Svendsen came to town. You may imagine that made me happy because it wouldn't be good to come without knowing where to go. But thank God, I've now come to Ole and Birgit and they are so nice to me. They had waited for me a long time. The voyage was nice and I wasn't sick like most of the others. Ingebjørg Strand and her boys were not well. I could see that it wasn't good to be seasick and it is something you cannot really imagine. But we had good luck with the weather on our voyage. We had a gale one evening; it wasn't really a bad one but enough to make the cups and suitcases roll from one wall to the other. Ingebjørg and I laughed and three Swedish girls prayed to God for help and read in the hymnbook and wept, making great music. In one cabin they cried and prayed to God and in the other they swore and were boisterous. The voyage was long, ten days. We came to Quebec on the twenty-first and there we were separated. I had to go through Canada via Winnipeg and the others went via St. Paul and after that I was all alone, but things worked out better than I had feared. I was left on the platform when the others entered the train and the conductor said I was going on another train. Ingebjørg cried but I was brave and decided that there was nothing I could do about it. I had to wait for two long hours after the others had left. There weren't many who spoke so I could understand them and in my ears it was like chickens cackling to each other. But I managed and now I'm here and it has been good. Right now they are making me two dresses. Mother, you should see and hear how good Birgit is to me. It is easy to come to America when you are received by such people. The day after I arrived I went to town with Birgit and Albert and bought a new hat and material for a dress. For fun I'll send you a piece of the material. You may think I'm too fancy with such a dress, but it isn't necessarily so. It's nice to be like the others. I must say that those who receive newcomers have to be patient as they can't do anything and don't know anything about how things are. It isn't like in Norway where food is portioned. All kinds of food are set on the table and then you can eat as much as you want. It is soon the Fourth of July and then we'll have a celebration. You've heard about this before but I'll write to you again after we have celebrated. There is so much to write about but I'll have to say a little each time. They liked the brooch I brought for Lovise, yes that is the name of the girl it was for. And they also liked the ring I bought in Kristiania for eleven *kroner.* I should have brought more brooches; I could have made some money, but you can perhaps send some to me. One thing I miss is my belt. I have a dress that is worn with a belt and this is why I would like to have it. There are other things I could have taken with me now that I know more. Birgit often says that she should have remembered to write that I should bring my Hallingdal costumes and I suppose I could. It would have been fun to have them. I suppose they have all been thrown away now but you may be able to find them. You must write to me about how things are at home and about all acquaintances and about Guri and Lars Sundre and their wedding and about those at Krosshaug. There must be much news since I left. Tell Kari Larsgaard that it would have been fun if she had gone with me last spring. I've often wished it were so. Give my regards to them all, to Anne Plassen, Birgit and Margit Sundre, Margit Sandestølen, Syver Jegermoen, Tore Plassen, Hans Kaasalien, and others who may ask about me. I'll soon write to uncle and then you'll hear more about me. I may send you a photograph when I get them. We took them in Kristiania but they haven't arrived yet. I don't have more to write about now. My regards to all. I hope that this will find you well and satisfied with what you have.

Don't forget to give my regards to Thor and Ingebjørg Ulshagen. I'll write to them later. I forgot to bring my vaccination certificate, and I hope you'll send it in a letter. The doctor on the ship gave me a slip of paper but I would like to have mine nevertheless. The weather is nice and they say that the fields look nice if we don't have any accidents. Ole is well and he is now a cowherd but all he has to do is to fetch them for milking and they are not far away. Well, this is the end; more some other time. Please write to me; I'm waiting.

SIGRI NILSEN

To father.

I will write about the matters concerning Kari Sundre separately. She has now gone from us to her cousin who is married to T. Dengerud. [Unreadable sentence.] She didn't want to admit it but we took her to the doctor and he said that you have been pregnant for five to six months. You will give birth in August, he said, and then everything was clear. She wrote to T. Dengerud asking if she could come to him and after she had a letter from them she left two weeks ago. I have been waiting for a letter from her. Will you tell her mother? Don't you think it would be best that you talk to her before she hears gossip? That would be worse than hearing the truth from you. Would you also find out something for me? As you know, Botolf Hefte was interested in me in Norway and he still is. I get a letter from him almost every week asking me to come to Iowa, but I won't. Ole E. Sumbren has had the same intentions. But I won't; and do you know why? Niels Svendsen is the man I intend to live with for the rest of my life if you are not against it. We are closely related but this is also true of many others and he is a man that I think I will live with in harmony. He has said that there is no one else for him and that we must go through life together. You may be thinking that he will behave as he did with Guri Noss, but he won't and he has promised. But we haven't told this to anyone and will keep it to ourselves until we hear from you. You mustn't let anyone see these pages as they are kept separate. Please don't let anyone hear of this.

I plan to go away in the fall to take a three month tailoring course. I think I'll begin in October. It isn't so easy to be off in service all the time either. Even and I will soon write to Ole. They often write to us. We don't write so often but there isn't really all that much to write about from here. Would you please thank B. Vangen? I received her letter a few days ago. She says that they have received what they had owing from us. Write soon and and I'll write back. If you haven't written before you get this you will probably have another one before we get anything from you. Farewell to all of you.

SIGRI AND EVEN

Father and mother!!!

As you wished to see the one I've selected as my life companion I'll send you this now, but you shouldn't tell anyone about our relationship until you have more precise information from us. This has been taken from a photograph that was a little damaged, as you can see. You may wonder what has been written in the corner of the envelope but it only means that it will be returned to me if it doesn't get to you. Well, this is all I have to write to you this time so I'll end my letter with greetings to all who wish to have greetings from us here at Svendsen's.

Old Svendsen doesn't want to use his land this summer. He thinks he is too old to have so much trouble. Ole and Albert will be working the land this summer. For fun I'll tell you what animals Nils has: four horses, two cows, one pig, ten hens, but no cat, but he'll have to get one if I am to be here. Enough of this.

· —— ·

This letter marks the beginning of a second chapter of letters to the farm Gudmundsrud in Aal. Nils Nilsen's sister Gro had emigrated in 1862 after marrying Ole Svendsen from the farm Skrattegard in Aal. Gro Svendsen's letters have been translated and edited by Pauline Farseth and Theodore C. Blegen as *Frontier Mother: The Letters of Gro Svendsen* (Northfield: NAHA, 1950). Gro died in 1878 and Ole later married Birgit Olsdatter from the farm Gjeldokk in Aal. According to the 1880 census Ole Svendsen then lived in Traill County, N. Dak., and had these children: Nils (fifteen), Carl (fourteen), Ole (thirteen), Albert (eleven), Stephen (nine), Birgit (seven), Sarah (three), and Gurine (two). Two of Gro Svendsen's brothers had also emigrated, both named Ole after two grandfathers and called Big Ole and Little Ole. The latter, a pastor in Scandinavia, Wisc., brought three of his nephews with him to the United States in 1891 on his return from a visit. Sigrid and her younger brother Even went on to their uncle Ole Svendsen in North Dakota and Olaf (who was then fifteen and soon became Nelson) lived with his uncle in Wisconsin. A third brother, Nils, emigrated in 1895 and eventually returned to Norway around 1907. Even wrote on 4 January 1892 (Nor. ed. V:241). There are many letters from Sigri and her brothers as well as her uncles Ole. Typically, the parts of this letter addressed specifically to her parents were on separate sheets; they had contents of a more personal and private nature and were not meant for the wider readership of most immigrant letters. NE V:230

· —— ·

1891 — LETTER 2:269

FROM: Elise Wærenskjold, *Prairieville, Texas, 26 July 1891*

To: Thorvald Dannevig, *Lillesand, Aust-Agder*

⊶⇌◉⇌⊷

Dear Thorvald,

Thank you so much for your friendly letter and all your information. The reason I haven't written is that you wrote that you were going away; but when I saw in your sister-in-law's letter that you were at your dear uncle's funeral I didn't want to postpone it any longer. My old friend who wished to move back to Norway will have to remain in Texas. She sold her farm for 2,000 dollars to a man who we believed would and could pay so she let her money remain in the farm at a ten percent interest. But now he won't pay her and she was forced to take back the farm. This is very awkward for her as a single person as she will have to get a good renter who not only will take good care of the farm but who will be nice to share her house with, because she cannot live alone. Since Niels moved from me I've lived with four different families; but I've been lucky and they have all been nice people and been kind to me.

Next week I'm going to my dear Otto and will also visit other friends, as this will not make any significant difference in the cost of my tickets. I've had the good fortune to retain my old friends and get new ones where I live. Yet again, thank you for your letter and the trouble you took. My warm regards from your sincerely devoted old friend,

ELISE WÆRENSKJOLD

· —— ·

This letter is not in Clausen 1961. EW's old friend is Ouline Reiersen and it seems that EW has written to Dannevig for information concerning her planned relocation. «II:254 »II:279 NE V:231

· —— ·

FROM: Karen Solem, *Norden, South Dakota, 18 October 1891*

TO: Ole Tobias and Amalie Ødegaard, *Nannestad, Akershus*

Dear brother and sister-in-law,

Right after dinner today I was ready to begin this sentence: I'm now really happy because I have an entire Sunday afternoon to myself and will for once be permitted to write a letter in peace and quiet. But then, when I had found my pen and paper, placed myself at the table, and thought out this sentence, one of my neighbor wives came visiting, *Mrs.* Frickson, and then I had to lay aside my writing and try to keep her company even though my thoughts were all the time at Sundby where I suppose you today are celebrating your firstborn's birthday. My congratulations to both Sigurd and Torolf and I must add Olaf who comes in three days. Thank you so much for the letter I received on Tuesday. It was so good to hear that all was well with you and with mother but I didn't like to hear that mother has to take care of Marie's children. That is surely too much for one so old; she has had enough of responsibilities.

It is now already Friday evening after I wrote the above and there is not much use in starting again now as it is soon eight o'clock, but I'll sit up for a while anyway waiting for Laurits who is in Canby today. I may as well tell you that he is there to buy a wedding gift for Hilda Fella who will be married in a week. The groom is Ole I. Mellom, son of one of the most respected farmers in this township. (And then Laurits came and interrupted me; he had bought a giant fresh pike and so I had to fry him a taste of it and then no more was done that evening.)

October 18

It is now three weeks since I began this letter that must be the strangest letter you've had from me. And what should I then begin with. We've been to a wedding, a christening and a funeral since I last wrote anything. It is two weeks since there was a christening at Johan's, a little daughter who was named Selma Augusta, and I was her godmother. They now have five children, four girls and a boy. The next Friday there was a wedding at Fella, a great affair of course. About 200 had been invited but I think only 125 came and for my part I found that enough since I was one of the three responsible for the cooking along with *Mrs.* Blegstad and *Mrs.* Sjønne Kjenstad, and we had more than enough to do. It takes a lot of work to feed so many mouths twice—thrice actually as the young people danced all through the night and all wanted to have breakfast before leaving. I was so tired and worn out after this that I was too tired to work for two days—as if that was of any help. They were given wedding gifts at a value of about 180 dollars, including two beautiful clocks, one from Johan and us, and since we only have an old one that belongs to grandfather we will take it back and buy them a dining table instead. We think they will stay at Fella this winter but he is planning to buy land.

Sunday after the wedding there was a funeral at our nearest neighbor's to the east. *Mrs.* Ingeborg Moen had died, mother of the boy who died of consumption last summer that I wrote to you about, or rather to mother. I didn't attend the funeral as I didn't feel well but Laurits, grandfather and Syver were there. On his way home Laurits invited the parson and a few other families so I had guests for supper even though our house was a mess. Happily I had baked waffles while they were gone and I had some cold *ludefisk* that I stewed along with anchovies, swiss cheese and cranberry jam and, not to forget, coffee—so I managed that *alright*. I have so much to write about that I almost forgot to write about the harvest. It is about a month since we had the threshing machine. We didn't get it done without an accident this time. They fire with straw here and it so happened that an ember from the steam engine set fire to a wheat stack that burned up in an instant as everything was so dry and we didn't have enough water at hand; even with twenty-five men trying it wasn't possible to put out the fire. One stack caught fire after the other and in all we lost two and a half stacks of wheat and an enormous stack of oats. It was terrible to see so much of our crop burn up; we had never had so much before, and it was even worse to feel the fear that the wind would change direction and the fire get to our houses. Then we would have lost everything in a moment. Many worked so hard they got sick but no lives were lost. They drove the machine out of the flames, the blankets worn by the horses caught fire and Laurits plowed with our horses right up to the fire and the fire was so strong that it was reflected on the plowshares and the horses's noses were singed, but in this way he saved two stacks of oats. It appears that the owners of the machine are responsible for it and they will have to compensate our loss, valued at 220 bushels of wheat and 180 bushels of oats. We haven't received anything yet as they haven't threshed for themselves, but even if we get this we'll still have a loss and it won't be like having our own crop. Just having all our straw burned up is a significant loss as we would have used it for our cattle through the fall season and also on nice winter days when we can let them out. We did get 615 bushels of flax but one third of this is for grandfather. We sold our flax right from the machine and got seventy-five cents a bushel, but the weight was poor so we only got 399 dollars. We've only sold one wagonload of wheat; the price now is only eighty cents but they say it will be one dollar and then we'll haul all we have at once. We had ten acres with corn but it was damaged by frost in early fall so we'll only have some for the hogs. We have harvested our potatoes and got some nice and clean ones, about forty bushels.

We have really nice fall weather. We recently had a little rain that was good for the dry soil. It would be nice if the dry weather continued because of the fall plowing. We should soon do something about this photography but I dread the long drive to Canby and I don't think I want to go there this fall. A Norwegian photographer is setting up shop in Toronto and I think we should try him when he is ready.

I'm quite shocked to realize that it is a year since I last wrote to Aunt Mathea and now I suppose there is little use in writing. I hear that Anna has been living with you and that she is doing poorly. It must be awful for her, poor thing, that she isn't strong. We thought of asking her to come to us as it is so difficult to get maids here, but there would be no point in it as she wouldn't be able to stand our strong climate. Laurits has also mentioned sending for Karl but I have disagreed as I knew how much he wanted to be a seaman.

My letter is getting long but that's how it has to be. I send greetings to you from Nicolai and Mina and I've promised to send you a photograph of their little son Kasper. The boy was one year on October 2 but this portrait was taken in early summer; it's a good likeness. I'm glad that you liked *Skandinaven*. We don't know what the European edition is like as it is supposed to be different from the one we receive every week so I'll probably write for a sample some time. This newspaper has four different editions. I don't think it is worthwhile for you to send us *Intelligensen* as I've never been interested in that paper and we get all the news anyway. *Skandinaven* often has pieces on politics and other happenings from their regular correspondents in Norway and Denmark. Give our regards to relatives, friends and acquaintances and our greetings go to all of you from your

KAREN

Marie and Nordt are asking me to say hello from them to your three little boys. Marie wants me to tell you that she is a good girl and that she is going to be even better. I'll soon have to write to mother. Don't wait too long before you write.

. —— .

> Marie was KS's mother's step-daughter. Aunt Mathea Kristoffersdatter Nilsen was a sister of KS's mother and Anna and Karl were her children. KS writes *blankettene*, using the English "blanket" as if it were a Norwegian word. The "European edition" of *Skandinaven* was aimed at readers in Norway and Denmark who for the most part got their subscriptions as gifts from friends and relatives in the United States. At this time this Chicago newspaper also had daily, biweekly and weekly editions. Karen wrote to her mother on 12 April, and concluded: "I should have written more but it is now very late and I'm so tired that I can hardly see what I write." «II:259 »II:273 NE V: 235

. —— .

1892 — LETTER 2:271

FROM: Ole Jørgensen Lie, *Necedah, Wisconsin, 8 January 1892*

TO: Marie Olsdatter Vigerust, *Dovre, Oppland*

As we have time today I will inform you about how things are here. The land is not as good as they write. I think that there are not many who write who tell the truth. You have to work much harder than in Norway so for my part I think it is better to be in Norway for the rich as well as for the poor, as it is so hot here during summer that it is almost impossible to be outdoors. But there is no lack of food and drink for any of your people here. But it is very difficult for them as Ole and Andreas and Ole Olsen are out in the forest to earn money and I have to do all the work on the farm. I tend five horses and eighteen cows and calves. So I always have enough to do and thank my God that I've been in good health since I came. But things are not good with my wife as she doesn't like it here. If her situation doesn't improve we'll have to send her back next summer. It doesn't make sense for her to go here and cry for the rest of her days. But all is well with Anna. She goes to the English school every day so I think she'll speak English quite well by spring. It is difficult here for Norwegians. If you meet someone on the road and he talks to you it is like hearing a sheep bleat. I can tell you from Ragnhild that she got a good position this winter. She is with a Norwegian woman and is paid one and a half dollars a week so by spring she will have more than the price of her ticket that Olianna sent to Norway.

I don't have more to write about for now. I can tell you that we are reasonably satisfied with our situation here. But I would not advise you to come to America as you would not like it here. They don't write as it is but I will write the truth and not tell any lies. You must write as soon as you get this letter so we can hear how things are in Norway. No more this time. Greetings from me. Give my regards to all who may ask about me. Farewell.

OLE JORGENSEN LIE

· —— ·

OJL, his wife, Anne (a sister of Marie Olsdatter Vigerust), and their children Anna and Andreas (who soon changed his name to Andrew) from the croft Snekkerlia, Ragnhild Olsdatter Vigerust, and other relatives in Dovre emigrated in 1891. In Necedah they were welcomed by a son, Ole Olsen Lee, and other relatives such as the siblings Jacob and Ole Olson and Olianna Hanson from Vigerust and Anne Norsby and her siblings from Nørstebø. Their children used the name Lee but it seems that OJL and Anne continued to spell their name Lie. They were sixty-four and fifty-eight in 1891. Anne's unhappiness with her new home developed into depression, and she and her husband eventually returned to Norway. NE V:242

· —— ·

FROM: Nels T. Olson, *Callender, Iowa, 2 February 1892*

TO: Gro Olsdatter Torvetjønn, *Rauland, Vinje, Telemark*

—◦═◦◎◦═◦—

Dear sister,

It is now more than twelve years since I spoke with you face to face. I've heard a little from you in letters from Gisle and Tor. Gisle sent me your address in his last letter, so I'll send you a few sentences and first of all let you know that we are all well. I would like to hear the same from you. We have already become a large family with eight children, six boys and two girls. The youngest girl is named Anne after old Ole Stenersrud's sister. I have long thought of writing to you but have put it off again and again and I suppose you have also thought of writing to me. In this we have both been negligent and we should both try to write more often to each other and I now demand an answer from you as soon as you have read my short letter.

We sent a *ticket* to Gisle and his wife—eighty-five dollars—so we expect them from Norway in late March. We sent it January 21. Since Gisle has so little it would be good of you to help him with a little travel money; there are many expenses on the journey. Or perhaps you will join them and come to America and if so you will be very welcome. I assume you'll be going over to Ødefjell to speak with Gisle and his wife. Svanaug and Jon have also planned to come but I don't know what they'll do. Gro, I must ask you if you are only a simple servant girl or if you have advanced somewhat in life so you don't have to do hard work all the time. If you do, then I would advise you to come to America even though you may not be the right age to learn to do things the American way. Cooking is very different here so it would take you some time to learn how to do it, but I think you would learn it soon enough. I won't write any more this time so you'll have to be satisfied with this brief note until I have a reply from you. But I can tell you that I like America and do not regret coming here. We would probably have done poorly if we had settled some place in Norway. We are not yet wealthy but we have more than our daily needs and we'll perhaps be wealthy if we have luck and God is willing. Tell us all you know from Møstrand. The next time I'll write more about America. Farewell in God. Best regards from us all. Your loving brother

NILS O. TORVETJØNN

. ——— .

NTO wrote to his brother Tor Olsen Bakken on 23 November 1891 (Nor. ed. V:238) about sending a ticket to their brother Gisle and asking him to help him on his way. Svanaug was a sister who was married to Jon Jonsen Neset. «II:264 NE V:244

. ——— .

1892 — LETTER 2:273

FROM: Karen Solem, *Norden, South Dakota, 15 February 1892*

To: Ole Tobias and Amalie Ødegaard, *Nannestad, Akershus*

⊹≡◉⇐⊹

Dear brother and sister-in-law,

Thank you so much for your welcome letter that I received a month ago. We were all so glad to hear that all is well with you and mother. Here everything is, praise God, fine and well. We have all had colds at different times this winter but this is nothing to be concerned about. The health situation is quite good all over the prairie around here but it is said that "La Grippe" has been visiting here and there. At Johan's the three youngest children have been poorly for some time but they are now well while Ragnhild has been so ill that she has been in bed, but she was a little better last night when Louis was there. We visited Nicolai and Mina yesterday; they had a little daughter last Friday so Mina was still in bed, but both she and the little one were doing well. Little Kasper is really nice and clever and that is good since he already has a sister.

Hilda Fella, who married Ole Mellom last fall, had a daughter January 16. All is well with them and with the others at Fella. I'm also expecting a little one in a few weeks. May God grant that it soon be done. I'm not all that strong right now but I'm glad that I have such an excellent maid—

Johanne Hansen who I believe I wrote was here a few weeks last winter. She is a daughter of Torvald Lerberg and Dorthea Aanesruddalen. Mother knows them well.

It is so strange that you have met one of father's former friends from his school days. When you mentioned T. Hansen I wished that you had given me his address since I've been looking for it for so long. But you may not have it? Give my regards to those of our relatives you may get in touch with in Holmestrand. I should have written to them but I've waited far too long. We didn't get any photographs taken last fall either but we must do it if we still are among the living next summer.

I had a letter with a Christmas card from Sally last Christmas. I think I've told you that she is married to Ole Fossum from Gjerdrum who is the son of a brother of grandfather's brother's wife at Highland Prairie, Fillmore County. So we are in a way related and of course we have been like sisters since the first time we met. Last year I received a photograph of her little girl who is now one year old. Sally is such a good and nice person and I have long wished that she and Amalie would get to know each other. Couldn't you invite her to visit you next summer? This would make her so happy and she could also stay for a while with mother. I wouldn't have written this if I hadn't been sure that she wouldn't be any trouble since I know well that Amalie has more than enough on her hands as it is. But don't be too concerned about this; it is merely something I have wished for; Sally has never mentioned it.

My letter seems to be getting quite long. You must realize that I have a maid, so I have a lot of time on my hands. Last night I also wrote two letters, one to my sister-in-law Anna on Highland Prairie; she and I are almost the only ones in our family who exchange letters between these two places. My other sister-in-law there, Carl's wife, is quite poorly—she has been ill for a whole year and is now so weak that she cannot get out of bed without help. And she is still a young woman, not much more than thirty. The other letter was to my cousin Karen who will be a bride tomorrow in Chicago. The groom's name is Gustav Hoch, a German by birth. They sent me such a beautiful invitation card that I would have sent it to you if I didn't so want to have it myself. Christine Nelp as well as her daughter Marie, who is now an adult, also live in Chicago. Marie is getting married next spring—well, if it doesn't all go wrong again. So we have people we can stay with if we should go to the World Exhibition in '93. Greetings from all here and your devoted daughter,

KAREN

Today we have very nice winter weather with enough snow for sleighs. It is quite cold at times and we have snowstorms. The wheat prices have not been as good as expected—rarely up to forty cents since last fall and we didn't get more than forty-four for what we've sold so far. Give my regards to Josefine Olsen. I realize that she hasn't lost her good temper since she sings children's songs with the little boys. Say hello to the little boys from Marie and Nordt. Marie has learned the letters and will soon get an ABC, and she is learning how to crochet—but she plays most of the time. Has mother received the ten dollars we sent her for Christmas? We would of course like to know. I have had greetings from mother and from my old teacher Olsen from Anton Hetager. Would you please give him my regards when you see him?

. ——— .

> This letter has been several days in the making. La Grippe was a common term for influenza. KS wrote a short note to her mother on 3 April 1892, telling her that she had had a daughter and that her name was Olga Alvilde. Her deceased father's former friend was Ole Pedersen Sunne. KS's father-in-law (always referred to as "grandfather") and his family had lived in Fillmore County before coming to Deuel County in South Dakota. Two of his sons still had farms there. «II:270 »II:285 NE V:245

. ——— .

1892 — LETTER 2:274

FROM: Rena Olson (Ragnild Olsdatter Vigerust)
Necedah, Wisconsin, 27 February 1892

TO: Marie Olsdatter Vigerust, *Dovre, Oppland*

⋅⇒◯⇐⋅

Dear sister Marie,

As it has been some days since I received your letter I must now reply. I and our relatives here are in good health and I was glad to see that this is also the case with you and yours. You know that my sister is very busy and needs many servant girls. She also wanted me to work there and I would have liked to do it but I was offered another position and thought that I could get to learn a little more. It was a Norwegian family. The husband was away from home. So there was a wife and two little girls, but then the husband returned and they no longer needed a maid. So I went to Olianna and now I'm at my cousin's, Rønnaug Norsby. I plan to visit my siblings who live out in the country. Last summer I worked for my sister and I think I'll be with her next summer too. The Norwegian family I worked for ate Norwegian food: rice porridge, cheese, and other things from the dairy. My brothers Jakob and Ole and Ole and Andrew Lee are still in the forest but we expect them home soon. Anne Lie is very dissatisfied. I for my part don't think she has any reason to be dissatisfied as they have a good house and all they need. They slaughtered two hogs and a calf and since then I've heard that they got two cows and they are said to have a good supply of flour and are able to buy what they need in the store. Anna is home this winter and goes to school. So I think she should be satisfied and not complain so much. I'll visit her and try to comfort her as well as I can, but I suppose it won't help much. We others are quite satisfied but I won't advise you to come when I see how things are with Anne. The only thing she talks about is returning to Norway.

You ask what we eat here. I cannot give you a full account. Let me first describe the meat that comes both first and last: beaf steak, mutton and veal, fried ham, chicken, and many other kinds. Fish is also much used and potatoes are served with every meal. For dessert there are pies and puddings. In the evening there is a lot of cake and sauces of berries and many kinds of fruit after they have eaten the other food. In the morning there are usually buckwheat pancakes in the winter but not during summer. Eggs are not used by the dozen but by the bucket. You must excuse my joke but eggs are used all day. In summer eggs are much used for breakfast and they are also used for baking. I'll soon send you the money I owe you. It is now long since Christmas but I will nevertheless tell you how it was. [...]

· —— ·

RO was fifty-four upon emigrating in 1891. She wrote a letter some months after her arrival (Nor. ed. V:237) saying that she had mostly lived with her sister and brother-in-law Olianna and Hans E. Hanson, who had a hotel or boarding house in Necedah. She is quite impressed by the prosperity of her cousin Ole Olson Lee from the croft Snekkerlia. At some point she changed her name from Ragnild Olsdatter Vigerust to Rena Olson. The cheese used by the Norwegian family was made by boiling whey (*gub* or *gumme*). RO does not seem to understand that Anne Lie (the mother of Ole, Andrew, and Anna Lee) was not merely dissatisfied but that she suffered from depression. For "cake" and "sauce" she had no Norwegian words and wrote what she had heard: *kig* and *sas*. She did not write "bucket" (or *bøtte*) but *skjeppe*, an old unit of volume corresponding to 17.4 liters. The conclusion of the letter has been lost. In margins RO asks about possible new emigrants and sends her greetings. There are also a few words of greeting signed by Anne Norsby. NE V:246

1892 — LETTER 2:275

FROM: Iver Andersen Lee, *Mayville, North Dakota, 4 April 1892*

To: Anders Olsen and Anders Andersen Lie, *Hedalen, Sør-Aurdal, Oppland*

Dear father and brother,

I've long had a desire to hear from you and write to you. It is more than a year since I wrote and I've had no reply. One of the letters may have been lost. But I've had some news from Hedalen, most recently from Marie Bruskerud. She told about the sudden death of Torkel Nordhagen. I haven't heard anything from you but hope that you're all alive and in reasonably good health. I don't know whether you've heard anything about me since I last wrote. I can tell you that my wife and I have had a little daughter and her first birthday was last March 17. She is in good health and is growing slowly but steadily. She can walk with support but hasn't tried on her own yet. She was christened Kari and of course she sends you her best regards. My wife and I are in good health but last winter I was poorly for awhile. I don't know for sure whether it was rheumatism or la grippe or influenza that we've heard so much about in recent times. I was in bed for about a week and then got better but later I had several minor relapses. For a long time, however, I've been as strong as before.

Times are as usual in that they bring us both hope and discouragement. All in all we've had good times these last couple of years. Last year's crop was the largest ever in American history, but, as they say, a large business needs large sums. There was a large crop but it led to large expenses and much waste. Wages were unusually high since it was so difficult to save the large crop. Twice as much labor as usual was needed for harvesting and threshing. On top of this we had an unusually wet fall that caused such delays that about one third of the crop here in the Northwest remained unthreshed through the winter. Some of it is in *shocks*, that is about eight to twelve sheafs placed in a heap out in the field, and some is in *stacks*, that is in a heap much like you pile up leaves in the fall. I am among those with an unthreshed crop but at least I got it stacked in time. I fear, however, that the crop that has been out all winter is more or less damaged. How much this may be we won't know until we've threshed it and that can't be done until we have finished spring plowing and planting. On top of this is the loss from not having had it threshed last fall when the price for wheat was about eighty cents a bushel. For some time now it has been about sixty cents and it may be even lower before we have threshed our wheat and hauled it to town.

Our weather has been very unstable. Early last fall we had a snowstorm that stopped our threshing as the snow had gone far into the stacks. From Christmas we had a long stretch of bitter cold and since then we've had periods of mild weather followed by cold periods. We had another snowstorm March 8 and 9. It was the worst we've seen even though I've lived long enough on the Dakota prairie to have seen quite a few storms. It's been sad to read about the lives that have been lost and the damage that's been done. It began in the late afternoon of the eighth and we were lucky that it began so late in the day. Had it begun earlier when most people were out many more would have died because the weather had been so nice the day before that many were out on the roads. The wind was strong enough to shake the largest houses. I was up much of the night because I didn't feel safe enough to go to bed. I sat there looking at how everything hanging on the wall moved because the house was shaking. Several houses blew down that night and some roofs were blown off. The next morning I found the roof of my cowshed in pieces all over the field. My animals were unhurt except for some chickens that had frozen to death.

I don't have much news for you. You may have heard that Amund Rustebakke is dead. He died last winter of influenza. One of his brothers, Guttorm, lives not so far from here but you may not know him. I've had several letters from my brothers Ole and Mikkel this winter. Mikkel has long spoken of coming out west to see me and he was determined to come last fall to see whether he would like it here, but then his wife had twins and he had to stay at home.

Spring work has not yet begun. We've had mild weather for some time but it has been so wet that it hasn't been possible to do any work out in the fields or anywhere else and it seems it will get even wetter as it has rained about every other day for a week or more and last night and today we've had a lot of snow. We haven't had such a wet spring for many years and both fields and roads are such that we'll not have any traffic for a long time.

I must conclude, but when I've done my spring work and threshed my crop I'll write again so you can hear how I'm doing. May these lines find you in good health. I know, father, that you can no longer be counted among those who are physically sound and well and I know that you sit there bent down with the weakness of old age, but may God grant you spiritual strength to carry your cross to a victorious conclusion, for then the hand that has lain the cross on you will exchange it for the imperishable crown of salvation. With this my best regards to all who hear or read this letter from

IVER A. LIE AND FAMILY

. ——— .

What we now call the Midwest was then still the Northwest. In Wisconsin, IAL's brother Mikkel's wife was Ingrid. «II:262 »II:283 NE V:247

. ——— .

1892 — LETTER 2:276

FROM: Halvor Hansen Ulsness, *Lowry, Minnesota, 10 April 1892*

To: Nils Andreas Olsen Brusli, *Tørdal, Drangedal, Telemark*

My good friend!

It seems that our correspondence has stopped entirely but my longing to hear from you makes me take it up again. I'm glad to be able to report that we are all well. When we have health we are often unable to appreciate it if we don't consider those who are without this benefit. This should make us think and give our thanks to Him whose grace allows us to enjoy these benefits. Last winter my son Hans took a course at the English school in Glenwood but a few weeks ago he came home to help me with the spring plowing and planting. Some time ago I finally I got the deed for my land but it cost me a little more than 1,100—eleven hundred—dollars. My oldest daughter Signe has often been away in service. Now she is working for my nearest neighbor, a man from Gjerpen and gets one dollar and seventy-five cents a week. My second daughter Mari Johanne is at home and is preparing for her confirmation. Our youngest daughter Nelle Olette is thriving; she speaks English almost as well as Norwegian.

We had a very good crop last year and this gave many farmers a good boost. I hadn't broken so much land and got 600 bushels of wheat, 200 of barley and oats and what we need of potatoes. I've had to buy many things that are quite expensive. Last year I bought a selfbinder that cost 135 dollars and this year a drill harrow for eighty-five dollars. I also had to buy a harness for thirty-four dollars and a horse for eighty dollars. So you may imagine that my debt is considerable, but with God's help I hope to be able to repay it. I now have four horses, nineteen head of cattle, three sheep, three pigs and about forty chickens.

Torbjørn and Guro and their family are doing well. It's only a mile from my house to his. There is so much I would have liked to tell you Nils but this will have to be enough for now. Loving regards to you and your family and your old mother from us. Please give our regards to all at Homli and to Margit's brothers Hans, John, Tor and Halvor. I hope you'll send me a long letter as soon as you have received this and tell us a little about those mentioned above as well as about your neighbors, how Harald Bjørnejordet is doing etc. You may imagine that I'm longing for a letter from you.

As for politics I can tell you that I subscribe to *Skandinaven* so I know all things of importance in Norway. Some time ago I read a letter to the editor from Ole Torjusen that Nils Sandvik was dead and he asked for his son's address. A few days ago my son had a letter from Nils Nordbø. They are doing well, are farming on shares and planting on 110 acres. This must be all for now.

HALVOR H. ULSNESS

· —— ·

HHU wrote *ded* (deed). Gjerpen is now part of Skien, a town in Telemark. Immigrant newspapers such as *Skandinaven* in Chicago frequently printed correspondence from Norway. «II:258 NE V:248

· —— ·

FROM: Andrew Lee (Andreas Olsen Snekkerlia)
Necedah, Wisconsin, 18 April 1892
TO: Marie Olsdatter Vigerust, *Dovre, Oppland*

Dear Aunt,

As I have time today I must write you some words again. I wrote last winter but haven't received any reply and this surprises me. Well, I must first tell you how we live in this far distant country. Our situation now is not good. Father is very ill. It is the same illness as before but it is now very bad. He has no peace day or night. He has to walk around at night as well as during the day so I don't think he'll survive this time. We have tried a doctor but it didn't help and he is getting worse and not better. And mother goes on here unhappy and dissatisfied and only wants to return to Norway. She paces and weeps all the time. There is no help in trying to talk to her. We'll have to send her back to Norway next spring. I will go with her if I live and have my health because I won't see my mother in this situation. I think I've made enough money to manage the journey. Our emigration was a bad thing for my parents. Except for our parents we are all well.

I like it so much here that I won't stay long in Norway should it happen that I come there. Last winter I was in the forest for four and a half months. I got twenty-two dollars a month and free board. All in all I got one hundred and three dollars. Brother Ole was there for three months. He was paid twenty-six dollars a month. I came home from the forest March 10 and I'm now working on a railroad not so far from home. It is so close that I sleep and eat at home. I have thirty-two dollars a month. We begin work at seven in the morning and work til noon when we have dinner and then work from one to six. We work ten hours without a break. I bring my dinner to work. These are not long hours but the work is hard.

Anna and Ragnhild work in town for Olianna. They are in good health. I must tell you that Bjørner Norsby has recently held his wedding. His wife is Norwegian and her name is Inger Lise. I must now end this short note with greetings to you and your mother and sister from all of us. You must write as soon as you've read these simple sentences and tell me all the news you know and who is working around on the farms. Jakob and Ole and their families send their regards. They are all well. Farewell.

ANDREI LIE

Don't show this letter to strangers.

. ——— .

> AOL, son of Anne and Ole Lie from the croft Snekkerlia in Dovre, emigrated with members of his family and other relatives from Dovre in 1891. He soon changed his name to Andrew Lee, as he explained in a letter to his mother's sister on 2 August 1891 (Nor. ed. V:232) where he gave an account of their journey. He first signed himself "Andrias Snidkerlien" and then added: "My address is *Endru Lie* as Andrias is *Endru* in English." He then signed a second time as *Endru Lie*. He soon learned the correct spelling of his new name and also, as did his siblings, spelled his last name Lee. His older brother Ole had emigrated some years before and there is a letter to his aunt sent from a lumber camp on 23 November 1884 (Nor. ed. IV:252). Anna Lee is Andrew's sister and Ragnhild (who changed her name to Rena Olson) and Olianna Hanson are his aunts, sisters of his mother and of Marie Olsdatter Vigerust. Bjørner Norsby Americanized his name to Barney. Jakob Olson was a brother of Marie Olsdatter Vigerust. «II:271 NE V:249

. ——— .

1892 — LETTER 2:278

FROM: Ingeborg Larsen, *Moscow, Idaho, 17 May 1892*

To: Ole Henriksen and Henrik Olsen Stokkenes, *Eid, Sogn og Fjordane*

⤜◉⤛

Dear father and brother and family,

I have now received your long awaited letter. Thank you so much. I'm sorry you didn't get my Christmas letter because I wrote one and enclosed a receipt for the money to Lotie. I see that my dear father has a mortal illness. I wish you could say, "For to me to live is Christ, and to die is gain." Oh, father—do not go to bed this evening before you accept the Lord. Let Jesus have you born again in spirit and be new every day in his image. Is a little swearing and mindless intercourse with ungodly friends acceptable to God? No—we should have a new life. We are told to wander as Jesus wandered. Read the sixth, seventh, and eighth chapters in Paul's letter to the Romans. But let not this suffice. Read the verses in the seventh chapter, but look more carefully in the eighth. "There is therefore now no condemnation for those who are in Christ Jesus and who do not live according to the flesh but to the spirit." The flesh leads us into sin but we must crucify the flesh every day. The fifteenth verse and on is a Christian's beginning. Christ cannot save us until we have accepted Jesus. And then we will have both the strength and the desire to do God's will. It is written that our deeds shall follow us. What would heaven be like if the drinker and the swearer, hate and envy and all such should inherit the Kingdom of God. Oh, no! We haven't tasted intoxicating drink since we came here three months ago. A woman gave a lecture on total abstinence. We all signed up without knowing of each other. That must be true obedience to the spirit! We have a good time in the English Methodist church in Moscow. We go to their meetings every evening. There is a great awakening here—one hundred are said to have asked for intercession. Thanks to the Lord who has taught me to understand the language they speak there.

As we have written earlier we now live in Moscow. We have a nice house as you will soon see in a photograph we will send you. Lotie now works for four and a half dollars a week. Oluf goes to school. Larsen is out on our land plowing. I tend two cows. Oluf goes with some of the milk selling it to the houses. My plan is to have chickens if we get up a fence. Amund is out on our land and makes his own food, eating and sleeping there. He has binoculars and from a small hill he can see all of Moscow—it is as far as from your house to "*Stykkje-bakken*." It is called Paradise Hill. He goes up there on Sundays and sits looking through his binoculars. We let the upstairs room for three months last winter for 10 dollars a month, but then the husband died and the wife and daughter left to find work. A sister, an old lady, went to become a schoolteacher—and so this family was spread.

Dear brother, will you buy a ring and a brooch for Larsine and pay for it with her own money? Both must be of gold. Have someone with good taste buy them. She so often says that she has nothing in memory of Norway, not even of her father. Please get this done as soon as possible. Send it in my name: Mrs. Ingeborg Larsen, Moscow, Idaho, USA. As for the size of the ring, try it on Karoline. Think of a little lady, a small hand, not one that is worn with work. Congratulations on your little daughter. I can no longer keep track of how many nieces I have. May you have the grace to bring them up for the Lord. You seem to think I will return to Norway, but I think you should come to the World Exhibition in Chicago next summer. Then we can meet each other there.

Dear father. Make sure of your relationship with God so you can sing in joy, "I am flying home to Jesus to praise God among the angels." Then we will meet again in Jesus, some today and some tomorrow. Praise be the Lord. Your sister and daughter

INGEBORG LARSEN

· —— ·

Lotie (Larsine) is a daughter from her first marriage to her present husband's brother and the money must be of her inheritance. IL quotes from Philippians 1:21. Her quotation from Romans 8 is not accurate. The Methodist church in Moscow is called English because of the language. In 1910 the funeral for IL was in the Moscow Methodist Church. «II:194 NE V:250

· —— ·

1892 — LETTER 2:279

FROM: Elise Wærenskjold, *Prairieville, Texas, 29 July 1892*

TO: Thomine Dannevig, *Lillesand, Aust-Agder*

⊷⟾⟾⟾⊶

My dear, good Thomine!

I don't have so much to write about but I will send you a few lines hoping to get a long and good letter from you. I suppose you are in your home in Lillesand as you now are enjoying such a nice summer in Norway. Last year your health was not good but I hope that you were able to spend the winter months with your children and that you now are well. You cannot imagine how often my thoughts are in Lillesand and in the Moland parsonage where I spent my happiest days. Is the old parsonage still standing?

And how do things now look at Møglestue? Has the beautiful garden been kept up? Does the school for needlework still exist? How is Stina Normann doing? If you ever see her please give her my regards and tell her that I would appreciate a letter from her. Please also give my regards to Thomine Arentz and Nicoline. It is so strange to think of how few are left of my old friends and acquaintances.

My life continues in its old monotonous way but I am grateful to God that he gives me the strength to take care of my home and cultivate my garden and that I can travel on my own to my dear Otto. Walking is more difficult than it used to be so I am rarely able to visit Ouline Reiersen even though I would like to spend time with her. She also finds it difficult to walk far, but she is doing well and has a comfortable home. She sends her friendly regards.

On May 5 Niels's little girl arrived in a great hurry, indeed in such a hurry that she was there before either the neighbor woman or the doctor could come. But everything went well and she is a really good little girl. Our Pastor Rystad baptized her in the parents' home and there the strange thing happened that five old women were godmothers as the men and the young woman who had been asked to be sponsors did not have time to come. Rystad came on May 14 but on the fifteenth and seventeenth when we were supposed to have church services it rained so much that they could not he held. The pastor is here only eight days at a time and this is far too little, especially for the young people who are to be confirmed.

I suppose you have seen in the newspapers how many catastrophes we have had this year in America, some caused by storms and cyclones and some by flooding. We have had more rain and wind than usual but, thank God, we have not had more damage here than the destruction of quite a few fruit trees. It seems that we will have a very good harvest.

I hope that Thorvald will be so kind as to mail the enclosed letters with the correct addresses. I know neither their nor Thorvald's addresses so I'm sending them to you. Please let me have Thorvald's address when you write to me. I will begin to wait for your letter in two months. I suppose you now have had your first taste of new potatoes and here we are harvesting them. I ate my first new potatoes in late April and peas, carrots and asparagus from the middle of March to the middle of May. I will now conclude with loving regards to you and your children and grandchildren. Could you please send me a portrait of Niels's wife and children? Farewell! This is the wish of your old friend,

ELISE WÆRENSKJOLD

In Clausen 1961, 152–153 this letter has no references to friends in Lillesand. «II:254 NE V:254

1892 — LETTER 2:280

FROM: Anna Lee, *Necedah, Wisconsin, 25 September 1892*
TO: Marie Olsdatter Vigerust, *Dovre, Oppland*

Dear Aunt,

I must take up my pen and write a few words and tell you how I am. I'm well and in good health and would like to hear the same good news from you. Mother is the same or a little better. She is now able to make house for Ole and Andreas. I'm working for a German family but they speak only English and I can understand all they say and it's good to work there. They are only four and it is close by Hanson's. Ragnhild has sent fifteen dollars and if this is too much you are to have the remainder. She works for Olianna and is very busy. There are eighteen beds to be made every day and she does laundry twice a week and you must realize that this is a huge laundry as they use two sheets on every bed. But they only wash one of them every week and the pillows are small. There is one for each person and the beds are so large that the blankets are folded three times on each side. Would you please try to get the address for Gunhild Jellien? I must now end this brief note with greetings from us all. Please say hello to Ingri Stigen from me and Ragnhild. You must forgive me for not writing more because when I came up to Hanson's Ragnhild wanted me to write immediately that she has sent the money. Give my regards to all at Slette and to Ole Bersangaard. Dear, please write to me right away. I wish I could have talked with you. Well, I must stop now and go home to make supper. Write immediately. Sincerely,

ANNA LEE

· ——— ·

Marie Olsdatter Vigerust, Ragnhild Olson (who called herself Rena), and AL's mother Anne Lie were sisters. Ole and Andreas (who changed his name to Andrew) were AL's brothers. The money returned by Ragnhild was for her ticket. «II:271 NE V:257

· ——— ·

1892 — LETTER 2:281

FROM: Andrew Lee, *Eau Claire, Wisconsin, 14 October 1892*

TO: Johan Peter Eriksen and Ingborganna Andersdatter Lian
Verdal, Nord-Trøndelag

⊷⟹⟸⊷

Dear parents!

I must ask you to forgive me for not writing for so long but I have some excuses: yesterday I came home from North Dakota where I've been for a couple of months and there I couldn't write or, rather, I couldn't get a letter mailed. The mills here closed because of a strike among the workers so I went to Dakota. I worked in a little town called Grafton. On my way home I stopped for a few days in Minneapolis and looked at the city's curiosities but I didn't see anyone I knew. In Dakota I worked for someone who had a threshing machine and I liked it there. In a week or so I'll be going back to the forest. I have no news worth mentioning. All is as usual. You can give the other portrait I sent you to whoever you wish if anyone wants it. This is all I now have to write about. Give my regards to all acquaintances and regards to you from me. I'm sending you some money today. Please forgive me for not having sent some earlier but better late than never. Don't write until you get my address in the forest.

ANDREW LEE

· ——— ·

AL wrote a brief letter to his parents on 20 June and was also then sorry that he had not written for so long. «II:266 NE V:258

· ——— ·

FROM: Rakel Tonnette Thorkelson (Rannestad)
Willmar, Minnesota, 1 December 1892

To: Osmund Atlaksen Ovedal, *Sirdal, Vest-Agder*

⤙⟹⟸⤚

Dear and unforgetttable brother and family,

I will take up my pen to write a few words and let you know that we are all well which is one of the best goods that we may wish for ourselves here on earth and with God's help I hope to hear the same from you. The boys have been away working this summer. Theodor has worked for a man since before Christmas. He has been home for two months but now he has returned to the same man and will be there this winter. Last summer he made two hundred dollars. Albert has been away for four and a half months and has made sixty-six dollars. I think he'll stay home this winter and go to English school. I sold my land one year ago and got 1,000 dollars for it. I had a large debt. I've bought a lot in town and built a house for myself. I owe a little on it but I hope the boys will help me now that they are so big. We live upstairs and I've rented the rooms downstairs for eighty-nine dollars a month to a man and wife. They are Irish.

I'll send Bolette and Ingeborg a small handkerchief each for Christmas and Karen Bertine will send them a small rug. Thank you for the portrait you sent us. It was very nice. We must try to send you some in return. We haven't had any taken yet. All you know around here are doing well. I visited Ole Salveson last Sunday and they are doing well. They just had a little boy who is now two weeks old. They have three girls and two boys and they are all well. Kolbjørn Pedersen Rannestad has also sold his land and has built a house in town not so far from us. Syvert and Syverine Konstadli and their family are doing well. I will send two letters at once since I don't dare put too much in one letter. I hope you will get them for Christmas. I must wish you a Merry Christmas and a happy New Year.

I mustn't forget to ask you to please pay Nils Andreas Jødestøl for a book I borrowed from him at the time he was here. When he wrote to Ole Salveson for his suitcase both books were with me and in his rush

Ole couldn't get them. It is Johann Arndt's *True Christianity*. I spoke with Ole about the book but he said I could keep it and I would like to pay for it. I suppose I could send the money but I don't know how it would be with such a small amount. It isn't long since I had a letter from Ingeborg Helena, daughter of Sigbjørn. They are doing well but Berent Anton, the next youngest son of Sigbjørn went to Tennessee last June and they haven't heard from him since. I had a letter from Berte Tonette recently. She is also doing well. I suppose you've heard that the wife of mother's brother died some time ago. Karen Bertine is going to English school. She sends her regards to Bolette and aunt Ingeborg and thanks them for the portrait. She says to tell Bolette and Ingeborg that she is going to her aunts Sara and Siri next summer. In conclusion, my best regards to you all from all of us. Farewell in the Lord. Your sister

RAKEL T. TORKELSON

. ——— .

RT is a widow and has two sons and a daughter (Karen Bertine). Bolette and Ingeborg are the daughters of Osmund at Ovedal. Siri, Sigbjørn, Berte Tonette, and Sara are siblings in Wisconsin. RT's mother's brother was Haavard Sigbjørnsen Ovedal and his widow was Karen Tonette. Johann Arndt (1555–1621) was a German Lutheran theologian. His *Wahres Christentum* was first published in 1605–1610 and was translated into many languages. «II:241 NE V:260

. ——— .

1892 — LETTER 2:283

FROM: Mikkel Andersen Lee, *Mount Vernon, Wisconsin, 3 December 1892*

To: Anders Olsen and Anders Andersen Lie, *Hedalen, Sør-Aurdal, Oppland*

⭒═◉═⭒

Dear father and brother and family,

It is with me as with the boy who was away for too long and didn't dare go home. I'm almost afraid to write but I'll have to try. I don't have much news. Herman Klemmetsrud died last fall of cancer of his tongue. The doctor cut off a piece but the cancer attacked his throat and then death brought an end to his suffering. Uncle Ole sends his regards saying that he is in good health and lives like a hawk in a flock of chickens. Beret Lie also asks me to say that she is in good health and doing well. She has a pension of twelve dollars a month from her husband. Uncle got his pension for participating in the Civil War and she will receive his pension for as long as she lives. Our aunt is also in reasonably good health as are Olaug and her brother Ole Børtnes. Brother Ole is in good health and still works as a schoolteacher and precentor in addition to his carpentry. I recently had a letter from brother Iver who says that he and his family are in good health and that they had a good crop. I and my family are all in good health. My twin daughters are growing and thriving and have begun to walk. We had an average crop this year. Kari, Anders and Oline go to English school about seven months of the year. They speak English among themselves and I don't understand much of what they are saying. It is with me as it was with Uncle Tom who was a pastor and couldn't read and when he was fifty his oldest son taught him to read. I'm an American citizen and don't know the American language. I'll have to learn it from my children. This is the only way I can learn it.

I have five cows, two heifers, six sheep, forty to fifty chickens, four turkeys, two pigs, and two horses. My letter will be short as I don't have so much to write about but my thoughts of my old father make me send you a few words. I know for sure that father's thoughts are often here with us and that he wonders how we live and when his thoughts return I'm also sure that they rise up to God and carry us in the arms of his prayers and for this and all his goodness I give him my and my family's loving gratitude. The Lord will be standing by your deathbed and give you words of comfort and lead your soul to the heavenly Kingdom. I, tired pilgrim, need comfort. It is written that when the Prophet Elijah was persecuted by Jezebel and the priests of Baal and had to flee into the desert, he wished for death and sat under a juniper tree and prayed, "It is enough; now, O Lord, take away my life, for I am no better than my ancestors." Then he lay down under the tree and slept, and see, there was an angel of God who touched him and said, "Get up and eat." "He looked, and there at his head was a cake baked on hot stones, and a jar of water. He ate and drank, and lay down again. The angel of the Lord came a second time, touched him, and said, 'Get up and eat, otherwise the journey will be too much for you.' He got up, and ate and drank; and he went in the strength of that food forty days and forty nights to Horeb the mount of God. At that place he came to a cave, and spent the night there." This is in 1 Kings 19:4–9. Of this we can see that the people of the Lord do not walk through this world on roses. Luther says somewhere, Lord, I am tired and can do no more. May those who come after me do better. Amen. So I must also conclude that I'm too tired to do any more today. I can hear the clock already striking ten so I must wish you a happy Christmas and a good and blessed New Year. Give my regards to Mikkel Sørlie, Erik Lia, Erik Klemmetsrud and family, Kristofer Ruste and family, Tidemann Ruste, Mikkel Lisbraaten, my aunt and her family, Ole Jørandby and family, and first and last father and brother and family—you are all greeted from me and my family. Sincerely,

M ANDERSEN LIE

· ——— ·

Enclosed is a small sheet with a few sentences in dialect, the language spoken among members of this family. MAL wrote on 11 December 1891 (Nor. ed. V:239), mainly with reflections on his father's old age and illness. He also wrote on 28 November 1893 (Nor. ed. V:291), saying that he had been called to be precentor in a neighboring congregation but that he had referred them to his brother Ole. He enclosed the twenty-eight paragraph constitution for the Springdale Norwegian Lutheran Congregation. «II:275 NE V:261

· ——— ·

1892 — LETTER 2:284

FROM: Jacob Hanson Hilton, *Socorro, New Mexico, 15 December 1892*

To: Hans Jakobsen and Anne Olsdatter Hilton
Kløfta, Ullensaker, Akershus

Dear parents,

As Christmas is soon here I'll have to send you a little present. It's not much but still the best and dearest I have: a photograph of my two children Annie and Joseph. We should have had them taken earlier but the photographer has been too busy. I wish you could have had them for Christmas, but better late than never. The silk kerchiefs are from my wife to each of the girls and I hope they will arrive safely. It's so often that such things don't get through by mail and I don't know why. It's so long since I've heard from any of you in my dear home that I don't quite know what to write about. I have no news of significance except that two weeks ago I bought the town's only saddler's business so I now have two men working for me, one a saddler and harnesser, the other a shoemaker, and they are the only ones in town and I hope it will stay that way. Next year I've planned to let my farm out in the country and move back to town as it's too much work for me to go into town every morning and back again in the evening. I have to be up at five to tend and milk the cows, and two horses, a pig, thirty chickens and eight ducks; all have to be watered and fed before I go to town because we have no servant to help us and my wife is busy with the home and the children. I'm rarely home before nine or nine thirty as the store has to be kept open till eight thirty or nine since all the others do the same. This has gone on for two years and I'm tired of it. Times here are very bad. All the stores sell shoes and boots along with everything else since they believe that the shoe business is profitable. This is why I had to add on another business in order to pay for my bread and expenses.

How is everything in the dear home? I suppose Oluf and Dorthea have married. I saw in Karen's letter that it would be this fall but that is all I've heard. I haven't heard from Oluf for several years. I don't know why; perhaps he doesn't bother to write. I've often thought that if I should one day have the luck to be able to sell my business here, then I'd take my whole family and sail to Norway for yet another visit. But I dare not think too much about it since it is so doubtful whether the times here will improve. My wife often says that she would <u>so much</u> like to go to Norway and every time I get a letter she wants to go right away. She reads all the letters I get from home and understands everything she reads, and when I speak to her in Norwegian she answers correctly—but in English. Joseph can say that he is "*en snil nosk* [sic] *gut*." I'll have to end now with loving regards from us all, hoping that we will some time meet on Norwegian soil at Hilton. And in conclusion, loving greetings from your son

JACOB

· —— ·

Oluf Hilton married Sina Streiff, heiress to one of the largest farms in Ullensaker, and Anne Dorthea married Jakob Finsen who in 1893 took over Christopher Jacobson's general store at Kløfta. Joseph's few words of misspelled Norwegian may be translated "a good Norwegian boy." The last preserved letter from JHH is dated 13 December 1893.

It is his shortest letter: a few words about the photograph of his new daughter Bertha and a sentence on the bad times in the United States. He now does all the work in his shop. «II:232 NE V:262

· ⎯⎯⎯ ·

1892 — LETTER 2:285

FROM: Karen Solem, *Norden, South Dakota, 26 December 1892*

To: Ole Tobias and Amalie Ødegaard, *Nannestad, Akershus*

◦➤≡◉≡◀◦

My dear brother and sister-in-law,

Today is the First Day of Christmas and it is so bitterly cold that Louis had to go alone to church. All three children are sitting on the floor playing with their nuts, candy, popcorn, and apples that *St. Claus*, Father Christmas, has filled their stockings with during the night. They also got many toys so they're really busy today. One of my Christmas presents was a beautiful album that cost five dollars with space for fifty-two cabinets. It was given to me by *Mr.* Eriksen who lived here last summer. He of course knew that I had good use for it and it is already half full. I was just reading "For Women" in *Skandinaven* and found a piece about letter writing and this made me cast aside the newspaper and find my pen and paper. When I received your long awaited letter last fall I was firmly determined to write back at once since I thought I had a thousand and one things to tell you but time has run away with me and it is now Christmas. Thank you so much for the photographs. It is nice to see them as they grow and change and even better to see Toralf for the first time. He's such a sweet boy; I could hardly believe that it is he sitting there with the others. Nicolai got the photograph of Toralf, Johan got the one with all three, and I kept the two others. Send as many more as you like and I'll pass them on to, for instance, Fella, Christian and Carl in Fillmore County, my cousin Carrie in Chicago and Uncle in Peru. They would all be happy to have a photograph of the little boys and of you too, and I'm sure you would get many in return. Since we're talking of photographs, let me mention something I've thought about for a long time. Wouldn't it be possible to take mother to Kristiania and get a good photograph of her alone? Dear Tobias, please do this before it's too late. Now may be the time to again ask you to excuse me for not sending the photographs I've promised for so long, but this time I'll only say: be patient, you'll have them some day.

I had a letter from Cousin Anna a long time ago. She seemed to be quite happy where she is so I don't think I'll invite her to come here any more. I'll have to try to write to her during Christmas. I have no plans to go anywhere this Christmas; it is so much trouble to pack up the three little ones and there is also the risk that they will get ill so it is bad entertainment to go visiting with small children. On December 14 there was a great wedding. The groom and bride were *Mr.* Ole Halvorsen and *Miss* Emma Melha. She is a teacher and he has a lumber and hardware store in Brandt. The wedding was in the bride's home. The bride was in white as were two adult bride's maids. The band played for about 145 people. There were many nice presents, no dancing but the young people entertained themselves in various ways. We were there until the morning of the next day. The children caught colds on our way home as we had a seven mile drive. You will of course be meeting Olaus Thompson and Ludvig Hetager who left from here about a month before Christmas. I wasn't able to speak with either before they left. Louis met Ludvig in Brandt and he promised to visit us but I assume he didn't have time and that must be *all right.*

The Second Day of Christmas
Today we have what they usually call nice weather as there is no wind even if it is quite cold. There will be a *"surprise party"* for Christian Kjønstad this afternoon. He is fifty and his siblings and children have decided to surprise him with presents. As Nicolai is married to his daughter we are sort of in the family so we are invited, but as I've said before I don't like to be cold but rather be at home alone with the children, so we sent grandfather in our stead. Our presents are: an illustrated Bible, a lamp to hang from the ceiling, and a bookcase.

I wish I had more time to write when I at times get my *"inspirations."* Then my letters could have been a little more interesting and not so lifeless. But when you are so *"crowded"* in your daily striving that you can hardly think of anything but cooking, sewing, knitting, cleaning, and the thousand and one things that are ready to overwhelm you, from where will you then have your thoughts of the beautiful, the exalted or even, if I may so, the romantic. Yes, from where? Well, my English paper *The Housekeeper* is wonderful; it is about the best company I have. It expands my view of life and often makes me take up something new and makes me exclaim: "Well, I won't be old until I'm fifty."

Dear brother, I've written a good deal that I shouldn't have done. You must use your *common sense* and not read it aloud to too many. Tell mother that I talked with Nils Engelstad at the wedding and he told me that his mother was much better now than when we were there. Michael Engelstad sends his regards. He is quite sickly poor fellow and has suffered from a bad nervous disease for several years. He told me about some of the tricks you and he had done when you were boys and that you once dug a hole and covered it with twigs, grass and sand as a trap for father, and you succeeded.

I'll have to end this soon. All is well with all here. Peder Fella has gone on a visit to Fillmore County for a few weeks. We have no snow. Times are so-so. Christmas will be long past when you get this letter so I can only hope that you have had a blessed and merry Christmas. Marie and Nordt tell me to say hello to the little boys. Olga is crying so this must come to an end. Give my regards to all relatives and acquaintances, to Hans and his family and, not to forget, Josefine Olsen. I have a nice lace pattern that I'll send to her. I promised to write to her when I said farewell to her halfway between Kleppe and Larsen the shoemaker. I haven't and I hope she doesn't resent this. Oh, how well I remember her last words to me … And give my regards to mother. Greetings to you both and to your little boys from all of us, your devoted

KAREN

My best wishes for the New Year. *I should like very much to write you a few lines in secret if you could tell me that nobody else was going to see it, if so, only answer: Yes.*

· ——— ·

KS added *nuts* and *candy* in parentheses after the Norwegian words. Cabinets (spelled with a k) is the word used by KS. Nicolai, Johan, Christian and Carl were her brothers-in-law; the widower Per Fella had been married to a sister-in-law; Carrie (also called by her Norwegian name Karen) Hoch was a cousin married to a German in Chicago; her Uncle in Peru was Ole Christophersen; her cousin Anna in Norway was a daughter of Mathea Kristoffersdatter, a sister of KS's mother. KS's father was Ole Pedersen Sunne; her stepfather Olaus Olsen. Hans Olausen was her stepbrother. Her brother evidently understood some English and the last words in English were for him alone. KS had written to her mother 6 November 1892. «II:273 NE V:264

· ——— ·

REFERENCES

Bjerke, Robert A. 1994. *Manitowoc-skogen: A Biographical and Genealogical Directory of the Residents of Norwegian Birth and Descent in Manitowoc and Kewaunee Counties in Wisconsin from the First Settlement to 1900.* Manitowoc, Wisconsin, 1994. (Available at www.rbjerke.net/wp-content/files/Manitowoc-skogen.pdf)

Bjork, Kenneth O. 1958. *West of the Great Divide: Norwegian Migration on to the Pacific Coast, 1847–1893.* Northfield: NAHA.

Blegen, Theodore C. 1931. *Norwegian Migration to America 1825–1860.* Northfield: NAHA.

———. 1940. *Norwegian Migration to America: The American Transition.* Northfield: NAHA.

———. 1955. *Land of Their Choice: The Immigrants Write Home.* Minneapolis: University of Minnesota Press.

Clausen, C. A. 1961. *The Lady with the Pen: Elise Wærenskjold in Texas.* Northfield: NAHA.

Engen, Arnfinn. 1983. "Emigration from Dovre, 1865–1914," *Norwegian-American Studies* 29, 210–252. Northfield, NAHA.

Fra Amerika til Norge. Volumes 1–3 edited by Orm Øverland and Steinar Kjærheim. Oslo: Solum Forlag, 1992 and 1993. Volumes 4–7 edited by Orm Øverland. Oslo: Solum Forlag, 2002, 2009–2011. (In this edition these volumes are referred to as Nor. ed.)

Hansen, Karen V. 2013. *Encounter on the Great Plains: Scandinavian Settlers and the Dispossession of Dakota Indians, 1890–1930.* New York: Oxford University Press.

Hustvedt, Lloyd. 1979. *Guide to Manuscripts Collections of the Norwegian-American Historical Association.* Northfield: NAHA.

Joranger, Terje Mikael Hasle. 2000. "Emigration from Reinli, Valdres to the Upper Midwest," *Norwegian-American Studies* 35, 153–196.

Lovoll, Odd S. 2010. *Norwegian Newspapers in America: Connecting Norway and the New Land.* St. Paul: Minnesota Historical Society Press.

Leiren, Terje. 1987. *Marcus Thrane: A Norwegian Radical in America.* Northfield: NAHA.

Malmin, Rasmus, O. M. Norlie and O. A. Tingelstad. 1928. *Who's Who among Pastors in all the Norwegian Lutheran Synods of America, 1843–1927.* Minneapolis: Augsburg Publishing House. (Information about Lutheran pastors is from this volume.)

Nelson, E. Clifford and Eugene L. Fevold. 1960. *The Lutheran Church among Norwegian-Americans: A History of the Evangelical Lutheran Church.* Two volumes. Minneapolis: Augsburg Publishing House.

Norlie, Olaf Morgan. 1918. *Norsk Lutherske Menigheter i Amerika, 1843–1918.* Two volumes. Minneapolis: Augsburg Publishing House. (Most information about Norwegian-American Lutheran congregations is from this work.)

———. 1924. *School Calendar 1824–1924: A Who's Who among Teachers in the Norwegian Lutheran Synods of America.* Minneapolis: Augsburg Publishing House.

Øverland, Orm. 1989. *Johan Schrøder's Travels in Canada 1863.* Montreal: McGill-Queen's University Press.

———. 1996. *The Western Home: A Literary History of Norwegian America.* Northfield: NAHA and Champaign: University of Illinois Press, 1996.

———. 1996. "Learning to Read Immigrant Letters: Reflections towards a Textual Theory," in Øyvind Gulliksen et. al. eds., *Norwegian-American Essays 1996.* Oslo: NAHA-Norway.

———. 2002. "Letters as Links in the Chain of Migration from Hedalen, Norway to Dane County, Wisconsin, 1857–1890." Todd W. Nichol, ed., *Interpreting the Promise of America*, 79–103. Northfield: NAHA.

———. 2009. "Intruders on Native Ground: Memories of the Land-Taking in Norwegian Immigrant Letters." Udo Hebel, ed., *Transnational American Memories*, 79–103. Berlin and New York: DeGruyter.

Rene, K. A. 1930. *Historie om Udvandringen fra Voss og Vossingerne i Amerika.* Madison, Wisc.

Russell, Charles H. 2006. *Undaunted: A Norwegian Woman in Frontier Texas.* College Station: Texas A&M University Press.

———., ed. 2010. *Light on the Prairie: New Writings of Elise Waerenskjold.* Houston, Texas: Shining Brightly Books.

Svendsen, Gro. 1950. *Frontier Mother: The Letters of Gro Svendsen.* Translated and edited by Pauline Farseth and Theodore C. Blegen. Northfield: NAHA.

Syversen, Odd Magnar. 1982. *Norge i Texas: Et bidrag til norsk emigrasjonshistorie.* Stange, Norway: Stange historielag.

Ulvestad, Martin. 1901. *Norge i Amerika med Kart.* Minneapolis.

———. 1907. *Nordmændene i Amerika: Deres Historie og Rekord.* Minneapolis.

———. 1913. *Nordmændene i Amerika: Deres Historie og Record.* Vol. 2. Minneapolis.

Wist, Johs. B. 1914. *Norsk-Amerikanernes Festskrift 1914.* Decorah: The Symra Company.

Zempel, Solveig. 1991. *In Their Own Words: Letters from Norwegian Immigrants.* Minneapolis: University of Minnesota Press.

Information on many letter writers and their contexts may be found at a number of websites. The following sites have been used:

Census reports

The Norwegian census data from 1801, 1865, 1875 (incomplete), and 1900 are available at arkivverket.no/Digitalarkivet

The site of the Norwegian-American Genealogical Center & Naeseth Library includes some census data on Norwegian immigrants (for instance in the Wisconsin 1850 and 1880 census) as well as other information: www.nagcnl.org/index.php

Immigrant ships

The Norway Heritage website offers information on immigrant ship sailings and passengers: norwayheritage.com/

Some other specialized sources

For quite comprehensive information on the population of Ål in Buskerud see the online edition of Thor Warberg, Nye Ål bygdebok (in progress): www.aal-bygdebok.no/register.htm

Some may also find the website of the Norwegian Institute of Local History useful: lokalhistoriewiki.no/index.php/lokalhistoriewiki.no:Hovedside

Book design by Holmes Design, Northfield, Minnesota.

The interior type is set in a version of Sabon, a typeface designed by the German typographer Jan Tschichold (1902–1974). Sabon's design is based upon the original letter forms of Claude Garamond and Robert Granjon. Tschichold named his typeface for the Frankfurt type-founder Jacques Sabon, who died in 1580.

Printed by Bolger Printing, Minneapolis, Minnesota.